The Sommelier Prep Course

The Sommelier Prep Course

AN INTRODUCTION TO THE WINES, BEERS, AND SPIRITS OF THE WORLD

Michael Gibson

JOHN WILEY & SONS, INC.

This book is printed on acid-free paper. ♾

Published by John Wiley & Sons, Inc., Hoboken, New Jersey

Published simultaneously in Canada

For general information on our other products and services or for technical support, please contact our Customer Care Department within the United States at (800) 762-2974, outside the United States at (317) 572-3993 or fax (317) 572-4002.

Wiley also publishes its books in a variety of electronic formats. Some content that appears in print may not be available in electronic books. For more information about Wiley products, visit our website at www.wiley.com.

Library of Congress Cataloging-in-Publication Data:

Gibson, Michael.
The sommelier prep course : an introduction to the wines, beers, and spirits of the world/Michael Gibson.
p. cm.
Includes index.
ISBN 978-0-470-28318-9 (pbk.)
1. Sommeliers--Vocational guidance. I. Title.
TX925.G53 2010
641.2--dc22

2009018427

Printed in the United States of America
14

Contents

Preface

While there are hundreds of wine books in publication, there are few true wine textbooks. The textbooks that do exist, while informative, are geared toward semester-length courses and go into great depth on the subject matter, making them cumbersome for introductory learners. Few, if any, of the texts also offer information about beer and spirits.

The Sommelier Prep Course is a wine textbook that takes a topical approach to wine, beer, and spirits, focusing on the information that is most important at the introductory level. It is intended for use either as a text for introductory- to intermediate-level wine classes or as a self-guided introduction to wine for industry professionals. The goal of *The Sommelier Prep Course* is to build a strong foundation of knowledge about wine and other alcoholic beverages—not to be an exhaustive study on the subject. This book provides a base for educators to add to and customize depending upon their focus.

The idea for this book comes from more than six years of experience as the lead instructor for wines and spirits at the Le Cordon Bleu College of Culinary Arts—Scottsdale (formerly Scottsdale Culinary Institute). During my tenure, I had to quickly learn how to pack a lot of information into a short period of time. I have tried to fine-tune my curriculum to introduce students to the topic, and the results of those experiences are mirrored in this text.

I would like to thank all of the people at John Wiley & Sons who embraced my ideas for a new book about wine and helped me through the process, especially Rachel Livsey, Christine McKnight, Shannon Egan, Michael Olivo, Jeff Faust, and Laura Ierardi, who all helped me turn it into a reality.

Finally, I would like to thank my family for their encouragement, patience, and understanding as I completed this project. Without them, it would have been impossible for me to have written a single chapter. They will never know how grateful I am for their belief in me and their support. This book is dedicated to them.

I hope that you enjoy reading *The Sommelier Prep Course* as much as I have enjoyed the research and writing.

Cheers!

Michael Gibson

The Sommelier Prep Course

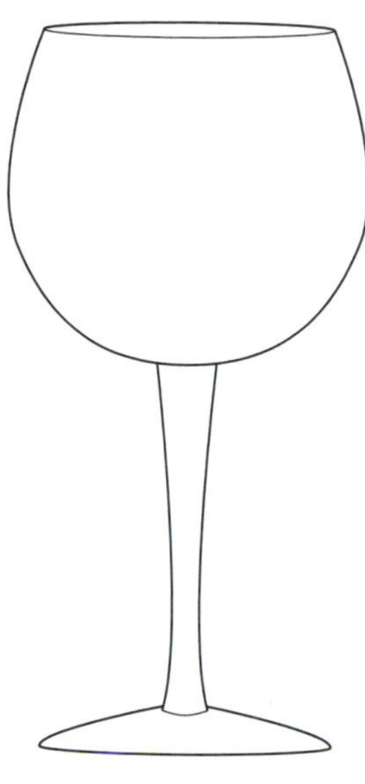

CHAPTER 1

Wine Basics: Fermentation, Grapes, and the Flavor of Wine

Wine rejoices the heart of man and joy is the mother of all virtues.

—**JOHANN WOLFGANG VON GOETHE,** German author and playwright

When one is beginning to learn about wine, many questions must be answered: What is wine? How is wine made? Why are grapes used to produce wine? Why do certain wines taste the way they do? In this chapter, these important questions will be answered. The topics introduced in Chapter 1 include:

- A definition of wine and a brief discussion of the raw materials used to produce it and the process by which it is produced: alcoholic fermentation.
- A discussion of *Vitis vinifera,* the wine grape; including where it came from, how it has been developed into its modern form, and what characteristics it possesses that make it important to the production of wine.
- The three impacts on a wine's flavor: grapes, viticulture and *terroir,* and viniculture.

What Is Wine?

For thousands of years, even predating the beginnings of Western civilization, humans have been converting the juice of grapes into **wine.** Today, wine is more popular than ever, with premium wines being produced and consumed all over the world. Wine can be defined many different ways depending upon how it is used. We use wine to celebrate, to add to the enjoyment of food, and to foster conversation. Some people collect and store wines, waiting for the perfect moment to remove the cork. Others buy wine for its health benefits. Wine has been written about by some of the world's best-known poets, authors, and playwrights. It is mentioned more than any other type of food or beverage in the Bible. Wine is intertwined throughout the history of mankind, and continues to be an important part of daily life and custom in many parts of the world today. Whatever our reasons for drinking it, learning to better understand wine—what it is, how it works, where it comes from, why it tastes the way it does, and how it best matches with foods—can enhance our enjoyment of all types of wines.

> **Wine**—A **fermented beverage** produced from the juice of any fruit, usually grapes.

Although wine means many different things depending upon whom you ask, we need to have a working definition of wine to truly understand it.

Two things need to be understood for wine to make sense: the raw material used for its production and the process by which it is produced.

FRUIT: THE RAW MATERIAL OF WINE

The sugar found in fruit is the raw material used to produce wine, and technically, wine can be produced from the juice of any fruit that contains sugar, not just grapes. While grapes are synonymous with wine, there are several other types of fruit whose juice is fermented into wine. The most common fruit wines are made from apples (called cider), pears, plums, and berries. That said, the vast majority of wines produced in the world each year are made from grapes, especially one specific species of grape: ***Vitis vinifera,*** or the "wine grape." This species has been shaped over the course of thousands of years into the perfect fruit for fermentation.

ALCOHOLIC FERMENTATION: HOW WINE IS PRODUCED

Regardless of the beverage being produced, all alcoholic beverages must at some point go through the process of **alcoholic fermentation.** This process is the only way that humans can create alcohol for consumption. Alcoholic fermentation is a biological process that occurs in nature every day. In fact, it is an initial stage of the spoilage process, as a microorganism breaks a compound down into smaller parts during this type of fermentation.

Humans have spent hundreds, if not thousands, of years attempting to control and understand this process, but it was not until the 1850s that Louis Pasteur used a new invention, called a microscope, to determine the exact process of alcoholic fermentation.

The Formula for Alcoholic Fermentation

Sugar + Yeast = Ethanol + Carbon Dioxide + Heat

So, when **yeast** comes in contact with sugar, it consumes the sugar molecules, breaking them down into two major waste products: **ethanol** and **carbon dioxide.** The process also produces heat due to the yeast's metabolic activity (see the diagram below).

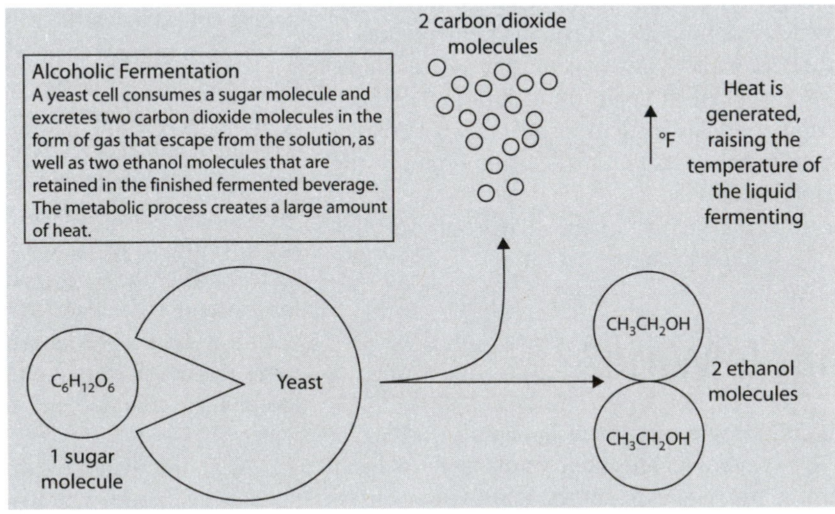

Alcoholic fermentation.

Practically any source of sugar can be fermented, and for wine, the two fermentable sugars from grapes and other fruits are fructose and glucose. The sugar source that goes through fermentation is what determines the type of beverage produced. For example, fruit juice that is fermented produces wine, a mixture of barley and water that is fermented produces beer, and a mixture of rice and water that is fermented produces saké. We typically describe wines based on the actual **varietal** of grape used to produce them. A varietal is the particular subspecies or type of grape (e.g., Chardonnay, Merlot, Zinfandel, etc.). Since the grape is the sugar source, its characteristics are carried over into the finished wine after fermentation.

Yeast is a single-celled fungus that feeds on sugars and simple carbohydrates. A specific species of yeast is used to conduct most alcoholic fermentations, whether one is making a fermented beverage like wine or the base for a distilled beverage like the mash used to produce a whiskey. The scientific name for this species is ***Saccharomyces cerevisiae.*** It is sometimes referred to as budding yeast, brewer's yeast, or baker's yeast. (*S. cerevisiae* is also the species of yeast used to make dough rise when baking breads.)

Ethanol, or ethyl alcohol, is the product of fermentation that separates grape juice from wine. It is the alcohol found in all alcoholic beverages, from beer to vodka. Although it is slightly toxic to humans (which is often felt in the form of a hangover after consuming large amounts of alcohol), ethanol is what causes alcoholic beverages to have intoxicating effects. Ethanol plays a major role in the flavor profiles and characteristics of wines and other alcoholic beverages, as it has a distinctive, almost perfumed aroma and slightly sweet taste, and produces a slight burning sensation on the palate. The more sugar in a liquid being fermented, the higher the ethanol levels produced during fermentation.

The other physical product of alcoholic fermentation is carbon dioxide (sometimes referred to as CO_2). Carbon dioxide is an inert gas (meaning it rarely reacts with other compounds); as fermentation proceeds, the beverage being fermented almost looks like it is boiling, as carbon dioxide bubbles are generated and break the surface of the liquid. For most alcoholic beverages, this gas is simply allowed to blow off into the atmosphere, and has no impact on the final flavor or characteristics of a product. The exceptions to this are carbonated beverages like Champagne, other sparkling wines, and some beers. For these beverages, a portion of the carbon dioxide produced is captured and allowed to dissolve into the solution. When the container holding that beverage is opened, the carbon dioxide begins to escape and produces the tiny bubbles that make these beverages carbonated.

As a result of this churning and active biochemical reaction, where yeast cells are metabolizing sugars and asexually reproducing as their cells split, the temperature of the liquid being fermented is raised. Thus, heat is the final product of alcoholic fermentation. It is not unusual for an uncontrolled fermentation to cause a liquid to rise to over 100°F. The warmer a fermentation, the quicker the yeast metabolizes sugar; and in this mad rush, several biochemical products are created by the yeast, which can have a major impact on the flavor of a finished product. Throughout most of history, winemakers could not control this heat because they lacked technology such as refrigeration. As a result, most alcoholic beverages had foul flavors resulting from the yeast metabolizing sugar too quickly. Today, winemakers ferment wines in temperature-controlled rooms or tanks. This allows them to maintain the exact temperature at which they want their wine to ferment, depending upon the characteristics they wish to bring out in each individual wine.

Why Does Bread Have Holes in It?

The *Saccharomyces cerevisiae* species of yeast is not only used in the wine, beer, and spirit industries for fermentation; it is also the main yeast used by bakers to make bread dough rise. The yeast is added to the dough and begins to feed on either sugars found in the flour or sugar added to the dough. While small amounts of ethanol are produced (and subsequently burn off when the bread is baked), large amounts of carbon dioxide gas are also produced, forcing the dough to rise and creating the holes found in bread after it is baked.

Why Is Wine Made from Grapes?

Although wine can be produced from the juice of any fruit, more than 95 percent of the wine produced in the world each year is made from one species of grape called ***Vitis vinifera,*** or the "wine grape." There are several different species of grapes, but *Vitis vinifera* has been specifically bred for thousands of years with one purpose in mind: the production of wine. Humans have been manipulating and developing *Vitis vinifera* for centuries, helping it to evolve into what it is today.

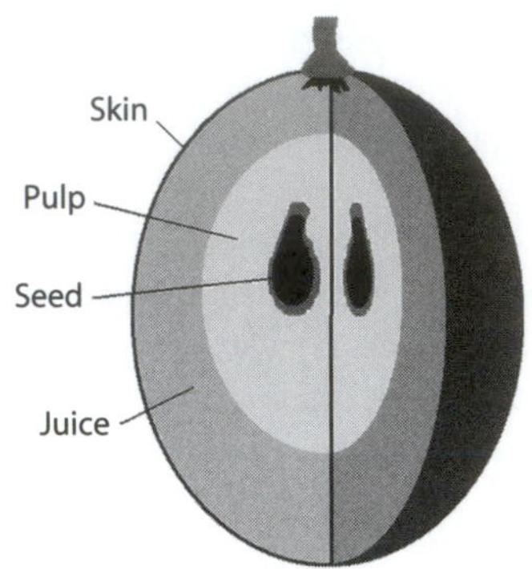

Cross section of a *Vitis vinifera* grape.

Can Wine Be Made from Grapes Bought at the Store?

While table grapes can (and sometimes are) grown for wine production, they are almost always of a different species than *Vitis vinifera*. Many table grapes belong to a species of vine called *Vitis labrusca. Labrusca* vines are native to North America and include the popular varietals Concord and Red Flame. While *labrusca* grapes make good juice and jelly and taste good eaten raw as a snack, for the most part the wines they produce are considered inferior to those made from *vinifera* vines. In fact, wines made from *Vitis labrusca* grapes are known for a distinctive foxy characteristic—reminiscent of fox urine!

The origin of *Vitis vinifera* lies in ancient Mesopotamia (modern-day Iran and Iraq) and surrounding areas. The first wines are believed to have been accidentally produced between seven thousand and nine thousand years ago during the Neolithic Era by hunter-gatherers who would have harvested *Vitis vinifera* grapes when they were in season. If there was an abundance of grapes, they would have stockpiled them in clay jars or animal skins to consume later, and if all of the grapes could not be consumed quickly, those left over would begin to spoil. Because alcoholic fermentation is one of the initial stages of the spoilage process, the result would be an extremely crude wine full of grape skins, seeds, and pulp. These first wines would not have tasted very good, but when consumed, they changed the way these nomads felt and brought on the intoxicating effects of ethanol—a magic potion of sorts. The rest is history.

When one takes a look at the physical characteristics of the grape, it is not surprising that grapes would have produced the first wines (see the diagram above). A grape is, more or less, a small sack of sugar-rich juice, surrounded by a thin membrane that has wild yeast clinging to it. A grape is basically a fermentation time bomb—it is not a matter of if a grape will start turning into wine, it is more a matter of when.

Nevertheless, wild *Vitis vinifera* grapes do not have any inherent characteristics that make them better suited for wine production than other grape species. It was only through the domestication and selective breeding of this species that we have such a specialized wine grape today. There were not wild Riesling vines or wild Pinot Noir vines growing in Mesopotamia; these are grape varietals that have been developed over time.

The first step in this developmental process was **domestication**, accomplished when agriculture was applied to *Vitis vinifera* as early cultures began to plant seeds in vineyards outside of the plant's native homeland. As grape vines began to be grown in this manner, humans quickly gained control over the

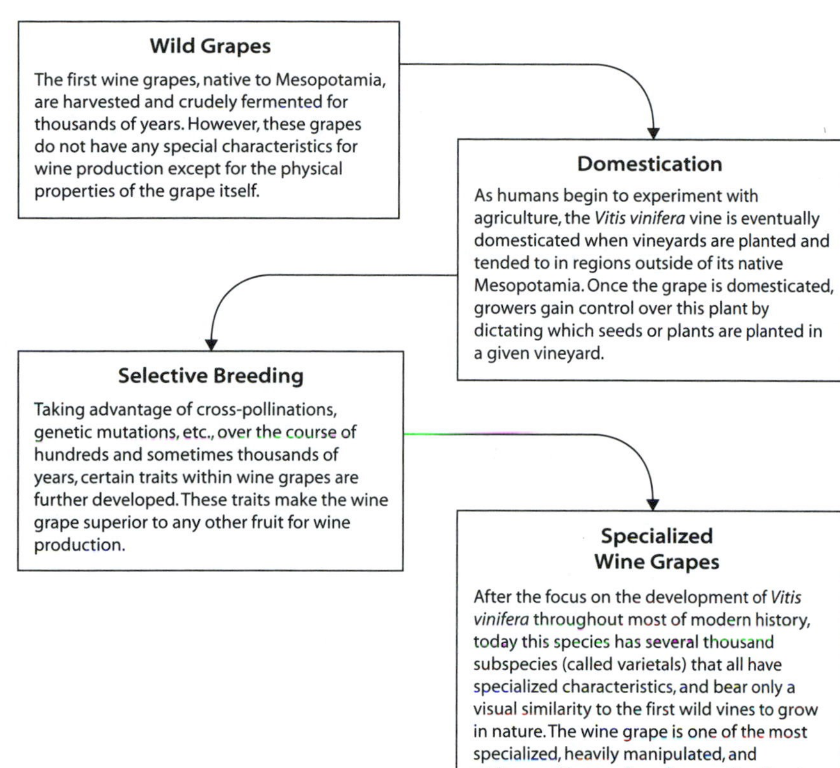

The evolution of the wine grape.

species, deciding how it would be grown, which seeds would be planted, and which vines would be allowed to propagate new vines. Once control over *Vitis vinifera* was established, selective breeding of the wine grape could begin.

Selective breeding is when certain vines are selected to produce the next generation of vines due to their characteristics, qualities, and agricultural adaptability. This next generation might then produce subsequent generations of plants, maintaining that set of genetic traits. In the case of *vinifera* vines, this began slowly, starting with agricultural decisions made out of necessity. If you planted ten vines in a new vineyard, and only one of those vines could survive, that would be the vine whose seeds would be planted throughout the rest of that vineyard. Whatever the reason for that one vine's survival, it would be those individual characteristics and that vine's genetic line that would be allowed to perpetuate over time.

Selective breeding is not something that occurs overnight, and it took hundreds if not thousands of years to produce some of today's grape varietals. Some were the result of isolating and continuing traits in a vine, as discussed above. However, many were simply the result of taking advantage of lucky mistakes and quirks in nature. Several of the popular grape varietals we know today originated as genetic mutations.

Consider wine grapes with no pigment in their skin. For the most part, wild *vinifera* vines are all red-skinned. The white-skinned grapes we use today are the equivalent of albino grapes—the result of a genetic mutation. Pinot Blanc (a white-skinned grape) is a varietal that resulted from a mutation of Pinot Noir vines. In nature, these grapes without pigment, which are weaker genetically, would probably never propagate to continue their genetic line. However, if a grape grower is in charge of a vineyard, he or she is in control of the plants in that vineyard and could make the decision to plant only seeds from a vine that produced albino grapes. Over the course of subsequent generations, that trait would become inherent in that grape grower's vines.

Crosses, or a pollination of one varietal plant by a different varietal, have also added to the abundance of grape varietals we have today. These can happen either on purpose as a result of plant science, or by accident out in a vineyard. It is believed that Cabernet Sauvignon is the result of the accidental cross-pollination of the Cabernet Franc varietal and the Sauvignon Blanc varietal (hence, Cabernet Sauvignon). Pinotage is a South African grape varietal that was created by a plant scientist in the 1920s when he crossed the Pinot Noir varietal with a grape varietal called Cinsaut.

Regardless of how selective breeding has occurred, the end result is at least 3,500 (although some estimates reach as high as 10,000!) different subspecies of *Vitis vinifera*—each distinct and very different from the original wild vines from which it descended. In addition to the number of varietals produced, important characteristics were also developed into the *Vitis vinifera* species to make it ideal for the production of wine. This is the reason that wine today is synonymous with the wine grape.

How Many Grapes Are in a Bottle of Wine?

As far as how many wine grapes it takes to produce one bottle of wine, the answer can vary greatly depending upon the style of wine being produced and the varietal or varietals that are being used. For the production of most dry wine, it will take approximately 2½ pounds of grapes to produce a full 750-milliliter bottle of wine, which works out to roughly 600 to 800 wine grapes. Some sweet dessert wines are made from shriveled, concentrated grapes, and these wines can use well more than twice the normal amount.

Characteristics of the Wine Grape

While the multitude of wine grape varieties means we have almost countless characteristics within the entire species, there are certain characteristics that all wine grapes share. These characteristics are what make wine grapes ideal for wine production, and include high **sugar** content; high levels of **acidity**; large concentrations of **tannins**; a built-in supply of yeast for **easy fermentation**; and the fact that grapes are **biochemically complex,** leading to a complexity of flavor.

SUGAR

Wine is a fermented beverage, and sugar is the basic building block needed for an alcoholic fermentation. It makes sense that wine grapes, being bred only for the purpose of producing wines, would have large amounts of sugar in their juice. Not surprisingly, *Vitis vinifera* grapes typically contain extremely high levels of sugar; in fact, ounce for ounce, wine-grape juice is the sweetest juice of any fruit. The more sugar a liquid contains, the more ethanol is produced. While most fruits would produce wines that topped out at roughly 10 percent alcohol by volume, wines made from wine grapes can naturally weigh in as high as 17 percent alcohol by volume.

ACIDITY

While sugar is important to fermentation and wine, if that sugar has nothing to balance out its sweetness, the resulting wine will taste overly or sickly sweet. Imagine eating a bowl of sugar or drinking a glass of

How Acidic Is Wine?

Acidity is often measured using the pH scale, where the lower the pH of a substance, the higher the concentration of acidity. The pH of most wines ranges from 2.9 to 3.8, making wine an extremely acidic beverage. Compare that to the pH of lemon juice, which is 2.4.

simple syrup (concentrated sugar water). Even if you have a sweet tooth, that probably sounds extremely unappetizing (or like a stomach ache waiting to happen). Is there a way to balance all of that sweetness? For wines, and a large variety of other products from certain candies to soft drinks, the balance comes in the form of acid.

In the same way that the sweetness of sugar needs to be balanced, so too does the sour flavor of acid. While you probably would not want to drink a glass of simple syrup, a glass of lemon juice is probably also unappealing. If you were to mix the two together, however, you would have lemonade. The high level of acidity found in the juice of wine grapes is therefore the next important characteristic for making wine. Not only do wine grapes contain a high level of acidity, but also an array of different acids. (The three main acids found in wine grapes are tartaric, citric, and malic.) This acidity helps balance out the inherent sweetness of *vinifera* juice, and is also one of the most important reasons that wine is such a good match for food.

TANNINS

The skins, seeds, and stems of wine grapes contain unusually high concentrations of **tannins.** Tannins are long-chain phenols found in all plant life, but very rarely in fruits. (Tannins are also found in large concentrations in tea leaves and the wood of trees.) All grapes have tannins in their skins, whether they are wine grapes or table grapes, but wine grapes tend to have higher concentrations. The main reason that wine grapes are so tannic is their size; wine grapes are much smaller than most table grapes, and that means that they have a larger skin-to-juice ratio.

These tannins are not something that you taste when you drink wine, but rather something you feel—a sensation of astringency. Astringency is best described as a drying out of the palate. Wines with high tannins might make you feel like your tongue is fuzzy, or almost like your teeth have socks on. Imagine chewing on table grapes until all of the juice and sweetness is gone, and all you are left with is the skins on the palate. As you continue chewing these grape skins, you will feel the astringency of the tannins found within them. While this may sound like a strange sensation, it is tannins that give a red wine its structure (tannins are not easy to detect in white wines because of how they are made), and they add a degree of complexity to wines made from wine grapes that is not found in wines made with other kinds of fruit.

EASY FERMENTATION

When you buy grapes at the store, very rarely are they shiny; instead, they are coated with a powdery residue. Wine grapes are no different, and when they are harvested, this powdery residue (called a bloom) clings to their skins. This bloom is composed mostly of wild yeast cells clinging to the grape. Yeast is a single-celled organism, and thus does not have a brain, but it is not stupid. These yeast cells cling to the grapes in a dormant state, knowing that at some point the grape will be separated from the vine and when its skins are damaged or begin to break down, sugar will be exposed. This will allow the yeast cells to start fermentation and asexual reproduction, fulfilling their biological drive to produce more yeast cells. This means that by their very nature, wine grapes are very easy to ferment (remember that it is already easy to extract the sugar-rich juice of grapes). All you have to do to make wine is take some grapes and either crush them to extract their juice or allow them to sit until spoilage begins to split the skins of the grapes. This ease in starting fermentation is probably why the grape was the focus of winemaking efforts early on in history.

BIOCHEMICAL COMPLEXITY = COMPLEXITY OF FLAVOR

With all of the genetic manipulation *Vitis vinifera* has gone through over the course of thousands of years of selective breeding, it is safe to assume that the juice of these grapes is biochemically complex. Not only were physical characteristics such as sugar content and acidity magnified, but so too were chemical components that make up the flavors found in these grapes. Certain varietals were developed because of the aromas and flavors they produced in the resulting wine. If you could grow grapes that were reminiscent of apricots or peaches, your wine would be unique, gaining you a competitive advantage. The more of these flavor compounds wine grapes contained, the more complex the wines made from them became; and, as in most things involving food and beverages, the more complex the flavors of a product, the more high-quality it is considered.

The end result is a complexity of flavors produced by wine grapes that you find in no other fermented beverage. If you try a hard cider made from apples, the dominant flavor of the cider will be apples. Wines made from raspberries or blackberries will taste like raspberries and blackberries, respectively. Even wines made from other species of grapes (such as Concord grapes) taste like grapes.

Wines made from wine grapes will have many flavors, from apples and pears to lemons, limes, grapefruit, tropical fruits, berries, dried fruits, artificial fruits, and more. The one flavor rarely found in wines made from wine grapes, however, is the flavor of grapes. Those flavors have for the most part been bred out of the wine grape. If you taste a Sauvignon Blanc–based wine and smell and taste grapefruit, it is not because the winemaker added grapefruit to the wine. It is because the same biochemicals that make a grapefruit taste and smell like a grapefruit are also found in that specialized *vinifera* varietal. It was bred to taste that way.

Although it is not necessary or important for a wine enthusiast to understand the science behind the development of this biochemical complexity, it is important to understand that wine grapes are complex. This complex biochemistry is what leads to a complexity of flavor in wines made from wine grapes, and is probably the most important characteristic making *Vitis vinifera* the most important fruit for wine production.

These wine bottles are labeled by the name of the main grape varietal used in their production, a common practice in most wine-producing regions outside of Europe.

Why Does My Wine Taste Like This?

When tasting and discussing wine, it is important to be able to identify and describe what you taste. Far more important, however, is having an understanding of why that particular wine tastes that way. This may be the most important thing you ever learn about wine, and I cannot emphasize this point enough—even though wine is an extremely complex beverage, ***the influences that shape the flavors found in any wine can be broken down into just three parts:***

The **grapes** used to make the wine;

Viticulture and ***terroir,*** or the agricultural decisions made while the grapes were growing and the specific environment where those grapes were grown; and

Viniculture, or the winemaking practices and procedures used to produce the wine.

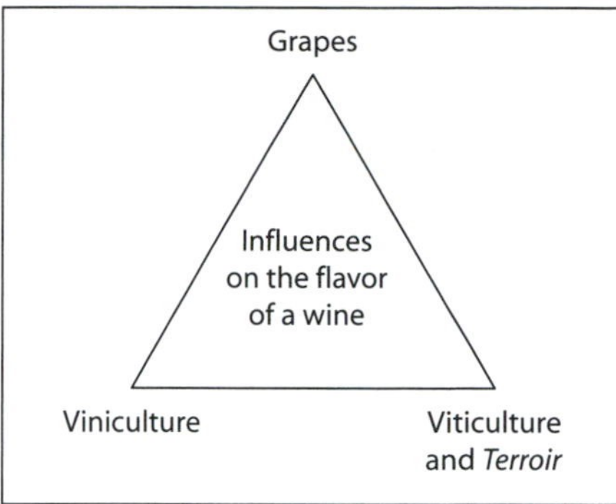

The three influences on the flavor of a wine.

GRAPES

The grape varietal or the blend of varietals used to produce a wine will have the largest influence on the flavor of most wines. Since grape juice is the basic building block of a wine, the flavors and characteristics of the juice from particular varietals of grapes or blends of grapes will be retained in the finished product. For instance, a wine made from Pinot Noir grapes should display flavors of cherries, cranberries, and earthiness because those are flavors that the Pinot Noir grape inherently imparts. Sauvignon Blanc grapes, on the other hand, will produce a wine that has flavors of grapefruit, tropical fruit, and freshly mowed grass because those are flavors found in the juice of Sauvignon Blanc grapes. Important wine grape varietals and the characteristics they impart will be discussed in Chapter 5.

VITICULTURE AND *TERROIR*

The art and science of growing grapes is referred to as **viticulture**, and grape growers have an influence on the quality and characteristics of the fruit they grow based on agricultural decisions they make in their vineyards. Vines can be trained to maximize the exposure of their leaves to the sun, speeding up photosynthesis. When irrigated, vines are allowed more access to water. Regardless of which procedures are applied, how particular vines are actually grown can determine, to some degree, the flavors and characteristics that these grapes will impart to a finished wine.

It is not just the processes and procedures that grape farmers utilize in their vineyards that can affect wine grapes, but also the influence of the actual vineyard on the vines. There is an important reason that wines made in two different places from the same grapes can taste very different from one another, even if the winemaking practices used to produce them are identical. This difference can be summed up by the French term ***terroir***, which describes the unique "taste" of a specific place.

> ***Terroir*** Directly translated, the French word *terroir* means "dirt" or "earth." When applied to wine, however, *terroir* is short for the French term *goût de terroir* (taste of the earth). This term describes the impact of the environment on a particular wine—the flavors that the vineyard itself contributes to a wine.

Terroir encompasses all of the environmental impacts on a grapevine as it produces fruit each year, from climate, to soil conditions and chemistry, to the geography of the vineyard. These environmental factors make the flavor of the fruit grown in each individual vineyard site unique. For example, a Cabernet Sauvignon–based wine from California's Napa Valley will tend to be higher in alcohol, more full bodied, and lower in acidity, and will have more powerful fruit flavors than a Cabernet Sauvignon–based wine from the French region of Bordeaux. This is due to the *terroir* of Napa Valley; the climate there is warmer than the climate of Bordeaux. A warmer climate causes the grapes to ripen more, which produces these characteristics in the resulting wine. The two wines would be made from the exact same grapes, could be treated exactly the same in the winery, and would still end up tasting very different. The role of *terroir* and viticulture will be discussed in detail in Chapter 3.

WINEMAKING

While viticulture is the art and science of growing grapes, **viniculture** is the art and science of making wine. The decisions and practices that a winemaker uses when producing a wine have a huge impact on the flavors found in that particular wine. As the science of winemaking is better understood, winemakers can have a greater influence on the flavors and characteristics found in a finished wine.

Have you ever tried a California Chardonnay that tasted buttery? That flavor does not come from the Chardonnay grape, nor is it a flavor that is imparted from the particular vineyard in which the vines grow; rather, it is a flavor produced by a winemaking procedure that happens after a wine has been fermented. If you store a wine in an oak barrel for twelve months, the flavor of the wine will change. A winemaker must decide how to complement or manipulate both the flavors that come from the grapes they are using and the flavors that result from how and where those particular grapes were grown. The role of winemaking and viniculture will be discussed in Chapter 4.

Summary

Wine is one of the world's most important products, and has been a part of Western culture for thousands of years. And, while the topic of wine may seem daunting at times, it really is a simple beverage. Regardless of price, pedigree, or hype, all wine is simply the fermented juice of fruit. The fruit used to produce most wines is the wine grape, *Vitis vinifera*, which has been developed for thousands of years to possess the important characteristics needed for wine production. Finally, the flavors found in every wine you will ever taste are a result of only three influences: grapes, viticulture and *terroir*, and viniculture. With that in mind, you now possess a strong foundation for understanding wine. In the chapters that follow, you will gain information that will build on that foundation.

Review Questions

1. Wine can be produced from any fruit, not just grapes.
   A. True
   B. False

2. The correct formula for fermentation is:
   A. Sugar + Yeast = Methanol + Carbon Dioxide + Heat
   B. Sugar + Yeast = Methanol + Sulfur Dioxide + Heat
   C. Sugar + Yeast = Ethanol + Sulfur Dioxide + Heat
   D. Sugar + Yeast = Ethanol + Carbon Dioxide + Heat

3. The scientific name for the yeast used in wine fermentation is:
   A. *Vitis vinifera*
   B. *Saccharomyces vinifera*
   C. *Saccharomyces cerevisiae*
   D. *Vitis cerevisiae*

4. The specific type of alcohol found in wine, beer, and spirits is:
   A. ethanol
   B. methanol
   C. isopropyl
   D. butanol

5. The warmer a fermentation, the faster the yeast ferments.
   A. True
   B. False

6. The scientific name for the wine grape is *Vitis vinifera*.
   A. True
   B. False

7. Which of the following is not a specific characteristic of wine grapes?
   A. High sugar levels
   B. High acid levels
   C. Pest resistance
   D. Biochemical complexity

8. The juice of wine grapes is sweeter than the juice of any other fruit.
   A. True
   B. False

9. The tannins found in wine grapes serve to balance out the sugar in resulting wines.
   A. True
   B. False

10. Which of the following does not have an impact on the flavor of wine?
   A. Grapes
   B. Price
   C. Winemaking
   D. *Terroir* and viticulture

Key Terms

wine
fermented beverage
alcoholic fermentation
yeast
ethanol
carbon dioxide
varietal
Saccharomyces cerevisiae
Vitis vinifera
domestication
selective breeding
sugar
acidity
tannins
biochemical complexity
viticulture
terroir
viniculture

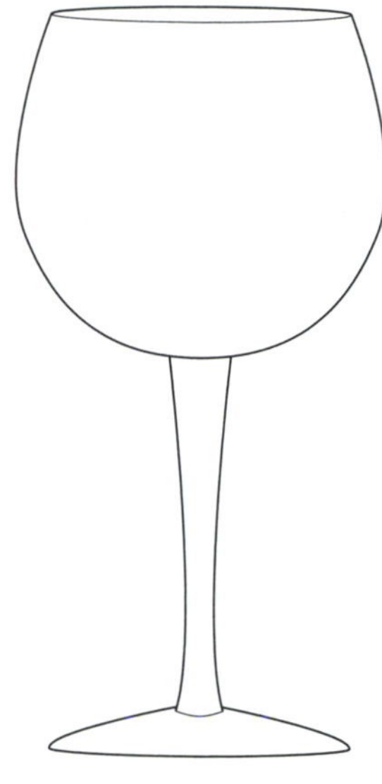

CHAPTER 2

A Short History of Wine

Fermentation and civilization are inseparable.

—**JOHN CIARDI,** American poet

Wine has been produced for thousands of years and is completely intertwined with the history of Western civilization. This chapter covers the early history of wine: how the first wines were accidentally discovered and how ancient cultures such as the Egyptians, Greeks, and Romans impacted wines, winemaking, and wine's spread throughout Europe.

We also discuss the modern history of wine, including the evolution of wine during the Dark Ages and Middle Ages, the worldwide spread of wine and wine grapes, scientific discoveries suchas the role of yeast in fermentation, France's long-time domination of premium wine production, the emergence of winemaking in California, the Spurrier Tasting of 1976 that ushered in an era of premium wine production around the globe, and finally, where wine and the international wine industry are today.

The Ancient World

THE NEOLITHIC ERA: THE FIRST WINES

The origins of wine are shrouded in mystery, as this fermented beverage was first produced well before the beginnings of recorded history. The oldest fossilized evidence of the *Vitis* genus, better known as the grape vine, dates back more than sixty million years. The specific species of grape vine we know today as the wine grape, *Vitis vinifera,* dates back at least ten million years. *Vitis vinifera* is native to the eastern Mediterranean regions known as **Mesopotamia**—the Fertile Crescent between the Tigris and Euphrates rivers and beyond, including modern-day Iran and Iraq as well as portions of Turkey and Syria.

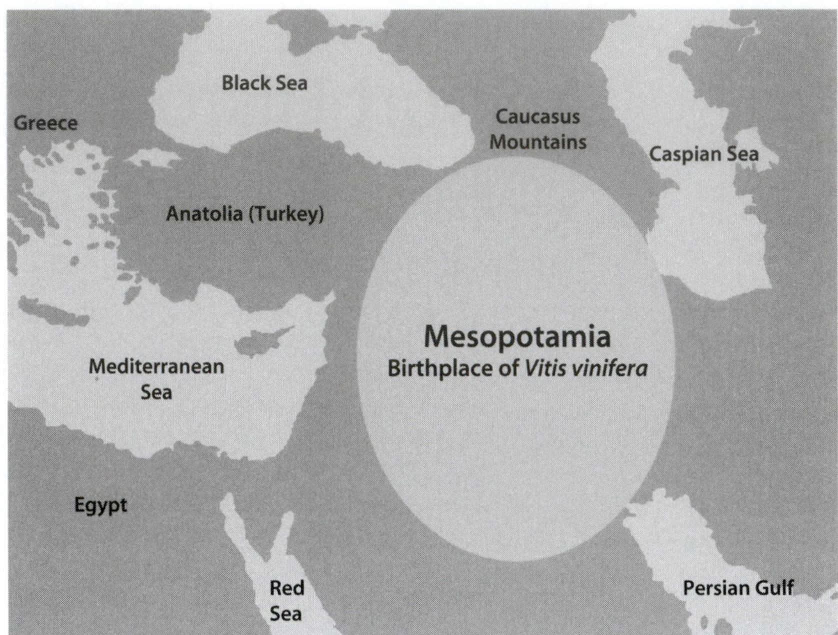

The area considered to be the birthplace of the *Vitis vinifera* species.

Most historians agree that the first wines were accidentally produced during the late **Neolithic Era,** probably between 5000 B.C. and 7000 B.C. This was the age of the hunter-gatherer in Mesopotamia, which is credited as the cradle of Western civilization.

No one is quite sure how the first wines were produced, but more than likely, it was an accidental event with a positive outcome. Life was not easy for a hunter-gatherer in ancient Mesopotamia. Nomadic tribes waged a daily battle for survival as they foraged, hunted, and gathered enough food to sustain their members. ***Vitis vinifera*** vines grew wild in the region, so it is safe to assume that these hunter-gatherer tribes would have harvested grapes from these vines when they were in season. Whatever could not be consumed immediately would have been placed in clay pots and animal-skin containers.

If a surplus of grapes was harvested, the grapes that could not be consumed by a tribe quickly would begin to spoil, and alcoholic fermentation is one of the early stages of the spoilage process. When the skins of these grapes began to split and their sugar-rich juices were exposed, wild yeast clinging to the skins or floating around in the air would have begun alcoholic fermentation. Upon opening a clay pot or animal-skin container filled with these now fermenting grapes, the hunter-gatherer would have been greeted with an extremely crude version of wine.

A waft of carbon dioxide would be followed by the sight of a mixture of fermented grape juice along with the skins, stems, seeds, and pulp of the grapes. This liquid would have begun to dissolve the clay pot, leaving a layer of mud at the bottom. The wild yeast, upon completing the fermentation of the grape sugars, would produce a thick, scummy mass floating on the surface of the murky liquid.

While this would be discarded today, hunter-gatherers could not just throw away food, so someone would have had to give it a try. They would probably use a rudimentary straw, such as a hollow papyrus reed, to drink the wine. After jamming the straw through that thick foamy mass of yeast on the surface, they could drink the liquid below.

Did these first wines taste good? Certainly not! They would have tasted like spoiled grapes and the uncontrolled fermentation would have created several off flavors. However, taste was not what was important. The intoxicating and euphoric effects brought on by the alcohol in these crude wines would have made these beverages magic potions for early people—a gift

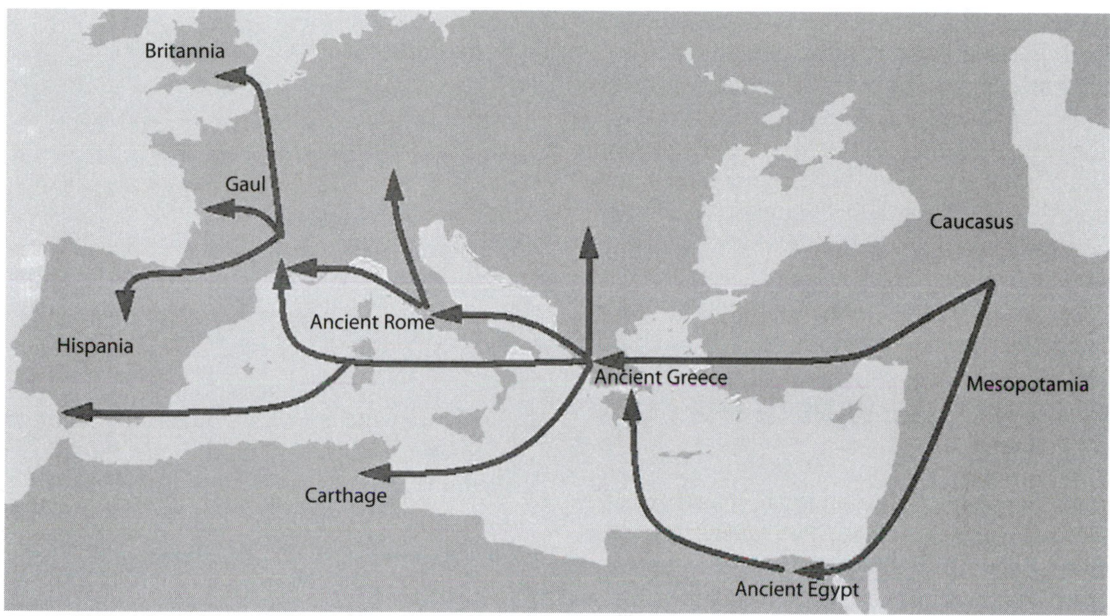

The spread of *Vitis vinifera* and winemaking in the ancient world.

from the gods. It would not have taken long before these tribes began making wines on purpose, possibly even speeding up the process by smashing the grapes after putting them into containers.

With the dawn of agriculture, these hunter-gatherer tribes began to settle. With the ability to grow much of their own food, not everyone in the tribe had to hunt and gather food each day. Individuals could focus on building tools and permanent shelters, and eventually developing their language and the written word. Fermented beverages, including wine, played a role in daily life along the way. These small encampments eventually turned into villages, and villages turned into cities. Civilization in the western world had begun, and the first major cultures in western civilization rose to power in Mesopotamia.

EARLY MESOPOTAMIAN CULTURES: THE DAWN OF WINEMAKING

As civilization began to flourish in Mesopotamia around 5000 B.C., organized winemaking began to be practiced there. Several cultures, including the Mesopotamians, Sumerians, and Phoenicians, helped to develop the process of winemaking and spread a wine culture into neighboring regions and beyond.

It is believed that *Vitis vinifera* was first domesticated in the areas of Mesopotamia north of the Caucasus Mountains of modern-day Georgia during the Bronze Age, in roughly 3000 B.C. This would have allowed for the development of vineyards capable of producing enough grapes for wide-scale production of wine. With several fledgling cultures beginning to grow throughout these regions, wine was quickly established as an important beverage.

Without an understanding of fermentation science or proper sanitation, these wines did not last long. Wine at this point was seasonal, available only for a few weeks after it was produced before it would begin to spoil. Containers used to store wine would probably have been earthenware or animal-skin vessels, which could taint the wine and allow for rapid oxidation and deterioration. The murky and crude wines of Mesopotamia were often flavored with a variety of spices, herbs, and sweeteners in an attempt to mask off flavors generated during uncontrolled fermentations. Despite all of this, wine was a beverage often reserved for royalty, religious figures, and a privileged few. The drink of the masses was beer.

As Mesopotamian cultures spread, winemaking and grape growing were introduced to other regions of the eastern Mediterranean. Most importantly, wine eventually made its way to two important civilizations that further advanced its quality and elevated its status as a revered beverage. To the east, wine was spread to the Hellenic culture of ancient Greece; and to the south, wine made its way to the Nile River Delta and ancient Egypt.

King Tut: Wine Connoisseur?

During the excavation of the tomb of King Tutankhamen in the 1920s, several vessels were discovered. Scientific testing on the residue found in these vessels proved that they had once contained wine. In fact, there were several different types of wine identified, including white and red wine. The ancient Egyptian king apparently wanted to make sure he had a well-stocked wine cellar in the afterlife.

THE EGYPTIANS: WINE IN THE AFTERLIFE

Ancient Egyptian civilization began sometime before 3000 B.C. and flourished for more than three thousand years in various forms. Hieroglyphic and archaeological evidence prove that wine was an important part of Egyptian civilization almost from its beginning. As in other early cultures, wine was not a common beverage in ancient Egypt; it served mainly a ceremonial role, and would have only been enjoyed by pharaohs, nobles, and religious priests. The vast majority of Egyptians would never have had access to wine, and instead drank the far more common fermented beverage of the time, beer.

Many superstitions surrounded wines and winemaking, and the process of fermentation was believed to be a gift granted by the gods. The deity known as **Osiris** was responsible for wine and the harvest, along with life, death, and the afterlife. Wine was considered a vital provision for the afterlife, and vessels containing wine residue have been discovered in several Egyptian tombs. Some of these vessels were even engraved with the name of the winemaker and the region in which the wine was produced.

While wine was important to the Egyptians, the wine grape vine was not native to the region. This means that grape vines were brought to Egypt by another culture, or Egyptians brought vines back from journeys into Mesopotamia. In either case, the fertile lands of the Nile River Delta proved to be quite hospitable to *Vitis vinifera*. Soon, large advanced vineyards were planted throughout ancient Egypt, and wine production was studied and improved. The storage of wine was still difficult, though, so it spoiled quickly and was often available only during certain parts of the year. The Egyptians' success with winemaking was eclipsed by only one other culture during their early reign—the ancient Greeks.

THE GREEKS: WINE IS INTRODUCED TO EUROPE

The origins of winemaking in the area known today as Greece may date back more than six thousand years. Clearly these were the first wines produced in Europe. During the golden age of ancient Greece, wine was enjoyed year-round and became a part of daily life not just for kings and nobles, but for most levels of society. Many of the winemaking practices that are still used today were developed first in ancient Greece.

With the introduction of the wine grape vine to Greece, probably in the region of Macedonia, wine quickly became an important beverage. The Greeks had a god of wine and revelry named **Dionysus,** who was believed to be responsible for the conversion of grape juice into wine. Temples were built throughout ancient Greece for Dionysus, and priests, winemakers, and cults worshipped him. Large and often quite rowdy religious festivals were celebrated each year to honor this god and secure a good harvest. The annual cycle of birth, growth, and harvest played a large role in the myths and legends of the time, and these themes are even echoed in Christian theology.

Grape growing saw several advances during the time of the ancient Greeks. They developed advanced trellising systems and vineyards, attempting to improve the raw materials used to produce wine. In addition, many varieties of wine grapes were bred in ancient Greece, and the descendants of these early varietals are still grown in modern-day Greece and other parts of Europe. One of the most important advances the Greeks made in winemaking was in its storage. Tall and large pottery vessels called **amphorae** were used to store liquids, including wine. To keep the wines from spoiling, a layer of olive oil was floated on top of the wine, effectively serving as a barrier for oxidation. This meant that wines could actually be aged and matured. For the first time, wine was not just a beverage relegated to limited consumption during a few short weeks of the year. Wine quickly became more and more common, and eventually this beverage that had been enjoyed only by a relative few was available to all who could afford it.

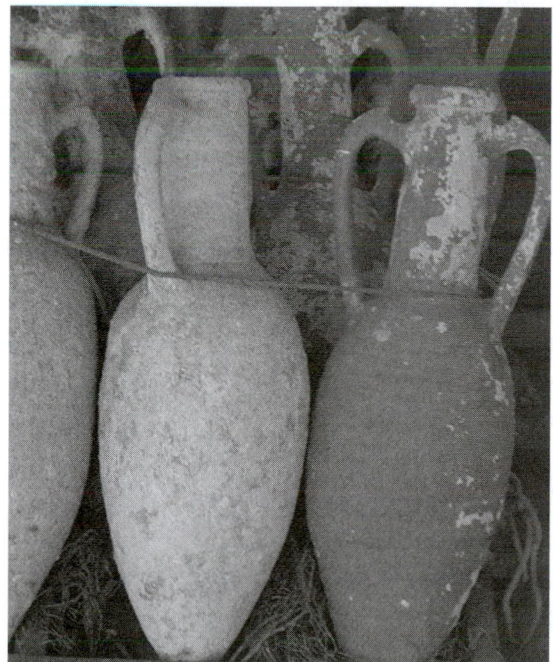

Vessels called amphorae were used to store and age wines in ancient Greece.

Wine had finally become a commodity, and wines began to be traded and shipped amongst the city-states of ancient Greece and beyond to other cultures in the Mediterranean. As the Greeks' culture spread throughout Europe, they introduced wine and the vine to several of their new colonies. These regions included parts of southern France (near the modern-day city of Marseilles), the Iberian Peninsula (home to Portugal and Spain), and a neighboring land that the Greeks called ***Enotria,*** meaning "land of wine." This region was named for the fact that vines thrived wherever they were planted there, and because it was the source of some of the best wines produced in ancient Greece. Spreading wine to this land was important because a fledgling culture soon started there that had a love of wine from the beginning. We know *Enotria* today as Italy, and the fledgling culture eventually became the most important ancient civilization in Europe: Rome.

THE ROMANS: THE GOLDEN AGE OF ANCIENT WINE

As the ancient Romans rose to power, they not only adopted the Greeks' love of wine, but also their system of mythology and religion. Rome also had a god of wine, named **Bacchus,** who was very similar to the Greek deity. As with the ancient Greeks, the Romans believed that Bacchus was responsible for wine and that divine intervention caused its production. Temples and worshippers abounded throughout the Roman Empire, due to the great importance placed on wine.

No other ancient culture was more important to the advancement of wine's quality and the spread of its production and usage in Europe. As the Roman Empire expanded, new areas of winemaking were established. The Romans spread wine throughout modern-day Italy, France, Spain, Portugal, Germany, and beyond. Wine's role in European daily life and customs is due in large part to the influence of the Romans, thousands of years ago.

The Romans made several advancements in both grape growing and winemaking. Full-scale selective breeding of wine grape vines developed several new

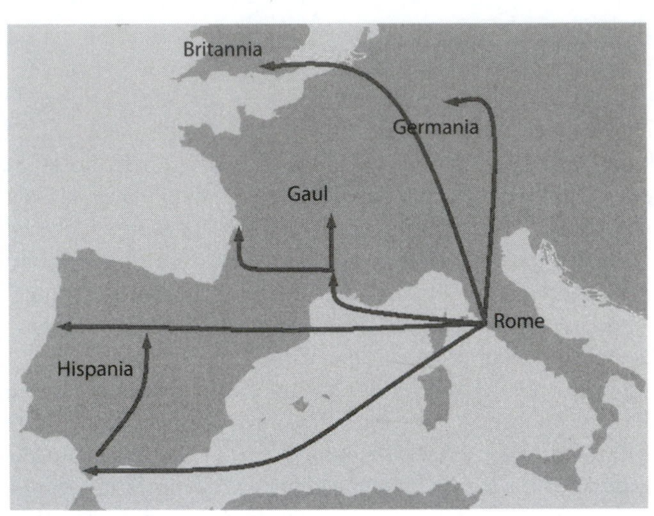

The spread of wine through the Roman Empire.

varietals, many of which are the ancestors of grapes we use today. Pests and diseases in vineyards were identified and treated, and advanced systems of trellising and vineyard maintenance were established. Roman winemakers were probably the first to have a basic understanding of ***terroir***, identifying different areas of quality growth and matching specific grape varieties to their ideal growing conditions.

Pompeii and Wine

The city of Pompeii was considered a vacation destination for the wealthy and fashionable nobles of ancient Rome. It was surrounded by both villas and vineyards where some of the most sought-after wines of the Roman Empire were produced. The eruption of Mount Vesuvius in A.D. 79 smothered the city and nearby areas in ash, destroying the city itself as well as the winemaking properties, yet preserving for archaeologists vivid evidence of the role and importance of wine for the Romans. Hundreds of wine bars or taverns (called *thermopolia*) have been unearthed in the ruins of Pompeii. The prices and descriptions of the wines sold at these wine bars can still be found painted on many of the walls. In addition, thousands of amphorae and other wine containers were unearthed.

Winemaking also improved greatly in the Roman Empire. Amphorae were replaced with wooden barrels and bottles made of glass. Presses were developed to more efficiently remove the juice from grapes prior to fermentation. Several additives were used in wine to cut acidity and add flavor. Wines were even sometimes allowed to age in contact with the sediment they produced during fermentation—a precursor to the modern practice of ***sur lie*** aging.

This was truly the pinnacle of wine and winemaking in the ancient world. Never before had the quality of wine been so good, nor had its importance been spread so far. The Romans had an undeniably lasting effect on wine culture, but all good things must come to an end—and in A.D. 476, the Roman Empire came to a crashing end and Europe was plunged into darkness.

The Modern World

THE DARK AGES: MAINTAINING A WINE CULTURE IN EUROPE

After the fall of the Roman Empire, Europe entered a period known as the Dark Ages. This was not a good time to be alive. Disease and pestilence spread throughout the continent. With no government to offer protection to the citizens, roving bands of Germanic barbarians sacked and pillaged their way across Europe. Food shortages were common and water supplies were polluted to the point that people began to get sick and die from drinking water. For the first time in centuries, the average European had to fight for basic survival.

With all of these challenges, many aspects of daily life enjoyed during the Roman era began to fade—most of them cultural elements like art, literature, architecture, music, cuisine, and winemaking. There was only one group powerful enough during the Dark Ages to preserve some of these cultural aspects in Europe: the Catholic Church. Winemaking was especially important to the Church, and wine and a wine culture were maintained and in many cases strengthened in Europe during these bleak times because of this fact.

There were many reasons the Church became heavily involved in winemaking during the Dark Ages, the most important of which was that they were already involved in wine production prior to the fall of Rome. Wine was needed to conduct their religious ceremonies, so most of the Catholic churches and monasteries located throughout Europe already had vineyards and winemaking facilities. With water supplies often polluted, this wine could also serve as a safe beverage for Europeans. Since wine was produced from grape juice, it was considered safe and healthy for the young and old alike.

The influence of the Catholic Church on winemaking in Europe and even in the Americas is still felt today. Many of the top vineyards and wine regions of Europe were first planted or maintained by the Church during the Dark Ages, Middle Ages, and Renaissance, and the Church certainly controlled wine production in Europe during these times. Missionaries in the Americas would eventually be the first to plant wine grapes in the New World. Many of the daily customs of drinking wine in Europe are a result of the connection between wine and the Catholic Church.

Wine and Christianity

Wine has played a very important and symbolic role in the Christian religion from its ancient beginnings to modern day. Wine is mentioned more than any other food or beverage in the Bible, with more than 150 direct references to wine in this holy book. Noah's first act after the flood waters receded and his ark was set aground was to praise God by planting a vineyard. Jesus turned water into wine at the feast of Cana.

Wine is also used in the religious ceremonies of the Catholic faith as a symbol of Christ's blood. Much of the symbolism here involves the fact that wine is constantly renewed with each vintage, as Christ was resurrected after his death. This started at the Last Supper, when Jesus passed a chalice filled with wine to the Apostles to drink to his remembrance.

"This cup is the new testament in my blood: this do ye, as oft ye drink it, in remembrance of me."
—1 Corinthians 11:25.

THE MIDDLE AGES AND THE RENAISSANCE: A NEW AGE

During the Middle Ages, new European nations such as Spain, France, Portugal, and England began to emerge. Winemaking was still widely controlled by the Catholic Church, but a new secular wine trade was established. These winemakers and merchants considered wine a profession, and soon it became an important commodity traded throughout Europe. This was especially true for many northern regions of Europe that had to import wines for personal and religious use, because their climates were too cold to grow their own grapes.

For these wines to be shipped around Europe, new techniques and technologies were established to increase the shelf life of wine. Interaction with Muslim cultures during the Crusades and the Moorish conquest of Spain introduced Europe to distillation. It was not long before wines were being fortified with grape-based spirits because of their preservative abilities. Several notable wines produced in Europe

The English Love Affair with French Wine Begins

In 1152, Henry II of England married Eleanor of Acquitane in a royal wedding. Her dowry was control of southwestern France, including the area today known as Bordeaux. For almost three hundred years, wine from this region was considered the drink of the English royal court, until France finally reclaimed its lands. England became a nation of wine drinkers (amongst several other beverages) and their link with the red wines of Bordeaux, which they called "clarets," was solidly forged.

are still fortified today, including Port and Madeira from Portugal, Sherry from Spain, and Marsala from the Italian island of Sicily.

In the 1600s, a new innovation in wine storage was introduced: the **cork.** While bottles had been used to store wine since the time of the Romans, most wine was stored and shipped in wooden barrels. Bottled wine spoiled much more quickly than wine in barrels, as the different materials used to seal the bottles worked poorly. Stoppers made of cork, produced from the bark of the cork oak tree, changed all that. Due to its elasticity and airtight structure, cork was the ideal material to seal bottles. With the introduction of the cork, fortification was no longer a necessity, and many winemakers stopped the practice.

Wine flourished in Europe through the Middle Ages and into the Renaissance. Quality improved dramatically, imports and trade throughout Europe increased significantly, and several of today's top wine regions were established. The most important beverage in Europe was firmly cemented as part of the continent's culture, and soon it would be spread into areas of the world about to be discovered.

THE AGE OF CONQUEST: THE WINE GRAPE IN THE AMERICAS

World history was changed forever when the explorer Christopher Columbus got lost looking for a quicker trade route to the East Indies in 1492. On his voyage, commissioned by the Spanish, he stumbled on two continents blocking his route: North and South America. Believing that these new lands were rich with mineral wealth, the monarchs of Europe raced to conquer as much of the Americas as possible.

The first wave of Europeans sent across the Atlantic were conquistadores and soldiers, who landed and conquered as much as they could. By far, the Spanish were the best (or worst) at this, eventually claiming Central America, Mexico, all of South America except for the Portuguese colony of Brazil, and large areas of what is today the American Southwest and Southeast. They brought wines with them, but they were quickly consumed or eventually spoiled. The second wave of settlers sent to the Americas had a more significant impact on the history of wine.

This second wave was made up of several groups. Enterprising ranchers and farmers came to claim large tracts of land. Miners and prospectors arrived to search for gold and silver. Political officials came to establish colonial governments. Finally, Catholic missionaries came to minister to the Europeans colonizing the New World and to save the souls of the indigenous people of the Americas.

These missionaries began establishing Catholic missions and churches throughout the Spanish colonies, and you cannot have a Catholic mass without wine to offer for the Sacrament. That meant they arrived in the Americas with a Bible in one hand and ***Vitis vinifera*** grape seeds in the other. Establishing vineyards in the New World was an important priority.

Wine Arrives in California

California is known today as one of the world's most important wine-producing regions, but winemaking did not arrive there until Spanish monks began building a series of missions throughout the area. The first wine grapes are believed to have been planted in what is today the state of California near the Mission San Diego in 1768.

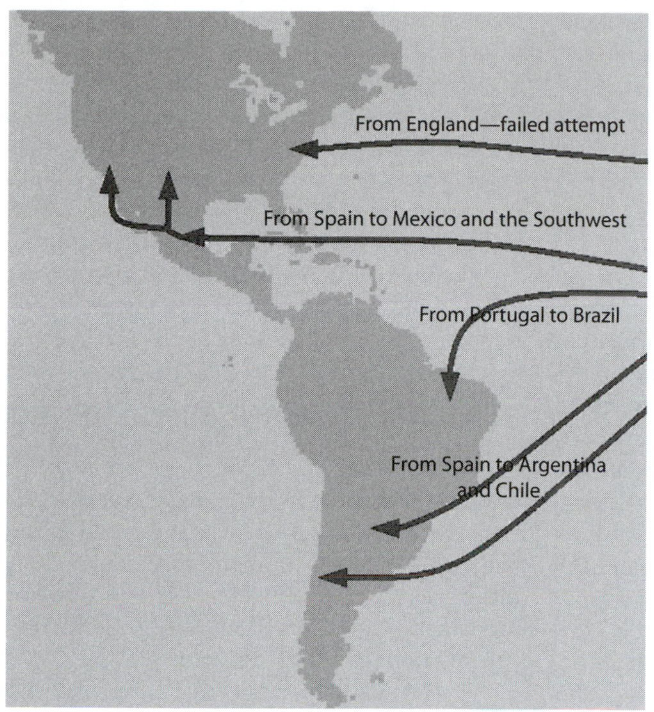

The spread of wine to the Americas from the late 1500s to the 1700s.

The most important variety of grape planted in the New World during the early colonial era was known by many names. It was called Criolla in Argentina, Pais in Chile, and Mission in Mexico and what eventually became the American Southwest. The first *Vitis vinifera* vines were planted by Spanish missionaries in what is today the United States in the 1590s, most likely in modern-day New Mexico.

COLONIAL TIMES: SUCCESSES AND FAILURES

Although the wine grape species had been developed and cultivated in Europe for thousands of years, it adapted quite well to the conditions found in many parts of the Americas. Early wine industries were established in several Spanish colonies including Chile, Argentina, and Mexico. Hernando Cortez, the Spanish general who had conquered the Aztecs in Mexico, was named the new ruler of that region by the Spanish Crown. One of the first official proclamations he made concerned new plantings of grape vines by newly arriving European settlers who were being granted holdings of land to farm or ranch. A colonial wine industry quickly developed in Mexico and became so successful that the Spanish government eventually outlawed it, after winemakers back in Spain protested that it cut into their profits.

New England had a climate suitable to the *Vitis vinifera* species but the British colonists, unlike the Spanish colonists in other regions of the Americas, were wholly unsuccessful at getting these vines to grow. Although England had long been a large consumer of wines, the country lacked the size and climate to practice large-scale grape growing. The English had always relied on other European nations, especially France, for their supplies of wine. Unfortunately, throughout most of the Middle Ages and into the colonial era, England and France were often at war with one another. These conflicts always resulted in England being cut off from French supplies of wine. In an effort to source new wines that could meet the market demands, English merchants scoured Europe for substitutions. With the colonization of the eastern coast of North America, England came to control a large landmass with a temperate climate suitable for grape growing. Wild species of native American grape vines grew throughout the colonies, leading the English to believe that they could grow the wine grapes of Europe on English soil.

This could have been the solution to all of England's difficulties in producing and securing wine, except for one thing: The wine grape vines they planted throughout the New England colonies always quickly wilted and died. Vines planted in areas where native vines thrived seemed to get wiped out the quickest. No solution presented itself during these colonial times, although several attempts were made. New England began concentrating on producing cider, beer, and rum, instead of wine. The British colonies of Australia and New Zealand eventually began producing wines, and attempts in New England were soon forgotten. The true cause of the British failure to get vines growing in the colonies would not be learned for another couple of hundred years, when it showed up in European soil.

FRANCE: WINE DOMINATION

With wine grape vines first being planted on its soil by the Greeks and Romans, France has a long and proud history of wine production. Throughout the Middle Ages and beyond, the wine regions of France were surveyed and studied. Diligent grape growers began developing grapes that were perfectly suited to the diverse *terroir* of the country. Styles of wine and winemaking techniques were slowly perfected as generations of winemakers dutifully strove to make better wines.

Wine may have been as important to other nations in Europe as it was to the French, but no other nation worked so hard or cared so much when it came to making better wines. This commitment to quality eventually led to wines that had no equal anywhere else in the world. From the 1600s on, France was the undisputed world leader in quality wine production. Certain individual wines from other parts of the world were considered of high quality, but these were few and far between. Across the board, France was producing top-quality wines of all different flavor profiles and styles.

It was soon believed that there was something special about France when it came to wine—something not found anywhere else. For almost four hundred years, France produced well over 90 percent of what the world considered premium wine, and they still make considerably more than any other country today. The dominance of French wine was soon accepted as fact, and this dominance would go unchallenged even throughout most of the twentieth century.

SCIENTIFIC ADVANCES IN THE 1800s

As the Industrial Revolution swept through Europe during the middle of the 1800s, several scientists began to apply new principles and methods to winemaking. The discoveries they made and techniques they perfected ushered in a modern era of winemaking. The two most important of these scientists were **Jules Guyot** and **Louis Pasteur.**

Dr. Jules Guyot was a French physician who had an avid interest in agriculture and wine. Through much research of traditional grape growing methods and fieldwork, he developed several agricultural techniques to improve the cultivation of wine grape vines and the quality of the fruit they produced. Much of his work was concerned with how grapevines should be grown, pruned, trellised, and cared for. He published three important works of his findings that paved the way for modern viticulture. There are several pruning techniques named in his honor that are still widely used throughout the world today.

Famous for his findings that led to the development of the pasteurization process, the French chemist Louis Pasteur also made one of the most important discoveries ever about wine and other fermented beverages. Throughout millennia, the actual source of alcoholic fermentation had remained completely unknown, and was attributed to everything from divine intervention to spontaneous development. With a background in chemistry and the study of microorganisms, Pasteur was able to prove in 1857 that microscopic yeast cells were actually responsible for fermentation. This finding allowed winemakers to improve sanitary conditions, control fermentations, and propagate better strains of yeast for winemaking.

Throughout most of history, winemaking techniques had simply been passed down through generations and no scientific understanding was involved. The advances of Guyot, Pasteur, and others, turned winemaking and grape growing into sciences. The wine industry in the mid-1800s was on the threshold of a new era, but that was all overshadowed by a frightening new development that threatened to wipe out the wine grape vine altogether.

GLOBAL DEVASTATION: THE WINE GRAPE FACES EXTINCTION

Part of the heritage of the discovery of the New World by Europe was the adoption of several plants, fruits, and vegetables native to the Americas. Imagine modern European cuisine without tomatoes, peppers, potatoes, corn, chocolate, and vanilla, all of which were brought to Europe from the New World. Along these same lines, nineteenth-century winemakers decided to experiment with native American grape vines.

In the early 1860s, a group of winemakers from southern France had several native vines from the east coast of the United States dug up and transplanted into their vineyards. They were attempting to find out if a species of vine known as ***Vitis labrusca*** (a species of table grape native to a region stretching from New England to the Mississippi River valley) could yield quality grapes for wine production on French soil. Unknowingly, they had just unleashed one of the greatest ecological disasters mankind has ever known.

Early results of this experiment were mixed: the vines thrived in the soils of southern France, but the wines they produced were of low quality. The experiment was ultimately considered a failure, and winemakers in the region quickly forgot about it when they found their own *Vitis vinifera* vines in nearby vineyards suddenly beginning to wilt and die. This soon changed from an isolated, local problem into a regional crisis, as vineyards throughout the top wine regions of southern France were affected and their vines began to unexpectedly die.

Over the course of the next two decades, this problem spread into central France and then on to the rest of Europe and the New World. Winemakers were faced with a global epidemic that many feared meant extinction for the wine grape and the end of wine. The cause of this epidemic was eventually discovered to be a tiny insect called ***phylloxera.***

Native to the soils of the eastern United States, *phylloxera* is a nearly microscopic insect related to the aphid that feeds on the roots and leaves of grape vines. Over centuries, vines native to North America like *Vitis labrusca* had developed a defense or resistance to *phylloxera* in the form of very thick bark on their roots. Developed in complete isolation from any similar pests, *Vitis vinifera* vines had no such resistance. *Phylloxera* damaged their root structure and, along with infections the roots developed, the *phylloxera* quickly starved the vines of nutrients and water until they died.

It is believed that *phylloxera* found its way to Europe in the soil packed around the roots of those first, experimental American vines planted in southern France. At the time, vine nurseries in central France served as the source for transplanted wine grape vines sent all over Europe as well as to emerging wine regions around the globe such as California, Australia, and South Africa. Thus, after *phylloxera* finally spread into central France, it was subsequently spread throughout the wine-producing world. The only wine-producing country in the world that has not seen the spread of *phylloxera* is Chile, due in large part to its isolation and the sandy soils common there, which *phylloxera* avoids.

By the time the cause of this epidemic was discovered, it was almost too late for winemakers. Vineyards throughout the world were rapidly infested and

An insect called *phylloxera* wiped out many of the top wine regions of the world in the late 1800s. Illustration by Matt Gibson.

destroyed. Several methods were used to fight *phylloxera* with little to no success. To this day, there is no known cure for *phylloxera* and it still infests vineyards throughout the winemaking world.

As winemakers feared the worst, a solution would eventually present itself in the late 1880s. The classical wine grape of Europe found salvation in the most unlikely of places: Denison, Texas.

TURN OF THE TWENTIETH CENTURY: THE WINE WORLD REBOUNDS

Several attempts to thwart the *phylloxera* epidemic were made throughout Europe and the rest of the world. Everything from flooding vineyards to burying live toads under vines was tried, but none of these methods were successful. Top scientists and viticulturalists believed that the solution might be found in developing hybrids of wine grape vines crossed with native American grape vines, although the wines were of doubtful quality. Eventually, attempts were made to use **grafting** as a possible solution.

For hundreds of years, grafting had been a part of the agriculture of the vine. A cutting from one vine could be grafted onto the rootstock of another, and if properly done, the two would grow together into one plant. This worked for vines of the same species, and even for vines of different, related species. If a **resistant rootstock** could be found that could survive *phylloxera* and thrive in the soils of France and Europe, *Vitis vinifera* cuttings might be grafted onto them, effectively getting around the *phylloxera* epidemic. Many rootstocks were tried, but with little success.

Thousands of miles away from the vineyards of France are the dusty plains of northeastern Texas: home to the city of Denison and, in the late 1800s, a horticulturalist named **Thomas Munson.** Educated in agricultural sciences at what would become the University of Kentucky, Munson specialized in grape cultivation and eventually moved to Denison. There he developed and bred dozens of grape varietals and gathered an extensive collection of native American vines.

Munson worked diligently to cultivate native vines to survive different soil types and conditions. His work was geared toward increasing the quality of the fruit these native vines produced, but it eventually led to the solution to the *phylloxera* problem. The ability of the rootstocks he had developed to resist *phylloxera* and to adapt to a variety of different soils made them the ideal base onto which to graft cuttings of wine grape vines. By the late 1880s, thousands of bundles of north Texas rootstocks were being shipped to France and the rest of the winemaking world, and grape growers began grafting their wine grape vines to them.

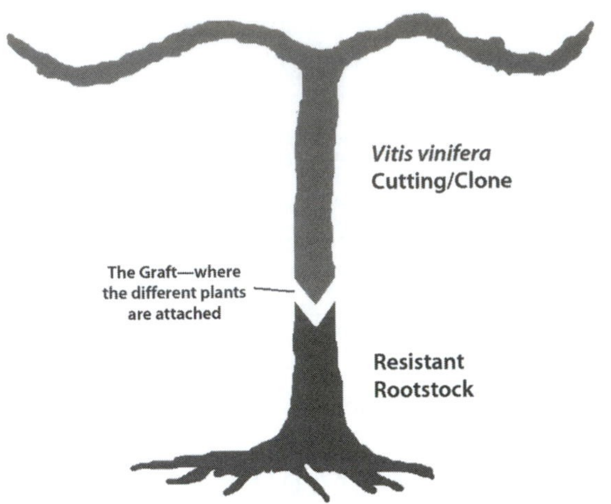

The grafting of wine grape cuttings onto resistant rootstock.

Munson was named a *chevalier,* or knight, in the French Legion of Honor for his efforts that saved the blight-stricken vineyards of Europe, and Denison, Texas, now has an unusual sister city: Cognac, France. Replanting on resistant rootstock took place around the world, and winemaking returned as best it could to normalcy. France returned to her place as the most important wine country at the turn of the new century, producing most of the premium wine in the world. The rest of the winemaking regions of Europe replanted and once again began producing their wines—some important and noteworthy, but most simple and rustic. New World winemakers reestablished their vineyards and continued producing their typically industrial, bulk wines. Although this had been the status quo for hundreds of years, things were about to change.

EARLY CALIFORNIA: DIFFICULT BEGINNINGS PAY OFF

While it is considered the premier winemaking region of the United States today, if not the top region outside of Europe, California has experienced several setbacks and a difficult start at winemaking. Through the 1800s and early 1900s, the bulk of winemaking in the United States occurred on the East Coast and especially in the Midwest. California's importance is only a recent development.

Although the state has a winemaking tradition dating back hundreds of years to the establishment of Catholic missions, the first commercial winery in California did not open until the late 1830s. Wine grapes were not planted in the northern California regions known today for quality production until the 1850s, after the gold rush began.

Almost before commercial winemaking had a chance to get started in places like Napa Valley and Sonoma, vines imported from France spread ***phylloxera*** to the state, wiping out several vineyards. Vines were eventually replanted around the turn of the century on resistant rootstock in California, as in the rest of the world. Throughout the first two decades of the 1900s, California winemaking began to gain momentum. Just as the state's bulk-wine industry was ready to challenge top producing states of the Midwest, it was attacked once again, this time by something far worse than invading insects: righteous politicians.

On January 17, 1920, **Prohibition** began in the United States. The Eighteenth Amendment to the U.S. Constitution, known as the Volstead Act, made the "manufacture, sale, and transportation of intoxicating liquors" a federal crime. Thousands of winemakers were immediately put out of business. Vineyards were dug up and replanted with new crops and wineries permanently shut their doors. The only legal loophole was for the production of sacramental wines sold to the church, but there were very few of these contracts.

When the repeal of Prohibition finally occurred in late 1933, the California wine industry was in ruins. While there were millions of thirsty Americans who would have loved a bottle of wine, they could not afford it. The Great Depression was in full swing and wineries had few customers and little money to renew production. California's wine industry would not begin to get back on its feet until World War II dragged the United States and the rest of

Agostan Haraszthy—The Father of California Winemaking

One of the most colorful figures in the history of California wine was Agostan Haraszthy, a Hungarian-born noble who moved to the United States in the 1840s. First settling in Wisconsin, he eventually moved to California in 1849 after the discovery of gold. Haraszthy settled in San Diego, where he became the first sheriff of San Diego County. He moved to San Francisco after being elected a state assemblyman in 1851, and he began to purchase land to grow grapes and make wine. In 1856, Haraszthy purchased some land in Sonoma County, where he planted vineyards and established the Buena Vista winery.

After much success making wine, he published a guide to growing grapes and winemaking called "A Report on Grapes and Wines of California." Known as one of the best winemakers in California at the time, he was sent to Europe in 1861 by the state's governor on a mission to study European winemaking techniques and to gather grapevine cuttings from European vines. He returned several months later with over 100,000 cuttings from more than 350 different grape varietals! This was the first time many of these varietals had ever been introduced to the state. The introduction of the Zinfandel vine to California is often credited to Haraszthy, although this is disputed.

Haraszthy was as colorful in death as he was in life. In 1868, he left California for Nicaragua in order to start a sugar plantation and rum distillery. A year later, he fell into a river on his property, and there are disputed reports that he was attacked and eaten by alligators. In 2007, Agostan Haraszthy was named to the Vintners Hall of Fame by the Culinary Institute of America.

the world out of the depression era. Starting in the 1950s, however, the state's rise to the top of American winemaking would be incredibly fast and surprising.

As winemakers around the United States began to emerge from Prohibition and the depression, California was thrust into a position of dominance due to several unrelated circumstances. There was a huge demographic shift in the United States during the depression era, as people moved west from eastern and midwestern states in search of work, meaning that California had an abundance of labor and consumers. This allowed California's wine industry to reestablish itself faster than those in other parts of the country traditionally known for wine.

With a period of relative prosperity beginning in the 1950s, Americans could afford to purchase wines again. At the same time, hundreds of thousands of U.S. troops had just served tours of duty in Europe, where they got a taste for wine. These facts combined to create a huge new demand for wine in the United States, and California was in the right place at the right time because it was able to rebuild its wine industry quickly. While California ranked third among U.S. states in wine production in 1950 (behind Missouri and Ohio), the state now produces roughly 90 percent of American wine six decades later!

Did winemakers produce top-quality wines in California during the 1950s? No. Mass-produced bulk wines were the norm, with grapes selected for their quantity of yield rather than the quality of their wines. Many of these generic table wines were given the names of famous wines and regions of Europe, like Chablis, Burgundy, and Chianti; but they were made from inferior grapes using basic techniques, and paled in comparison to the originals. Quality wines were produced almost exclusively in Europe, especially France, during this time; standards for California were much lower.

Several things changed in the United States during the 1960s, not the least of which was wine production in California. For most winemakers, bulk wines continued to make up the vast majority of their offerings. During this decade, however, a handful of winemakers began to do curious things in their vineyards and wineries. High-quality French grapes were planted and modern French winemaking techniques were adopted. The goal of these winemakers was almost universally considered impossible: they wanted to produce top-quality, premium wines similar to those produced in France. While the majority of the winemaking establishment scoffed at these practices and winemakers, an event would occur just a few years later that would prove that this goal was not impossible, but within reach.

THE JUDGMENT OF PARIS: THE DAY EVERYTHING CHANGED

French domination of premium wine production had been unquestioned for hundreds of years leading into the 1970s. This all changed on May 24, 1976, when an informal wine tasting competition took place in Paris, France. Today known as the **Spurrier Tasting** or the **Judgment of Paris**, this event changed the international wine industry forever.

Steven Spurrier was an Englishman who made his living as a successful wine merchant in Paris, selling premium French wines. He established the first private wine school in the city and taught classes to everyone from American tourists to French sommeliers. In 1976, he arranged a media stunt of sorts: a wine tasting competition connected to the American bicentennial events in Paris that year, to bring attention to his wine shop and put to rest the idea that wines from upstart regions around the world could compare to what France had to offer.

The competition was certainly not set up to be fair. Spurrier had a vested interest in the French wines winning, and although he was confident that this would be the case, he took several precautions to make sure. The French wines entered into the competition were from some of the most famous, world-renowned winemakers and wine estates from the country's two most important wine regions: Burgundy and Bordeaux. These were pitted against the wines of California wineries, many of which had been in existence for only a few years. The tasting took place in Paris, and all of the official judges were French—from leading wine authorities and authors to sommeliers and famous winemakers.

In an effort to compare similar wines, two major grapes and styles were selected to be judged. California Chardonnays competed against white wines from Burgundy, generally considered France's most important white wine region. Chardonnay is the only grape legally allowed to be used in the production of Burgundy's top white wines, and the grape had been first developed in Burgundy several hundred years earlier. For red wines, some of the top Cabernet Sauvignon–based wines of Bordeaux were put head to head with California Cabernet Sauvignons. As with the white wine matchup, Cabernet Sauvignon was a grape that had originated in Bordeaux hundreds of years earlier, and wines produced primarily from this varietal in Bordeaux were considered some of the top red wines produced in the world.

The competition was set up as a blind tasting, so the judges did not know which wines were being tasted as they were presented. Opinions of the different judges varied widely, but when the overall results were tallied the winners turned the wine world upside down.

The top white wine chosen was the 1973 Chateau Montelena Chardonnay made in Napa Valley, California. In fact, most of the high-scoring white wines were California Chardonnays. The top-scoring red wine selected was the 1973 Stags Leap Cellars SLV Cabernet Sauvignon, also from Napa Valley. To add insult to injury, competing against some of the top red wines in the world that had been produced for hundreds of years, that was the first year the Stags Leap winemaker had ever made wine from grapes grown in that particular, immature vineyard!

The French judges and the wine industry were stunned. Centuries of French dominance over premium wine production had finally been challenged, and were defeated by one of the least likely sources. Winemaking around the world would never be the same. In wine-producing countries both traditional and new, winemakers now believed that they too could produce premium wine. Higher-quality grape varietals were planted, modern winemaking techniques were adopted, and wines of surprising quality were made in places where this was previously thought impossible. The wines of California were suddenly thrust into the limelight, and a quality revolution swept the winemaking world.

The Judgment of Paris—Part Two

After the Spurrier Tasting took place in 1976, the French predictably cried foul. Many French winemakers claimed that because of the way they are made, California wines were meant for immediate consumption, while French wines would improve with age, only then showing their best qualities. In 1986, a group of French and this time American wine critics, writers, and authorities convened to reenact the first Spurrier Tasting with the same wines from the original vintages, only they had now been matured for ten years. After tabulating the results, California wines still came out on top and actually did better overall than they had in the original tasting!

Though it may be mere coincidence, the late 1970s and early 1980s were a time of major change in the wine world. France eased regulations for certain classifications of wine in an attempt to better compete against other wine-producing countries in the late 1970s. Tuscan winemakers began experimenting with nontraditional grapes and blends that eventually became the "super Tuscan" wines. Australia, New Zealand, and Chile all modernized their wine industries and began producing better quality, single varietal wines. Spanish winemakers began experimenting with modern techniques and new styles of wine. Millions of dollars began rolling in as people invested in northern California wineries. The Spurrier Tasting may not have caused all of these events to happen, but at the very least it marked the beginning of a new age of winemaking around the world.

MODERN DAY: YOU ARE HERE

Although it has taken thousands of years of wine production around the world to arrive where we are today, this is truly the golden age of wine history. Never before have so many quality wines been produced in so many different regions around the world. Several grape varietals have been made famous as they spread to countries not traditionally known for wine. Wine is more popular today than ever before, and the future looks bright for the winemakers practicing their craft throughout the world.

Summary

The history of wine is long, colorful, and completely intertwined with the history of Western civilization. All of the major cultures and events throughout western history have shaped the modern-day wine industry and culture. From wine's humble beginnings in the Neolithic period to the top-quality varieties being produced around the globe today, wine has been a constant part of human life.

Review Questions

1. Bacchus was the Roman god of wine.
- **A.** True
- **B.** False

2. *Phylloxera* is a(n):
- **A.** disease
- **B.** Greek vessel for storing wine
- **C.** grape variety
- **D.** insect

3. What year did the Spurrier Tasting take place, when California wines beat French wines in a blind tasting competition?
- **A.** 1920
- **B.** 1961
- **C.** 1976
- **D.** 1980

4. Which procedure effectively solved the problem of *phylloxera*?
- **A.** Irrigation
- **B.** Grafting
- **C.** Cross-pollination
- **D.** Fruit set

5. The first people to plant wine grapes in the Americas were Spanish missionaries.
- **A.** True
- **B.** False

6. Wine and the wine grape's origin lie in:
- **A.** Portugal and Spain
- **B.** France and Italy
- **C.** Iran and Iraq
- **D.** Chile and Argentina

7. The ancient culture that spread wine throughout Europe was:
- **A.** the Egyptians
- **B.** the Greeks
- **C.** the Aztecs
- **D.** the Romans

8. Who kept a wine culture alive in Europe during the Dark Ages?
- **A.** The French
- **B.** The Roman Empire
- **C.** The Catholic Church
- **D.** Spanish conquistadores

9. Who discovered the role of yeast in fermentation?
- **A.** Louis Pasteur
- **B.** Thomas Munson
- **C.** Jules Guyot
- **D.** Steven Spurrier

10. California has dominated American wine production since the gold rush began in 1849.
- **A.** True
- **B.** False

Key Terms

Neolithic Era
Mesopotamia
Osiris
Dionysus
amphorae
Enotria
Bacchus
cork
Jules Guyot
Louis Pasteur
Vitis labrusca
phylloxera
grafting
resistant rootstock
Thomas Munson
Prohibition
Spurrier Tasting
Judgment of Paris
Steven Spurrier

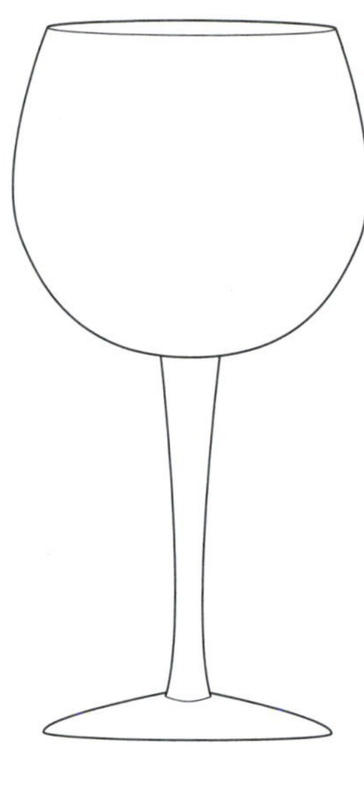

CHAPTER 3

Viticulture: The Art and Science of Growing Grapes

The sun, with all those planets revolving around it and dependent on it, can still ripen a bunch of grapes as if it had nothing else in the universe to do.

—**GALILEO GALILEI,** Italian astronomer and philosopher

Viticulture is the art and science of growing grapes. Agricultural decisions made in the vineyard have an enormous impact on the quality, quantity, flavor, and price of every wine produced. Many believe that a wine is not made in the winery, but rather in the vineyard, where viticultural decisions and factors reign supreme. This chapter discusses the specifics of the *Vitis vinifera* vine, typical agricultural decisions in vineyards over the course of a season, how the vineyard site can affect the flavors and qualities of a wine grown there, organic and biodynamic viticulture, and how stress and other factors affect quality.

Vitis vinifera: The Wine Grape Vine

All species of grapevines fall within the *Vitis* genus, a grouping of flowering vine plants that produce berries called grapes. Fossilized remains of prehistoric grapevines have shown that this genus evolved tens of millions of years ago. Many of the roughly sixty different species of this genus are native to Northern Hemisphere regions including the United States.

The species of the *Vitis* genus are the most widely planted agricultural crop on Earth. There are more than 20 million acres of vineyards planted with grapevines, the majority of which are intended for the production of wine. *Vitis vinifera* is the most planted grape species and is found on every continent in the world except Antarctica.

One of the first developments toward domesticating *Vitis vinifera* was the selection of hermaphroditic vines that could **self-pollinate.** Throughout time, many ancient cultures including the Egyptians, Greeks, and Romans played a part in developing *Vitis vinifera* into what it is today. This species has several characteristics that make it unique. Some of these are considered assets and explain why *Vitis vinifera* produces such high-quality wines, and others are major drawbacks that have even threatened the existence of the vine throughout history.

Characteristics of the *Vitis vinifera* Species

PROS	CONS
Develops extremely high sugar content	Susceptible to pests and diseases
Has high levels of acidity	Prone to mutation
Contains large concentrations of tannins	Grapes degrade quickly after harvest
Has complex flavors	Weak structure is easily damaged
Has minimal nutritional requirements	Sensitive to extremes of climate
Self-pollinates	

Major Grape Species that Can Be Used for Wine Production

Vitis vinifera—This species is native to the region of Mesopotamia and the southern Caucasus, and was mostly developed and bred in Europe. This is the predominant grape species used for wine production.

Vitis labrusca—Native to the east coast of North America, this species is predominantely used for juice and jelly, although it is sometimes used in the production of wine. The most famous varietal is the Concord grape.

Vitis aestivalis—Sometimes called the "summer grape," this species is native to the eastern United States and was one of the original native vines used for wine production in the New England colonies. Sometimes used for wine production still today, especially in the midwest United States. The most famous varietal is the Norton grape.

Vitis rotundifolia—Known as the Muscadine grape, this species is native to the southeastern United States and is commonly used to produce wine, jelly, juice, and raisins.

Vitis riparia—Native to central and eastern North America from Canada to Mexico, this species, also known as the "riverbank grape," is sometimes used for wine production. Its resistance to *phylloxera* as well as several other pests and diseases make its rootstock ideal for grafting vulnerable *Vitis vinifera* cuttings. It is also used for juice and jelly.

Although the *Vitis vinifera* species is not perfect, its positives far outweigh any difficulties in growing and tending to these vines. This species is one of the most specialized, manipulated, and heavily bred plants in the world. It is through the thousands of years of care and development that *Vitis vinifera* has become so important to winemaking in modern times.

WHERE DO GRAPEVINES GROW?

The facts that *Vitis vinifera* is a plant and that wine is an agricultural product are often overlooked. Like all other plants, it can live only in a certain temperature range and can adapt only so much to extremes in climate. The ability to produce wine in a given region depends more on that region having conditions suitable for growing grapes than on an individual's desire or agricultural prowess. Simply put: the areas of the world that produce wines do so because they can grow wine grapes.

Vitis vinifera vines grow best in mostly **temperate** conditions. Extremes of either heat or cold can be withstood by only a handful of specialized varietals. If the average temperature is too hot, the grapes will ripen too quickly and will not develop balance, if they form at all; vines will remain completely dormant and will not produce foliage or grapes if the average temperature is too cold. This limits the growing of wine grapes and the production of wine to areas of the world that are:

- Far enough away from the equator, where regions are closest to the sun and climates are hottest, and
- Far enough away from both the North Pole and the South Pole, where the regions are furthest from the sun and climates are coldest.

Taking this into account, wine production is typically limited to the areas of the globe between the 30th parallel and the 50th parallel of latitude in both the Northern and Southern Hemispheres.

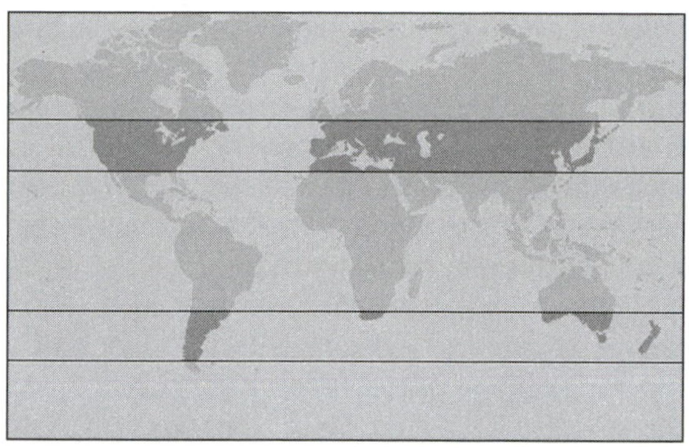

The temperate zones between the 30th and 50th parallels of latitude highlighted on the continents of the world.

VINE ANATOMY

A *Vitis vinifera* vine has several key components that allow it to grow and produce fruit:

Canopy This term applies to the vine's leaves and shoots, which often need to be controlled through different practices to shade the grapes, maximize leaf exposure to the sun, or allow air circulation.

Grape Clusters/Bunches The mature fruit of a grapevine form groupings of grapes called clusters or bunches.

Flowers The grapevine flowers in the spring. These flowers are quite small and form in groupings off of shoots. This is the reproductive portion of the plant that typically self-pollinates before eventually forming the individual grapes.

Leaves The leaves of the vine capture energy from the sun, which causes photosynthesis to take place. Water and carbon dioxide are converted into sugar and oxygen through the actions of chlorophyll. This provides energy for the vine to grow, and allows the grapes to ripen and build up sugar content. Interestingly, each varietal has a uniquely shaped or patterned leaf, and many varietals can be identified simply by this shape.

Shoots Shoots are the branches that shoot off the head and cordons of a vine. They form from tiny buds in the early spring and are the areas of the vine where leaves, flowers, and eventually grapes form.

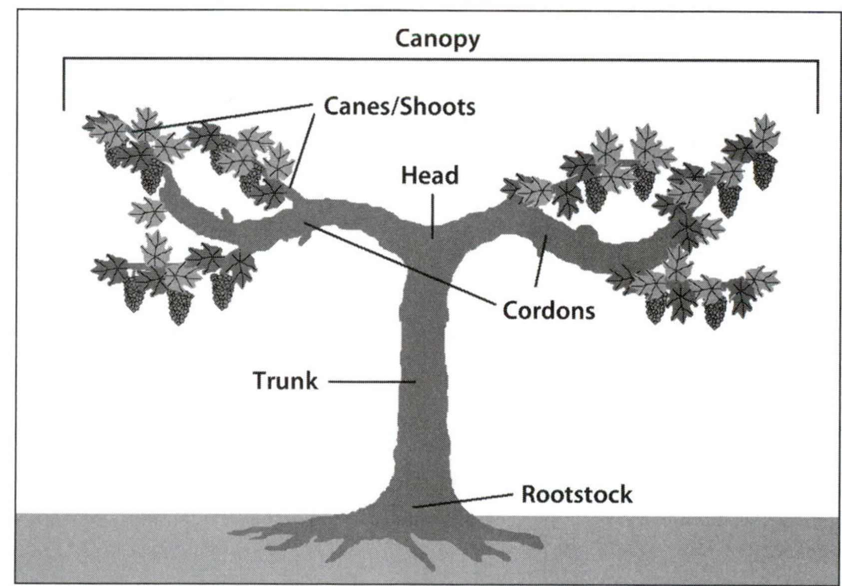

Anatomy of a *Vitis vinifera* grapevine.

Canes After the harvest, the shoots dry out and turn hard and woody. At this stage they are often pruned from the vine; however, they can be trained along a wire or some other trellis material away from the plant. If allowed to develop and thicken, canes will turn into cordons, becoming permanent parts of the vine.

Cordons Cordons are permanent branches of the vine, starting at the head and often trained in a horizontal fashion away from the trunk. Similar to a main branch of a tree, this is where the majority of the shoots will form and grow.

Head The top of the vine where shoots can form, or from which cordons originate if trellised, is called the head.

Trunk The trunk is the straight part of the vine that extends up from the rootstock and turns into the head. Transporting water and nutrients from the roots up to the head, cordons, and canopy is the main function of the trunk.

Rootstock The rootstock is the portion of the vine that extends into the ground and pulls water, nutrients, and minerals out of the soil. For most *Vitis vinifera* vines, the trunk and vine are actually grafted onto the rootstock of another plant, typically of another species.

VARIETALS, MUTANTS, CROSSES, HYBRIDS, AND CLONES (OH MY!)

With agriculture being practiced on the *Vitis vinifera* vine over thousands of years, many different subspecies or **varietals** have been developed. In some wine-producing regions, wines are labeled by the specific grape that was used in their production. Chardonnay, Merlot, Zinfandel, and Sangiovese are all different *Vitis vinifera* varietals you might find on a label from California, for instance. Other winemaking regions label their wines by the name of the region itself, but there are almost always restrictions on the type of varietals they may plant in their vineyards.

Varietals or grape varieties are basically vines that produce grapes with distinct and unique characteristics. Estimates vary on the number of varietals of *Vitis vinifera* that are grown in the world today, but the figures are all quite high—usually between 3,500 and 10,000! There are several different ways that these varietals have been bred or have naturally evolved. Some varietals have been generated by simple genetic **mutation.** This is nothing more than a vine that has developed different characteristics, flavors, or qualities from an imperfect genetic reproduction. Many vines are prone to mutation, especially Pinot Noir. Pinot Grigio, Pinot Blanc, and Pinot Meunier are all different mutations of the Pinot Noir vine.

Other varietals are the result of crosses. The genetic crossing of two different varietals will generate what is known as a **cross.** If the pollen of one varietal is used to pollinate the flowers of another, the resulting seeds in the grapes produced through reproductive action will be different from the seeds of the two parent vines. They will have genetic material from both parents, but will be different from both parents as well. Some of the most important grapes used today are crosses. Cabernet Sauvignon is a cross between Cabernet Franc and Sauvignon Blanc. Pinotage is a cross between Pinot Noir and Cinsaut. Crosses can happen in nature, but grape scientists and viticulturalists have produced most of the crosses that are commercially viable.

A **hybrid** is similar to a cross, except that the two plants involved are of different but related species. In wine regions of the east coast of the United States, it is not uncommon to see hybrids planted in wine vineyards. Several different hybrids were developed in the late 1800s and early 1900s between *Vitis vinifera* vines and heartier native American grape species to produce vines that could survive rough conditions yet still produce quality wines. Most hybrids produce inferior wines, but there are a few quality exceptions such as Seyval Blanc and Vidal Blanc.

Clones may bring up images of dark laboratories and mad scientists, but in the winemaking world, a clone is nothing to be afraid of. A clone is basically a vine that is an exact DNA copy of another, achieved through asexual reproduction. Most grapevines you see in vineyards start as cuttings from existing vines that are propagated into new plants. The new vines are copies of the old vines, or clones.

Many varietals have several different clones, and some have hundreds or more.

Clonal selection involves selecting the best genetic material available for the varietal you wish to use, and propagating it in your vineyard. Some clones are used because they produce certain flavors, while others are chosen for their ability to withstand certain climate and soil conditions.

SEASONAL CYCLE OF THE VINE

The *Vitis vinifera* vine is a perennial plant that goes through a growing cycle each year in which it forms leaves, flowers, and fruit in the warm growing period, and then dies back after the fruit has matured. The next year the cycle will repeat itself. This cycle is dependent upon and revolves around the different seasons.

Dormancy During the cold winter months, a grapevine is dormant. There are no outward signs of growth or life, but that does not mean that things are not occurring inside the vine. If the ground is not frozen, the vine will pull water and nutrients from the soil, building up energy for the spring when new growth will form.

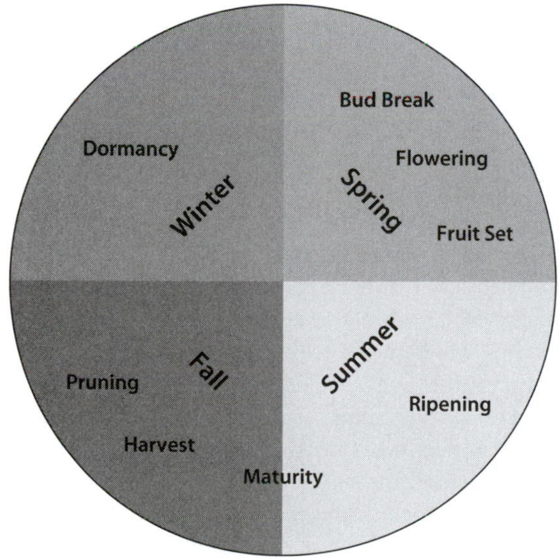

The seasonal cycle of a grapevine.

Bud Break This is the period when buds begin to form on either the head or the cordons of a vine. Bud break is the first outward sign of life after dormancy and occurs when temperatures begin to rise in the spring. These buds will eventually turn into shoots that form leaves within a few weeks. These leaves will allow the vine to speed up growth as photosynthesis begins.

Flowering Several weeks or even a couple of months after bud break begins, tender green tendrils will grow off of the shoots in between the leaves and will form a branched cluster of small flowers called a ***panicle***. These small flowers will then self-pollinate. Strong winds, heavy rains, or extreme temperatures will have a detrimental effect on the pollination.

Fruit Set Once the flowers have pollinated, each individual flower will form a small grape. This is the stage called fruit set, which usually occurs in late spring. When first developing, these baby grapes will be hard, tiny, and green. They will contain only minimal amounts of sugar and have extremely high levels of acid.

Ripening As the small grapes begin to grow larger, sugars, flavor compounds, and water will begin to form inside. A little over a month after fruit set, the grapes will go through a change called ***veraison***. This is when the color of the grape changes and turns red for varietals with pigment in their skin, and the grapes soften, allowing for the flow of water and sugar from the leaves. As sunlight hits the leaves of the vine, photosynthesis creates sugar in the plant, which starts sending it to the grapes. As the grapes begin to ripen, sugar builds in the grapes and the high acidity starts to drop out.

Ripening is one of the most important aspects of viticulture and will affect three of the major characteristics of a finished wine:

- Acidity in grapes translates into acidity in a finished wine, which can be felt on the palate and tasted. The less ripe a grape, the higher acidity the resulting wine will have.

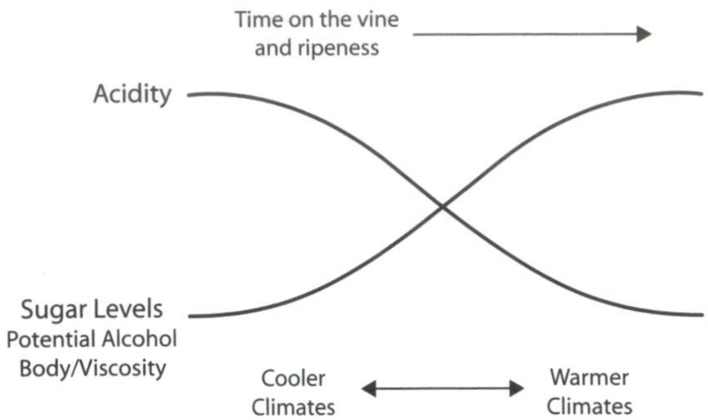

The inverse relationship between sugar and acid during ripening.

- At the same time, sugars in a grape will eventually be converted into alcohol through fermentation. The more sugar found in the grapes, the more potential alcohol can be produced in a resulting wine.
- Sugar and other compounds dissolved in the juice of a grape also contribute to the density or thickness of the juice. Riper grapes have thicker juice and will produce a thicker or heavier wine.

Grapes grow riper the longer they are allowed to hang on the vine, and this period is referred to as **hang time.** The length of the ripening period will be determined mostly by climatic conditions, with warmer climates allowing for longer hang time and cooler climates dramatically shortening the ripening period. Therefore, if the same type of vine was planted in two different climates, the grapes grown and ripened in the cooler climate would have much higher acidity, lower alcohol content, and less body than the grapes of the same vine planted in a warmer climate. Understanding how ripeness and climate can impact characteristics in a wine is vital for wine tasting and analysis.

Maturity As the grapes become ripe, other physical changes will take place inside them as the seeds come to reproductive capacity. Flavors develop, pigments darken, and tannins mature and begin to soften. Many viticulturalists determine the time to **harvest** their vineyards based on these characteristics related to the physiological maturity of the grapes, rather than simply the sugar content. For instance, if a winemaker wanted to produce a red wine with softer tannins, he or she could allow the grapes to have a longer hang time. Full maturity usually occurs in the late summer to late autumn months, depending upon the climate of the region in which the grapevines are growing.

Rain or irrigation just before the harvest would be potentially damaging, as the roots would suck in this water and send it to the grapes. This would cause them to swell, diluting their sugar and flavor. A wine made from grapes in this condition would taste simple and watered down.

Once the grapes are deemed ready or nature forces a grower's hand, the grapes are harvested by cutting the bunches from the vine. The total time from bud break to harvest is typically four to six months.

After building up energy stores in the vine, leaves will drop from the vine and all of the new growth will turn from green to brown and begin to harden and become woody. Much of this new growth is often pruned or trimmed from the vine to protect the plant from damage over the winter and to encourage new growth to form during the next spring. The combination of the loss of foliage and cooling temperatures as winter approaches forces the vine back into a period of dormancy and the cycle begins again.

Wine grape vines can have incredibly long life spans during which they will produce grapes. It typically takes three to five years for a vine to completely establish itself and begin to produce commercial-quality fruit. From the ages of ten to thirty years, the vine will be in a period of prime production and will produce higher yields of fruit than at any other point in its life span. That said, wine grape vines can often live to be one hundred years old or more! Many wineries that make wines from older vines will label the wine with the designation "**Old Vines**" or, in French, ***Vielle Vignes.*** The actual age of the vines will sometimes be listed as well.

The World's Oldest Grapevine

According to the *Guinness Book of World Records,* the oldest living grapevine in the world is located in the city of Maribor, Slovenia. It is known simply as the "old vine," and genetics testing and other evidence have confirmed the fact that the vine is over four hundred years old! Each year, grapes from the vine are harvested, fermented, and bottled in tiny bottles to be given as ceremonial gifts from the city's government.

VINTAGE DATING

The annual growing cycle of vines is referred to as a **vintage** in the wine industry. If a wine is made from grapes that were harvested in the same year, it will almost always list a vintage year on the label. This year has nothing to do with the date the wine was made, produced, aged, or released—it simply refers to the year the grapes were grown and harvested.

A wine label listing a vintage: the year in which the grapes that produced this wine were harvested.

This vintage can tell you a lot about a wine. Obviously it lets you know how old the wine is, giving you an idea as to its maturity level depending upon the style. With a little research or knowledge, you can also ascertain what the climate was like during the vintage year in the region from which the wine came. Climate can have a major impact on the characteristics and quality of grapes, and this will affect the wine that is produced from them.

Some wines are bottled without a vintage date, and are referred to as **non-vintage** or NV for short. A more appropriate term might be "multi-vintage" as these are wines made from more than one year's harvest (a term that some winemakers in Champagne, France, are actually beginning to adopt). This is done in some cases to produce inexpensive wines, but some of the world's greatest wines are also non-vintage. Top examples of non-vintage wine include most Champagne, several styles of Port, and all Sherry.

Vintage Charts

Several groups and publications produce vintage charts. These are commonly tables that list the major wine-producing countries and regions of the world, and assign each a score or grade for every vintage based on overall growing conditions in that area for that year. These charts often go back several vintages and are a good tool to use when selecting or purchasing wine. Often, they will also list whether a wine from a certain vintage and region is ready to drink, should be aged for a longer period of time, or is past its prime. That said, vintage charts have their limits, as the abilities of a winemaker or grape grower can overcome a poor vintage, and bad wines can be produced in great vintages. A simple search of the term "vintage chart" will yield hundreds of examples on the Internet, or look in some of the more popular wine publications.

Agricultural Decisions and Practices

Viticulture involves making several agricultural decisions in a vineyard, including what type of grapes should be grown, how they will be grown and shaped as the plants mature, and how the vines should be maintained through their life cycle. Most of these decisions must be carried out using various viticultural practices, many of which have been developed and perfected over thousands of years. The competency of a grape grower or viticulturalist can be seen in how he or she utilizes judgment, scientific knowledge, the wisdom of experience, and technical skill to fully realize the potential of a vineyard.

GRAFTING AND PROPAGATION

The natural way for a *Vitis vinifera* vine to **propagate** is to grow from a seed. This is the way wild *Vitis vinifera* vines reproduce and form new plants in nature, and the way new vineyards were established for thousands of years. Modern viticulture takes a much different approach, called grafting. Grafting is an agricultural technique for propagating certain plants that involves taking a **cutting** from one plant and grafting or attaching it to another. In viticulture, this most commonly involves taking a cutting from a donor vine called a **mother vine** and attaching it to the rootstock of another plant, using a special V-shaped cut that fits both pieces firmly together. After a period of time, the two parts will eventually grow into one plant. If done correctly, there will be no noticeable difference in quality of the wine produced from the grafted vine's grapes.

Using this procedure, a grape grower can have the best of both worlds. A specific rootstock can be chosen or developed that is suited to the soil and climate conditions of a particular growing site. At the same time, the cutting selected for the graft can be chosen for the flavors or characteristics it can produce in a wine. Due to the fragile nature of *Vitis vinifera* rootstock when exposed to some pests and diseases, wine grapes are often grafted onto rootstock from similar but more resistant species of vines. Rootstock from native American grapevines is used throughout the world due to its resistance to certain pests, including an insect called *phylloxera* that threatened the existence of the *Vitis vinifera* species in the late 1800s (see page 23).

Grapevine nurseries have been established around the winemaking world to propagate vines. When planting vines in a vineyard, many growers will get the rootstock established first, before grafting cuttings to those rootstocks. This requires special tools and the hands of a surgeon to ensure that the graft takes. Because of this, most growers plant vines that have already been grafted at the nursery, called **bench grafted** vines.

TRAINING, TRELLISING, AND CANOPY MANAGEMENT

Once vines have been established in a vineyard, they are often trained or formed into a particular shape by attaching new growth to trellises and other structures. There are many reasons to train vines, most notably to control their rate of growth, exposure to the sun and air circulation around the vine, and to make it easier to access the vine and its grapes. In ancient times, vines would often be trained up trees to maximize their reach and production capacity while keeping them off the ground. If a vine is not trained, it will grow into a thick bush, often referred to as a bush vine.

Today, the most common means of **training** a vine is to use a trellis system. As the vine develops shoots, these can be trained along wires or stakes. After harvest, these shoots become hard and woody and make strong branches called cordons. New shoots can grow on these cordons in subsequent vintages.

The most common means of **trellising** involves creating a vine with a T-shape. This is done by planting posts at the end of vine rows and then running wires between them. As the vines grow and develop, the cordons are established on the wires. This will eventually result in a row of T-shaped vines that are easy to maintain and harvest. There are innumerable ways to train vines along trellises: from double Ts to V-shaped vines, or even just on tall sticks or posts planted into the ground next to each vine. The type

Young vines being trained along a wire trellis.

selected often depends on the vineyards, varietal, and growing conditions.

The canopy of a vine is made up of the leaves and shoots that shade and protect the grapes. **Canopy management** is an important task in most vineyards. It involves pruning the canopy to create a desired result. Pruning can occur after the harvest to prepare the vine for the next season's growth, or it can be done during the ripening period to maximize sun exposure of the grapes and ensure full ripening. A properly managed canopy will ensure a healthy vine and quality grapes.

FIGHTING PESTS AND DISEASE

One of the most important aspects of viticulture is maintaining healthy vines. Throughout history, several different insects, diseases, and fungi have wiped out entire vineyards—sometimes even whole regions. The *Vitis vinifera* vine has been bred for several characteristics over time, but very little of that had to do with resistance to pests and diseases.

There are a frightening number of different maladies and pests that would love to destroy a grapevine (e.g., *phylloxera*, see page 23). Viticulturalists practice several different methods to either eradicate or at least control these pests.

The simplest means of controlling some vineyard plagues is to practice responsible and commonsense viticulture. Humid conditions can provide

Insect Invader in California: The Glassy-Winged Sharpshooter

In the early 1990s, an insect called the glassy-winged sharpshooter was detected in Southern California. This leafhopping insect, native to the southeastern United States, has the ability to spread Pierce's disease to wine grape vines as it eats their foliage. Pierce's disease is a bacterial infection transmitted to the vine, for which there is no known cure. This invasion caused millions of dollars' worth of damage to vineyards in Southern California before finally being contained. The glassy-winged sharpshooter is just another example of the vulnerability of *Vitis vinifera* vines to pests.

the potential for mildews and fungus infestations. Simply trimming canopies to encourage airflow through the vines can mitigate this effect. Grafting of vines has also certainly helped in the battle against many dangerous insects. Rootstocks have been developed that can fight off or at least stand up to several of these pests.

Several different soil agents and chemical mixes have been developed to stop disease and microbial threats as well. Copper sulfate mixed with lime, known as Bordeaux mixture, is effective in stopping certain types of mildew and fungi that plague vines. Many different insecticides, fungicides, and antimicrobial agents—both chemical and natural—are utilized in vineyards throughout the world. One way or another, a viticulturalist must protect his or her vines.

Major Organic Certifying Bodies

Certified organic agriculture and viticulture are both highly regulated practices which must follow strict guidelines. There are several regulating bodies that certify vineyard operations and wineries as organic, and many major wine-producing countries have developed their own. Below is a list of some of the major certifying bodies (and the certifications they award) from around the world.

- International: ECOCERT—Certified Organic
- United States: United States Department of Agriculture—USDA Certified Organic
- France: French Ministry of Agriculture—Agriculture Biologique (AB) certification
- Australia: Biological Farmers of Australia—Australian Certified Organic (ACO)

ORGANIC, SUSTAINABLE, AND BIODYNAMIC VITICULTURE

With the modern popularity of organic and sustainable agriculture in the world today, it should come as no surprise that it impacts the wine world as well. Many wineries now produce and label wines as organic, made from organically grown grapes, sustainably grown, and biodynamic. The "greening" of the wine industry is a very present trend. Organic and other viticultural practices may seem like modern practices, but in reality they usually simply involve growing grapes the same way they have been grown for thousands of years—naturally.

The basics of **organic viticulture** involve growing vines and harvesting grapes without the use of chemical fertilizers, pesticides, or fungicides. These chemicals can have a toxic effect on many of the microorganisms that live in healthy, fertile soil, and can actually end up in a wine as a residue. Organic viticulture aims to build the soil by using natural fertilizers like manure and compost while discouraging insects, pests, and disease through natural means, such as planting certain crops in between the vines.

Wines can be labeled "made from organically grown grapes" if they were produced from grapes grown in this manner, but to be considered "organic" wines, these practices must also extend into the winery. For a wine to be considered "organic" or "made from organically grown grapes," the grape grower and/or winemaker must follow strict guidelines laid down by an official certification body. There are several different regional certifying bodies that can award organic certifications to wines and vineyards, each with its own detailed regulations.

Sustainable viticulture is very similar to organic grape growing, except that there are not as many strict regulations and definitions that control its practices. The main focus is on the overall environment of a vineyard, area, and region—taking advantage of the natural ecosystem and making the most of nonrenewable resources. Care is taken to protect and work in concert with the environment while still maintaining economic viability. There are no major certifying bodies for sustainable viticulture, so it is often a distinction that grape growers practice voluntarily and define themselves.

Another popular buzzword in viticulture today is **biodynamics.** This newly popular approach to viticulture traces its roots back to 1929, when an Austrian named Rudolph Steiner proposed unique techniques to be used in the vineyard. Biodynamic viticulture is similar to organic viticulture, except that it prescribes

Major Biodynamic Certifying Body

Biodynamic certification for viticulture and agriculture is highly regulated, and a vineyard operation must meet strict guidelines to receive this type of certification. There is one major certifying body and certification for biodynamics:
Demeter International—Certified Biodynamic.

that many vineyard activities, such as pruning and harvesting, be conducted according to the phases of the moon and planets. Several different soil additives are used during certain times of the year to build the health of the vineyards and improve the quality of the vines.

There is no evidence to support a clear increase in the quality of wines made through the use of organic, sustainably grown, biodynamic, or any other viticultural philosophies or practices. However, there is one definite positive effect: subscribing to any of these disciplines results in a grape grower getting to know his or her vineyards better. The more a grape grower knows and understands a vineyard, the greater chance he will have to bring out the best in it. And that can be proven to produce better wines.

STRESS AND OTHER FACTORS AFFECTING QUALITY

Several factors affect the quality of grapes a vine will produce, including the varietal chosen, clonal selection, proper maintenance of the vines and vineyard, and even the age of the vines. The growing conditions found in a vineyard site will also play a role in the quality of the grapes. Those conditions often determine the amount of **stress** a vine is under, and stress can be linked directly to quality.

Imagine a vine planted in ideal conditions: fertile soils, ample access to water, and a pleasant temperate climate. That vine would be growing in a low-stress environment. With no threats to survival, water, or nutrition, the vine would grow vigorously and would produce a large quantity of grapes.

Now think about another vine growing in a different vineyard or region. This time the vine is planted in a soil that weeds do not even want to grow in, it is an arid region and the vine gets water only when it rains, maybe there is harsh weather, or it might be planted on the side of a steep slope. Whatever its troubles, you now have a vine in a high-stress environment. This vine will focus much of its energy on survival, and will be able to produce only a low yield of grapes.

Which vine will produce a higher-quality wine? More often than not, the vine in the high-stress environment will make better wine. This is because both vines have the same relative amount of flavor to contribute to their grapes. The vine growing in the low-stress environment can produce many more grapes, and this flavor will be spread out amongst all of them. This will result in grape juice that seems diluted or watered down. Complex flavors may exist, but they will not be detected because they are in such small concentrations.

The vine growing in the high-stress environment, on the other hand, will have concentrated its entire flavor into just a small number of grapes. These grapes will be intensely flavored, and will produce wines that seem complex because the different flavor compounds are all in large concentrations. This will be the better wine.

Stress most often comes from the vineyard, and from the way growing conditions naturally limit yield. Many of the top vineyard sites in the world are areas in which no other crop besides grapevines could grow. Besides environmental factors that affect stress and quality, viticultural techniques can be used to create stress on vines. There are several ways this can be accomplished:

Dry Farming This is the practice of growing vines without using irrigation. Many areas that receive ample rainfall do not have to worry about irrigation, but in those regions that do, limiting irrigation water will put vines under very stressful conditions.

Old Vines The older a vine gets, the more its production slows. Wines made from old

Label Term: Old Vines

The term "Old Vines" or "Old Vine" is often found on labels of wine that are produced from older grapevines. While there are no official regulations governing the use of this term, most winemakers will only list it if the vines that produced the fruit for the wine are at least thirty-five years old. Below is a list of the term in other languages:

- *Vieille Vignes*—French
- *Vigna Vecchia*—Italian
- *Viñas Viejas*—Spanish
- *Alte Reben*—German

vines are typically more intense, complex, and concentrated than those from younger vines in the prime of their production.

Green Harvest If causing stress on vines is not possible, growers can simply lessen the yields themselves. The practice of green harvesting involves cutting off a percentage of a vine's grapes when they first form during or just after fruit set. This will force the vine to send energy, sugar, and flavor to the remaining grapes, concentrating their flavor.

Limiting yields to produce top-quality wines is a common practice in Europe, and it is catching on throughout the winemaking world. It does not make sense to cut off half your grapes or dry farm your vines if you are producing a simple bulk wine, but it is sometimes a necessity for premium wine production.

Terroir: The Taste of a Place

As discussed in Chapter 1, *terroir* is a French term which describes the unique taste of a specific place when discussing wine. The overall effect that a vineyard has on the vines growing there depends on the sum total of the environmental impacts on that vineyard. These impacts are mostly determined by nature and include climate, soil type and composition, and terrain. Human interaction can also impact *terroir*, but there is only so much a viticulturalist can do.

Every aspect of climate can affect the growing conditions of vines in a specific site. Even something as basic as the average temperature in a region can impact ripeness levels in grapes, which shape the acidity, alcohol, and body of a wine. Other weather influences include:

Rainfall How much does it rain and when does it rain during the year? Rains in the winter and spring are ideal for sparking vigorous growth, while rain in the summer months slows down ripening, and rain just before the harvest can waterlog the grapes and dilute their flavors.

Wind Strong winds force a vine to spend energy on developing a strong structure rather than ripening grapes. This will limit ripeness and maturity in grapes. During the spring, winds can cause a poor or varied fruit set as the flowers try to self-pollinate.

Fog and Cloud Cover Lack of sunlight in cool regions can cause ripening to become sluggish, resulting in underripe flavors in grapes. In warm climates it can regulate ripening, allowing grapes to come to maturity at a more regulated pace and leading to better quality.

Daytime versus Nighttime Temperatures The combination of warm days and cool nights will also help regulate the ripening of grapes and allow them to develop better. Technically referred to as **diurnal temperature** variation, this difference allows grapes to develop sugar content and flavor concentration during the heat of the day, while maintaining a balanced acidity as the grapes cool down at night.

If the dirt you grew plants in did not matter, then why would they sell potting soil? The answer is that the type and physical composition of the soil you grow plants in does matter. Soil type and composition can also have huge impacts on *terroir*:

Drainage If a vineyard has clay soil that holds onto moisture, it will have more access to water than a vineyard with sandy soil, where the water will quickly drain away. Drainage can contribute to vigorous growth of a vine or it can limit that growth, based on the amount of irrigation vines receive. In a vineyard with clay soil, vines will receive more water and will grow more vigorously, while vines planted in sandy soil will struggle due to lack of water.

Fertility The more nutrients found in a soil, the faster the vines planted in that soil will grow and the more vigorous they will be. In commercial vineyards producing a vast quantity of wines, fertile soils equal larger yields. Many premium wines from around the world are planted in nutrient-deficient soil for just the opposite effect. The soil will cause the vine to struggle, producing fewer but more flavorful grapes.

Physical Makeup The minerals and trace elements that comprise different types of soil will impact growing conditions and flavors in grapes. The wine grape has an interesting ability to pick up the flavors of certain minerals and translate them into your glass. Rieslings can be very different in flavor based on the type of soil in which they are planted. Most of the vineyards of Burgundy, France, are planted on a special type of limestone soil that gives them a unique, mineral flavor. Subsoils under the surface often come into play, as a vine can dig 50 to 60 feet down with its roots, looking for moisture and nutrients.

Surface Effects Soils do not only have an impact underground where the roots are located; what is on the surface matters as well. The chalk in the soil of Champagne, France causes the dirt there to be nearly white in color. This causes the soil to reflect the sun's rays back to the vines, helping to further ripen grapes in a cold climate. Many of the most highly prized vineyard sites in Germany are planted in slate soils. Slate is a black rock that absorbs energy from the sun all day and then rereleases it back to the vine in the cooler evening hours in the form of heat.

The terrain of a vineyard or growing site can also impact how the vines grown within it develop and ripen. Topography, shape, and location are all important aspects of vineyard sites, and many top wines are famous because of the terrain of their vineyards. Terrain can affect *terroir* in many ways, including:

Orientation Heat can help grapes ripen, but it is exposure to sunlight that does most of the work. Vines have been planted on or around slopes and hills for millennia, in an effort to minimize or maximize exposure to sunlight. The most highly prized vineyards in Germany are planted on the south-facing, steep slopes of river valleys to maximize sun exposure and generate more ripeness. Grape growers in warm climates often do just the opposite and plant their vines where direct sunlight can be partially blocked to avoid overripening their grapes.

Elevation There are a handful of wine grape vineyard sites near the equator, where conditions should be too hot for *Vitis vinifera* vines to survive. What they all have in common is that they are located at high elevations, where the climate is cooler.

Low-Lying Areas Valleys and low-lying areas are common places to establish vineyards and practice agriculture. One of the main reasons for this is that soils are almost always more

Argentina: Winemaking in the Sky

Most of the winemaking regions of Argentina are found high up in the Andes Mountains, one of the tallest mountain ranges in the world. It is not unusual to find vineyards planted at elevations of more than 3,000 feet, with an enterprising few winemakers planting them at over 5,000 feet above sea level. These heights keep vines out of the hot, muggy conditions found in the valleys below, allowing grapes to slowly ripen and maintain a balancing acidity.

fertile and moisture is more accessible in lower-lying areas, because nutrients in the soil and rainwater runoff will wash down from the higher areas that surround them. You never hear anybody talking about fertile mountaintops.

Large Bodies of Water Vineyard sites are often planted near oceans, seas, lakes, and rivers. The reason is not for the scenic views but rather for the tempering effects these large bodies of water have. Since water is denser than air, it heats up and cools down much more slowly. A large body of water will act like a layer of insulation, keeping temperatures from rising or lowering drastically.

Terroir is neither a guarantee of better wines nor a death sentence for a grape grower. Human interaction and viticultural practices can to a certain extent accentuate or diminish certain effects of *terroir.* A grape grower can always irrigate a vineyard that did not receive enough rainfall, or fertilize soils that lack nutrients. Leaf thinning can be used to mitigate too much exposure to sunlight, and planting trees and other large plants can block excessive winds.

A good grape grower should not seek to control *terroir,* but rather simply understand the *terroir* of his or her particular growing area and adapt to it. In large part, this is why the French are so successful at making good wines. They know their *terroir.*

Terroir is a French concept, and has been used to establish France's complex system of appellations, or regions of origin, and quality classifications known as the AOC laws. Basically, the quality of a wine is determined by where it is grown. Those areas that have historically been shown to produce top-quality and distinct wines have been given official boundaries and assigned their own unique designations. This is possible in France because grape growers have spent centuries studying the many vineyard areas throughout the country, and the ideal grapes are matched up to the conditions found in that particular place.

Summary

The art and science of viticulture has come a long way in nine thousand years. Never before in the history of winemaking have there been so many important varietals grown using such high-quality techniques and practices. The fact that wine is an agricultural product is often lost on wine drinkers, but what happens in the vineyard has as much to do with what ends up in the bottle as what happens in the winery.

Review Questions

1. The more stress a grapevine is under, the more grapes it will produce.
   - A. True
   - B. False

2. Grapes grown in a warm climate will produce wines with ______________ than a wine from a cool climate.
   - A. more acid and less alcohol
   - B. more acid and more alcohol
   - C. less acid and more alcohol
   - D. less acid and less alcohol

3. *Terroir,* when referring to wine, describes the unique "taste" of a specific place.
   - A. True
   - B. False

4. The name of the genus made up of grapes is called:
   - A. *Vinis*
   - B. *Vitis*
   - C. *Labrusca*
   - D. *Rotundifolia*

5. Although grapevines are in a period of prime production between ten and thirty years of age, they can live to well over one hundred years old.
   - A. True
   - B. False

6. The art and science of growing grapes is called viticulture.
   - A. True
   - B. False

7. A vintage date on a bottle of wine signifies the year the:
   A. wine was released
   B. wine finished fermenting
   C. wine finished oak aging
   D. grapes were harvested

Match the following terms to their proper definition.

8. Clone	A. Reproduction between two plants of the same species
9. Varietal	B. Reproduction between two plants of different species
10. Cross	C. A subspecies
11. Hybrid	D. An exact genetic copy

12. Attaching a plant to the rootstock of another is called ___________.
   A. training
   B. pruning
   C. green harvest
   D. grafting

Key Terms

self-pollinate	hybrid	maturity	training
temperate climate	clone	harvest	trellising
canopy	clonal selection	Old Vines	canopy management
grape clusters	dormancy	*Vielle Vignes*	organic viticulture
shoots	bud break	vintage	sustainable viticulture
canes	flowering	non-vintage (NV)	biodynamics
cordons	fruit set	propagation	stress
rootstock	ripening	cutting	dry farming
mutation	*veraison*	mother vine	green harvest
cross	hang time	bench grafted	diurnal temperature

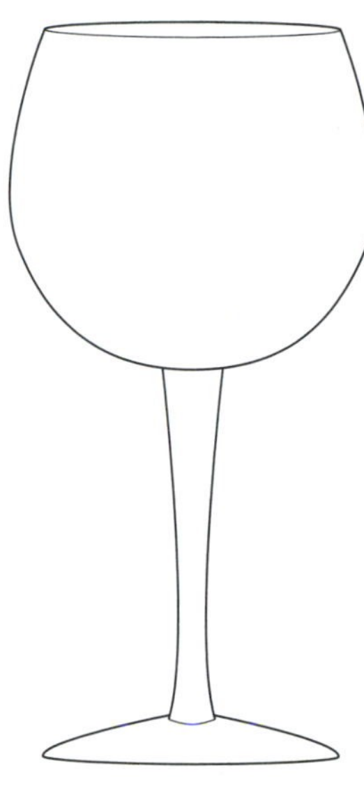

CHAPTER 4

Viniculture: The Art and Science of Making Wine

Wine is a living thing. It is made, not only of grapes and yeasts, but of skill and patience. When drinking it remember that to the making of that wine has gone, not only the labor and care of years, but the experience of centuries.

—**ALLAN SICHEL,** French author and wine merchant

Viniculture refers to the decisions made and procedures performed in the winery that help shape the flavors, quality, and characteristics of wines. This chapter will make the winemaking process easy to understand, explaining the path from grapes to glass for the three major styles of wine produced: table wines, sparkling wines, and fortified and dessert wines.

Table Wine Production

Table wine is the most commonly produced kind of wine in the world. It is often what most people refer to when they talk about wine. The term "table wine" means a wine that is mostly dry and still—that is, it contains little to no sugar when bottled and has no carbonation. A wide variety of different table wine styles exists and they can be white, red, or rosé. When used in this chapter, the term table wine should not be confused with the official quality classification of the same name found in most European countries.

A majority of the wines commercially available today fall into this category, and as a result, this will be the most detailed section of this chapter. The path that winemaking takes can be divided into six distinct stages: the harvest, grape processing, fermentation, bulk aging, clarification and conditioning, and bottle aging. This chapter will not go into great detail on the science and technology of winemaking, but rather will simplify and explain the major decisions winemakers make during the production of red, white, and blush wines, and their impacts on a finished wine.

THE HARVEST

Although often considered part of viticulture or grape growing, the harvest is also where viniculture begins. Technically, the harvest involves picking the grapes for a particular wine or from a particular vineyard when they are ripe. This, however, is a very simplistic view, considering how many of wines' characteristics are dependent upon the ripeness of the grapes used.

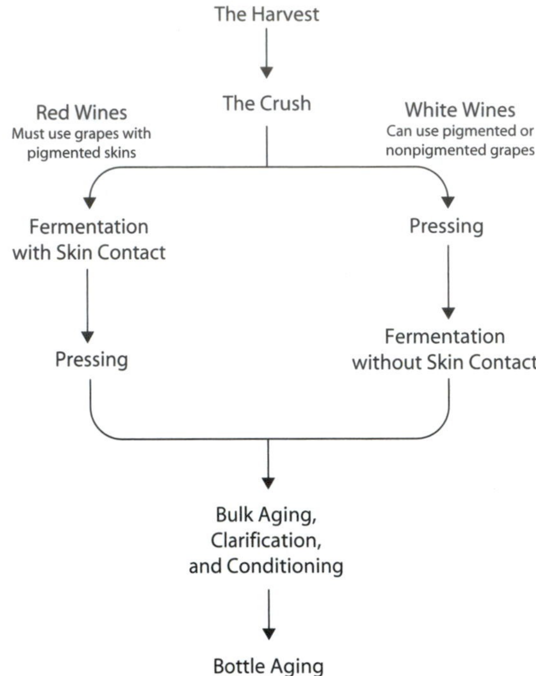

The stages of table wine production.

To Pick or Not to Pick—That Is the Question!

One major question must be asked prior to the harvest, and that is: How ripe is *ripe*? Ripeness is a matter of personal (and in this case, professional) preference; and two winemakers could have completely different views on when grapes are ripe. Maybe the winemaker's vineyards are in a warm climate where overripeness can be a problem, and he or she intends to produce a wine that still has some natural acidity in it. If that is the case, that winemaker's idea of ripeness might be harvesting the grapes early, prior to massive drops in natural grape acids. Those grapes are ripe to that winemaker, but other winemakers might consider those grapes underripe.

If a winemaker wanted to produce a higher-alcohol, full-bodied wine in a cooler environment, he or she would need to allow the grapes more hang time in the vineyards to ensure more buildup of sugar in the grapes. These grapes would be ripe to that particular winemaker; however, other winemakers in that region might consider those grapes overripe.

What will answer the question, how ripe is *ripe*? is the style of wine that is being produced. Most winemakers would like to work backward here, first deciding on the style of wine they hope to produce, and then using the characteristics of this envisioned wine to guide them in determining the optimum ripeness they need in their grapes. This is great if the winemaker owns or controls the vineyards. But if the wine is being made from grapes the winemaker has purchased from a third-party grape grower, the style of wine will need to be determined by how ripe those purchased grapes are when they are delivered. This is one reason that wines produced from estate-grown fruit (grapes grown in vineyards the winemaker owns or controls) tend to be higher in quality than those that are not.

Hand Harvest versus Mechanical Harvest

Once the optimum ripeness has been achieved in the vineyards, the true work of the harvest begins. The grapes must be picked from the vines and transported to the winery for the winemaking process to continue. How those grapes are to be picked, though, can also have large ramifications on a finished wine.

There are two basic methods of harvesting grapes: **hand harvesting** and **mechanical harvesting.** Hand harvesting consists of workers moving through a vineyard and picking bunches of grapes, which are then graded, sorted, and sent to the winery. If quality is the ultimate goal of a winemaker, then hand harvesting is the best method to employ. Hand harvesting involves using people with eyes and brains, moving through the vineyard to pick grapes. They can make decisions about what to pick and what not to pick as the harvest is conducted, ensuring that only those grapes that are ready to be picked are cut from the vines. Some of the vineyards responsible for extremely high-quality wines can be harvested more than once (in some cases vineyards can be harvested nine or ten separate times), in which case only perfect grapes are selected to be picked each time. This results in the highest-quality raw materials for winemaking.

Hand harvesting does have its drawbacks, however. Those workers going through a vineyard need to be paid for their services, and a slow, methodical harvest is not very efficient. If efficiency is the goal (often the case for large commercial wineries simply because of the large number of vineyards that need to be harvested), then hand harvesting may not be practical. Similarly, if economic control is a concern (for example, many Australian wineries will not utilize hand harvesting because minimum wage there is over $15 an hour), then another method needs to be utilized to harvest vineyards: a mechanical harvest.

A mechanical harvest is one in which a piece of farming equipment is used to remove the grapes from the vines. This is typically done with a modified tractor that has arms that reach out and grab the vines, shaking them and causing the bunches of grapes on the vine to fall to the ground. These bunches can then be gathered up into bins and sent off to the winery.

There are major drawbacks to this method—damaged or bruised fruit, and gathering underripe and rotten grape bunches as well as sticks, rocks, and other matter. However, it is very fast and efficient, and it involves much less labor and money than hand harvesting. Again, depending on the style of wine being produced, each winemaker decides which method to utilize, unless the decision is made for them out in the vineyard—uneven terrain, for example, would prohibit the use of farm machinery; while thousands of acres of vines would make hand harvesting impractical. Regardless of the method used, though, once the harvest has been completed the grapes are taken to the winery, and the next stage of the winemaking process, the crush, begins.

PROCESSING THE GRAPES

Once the grapes have been harvested and delivered to the winery, they are classified, weighed, and sorted, and final quality-control checks are made before they are crushed. It is at this point that we start to see major differences between the ways white wines, red wines, and rosé or blush wines are produced.

The Crush

Once sorted, the first step in processing grapes for wine production is **crushing.** This process usually consists of gently breaking the skins of the grapes to release their juices in a piece of equipment called a crusher. The resulting mixture of grape juice and grape solids (such as the skins, stems, seeds, and pulp) is referred to as **must.** For most red wines and a few whites, the stems of the grapes or grape bunches will also be removed at this point using a crusher equipped with a destemmer. The destemmer removes large particles (mostly stems) while the must is being produced. These stems contain large concentrations of tannins and, often, green-vegetable flavors.

Great care is usually taken at this point to avoid excessive **oxidation,** which could degrade the quality of the must. Oxidation is the result of oxygen acting on a substance. Think about how the color, flavor, and aroma of an apple's flesh can be affected when the apple is cut in half and allowed to sit out on a counter, exposed to oxygen. Winemakers use different techniques to slow oxidation, such as chilling the must because oxidation works much more slowly at colder temperatures. Regardless, most winemakers work quickly to process the grapes into must and then begin **fermentation.**

Sulfites

While sulfites are naturally occurring compounds found in most grapes, many winemakers add sulfites—mostly in the form of sulfur dioxide powder—to the grapes just prior to crushing or to the must after crushing, to act as a preservative, slow oxidation, and inhibit the growth and metabolism of unwanted microorganisms such as bacteria and wild yeasts. This is often done when the winemaker plans to use a cultured yeast strain to conduct his or her fermentation. Sulfite warnings appear on wines sold in the United States when they contain more than 10 parts-per-million of sulfites, because there is a small percentage of the population that is extremely allergic to them.

Foot Treading: Stomping the Grapes

Besides the mechanical method, another possibility exists for crushing grapes, although it is not commonly used today, and that is foot treading. Foot treading consists of placing the harvested grapes into large, shallow vats called *lagares* and having workers remove their socks and shoes, roll up their pants, and systematically march back and forth over the grapes, slowly crushing them and exposing their juices.

While it was common in the past, foot treading has mostly been abandoned in favor of using far more efficient mechanical crushers. Foot treading may be gentler to the grapes than using a crusher, but it is much less efficient and allows excessive oxidation to occur. The only wine that is still almost always produced through foot treading is vintage Port. Because it is a sweet red dessert wine, it is best to limit the amount of tannins and bitter compounds extracted from the grape skins for a vintage Port wine.

Processing Must for White Wine Production

Since the juice of nearly all grapes is clear, white wines can be produced from grapes with or without pigments in their skins. It is absolutely possible to produce a white wine from black-skinned grapes, as long as the skins are removed before the juice begins to extract pigment. While not common, there are some classic white wines produced from grapes that have pigment in their skins. Pinot Grigio, also known as Pinot Gris, is one example. It is not uncommon for Pinot Grigio grapes to be partially or fully pigmented; however, this varietal is almost always produced in a white style. Most Champagne is actually produced from black-skinned grapes, even though the vast majority of Champagne is considered white wine. How is this possible? The skins are removed from the juice quickly using a process called **pressing.**

The process of pressing for white wines involves removing the grape juice from the solid matter—skins, stems, seeds, and pulp. Pressing usually occurs immediately after the grapes are crushed for most white wines. Regardless of whether black- or white-skinned grapes are being used, the skins must be removed before fermentation for white wines, to limit the amount of tannins, bitter flavor compounds, and pigments that can be extracted into the juice. Pressing is usually conducted in either a basket press or a bladder press.

Both a basket press and a bladder press serve to squeeze the must, releasing the juices. A basket press is a vessel into which the must is placed, and then a wooden or metal plate is slowly lowered down into the vessel using a screw drive. This will eventually squeeze all of the juice through a grate located at the bottom of the press, which allows the now clear juice to leak out, while holding back the grape solids. A bladder press works in much the same way, except that an inflatable bladder (basically, a large balloon) at the top of the press is filled with air, slowly expanding, filling the space in the press, and squeezing the juice away from the solids. Because they handle the grape solids more gently, causing them less damage and therefore leaching less bitterness and tannins into the juice, bladder presses are becoming a more popular option today.

After this clear juice is collected, fermentation of a white wine begins as yeast (either residual wild yeast from the skins of the grapes or cultured yeast introduced to the clear juice) begins to ferment the sugars into alcohol and carbon dioxide.

There are a few exceptions to the way this processing can take place for white wines. Some top-quality white wines are made from free-run juice. This is the juice that simply runs through the grate at the bottom of the press before any pressure is applied to the must. This juice will produce wines with softer characteristics and pure flavors because very little of the bitter flavor compounds or tannins from the grape solids will be dissolved into it. In some cases, if a winemaker is using very aromatic white-skinned grape varieties or trying to produce a more full-flavored white wine, the juice may be allowed to remain in contact with the grape solids for a short period of time. After this period, the juice is pressed away from its solids and moved on to the fermentation tanks.

Processing Must for Red Wine Production

When producing a red wine, a winemaker has to use black-skinned grapes. The only place where grapes contain pigment is in their skins, and without these dark-colored skins, it would be impossible to produce a red wine. Therefore, fermentation commences for a red wine immediately after crushing occurs, with the must still containing the skins, seeds, pulp, and sometimes stems, mixed together with the grape juice. As fermentation begins, pigments (as well as tannins and flavor compounds) are leached from the skins and other solids, causing a wine produced in this manner to become colored. Since red wines need the pigments, tannins, and bitter compounds from the skins and other solid particles, pressing of red wine occurs either well into or after the process of fermentation, which helps to extract these compounds.

In a nutshell, that is the primary difference between the production of white wines and red wines: red wines are fermented with skin contact and white wines are fermented without. Following this stage of processing the grapes, whites and reds return to the same path, so, in a way, this stage is what truly defines the type of wine being produced.

Processing Must for Rosé or Blush Wine Production

Rosé or blush wines, like red wines, must be produced from black-skinned grapes. The process for producing most rosés begins very much like the process for producing a red wine. After crushing, either the grape juice is allowed to stay in contact with the solid particles of the grape (the skins) for a short period, or fermentation is commenced with the skins included, allowing the pigment to be extracted. Once the appropriate pink color has been achieved in the juice or in the fermenting wine, the must is pressed so that no further pigments (or other compounds) can be extracted. The rosé is fermented in exactly the same way as a white wine from this point, with no contact with grape solids, until fermentation is completed. So, in effect, most rosés begin like a red wine and finish like a white wine.

Two other possibilities exist for producing rosé wines: a process known as *saignée* or "bleeding," and blending. The *saignée* method produces a rosé wine as a byproduct of red wine production. If a winemaker wishes to impart more tannins and stronger flavors to a red wine, he or she can bleed off some of the pink-colored wine during the early periods of fermentation. This increases the grape solid–to-juice ratio for the red wine, producing a more vibrantly colored, tannic, and strongly flavored red wine. The pink-colored wine that was bled off is then fermented separately into a rosé wine. Blending, on the other hand, is simply mixing a portion of red wine into a white wine to impart color. This method is rarely used today.

Where to Find the World's Best Rosé Wines

Most Americans think about the pink, sweet White Zinfandels of California when rosé wines are mentioned, but these blush wines are often nothing more than simple and cheap. Most wine experts would agree that the world's greatest rosés are produced in southern France. Here, winemakers specialize in dry, sometimes even slightly tannic rosé wines with complexity, elegance, and character. Several wine regions in Languedoc-Roussillon, the Rhône Valley, and Provence are quite famous for their rosé wines.

FERMENTATION: TURNING GRAPE JUICE INTO WINE

Regardless of how the grapes were processed, once they have gone through this stage they are quickly moved to fermentation tanks and the next stage of winemaking—fermentation—commences.

Fermentation itself is one of the most important aspects of the winemaking process—it is what converts grape juice into wine. The process, as detailed in Chapter 1, is very simple. Sugars in the grape juice are consumed by yeast cells, and as the yeast uses the energy from these sugars to asexually reproduce, it excretes the waste products of ethanol and carbon dioxide. Heat is also generated as this active biochemical process occurs. As with most of the steps in winemaking, fermentation is a simple process that entails very complex decisions on the part of the winemaker to produce the best wine possible.

Wild Yeast versus Cultured Yeast

One of the biggest decisions a winemaker needs to make about the fermentation process is how it should occur. Wild yeast clings to the skins of wine grapes as they grow, and this yeast can be used to ferment the wine. However, many winemakers choose instead to use cultured yeast purchased from a laboratory to conduct their fermentations. If wild yeast is naturally occurring and does not cost anything, why would a winemaker choose to buy a yeast strain and use that to conduct the fermentation? The best answer is control.

There are literally thousands of different yeast strains found in nature, and each of them will produce different characteristics in a wine. An obvious reason to select a cultured yeast strain instead of using wild yeast is flavor. Other reasons include the potential lack of enough yeast cells to quickly begin fermentation, and the presence of bacteria or other microorganisms along with the natural yeast, which could negatively impact the fermentation. Remember, the only ingredient used to produce a wine other than grape juice is yeast, so this can be an extremely important decision. For the most part, wild yeast is more widely used in Europe, where thousands of years of winemaking tradition have led to the identification of beneficial yeast strains. Outside of Europe, a lack of tradition and a focus on technology and science lead to the heavier use of cultured yeast.

Fermentation Temperature

Besides deciding which yeast to use when conducting fermentation, another major winemaking decision is the temperature at which that fermentation will take place. The metabolic activity of the yeast generates heat, which, if not controlled, can rise to levels at which off flavors can be generated in the wine. Fermentation is simply a controlled form of spoilage, after all. If the heat is not controlled, the fermentation can become too vigorous and produce foul-tasting compounds. Winemakers typically control the heat of fermenting wine by conducting the fermentation in temperature-controlled tanks, vats, or rooms. A winemaker can and should determine the temperature at which fermentation will be conducted, because even a few degrees difference can have major impacts on the flavor and characteristics of a finished wine.

Yeast is a living organism, and most yeast strains will tolerate only certain temperature ranges. For premium wine production, this temperature range will usually fall somewhere between 50°F and 95°F. Temperatures below 50°F will cause the yeast to go dormant and stop fermentation, while above 95°F the yeast will create spoilage flavors.

Warm fermentations are often concluded quickly, lasting only a week or two. Cool fermentations progress more slowly, lasting from two weeks to a month or more. Cooler fermentations are conducted from roughly 50°F to 60°F, where the yeast metabolizes sugar slowly, producing very few and slight fermentation flavors. This is the practice typically used for delicate white wines that could be masked or muddled by the addition of flavor. More robust whites and almost all reds are fermented at warmer temperatures, from 60°F to 95°F. Warm fermentations cause the yeast to rapidly metabolize sugar, extracting more components from grape skins and solids for red wines, and often creating fruity flavors and alcoholic notes for reds and whites. For a strongly flavored wine, this additional flavor adds complexity.

Materials for Fermentation

The final major decision a winemaker needs to make is the type of material in which a wine will be fermented. Most wines go through fermentation in stainless-steel vessels because they are easy to clean and sanitize after use, will not react with the wine during fermentation, and are ideal for temperature control. For certain styles, especially California-style Chardonnays, fermentations are conducted in oak barrels. This is often done in temperature-controlled rooms or caves, and will impart strong, oaky flavors to a wine.

BULK AGING

Once fermentation has concluded, a winemaker has technically produced a wine. This wine is only at the beginning of the winemaking process, however, and may have to wait several months or years before it is finished and ready to drink. During much of this time, the wine will go through the stage of **bulk aging.** While the wine could be immediately bottled after fermentation, there are several reasons why it should spend a period aging in bulk first:

Maintaining Consistency Most wines are fermented in several vessels, not just one. Aging in bulk allows these different components to mix prior to bottling to maintain a consistent product.

Blending By aging in bulk, multiple wines from different vineyards, grape varieties, or winemaking practices can be allowed to develop on their own. At a certain point, their characteristics can be weighed and they will be blended together in certain proportions.

Allowing Flavors to Mellow/Mature Fermentation is an active biochemical reaction. When a wine comes out of fermentation, its flavors can be quite harsh and biting. Exposure to oxygen and/or time during bulk aging allows these characteristics to soften.

Harmonizing Flavors Think about potato salad: The first day a potato salad is made it is good, but it is always better the second day. Why? Because its flavors come together; they marry, meld, and harmonize. Aging a wine in bulk has the same effect.

Manipulating the Wine If a wine were bottled immediately after fermentation, the only thing that a winemaker could do to it is allow it to age in the bottle. Aging in bulk allows a winemaker to have access to the wine so that all manner of different winemaking practices can be employed, and it allows the wine to form sediment and be clarified.

The type of vessel used to age a wine and the materials used to make that vessel can also have a major impact on the taste of a finished wine.

Nonreactive versus Reactive Materials

One of the largest influences a winemaker can have on the flavors and characteristics of a wine is choosing the type of material the wine is aged in during the bulk aging stage. The two major categories of materials used for bulk aging are **nonreactive** and **reactive.**

A nonreactive material will not interact with a wine it comes in contact with. It will remain completely neutral, not adding any flavors or aromas. The most common nonreactive material used in wineries for bulk aging is stainless steel, although some winemakers use concrete vats, glass-lined tanks, or sometimes even wood barrels lined with paraffin wax or some other neutral sealant.

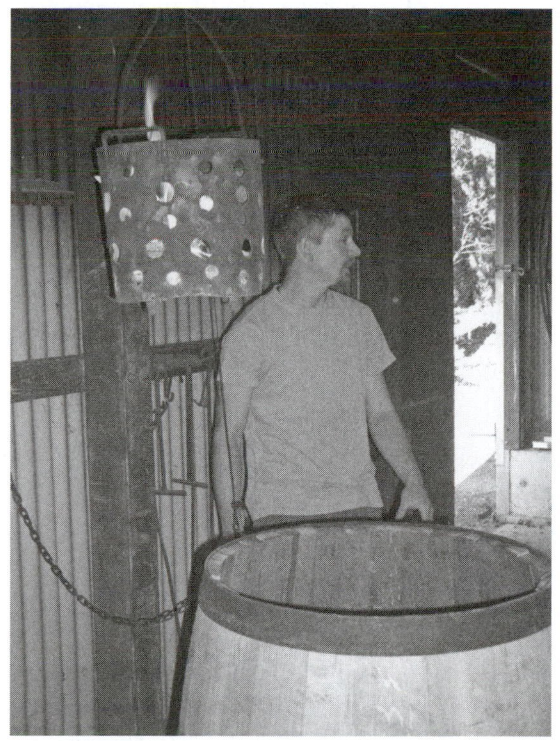

A cooper building an oak barrel for aging wine.

A reactive material, on the other hand, will interact with and react to wine it comes in contact with. It can change the aromas, flavors, and even color of a wine. The most common reactive material used in wineries for bulk aging is wood, usually in the form of oak barrels.

Therefore, the major decision involving bulk aging is whether to age the wine in oak barrels, stainless-steel tanks, or some other type of aging vessel. It is a misconception that all wines are aged in oak barrels, as a large percentage of wines will never see the inside of a barrel. This decision is most often made based on the style of wine being produced.

Oak can contribute strong flavors to a wine that can mask softer ones. Often, the freshness and fruitiness of a wine can be dulled if it is aged in oak. Generally, delicate white wines are the ideal candidates for aging in stainless steel or some other nonreactive material. More robustly flavored white wines and almost all reds will be aged in oak because they can stand up to the flavors that come from the barrel. **Oak aging** just adds to their complexity, complementing but not dominating other flavors. Wines aged in stainless steel are usually bottled much sooner than wines aged in oak barrels.

Oak Aging

Most wines that are aged in wooden barrels are aged in oak. Barrels made from wood were first utilized by ancient Roman winemakers to store and age wines. Chestnut, pine, redwood, apple wood, cherry wood, and even acacia have been and are still used to make wine barrels, but none of them have the same combination of properties that make oak such a viable material for aging and storing wine. Often these other woods will leach excessive tannins or off-putting flavors or colors into the wine. Through thousands of years of trial and error, oak has come to be the standard type of wood used to make wine barrels. There are three major reasons why:

Physical Properties Oak is a hard wood and can stand up to significant abuse. It is nonporous so it will not leak, yet it still allows a small amount of oxygen to permeate into the wine, causing a mellowing and maturing effect. It contains tannins, which can add texture and structure to wines, and it is malleable or flexible under the right conditions—an important fact, since the staves or boards that make up the rounded curves of a barrel are not carved into that shape, but bent into it.

Availability Old-growth oak forests and major barrel-making facilities (called cooperages) are found in two of the world's top four wine-producing countries: France and the United States. This means the barrels are made relatively close to where the wineries need them. Slovenia and a few other Eastern European regions also provide a comparatively inexpensive supply of oak barrels for winemaking, but these are not held in the same high esteem as French or American oak barrels.

Taste The most important reason that oak is used to make wine barrels is that it contributes positive flavor characteristics that are either leached from the wood itself or produced through the process of oxidation.

As for the flavors that oak aging contributes, they fall into two major categories: wood flavors and oxidation flavors. Wood flavors are attained by the wine coming into physical contact with the barrel, leaching compounds and flavors from the wood. These flavors can differ widely based on the type of wood used, the age of the barrel, and the skills and techniques of the cooper—the artisan who makes the wooden barrels.

> **Cooper**—An artisan who produces wooden barrels.
>
> **Cooperage**—Either the facility where wooden barrels are produced, or the art of barrel making.

The most common flavors from oak aging are those associated with the wood itself and with how the barrels are made. General wood flavors would include those reminiscent of oak, cedar, pencil shavings, sawdust, or a cigar box. Warm vanilla notes are also common, since oak contains some of the same compounds found in vanilla beans. Depending on where the oak for a

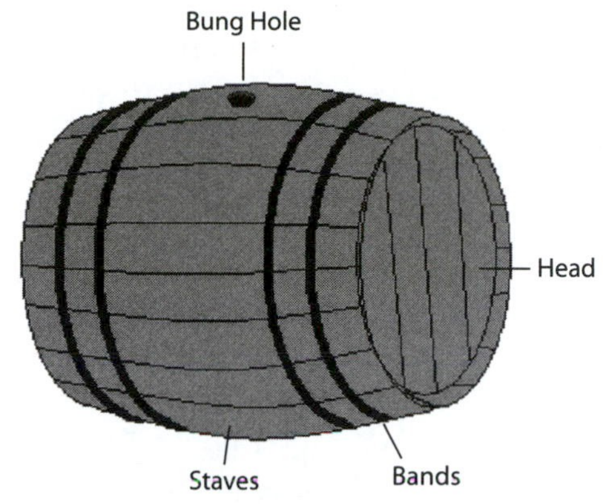

The anatomy of an oak barrel.

barrel is grown, it might contribute flavors such as cinnamon, cloves, nutmeg, black pepper, toasted coconut, or even dill.

The process of making a barrel can also play a role in the flavors it contributes. When bending the staves of a barrel into shape, they have to be heated—usually by steam on the outside of the barrel and direct fire on the inside. This will lightly to heavily toast the inside of the barrel, which can ultimately contribute to wood flavors like smoke, campfire, toasted bread or nuts, coffee, and/or dark chocolate.

Oxidation flavors do not come from the barrel itself, but from how the barrel is made. An oak barrel is made to be watertight, but not airtight. Over the course of a year, an oak barrel filled with wine can see anywhere from a 2 percent to a 5 percent loss due to evaporation. (The missing wine is called the "angel's share.") If wine can vaporize into a gas and escape from the barrel, that means that gasses can also get into the barrel—most importantly, oxygen.

Over time, oxygen will penetrate a barrel and begin oxidizing a wine. This will slowly change the color of a wine, as well as its flavors and aromas. Oxidation aromas in wine are usually reminiscent of caramelization—caramel, butterscotch, honey, brown sugar, burnt sugar, or even molasses. Depending upon style, these are generally considered positive characteristics. If a wine is allowed to overoxidize by spending too much time in a barrel it can pick up negative, stale characteristics.

As with most of the other steps in the winemaking process, a multitude of decisions must be made by a winemaker who decides to age his or her wines in oak barrels. The following are some of the more important decisions.

Factors Affecting the Strength and Type of Oak Flavors in Wine

Length of Aging Wines aged for longer periods of time in oak barrels will pick up more flavor than those aged for short periods. The longer a wine is in the barrel, the more it will draw out of the wood and be impacted by oxidation. Most wines are only aged for several months in oak, although some can be aged for many years or more, depending on style.

New Oak vs. Used Oak The fewer times a barrel is used, the more flavor it has to contribute. As a wine ages in an oak barrel, it pulls flavor from the insides of that barrel. Subsequent wines in the same barrel simply have much less access to flavor, as it has already been leached away. Crystals and other sediment deposits can also form inside a barrel (most commonly from tartaric acid in wine that converts into tartrate crystals), blocking the pores of the wood and further limiting the flavor compounds that the wine can access.

French Oak vs. American Oak Due to different growing conditions, the actual source of the wood used for a barrel can play into the types of flavors it might contribute. The two major sources of oak are France and the United States. French oak is far more commonly used for higher-quality wines. It contributes elegant vanilla notes and flavors of baking spices like cinnamon, cloves, and nutmeg. American oak is not as widely used in winemaking because it has more aggressive flavors like a strong vanilla character, toasted coconut, and dill. In some cases, winemakers will use barrels from sources other than France or the United States to age their wines, especially Slovenian oak barrels. These tend to be more neutral in character and affordable in price.

Barrel Size Oak barrels can range in size from just a few gallons to hundreds of gallons. Smaller barrels will impart stronger flavors than larger ones. Larger barrels contain so much volume that only a small percentage will ever come in contact with the wood, while small barrels have a much higher surface area–to-wine ratio. The standard-sized wine barrel most commonly used is called a ***barrique,*** and can hold 50 to 60 gallons of wine.

Level of Toast When an oak barrel is pieced together, the staves are often toasted on the inside while direct flames help to make the wood more flexible. The level to which a barrel is toasted can change the flavors it contributes. Slightly toasted barrels will give a wine flavors of toasted bread or nuts. Heavily toasted barrels might make a wine reminiscent of roasted coffee beans or dark chocolate.

CONDITIONING, CLARIFICATION, AND BLENDING

Conditioning, clarification, and blending processes most often occur near the end of bulk aging or after bulk aging is complete. However, they can also take place before or during the bulk aging stage, and in some cases even during fermentation. The different methods involved draw from a wide range of scientific applications and winemaking experience. These are the practices a winemaker has the most control over, and can significantly shape the characteristics and flavors of a finished wine.

Conditioning

The **conditioning** stage of the winemaking process involves manipulating a wine's characteristics through physical, chemical, and biological means. Several different techniques can be utilized, with the ultimate goal of accentuating certain characteristics and diminishing others. Conditioning most often occurs in or around the bulk aging stage, depending upon what method or methods are being employed.

Heavy manipulation of wines is most commonly practiced in non-European countries, which focus more on the science of winemaking than on tradition. Many European winemakers limit these practices (or they are limited by law) because they strive to show off what the land can produce more than their skills in winemaking. Below is a list of common conditioning practices, although many others are also used.

Important Conditioning Practices

Acidification Natural grape acids can be added to a wine to make it more acidic or to balance out residual sweetness.

Sur Lie* Aging/Aging on the Lees** After fermentation concludes, yeast cells can be suspended in the wine. When the wine is transferred to bulk aging vessels, this spent yeast, or **lees,** will eventually sink to the bottom of the vessel, forming sediment. Most wines will quickly be racked away from this sediment, but if allowed to remain in contact with the lees for an extended period, the wine is said to be aging ***sur lie, French for "on the lees." Wines that go through *sur lie* aging will often pick up rich earthy and nutty notes, and develop a creamy, thick mouthfeel. This is most commonly done for California-style Chardonnay and other white wines.

Battonage The practice of ***battonage*** is almost exactly the same as *sur lie* aging except that the lees are stirred periodically, causing the spent yeast cells to become suspended in the wine again. This accentuates the characteristics developed during *sur lie* aging.

Malolactic Fermentation A **malolactic fermentation** is a secondary fermentation caused by introducing a specialized bacteria strain into the wine (although it may naturally start on its own). This bacterium breaks down malic acid—the same tart acid found in green apples—into lactic acid, the much softer acid found in sour cream and milk. In addition, malolactic fermentation creates a biochemical compound called diacetyl—the same organic compound that gives butter its distinct flavor.

The purpose of this process is to soften the acidity of a wine and add rich, buttery flavors. Almost all reds go through malolactic fermentation, although it is more easily identified when used in white wines, especially those made with Chardonnay grapes.

Clarification

All wines should be clear, or free of suspended particles. Cloudiness or haziness is considered a major flaw, often a sign that the wine was poorly made and/or improperly stored. When analyzing a wine, clarity is the very first characteristic that needs to be assessed as an initial quality-control check.

The haze in wine is caused by suspended particles floating in the wine, too light to sink to the bottom. These can be spent yeast cells, grape solids, or even solid particles that form from liquid substances during aging. Regardless of what causes wines to be hazy or cloudy, clarity must be addressed by the winemaker, and several methods are used to clarify wine. During **clarification,** the winemaker will attempt to use the most gentle means possible, as clarification methods can also strip flavor out of a wine if too aggressively employed. Below is a list of the three most important clarification techniques.

Major Methods of Clarification

Racking As suspended particles in a wine settle to the bottom of the aging vessel, the wine above this sediment is gently transferred from that vessel to another, leaving the sediment behind. Over the course of time, many wines will lose all traces of cloudiness after racking. Racking is often done at the same time wine barrels are being topped up to replace wine lost due to evaporation. This is the most gentle and preferred method of clarification.

Fining Certain compounds (known as **fining agents**) have a tendency to bond with the suspended particles in a wine, forming larger particles. These are too heavy to remain suspended, so they sink to the bottom, forming sediment. This sediment is then removed the next time the wine is racked. Some of the most common fining agents used are egg whites, bentonite clay (a fine powder), Irish moss (freeze-dried seaweed flakes), and gelatin. Each removes haziness from a wine without leaving residual flavors. Fining is not the most aggressive way to clarify a wine, but some winemakers choose not to fine if they do not have to, because they feel it strips flavor from a wine.

Filtering Filtering a wine to clarify it is very aggressive and can strip significant amounts of flavor. Basically, the wine is forced through some sort of substrate (often diatomaceous earth, a fine powder which is commonly used to filter liquids) with openings large enough for the wine to pass through but too small for suspended particles, which it traps. Filtering is used only as a last resort for premium wines, or to ensure stabilization and consistency in bulk wines.

Blending

Successful winemaking often involves **blending** multiple components together into one finished wine. Blending is often regarded as an art form, and a serious palate and winemaking experience are necessary. All sorts of components can be blended together, including lots or batches of wine made using different grape varieties, vintages, winemaking practices, and zones of *terroir.* Most blending is conducted just prior to bottling, so the qualities of the different components can be assessed. The overall goal is to create a wine that is greater than the sum of its parts. Blending can be used to balance certain characteristics in a wine, to add complexity, or to maintain a consistent style over time. Many of the world's most important styles of wine are blends.

BOTTLE AGING

Once bulk aging comes to an end, the final blend has been determined, and all clarification and conditioning practices have been finished, the wine is bottled. This is usually done on a mechanized bottling line. Bottles are purged with an inert gas to expel oxygen, filled with wine to an exact level, sealed with a cork or other closure, and labeled. Although it is now in the final package it will be sold in, the wine still must go through the final stage of the winemaking process: **bottle aging.**

When bottled, the wine contains a small amount of dissolved oxygen. This oxygen will slowly interact with and oxidize the wine over time, mellowing and maturing it, while other components in the wine also impact one another. If the bottle is not opened at or prior to its peak of maturity, the oxygen will eventually break the wine down until it is overoxidized, its flavors are dull and stale, and it is considered dead.

The time it takes for a wine to reach its peak once it is bottled can vary widely. It depends upon several factors, including the type of grapes used, the climate in which the grapes were grown, the vintage they were harvested, the style of wine produced, and the winemaking practices used. The statement that "all wines get better with age" is not always true. Some wines require decades in the bottle to reach maturity, while others require only a short period of a couple of months or less.

Wine bottles being aged in a winery's cellar, slowly maturing before they are labeled and released.

What will determine the aging potential of a wine are the characteristics it possesses. The main characteristics that can increase this aging potential are high levels of acidity, alcohol, residual sugar (sweetness), and/or tannins. Each of these com-

How Long Should You Age a Wine?

Here are some examples of the aging potential of certain styles of wine.

WINE STYLE AND CHARACTERISTICS	AGING POTENTIAL
Dry white wine with low acidity and low alcohol content (e.g., Italian Prosecco, Portuguese Vinho Verde)	Months
Dry white wine with high acidity and low alcohol content (e.g., dry German Riesling, Italian Pinot Grigio)	1–3 years
Dry white wine with low acidity and high alcohol content (e.g., California or Australian Chardonnay)	1–3 years
Dry white wine with high acidity and high alcohol content (e.g., white Burgundy, Alsatian Riesling, vintage Champagne)	Several years
Semisweet white wine with low acidity (e.g., semisweet Gewürztraminer)	1–3 years
Semisweet white wine with high acidity (e.g., semisweet German Riesling, especially Kabinett and Spätlese)	Several years
Dessert white wine with low acidity (e.g., Italian Moscato d'Asti)	1–3 years
Dessert white wine with high acidity (e.g., German Trockenbeerenauslese, French Sauternes)	Decades
Dry red wine with low tannins, low acidity, and low alcohol content (e.g., French Beaujolais)	1–3 years
Dry red wine with low tannins, high acidity, and low alcohol content (e.g., red Burgundy, Oregon Pinot Noir)	Several years or more
Dry red wine with high tannins and high alcohol content (e.g., Italian Barolo, red Bordeaux, California Cabernet Sauvignon)	Decades
Fortified dessert wine with extreme sweetness and alcohol content (e.g. Madeira, vintage Port)	Decades

ponents acts as a natural preservative, slowing the maturation process down at a rate dependent on their concentration or presence.

Bottle aging used to be the responsibility of the consumer, and wineries would release wines for sale immediately after bottling. In today's world of instant gratification, however, this responsibility has shifted to the winemaker. Since the vast majority of wines are now consumed just a few days after purchase, winemakers know that they need to age their wines themselves to ensure that at least a minimal amount of maturity has been achieved. This is a winemaking decision that can have a major impact on the quality of wine when it is actually consumed. Released too early, wines might taste harsh and aggressive; too late, and they might pass their peak as they wait to be purchased.

As a result of these changing practices, wine is made differently today than in times past. Winemakers do not make any money on wine that sits in their cellars waiting to be released. Therefore, today wines are commonly made using various techniques that speed up the aging process, from extending the bulk aging stage to pumping pure oxygen into a wine before bottling. The faster a wine can go through bottle aging, the faster it can get to market. This means that most wines are not intended to be significantly aged above and beyond the bottle aging conducted at the winery. The vast majority of wines sold today will actually be ***negatively*** impacted by five or more additional years of aging!

Once the bottle aging stage is complete, the wines are packaged in cardboard boxes or wooden cases. They are often sold to brokers or distributors, and then sold to retailers, where they are finally purchased by the end consumer, and at long last the journey from grapes to glass is over.

Sparkling Wine Production

There are a wide variety of sparkling wines produced throughout the world. **Sparkling wine** contains dissolved carbon dioxide, which is released from the wine upon opening the bottle. The carbon dioxide causes sparkling wines to range from slightly fizzy (called ***pétillant*** in France and ***frizzante*** in Italy) to intensely frothy. The beginning of the production process is the same as that of a normal table wine. Once the still base wine has been produced, various methods are used to create and capture the carbon dioxide bubbles. The top methods include ***méthode champenoise,*** the **Charmat method,** the **transfer method,** and **force carbonation.**

A selection of sparkling wines from around the world.

MÉTHODE CHAMPENOISE

Champagne, produced in the Champagne region of northern France, is the world's best-known sparkling wine—and the method used to produce it has been adopted by most premium sparkling wineries. In Champagne, this production method is known as ***méthode champenoise,*** or the "Champagne method." In other areas of the world, it is called ***méthode traditionale*** (spelling variations include ***tradition*** and ***traditionelle***), the "traditional method," and is used for the production of Cava in Spain and most top California sparkling wines. It is considered the most natural and top-quality method for producing sparkling wines, and is made up of four basic stages: primary fermentation, secondary fermentation, **riddling**, and **disgorgement**. Sparkling wines made this way are sometimes labeled "Fermented in This Bottle."

Primary Fermentation: Creating a Base Wine

The first step in *méthode champenoise* is to create a base wine that is dry and still; that is, that contains no sugar or carbonation when the primary fermentation is completed. The overall goal of this stage is to create alcohol, and it is very similar to the production of a table wine. The grapes are crushed, pressed, and fermented, and the carbon dioxide is simply released into the atmosphere. Aging can take place in oak barrels or stainless-steel tanks. After the aging period has run its course, different component wines can be blended together to create the ***cuvée,*** or final base, for the sparkling wine.

Secondary Fermentation: Making Bubbles

After the base wine has been produced and blended, it is then poured into bottles. The bottle that is filled with the base wine will almost always be the same bottle that the wine will be sold in. A mixture of an exact amount of yeast and sugar, called ***liqueur de tirage,*** is then added to the bottle. The bottle is then capped off with a crown cap (similar to the caps used on beer bottles) and a secondary fermentation ensues.

This secondary fermentation is conducted to create the carbonation of the wine. As the yeast begins to consume the sugar from the *liqueur de tirage,* it will begin to produce a small amount of alcohol as well as a lot of carbon dioxide. The amount of sugar added will determine exactly how much carbon dioxide is produced. Since the carbon dioxide cannot escape from the bottle because it is capped off, the gas will begin to build up pressure in the bottle and eventually dissolve into the wine. There can be an incredible amount of pressure in a sparkling wine, typically 115 pounds per square inch (psi)—more than the amount of pressure found in the tire of an eighteen-wheeler! Once this secondary fermentation is completed, the sparkling wine has been produced, but still needs to be finished.

How Many Bubbles Are in a Bottle of Champagne?

The Champagne house called Bollinger has determined through careful measurement and advanced mathematics that there are roughly 56 million bubbles in a single bottle of Champagne!

After consuming all of the sugar from the *liqueur de tirage,* the yeast will eventually starve and die. These spent yeast cells will sink to the bottom of the bottle and form sediment, called lees. Similar to *sur lie* aging for table wines (although this is usually done in a large tank or barrel for table wines), many winemakers allow their wines to age in contact with the lees in the bottle, as it gives the resulting wines a creamy mouthfeel and adds rich, yeasty flavors. This is one of the main differences between wines made using the *méthode champenoise* and wines produced using other methods.

Once this aging period is over, the wine will be ready to drink, except for one major challenge: the spent yeast cells need to be removed from the bottle without losing the carbonation.

Riddling: Do the Twist

To remove the lees from a bottle of carbonated wine, this sediment is forced into a compact clump or "plug" that rests on the inside of the cap at the mouth of the bottle. Since the lees can stick to the inside of the bottle, forming this yeast plug is not as easy as simply turning the bottle upside down and waiting for gravity to do the work. Instead, the bottle must be kept in almost constant motion as the lees are slowly coaxed into the neck of the bottle.

Riddling (called *remuage* in French) is the means of forcing the yeast down into the neck of the bottle, and it can be a laborious process. Traditionally, the bottles are placed in ***pupitres*** (riddling racks) that resemble A-frame sandwich boards that have been drilled with holes just larger than the circumference of the neck of the bottle. Over time, the angle of these bottles is increased until they are eventually almost completely upside down. To ensure that the yeast does not stick during this gradual process, each bottle will receive a quarter twist daily until the yeast plug is formed.

While this hands-on approach is still widely used by traditional sparkling wineries, many conduct the riddling phase more quickly in a piece of equipment called a **gyropallet.** In a gyropallet, the bottles are stacked upside down and then slowly rocked back and forth. This causes the yeast to quickly slip down the insides of the bottle, forming a yeast plug in days rather than weeks. Regardless of how it is accomplished, once the yeast has been forced into the neck of the bottle and into a plug, it is ready to be removed.

Disgorgement: Finishing the Sparkling Wine

The final stage of *méthode champenoise* is disgorgement (*dégorgement* in French)—when the yeast plug is removed and the wine is made ready to age or sell. It begins by dipping the neck of the bottle into a freezing liquid, causing the wine that surrounds the yeast plug to freeze. When this wine turns to ice, it effectively prevents the yeast from falling back into the wine when the bottle is turned right side up.

Once the bottles are upright, the cap sealing the bottle is popped off. The pressure from the wine then forces the frozen yeast plug violently out of the bottle. Before the carbonation has an opportunity to escape, the wine is "dosed," which means liquid is added back to the bottle to the appropriate fill level before the bottle is corked. This **dosage** is referred to as ***liqueur d'expédition,*** and it is made up of still wine that will sometimes be blended with pure cane sugar. A sweetened dosage is how a sparkling winemaker produces a sweeter Champagne or sparkling wine, and is documented on the bottle with terms like *brut, extra dry,* and *doux,* depending upon how much sugar is added.

Following dosage, the bottle of sparkling wine is corked. Most sparkling wine bottles use a much larger cork than normal to help hold in the pressure. To ensure that the cork remains in the opening of the bottle, it is often attached with a wire cage that grips the cork and the extended rim around the neck of the bottle.

Sparkling Wine Bottles and Pressure

It is important to always take precautions when opening a bottle of sparkling wine, as there is often well over 100 pounds per square inch (psi) of pressure inside the bottle—corks have been clocked at speeds of over 100 miles per hour leaving bottles! This is why Champagne and sparkling wine bottles are made of thicker, heavier glass than other wine bottles; a special, larger cork is used to seal the bottle; and a wire cage must be utilized to hold the cork in the bottle.

THE CHARMAT METHOD

While the vast majority of the world's top sparkling wines are produced using *méthode champenoise/ traditionale*, there are several top-quality examples (and many poor examples) produced using the Charmat method. Sometimes called *cuve close* or the tank method, this is a much quicker and less expensive means of producing a sparkling wine. Some of the top examples of sparkling wines produced using the Charmat method include Prosecco, Asti, and Moscato d'Asti—Italy's most important sparkling wines—as well as German Sekt and many American sparkling wines.

The Charmat method is similar to *méthode champenoise* in that a double fermentation takes place: the first to make a base wine and the second to create carbonation. The major difference between the two is that for the Charmat method, the secondary fermentation takes place not in a bottle, but rather in large, pressurized, stainless-steel tanks. Once the secondary fermentation is completed, the wine is bottled under pressure to maintain its carbonation level.

The use of pressurized tanks means that the wine is not in close contact with the spent yeast once the fermentation is over, as it would be if the fermentation had taken place in the bottle. This method leads to wines that do not have a marked yeasty character; it is more about a pure expression of the fruit. The bubbles in a sparkling wine produced with the Charmat method are different as well. Instead of very tiny bubbles, the Charmat method produces larger bubbles which do not last as long.

TRANSFER METHOD

Although not as commonly utilized as it once was, the transfer method is another means of producing a sparkling wine. It is basically a variation of *méthode champenoise,* where a base wine is individually fermented inside the bottle. Once the secondary fermentation has concluded, the wine will often go through a bottle aging period before clarification begins, and the transfer method begins to alter course from *méthode champenoise*. Instead of riddling and disgorging the bottles to remove the spent yeast, the bottles are instead emptied into a pressurized vessel through a special process. This causes the wine from all of the bottles to be blended together. It is then clarified under pressure and then rebottled and dosed. Sparkling wines made in this fashion will often be labeled "Fermented in *The* Bottle" instead of "Fermented in *This* Bottle."

FORCE CARBONATION

The least desirable means of producing a sparkling wine is force carbonation. In this method, the carbonation is not created by the natural activity of yeast consuming sugar and producing carbon dioxide. Instead, a base wine is put into a large, stainless-steel tank that has carbon dioxide gas pumped into it under pressure. As the gas has nowhere to escape from the tank, it will eventually dissolve into the wine. Typically, only lower-quality sparkling wines are produced in this manner.

Fortified, Semisweet, Sweet, and Dessert Wine Production

There are several methods used to produce sweet wines and **dessert wines** in a multitude of different styles. What all these wines have in common is that they contain residual sugar. This can be natural sugar from the grapes retained through different winemaking techniques or sugar that is added to the wine after fermentation. For a wine to technically qualify as a dessert wine, it must contain at least 5 percent residual sugar, although sugar levels can reach much higher.

The most common styles of sweet wines and dessert wines and the methods used to produce them are discussed in this section, including: **fortified wines** (which are typically sweet but can also be dry), sweetened wines, **late harvest** wines, **botrytised** wines, and **ice wines.**

FORTIFIED WINES

Before the invention of the cork to seal wine bottles, the majority of the world's wines were fortified. The term "fortify" means to add something or make something stronger. In the case of fortified wines, this means that high-proof brandy is added to a wine. Brandy is the obvious choice of spirit for a fortification since it is distilled wine. This addition of a neutral, distilled spirit substantially boosts the alcohol content of a wine, increasing its shelf life and aging potential. These wines are often finished at anywhere from 15 percent alcohol by volume (abv) to 20 percent abv and beyond.

A selection of fortified wines.

Fortified wines range in style from bone dry to syrupy sweet, and are made in a variety of ways. The sweetness level is often determined by when the wine is fortified. To make a sweet fortified wine, the brandy is added at some point during fermentation. This raises the alcohol content to such a degree (usually 18 percent abv or more) that it kills all of the yeast fermenting the wine. With the yeast gone, the remaining natural sugar from the grapes is left behind to sweeten the wine. This is the manner in which Port is produced, as well as most Madeira and Marsala wines.

The brandy used to fortify a wine also can be added after the fermentation has been completed. This will result in a very dry, high-alcohol wine. Some sweet fortified wines are made in this manner and have concentrated grape juice added after fortification to act as a sweetener. Sherry is the top example of a fortified wine that is fortified after fermentation.

SWEETENED WINES

A wide variety of semisweet wines, and sometimes even dessert wines, are produced simply by adding sugar to the wine after fermentation has been completed. The most common sweetening source is unfermented grape juice added after the spent yeast has been removed from the wine. This is very common for semisweet wines in Germany, where this sweetener is called ***süssreserve,*** or "sweet reserve." Wines are commonly sweetened there and in other cold wine regions of the world in an attempt to mask high levels of acidity—think of adding sugar to lemon juice to make lemonade.

In some cases, dessert wines are produced by adding sweetness, but they are processed differently because plain grape juice is not sweet enough to add the sugar content necessary for a dessert wine. Instead, dessert wines are sweetened with unfermented grape juice that has been cooked down and concentrated into a rich, sweet syrup. Sweet styles of Sherry are sweetened using this method.

LATE HARVEST WINES

The term "late harvest" refers to wines made from grapes picked late in the ripening season, after most vineyards have already been harvested. This extra time on the vine allows higher-than-normal sugar levels to build up in the grape. The result is a base for either high-alcohol wines if fermentation is entirely completed, or more often for sweet wines that have their fermentations ended early to retain natural, residual sugar.

Sweet late harvest wines are produced widely around the world, often in cooler climates where normal ripeness is minimized. The natural acidity found in wines from these regions helps to balance out the residual sweetness. These wines often have concentrated, ripe fruit and honey flavors. Some of the more common grape varieties used to produce late harvest wines include Riesling, Gewürztraminer, and Sémillon.

Germany is famous for late harvest wines, and even has an official category for them called *Spätlese,* which literally translates to "late picked." In the Alsace region of France, wines made from late harvested grapes are labeled ***Vendange Tardive,*** which literally translates to "late harvest," although these wines are often fermented completely dry. In most non-European wine-producing countries, wines will simply be labeled "Late Harvest" or "Late Harvested."

Late harvest grapes also act as the base for other styles of dessert wines. Both botrytised wines and ice wines begin with late harvest level grapes, though in both cases something additional happens to those grapes to help concentrate their sugar levels even more.

BOTRYTISED WINES

For most wines, a vineyard full of grapes infected with a mold called ***Botrytis cinerea*** would mean disaster. If, on the other hand, botrytis infects certain types of ultraripe, thin-skinned grapes under perfect climate conditions, then a winemaker can produce some of the greatest and sweetest dessert wines in the world. Botrytis is a mold that lives in cool, moist climates, growing on and attacking produce. If you have ever had a gray, fuzzy mold grow on strawberries or other fruits in your refrigerator, then you have seen botrytis at work.

Often called "noble rot," botrytis forms on grapes left to overripen, eventually enveloping them completely. It begins to pierce the skin of the grapes, removing water from them. These now-shriveled grapes have a concentrated juice left behind that is rich in sugar content and flavor. Natural acids remaining in the grape juice serve to balance out the concentrated sugar. Once the grapes are crushed, this thick juice can be pressed away from the grape solids (including the botrytis clinging to the skins) and partially fermented to retain high amounts of residual sugar. Often, the resulting wines will be intense and elegant with flavors of ripe stone fruits and honey, as well as a sweet corn characteristic contributed by the botrytis itself.

In the United States and other regions outside of Europe, there has been an increase in production of botrytised wines, with some examples rivaling the best of Europe, although these are often produced from grapes that have been artificially infected with botrytis cultures. California and Australia currently lead the way in these styles of wines, using a wide range of grapes from Sémillon to Riesling.

Other Names for Noble Rot

Noble rot is known by many different names throughout Europe, where by law it must form naturally on grapes, and it is used to make some of that continent's best dessert wines:

- Called *pourriture noble* in France, noble rot is used to make the sweet white wines of Bordeaux, including the famous wines of Sauternes, as well as Alsatian wines labeled "Sélection de Grains Nobles."
- It is referred to as *Edelfäule* in Germany, where there are two official ripeness categories that can be produced from botrytised grapes: Beerenauslese (BA) and Trockenbeerenauslese (TBA).
- In Hungary, *Aszú* is the term for noble rot, and the sweet wines of Tokay are also made with botrytis-infected grapes—including Tokay Essencia, one of the sweetest wines in the world.

ICE WINES

Ice wine, called *Eiswein* in German, is a style of dessert wine produced from partially frozen late harvest grapes. Vineyards are often harvested at night for ice wine, when the temperature dips well below freezing. Due to their high sugar content, ultraripe grapes can be harvested in a partially frozen state, as much of the water content of the grape juice has turned into ice crystals. If the grapes can be crushed and pressed before they thaw, then the ice crystals will be removed along with the other grape solids. This will concentrate the sugar content, acidity, and flavor of the grape juice, creating a perfect base for producing a balanced, intense dessert wine.

Ice wines were first produced in Germany, and the country is still home to some of the best. An official ripeness category was established for these wines called *Eiswein,* and they are produced from late harvest level grapes that may or may not have been infected with botrytis. Besides Germany, other major ice wine producers include Austria and Canada, which produces more ice wine than any other country in the world today.

Summary

There are a dizzying number of different wine styles produced in the world, most of which are significantly impacted by the winemaking or vinicultural techniques used to produce them. Table wine is the most common style of wine, and its production follows a fairly consistent path, from harvesting and crushing grapes, to fermenting the grape juice into wine, to finishing the wine through aging and conditioning. Sparkling wines are also produced in a number of different ways, although the traditional production methods used to make Champagne are generally considered the best. Finally, wines can be sweetened using several different techniques, from adding high-proof brandy to concentrating the sugar of grapes in the vineyard. Viniculture truly is both an art and a science.

Review Questions

1. If a winemaker is producing a top-quality wine, which method would he or she most likely select to harvest the grapes?
   - A. Hand harvesting
   - B. Mechanical harvesting

2. The primary difference between the production of red wine and white wine is that:
   - A. red wines are fermented at cooler temperatures than white wines
   - B. red wines are aged in oak barrels and white wines are not
   - C. red wines are fermented with their skins, white wines without
   - D. red wines are fermented with wild yeasts, white wines with cultured yeasts

3. The stage of the winemaking process during which solids (such as skins, seeds, and stems) are separated from liquids (either juice or wine) is called:
   - A. pressing
   - B. crushing
   - C. fining
   - D. fruit set

4. White wines can be produced from red grapes.
   - A. True
   - B. False

5. All wines should be clear.
   - A. True
   - B. False

6. Which of the following characteristics in a wine will *not* prolong its aging potential?
   - A. Alcohol
   - B. Body
   - C. Tannins
   - D. Sugar

Match the following winemaking practices to their appropriate description.

7. Fining	A. Clarifying a wine by moving it away from sediment
8. *Sur lie* aging	B. Stirring up sediment and dead yeast cells
9. Racking	C. Adding a substance to a wine to remove cloudiness
10. *Battonage*	D. Allowing a wine to age in contact with its dead yeast

11. Sparkling wines made using *méthode champenoise* will ultimately go through two separate fermentations: one in bulk and one in the bottle.
    - A. True
    - B. False

12. Outside of the Champagne region of France, *méthode champenoise* is more correctly called ________.
    - A. the Charmat method
    - B. force carbonation
    - C. *méthode traditionale*
    - D. malolactic fermentation

13. Fortified wines are made stronger by:
    - A. the use of grapes affected by *phylloxera*
    - B. the addition of sugar
    - C. the addition of high-proof brandy
    - D. the addition of extra yeast

14. Botrytis is a:
    - A. special yeast strain used to produce sparkling wines
    - B. type of red-skinned grape grown in Germany
    - C. mold that attacks grapes and concentrates their sugar content
    - D. process of adding sugar to fermenting wine to boost alcohol

Key Terms

table wine
hand harvesting
mechanical harvesting
crushing
must
oxidation
fermentation
pressing
bulk aging
reactive
nonreactive
oak aging
new oak
used oak
French oak
American oak
barrique
conditioning
acidification
lees
sur lie aging
battonage
malolactic fermentation
clarification
racking
fining
fining agents
filtering
blending
bottle aging
sparkling wine
méthode champenoise
Charmat method
transfer method
force carbonation
méthode traditionale
riddling
disgorgement
cuvée
liqueur de tirage
pupitres
gyropallet
dosage
liqueur d'expédition
dessert wine
fortified wine
late harvest
Botrytis cinerea
botrytised
ice wine

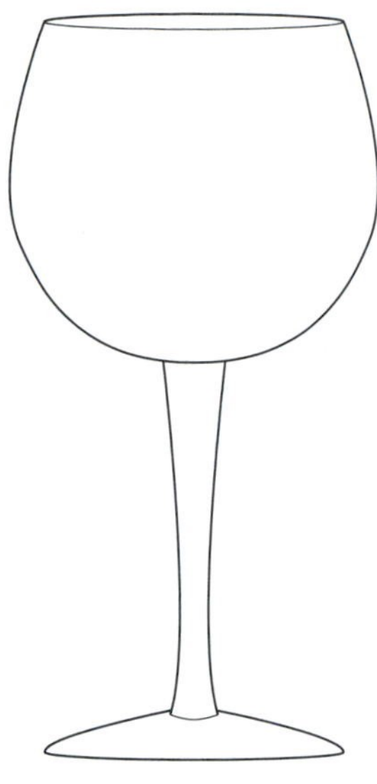

CHAPTER 5

Wine Grape Varieties

I am certain that the good Lord never intended grapes to be turned into grape jelly.

—**FIORELLO LA GUARDIA,** former Mayor of New York City

This chapter discusses the major characteristics of the world's most important wine grape varieties. It is estimated that there are between 3,500 and 10,000 varieties of *Vitis vinifera* that cover an enormous range of flavors and characteristics. This chapter focuses on the most prominent grape varieties that produce the world's best wines. The most important grapes that are grown widely around the world are discussed in detail, while other important regional grapes are also covered.

International Grape Varieties

There are literally thousands of wine grape varieties used to produce wine today, most of which were developed in various wine regions throughout Europe. Over the course of time, the vast majority of these grapes have continued to be planted solely in their native soil. Yet there are certain grape varieties that have gained international popularity and have been adopted in many other winemaking regions around the world. With the expansion of viticulture into the New World, important grape varieties had to be imported because there were no native *Vitis vinifera* vines in these regions.

We will refer to these grapes capable of producing world-class wines that are grown widely around the world as **international grape varieties.** There are eight international grape varieties, four that produce white wines and four that produce red wines. These eight grape varieties are **Riesling, Sauvignon Blanc, Pinot Gris/Grigio, Chardonnay, Pinot Noir, Syrah/Shiraz, Merlot,** and **Cabernet Sauvignon.** The following section discusses the characteristics found in the wines these grapes produce, as well as where they are successfully grown.

WHITE INTERNATIONAL GRAPE VARIETIES

Riesling

Common aliases: Johannisberg Riesling and White Riesling (some U.S. wineries).
Origin: Germany

Preferred growing conditions: Does best in cool to cold climates.
Body: Ranges from very light when made in a dry style, to thick and syrupy when made into a superripe dessert wine.
Acidity: Very high.
Style: Most tend to be dry to slightly sweet table wines, as many winemakers add a touch of sweetness to mask the high acidity of the grape. In certain conditions, however, it can be made into extremely sweet dessert wines.
Aging regime: Almost always aged in stainless steel and should not have characteristics of oak.
Varietal characteristics: Riesling is a grape that very effectively translates *terroir,* such that it does not have consistent varietal characteristics—it can range from heavily mineral to lush and fruity, depending upon growing conditions. If any generalizations can be made: younger Rieslings tend to show floral characteristics, while aged Rieslings tend to show honey and petrol (gasoline) notes.

The Riesling grape is considered the chameleon of the winemaking world for its ability to translate *terroir* and change characteristics based on where it is grown. This quality, along with the grape's natural affinity for food, make it a favorite amongst many wine professionals.

Stylistically, Rieslings can also vary widely—sweet or dry, slightly sparkling or still, table wine or dessert wine. It is one of the few grape varieties in the world that can produce both world-class sweet wines and dry wines. The one characteristic in Riesling that is always present—regardless of where it is grown or the style in which it is produced—is a central core of acidity.

Riesling traces its roots back to Germany more than five hundred years ago, and many of the best Riesling wines are still produced there. In the cool climate of Germany, Riesling grapes can produce ultralight, dry wines with piercing acidity. When climate conditions are right, they are capable of producing richer late harvest wines, and, in some cases, extremely decadent dessert wines that possess a balancing acidity.

The best Rieslings produced outside of Germany would arguably be those produced in the French wine region of Alsace. Located along the German border (in fact, Alsace used to be part of Germany), Alsace is home to mostly dry, fuller-bodied Rieslings than those in Germany. Besides Alsace, several other cool-climate wine regions in Europe grow the Riesling grape, most notably Austria. Outside of Europe, Riesling is quite popular in cooler wine regions. Top-quality Rieslings are produced in cooler areas of California, Washington State, New York State, Australia, New Zealand, and Canada. The prominent style in these areas is fruity and dry, though semisweet and dessert styles can also be produced.

Sauvignon Blanc

Common aliases: Fumé Blanc (California).
Origin: Disputed—both Bordeaux and the Loire Valley of France claim to be its place of origin.
Preferred growing conditions: Grows best in temperate to cool climates.
Body: Light to medium.
Acidity: Medium to high.
Style: Almost always made into dry table wines.
Aging regime: Can be aged in either oak or stainless steel depending upon the style of wine the winemaker is shooting for. Most French Sauvignon Blanc is made without the presence of oak.
Varietal characteristics: Grapefruit, tropical fruits, gooseberries, freshly cut green grass, herbs, and cat urine.

While the true origin of Sauvignon Blanc is unknown, it is a grape variety with very distinct varietal characteristics. It is generally produced into lighter-bodied, acidic, and dry white wines reminiscent of ripe grapefruit and gooseberries. The term *Sauvignon* is actually derived from the French word for "wild" or "savage"—a nod to the typical grassy and herbal notes often present in wines produced from this varietal. With its central core of acidity, Sauvignon Blanc is a wonderful accompaniment to a wide range of foods.

The top 100 percent Sauvignon Blanc–based wines are produced in the Loire Valley of France, most notably near two villages famous for the grape variety, Sancerre and Pouilly-Fumé. Loire Valley Sauvignon Blanc is the textbook version: light, clean, acidic, and intensely grassy and herbal. These wines are all aged in stainless steel or neutral oak to preserve the freshness of their flavor characteristics.

New Zealand produces their Sauvignon Blanc in a similar fashion, rarely allowing it to be aged in oak barrels. The unique *terroir* of this island nation produces white wines with bright grapefruit and tropical notes, which has made this grape the most important grown in that country. Worldwide vineyard acreage planted to Sauvignon Blanc was beginning to decline before New Zealand's versions gained international attention, reversing this trend.

California winemakers produce Sauvignon Blanc in two distinct styles. Many winemakers produce clean, light versions aged in neutral oak or stainless steel that focus on fruit flavors. Others approach it similarly to Chardonnay, heavily manipulating the grape by barrel fermenting and using new oak barrels for aging. Malolactic fermentation can also be used to soften up its acidity and to add a rich, buttery characteristic. Fumé Blanc is a term sometimes used in California for Sauvignon Blanc. Originally coined by famous California winemaker Robert Mondavi to denote his Sauvignon Blanc wines aged in oak barrels, the term was never trademarked. Since then it has become a legally approved synonym for the Sauvignon Blanc grape in California, and has been adopted by many wineries throughout the state for Sauvignon Blanc regardless of how it is aged.

Bordeaux is famous for its Sauvignon Blanc–based wines, although the grape is blended with other varietals. It is classically blended with the white Sémillon grape in the region to produce both dry and sweet styles of wine. In the subregions where Sauvignon Blanc plays the starring role in a blend, such as Graves and Pessac-Léognan, Sémillon is added to soften up the sharp acidity and add a roundness to the wine. In other areas like Sauternes and Barsac, where Sémillon is dominant, the classic style would be a sweet, botrytised dessert wine. In these wines, Sauvignon Blanc brings a vibrant, balancing acidity to the richness of the Sémillon.

Pinot Gris/Pinot Grigio

Common aliases: Rülander (Germany/Austria).
Origin: Burgundy, France.
Preferred growing conditions: Does best in temperate to cool climates.
Body: Light to medium.
Acidity: Medium to high.
Style: Mostly produced into dry table wines.
Aging regime: Wines labeled Pinot Gris will usually be aged in oak barrels, while those labeled Pinot Grigio are almost always aged in stainless steel or neutral barrels.
Varietal characteristics: *Pinot Gris:* ripe apples, peaches, almonds, cream; *Pinot Grigio:* green apples, citrus, minerals, and spice.

Although Pinot Gris and Pinot Grigio are two names for the same grape variety, there tend to be major style differences depending upon how the wine is labeled. Pinot Gris is the French name for the grape variety (Pinot Gris means the "Gray Pinot"), and the French style of producing this wine yields rounded, medium-bodied, oak-aged whites. Pinot Grigio is the Italian name for this grape variety (*grigio* is the Italian word for gray), and Italian-style Pinot Grigio tends to be crisper and higher in acidity, and is never aged in oak. For the most part, winemakers around the world will label their wines either Pinot Gris or Pinot Grigio based on the style that they emulate.

Pinot Gris/Grigio is a genetic mutation of the red-skinned Pinot Noir grape, although it is almost always produced into a white wine (there are a handful of rosé wines produced). In the vineyard, the grapes themselves can range from green to deep purple, even on the same vine! Because of these varying levels of pigmentation, winemakers produce white wines from the varietal by removing the skins prior to fermentation.

The grape originated in Burgundy, but it is no longer grown there; Alsace is actually the most

Pinot Grigio is Italy's top wine export to the United States.

important French region for Pinot Gris today. Alsace is home to the classic Pinot Gris style of the grape, which is also the style of choice in Germany, Oregon, and amongst most California producers. The classic Pinot Grigio style originated in northeastern Italy in the area of the ***Tre Venezie*** (the three neighboring regions of Veneto, Trentino-Alto Adige, and Friuli-Venezia Giulia). Italian Pinot Grigio is the most popular imported wine sold in the United States today.

Chardonnay

Common aliases: Morillon (Austria).
Origin: Burgundy, France.
Preferred growing conditions: Grown in almost every growing condition possible, although the best wines are grown in temperate to cool climates.
Body: Medium to full.
Acidity: Low to medium, depending upon style.
Style: Almost always made into dry table wines.
Aging regime: Almost always aged in oak.
Varietal characteristics: *Old World style:* citrus, green apples, olives, nuts, minerals; *New World style:* pears, apple pie, pineapples, toffee, butter, vanilla, and spice.

Chardonnay is the most popular white grape varietal sold in the United States, with more California Chardonnay being sold than any other white wine. The grape is grown in almost every wine-producing country in the world because it sells well and adapts to a wide variety of climates and conditions. Chardonnay-based wines tend to be fuller-bodied and softer in acidity than most other white wines. The grape's somewhat neutral characteristics lend themselves well to heavy manipulation in the winery, such as barrel fermentation, extreme oak aging, and malolactic fermentation.

The native homeland of Chardonnay is Burgundy, France, and it is decidedly the most important white grape still grown there, producing some of the world's best white wines. There are a variety of different Chardonnay styles produced in Burgundy. In the northern subregion of Chablis, the grape tends to produce lean, acidic, mineral-laden wines. In the Côte d'Or, considered the top Burgundy region for Chardonnay, the wines are rich and complex, with more pronounced oak characteristics. In southern Burgundy, the subregion of Pouilly-Fuissé produces a softer, fruitier style.

Chardonnay can also be used to produce sparkling wines, and is the only white grape variety that can legally be grown in the French region of Champagne. Here the grape never fully ripens as it does in Burgundy, and therefore it produces a very light and acidic wine that is used as a base for sparkling wine. When a Champagne is made from 100 percent Chardonnay grapes, it will be labeled "blanc de blanc"—a white wine made from white grapes. Chardonnay is also one of the top grapes used to produce sparkling wines in California, and is gaining popularity as a component in Spanish Cava.

Chardonnay is a grape that has spread far and wide from its native homeland of Burgundy, as evidenced by this Australian bottling.

California has become the world's second most important producer of Chardonnay after Burgundy. The top-selling style of white wine in the United States is California Chardonnay. The classical style of Chardonnay produced in California is soft, rich, oaky, and buttery, due to heavy manipulation in the winery. While this is the dominant style, many winemakers in California are beginning to take a less aggressive approach to the grape, similar to the winemaking techniques used in Burgundy. With a climate more similar to Burgundy than California, Oregon has also become a serious domestic producer of Chardonnay.

Various styles of Chardonnay are also produced in Australia, from rich and creamy to lean and unwooded. The top regions in the country for the grape are in western Australia and Victoria. Chardonnay is also grown well in all of the recognized wine regions of New Zealand, and is gaining popularity in South Africa, Argentina, and Chile.

RED INTERNATIONAL GRAPE VARIETIES

Pinot Noir

Common aliases: Spätburgunder (Germany and Austria), Pinot Nero (Italy).
Origin: Burgundy, France.
Preferred growing conditions: Does best in temperate to cool climates.
Body: Light to medium.
Acidity: Medium to high.
Pigmentation: Thin.
Tannins: Low.
Style: Dry red table wines.
Varietal characteristics: Cranberries, cherries, wet earth, tobacco, leather, smoke, spice, and barnyard.

Although Pinot Noir is one of the most finicky and notoriously difficult wine grape varieties to grow, it is widely planted because of its ability to produce superior-quality wines. These wines can be elegant and full of finesse, yet at the same time intense and concentrated. One of the greatest attributes of Pinot Noir is its ability to translate and showcase *terroir*—it truly speaks of the earth it was grown in. This ability has made wines produced from Pinot Noir grapes grown in ideal conditions some of the most sought after and expensive in the world, sometimes costing several thousand dollars a bottle.

Pinot Noir originated in the cool environments of Burgundy, located in central France. Due to its cooler origins, Pinot Noir is unlike any of the other red international grape varieties. A central core of acidity is what drives Pinot Noir, and makes it one of the world's most versatile wines with food. It ripens relatively quickly in a cooler environment, in part because the grapes have very thin skins in comparison to most other red grapes. This leads to wines that have minimal pigmentation and very soft tannins. While tannins are the foundation of many other red wines, acidity serves that purpose for Pinot Noir. This grape is rarely blended with others when producing a wine because it is so complex on its own. Besides bright red fruits, Pinot Noir is often quite smoky, spicy, and earthy.

With a natural tendency to mutate, Pinot Noir has spawned hundreds of different clones, and several different grape varietals. Mutations of Pinot Noir include Pinot Blanc, Pinot Gris (Grigio), and Pinot Meunier. There are even some grape scientists who believe that Chardonnay is a descendant of Pinot Noir.

Most wine experts would agree that, although it is widely planted, the top examples of Pinot Noir–based wines still come from the grape's native homeland of Burgundy, France. Burgundy's cool, continental climate, when combined with the unique, limestone-rich soil of the region, is ideal for growing Pinot Noir grapes. Many villages and vineyards throughout Burgundy have become famous for their versions of 100 percent Pinot Noir wines. Burgundian Pinot Noir tends to be very intense and complex at its best, with defining earthiness and often even barnyard characteristics. Some of the most legendary and expensive wines in the world are Pinot Noirs from Burgundy.

This grape is planted in significant acreage throughout other regions of France, but if there is an area in the country besides Burgundy that produces world-class wines with the Pinot Noir grape, it is Champagne. These wines bear little resemblance to the Pinot Noir–based wines of Burgundy; instead, in Champagne the grape is responsible for some of the world's best sparkling white and rosé wines. Pinot Noir has long been grown in Champagne; besides Chardonnay, the only other grape legally grown in the region is one of Pinot Noir's descendants, the red-skinned Pinot Meunier. Many of the Champagnes labeled "Blanc de Noirs" are made partially or wholly from Pinot Noir grapes. Pinot Noir is also turned into top-quality sparkling wines in cooler regions of California.

Pinot Noir has spread beyond the borders of Europe and has been readily adopted in several regions around the world, including California and Oregon in the United States and the island nation of New Zealand. These Pinot Noir wines tend to be more fruit driven, with soft hints of earth to help

A selection of California wines made from Pinot Noir grapes, an ideal varietal for cooler-climate regions.

balance them out. Often far riper than their French counterparts, they nonetheless speak of the vineyards in which they are grown. Several other wine regions around the world have begun to grow Pinot Noir in earnest, especially cooler areas of Australia and Chile—with exciting wines showing their promise.

Syrah/Shiraz

Common aliases: None.
Origin: The Rhône Valley, France.
Preferred growing conditions: Does best in warm to hot climates.
Body: Medium.
Acidity: Medium to low.
Pigmentation: Medium to thick.
Tannins: Moderate.
Style: Dry red table wines.
Varietal characteristics: Blackberries, raspberries, jam, leather, black pepper, smoke, and meaty/gamey.

Of all the international grape varietals, Syrah was developed in the warmest region. The Mediterranean climate of the Rhône Valley of southern France is the native homeland of this powerful, intense grape varietal. Syrah is also known as Shiraz in certain parts of the world, particularly South Africa and Australia. As evidenced by Pinot Gris/Grigio, it is not unusual for a grape to have more than one name—although it is unusual for more than one to be commonly used around the world.

Prior to modern DNA testing, there were many wine authorities and historians who argued that the Syrah grape actually originated in Persia, near the ancient city of Shiraz. It could have been brought to France by an ancient culture such as the Romans or even by returning French knights during the Crusades. All the while, the French argued that the grape was indigenous to France. DNA tests performed on Syrah proved that the French were indeed correct and that the varietal is a descendant of two obscure French grapes, Mondeuse Blanche and Dureza.

Syrah is a varietal capable of producing several styles of wine, although the two most important are leaner versions with intense earthy and almost meaty flavors, and fuller versions packed with opulent, superripe dark fruit. Syrah's affinity for warmer growing regions can lead to wines of higher alcohol and extract than many, although the structure of wines made from the grape are rarely over the top in terms of tannins and body. This makes for a wine that can be extremely powerful, yet approachable at the same time. Commonly blended with other grapes, Syrah adds richness and depth to many blends.

Some of the greatest Syrah-based wines produced today still come from its place of origin, the Rhône Valley of France. Separated from the Mediterranean coast of southern France by the region of Provence, the Rhône Valley is home to a warm, balmy climate in which this grape thrives. The northern regions of the Rhône Valley produce the most important examples of Syrah, and winemakers in these regions cannot legally grow any other red grape varietal. These wines tend to be powerful and deeply flavored with dark berries, fresh cracked peppercorns, and a smoky meatiness. Although also grown in the southern regions of the Rhône, Syrah is typically used there only as a component in blends of a large variety of other grapes.

Australia's warm, sunny climate has become a second home for Syrah, referred to as Shiraz in the land down under. This grape has had such success in Australia that today it is easily the country's most widely planted grape variety. Shiraz has seen a serious boom in popularity around the world due to Australian Shiraz, especially in the United States. The only foreign wine that U.S. wine drinkers consume more than Australian Shiraz is Italian Pinot Grigio! Shiraz in Australia is usually very ripe and loaded with jammy, berry fruit flavors.

Other regions of note growing Syrah/Shiraz are California and South Africa. In California, the grape is typically known as Syrah, and is capable of producing rich red wines. It is currently the fastest-growing grape varietal in California in terms of new acreage being planted. In South Africa, the grape is known as Shiraz, and it quickly took to this area's warmer climate. South Africa's Shiraz-based wines are leaner and more earthy in general than Australian or Californian versions, but at their best can exhibit the same intensity and power this grape is known for.

Merlot

Common aliases: None.
Origin: Bordeaux, France.
Preferred growing conditions: Widely grown in many climates due to its popularity, although it does best in temperate to warm climates.
Body: Medium to full.
Acidity: Low.
Pigmentation: Thick.
Tannins: Moderate to high.
Style: Dry red table wines.
Varietal characteristics: Blueberries, black cherries, plums, chocolate, spice, cedar, and vanilla.

Merlot is a grape that serves several purposes. It can be used as a base for some of the world's richest, most powerful, complex red wines. On the other hand, it can be made in a simple, fruity style meant for easy consumption. Regardless of style, however, Merlot is easily one of the world's most popular and recognizable grape varieties.

The name Merlot comes from the French word *merle,* which means "blackbird." This is a reference either to the grape's dark color when ripe, or to the propensity of blackbirds to feast upon ripened Merlot grapes when they migrate south for the winter in the region where the grape originated, Bordeaux, France. Bordeaux is home to a temperate climate, and this means that the Merlot grape, which came from this region, is rather adaptable to a wide variety of vineyard sites. Merlot is grown widely around the world, but unfortunately this is due to the grape's popularity, and not the particular conditions that are found in some of these regions. When matched up with the right conditions, and when grown in a serious manner, Merlot is capable of producing deeply concentrated red wines. Its thick skins can lend themselves to a highly tannic wine with a heavy amount of pigmentation. Often, Merlot showcases fruit in its youth, especially ripe, dark berries.

For intense structure and depth, Merlot is considered at its best when grown in the Right Bank area of Bordeaux, France. Located along the Atlantic coast, Bordeaux can be divided into two major regions: the Right Bank (eastern side) and the Left Bank (western side) of the Gironde River, which flows through the appellation. Merlot is better suited to the Right Bank of Bordeaux because the climate is slightly warmer and the soil is made up of rich clay. This area is where the most legendary Merlot-based wines in the world are produced. Fully structured and intense, these wines are built to last through significant aging. Merlot is also grown on the Left Bank of Bordeaux, but here it is often delegated to be a minority component of a blend, often dominated by Cabernet Sauvignon.

Merlot is also grown in many important wine regions outside of Bordeaux. California is home to some of the best, most serious Merlot in the world, although the grape is also commonly used in California to produce basic, fruity reds. Washington State has also planted significant amounts of Merlot, and because it has a more temperate climate than California, typically produces a drier, earthier style. Merlot is also widely planted in the wine regions of Chile, Argentina, Australia, South Africa, and even New Zealand. Many unique and critically acclaimed wines are being produced in Tuscany, Italy, where the grape is a favorite in nontraditional wines called super Tuscans. All evidence points to the lasting popularity and growing acreage of this grape variety.

Merlot is the most important grape grown in the French wine region of Saint-Émilion, a subregion of Bordeaux, where this variety originated.

Cabernet Sauvignon

Common aliases: None.
Origin: Bordeaux, France.
Preferred growing conditions: Grown in almost every growing condition possible, although the best wines are grown in temperate to warm climates.
Body: Full.
Acidity: Low to medium.
Pigmentation: Thick.
Tannins: High.
Style: Dry red table wines.
Varietal characteristics: Black currants, plums,

black cherries, mint, bell pepper, cedar, vanilla, and musty/wet dog.

Many would consider Cabernet Sauvignon to be the world's most important red grape variety. It is widely recognized, capable of producing world-class wines in a range of different wine regions, and fairly easy to grow. The grape is actually a result of a natural cross between two grape varietals indigenous to Bordeaux, France: Cabernet Franc and Sauvignon Blanc.

Cabernet Sauvignon–based wines are typically about two things: power and structure. This grape has very thick skin, which leads to wines with intense tannin levels and almost opaque pigmentation. These wines typically possess the dark, brooding fruit it acquired from its Cabernet Franc heritage, as well as herbal and vegetal notes that it gets from Sauvignon Blanc. The wines produced from Cabernet Sauvignon are often built to age for extended periods, as the tannins slowly soften and more complexity is achieved.

Blending is quite common when using Cabernet Sauvignon. In the most important forms of these blends, Cabernet Sauvignon plays the starring role and sets the foundation for the wine. Softer blending grapes, especially Merlot, are added to soften the edges of the blend and to add fruit. Cabernet Sauvignon can also be used to add power to blends when used in smaller portions or to make a wine heartier.

While the ultimate source for Cabernet Sauvignon can be debated, the most important region in the world for this grape has historically been its native homeland of Bordeaux, France. On the Left Bank of Bordeaux it finds a perfect combination of temperate climate and gravelly, well-draining soil. Here, Cabernet Sauvignon plays the starring role in some of the most famous wines produced on Earth. Merlot and other blending grapes are added to soften them up as mentioned above, but the structure and power of the Cabernet Sauvignon drives these wines. On the Right Bank of Bordeaux, the grape is often added to Merlot-based wines to lend tannins and structure.

Cabernet Sauvignon is the grape that made California winemaking famous, and is the most widely grown red wine grape variety in that state today. California Cabernet Sauvignon from the top appellations is capable of intense concentration, full tannins, and rich fruit. Many California producers blend small quantities of other grape varieties into their Cabernet Sauvignon–based wines (especially Merlot) in a similar fashion to the winemakers of Bordeaux. Although not as well known, the grape is also responsible for the most important wines of Washington State. The temperate climate of eastern Washington is ideal for the grape, and a style more similar to that of Bordeaux than California can be produced there.

In Chile's top wine regions, Cabernet Sauvignon was originally grown by transplanted French winemakers attempting to recreate the wines of their home. Although often simple and soft, Cabernet Sauvignon can produce intense and powerful wines in Chile. Argentina has also followed its South American neighbor's lead and grows significant amounts of good, and often great, Cabernet Sauvignon. Other areas for quality production of Cabernet Sauvignon include regions of Australia, South Africa, New Zealand, and Southern France.

Although Italy is an extremely traditional winemaking country with thousands of indigenous grape varietals, Cabernet Sauvignon has also found a home there. In Tuscany, the grape has long been used in small percentages in Sangiovese-based wines to add structure and richness, especially in Chianti and Chianti Classico. Realizing the quality of the Cabernet Sauvignon and its potential in the region, winemakers used this grape to lead the super-Tuscan revolution in the 1970s and 1980s, and it is now often used as the main grape in many of these nontraditional wines.

Other Important Grape Varieties

The international grape varieties are not the only grape varieties used to produce top-quality wines. There are dozens of other varietals capable of producing wines that are the equals of wines made from the international grapes, but that are limited to just one or a few different wine regions. The vast majority of wine grapes grown around the world fall into this category—for example, California's Zinfandel grape or Spain's Tempranillo. These important grape varieties produce a multitude of different wine styles and flavor profiles.

> The following grape icons appear throughout the book to identify which grape varietals produce red wines and which produce whites. Do not forget that in some cases, red-skinned grapes may be used to produce white wines. These grape icons identify the color of wine produced from each grape, not necessarily the color of the grapes themselves.

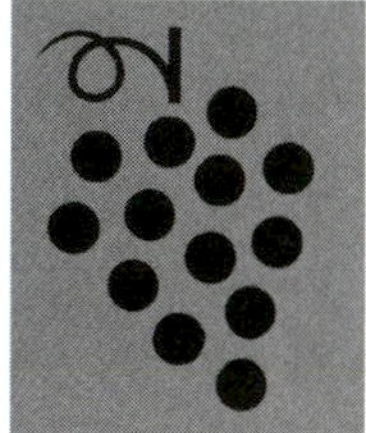

Red wine grapes.

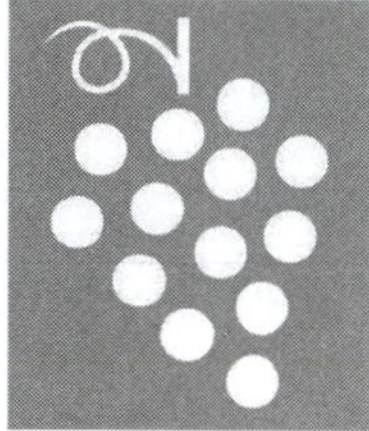

White wine grapes.

AGLIANICO Produces hearty and dense red wines in southern Italy, most importantly in a wine called Aglianico del Vulture.

ALBARIÑO Exciting white grape variety that has gained attention in northwestern Spain, producing dry, light-bodied, stainless-steel aged, fruit-forward wines, especially in the region of Rías Baixas. Also known as **Alvarinho** in Portugal.

ALIGOTÉ Lesser known and considered a second-rate white grape of Burgundy, where it is grown in small quantities to produce dry, crisp whites.

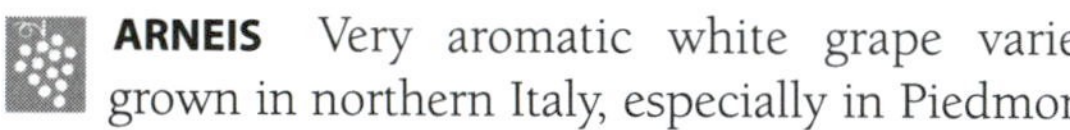

ARNEIS Very aromatic white grape variety grown in northern Italy, especially in Piedmont.

BARBERA Workhorse red grape variety grown throughout Italy and gaining acceptance in California. Barbera tends to produce wines of moderate body and tannins, good acidity, and red fruit flavors. It ranges in style from simple and rustic to extremely intense and complex. The best examples come from the northern Italian region of Piedmont, especially Barbera d'Alba and Barbera d'Asti.

BLAUFRÄNKISCH Light and fruity red grape variety grown in Austria, as well as in Germany and Washington State (both regions use the name **Lemberger**), and in Hungary (where it is known as **Kékfrankos**).

CABERNET FRANC One of the blending grapes of Bordeaux, this widely grown red grape is also produced as a single varietal. Cabernet Franc is one of the parents of Cabernet Sauvignon, and has similar body, power, and tannin structure to a light Cabernet Sauvignon wine. Often produces dry red wines reminiscent of dark fruit, green bell pepper, and herbs. Rarely plays a leading role in top red wines in Bordeaux and California, but rather is used as a blending grape to add complexity to Cabernet Sauvignon– and Merlot-based wines. The most important Cabernet Franc–based wines come from the Loire Valley of France, especially Chinon and Saumur. Also called Bouchet.

CARIGNAN Red grape variety producing rich, earthy, full-bodied red wines. Grown in Spain and in small quantities in California, but the best examples are found in southern France, especially Corbières.

CARMENÈRE Sometimes referred to as the "lost grape of Bordeaux," this powerful red grape used to be one of the most important grapes of Bordeaux. The *phylloxera* epidemic of the mid-1800s practically wiped the grape out in France, but some survived after being transplanted to Chile, where it is widely grown today. Carmenère produces structured wines with deep, dark fruit and earthy flavors. Also called **Grand Vidure.**

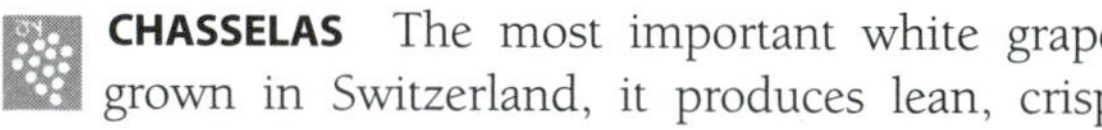

CHASSELAS The most important white grape grown in Switzerland, it produces lean, crisp white table wines. Significant acreage is planted in the Loire Valley of France as well. Also called Fendant.

CHENIN BLANC Important white grape variety that originated in the Loire Valley of France. The grape is used mostly to produce dry to slightly sweet table wines, depending upon the growing conditions from which the grapes were harvested. However, it can also produce extremely sweet dessert wines. Chenin Blanc wines tend toward fruity flavors such as melon, red apples, and tropical fruits, and the use of oak aging is kept to a minimum. The highest-quality wines still come from the Loire Valley, specifically Vouvray and Savennières. The grape was more widely grown than Chardonnay in California up until the 1980s, and is still widely grown there. The top-producing region for the grape today is actually South Africa, where the grape is sometimes called Steen.

CINSAUT/CINSAULT Red grape variety originated and still widely grown in southern France; produces earthy, smoky red table wines.

CORTESE White grape variety grown in the northwest Italian province of Piedmont; used to produce dry, crisp white table wines such as Gavi.

CORVINA Cool-climate red grape variety that produces smoky, earthy red wines in northeastern Italy, specifically Valpolicella in Veneto. Can produce powerful, high-extract wines when the grapes are dried and raisined prior to winemaking to produce a wine called Amarone della Valpolicella.

DOLCETTO Northern Italian red grape variety that produces soft, silky red wines reminiscent of ripe, red fruits. The best examples come from Piedmont, especially Dolcetto d'Alba.

FURMINT White grape variety capable of extreme ripeness levels and susceptible to botrytis. Most commonly used to produce lush, sweet, late harvest/botrytised wines, most famously Tokaji, in its native Hungary.

GAMAY The red grape variety of the French wine region of Beaujolais, Gamay produces light, fruity red wines that often exhibit floral notes. Although it is also grown in the Loire Valley, and is sometimes used as a minor blending grape in Burgundy, the very best Gamay is grown in top villages of Beaujolais. It is also the grape used to produce Beaujolais Nouveau wines: short-lived, extremely soft red wines intended to celebrate the French wine harvest each year.

GEWÜRZTRAMINER Extremely aromatic white grape variety that originated in northern Italy. The name refers to a "spicy" grape in German, and Gewürztraminer-based wines have a strong perfumed, spicy flavor profile reminiscent of lychee fruit, rose petals, and white pepper. It is primarily made into dry or slightly sweet table wine, although it can be produced in many different styles, even extremely sweet dessert wines. The best examples of Gewürztraminer are produced in Germany and in the French

Dolcetto is an important red wine grape grown in Piemonte (Piedmont), Italy, where these Dolcetto d'Alba wines were produced.

wine region of Alsace, although the grape has been adopted in California and Washington State.

GRENACHE This red grape variety originated in Spain (where it is called **Garnacha**), but was raised to its pinnacle in southern France. Grenache produces medium-bodied red wines that usually exhibit red fruit and strawberry jam characteristics, and also tend to have a high level of alcohol. It favors warmer climates and is often used in blends with other warm-climate grape varieties such as Syrah and Mourvèdre. It is the main grape used in the production of red wines in the southern Rhône Valley of France, most notably Châteauneuf-du-Pape and Côtes-du-Rhône. The grape is also widely grown in Provence, Rioja and Priorato, Spain, Australia, and California. Although most commonly used in blends, it is becoming more popular to use Grenache as a single varietal, especially if it comes from old vines. The grape is also used to produce some of the highest-quality rosé wines in the world (with the most classic example being Tavel from southern France) as well as fortified dessert wines (most notably the softly sweet Banyuls, also from southern France).

GRÜNER VELTLINER The most important grape variety in Austria, Grüner Veltliner produces light, dry to semisweet white wines reminiscent of lime zest and white pepper.

Spain is the native home for the Garnacha grape, known as Grenache in France.

LAMBRUSCO Rustic red grape variety grown in northern Italy, especially in Lombardy, where it is used to produce sweet, sparkling red wines.

MALBEC Although Malbec is seen merely as a workhorse blending grape in its native France, it is considered at its best when grown in Argentina. Malbec produces deeply colored, dense, structured red wines with flavors of dark fruits. In France, it is a minor blending grape in Bordeaux (where it is known as **Cot**) and is the main grape used to produce the dark, rich wines of Cahors (where it is known as **Auxerrois**).

MALVASIA Malvasia is actually a close-knit family of different grapes rather than one varietal. The grapes themselves can be white, pink, or red, and mostly produce soft, sweet wines. Grown throughout southern Italy.

MARSANNE Hefty white grape variety that favors warmer climates and produces soft, full-bodied white wines with ripe melon and stone fruit characteristics. Often blended with the Roussanne grape, Marsanne is most widely known for rich white wines from the northern Rhône Valley of France (where it can also be blended into red wines in small percentages to increase aromatics). Other areas for Marsanne production include California and Australia.

MAVRODAPHNE/MAVRODAFNI Important Greek grape variety used to produce sweet, fortified red wines in the region of Achaïa.

MELON DE BOURGOGNE White grape variety that produces very crisp, light-bodied wines. The most important wines produced from this grape come from the westernmost district of the Loire Valley of France called Muscadet.

MOURVÈDRE A powerful red grape variety producing dense, tannic wines with dark fruit and gamey characteristics. Mourvèdre is most commonly used in red blends, whether in the Grenache-based wines of the southern Rhône Valley, in the

G.S.M. wines of Australia along with Shiraz and Grenache, or in a variety of red wines from Provence. The most notable Mourvèdre-based wine comes from a region called Bandol in southern France.

MÜLLER-THURGAU Lower-quality German grape variety most commonly grown for mass-produced white wines. It is widely grown in Germany for its ability to ripen quickly and produce a lot of fruit in a cool climate. The main grape used for the German wine Liebfraumilch, Müller-Thurgau is also finding a small foothold in cooler regions of Oregon and Washington State.

MUSCADELLE A minor white blending grape grown in Bordeaux, where it is used in small percentages to add aroma to the dry wines and especially to the sweet, botrytised wines of the region. Muscadelle is also grown in Victoria, Australia, where it is used for thick, sweet fortified wines.

MUSCAT A collection of almost two hundred related grapes rather than a single grape variety, Muscat is one of the oldest grapes used for wine production today. Muscat grapes can range from deeply pigmented, dark-skinned grapes to completely white grapes on the vine, and can produce an array of different styles. While styles of Muscat can vary widely, most will be reminiscent of ripe, musky fruit and fresh grapes (this is one of the few wine grapes that produces wines that taste like grapes!), or, if fortified, dried fruit and raisins. The most important Muscat variety is called **Muscat Blanc à Petits Grains,** and it is responsible for most of the world's top-quality Muscat-based wines. This variety is known by several names around the world, including **Moscato** in northern Italy, **Brown Muscat** in Australia, and **Muscat Canelli** in California. Muscat can produce wines that vary from bone dry to syrupy sweet, and range in style from light table wines to sweet sparkling wines, to dense fortified wines. In the northwestern Italian region of Piedmont, it is the grape responsible for the sweet sparkling wines of Asti. In southern France, the grape is used to produce a variety of sweet wines that can sometimes be fortified, especially Muscat de Beaumes-de-Venise from the Rhône Valley. In the New World, Muscat is often used to produce late harvest wines and dense, dark fortified wines in California.

NEBBIOLO The name Nebbiolo means "little fog," and refers to the thick fog that forms in many of the vineyards of Piedmont, Italy, where this variety originated. This red grape is responsible for some of the most sought after and important wines produced in Italy today, including Barolo and Barbaresco. Wines produced from this grape variety tend to be rich and powerful, with high levels of acidity, alcohol, and especially tannins. Due to their tannic structure, wines produced from Nebbiolo grapes tend to see extended periods of oak aging. The grape, while responsible for world-class wines in Piedmont, has not been successfully grown in any other areas around the world, although many have attempted.

PALOMINO A white grape variety grown mostly in southern Spain that produces bland table wines but spectacular fortified wines. Palomino is the primary grape used in Jerez, Spain, for the production of Sherry.

PETITE SIRAH Although it is possible that Petite Sirah is a distant relative of the Syrah grape, the two should not be confused with one another. Petite Sirah is known as Durif in its native France, where it is considered a rustic, workhorse red grape variety. Most high-quality Petite Sirah is actually grown in California today, where it can be used to make red blends heartier or can be produced into a single varietal wine. The grape produces full-bodied, extremely deep-colored red wines with a powerful tannin structure, and a flavor profile reminiscent of ripe/cooked fruit and pepper.

PETIT VERDOT One of the blending grapes used for the production of red Bordeaux wines, Petit Verdot contributes color, tannin, and spicy flavors to these wines. While it is most commonly used around the world as a component in red wine blends, it is increasingly being used in the production of single varietal wines, especially in California.

PINOT BLANC This white grape variety is a relative of the Pinot Noir grape, and is generally used to make crisp, higher-acid table wines. Often compared to Chardonnay, the grape produces wines that are not as dense or complex, but that do exhibit fruity and aromatic characteristics. Pinot Blanc is grown in the French region of Alsace, in California, and in Italy (where it is known as Pinot Bianco).

PINOT MEUNIER A genetic mutation of Pinot Noir, this grape's name means the "miller's pinot," a reference to the fact that the underside of the vine's leaves are white and look like they have been dusted with flour. Although it is a red-skinned grape variety, it is most commonly used as a blending grape in the production of sparkling white wines, most notably Champagne.

PINOTAGE This red grape variety was developed for the South African wine industry in the 1920s, and is a genetic cross between Pinot Noir and Cinsaut (known as Hermitage in South Africa). Its production today is almost entirely limited to South Africa, where it produces lighter-bodied red wines that are often earthy and smoky.

PROSECCO White grape variety grown in the Veneto region of northeastern Italy, where it produces fruity, crisp sparkling wines of the same name.

ROUSSANNE A white grape variety that is at its best in warmer climates, Roussanne produces delicate wines that can often show flavors of peaches and other stone fruits. The grape is often blended with Marsanne and acts as a balance for that grape's heavy, musky flavors. Roussanne is also blended in small percentages into the red wines produced throughout the Rhône Valley of France (especially the reds of the northern Rhône and Châteauneuf-du-Pape in the southern Rhône), adding aroma and acidity. Winemakers in California and Australia are beginning to experiment with this grape.

SANGIOVESE The most widely grown grape in Italy and the most important in the region of Tuscany, this grape's name means "blood of Jupiter." Sangiovese is responsible for most of the top-quality red wines produced in Tuscany, including Chianti and Chianti Classico, and also provides the base for several super Tuscan wines. Two important clones of Sangiovese are used to produce other top Tuscan wines: **Brunello,** which is used in the production of Brunello di Montalcino, and **Prugnolo,** which is used to make Vino Nobile di Montepulciano. Wines made from Sangiovese are more acidic than they are tannic, and this is one of the reasons that they have such a natural affinity for food. On its own the grape will produce light- to medium-bodied wines that emphasize red fruit flavors and are reminiscent of clay and wet earth. It is commonly blended with heavier red grape varieties (including Cabernet Sauvignon) to make it heartier, richer, and more tannic. Sangiovese has in recent years become more popular in California, and interest is definitely growing.

SCHEUREBE One of the most widely planted white wine varietals in Germany, Scheurebe is a cross between Riesling and Sylvaner. The grape is similar to Riesling in many ways, but often lacks its complexity and purity of flavor. It can be used to produce everything from dry, fruity white wines to sweet, botrytised dessert wines.

SÉMILLON Sémillon is probably best known as one of the blending grapes for the production of white wines in Bordeaux, France. The grape is most commonly blended with Sauvignon Blanc, and is made into two distinct styles in Bordeaux. When used to produce dry table wines, it serves to round out and soften the blend. It can also be the dominant grape variety in the sweet, botrytised wines of Bordeaux, which are rich in honey and apricot flavors, especially Sauternes and Barsac. The grape is widely grown in other parts of the world, producing mostly neutral table wines except in Australia, where it is one of their most important white grapes and is capable of producing exciting, complex dry white wines.

SYLVANER A white grape variety grown throughout Germany, producing mostly simple, dry to semisweet table wines.

TANNAT A high-tannin red grape variety that produces rich, structured wines reminiscent of red fruits and jam. Tannat is grown in several regions of southern France, where it can be used as a component of a blend or as a single varietal (most notably Madiran). Some of the most exciting wines made from the grape, however, are now being produced in the South American country of Uruguay.

TEMPRANILLO The hearty red grape variety producing the top traditional red wines in Spain. Tempranillo produces red wines that can be intensely structured and long lived, and that have a natural affinity for oak aging. The wines are often reminiscent of cherries, leather, and earth. Grown throughout Spain, the grape is by far that country's most important, and is either made into single varietal wines or used as the main grape into which Garnacha and Cabernet Sauvignon are commonly blended. It is known by several names including **Tinto de Toro** (in Rueda, Spain), **Tinto Fino** (in Ribera del Duero, Spain), and **Tinta Roriz** (in the Douro Valley of Portugal, where it is a major component in many top Port wines). The most important growing regions for the grape variety are in north-central Spain and include Rioja and Ribera del Duero. It is increasingly being grown in Argentina and California today.

TORRONTÉS Aromatic white grape variety responsible for the most interesting white wines being produced in Argentina today. It produces intensely perfumed wines, which are rarely aged in oak.

TOURIGA NACIONAL This rustic red grape variety is responsible for the top dry red wines of Portugal, and serves as the main grape used for the production of Port. Touriga Nacional produces mostly structured, simple, rustic wines reminiscent of plums and chocolate on its own, but is more commonly the star of a red blend, where it lends power.

TREBBIANO A white grape variety grown widely throughout Italy and also in France (where it is called **Ugni Blanc** and is mostly used for a base in brandy production, including Cognac). It produces mostly bone-dry, highly acidic wines that are crisp and, at their best, extremely refreshing.

VERDELHO An important white grape variety used in the production of top-quality fortified Madeira wines. The grape is also capable of producing fruity, dry white wines in Portugal and especially Spain, where it is commonly called **Godello**.

VIOGNIER The most important white grape variety grown in the Rhône Valley of France, Viognier is capable of producing full-bodied, powerful, high-alcohol white wines. It is an extremely aromatic variety when fully ripened, demonstrating intense peach, apricot, and honeysuckle aromas. The best Viognier-based wines come from warmer climates such as its native homeland of the Rhône Valley (where it is used in the production of Château-Grillet and Condrieu), California, and Australia. It is commonly blended in small percentages into Syrah- and Shiraz-based wines, lending additional aroma and character to those wines in both France and Australia.

VIURA An increasingly important white grape variety in northern Spain, where it is used in the white wines from Rioja and also as the base for most sparkling Cava (where it is known as **Macabeo**). It tends to produce floral, high-acid white wines.

XINÓMAVRO One of the top red wine grapes of Greece, Xinómavro (meaning "sour black") produces light-bodied, high-acid red wines reminiscent of red fruits.

ZINFANDEL A red grape variety that is widely considered by many to be California's grape because it is not widely grown anywhere else in the world. Its origins shrouded in mystery, it was only recently determined that Zinfandel is actually a Croatian grape variety called Crljenak. This grape is used to produce a variety of different styles including semi-sweet blush wines (called White Zinfandels) and even late harvest, port-style wines, but the most important are dry, intense, high-alcohol red wines. At its best, Zinfandel produces intensely colored, powerful red wines that have strong blackberry, pepper, and jam flavors. It is commonly aged in American oak, and therefore shows the flavors of dill and coconut. Although these wines are all about impact and power, they are not as tannic or structured as some other heavy red wines. Zinfandel is grown throughout California, with some of the better examples being produced in Sonoma County and Paso Robles. The only other regions in the world producing significant amounts of this grape variety are southern Italy and Sicily, where it is known as **Primitivo.**

Summary

For many wines, the most important impact on their flavors and characteristics is the variety or varieties of grapes used in their production. Over thousands of years, an amazing array of grape varieties has been developed as farmers, viticulturalists, and winemakers have worked to adapt *Vitis vinifera* to different climate zones, soil types, and wine styles. Through their work and with a great deal of help from nature, this species of grape has become the ideal fruit used for the production of wine.

Review Questions

1. The only international grape variety to have originated outside of France is:
   - A. Chardonnay
   - B. Merlot
   - C. Riesling
   - D. Syrah

2. The international white grape variety that has the heaviest body and lowest acidity is:
   - A. Riesling
   - B. Sauvignon Blanc
   - C. Pinot Grigio
   - D. Chardonnay

3. The words Gris and Grigio both mean gray.
   - A. True
   - B. False

4. The international red grape variety with the lowest amount of tannins, thinnest skins, and highest acidity is:
   - A. Pinot Noir
   - B. Syrah
   - C. Merlot
   - D. Cabernet Sauvignon

5. Another name for the Syrah grape is:
   - A. Shazaam
   - B. Petit Sirah
   - C. Merlot
   - D. Shiraz

Match the following international grape varieties to their typical varietal characteristics. ***Some answers may be used more than once, and some not at all.***

6. Riesling
7. Sauvignon Blanc
8. Pinot Grigio/Gris
9. Chardonnay

- A. Grapefruit, grassy, herbal, and hints of cat urine
- B. Pear, pineapple, buttery, oaky, and spicy
- C. Floral, depends upon *terroir*
- D. Green apple, citrus, and mineral

10. Pinot Noir
11. Syrah
12. Merlot
13. Cabernet Sauvignon

- A. Blackberries, meaty, smoke, and black pepper
- B. Black currant, mint, bell pepper, and wet dog
- C. Blueberries, cherries, chocolate, spice, and vanilla
- D. Cherries, cranberries, earth, spice, and barnyard

14. Which international red grape variety originated in the warmest climate and shows characteristics such as medium tannins, acidity, and body?
   - A. Pinot Noir
   - B. Syrah
   - C. Merlot
   - D. Cabernet Sauvignon

Key Terms

international grape varieties
Riesling
Sauvignon Blanc
Pinot Gris/Pinot Grigio
Chardonnay
Pinot Noir
Syrah/Shiraz
Merlot
Cabernet Sauvignon
Aglianico
Albariño
Alvarinho
Aligoté
Arneis
Barbera
Blaufränkisch
Lemberger
Kékfrankos
Cabernet Franc
Carignan
Carmenère
Grand Vidure
Chasselas
Chenin Blanc
Cinsaut/Cinsault
Cortese
Corvina
Dolcetto
Furmint
Gamay
Gewürztraminer
Grenache
Garnacha
Grüner Veltliner
Lambrusco
Malbec
Cot
Auxerrois
Malvasia
Marsanne
Mavrodaphne/Mavrodafni
Melon de Bourgogne
Mourvèdre
Müller-Thurgau
Muscadelle
Muscat
Muscat Blanc à Petits Grains
Moscato
Brown Muscat
Muscat Canelli
Nebbiolo
Palomino
Petite Sirah
Petit Verdot
Pinot Blanc
Pinot Meunier
Pinotage
Prosecco
Roussanne
Sangiovese
Brunello
Prugnolo
Scheurebe
Sémillon
Sylvaner
Tannat
Tempranillo
Tinto de Toro
Tinto Fino
Tinta Roriz
Torrontés
Touriga Nacional
Trebbiano
Ugni Blanc
Verdelho
Godello
Viognier
Viura
Macabeo
Xinómavro
Zinfandel
Primitivo

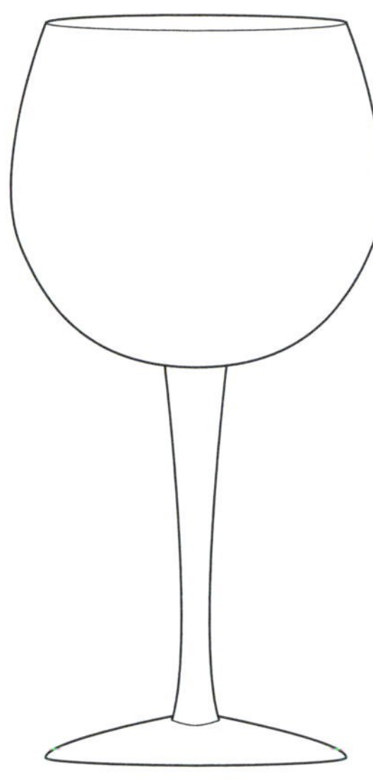

CHAPTER 6

Food and Wine Pairing

A meal without wine is like a day without sunshine.

—Italian proverb

One of the most important aspects of wine is its affinity for food. This chapter takes a commonsense and scientific approach to pairing food and wine. Pairings based on body, flavors, and characteristics of wines are discussed in detail, and wine tasting exercises are included to help illustrate both positive and negative pairings.

Pairing Guidelines

Pairing food and wine should not be viewed as an exact science, a magic trick, or even a lucky coincidence. Wine has a natural affinity for food that cannot be matched by that of any other beverage; however, to produce a great pairing, you must have at least a basic understanding of the characteristics of both wine and food. With this understanding in mind, there are certain guidelines that can help maximize the marriage between wine and food. These guidelines should not be seen as hard and fast rules, but rather as a group of factors that can help you create a solid match.

MATCH QUALITY

When pairing wine and food, you must always take into account the quality of the wine and the quality of the dish. A complex dish made for special occasions deserves a complex and special wine. On the other hand, simple, everyday dishes match best with simple and easy-to-drink wines. Putting a simple wine with a special dish would be as unsuccessful as squeezing ketchup onto filet mignon. If you are going all out on a meal, with the highest-quality ingredients turned into a dish possessing intensity and complexity, then you owe it to yourself to find a wine that fits the bill.

- Special-occasion dishes with special-occasion wines
- Everyday dishes with everyday wines

MATCH POWER AND WEIGHT

Imagine you are at the dinner table and are served a dish of delicately seasoned scallops along with a peppercorn-encrusted, smoked venison chop.

As you begin to eat, you take a bite of the scallop, a bite of the chop, a bite of the scallop, a bite of the chop, and so on. What will the outcome be? Very quickly, you will no longer taste the scallop. The same thing will happen if you pair a wine to a dish with the same inequality in power. If you pair a Cabernet Sauvignon with those scallops, all you will taste is the power of the wine. If you pair a soft Riesling with the smoked venison chop, all you will get is the smoky meat. Always take the relative power and weight of a wine and dish into account when making a pairing. The whole point of food and wine pairing is to make both the food and the wine taste better. If you cannot taste one or the other, then you are defeating the purpose.

- Heavy dishes with heavy wines; robust dishes with robust wines
- Light dishes with light wines; delicate dishes with delicate wines

LOOK INTO THE MIRROR

One of the easiest ways to make a wine and food seem to have a natural affinity for one another is to use **mirroring** when you pair. Mirroring involves pairing two similar characteristics to bring out that shared characteristic. If you have a peppery dish and want to emphasize the spicy pepper flavors, then pick a wine that has peppery characteristics, like a Zinfandel. If you have an earthy mushroom dish and want to bring out that essence, pick an earthy wine like a red Burgundy. It is no mistake that a rich, buttery California Chardonnay has a natural affinity for lobster, which is also rich and buttery. One of the easiest ways to guarantee mirroring in a pairing is to use the wine you are serving as an ingredient in the food as well. It makes pairings seem like they are meant to be together.

Mirror flavors and characteristics that a dish and a wine have in common.

USE WINE TO FIGHT FAT

While fat is what gives a piece of meat a lot of its flavor, it can actually coat your tongue and get in the way of tasting that flavor when you eat. Imagine biting into a piece of gristle while eating a steak: it will completely mute the flavor of the meat and dish. Practically every dish has a certain amount of fat in it, and when pairing wine, you should always take that fat into consideration. There are two ways to neutralize the fat in a dish and bring out more of the food's flavor using wine pairing: acid and tannins.

Lighter dishes with high levels of fat, such as salmon, poultry, cream sauces, and pork, are best paired with wines high in acidity. Think Riesling, Sauvignon Blanc, and Pinot Noir. The acid in these wines will act like a knife that cuts through the fattiness in a dish, revealing more of its flavor. At the same time, the fat in the dish will neutralize much of the acidity in the wine, dulling the knife and making the wine less tart.

Heavier dishes with high levels of fat need heavier wines, and typically, the heavier the wine, the lower the acidity. Therefore, a different way to contrast fat is needed. These types of dishes are best paired to wines high in tannins, such as Cabernet Sauvignon or Merlot. The tannins in the wine act like a brick wall that stands up to fat. As tannins settle on the surface of the tongue, they physically block fat. While this is occurring, the fat also helps to lessen the presence of the tannins, so the wine will soften.

Use acid and tannins to contrast fat in a dish.

- Acid cuts through fat
- Tannins stand up to fat

FLAVORS WORK TOGETHER

Our sense of taste is a very interesting thing, indeed. Flavors on the palate change the perceptions of flavors that follow them in a dramatic fashion, and can make or break a food and wine pairing.

One experience with the way flavors work together that everyone can understand is what happens when you brush your teeth and then make the mistake of drinking orange juice. Yuck! The sweetness of the toothpaste actually changes the perception of how we taste the orange juice, effectively stripping it of any sweetness. By understanding how flavors work together, you can feel confident choosing certain wines for certain foods.

In the simplest terms, salty and sour flavors bring out the positive characteristics and flavors of a food or wine. Bitter, sweet, and savory flavors bring out the negative characteristics and flavors. Chefs understand this, and it explains why almost all sauces are either salty or sour. We season with salt and squeeze lemon onto a vast assortment of foods. There is a reason that they serve salty cheeses at a wine tasting—they are trying to sell wine! Use these changes in perception to your advantage. To make wines taste better, pair them with foods that have salty or sour flavors. To make foods taste better, wines that are high in acidity and have sour flavors work best.

- Salty and sour flavors bring out the positive characteristics of flavor.
- Sweet, bitter, and savory flavors bring out the negative characteristics of flavor.

THINK LOCALLY

Wine has been around for thousands of years, and throughout most of its history, people were not as mobile as they are today. If you were born in Tuscany a hundred years ago, you most likely lived your life in Tuscany and died in Tuscany. You lived your entire life eating the foods of Tuscany and drinking the wines of Tuscany. Common sense dictates that the wines and foods of a region pair together well. Just because we live in a time when you can jump on a computer, book a ticket to Paris, and be in Europe tomorrow, does not mean that we should forget about the roots of wine and food. If you are serving a regional dish, pair it with a wine from that region. They were made to go together.

Pair regional wines with regional dishes.

SEE THE WHOLE PICTURE

Many times, pairing suggestions are far too simple, and concentrate on pairing a wine to the wrong component of a dish. It is common to hear simple suggestions like: "pair Pinot Noir with duck or Cabernet Sauvignon with lamb." While these can be good suggestions, a good wine pairing takes into account more than just the meat or protein served in a dish. How many different ways can duck be prepared? How many recipes could you find for lamb? When pairing food and wine, you need to see the big picture. Pair the wine not only to the protein, but also to the sauce, vegetables, and starch in a dish. By taking the entire dish into account, you will select a wine that pairs much more successfully with the whole plate.

Take all components of a dish into account (meat, sauce, etc.) when selecting a wine.

SUCCESS WITH SPICE

It can be tricky to select a wine to go with a spicy dish. This is because spiciness in a dish is not something we taste, it is something we feel. A jalapeño pepper is hot because it physically irritates the surface of the tongue. When pairing wines with spicy dishes, you always need to take this into account. Your best bet with spicy foods is to pair them with a slightly sweet wine. The sweetness in the wine will tame the heat of the dish and bring out more of its flavor.

Wines to avoid with spicy dishes are those wines that also irritate the surface of the tongue. Tannins are a component of red wines that irritate the soft tissues in the mouth, causing a sense of dryness on the palate. Adding this irritation to the irritation caused by spicy foods will actually make the food hotter and the wine more tannic. Stay away from the atomic hot wings with a glass of Cabernet Sauvignon!

- Spicy foods pair best with slightly sweet wines.
- Spicy foods are a bad match for high-tannin wines.

THE SWEET LIFE

Thinking back to our earlier discussion of toothpaste and orange juice, you need to be careful when pairing wines with desserts. The simple rule of thumb is to always make sure that the wine you are serving with a dessert is sweeter than the dessert itself. Most sweet wines have a very intense level of acidity to balance out their sweetness. If that sweetness is stripped away from the wine, all that will show is that stark, raw acidity. By ensuring that your dessert wine is sweeter than your dessert, you ensure that the wine will retain its natural sweetness and complement the dish, rather than turn into battery acid.

Dessert wines should always be sweeter than the dessert they are served with.

RULES WERE MADE TO BE BROKEN

The one food and wine pairing rule that most people have heard of is to pair whites with whites and reds with reds; pair white wines to white meats such as fish and poultry, and pair red wines to red meats such as lamb and beef. In general terms, this rule is not so bad, but it should not be regarded as gospel by any means.

Typically, lighter white wines will go well with lighter dishes such as seafood, but big, full-bodied whites like Viognier or Chardonnay could overshadow the lightness of a fish's flavor. Strongly flavored fish dishes or chicken with bold flavors could run over lighter white wines. A soft Pinot Noir may not have enough power to stand up to a hearty beef stew.

Avoid broad generalizations like pairing colors (white with white and red with red) because there are so many variables in different foods and wines. It is better to think in specific terms about a dish (such as the body, quality, power, and specific flavors discussed above). If you stick too closely to food pairing rules, they can limit your creativity and options when putting a match together. Besides, there are some great pairings between red wines and fish, and some beef dishes are best complemented by a white wine.

The best thing about pairing wine and food is that it is always an interesting experiment in matching things. Sometimes it works so well that you will remember the match and speak of its greatness forever. Other times, you end up with a decent match, but nothing special. Realize that there are no perfect food and wine pairings out there. Everyone tastes things differently, and not everyone likes the same combinations. Have fun with pairing, be willing to break any of the rules, and, most importantly, drink what you like. The truth about pairing wine and food is that most wines go with most foods. In reality, it is easy to match them. Be willing to experiment, try new things, and turn defeat into victory.

Try These Pairings

On the following page is a table showing some suggested food and wine pairings. By no means should you consider these suggestions as the only wines that can be used for these types of foods—this is intended as a starting point for a delicious journey!

	Lighter and Acidic Preparation	Rich and Creamy Preparation	Spicy Preparation
Clams/Shellfish	Champagne	White Burgundy	German Gewürztraminer
Crab/Lobster	Spanish Albariño	California Chardonnay	Alsatian Riesling
White Fish	French Sauvignon Blanc	Oregon Pinot Gris	French Chenin Blanc
Oily Fish	New Zealand Sauvignon Blanc	Valpolicella	Beaujolais
Chicken	Italian Pinot Grigio	California Sauvignon Blanc	Viognier
Duck	Italian Barbera	Red Burgundy	Australian Shiraz
Pork	French Rosé	Chianti Classico	Grenache
Beef	New Zealand Pinot Noir	California Cabernet Sauvignon	Argentine Malbec
Lamb	Red Bordeaux	California Merlot	Spanish Tempranillo
Game Meats	California Pinot Noir	French Syrah	Zinfandel

Summary

Food and wine have a natural affinity for one another. Through a basic understanding of how the sense of taste works and the application of some common-sense guidelines, it is easy to match wines and foods.

Review Questions

1. It is always best to pair a high-quality wine with lower-quality food to accentuate the wine.

- **A.** True
- **B.** False

2. If trying to make a pairing using the concept of mirroring, the best match to a crisp, dry Pinot Grigio with green apple and mineral flavors would be:

- **A.** a rich, buttery lobster dish
- **B.** a braised beef dish with a red wine reduction
- **C.** a light pork dish served with an apple compote
- **D.** seared shrimp in a garlic cream sauce

3. Which two characteristics in wine are best when paired with dishes that have a high fat content?

- **A.** Sugar and acid
- **B.** Acid and tannins
- **C.** Sugar and tannins
- **D.** Alcohol and sugar

4. It is always a good idea to match full-bodied wines with heavy dishes.

- **A.** True
- **B.** False

5. Which two taste sensations bring out the positive flavor characteristics of a food or wine?

- **A.** Sour and salty
- **B.** Sour and bitter
- **C.** Sweet and salty
- **D.** Sweet and bitter

6. In almost every case, the determination of a wine pairing should be based only on the protein (meat) component of a dish.

- **A.** True
- **B.** False

7. When pairing sweet wines with desserts, it is always best for the dessert to be sweeter than the wine.
   A. True
   B. False

8. It is best to avoid red wines with strong tannins when making a pairing with spicy foods.
   A. True
   B. False

9. It is never a good idea to pair white wines with red meats and red wines with white meats.
   A. True
   B. False

10. Spicy foods are best matched with:
   A. dry, white wines
   B. sweet, white wines
   C. dry, red wines
   D. sparkling wines

Tasting Exercise

DETERMINING HOW FLAVORS AFFECT ONE ANOTHER AND WINE

Wines Needed

You will need to get three different styles of wine to taste during this exercise. You will need enough wine so that you can take at least six sips, matching the wine with each of the food items below (roughly 1½–2 ounces of each). The wines should be poured into three separate glasses. It is also important to have water to cleanse your palate between tastes, as well as a vessel that you can spit into.

Wine Style	Example
A soft, sweet white wine	A semisweet Riesling
A dry, high-acid white wine	A cooler-climate Sauvignon Blanc
A dry, tannic red wine	A Cabernet Sauvignon

Foods Needed

You will need food items that exaggerate the five taste sensations. Examples have been given, but feel free to substitute what is readily available. You should have enough of each food item that you can taste a bite of each three times, matching it with all three wines.

Taste Sensation	Example
Sweet	Grapes cut in half and dipped in sugar
Sour	Lemon wedges
Bitter	Walnuts or baking chocolate
Savory	Unseasoned crab meat
Salty	Monterey Jack cheese cubes that have been dipped into kosher salt on one side

The Exercise

The goal of this exercise is to see the impact that the five taste sensations found in food have on different types of wine. Each wine should be tasted separately and combined with all of the possible food items before moving on to the next wine style. First, each wine should be tasted on its own to determine its main flavor and mouthfeel characteristics, such as acidity, presence of bitterness, dryness, presence of fruity flavors, and tannins (for the red).

Once this baseline has been established, move on to combining the wine with the sweet food item. Take a bite of the sweet food item and chew it until a very sweet flavor registers on the palate. Either spit the food out or swallow it, making sure that you have no more of the food item in your mouth. You simply want the perception of that taste sensation to remain on the palate. Now try another sip of the wine with the sweet flavor in your mouth. What happens to the characteristics of the wine? Does it change the way it tastes and feels on the palate? Is this a good combination, bringing out the positive characteristics of the wine, or does the match make the wine more acidic, bitter, less sweet, stripped of flavor, and/or tannic?

Once you cleanse your palate with a drink of water, move on to the next food item (in this case, the one representing the sour taste sensation), and combine this with the wine as explained above. Work your way through all of the flavor sensations

Wine Style	No Food	Sweet	Sour	Bitter	Savory	Salty
Soft, Sweet White Wine						
Dry, High-Acid White Wine						
Dry, Tannic Red Wine						

Food and wine pairing exercise chart.

(next would be bitter, followed by savory, and finally salty) before moving on to the next wine style. At this point you should repeat the exercise as you did for the first wine, tasting it on its own first and then moving through the different taste sensations.

Use the chart above to track your findings for each food and wine match-up.

Once you have tasted all of the combinations, what are your findings? Do red wines work differently than whites with the different flavors? Does sweetness in a wine change what happens when it is paired with different flavors? Which flavors in food had a positive impact on the wines? Which had a negative impact? How does seasoning and flavoring of food relate to how wine interacts with it?

Key Terms

pairing
match
quality
power
weight
mirroring

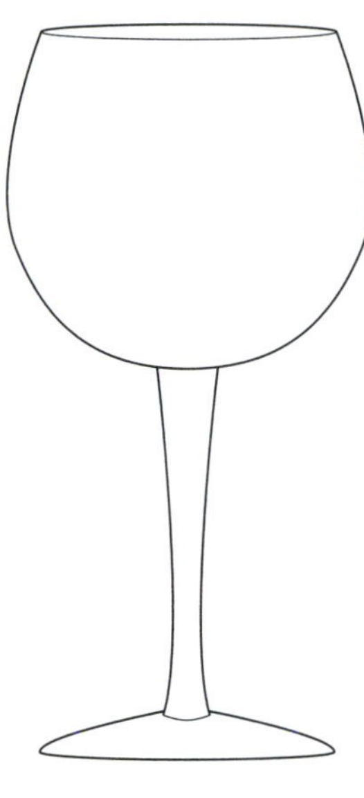

CHAPTER 7

Wine Tasting and Sensory Analysis

A person with increasing knowledge and sensory education may derive infinite enjoyment from wine.

—ERNEST HEMINGWAY

Being able to taste a wine and use your senses to analyze that wine is fundamental to an overall understanding of wine. Tasting and accurately describing a wine's characteristics is one of the most important, and most difficult, skills for a wine professional to master. Becoming a good wine taster requires focus, knowledge, and a solid connection with your senses. Everything that you sense about a wine, from the way it looks to the way it smells, tastes, and feels, can help you to draw conclusions about it, its quality, and its origins. In this chapter, we focus on how to prepare yourself for the sensory analysis of a wine, proper wine tasting etiquette, and the different types of tastings that you can conduct. Then, we discuss the step-by-step process for analyzing a wine using your senses of sight, smell, taste, and touch.

Wine Tasting Basics

Before jumping into a wine tasting, it is important that you know what you are doing, and place yourself in a situation where you can truly analyze and appreciate a given wine. The following is a list of wine tasting etiquette tips and considerations that can help you to focus your wine tasting endeavors and produce beneficial results.

TASTING WINE AND DRINKING WINE

We *drink* and *taste* wine for different reasons, which means we need to take a very different approach to each.

Why do people drink wine? There are several reasons: they like the way it tastes, they like how it pairs with food, they like the effects it has and how it makes them feel. These are all good reasons to drink wine, but when drinking a wine, the ultimate goal is usually to enjoy the wine. When a person is drinking a wine, very little thought or analysis goes into that wine, and that is fine. In reality, that is what wine is for: enjoyment. The most thought that generally goes into a wine when drinking it is the formation of a personal opinion about the wine: "I really like this wine" or "I do not really care for it." It all comes down to personal opinion when drinking wine.

When tasting wine, however, personal opinion and enjoyment are not very important. Tasting wine is done not to enjoy a wine, but rather to analyze the wine and come to a certain understanding about it and its characteristics. Tasting wine helps you to determine whether a given wine is typical of its style, what grapes were used to produce it, and what region it is from. It allows you to better understand the wine's quality—and in a business sense, to determine whether or not it would be a product to put on your wine list, or to suggest to a customer.

CONSIDER YOUR SURROUNDINGS

Always try to taste wine in a place that is free from distractions such as strong aromas (food, perfume, or cigarette smoke), loud noises, and interruptions. You want your focus to be on your wine, not your environment. Try to always taste in the same place and at the same time of day. Most wine professionals taste just before lunchtime, when the senses are heightened.

A SYSTEMATIC APPROACH

Separating personal opinion from facts in wine analysis can be difficult. Your mood and approach can hinder your ability to be objective when tasting. The best way to limit this problem is to use a systematic approach to tasting wines. When tasting wine, always judge using the same set of criteria in the same order. Using a tasting sheet like the one found on page 108 will help you to apply a systematic approach, and will force you to focus on wines objectively.

FOCUS ON YOUR SENSES

The only tools at your disposal to analyze a wine are your senses—after all, you are conducting a **sensory analysis.** The senses that you will directly use to analyze a wine are sight, smell, taste, and touch. You should make it a point to focus on each when tasting wine, and limit the amount of tasting you do if one of them is impaired (e.g., it is difficult to use your sense of smell if you have a cold and your nose is stuffed up).

LISTEN UP!

Your sense of hearing cannot be used to directly analyze a wine. (If your wine is talking to you, you probably have crossed over the threshold from tasting wine to drinking wine—and quite a bit of it!) However, by listening to other wine tasters, you can make yourself a better taster. It is very difficult when first learning to taste wine to have a vocabulary sufficient to describe it. Listening to the way others describe a wine can help you build your personal wine vocabulary, as well as put a name to the aroma or flavor you are trying to describe.

TO SPIT OR NOT TO SPIT?

One of the most obvious outward differences between tasting wine and drinking wine is that when tasting the wine, you should spit it out instead of swallowing. This may seem unnatural at first, but it is very important to stick to this policy when tasting wines. It is not only considered acceptable when tasting wine, it should be expected. The alcohol in wine will begin to dull your senses if you swallow the wine, and your senses are the only tools you have at your disposal to help you analyze wine. Once you begin to drink the wine, tasting and analysis cease.

TASTING MULTIPLE WINES

Whenever tasting more than one wine, it is always best to taste them in a specific order. So that one wine will not eclipse the wine that comes after it, arrange wines using the following guidelines whenever possible:

- White wines before red wines
- Lighter wines (in terms of body, alcohol, power, etc.) before heavier wines
- Sweeter wines are saved until the end of a tasting

To help lessen the effects of tasting one wine after another, it is always advisable to rinse your palate with water between wines.

TASTE BLIND

Tasting a wine blind is not a suggestion that you put on a blindfold or close your eyes when tasting. Rather, it means that you do not want to know what you are tasting in advance. Try not to look at the label or bottle of wine you are tasting before or while you are analyzing it. You should know very little or nothing at all about a wine you are analyzing, because you do not want perception or prejudice to get in the way of analysis. If you think you hate Merlot, and know that you are tasting a Merlot, you will have already made certain decisions about the wine before even looking at it. Remember, tasting is about analysis, and you must remain objective to be analytical.

YOU CANNOT BE WRONG!

One of the best things about tasting wine is that when properly analyzing a wine, you cannot be wrong in your assessment. Everybody smells and tastes things differently and uniquely based on how they are genetically hardwired, what they have been exposed to, and what their environment was and is like. If you smell something in a wine that no one else in a tasting group can smell, it does not mean you are wrong. To you, that aroma is present, and you should stand by your assessment.

On the other hand, realize that this means that no one else can tell you what a specific wine smells like or tastes like—not a wine critic, not the back of a label, not even a more experienced taster. As mentioned earlier, you should always listen to how others describe a wine, but ultimately it is up to you to determine your opinion of the characteristics of a wine.

Types of Wine Tastings

There are literally hundreds of different types of wine tastings that you can conduct or take part in, from an informal gathering of friends to formal meetings of wine professionals. In this section, you will be introduced to several types of tastings, all of which will encourage you to expand your knowledge of wine.

LED TASTING

A **led tasting** is when you already know something about a wine or its origins before you taste it. Led tastings are great for wine instructors trying to teach their students about a particular wine, region, grape, or winemaking technique. They can also be conducted on your own or in a group of other tasters by doing some research on a wine before tasting it. For example, if you wanted to learn more about the Merlot grape, you could taste a group of different Merlots from various wine regions. By reading up on the grape and those regions, what you taste will help to reinforce your knowledge of this grape and the growing conditions of the different regions. Led tastings are perfect for beginners, as there is an expert (whether in the form of a teacher, trained wine professional, or published resource) who can help describe why wine demonstrates its unique set of characteristics.

BLIND TASTING

For most of the serious professional wine organizations out there, eventually you will need to pass a **blind tasting** to achieve higher-level certifications. A blind tasting involves independently conducting a sensory analysis of a wine, and then drawing conclusions about that wine based on your findings. It is not uncommon for the taster to be asked to determine the age, origin, grapes used, and quality level for a given wine. To best prepare for professional blind tastings, you must practice regularly and understand the characteristics found in the world's most important wines and grapes. Simply being able to accurately describe a wine's different aspects is not enough, as you will need to apply your knowledge of wine to those findings. Sensory analysis of wine is discussed in detail in later sections of this chapter, and application of wine analysis is described in Chapter 8.

To practice blind tasting, it is best to work with a group of individuals who also want to learn more about wine or plan to go after professional wine certifications (to split the expense, if for no other reason). The wines should all be poured out of the view of the tasters. Upon receiving your wine or wines for tasting, you should conduct a sensory analysis and then attempt to apply that analysis to answer questions about the wine. After finishing a blind tasting with a group, discuss your findings to pick up ideas and knowledge that will make you a better wine taster.

VERTICAL TASTINGS

One of the most interesting tastings you can take part in is a **vertical tasting.** To conduct one, you will need to select a wine of which you can secure multiple vintages. The highlight of a tasting like this is seeing how the same wines made from the same vineyards and produced by the same winemakers can vary from one vintage to another. The differences you see, smell, taste, and feel are a result of the growing conditions during each of the vintages you taste. Warmer years might result in a spike in alcohol, body, and fruitiness; whereas cooler vintages will appear more lean and austere. Be sure to find a vintage chart for the region the wine comes from.

A vertical tasting is also an ideal way to illustrate how wines age. Take note of how the wines from older vintages differ from the wines from younger vintages. Color, aromas, tannin levels, and flavors, among other characteristics, will all change in a wine over time.

HORIZONTAL TASTINGS

A **horizontal tasting** is similar to a vertical tasting, except instead of tasting several vintages of one wine, you taste several wines from the same region and the same vintage. Imagine tasting five 2001 Cabernet Sauvignons from the Napa Valley, or four white Burgundies from 1999. Horizontal tastings can teach you to spot differences in how wines are made, as well as help you to better understand concepts like ***terroir,*** by showing how small differences in the vineyard (climate, soil composition, etc.) can affect a finished wine.

INDUSTRY TASTINGS

Industry tastings are typically held by wineries, wine brokers, or wine distributors to demonstrate their different offerings to consumers and retailers. These types of tastings are a great way to try a wide range of wines without having to make a huge monetary investment. It is important to remember a few important guidelines about industry tastings to maximize the experience. As you taste wines at an industry tasting, you should still focus on all of your senses when trying to describe a wine. Note taking is also fundamental to remembering the wines you taste, so you can review the characteristics of certain wines once the tasting is over or make an informed purchase of a wine you know you will enjoy. Although industry tastings are typically much less formal than other types of tastings, it is still important to remember the differences between tasting wine and drinking wine. You need to focus on your senses and spit if you are tasting—otherwise, you should treat the tasting as nothing more than a social gathering, and not as a tool to help you understand wine better.

Analyzing Wine with Your Eyes

You should always start the analysis of a wine by utilizing your sense of sight. This sense will start to reveal clues about the characteristics of a wine, as well as highlight certain components that need further analysis using all of your other senses as you continue to taste that wine. Sight can give you an idea about the age of a wine, whether or not it was made properly and stored properly, in what type of climate the grapes were grown, and even the type of grape or grapes used to produce the wine. You cannot come to any concrete conclusions about a wine using your sense of sight; rather, you can begin to form some opinions about a wine that can be later proven (or disproven) using your other senses.

CLARITY AND BRIGHTNESS

The first thing to look for when analyzing the visual appearance of a wine is whether or not the wine is clear, cloudy, or somewhere in between. Hold the wine up and slowly move the glass around over a white surface to determine whether you can see through it, or if the wine is cloudy and contains suspended particles. It is best to use a variable scale with cloudy on one end of the spectrum and clear on the other.

It is easy to analyze **clarity** and **brightness** for white wines, but for many red wines, it can be difficult to see through them because they contain pigments. For these wines, look through the edges of the liquid, where the wine meets the glass. This is where the volume of wine is the thinnest, and even for the deepest-colored wines you should be able to see through the liquid. If the edge is clear, the rest of the wine will be as well.

If a wine is clear, it is technically described as being **bright.** Cloudiness or haziness in a wine is a result of suspended particles in the liquid (not to be confused with sediment: small particles that sink to the bottom of a glass). This haziness should not be present in a wine that has been made properly or stored properly (winemakers use several methods for clarification). Older wines may have some haziness, but if the wine is younger or is excessively cloudy, be on the lookout for foul aromas and flavors when you later smell and taste the wine.

COLOR

The **color** of a wine can also tell you about some of its characteristics. Mainly, color is the first indication of age. Color changes are most likely the result of exposure to oxygen (think of what happens to the color of the flesh of an apple if you cut it open and allow it to sit on the counter for several hours). There are several factors that can alter the color of a wine, but the three most important are:

1. **Bottle Aging**—A slow oxidation and color change can occur over time as the wine interacts with the small amount of dissolved oxygen in the bottle.
2. **Barrel Aging**—Oak barrels are watertight, but they do allow for the wine to be exposed to large amounts of oxygen, resulting in a rapid oxidation and color change. The insides of a barrel may also have color from toasting that can be dissolved by the wine during the aging process.
3. **Residual Sugar**—Sweet wines tend to be darker in color because of concentration and because of the residual sugar in them.

When analyzing the color of a wine, it is always best to first assume that bottle aging is responsible, because color change due to bottle aging occurs at a regular and measurable rate, and is most easily identified using the sense of sight. It is very easy to later use your other senses to prove that barrel aging or residual sugar are responsible for the wine's color. If a wine smells and tastes heavily of oak aging characteristics, that would suggest that oak aging is the cause of the color. If the wine is very sweet when tasted, then residual sugar can be identified as the cause. While oak aging and residual sugar are easy to prove with your other senses, bottle aging is not as readily identified. Therefore, you should assume bottle aging until you can prove otherwise.

If bottle aging is responsible for the color of a wine, the regular rate at which that color changes over time can help you to identify how old that wine is. The juice used to produce white wines is clear, and you should expect that a young white wine (one to three years of age) will have the appearance of being either clear or light straw in color—basically, a very slight yellow color. As that white wine ages in the bottle and slowly reacts with oxygen, the color will become darker (just like an apple). As white wines gain some maturity (three to five years of age) their color will be more of a yellow hue, and once fully mature (five or more years of age) they should achieve a golden color. Once past their prime, white wines will turn brown as they begin to break down, overoxidize, and eventually spoil due to age. Therefore, a simple assumption can be made that white wines get darker as they age, and the darkness of each wine can give you an indication of how far along it is in the process, or the age of the wine.

The color of red wines is not as easy to interpret as the color of whites, because there are more factors affecting red wines' color. Remember that as far as color goes, red wines are simply white wines with pigmentation. The juice of black-skinned grapes is just as clear as the juice of white-skinned grapes. The color or pigmentation comes from the skins of the black-skinned grapes, which are allowed to remain in contact with the juice during fermentation. This allows the pigments to be dissolved into the solution of the wine along with tannins and flavor compounds. Therefore, the color of a newly made red wine follows this formula:

Red Wine = White Wine + Pigments

To properly analyze the color of a red wine, you must consider both the slow change of the clear liquid of the grape juice and the color of the pigments that slowly break down over time. This means that a young red wine (one to three years of age) will have a color reminiscent of the pigments found in the skins of black grapes—chiefly, a purple color, or at least strong hints of purple. As that pigment slowly breaks down, the color changes to a shade of red during middle maturity (three to five years of age). While aging continues, the pigment will continue to break down to a point where it allows the color of the slowly oxidizing white wine underneath it to be exposed. When that red wine reaches full maturity (five or more years of age), it will be golden in color with some amount of residual pigment still present. The result will be an amber or brick shade. Finally, when a red wine begins to age beyond its prime and become overoxidized, all of the pigmentation will have been broken down and the wine will appear brown (the same shade as a white wine that has reached the point of being dead!).

If a generalization can be made that white wines get darker as they age, the exact opposite generalization can be made for reds. As reds age and their pigments break down, they actually get lighter in color.

Be sure to document the color you see on your tasting sheet, so that you have this information when trying to come to a conclusion about a wine's age. While analyzing the color of a wine is an important step in determining the age of the wine, remember that it is only a part of the puzzle, and there are other factors you will use to come to a final estimate of a wine's age.

PIGMENTATION

Once you have analyzed the color of a red wine, the next characteristic to analyze will be the **intensity of pigmentation** (you will skip this step for white wines, as they have no pigmentation). The characteristic to measure is the amount of **pigment** present, not the color of that pigment. To apply this information, it is important to remember where the pigments that color a red wine come from: the grape skins. The thicker a grape's skins, the more pigments are contained in those skins. Therefore, a red wine that has a large amount of pigmentation and an intense or deep color must have been produced from grapes that have thicker skins. A red wine that lacks pigmentation must have been made from grapes that have thin skins.

To measure the intensity of pigmentation for a red wine, you should pick your glass up by the stem and tilt the glass at a 45-degree angle over a white surface with writing on it (use your tasting sheet or notes). While looking at the wine from above, you

Grape Pigments and Health

Many of the healthy benefits of the moderate consumption of red wine are caused by the pigments found in grape skins. These pigments are called **anthocyanins** and are strong antioxidants, helping to reduce the risk of cancer and other diseases, as well as maintaining healthy cardiovascular functions.

want to make note of how easy or difficult it is to see the words and letters through the wine. If it is very easy to read the writing while looking through the center of the liquid (like looking through a pair of pink- or red-colored sunglasses), you are analyzing a wine with very little intensity of pigmentation—a wine made from thin-skinned grapes. If the words are obscured, you have a wine that was made from medium-skinned grapes. When it becomes difficult or impossible to see through the middle of the wine to the writing below, then the wine was made with thick-skinned grapes.

Document how thick you think the grape skins are when analyzing intensity of pigmentation. Certain grapes have certain constant characteristics, including skin thickness. For instance, Pinot Noir has thin skins, Syrah has medium skins, and Cabernet Sauvignon and Merlot have thick skins. When further analyzing a wine and coming to overall conclusions about it, the intensity of pigmentation will help you to determine the possible variety of grape(s) used to produce that wine.

BODY, VISCOSITY, AND LEGS

When using your eyes to analyze the **body** or **viscosity** of a wine, you are answering a very simple question: How thick is the wine? The body of any wine is determined by the amount of dissolved solids contained within its liquid. To visually determine body, all you have to do is swirl your wine around the glass and notice two things: how it moves and how it clings to the inside of the glass.

Think about a wineglass half full of skim milk, and another half full of heavy cream. At rest, there is not much of a distinction between the two. Swirl both glasses, however, and you will see major differences. The skim milk will move quickly around the glass when swirled, reacting to every motion your hand makes. When you stop swirling the glass, the skim milk will rapidly sheet down the inside of the glass, falling back into the bowl of the glass. On the other hand, the heavy cream will move sluggishly around the glass when swirled, reacting only to major hand motions. When the motion stops, it will cling to the inside of the glass until large drops eventually form and slowly drip down into the bowl. Wines react in exactly the same way as their dairy counterparts. Light-bodied wines (those with fewer dissolved solids) will move around the glass quickly and sheet down the inside of the glass once the motion stops. Heavy-bodied wines (those containing larger amounts of dissolved solids) will move around the glass slowly, cling to the inside of the glass, and set up thick, slow-moving drips (called **legs** or **tears**) that will drop back down into the bowl of the glass. By analyzing the way a wine moves and the way it clings and sets up legs, a determination can be made and documented about the body or viscosity of a wine, from light to heavy or full.

While analyzing the body of a wine is important, what it can tell you about a wine is more important. Body is developed as dissolved solids and viscous compounds form in wine, and that begins all the way back at the vineyard. The raw ingredient used to produce wine is grape juice, and the main dissolved solid found in grape juice is sugar. The more sugar contained in the grape juice, the more body will be found in the resulting wine. (Other compounds and solids that are partially responsible for body will build up at the same time as sugar levels.) Sugar levels in grape juice are entirely dependent upon how ripe grapes get before they are harvested: more ripeness means more sugar.

There is only one way to achieve ripeness in grapes, and that is by allowing them to hang on the vine, so that sunlight, photosynthesis, and the grapevine can do their magic; the longer the ripening period, the riper the grapes. For longer ripening periods to occur, the vines must be growing in a warmer climate: grapes on a vine in Germany will never ripen as much as grapes on a vine in California during a normal harvest season. This means that more body in a wine is a result of the vine growing in a warmer climate. Lighter body is a result of using wine grapes ripened in a cooler climate. Body is your first indication of the type of climate in which the grapevines were grown.

There are a few caveats, however, about visually identifying body. While using your eyes can give you a very good idea about body in a wine, it is not the only way (nor the most accurate way) to measure it and come to a conclusion. There is no substitute for actually allowing the wine to come in contact with your palate while tasting it, and using your sense of touch to come to a final conclusion.

Residual sugar in sweet wines can also throw off your conclusions about body and climate. A sweet dessert wine will have a very heavy body, not always because of more ripeness in its grapes, but because of its residual sugar. Even dessert wines from very cold climates will be full-bodied. It is always best to use your visual analysis of a wine's body simply as an estimate of thickness and body. Verify that information by tasting and feeling a wine, which enable you to make a concrete conclusion.

BUBBLES/CARBONATION

Champagne and other sparkling wines can produce a delightful tingle on the palate as carbon dioxide gas is released while you take a taste; however, sight gives you your first indication that a wine is sparkling. Look for small **bubbles** that either cling to the bottom of your glass, or are generated in the wine as it rests in the glass. Ignore large bubbles that form on the surface of a glass of wine when it is poured—these are simply the result of the pouring action and surface tension. You should always document whether or not you see bubbles or **carbonation** in a wine, from effervescence all the way to a heavy carbonation.

More than likely, if you do see bubbles or carbonation in a wine, it is a white wine. Very rarely will a red wine be carbonated (a few exceptions being Lambrusco from Italy and sparkling Shiraz from Australia). For many red wines, it would be difficult to see small bubbles in the wine because of pigmentation. It is always best to assume no bubbles or carbonation in a red wine unless it is readily apparent.

Often, carbonation is found in wines from cooler to cold climates, adding mouthfeel to replace the lack of body these wines will display. Champagne, for instance, is the coldest and most northern classic wine region in France. A winemaker can literally trick your senses by adding a slight spritz to his or her lighter-bodied wines. Therefore, bubbles and carbonation are secondary indicators of climate. Their presence would more likely be found in wines from cooler, rather than warmer, climates.

SEDIMENT

Small particles or crystals that form in wine and sink to the bottom of the bottle or your glass are classified as **sediment.** Many compounds in wine can eventually form solid particles, especially tartaric acid, which forms into tartrate crystals; or proteins and tannins, which bond together to form particulate matter. In fact, sediment will form in almost every wine eventually, as long as it has a long enough period of time in which to form. This fact makes sediment the second visual indication of age, along with color. If you detect sediment in the bottom of a glass of wine you are analyzing, odds are that it is older—usually five years old or more.

Sediment is easy to identify in white wines, as you can see right through them. The pigment found in red wines poses an obstacle to detecting sediment, as it can block your view through the wine. You can either lift your glass above your head and look at the bottom of the glass from below (make sure you are coordinated enough to do this without ending up with a face full of wine!), or just follow this simple rule of thumb: Remember that pigments break down

Proper Wine Service: Decanting Wine

While sediment will not impact the flavors and aromas of a wine, it can be quite an unpleasant sensation to drink a wine that has heavy sediment. In a professional setting, wines that might contain sediment will often be decanted before they are served. Decanting is a process by which the wine is slowly transferred from the bottle to another vessel (commonly called a decanter), leaving the sediment behind. For instructions on decanting wine, see page 413.

over time, meaning young wine will have more pigmentation than older wine. Typically, if a red wine still has enough pigmentation so that you cannot see through it, then it is a safe assumption that the wine is not old enough to have formed sediment yet. This approach is much easier—and much less likely to result in a moment of messy embarrassment!

Analyzing Wine with Your Nose

Of all the senses used to directly analyze wine, smell is by far the most important sense you will use. Smell is so important that it actually should be called wine *smelling* rather than wine *tasting* (but no one would want to buy tickets to a wine smelling!). One of the reasons your sense of smell is so important is sensitivity. The average human can differentiate among approximately 10,000 different aromas! Compare that to the ability to detect only five taste sensations when relying on your taste buds: sweet, salty, sour, bitter, and savory. Your sense of smell is far more sensitive than your sense of taste.

Another reason for the importance of your sense of smell is the large role it plays in the flavor of a substance. While you might think that flavor is the way something tastes, in reality, the way it smells is far more important. Most food scientists will tell you that the flavor of a substance is made up of only 20 percent the way that substance tastes, and 80 percent the way it smells. Think about when you have a cold and your nose is stuffed up: can you taste anything? When you were a kid, and your mom wanted to give you a spoonful of medicine, what did you do? That's right: you held your nose so that you did not have to taste it.

HOW THE SENSE OF SMELL WORKS

Since smell is such an important part of wine tasting and analysis, it is important to understand how your nose works to maximize the amount of flavor and aroma you can detect. Aroma is detected when particles or molecules of a substance enter the nasal cavity and come in contact with the **olfactory epithelium.** This is a dime-sized piece of your anatomy located at the top of the nasal cavity. The olfactory epithelium is covered with microscopic hairs, called **cilia**; and when aroma molecules make contact with these cilia, an impulse is generated and sent to the olfactory bulb located in the brain, where it is registered as an aroma.

To better smell a substance, you need to maximize the number of aroma molecules/particles that come in contact with the olfactory epithelium. Imagine you are sitting at a wooden table. More than likely, you are not going to be able to smell that table. If you pulled out a chainsaw and began cutting the table into little pieces, you would be able to smell the table, because small particles of sawdust from that table would be released into the air and would enter your nasal cavity. For wine, the best way to force more aroma molecules into the air is to cause surface evaporation. This can be accomplished by rotating your glass, allowing the wine to form a thin residue on the inside of the glass, and allowing evaporation of this thin layer of wine to occur.

Another more common method is to swirl the wine around the inside of the glass. This will create an upside-down cyclone of aroma molecules to

Smell, Memory, and Mood

The sense of smell is closely linked to both mood and memory. It is not uncommon for certain aromas to bring back childhood memories or to affect one's mood. This is because the olfactory bulb along with the amygdala and the hippocampus make up the limbic system of the human brain, believed to be where emotions are processed and memories are created. When a scent is smelled for the first time, the brain will commonly link it to an event, place, or person. Many times, aromas found in wine can trigger certain emotions and memories, explaining why some aromas in wine are readily identified by certain people while others can fail to detect them at all.

form, which will be concentrated into the mouth of the glass. Many wine glasses are designed in a tulip shape, where the sides of the glass are far apart, and the bowl tapers into a smaller opening, to maximize this concentration of aroma molecules. Realize that this cyclone will not last indefinitely. You have a second or two before it will dissipate, so get your nose in there quickly, and reswirl the wine often when analyzing it with your nose. Do not be afraid to get your nose into the opening of the glass when you are smelling a wine.

The other important fact to consider when smelling a wine is that your sense of smell does not only work when you stick your nose into a glass; you can also pick up a lot of aroma using your **retronasal passage.** When you were a kid, did you ever have a mouthful of chocolate milk or apple juice when someone made you laugh? That's right: it came shooting out your nose! If this has happened to you, then you realize that there is a passageway from your mouth to your nose on the inside, called the retronasal passage. Just because you take a sip of wine does not mean you want to forget about smell. Make sure you breathe in and out of your nose while a sip of wine is on your palate. The warmth of your mouth will speed up surface evaporation in the wine, and it would be a real waste not to take advantage of all that aroma!

Who Knew? Different Usages of the Word *Nose*

Most people use the word nose to mean only the facial appendage that has two nostrils used to smell substances. In wine tasting, however, the term can be used in two other ways:

1. The sum total of the aromas detected in a particular wine can be described as its nose—e.g., "This wine has a wonderful nose!"
2. Some wine professionals even use the term as a verb to describe the act of smelling—e.g., "I picked up some hints of raspberry when I nosed the Pinot Noir."

INTENSITY OF AROMA

The first characteristic to assess and document using your sense of smell is the strength or intensity of the overall aroma. Do not confuse this with identifying or making a judgment about individual aromas. Aromas in and of themselves are neither strong nor soft. While you might think rose petals have a soft aroma, do not assume that the aroma of a wine is soft because you detect rose petals. If you were in a small room filled with 500 pounds of rose petals, it would suddenly become an extremely strong aroma. Instead, you should focus on how much total aroma you smell in a wine, how loud the aroma is. The best way to measure this is by using distance. If you swirl a wine, begin to bring it to your nose, and you can already smell it when it is still two feet from your face, that is a strong or intense aroma. Conversely, if you stick your nose completely into a glass after swirling the wine and you can still barely smell a thing, that is a soft aroma.

Strength or **intensity of aroma** can be used to help assess a wine's quality. Typically, wines that are of a higher quality will have more intensity of aroma. Just remember to base your judgment on the type of wine being tasted. For instance, reds will almost always have stronger aromas than whites.

IDENTIFYING INDIVIDUAL AROMAS

One of the most difficult skills to master when learning to analyze wines is identifying individual aromas. It is easy to hold a peeled banana in your hand, smell it, and come to the conclusion that it smells like banana; you have visual cues and memory helping you. It is another thing altogether to take a light straw–colored liquid, smell the liquid, and determine that it smells like bananas.

To identify wine aromas, it is always best to use a systematic approach, starting with broad aroma categories, and then refining your analysis by getting more exact about the specific aroma or aromas that you smell. Remember, humans can differentiate between approximately 10,000 different aromas. It is extremely difficult to smell a wine and immediately recognize a specific, individual aroma. You must start general and work toward more specific. It may seem that wine tasting professionals and seasoned wine veterans can literally pull these aromas from thin air, but in fact they are using the same systematic approach; they can just do it very quickly through years of practice.

To that end, you should realize that it would be almost impossible to take an initial sniff of a wine and immediately identify an individual aroma like lemon zest. It is possible, however, to immediately recognize a general fruity smell coming off of a wine. Once you have identified this smell as fruity, think about how many of those ten thousand different aromas you have just eliminated. Now, you can simply focus only on fruity aromas and get more specific. Is this fruity aroma reminiscent of tree fruits, tropical fruits, berries, dried fruit, or citrus? In this case, it would be citrus; now you have eliminated hundreds of other aromas you no longer need to think about, and you can get even more specific. What kind of citrus fruit? Oranges, grapefruit, limes, or lemons? For our example, the answer would be lemons. It may just be a general lemon smell, but you can still get more specific. Lemon juice, lemon oil, or lemon zest? In this case, it would be lemon zest. This is the way to truly arrive at a specific aroma.

Considering that the best way to identify most aromas is to start with broad wine aroma categories and then get more specific, it is good to know the four major categories of wine aromas.

Fruit and Floral Aromas

These represent aromas that generally come from the grapes used to produce a wine. Fruity aromas can remind you of citrus, berries, tropical fruits, tree fruits (like apples and pears), dried fruits, and even artificial fruit flavors. Floral aromas range from the smell of fresh flowers to the smell of perfume.

Earth and Mineral Aromas

Earth and mineral aromas are most likely a representation of the minerals and trace elements found in the soil of a particular vineyard, although some can come from the grapes themselves. This category represents aromas that are reminiscent of earth, wet dirt, minerals, vegetables, herbs, and plant matter. In general, white wines have more mineral aromas, while red wines tend to be earthier.

Wood and Spice Aromas

Wood and spice aromas develop in a wine through aging in oak barrels and exposure to oxygen during the aging process. These aromas will remind you of wood, smoke, roasted smells, spices, and caramelization.

Biological and Chemical Aromas

Aromas that have a biological or chemical quality are most likely derived from winemaking. Many can come from the fermentation process (especially in younger wines), while others develop through extended bottle aging (as a result of a slow oxidation and biochemical changes). These aromas can be reminiscent of several aromas you might not associate with wine, like yeast, butter, nail polish remover, vinegar, medicine, or even wet basement. While many of these aromas are considered major faults in most wines (such as mildew, hospital, and sulfur), a surprising number are actually positive aromas in certain wines, adding complexity and character. For instance, cat urine is considered a normal aroma for wines made from the Sauvignon Blanc grape, and top-quality Pinot Noirs from the region of Burgundy will often display barnyard aromas reminiscent of farm smells!

To ensure that nothing is left out, we should make sure that these four aroma categories represent the vast majority of wine aromas. Remember that 80 percent of flavor is aroma, and that our three main impacts on the flavor of a wine are the grapes used to produce a wine, the winemaking process that the wine goes through, and the *terroir* of a particular vineyard and viticultural decisions used in that vineyard. Fruit and floral aromas come from grapes. Earth and mineral aromas develop mostly because of *terroir* and what happens in the vineyard. Both wood and spice aromas and chemical

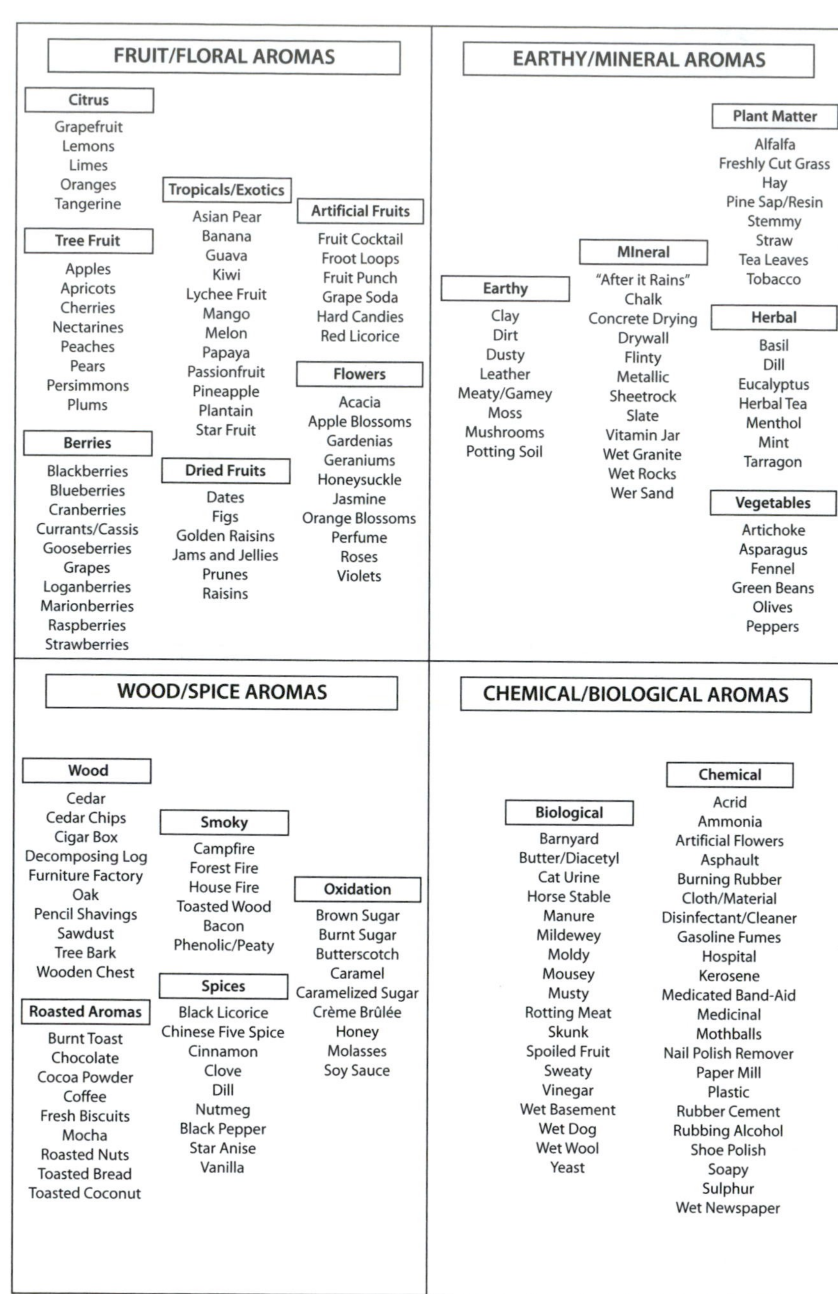

Individual aromas found in the four major aroma categories for wine. In each quadrant, aromas get more and more specific. Keep in mind, this is by no means an exhaustive list; rather it is a listing of common aromas.

and biological aromas come from different aspects of the winemaking process. Therefore, our categories do indeed represent the vast majority of aromas we would expect to find in a wine.

When documenting specific aromas found in a wine, it is also important not to lose sight of the relative strength of each aroma category. Some of these aromas may be subtle hints, while others may jump out of the glass at you as you nose the wine. Be sure to document not only the specific aromas you detect, but also which of the aroma categories is the strongest. This is an important piece of information that will help you to estimate the age of a wine when you are summing up your overall impressions.

AROMA COMPLEXITY

Be sure to take note of how complex or simple the nose is of a wine you are analyzing. A complex nose is one that has several layers of aromas; every time you stick your nose into the glass, something new is revealed. Simplicity of aroma is not inherently bad—a wine with a simple nose can still smell good—but it is important to note if a wine has relatively few aromas. **Complexity of aroma** will later help you to determine the overall quality of a wine.

ALCOHOL CONTENT

Ethanol is a volatile substance, and through evaporation, ethanol molecules convert to vapor form fairly quickly. This makes it possible for you to detect alcohol while smelling a wine. Imagine that you are blindfolded and someone places a shot glass full of beer and a shot of whiskey in front of you. Could you tell the difference between the two by just smelling both? Hopefully, it would be quite easy to detect the difference, and one of the main reasons is the difference in **alcohol content.** Airborne ethanol molecules will cause a tingling or warming sensation in the nostrils, as these fumes cause a slight irritation of the soft tissues inside your nose. Aromas such as rubbing alcohol also serve to indicate higher alcohol content in a wine. Later, when we actually taste the wine, similar sensations will help us to come to a solid assessment of alcohol content.

Analyzing alcohol content is important because it will help us further determine the type of climate in which the grapes for a particular wine were grown. Remember that sugar is the base ingredient that yeast converts into alcohol during the winemaking process. The more sugar is present in the grape juice, the stronger the alcohol content in a wine. This means that higher sugar content will be proportional to higher concentrations of alcohol. The only way a grape develops sugar is through ripeness, and, as discussed above, warmer climates produce riper grapes. Conversely, cooler climates result in lower sugar content, and therefore lower alcohol content. In this way, you can use alcohol content as part of your overall determination of climate.

Alcohol content measured by volume—known as **alcohol by volume** or **abv** (the measurement printed on wine labels)—will generally range from 7 percent to 20 percent, depending upon the style of wine and the climate the grapes were grown in. That said, the average alcohol content for all wines is roughly 13 percent alcohol by volume. While many examples exist at the extremes of high or low alcohol content, the vast majority of table wines will actually fall fairly close to the 13 percent mark, usually within 2 percent to 3 percent (10 to 16 percent abv). When you document alcohol content, keep this fact in mind and determine this characteristic accordingly.

Analyzing Wine with Your Palate

After analyzing a wine with your eyes and nose, it is finally time to analyze it with your palate, or mouth. When actually taking a sip of wine, realize that you are engaging three senses at the same time. You will taste the wine as it comes in contact with your taste buds, feel the wine as it comes in contact with the soft tissues of your mouth, and smell the wine as aroma compounds travel up to the nasal cavity from the mouth through the retronasal passage (be sure to breathe out through your nose). It is important to utilize all three of these senses to get an accurate assessment. Keep the following in mind while tasting a wine:

- **Take small sips.** You should take only small amounts of wine onto the palate when tasting. This will allow for maximum movement around the inside of your mouth, and maximum mixture with air. Avoid taking more than a half ounce of wine onto the palate at once.
- **Make sure the wine moves around in your mouth.** To get the full effect of tasting a wine, make sure the wine comes in contact with all the various surfaces of the inside of your mouth by moving it around on the palate. You can do this quite easily by chewing the wine. Simulate the movements you make while chewing food when you taste wine, and before you know it, the wine will make contact with all the surfaces it needs to. If you do not get the wine in motion, certain areas of the mouth closely associated with sensing different characteristics will be left out. For instance, acid is best sensed in the palate on the insides of the cheeks and on the sides of the tongue. If wine never comes in contact with these areas, you will not get an accurate reading on the acidity of a wine.
- **Allow your palate to adapt to a new wine.** It may take a sip or two before your palate adjusts to a particular wine, especially if that wine has strong or aggressive flavors. Take an initial sip of wine, move it around your mouth, spit it out, and immediately forget about what you sensed. Your next sip will give you a much more accurate assessment of a wine, as your palate will have adjusted to its characteristics.
- **Focus on individual characteristics with each sip.** After adapting your palate to a wine, make sure that you are focusing on a single characteristic as you take each sip. For instance, you should take a sip and focus solely on the body/viscosity of a wine. Then take a sip and focus on sweetness level. Continue this focus tasting on all of the characteristics you analyze with the palate and you will get a much more accurate assessment of a wine.
- **Do not forget to spit!** Keep your palate fresh and your senses sharp by spitting each sip of wine out after tasting.

BODY/VISCOSITY

The first characteristic to analyze on the palate is body/viscosity. Remember that you analyzed this characteristic already using your sense of sight, although coming in contact with a wine will give you a far more accurate assessment. As with measuring body/viscosity with your eyes, you are trying to answer the question: How thick is the wine? Wines that are heavy or full-bodied will seem thick and viscous on the palate. They will seem heavy on the tongue and will often coat the inside of your mouth. Lighter-bodied wines will seem thin on the palate. Again, a good analogy for the body/viscosity of a wine is to think about the sensations you would get from a sip of skim milk versus a sip of heavy cream. The texture of skim milk would be sensed on the palate similarly to a light-bodied wine, whereas heavy cream would be more similar to a full-bodied wine.

Body/viscosity should be measured and documented on a variable scale starting at light, moving through medium, and ending at heavy. For dry wines, body is directly proportional to the level of ripeness in the grapes used in its production—more ripeness equals more sugar, solids, and viscous compounds. With sweet wines, body is greatly affected by the level of sweetness. The sweeter the wine, the more dissolved sugar it contains and the thicker the body will become.

SWEETNESS

The juice of wine grapes is inherently sweet, containing extremely high levels of sugar. This sugar is consumed by yeast cells during the fermentation process, and if no sugar remains in a wine after fermentation, the wine is considered **dry.** Any sugar remaining in the wine is called **residual sugar.** While a majority of table wines are dry, there are a multitude of wines that range from having a hint of sweetness all the way to being syrupy sweet (think about drinking honey). When analyzing **sweetness,** you are trying to determine whether a wine contains any residual sugar, and if so, how sweet the wine actually is. Be sure not to confuse fruitiness with sweetness, however. We typically associate fruitiness with sweetness, and while many wines are fruity, that does not mean that they are necessarily sweet.

Sweetness Level	Description
Dry	No sugar
Semisweet	Just a touch of sweetness
Sweet	Fairly sweet, like fruit juice
Dessert wine (very sweet)	Like drinking honey

It is far more common to have a sweet white wine than a sweet red, and most of these sweet white wines come from cooler climates (the exception being white fortified wines such as Sherry, which actually come from quite warm climates). The winemaker either will reserve some of the natural sugar found in the grapes, or will add some sweetness to a wine (usually in the form of unfermented grape juice) just prior to bottling. Wines from cooler climates have a naturally high level of acidity due to shortened ripening periods, and this touch of sweetness is used to mask the high level of acidity. Whenever you detect sweetness in a wine, be sure to heighten your awareness of acid level in the wine.

ACIDITY

Wine grapes are acidic by nature, and that **acidity** will be present in a finished wine. You can detect acidity in wine with two of your senses: taste and touch. Acid tastes tart or sour, so the more of this sensation you detect, the higher the level of acidity. Acids also make your mouth water and cause a tingling sensation on the sides of your tongue, the insides of your cheeks, and the area where your jaws meet; the stronger the sensation, the higher the acidity. While both senses can be used to analyze acidity, it is best to rely on your sense of touch over your sense of taste. Winemakers can hide the sour flavors found in higher-acid wines by adding a touch of sweetness or not completely fermenting a wine. As mentioned in the "Sweetness" section above, sugar (even in very small concentrations) can mask acids, making a wine taste less acidic even if it contains a high concentration of acidity.

When tasting wines for acidity, keep in mind how acids in other foods affect your palate. Extremely high-acid wines should remind you of drinking something like lemon juice, whereas extremely low-acid wines will have a much softer impact on the palate, reminiscent of the acid found in sour cream or sour milk. As a general rule, the higher the acidity, the cooler the climate the grapes for that wine were grown in—less ripeness translates to higher acid levels.

INTENSITY OF FLAVOR

You can determine the **intensity of flavor** in a wine by analyzing how strong or intense the flavors are on the palate. Wines with low flavor intensity can seem soft, diluted, and watered down. Intensely flavored wines, on the other hand, will seem powerful, strong, and concentrated on the palate. A good analogy for intensity of flavor in wines is orange juice. If a wine with an average flavor intensity would be similar to a normal glass of orange juice, a wine with soft intensity would be like a mixture of half water, half orange juice. The flavor is the same, just watered down and diluted. A wine regarded as having a strong flavor intensity would be similar to orange juice concentrate: still the same flavor, but much more intense.

Intensity of flavor often depends upon the growing conditions in the vineyard. When grapevines are grown in a high-stress environment and struggle to survive, they produce less fruit than normal. This fruit, however, is much more concentrated and intense than the fruit from vines grown in a low-stress environment (see Chapter 3). Due to this relation to stress, intensity of flavor is most often used to help judge the quality of a wine.

TANNINS

Tannins are long-chain molecules found in red wines that come from the skins, stems, and seeds of grapes, as well as from contact with oak during the aging process. When judging tannins in a red wine, you are attempting to analyze the amount of **astringency** the wine possesses. Astringency is a tactile sensation: something that you feel. It is a sensation that makes it feel as though your palate is dry, even though you have just put a liquid in your mouth. Your tongue may suddenly feel fuzzy, or it might feel like your teeth have socks on. This sensation is a result of tannins irritating the soft tissues in your mouth. The more tannins a wine has, the stronger the astringent effects on the palate. These tannins will slowly break down over time, which is why many red wines are aged for longer periods than white wines, which have little to no tannin content because of the way they are made.

A wine with a high level of tannins should not be described as being dry. Instead it should be referred to as either **tannic** or astringent. Remember, dry is a term used to describe a wine with no residual sugar and actually has nothing to do with tannins.

Two important pieces of information have to be considered when analyzing tannins. The first is the amount of tannins present and the level of astringency, which will help to identify the grape varieties used to produce a wine. Wine made from grapes with extremely thick skins will have more astringency because there are simply more tannins available to be leached into the wine during the winemaking process. Thus, heavier tannin structure and higher astringency in a wine are the signs of a grape with thick skins, while lower levels signify that a thin-skinned grape variety was used.

Secondly, when analyzing tannins, it is important to note how aggressive the tannin structure is in a wine. As mentioned earlier, tannins break down over time: long-chain tannin molecules break down into smaller-chain molecules as the wine is slowly exposed to oxygen. Aggressive tannins, even in a wine that does not have a large concentration, will be abrasive and feel almost like sandpaper on the palate—a hallmark of a younger, underdeveloped wine. Older vintage red wines, even those made from grapes with thick skins and having larger concentrations of tannins, will seem softer—the astringency is still there, but it feels more like velvet on the palate. Document the overall impression you get from a red wine, taking into account both the amount of astringency and the aggressiveness of the tannins.

ALCOHOL CONTENT

Alcohol content can be analyzed with your nose and with your palate. When tasting a wine, alcohol causes a warming or burning sensation, especially near the back of the mouth and throat. This warming sensation will linger once the wine is spit out, or will be registered in the throat if the wine is swallowed. A wine that has too high an alcohol content is described as being **hot.** To analyze the content you must concentrate on the tactile sensation that the ethanol causes on the palate, as well as the effect it has on the retronasal passage.

Ethanol is a volatile liquid which readily vaporizes at room temperature; however, when warmed on the palate by your body heat, this volatilization becomes even greater. With a small amount of wine on the palate, you should force some air out of your nose. This will pull the ethanol vapors into your nasal cavity, where they can be sensed as fumes. By combining the strength of these alcohol fumes in the nose with the warming sensation on the soft tissue of the palate, a reasonable estimate of alcohol content can be determined. Remember that alcohol content should be documented between 7 percent abv and 20 percent abv, with an average of 13 percent.

FLAVOR PROFILE

When analyzing **flavor profile,** you are documenting the different, distinct flavors detected on the palate. The different flavors found in wines are the same as the aromas you might detect. Just like smell, there are four important categories of flavor: Fruit and floral flavors, earth and mineral flavors, wood and spice flavors, and biological and chemical flavors. Your sense of taste will further intensify these flavors by possibly adding sweet, sour, or bitter sensations. You should document the distinct flavors you detect and register on the palate.

It is also important to monitor if and how those flavors change. With many wines (almost all high-quality wines), the flavors change as the wine is in the mouth. There are three distinct stages that the flavor profile goes through: the **attack**, the **midpalate**, and the **finish.**

Attack

The first flavor sensations you pick up when taking a sip of wine are considered the attack. This lasts only a second or two before fading into the midpalate. For red wines, the attack generally ends when the tannins begin to be perceived. Typical flavors associated with the attack are bright and, often, fruity.

Midpalate

Once the attack begins to fade, new flavors emerge that make up the midpalate. This is often when more earthy/mineral and wood/spice flavors are detected. The midpalate lasts until the wine is spit out or swallowed.

Finish

After the wine has been spit out or swallowed, the flavors that linger make up the finish. Later, you will analyze the finish in terms of how long it lasts, but at this point you simply want to describe the flavor or flavors you detect during that time. Finish flavors are often spicy, toasty, or reminiscent of tart fruit.

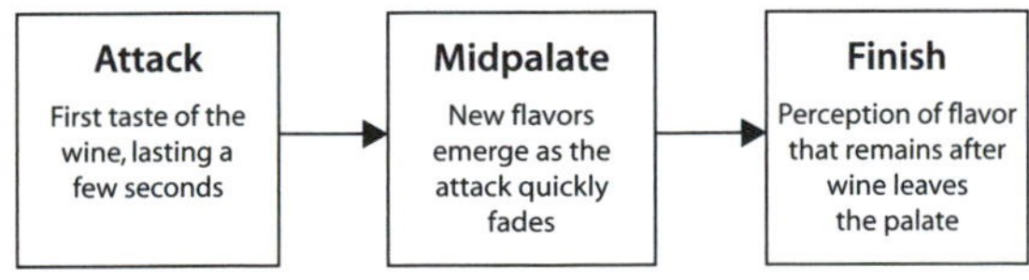

The progression of flavors on the palate.

FLAVOR COMPLEXITY

Similarly to when you smell the wine, you want to note the complexity of the flavors when you taste. Complex wines will have several distinct flavors that can be registered on the palate. Every time you take a sip, you register a new flavor. There are different and distinct flavors detected during the attack, midpalate, and finish. Simple wines tend to have only one or two distinct flavors. They may taste good, but they would not be described as complex. It is important to document the level of **flavor complexity** detected in a wine when tasting. This characteristic can later be used to help analyze the quality of the wine.

FINISH

The finish of a wine is a measurement of how long its flavor lingers in your mouth after the wine has been spit out or swallowed. Finish should be documented in terms of time. The flavor of a wine with a short finish will quickly dissipate and will no longer be registered in just a few seconds. You spit the wine out, and the flavor almost immediately goes away. A wine with a long finish will still be tasted even a minute or two after the wine is gone.

To analyze finish, concentrate on what you still taste once you have spit the wine out. Either using a timer or keeping time in your head, focus on how long that flavor lingers on the palate—the length of time you can still taste the wine. Document finish in the following manner: a short finish for a flavor that goes away in a matter of seconds, a medium finish for a wine whose flavor takes several moments to disappear, and a long finish for a flavor that lingers on the palate for a minute or more.

Analyzing finish is the final component in determining the quality of a wine. In general, higher-quality wines have longer finishes and lower-quality wines have shorter finishes. Higher-quality wines tend to have much more intense flavors than lower-quality wines, and these flavors will continue registering on the palate after the wine is spit out.

Summary

Tasting wine is a difficult skill to master, but a rewarding one to learn in an attempt to gain more knowledge about wine. To conduct a successful tasting and become a better wine taster you must understand how to taste a wine, attempt to maximize the ability of your senses, and minimize distractions.

Analyzing a wine involves focusing on the senses. You must first look at several characteristics, such as the color of a wine, possibly the pigmentation, and the way the wine moves and clings. Next, you smell the wine, documenting its intensity on the nose and the distinct aromas it produces. Finally, the wine is taken on the palate and the senses of taste, touch, and smell go to work analyzing tactile sensations as well as flavors.

Tasting wine is a skill. To become good at this skill, it must first be learned and then practiced. The more wines you taste, the easier it becomes to detect certain characteristics in wine. Correctly distinguishing the appropriate levels of body, alcohol, tannins, complexity, and finish in a given wine, properly determining color and brightness, and describing the aromas and flavors that you detect are the skills required to become good at wine tasting.

Tasting Sheet

Tasting sheets are often a helpful tool when tasting wines. They not only ensure that you assess all of the characteristics you are supposed to analyze in the proper order, but they also provide you with a written record of the wines that you have tasted. Below you will find a sample tasting sheet that can be copied and used to taste and analyze wines.

WINE:		APPELLATION:	
APPEARANCE		**NOSE**	
Brightness/Clarity:	cloudy ··········· | ··········· clear	Intensity of Aroma:	soft ··········· | ··········· intense
Color:		Fruit/Floral:	
Pigmentation:		Earth/Mineral:	
Body/Viscosity/Legs:	light ··········· | ··········· heavy	Wood/Spice:	
Bubbles/Carbonation:		Biological/Chemical:	
Sediment:		Aroma Complexity:	simple ··········· | ··········· complex
		Alcohol Content:	low: 7% ··········· | ··········· 20%: high
PALATE			
Body/Viscosity:	light ··········· | ··········· heavy		*Flavor Profile*
Sweetness:	dry ··········· | ··········· sweet	Attack:	
Acidity:	low ··········· | ··········· high	Midpalate:	
Intensity of Flavor:	soft ··········· | ··········· intense	Finish:	
Tannins:	low ··········· | ··········· high	Flavor Complexity:	simple ··········· | ··········· complex
Alcohol Content:	low: 7% ··········· | ··········· 20%: high	Finish	short ··········· | ··········· long
CONCLUSIONS			
Estimated Age:	1–3 yrs 3–5 yrs 5+ yrs	Possible Grape(s):	
Estimated Climate:	cold ··········· | ··········· hot	Estimated Quality:	low ··········· | ··········· high
Possible Origin(s):		Overall Impression:	1 2 3 4 5 6 7 8 9 10

Wine tasting sheet.

Review Questions

1. The reason one generally drinks wine is to enjoy it, while one tastes wine in order to analyze it.
   A. True
   B. False

2. It is always best to taste wine in a well-lit environment free from noise and obvious aromas.
   A. True
   B. False

3. It is always best to taste red wines before white wines.
   A. True
   B. False

4. A blind tasting refers to tasting a wine:
   A. with your eyes closed
   B. without analyzing the visual characteristics of the wine
   C. without knowing anything about the wine
   D. in a poorly lit room

5. A led tasting is one where:
   A. several vintages of the same wine are tasted
   B. an individual leads a group of tasters through the sensory analysis of a wine
   C. several different wines from the same region and vintage are tasted
   D. several wines are shown by a winery, broker, or retail establishment

6. A vertical tasting is one where:
   A. several vintages of the same wine are tasted
   B. an individual leads a group of tasters through the sensory analysis of a wine
   C. several different wines from the same region and vintage are tasted
   D. several wines are shown by a winery, broker, or retail establishment

7. A horizontal tasting is one where:
   A. several vintages of the same wine are tasted
   B. an individual leads a group of tasters through the sensory analysis of a wine
   C. several different wines from the same region and vintage are tasted
   D. several wines are shown by a winery, broker, or retail establishment

8. An industry tasting is one where:
   A. several vintages of the same wine are tasted
   B. an individual leads a group of tasters through the sensory analysis of a wine
   C. several different wines from the same region and vintage are tasted
   D. several wines are shown by a winery, broker, or retail establishment

9. Purple hints in a red wine are a sign of:
   A. acidity
   B. improper storage
   C. youth
   D. a warm climate

10. Sediment in a wine is typically a sign of:
   A. age
   B. improper winemaking
   C. grapes grown in a warm climate
   D. grapes grown in a cool climate

11. As white wines age, they get _______________ in color.
   A. lighter
   B. darker

12. As red wines age, they get _______________ in color.
   A. lighter
   B. darker

13. The *most* important sense we use when analyzing wine is our sense of:
   A. taste
   B. sight
   C. smell
   D. touch

14. To smell an aroma, the particles/molecules of the item you are smelling must become airborne.
   A. True
   B. False

15. We can use our sense of sight to evaluate acidity.
   A. True
   B. False

16. Intensity of aroma and intensity of flavor can be used as indicators of age for a wine.
   A. True
   B. False

17. Which of the following will *not* cause a white wine to turn golden?
   A. Extended bottle aging
   B. Aging in oak barrels
   C. Carbonation
   D. High levels of sugar

18. The amount of pigmentation a red wine has is an indicator of:
   A. grape skin thickness
   B. climate
   C. alcohol
   D. acid

19. A wine with high tannins would correctly be described as dry.
   A. True
   B. False

20. Which of the following is *not* one of the distinct stages the flavor of a wine goes through while it is on the palate?
   A. Finish
   B. Attack
   C. Forepalate
   D. Midpalate

Key Terms

sensory analysis
led tasting
blind tasting
vertical tasting
horizontal tasting
industry tasting
clarity
brightness/bright
color
intensity of pigmentation
pigments
anthocyanins
body
viscosity
legs/tears
bubbles/carbonation
sediment
olfactory epithelium
cilia
retronasal passage
intensity of aroma
aroma complexity
alcohol content
alcohol by volume (abv)
sweetness
dry
residual sugar
acidity
intensity of flavor
tannins
astringency
tannic
hot
flavor profile
attack
midpalate
finish
flavor complexity

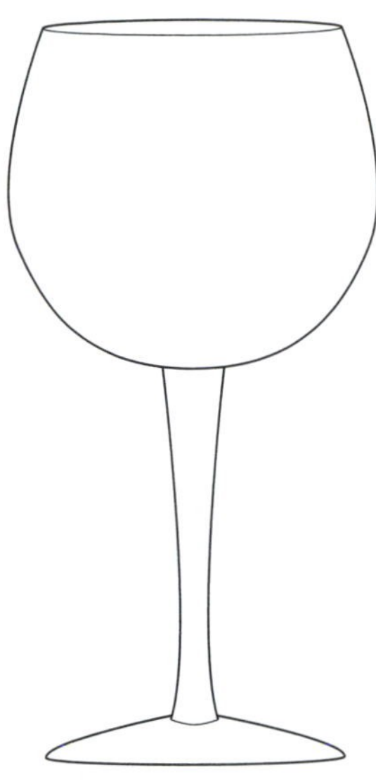

CHAPTER 8

Applying Wine Analysis

When it comes to wine, I tell people to throw away the vintage charts and invest in a corkscrew. The best way to learn about wine is in the drinking.

—**ALEXIS LICHINE,** French winemaker and writer

The skill of tasting and analyzing a wine is important, but it becomes much more valuable when the sensory impulses produced by that wine can be applied. Everything that you analyze in a wine can lead you to draw conclusions, including some of that wine's key characteristics. In this chapter, we focus on how to apply what we sense and document when tasting wines, and how to draw conclusions from it. Our focus is on determining a wine's age, the climate and place from which it comes, the type of grape or grapes used to make it, and its quality level.

Determining Age

To make an educated guess about the **age** of a wine, you need to focus on the visual and aroma characteristics you detected. Most wines age along a somewhat predictable arc, and will show their age in many ways. At a basic level, you should think of this age in terms of ranges. For example, attempt to determine if a wine is one to three years old, three to five years old, or five or more years of age. The two most important characteristics that can help determine age are color and dominant aroma category.

COLOR

A wine's color will change over time through bottle aging or barrel aging. The reason for this change is oxidation, which is slow and regulated inside a bottle and occurs much more quickly in the barrel. One other factor that might affect color is residual sugar, which can make wines darker. By the time you have completed a sensory analysis of a wine, you should be able to prove whether a wine received extensive oak aging or whether it contains residual sugar. If a wine has gone through an aging regime that included extensive oak aging, the wine will display clear barrel and oxidation notes. Residual sugar can be proved simply by detecting the presence of sweetness on the palate. If neither of these characteristics is detected, then the color of the wine is most likely a result of the slow oxidation that has occurred in the

Table 8.1 **Color of White Wines Based on Bottle Aging**

COLOR	PROBABLE AGE
Clear to light straw	1–3 years
Yellow	3–5 years
Golden	5+ years
Brown	Dead

Table 8.2 **Color of Red Wines Based on Bottle Aging**

COLOR	PROBABLE AGE
Purple/Purple hints	1–3 years
Red	3–5 years
Amber/Brick	5+ years
Brown	Dead

bottle. This happens at a fairly predictable rate for both white wines and reds (see Tables 8.1 and 8.2).

Regardless of what caused the color change in a wine, the color at the time of tasting will give you a starting point for determining age.

DOMINANT AROMA CATEGORY

As you analyze the specific aromas found in a wine, it is always important to document which of the four main aroma categories was perceived as the strongest. As wines age, their aromas go through several different transitions. When young, most wines will be strongly scented with fruit and floral aromas. The flavors from the grape are dominant. Also, it is not unusual to detect soft yeasty notes in a wine if fermentation was conducted recently.

Over time, the fruitiness begins to fade and the wine begins to smell more of earth and minerals. Subtle hints of biological and chemical aromas not associated with fermentation begin to develop. As a wine reaches maturity, which will take five years or more for the majority of wines, these chemical and biological aromas grow stronger, and it is not unusual to also begin to detect caramel notes, as the wine has been oxidizing slowly in the bottle over time.

The one wild card here is wood and spice aromas. Wines will pick up these notes only if they are aged in a barrel, which often impacts color. Aging in oak causes a wine to change colors prematurely, so the wine almost always looks older than it actually is. Be sure to keep this in mind if wood and spice dominate the nose. Caramelization aromas such as brown sugar or molasses, mostly caused by oxidation, are classic signs of this premature aging and color change.

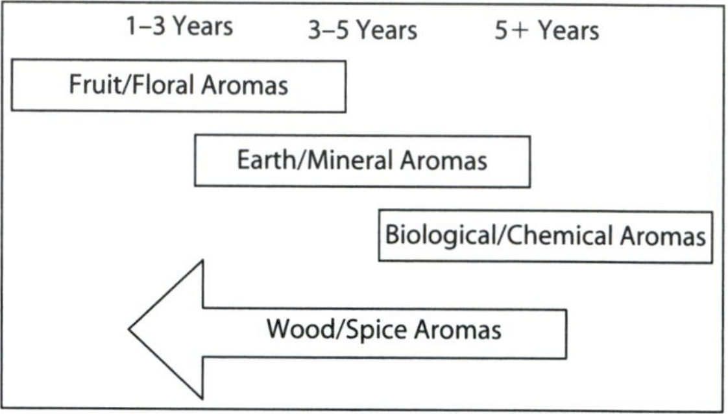

Dominant aromas at key age ranges. Note how wood/spice aromas would make you think to back up your assessment assuming oak aging and premature aging.

OTHER CLUES

Besides the two main characteristics that are used to analyze age, several others might help you to come to a final conclusion—chiefly, sediment and tannins.

Unless specifically treated in the winery, all wines should eventually develop or throw sediment. If sediment is noted in your glass, this points toward an older wine, typically aged five or more years. Because one of the main causes of sediment formation is tannins and proteins in a wine bonding and creating solid particulate matter, it is far more common to find sediment in older red wines than in whites.

Tannins are long chain molecules that are broken down into smaller chains over time and exposure to oxygen. Much of the purpose of aging a red wine is to soften the tannins prior to drinking.

If the tannins in a red wine are extremely aggressive, astringent, and harsh, that is often a sign that the wine is younger and the tannins have not yet broken down. If they are soft and refined, that will usually signify more maturity in a wine.

FORMING AN OPINION ABOUT AGE

To develop an estimate for age, the best place to start is with a wine's color. This will give you an assessment that can be either confirmed or disproved by the dominant aroma category and other indicators. Once you have determined an estimate based on color, you want to consider the aroma. As just discussed, the dominant aroma category can be used to help analyze age because aromas slowly change over time. If the wine appears young based on color, and aromas of fruit and flowers are the most dominant, you have a match. More than likely the wine you analyzed is in its youth: approximately one to three years of age. In the same way, wines that look older and have a coordinating dominant aroma category can be assumed to be older. If the color and dominant aroma category do not exactly match one another, then you need to consider a couple of possibilities:

- If wood and spice aromas dominate, the color change in the wine was probably rapid due to the increased amount of oxidation the wine was exposed to in a barrel. In this situation, it would be wise to back up your assessment. If the wine looks like it is more than five years old, it is probably more in the range of a three- to five-year-old wine. If it looks like it is three to five but has strong oak aromas, it may actually be quite young, between one and three years of age.
- Some wines are simply earthier than others due to the grapes, growing conditions, and/or winemaking practices used. It would be unlikely for a white wine that is clear or a red wine that has a strong purple color to be older, as these colors rapidly change. In this situation, color is probably your best guide.
- For red wines, if there is a question, let the tannins be your guide. If a red wine has the appearance of an older wine, yet it smells strongly of fruit, assess the tannins. If they are very harsh, then the wine is probably younger, and if they are softer, then the wine is most likely a little more mature.

Estimating age is not an exact science, and your estimate will not always be correct. If you evaluate the proper characteristics and consider your strongest argument based on the evidence at hand, though, you will be right much more often than you are wrong. With experience and exposure to several different wines of multiple ages, this process will become easier over time.

Determining Climate

Being able to determine the **climate** where grapes were grown for a wine you have just analyzed is not difficult if you understand the basics of viticulture and the stages a vine goes through during the growing season. The main characteristics to consider when you begin this assessment are acid, alcohol, and body.

During the summer months in a vineyard, grapes begin to ripen. As this occurs, organic acids in the grapes begin to break down while photosynthesis increases the grapes' sugar content. Nature typically determines how ripe these grapes will get before it is time to harvest, depending upon the climate. Warmer climates have longer growing periods and allow grapes to ripen to a fuller degree than cooler climates do. This means that in a warmer climate, the acid in grapes will break down to a lower degree and the sugar levels will increase to a higher degree than in a cooler climate. Three of the main characteristics we analyze during the sensory analysis of a wine will be impacted by this process: acidity, alcohol content, and body. (See figure on page 34.)

ACIDITY

The acidity in a grape when it is harvested will be translated into the wine that is made from it. Grapes grown in cooler climates should have much higher levels of acidity than those grown in warmer areas. If you analyze a single wine as having higher acidity, then the wine was probably made from grapes grown in a cooler climate. If you are comparing two wines that are similar to one another, such as two dry, light-bodied whites or two heavy reds, the wine with the more pronounced acid level will typically come from a cooler climate than the other wine.

ALCOHOL CONTENT

Ethanol is created by yeast cells as they metabolize sugar molecules. The more sugar present in grape juice, the higher the level of alcohol content produced, if the wine is fully fermented until dry. Warmer climates allow grapes to build up higher sugar content. If you analyze a wine as having a higher alcohol content based on the way it smells and the warming feeling it gives you on the palate, then the wine is most likely from a warmer climate. If you are comparing two similar wines side by side, the one that has a stronger presence of alcohol will most likely be from a warmer climate than the other wine.

BODY

In the same way that simple syrup is thicker than water because it has more solids (in this case sugar) dissolved into its solution, grape juice from riper grapes will be thicker than the juice from less ripe grapes. As sugar content builds up and other components develop in the grapes during the ripening period, the amount of dissolved solids in the juice produced increases, resulting in greater density. When fermented, this grape juice will be turned into wine that has the same thickness. If you analyze a wine as having a heavy body, it is more than likely from a warmer climate. When comparing two similar wines to one another, the wine that is thicker in body will more than likely come from the warmer of the two climates.

CONSIDERING SWEET WINES

Besides these three major characteristics that help to determine climate, it is important to also consider the sweetness of a wine. If a wine is sweet, that is not a sign that the grapes had high sugar content and you have tasted a wine from a warm climate. In fact, it is often a sign of a cooler-climate wine. Winemakers will often add sugar to a wine in the form of unfermented grape juice to mask high acidity. This is similar to adding sugar to lemon juice to make lemonade. If you detect residual sugar, concentrate on the tactile sensations that acids produce—your mouth watering, a tingling sensation on the palate, etc.—to determine whether there is a high level of acid in the wine. Also, remember that the body of a wine with residual sugar added will be thicker than that of a wine that was fermented dry. In effect, a sweet wine is a syrup, so it will seem thicker even if it has not come from a warm climate.

FORMING AN OPINION ABOUT CLIMATE AND BEYOND

Once you have considered each of the individual characteristics used to determine climate, it is time to put them all together and come to a conclusion. If all three of these characteristics point toward grapes grown in a warmer climate, then more than likely that is the case; and vice versa if all signs point toward a cooler climate. If there is a discrepancy, then the strongest argument, the one with the most characteristic evidence behind it, should be the one most strongly considered. One thing to consider here is that there are a wide range of climates between warm and cool. If you have assessed medium acidity, alcohol content, and body, then the wine probably came from a temperate climate.

After climate has been determined, certain general assumptions can be made about where a wine comes from, the **Old World** or the **New World.** The Old World refers to European wine-producing countries such as France, Italy, and Spain. New World refers to wine-producing countries located outside of Europe, such as the United States, Australia, and Chile. With climate as a starting point, you can begin to determine the wine's source. Typically, European countries have cooler climates than New World countries. Other clues might also point you in the right direction, including the fact that Old World wines tend to be more earthy and mineral-driven on the nose and palate, while New World wines tend to be more fruit-forward. Oak aging characteristics are also more present in wines from the New World, as winemakers there often put wines through heavier oak aging regimes than their Old World counterparts. For a more thorough look at differences between Old World and New World wines and winemaking, see Chapter 15.

At an advanced level and with experience and knowledge, you can use an estimate of climate as a key component in determining the origin of a wine. Once you have determined a climate and whether the wine is from an Old or New World country, you can apply several of the other characteristics you analyzed to this information to make an educated guess as to the wine's origin. This involves the application of a great deal of general wine knowledge, including what sorts of climates, grapes, and techniques are found in the various wine-producing regions of the world.

Determining Grape Varieties

With at least 3,500 different wine grape varietals grown throughout the world, determining which particular varietal or varietals were used to produce a particular wine can be a daunting task. Luckily, the vast majority of these grapes are quite uncommon, and only a few dozen are widely used as a single varietal or as a major component in common blends. Regardless, the task of determining the grapes used to produce a wine that you know nothing about except what your senses tell you is still very difficult. The ability to do so requires an extensive knowledge of the characteristics of different grapes, and the methods used to produce them into wine. It also involves understanding which characteristics to focus on.

For any grape identification, you need to first consider a few major characteristics such as body and acidity. From there, you will need to assess different characteristics depending upon the style of wine, red or white.

WHITE WINES

Different white wine grapes have different distinct characteristics, such as:

Residual Sugar—Only certain grape varietals are made into a sweet style; most will usually only be made dry.

Aging Regime—Oak aging is practiced only on certain white grape varietals. Many will never be aged in oak.

Determined Climate—Since you just determined the climate you believe the wine to be from, you might as well put that information to good use. In cooler climates, only certain white wine grapes will grow, and the same holds true for warm climates.

Varietal Characteristics—Different white wine grape varietals are noted for their distinctive aromas and flavors. For instance, Sauvignon Blanc is often noted for having grapefruit and grassy flavors, while Chardonnay will often show flavors of pears and butter.

RED WINES

Different red wine grape types will also have distinct characteristics when produced into wine, including:

Pigmentation—Grapes that have thicker skins will almost always produce wines with more pigmentation than those with thinner skins, since all the pigments found in a grape come from the skins.

Tannins—Thicker-skinned grapes will almost always produce more tannic wines than those with thin skins, because much of the tannin content in a grape is located in the skin.

Determined Climate—Only certain red wine grapes grow in warmer climates, and only certain red grapes grow in cooler climates.

Varietal Characteristics—Different red wine grape varietals are also noted for their distinctive aromas and flavors. For example, the Cabernet Sauvignon grape is known for strong black currant and plum aromas, while Syrah often is reminiscent of smoke, black pepper, and cooked berries.

FORMING AN OPINION ABOUT GRAPE VARIETY

Determining the specific grape variety used to produce a given wine is similar to detective work: the best way to do it is to use the process of elimination. If you taste a white wine and pick up the strong presence of oak flavors, then you can rule out certain grape varietals that are never aged in oak, such as Riesling. Pinot Noir is a grape that produces light-bodied wines and has naturally thin skins. If you analyze a wine with a full body, deep pigmentation, and high levels of tannins, you can be almost certain that it is not a Pinot Noir. Work through all the other characteristics before applying the varietal characteristics, however. These can often lead you down the wrong road, and with the complexity of different wine grapes, it would be hard to make a definitive decision about a specific wine grape based on flavors and aromas alone.

Determining Quality Level

When determining the **quality** level, it is important to remember that the quality of a wine is not based on how much you enjoy or dislike it. Quality is not subjective; it is based on certain characteristics and beliefs that have been developed over the course of history. You may not like foie gras or Roquefort cheese, but that has nothing to do with the quality assigned to those ingredients. When assessing the quality of a wine, you need to consider the intensity of aroma and flavor, complexity of aroma and flavor, and finally, the finish.

COMPLEXITY

Complex wines will have several distinct, detectable, and describable aromas and flavors. The more of these individual aromas or flavors you detect, the more complex and higher quality the wine. Complexity is generally considered the best determination of the quality of a wine.

INTENSITY

Intense flavors and aromas in a wine are often the result of fermenting grape juice with intense and

Wine Critics

Famous wine critics and wine publications that give their opinions on the quality of certain wines have a major impact on the wine industry today. Most assign scores to wines based on a 100-point scale (although many of these scales start at 50 points as the lowest possible score). A high score can often lead to commercial success, while low scores can have the opposite effect. While these rankings can be helpful in choosing wines, it is important to remember that these scores are based on what someone else thinks and many wineries do not submit their wines to be evaluated. Some of the major wine critics and publications today include Robert Parker Jr. (who publishes *The Wine Advocate*); Steve Tanzer (who publishes *International Wine Cellar*); *Wine Spectator; Wine Enthusiast; Wine & Spirits Magazine*; and *Decanter*.

concentrated flavors. Grapes often develop this intensity when the vines that form them are under stress. Much of this stress comes from environmental impacts, such as the nutrients in the soil or the amount of water available to the vine. But viticulturalists trying to produce the best grapes possible for wine production can also carry out different practices in the vineyard to place more stress on a vine, including green harvesting, dry farming, or using old vines. The more intense the flavors or aromas are, typically the higher the quality of the wine.

FINISH

The final component to use when determining quality is the finish. This is the measurement of the length of time the flavors in a wine linger on the palate before they finally fade away. A long finish will leave an impression on the palate that can last for up to several minutes. In general, higher-quality wines almost always have long finishes.

Professional Wine Certifications

There are several international organizations that offer professional wine certifications, almost all of which require candidates to pass a blind tasting evaluation as one of the criteria for higher-level certifications. Candidates must taste several wines and determine information about them including what we have covered in this chapter: age, climate, origin, grape varieties, and quality levels. Some of the more well-known certifying bodies and their higher-level certifications that include blind tasting and analysis as a criterion are listed below:

- The International Court of Master Sommeliers
  - Certified Sommelier
  - Advanced Sommelier
  - Master Sommelier (MS)
- The Society of Wine Educators
  - Certified Wine Educator (CWE)
- The Institute of Masters of Wine
  - Master of Wine (MW)

FORMING AN OPINION ABOUT QUALITY

After considering all of the characteristics that help determine quality, all that needs to be done is to put them all together. If all of the characteristics you assessed point toward a high-quality wine, then that is most likely the case. If not all of the characteristics point toward the same level, then the quality of the wine is somewhere between high and low and you need to look at how all of the different characteristics fit together. Quality is measured in a range from low to high; it does not have to be one or the other.

Summary

The ability to apply the sensory evidence you detect when conducting a wine tasting is not a fancy magic trick. Determining information about a wine using just your senses simply involves understanding certain information about wines, grapes, viticultural and vinicultural practices, and regional tendencies. The more one knows about wine, the easier it is to apply this knowledge to a glass of wine being tasted.

Review Questions

1. Which of the following characteristics is not useful when determining the quality of a wine?
   A. Complexity
   B. Tannins
   C. Finish
   D. Intensity

2. The more stress a grapevine is under, the more intensely flavored and concentrated the grapes it will produce.
   A. True
   B. False

3. Grapes grown in a warm climate will produce wines with ____________ than grapes grown in a cool climate.

   A. more acid and less alcohol
   B. more acid and more alcohol
   C. less acid and more alcohol
   D. less acid and less alcohol

4. Which of the following is *not* an indicator of the climate in which the grapes for a particular wine were grown?

   A. Color
   B. Body
   C. Alcohol
   D. Acid

5. Which of the following is *not* an indicator of age in a wine?

   A. Color
   B. Body
   C. Dominant aroma category
   D. Sediment

6. Tannin levels, pigmentation, and varietal characteristics are all good indicators of the grape varietal used to produce a red wine.

   A. True
   B. False

7. You are tasting a red wine that has a deep red color and soft tannins, and smells strongly of leather, tobacco, and wet dirt. How old is this wine?

   A. 1 to 3 years
   B. 3 to 5 years
   C. 5 or more years
   D. The wine is past its prime and breaking down

8. You are tasting a white wine that seems to have very little alcohol content, a sharp acidity, and a very light body. What climate did this wine most likely come from?

   A. Cool climate
   B. Temperate climate
   C. Warm climate

Key Terms

age
climate
Old World
New World
quality

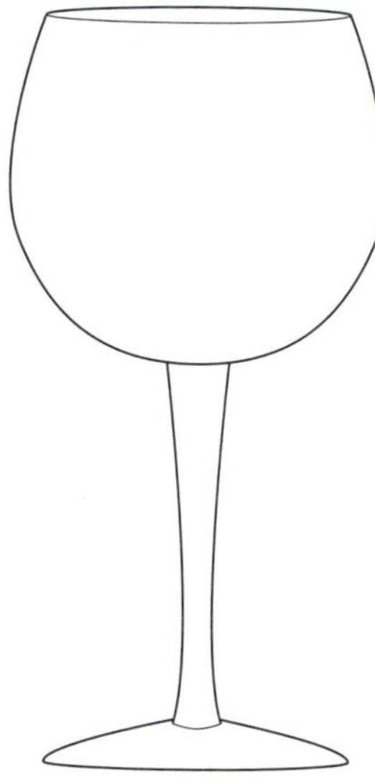

CHAPTER 9

The Wines of France

Wine is the blood of France.

—**LOUIS BERTALL,** *La Vigne*, 1878

France is the world's most important wine-producing country. No other country on Earth makes as much wine as France, and no other country produces as much premium-quality wine as France. This chapter discusses the importance and scope of French winemaking and the wine laws of France that have served as a model for all other wine-producing countries in the world, as well as the most important grapes grown and wines produced in the country. The most important wine regions of France are discussed in detail, including Bordeaux, Burgundy, the Rhône Valley, Champagne, the Loire Valley, and Alsace.

The Facts on France

CLIMATE

Located in Western Europe between the Atlantic Ocean and the Mediterranean Sea, France is home to a temperate climate overall. The country can be divided into three climate zones: a temperate-maritime climate in western France, a warm-Mediterranean climate in southern France, and a cool-continental climate in northern and central France.

TOP REGIONS

Classic Regions

- Bordeaux
- Burgundy
- The Rhône Valley
- Champagne
- The Loire Valley
- Alsace

Important Regions

- Languedoc-Roussillon
- Provence
- The Sud Ouest (Southwest)
- Jura
- Savoie
- Corsica

IMPORTANT INFORMATION

- France is the number one producer of wine in the world, typically producing more than 1.3 billion gallons of wine each year. In addition, France accounts for roughly 50 percent of all the premium wine produced in the world.
- Wine has been produced in France for more than 2,600 years.

- France is the most copied and emulated wine-producing region in the world, from grape varietals to winemaking techniques.
- The French wine laws, referred to as the AOC laws, are the oldest and strictest set of winemaking regulations in the world. They serve as the model for wine regulations in almost all other European countries. This system establishes various regions around France for winemaking and regulates how wines must be produced in each region.
- The AOC laws break up French wines into four quality classifications. These classifications are, from strictest and highest quality to loosest and lowest quality: *Appellation d'Origine Contrôlée* (AOC), *Vin Délimité de Qualité Supérieure* (VDQS), *vin de pays*, and *vin de table*.
- The top-quality wines of France are, with the exception of Alsatian wines, labeled by the region where the grapes were grown.

The History and Importance of French Wine

France is a country synonymous with wine. For thousands of years, winemakers in France have studied the land, developed hundreds of different grape varieties, and perfected classical styles of wine. Several groups and cultures have shaped French wine into what it is today.

The ancient Greeks are generally credited as being the first to plant wine grapes in France sometime around the sixth century B.C., roughly 2,600 years ago. After they settled and colonized the Mediterranean port known today as Marseilles, viticulture quickly flourished. After a few centuries of Greek rule, Gaul (as France was known at the time) came under the control of the Roman Empire.

The Romans served to elevate the quality of French wines with new grape varieties and winemaking techniques. Although vast amounts of wine were being produced near Rome, French wine began to be highly regarded amongst the wealthy and powerful in the Roman Empire. As the Catholic Church emerged and gained power near the end of the Roman Empire, its influence helped to spread winemaking from the south into areas of western, central, and northern France. After the fall of ancient Rome, the Church remained the primary producer of wine in France through the beginning of the Middle Ages, and its wines were the most highly regarded and sought after there.

As a monarchy was established in France in the Middle Ages, wealthy nobles set out to plant vineyards and produce wine in their land holdings. Wine regions with proximities to rivers and ports such as the Loire Valley and Bordeaux began to rise to power, as they could more easily transport their wines by ship to various markets in Europe. Quickly, the wines of France became accessible and revered throughout Europe.

One of the largest markets for French wine in the Middle Ages (and even today) was England. The popularity of French wine became even more ingrained in English culture when the French region of Bordeaux became an English landholding due to a royal marriage in 1152. In a similar fashion, Burgundy became part of the Dutch empire, and its wines were introduced to central European countries. Near the end of the Middle Ages, France won wars and regained control of these regions, but the rest of Europe was already hooked on its wines.

Heading into the modern era, France was the most important and powerful winemaking nation on Earth. It was widely believed during this time that France was the only country capable of producing top-quality wines. Scientific advances during the Age of Enlightenment in the 1600s and 1700s brought about major improvements to grape growing and winemaking in France.

In the 1790s, the French Revolution fundamentally changed the country. The noble classes and the Church were stripped of their vineyards and holdings, which were redistributed to the people of France. With little knowledge of producing wine, these new landholders had to quickly learn the viticultural and vinicultural practices that were part of the traditions of their regions.

The 1800s and 1900s saw amazing advancements and crushing setbacks for the winemakers of France. Following the *phylloxera* epidemic of the mid- to late nineteenth century, winemakers and grape growers replanted traditional vines using more modern methods. At the turn of the twentieth century, France once again reestablished itself as the world's most dominant winemaking nation. This dominance was threatened, however, as two world wars were soon fought on French soil. World Wars I and II had a devastating effect on France's classic wine regions, many of which became battle sites during these conflicts. At the end of World War II, France's wine industry was battered, but by no means destroyed. Replanting and rebuilding in the wine regions of France again quickly reestablished the French winemaking tradition.

Although the rest of the world is catching up to France in terms of quality and production today, the French are still the most important and prodigious producers of wine in the world. France is responsible for almost 20 percent of the world's total wine production today. It is not just the quantity of French wine that makes France important, however, but the vast amount of quality wine produced there. France produces roughly 50 percent of the world's premium wine. This means that one out of every two bottles of premium-quality wine sold in the world comes from France! The domination of quality wine production by France is steeped in history, but maintained by strict winemaking regulations and quality practices.

With all of this success, France has also become the most emulated winemaking region in the world. Grape varietals developed in France are grown in every other winemaking country in the world. French grape growing and winemaking techniques have been adopted as the international standard. The styles of wine that have become famous in France have spawned imitators throughout the winemaking world. Even the wine laws enacted in France in the 1930s serve as the model for winemaking regulations from Europe to the United States and beyond. As a result, the quality of wine produced around the world can mostly trace its roots back to the French. They have done more to develop wine and winemaking practices than any other civilization throughout history.

The Climate Zones of France

Much of the success of French winemaking has been determined and shaped by the climate of the country. Overall, France has a fairly temperate climate, which is ideally suited to the wine grape vine. That being said, the geography of the country creates a few distinct climate zones within France. These various climate zones are the reason that a country no larger in landmass than the state of Texas is able to produce such a wide array of wine styles, from a multitude of different grape varieties, all at a world-class level.

If the overall climate of France is temperate, then the actual climates found in the major wine regions of France start temperate, and then are shaped by their location and proximity to the Atlantic Ocean, the Mediterranean Sea, and the rest of the continent of Europe. These major geographical features divide France into three distinct climate zones.

Wine regions located along the western coast of France are greatly affected by the Atlantic Ocean. The Atlantic is an immense body of water, whose temperatures are regulated by its sheer volume as well as ocean currents. Throughout the course of the year, the Atlantic will not vary in temperature by more than a few degrees. This means that the Atlantic Ocean acts almost like a layer of insulation for the western coast of France, maintaining a temperate-maritime climate for the regions along the shore. In the winter it does not get too cold, and in the summer it does not warm up too much. The two classic French wine regions located within this temperate-maritime climate zone are Bordeaux and the western reaches of the Loire Valley, and it is also home to the important region of the Sud Ouest.

Another large body of water that impacts French coastal regions is the Mediterranean Sea. Much smaller and shallower than the Atlantic, the Mediterranean has very warm water temperatures. This does not insulate the regions of southern France; rather, it naturally raises the temperatures there. Along the French Riviera and neighboring regions you will find a warm-Mediterranean climate. The classic French wine region of the Rhône Valley is found in this climate zone, as well as the important wine regions of Provence and Languedoc-Roussillon, and the Mediterranean island of Corsica.

Central and northern France do not have a large body of water acting to temper or warm their climates. The major geographic impact on climate in those regions is not an ocean or sea, but rather the continent of Europe itself. Since solid ground can heat up or cool down faster and to a larger degree than water can, the wine regions in central and northern France have a climate that is dictated by their more northern latitude. You will predominantly find a cool-continental climate in this area of France. The classic French wine regions of Burgundy,

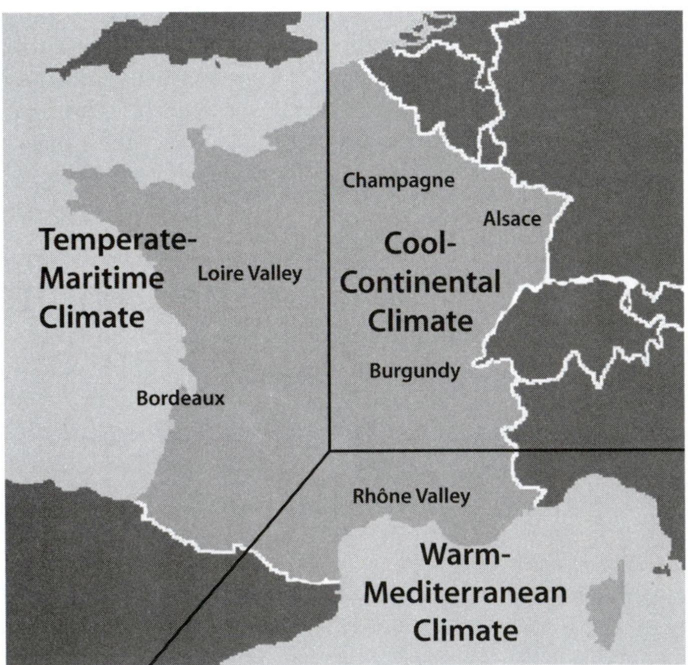

The major climate zones of France.

Alsace, Champagne, and the eastern reaches of the Loire Valley are all located in this cool-continental climate zone. Two important regions, Jura and Savoie, are also found in this climate zone.

How do these three major climate zones impact wines and winemaking in the various classic and important wine regions of France? The answer is growing conditions and ripeness. Different wine grape varietals thrive only in certain climate conditions. In cooler climates white wine grapes do best, while in warmer climates red wine varietals dominate. This is due to the fact that most red varietals need a longer time on the vine to fully mature. In a temperate climate, conditions are ideal for the production of white or red wine grape varietals. There are some obvious exceptions to this generality—such as the red wine grape Pinot Noir that thrives in cooler climates and the white wine grape Viognier that thrives in warmer ones—but understand that these grapes have unusual characteristics not commonly associated with other wines of the same color (i.e., the thin skins, delicate nature, and high acidity of Pinot Noir, and the full body and power of Viognier). The different grapes grown throughout the various wine regions of France are not dictated by chance or current fashion. Rather, they are carefully selected because of the climate and *terroir* found within that specific region. That is why you will find dramatically different grape varietals growing in wine regions that might be less than 100 miles apart. This is what explains the vast number of different grapes grown throughout the small country of France.

Besides grape varietals, the other major difference between wine regions in France is the style of wine they produce. Although style can be determined by winemaking, most winemakers in France strive to leave as minimal an impact on their wines as possible. In France the style of the wines is more heavily influenced by the vintage and the vines than by winemaking practices, and one of the most important aspects of the vines that shapes style is ripeness. In warmer climates, grapes simply get riper, while grapes will be less ripe in cooler climates. The ripeness of the grapes used to produce a wine drives three of the major characteristics that define any wine: acidity, body, and alcohol. The warm-Mediterranean climate of southern France will produce wines that are higher in alcohol, fuller-bodied, and lower in acidity. The cool-continental climate of central and northern France is responsible for producing wines with higher acidity, lighter body, and lower alcohol. Finally, a balance of body, acidity, and alcohol is what characterizes the style of most wines in western France.

French Wine Laws

France is home to the oldest and strictest wine laws in the world. These laws were shaped by traditions developed over hundreds of years as winemakers experimented with different grape varieties and winemaking techniques in the hundreds of unique wine regions throughout France. After centuries of trial and error, the French have figured out what they do best in their different wine regions, and the wine laws of France simply codify these traditions. First established in the 1930s, the French system of wine laws was made official to protect the important wines of France from fraud and to make the use of regional names illegal when the wines in question do not follow the traditions of their regions of origin. These laws serve the purpose of identifying and establishing the official wine regions of France, and dictating how wines can be produced in each region. The wine laws of France are regionally based because it is the land itself that determines how wine should be produced.

The French wine laws are generally referred to as the ***Appellation d'Origine Contrôlée*** or simply the AOC or AC laws. These laws break French wines up into different quality classifications based on where they are produced and how strict the winemaking standards are in those regions.

The lowest quality classification of French wine is ***vin de table***, which translates to "table wine." This category has the fewest restrictions placed upon it and these wines can be made from grapes grown anywhere in France. Labels for ***vin de table*** wines cannot mention any specific region or grape variety, simply "Vin Blanc" (white wine), "Vin Rouge" (red wine), or "Vin Rosé" (rosé wine), and "Produit de France" (Product of France). These wines are not very important, are rarely exported, and make up less than a quarter of French wine.

A step up in quality as well as in strictness of winemaking guidelines is the ***vin de pays*** quality classification. *Vin de pays* translates directly as "country wine" and refers mostly to wines made in important but not classic wine regions. Winemaking restrictions are relaxed in these regions, allowing flexibility similar to that found in the American wine laws. Wines are often labeled by the grape from which they are made, and winemaking techniques can vary widely. The most important *vin de pays* regions are in southern France, especially Vin de Pays d'Oc, where roughly 80 percent of the wines in this classification are produced. *Vin de pays* wines make up a little more than a quarter of French wine produced each year, and have recently increased in popularity in the United States and other international markets for their quality and value.

Just below the top quality classification of French wine is ***Vin Délimité de Qualité Supérieure***, or **VDQS**. This translates to "delimited wine of superior quality." VDQS is a temporary quality classification: it is for particular wine regions in France that aspire to move into the top quality classification. The VDQS designation means that the winemakers in the region are in a probationary period while their wines and winemaking are evaluated for quality and strictness. After a certain time period, the region will be either deemed worthy of a top classification or relegated back down to a lower classification. Less than 1 percent of the wines produced in France fall into the VDQS classification.

The highest quality classification in French winemaking is ***Appellation d'Origine Contrôlée*** (AOC)—the same term used to refer to the French wine laws. Translating to "area of controlled origin," this classification is home to the most historically important and classic wine regions of France. To ensure the quality of the wines from these AOC regions, the regulations are stricter than for any of the other classifications. Almost all of the wines that fall into this quality classification are named not for the grape variety used to produce them, but for the place name of the AOC region in which they are produced. This system of labeling wines by region is practiced in France because they have clearly defined regions where hundreds of years

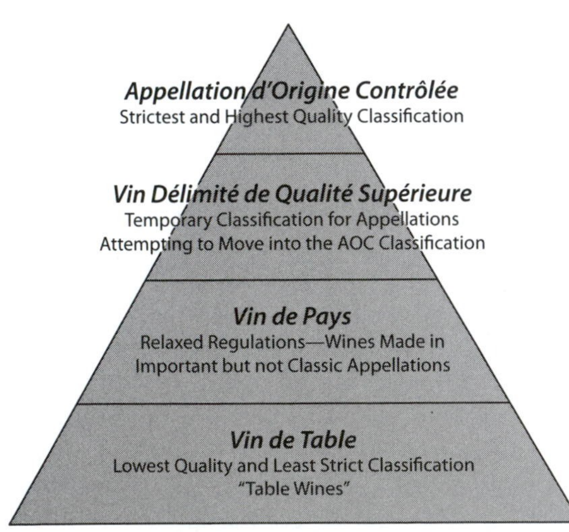

French quality classifications for wine.

French wines in the *vin de pays* quality classification are commonly labeled by grape variety, unlike the bulk of France's premium wine.

This label lists the term "Appellation Hermitage Contrôlée," meaning the wine is from the controlled appellation of Hermitage.

of winemaking tradition have determined the proper way to produce wine. When a winemaker produces a wine in an AOC region, he or she is growing the grapes best suited to that region's *terroir* and is utilizing the winemaking techniques that best complement what the region can produce.

When looking at a French wine label, the designation *Appellation Contrôlée* should appear if the wine comes from the top quality classification. Whatever region the wine comes from will be found between *Appellation* and *Contrôlée* (e.g., *Appellation Bordeaux Contrôlée,* etc.) and/or just above the term. This designation is an official guarantee from the French government that this wine is produced in this controlled appellation of origin.

The quality of French winemaking can be seen in the fact that roughly half of the wines produced in France fall within the AOC classification. AOC wines are by far the highest-quality, most sought after, and most expensive wines in France, if not the entire world. It is these AOC wines that have made France famous for wine.

In effect, a winemaker producing wine within an AOC region and using the place name of that region to label his or her wines is told what to plant, how to plant it, how and when to harvest, how much to harvest, how to make the wine, and how to age it! This may seem extremely restrictive, but in reality it is a luxury that other winemakers around the world can only dream of. The secret of French winemaking is that they have figured out what they do best from region to region, and they stick to it. Think of the

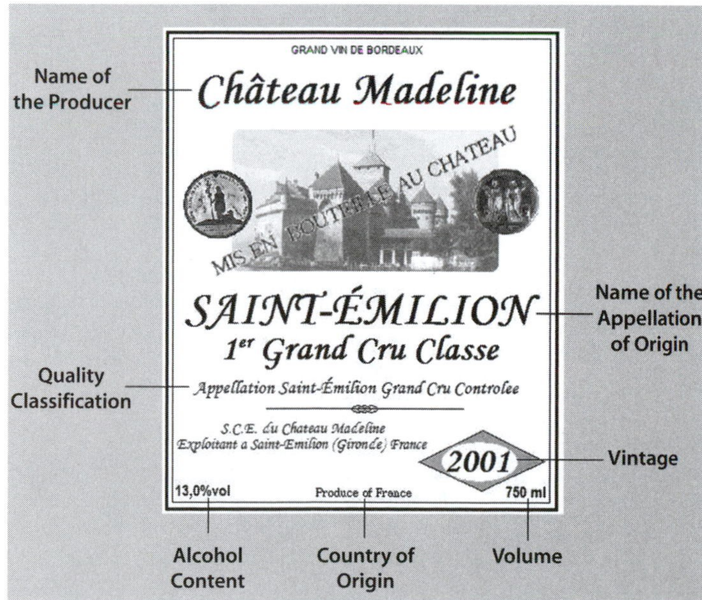

How to read a French wine label.

AOC laws as a recipe or formula that can be used to produce top-quality wines in a specific region. Follow the formula and you will make world-class wine.

The French government strictly enforces these AOC laws with the ***Institut Nationale des Appellations d'Origine*** **(INAO)**, but it is the winemakers of each AOC region itself who determine what the laws of that region are. This allows those winemakers to strictly maintain high standards across the board in their region, and to fine-tune the laws over time if a need is perceived. In this way, all winemakers of an AOC region have a stake in the wine laws. The reputation of each region must be upheld by every winemaker within that region. If everyone is growing the same grapes in similar *terroir* and using identical winemaking techniques, there should not be massive differences between any two wines made in the same AOC region. If you try one wine from an AOC region and like it, you will probably enjoy others from that region. Thus, if a winemaker produces a subpar wine in an AOC region, a consumer may perceive that all of the wines from that region are similar. In this way, one winemaker producing a subpar wine can hurt every other winemaker in that region.

There are hundreds of AOC regions located throughout France, but it is not necessary to memorize hundreds of different wine laws to understand French wine. It is important to note that most of these AOC regions are actually subregions of larger AOC regions. Bordeaux, for example, has more

AOC Regulations

To use one of the AOC place names, winemakers who grow their grapes in an AOC region must follow regulations regarding:

- **Origin:** 100 percent of the grapes used to produce a wine with an AOC designation must be grown in vineyards located within the specific boundaries of that region.
- **Approved grapes:** Wines with an AOC designation must be made only from the grape varietal or varietals approved in that region.
- **Harvest:** The AOC regulations govern the minimum and maximum alcohol content that can be found in the wines of a specific region, and this dictates when the grapes may be harvested, and at what level of ripeness.
- **Yield:** Winemakers using an AOC designation have a maximum amount of grapes, in weight, that they may harvest each vintage. This amount varies from region to region, but forces most winemakers to grow their grapes under stress. This serves to ensure higher-quality fruit, which should translate into higher-quality wine. It also means that the amount of supply found in a region is limited, helping to maintain prices and keeping winemakers from overfarming.
- **Aging regime:** Winemakers in an AOC region are told how long they must age their wines and what materials they can use to age them (new or used oak barrels, stainless-steel tanks, etc.).
- **Viticultural and vinicultural methods:** All aspects of how grapevines are grown, vineyards are planted, and wine is produced—including which methods are banned—are also governed specifically from region to region with an AOC classification.

Common French Label Terms

TERM	DEFINITION
Vin Rouge	Red wine
Vin Blanc	White wine
Vin Rosé	Rosé wine
Cru	Vineyard or growth. Commonly seen as "Grand Cru" (great growth) or "Premier Cru" (first growth), quality designations that refer to top wines and have different meanings in the various regions of France.
Sec	Dry
Doux	Sweet
Côte	Hill or slope
Clos	Walled vineyard, common in Burgundy
Château	Wine estate, common in Bordeaux
Domaine	Vineyard estate, common in Burgundy
Supérieur	Term used to indicate a wine of higher quality than minimum standards; often earned with higher alcohol content and/or lower yields.

France's classic wine regions.

than fifty AOC subregions within its borders, while Burgundy has more than six hundred! If an AOC is a subregion of a larger AOC region, then it must at a minimum follow the laws of the larger region of which it is a part. These AOC subregions can make their laws more restrictive than the larger AOC region's laws, but not looser. To generalize and make sense of French wine, you really need to learn about the laws of the large, classic regions of France, and then learn which subregions are found within them. Although there might be hundreds of these subregions, they are all growing the same grapes, have similar *terroir,* and have winemaking laws almost identical to the larger AOC regions because regulations are so strict. This means that the wines from various subregions within the same AOC region will taste similar—not the same, but similar. Knowing this, we will first learn about the classic AOC regions of France and how they make wine, and then learn about the subregions within each of them.

FRANCE'S CLASSIC WINE REGIONS

Bordeaux: The World's Most Successful Region

Bordeaux is arguably the most important wine region in France, if not the world. The wines of Bordeaux have been considered some of the best produced for hundreds of years. Wars have been fought over control of the region and ancient cultures celebrated its wines. Even today, Bordeaux wines are the most sought after and collected anywhere.

Although planted to the wine grape for thousands of years, Bordeaux first became important internationally in A.D. 1152, when Henry II of England wed Eleanor of Aquitaine, who controlled the region. With this royal marriage, Bordeaux officially came under the control of the English. Quickly, the wines of Bordeaux began being shipped to England and soon gained a large following there. Red Bordeaux is still popular in England today, where it is often called **claret.**

The English control of Bordeaux would last for a little more than three hundred years before the French reclaimed it at the end of the Hundred Years War. By that time, the English had been shipping Bordeaux wines around Europe, where they were extremely popular. The region's proximity to a major port city on the Atlantic only helped increase trade of Bordeaux wines in the subsequent centuries. It also gave Bordeaux a head start on landlocked regions like Burgundy for international trade. As its fame and reputation grew, so did the region. Eventually Bordeaux grew to be the largest top-quality region of France. With this growth came strict winemaking traditions employed to maintain the prestige of the region. By the 1800s and 1900s, Bordeaux's place as one of the world's great wine regions had long been secured.

Today, Bordeaux is considered the world's most commercially successful wine region, if not its highest-quality one. The secret to Bordeaux's success is the quantity of quality it produces. There are nearly 20,000 producers in Bordeaux annually making more than 150,000,000 gallons of premium wine. That accounts for a little more than 25 percent of France's premium wine production! To carry it one step further, remember that France produces half of the world's premium wine, meaning that the wine regions of Bordeaux produce more than 12 percent of the world's premium wine. That is easily more than any other wine-producing country on Earth.

Red wines dominate Bordeaux, and the two most important red grapes grown in the region—Cabernet Sauvignon and Merlot—have been transplanted widely around the world. Dry white wines are also made in Bordeaux, mostly from Sauvignon Blanc; and sweet white wines are made from late harvest Sémillon grapes infected with botrytis. Even a few rosés and sparkling wines are produced in the region. Most wines made in Bordeaux are blends. This is because Bordeaux is so large and has so many different areas of unique *terroir* that some varietals will thrive where others struggle, and in the end the sum will be greater than its parts.

Unlike Burgundy, where the wine regions are scattered and the vineyards divided, Bordeaux is home to a multitude of large, often historic, wine estates. A winery or estate in Bordeaux is known as a **château** and almost all of them use the term in their name. Château is the French word for "house" or "castle," so the name of a winery such as Château Margaux, for example, would translate to the "House of Margaux." Most of the wines produced in Bordeaux are made by châteaux that grow their own grapes on their property and make their own wines, although some wines are produced by ***négociants*** who buy grapes from growers.

All in all, the winemakers of Bordeaux live a charmed life. They have a pleasant climate, grow some of the world's most important grape varietals, and work amongst some of the most renowned wine estates in the world. The road to wine success has been paved with gold in Bordeaux.

The Facts on Bordeaux

CLIMATE

Located on the Atlantic coastline of southwest France, Bordeaux has a temperate-maritime climate that keeps conditions from getting too hot or cold throughout the year.

TOP WHITE GRAPES

- Sauvignon Blanc
- Sémillon

TOP RED GRAPES

- Merlot
- Cabernet Sauvignon

TOP REGIONS

Left Bank

- Médoc
- Haut-Médoc
- Graves

Right Bank

- Pomerol
- Saint-Émilion

Entre-Deux-Mers

DESSERT WINES

- Sauternes

IMPORTANT INFORMATION

- Bordeaux is the most commercially successful wine region in the world, producing more than 25 percent of France's top-quality wine.
- Almost all of the wines of Bordeaux are produced by blending different grapes. The major styles of wine produced in Bordeaux are powerful, dry reds made mostly from Cabernet Sauvignon and Merlot, dry white wines made mostly from Sauvignon Blanc, and lush dessert wines made mostly from Sémillon.
- Bordeaux is home to thousands of wine estates. An estate or winery in Bordeaux is referred to as a *Château*.
- The region of Bordeaux is broken up into two major areas for top-quality production, the Left Bank and the Right Bank of the Gironde estuary. Growing conditions and wine styles differ in these areas.
- There have been several attempts to classify the wines of Bordeaux, but there is no official classification governing all of the wines produced there. The most important system developed to date is the Classification of 1855, which ranked only a handful of top estates on the Left Bank.

IMPORTANT GRAPES OF BORDEAUX

Winemakers in Bordeaux believe in the philosophy that complexity is achieved by using more than one ingredient, and most of the wines produced in the region will be blends of two or more grapes. Depending upon where you are in Bordeaux, red wines will typically have a majority of Cabernet Sauvignon in the blend (especially on the Left Bank) or a majority of Merlot in the blend (especially on the Right Bank and for regional Bordeaux appellation wines). White wines are typically Sauvignon Blanc–based blends if they are dry and Sémillon-based blends if they are sweet.

Sauvignon Blanc

Bordeaux claims to be the native homeland of the Sauvignon Blanc grape, and no other white varietal is more widely planted there. When Sauvignon Blanc is used as the base for a white blend in Bordeaux, the resulting wine will be dry and acidic. Sauvignon Blanc is only used sparingly in the sweet wines of Bordeaux, often serving to balance the sweetness of the wine with its high level of acidity. Many of the dry, Sauvignon Blanc–based wines of Bordeaux will be aged in either stainless steel or neutral oak. Only the very best white blends are aged in new oak barrels. The main areas producing dry, Sauvignon Blanc–based wines in Bordeaux are the southern areas of the Left Bank and Entre-Deux-Mers.

Sémillon

The dominant white grape used in the production of botrytised, sweet white wines in a handful of Bordeaux appellations, Sémillon produces full-bodied, honey-laden wines. Sémillon is also blended into Sauvignon Blanc in small percentages when producing dry white wines in Bordeaux. Its rich character rounds out the Sauvignon Blanc in these wines, softening its acidity and adding body.

Cabernet Sauvignon

This red grape was first developed in Bordeaux hundreds of years ago, and although it is not grown as widely as Merlot in Bordeaux, Cabernet Sauvignon nonetheless plays a starring role in many of the region's top wines. Used as the main grape in the red blends of the Left Bank, Cabernet Sauvignon gives these long-lived wines intense tannins and structure. On the Right Bank and in the regional red wines of Bordeaux, it is often used as a blending grape to make Merlot-based or Cabernet Franc–based wines more robust.

Merlot

The Merlot grape is native to Bordeaux, and is used to produce some of the most important wines in the region. Merlot is by far the most widely used grape varietal in Bordeaux, planted on nearly 100,000 acres in the region. It often serves as the base for the soft and complex red blends of the top-quality communes of the Right Bank and most *Appellation Bordeaux Contrôlée* and *Appellation Bordeaux Supérieur Contrôlée* wines. On the Left Bank, where Cabernet Sauvignon dominates, Merlot is often used as a blending grape to soften tannin structures and add ripe fruit characteristics.

Other Notable Grapes

MUSCADELLE A minor white blending grape sometimes added to white wines to add lifted, floral notes.

CABERNET FRANC The most important of the minor red blending grapes in Bordeaux, and the only one that makes up the majority of the blend in some red wines in the region; often used in blends to soften the tannin structure and to add herbaceous and aromatic notes.

MALBEC A minor red blending grape that is used to add deep color, tannins, and dark fruit flavors; sometimes called Cot in Bordeaux.

PETIT VERDOT A minor red blending grape that is used to add color, tannins, and alcohol.

CARMENÈRE A red grape recently reintroduced to the region of Bordeaux. Carmenère is used in red Bordeaux blends to add color, soften tannin structure, and add red fruit and spice characteristics; sometimes called Grand Vidure in Bordeaux.

TERROIR AND IMPORTANT REGIONS

The large region of Bordeaux surrounds the city of Bordeaux, an important Atlantic port. Immense in scope, the region of Bordeaux encompasses nearly 300,000 acres of vineyards and produces more wine than any other classic French wine region. Proximity to the Atlantic Ocean tempers the climate of Bordeaux, which is considered temperate-maritime. Scattered throughout Bordeaux are a wide diversity of climate zones and soil types, which explains the use of several different white and red grapes in the region. In all, there are fifty-seven subregions found throughout Bordeaux.

A majority of the production in Bordeaux goes into simple, regional wines that are labeled as Bordeaux or Bordeaux Supérieur depending on quality and ripeness. These are of good quality, but they are not as important to the region as are the wines produced in the more specific communes of Bordeaux.

Flowing northwest through the middle of the region is the Gironde estuary, which empties into the Atlantic and is fed by two tributaries, the Dordogne River to the northeast and the Garonne River to the southwest. The Gironde and its tributaries divide Bordeaux into three major areas: the Left Bank, the Right Bank, and Entre-Deux-Mers.

Left Bank

The **Left Bank** of Bordeaux is located to the southwest of the Gironde estuary and Garonne River. The city of Bordeaux is located in the Left Bank along the Garonne River where it meets the Gironde. The Left Bank is more or less a peninsula jutting out into the Atlantic that has been built over millennia by eroded soil and earth washed down from the Pyrenees Mountains. The result is a soil made up of mostly gravel and sand that retains heat and drains very well, forcing vines to dig deep to find moisture. Since the Left Bank extends out into the Atlantic, the climate there is slightly cooler than in the more inland vineyards of the Right Bank. This combination of soil and climate is ideal for the Cabernet Sauvignon grape, and it is the main varietal used in most of the red blends on the Left Bank. The major winemaking regions located in the Left Bank are **Médoc, Haut-Médoc,** and **Graves,** although the general appellation of Bordeaux rings the outskirts of the top regions.

Médoc Stretching nearly 50 miles along the western banks of the Gironde estuary is the AOC region of Médoc. The region itself is divided into two major areas: the Bas-Médoc or "lower" Médoc to the north, and the Haut-Médoc or "upper"

How Bordeaux Got Its Name

The many rivers that cut through Bordeaux, along with its location on the Atlantic coastline, gave the region its name. The term Bordeaux is a contraction of *au bord de l'eau,* which means "along the water."

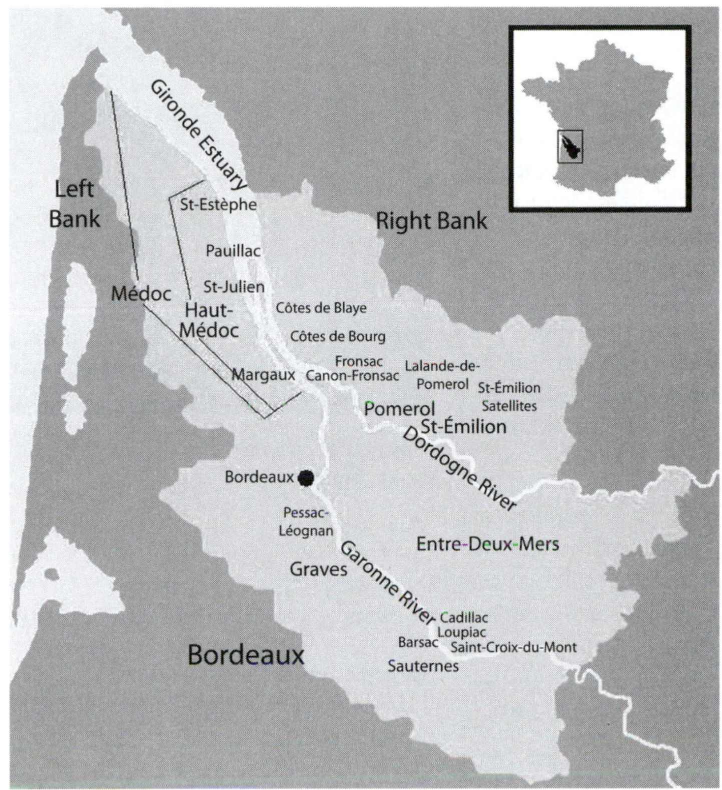

Bordeaux and its major appellations.

Médoc to the south. Most of the wines labeled "Appellation Médoc Contrôlée" are made by châteaux in the Bas-Médoc, the Haut-Médoc being a more important subregion dealt with in the next section. Cabernet Sauvignon is the dominant grape used for Médoc wines, and is often blended with Merlot and Cabernet Franc. Wines labeled with the Médoc appellation range in quality from basic to intense and complex.

Haut-Médoc Actually a subregion of the larger Médoc AOC, Haut-Médoc stretches north from the city of Bordeaux along the Gironde almost 15 miles. Soil conditions in Haut-Médoc are far superior to the rest of Médoc, and the quality of wine showcases this fact. Wines labeled "Appellation Haut-Médoc Contrôlée" are often high in quality. That said, the true renown of the region comes from the wines produced in four communes scattered throughout Haut-Médoc: **Margaux, Pauillac, Saint-Estèphe**, and **Saint-Julien**. These four AOC regions are considered by many to be the home to the greatest collection of top-quality wineries anywhere in the world. Two other communes of lesser status also found in Haut-Médoc are Listrac and Moulis.

Margaux Named for the village of Margaux, the appellation of Margaux is the southernmost of the four most important communes of Haut-Médoc. As with all of the other appellations in the area, Margaux wines are Cabernet Sauvignon–based. The region is home to more classified growth estates than any other in the Haut-Médoc, with the most important being the *premier cru* estate Château Margaux. Wines from

Margaux are often very elegant and smooth with soft tannins and intense aroma.

Pauillac Pauillac might be the most important appellation in all of Bordeaux, and its more renowned châteaux are some of the most famous wineries in the world. Sandwiched between Saint-Julien to the south and Saint-Estèphe to the north, almost every acre of the small appellation of Pauillac is owned by a classified growth estate. Of the five recognized *premier cru* estates on the Left Bank, three are found in Pauillac: Château Latour, Château Lafite-Rothschild, and Château Mouton-Rothschild. The wines of Pauillac are powerful, full-flavored, and long-lived.

Saint-Estèphe Saint-Estèphe is the northernmost of the important communes of Haut-Médoc, located just north of Pauillac. Of the four top communes, Saint-Estèphe is generally lesser known and is home to far fewer classified growth estates. Regardless, the region produces some of the most age-worthy wines in Bordeaux because of the powerful tannin structure they possess.

Saint-Julien Located just south of Pauillac, Saint-Julien is the smallest of all the important communes found in Haut-Médoc. The region produces very consistent, top-quality wines and is home to some of the most important classified growth châteaux in Bordeaux. Cabernet Sauvignon is the main grape grown in Saint-Julien, giving these wines great power and structure.

Graves Unlike Médoc and Haut-Médoc, which are exclusively red wine regions, Graves is an appellation with the ideal *terroir* for top-quality red and white wines. Graves is located just south of the city of Bordeaux, along the banks of the Garonne River. It is named for the gravelly soil found in the region (*graves* is French for gravel), which supports both white and red grape varietals almost equally well. In the 1980s, the northern portion of Graves was granted its own unique AOC designation, **Pessac-Léognan,** and this is generally considered to be the area where the best wines are produced. Both Cabernet Sauvignon–based and Sauvignon Blanc–based wines labeled "Appellation Graves Contrôlée" are often of good quality.

Many of the top wineries in the world are located in Médoc and its communes.

Pessac-Léognan Historically the best portion of Graves, Pessac-Léognan was granted its own AOC status just a few decades ago. It is home to top-quality Cabernet Sauvignon–based red wines that rival the best of Haut-Médoc and its communes, although they tend to be softer because Pessac-Léognan winemakers typically blend more Merlot into their wines. The only wine to receive *premier cru* status in the Classification of 1855 located out of the Haut-Médoc district was Château Haut-Brion, today found in Pessac-Léognan. Top-quality white wines made mostly from Sauvignon Blanc are also produced throughout the appellation.

Right Bank

Further inland, the Right Bank of Bordeaux is located east and north of the Gironde estuary and Dordogne River. The soils in the Right Bank contain far more clay than in the other regions of Bordeaux, which holds onto moisture and provides more fertile conditions for grapevines. This soil, combined with the weather conditions on the Right Bank, is more favorable for growing Merlot, which makes the base for most of the red wines of the region. Cabernet

Franc also does very well on the Right Bank, and is used as the lead grape in a handful of important red wines.

Most of the top regions found along the Right Bank of Bordeaux are in the eastern reaches of the area, just north of the Dordogne. Quality white and red wines are produced in the west, but they are mostly from large, lesser known AOC appellations such as the Côtes de Blaye and the Côtes de Bourg. Red wines are exclusively produced in the eastern regions of Canon-Fronsac, Fronsac, and Lalande-de-Pomerol—mostly Merlot-based wines of varying quality. The heart of the Right Bank, however, is made up of two very important regions where the world's best Merlot is produced: **Pomerol** and **Saint-Émilion.**

Pomerol Pomerol is the smallest of the top-quality communes of Bordeaux, and this limited supply has caused prices in the appellation to skyrocket. The vast majority of vineyards in Pomerol are planted to Merlot, which makes up a majority of most of the wines produced there. Insignificant amounts of Cabernet Franc and Cabernet Sauvignon are also grown and used as minor blending grapes. The wines of Pomerol are considered softer than those of the Left Bank, with more lush fruit and less tannin. Although the region has never been officially classified, Château Pétrus is generally considered the top estate; its wine rivals any produced in Bordeaux, and is by far the most expensive.

Saint-Émilion Saint-Émilion is named for the medieval village located in the center of the appellation. It is one of the oldest wine-producing regions of Bordeaux. The largest of the top-quality communes found in Bordeaux, Saint-Émilion produces far more high-end red wines than any other. Saint-Émilion wines are mostly made from Merlot, which tends to make them softer and more approachable at an early age than the wines of the Left Bank, although many structured wines are produced there. Left out of the 1855 Classification of Bordeaux, Saint-Émilion organized its own classification system, with estates in the top classification

The tiny Pomerol AOC produces the most expensive wines in Bordeaux.

being able to label their wines "Appellation Saint-Émilion Grand Cru Contrôlée." Of these, the two most important producers in Saint-Émilion, often compared to the top estates of the Haut-Médoc, are Château Ausone and Château Cheval Blanc. The appellation is ringed by four AOC regions that split from Saint-Émilion, known as the satellites: Lussac Saint-Émilion, Montagne-Saint-Émilion, Puisseguin-Saint-Émilion, and Saint-Georges-Saint-Émilion.

Entre-Deux-Mers

Entre-Deux-Mers translates to "between the seas" and is the name for a large appellation that dominates the island formed between the Dordogne and Garonne rivers where they feed the Gironde. While significant amounts of Merlot are grown in Entre-Deux-Mers, these are all bound for regional Bordeaux or Bordeaux Supérieur wines. Wines labeled "Appellation Entre-Deux-Mers Contrôlée" are exclusively dry, white wines of average quality that are mostly made from Sauvignon Blanc.

Bordeaux Dessert Wines

On either side of the Garonne River, south of Graves and the city of Bordeaux, are a collection of several wineries that specialize in producing botrytised dessert wines. With proximity to the river and cooler temperatures than other parts of Bordeaux, these regions are home to ideal conditions for grapes being infected with botrytis. As in other sweet wine–producing areas of France and the world, wines made from grapes infected with botrytis are usually lush and sweet, as this mold attacks grapes and removes their moisture. The thin skins and already rich character of the Sémillon grape makes it the most important used to produce this style in Bordeaux. Noteworthy sweet wines are produced in Barsac, Cadillac, Loupiac, and Sainte-Croix-du-Mont; however, the highest-quality examples almost always come from **Sauternes.**

Sauternes The southernmost of the sweet wine regions of Bordeaux, Sauternes is legendary for its late harvest, botrytised wines. When conditions are perfect, wines of dazzling richness and complexity can be produced. Sauternes wines are made only in the very best of vintages, and some years none is produced at all. When bad vintages occur, the wines are typically sold to large producers to be used as a component in simple regional Bordeaux wines. Several estates in Sauternes were included in the Classification of 1855, but only one received its own special status. The most important estate in Sauternes—Château d'Yquem—was given its own unique designation of *premier grand cru*, or "first great growth." Many consider it the most important wine produced in Bordeaux, white or red.

WINE CLASSIFICATIONS IN BORDEAUX

Several attempts have been made throughout Bordeaux's history to classify and rank its wines

Major Bordeaux Classifications

CLASSIFICATION OF 1855 (RED WINES)

Ranked sixty-one red wine–producing estates located mostly in Médoc and its subregions with the exception of one château in Graves. These rankings are broken up into five categories from *premier cru* (first growth) to *cinquième cru* (fifth growth). Wineries that are ranked in the 1855 Classification are often referred to as "classified growth" wineries. The five *premiers crus* are Château Haut-Brion (Graves/Pessac-Léognan), Château Lafite-Rothschild (Pauillac), Château Latour (Pauillac), Château Margaux (Margaux), and Château Mouton-Rothschild (Pauillac).

CLASSIFICATION OF 1855 (SWEET WINES)

The 1855 Classification also laid out rankings for the sweet white wines of Barsac and Sauternes. They were established into a hierarchy of three categories: *deuxième cru* (second growth), *premier cru* (first growth), and *premier grand cru* (great first growth). Of the twenty-six estates chosen for this classification, only one received *premier grand cru* status, Château d'Yquem in Sauternes.

CRU BOURGEOIS

A classification system established in the 1930s by the estates of Médoc that were left out of the Classification of 1855. There are almost 250 estates classified under the *cru bourgeois* system.

CRU CLASSÉ

In the 1950s, estates in Graves introduced the *cru classé* system of classification. There are no rankings in the *cru classé* system; it is simply a list of the best estates for red wines, white wines, or both in the region that include the designation on their labels. Château Haut-Brion is officially a member of this classification as well as the 1855 classification.

SAINT-ÉMILION CLASSIFICATION

Also in the 1950s, the estates of Saint-Émilion established a classification system. It established two ranks, *grand cru classé* (great classified growth) and *premier grand cru classé* (first great classified growth). To qualify, an estate must petition each year for the designation. Wines made in this classification are labeled "Appellation Saint-Émilion Grand Cru Classé." Two estates in the top ranking were given special status as category A estates: Château Ausone and Château Cheval Blanc.

based on quality. To date, no system has been developed that encompasses all of the estates and appellations of Bordeaux, and there likely never will be such a system. Instead, there are many classifications which cover different areas and wineries, and it can quickly get confusing.

It all started with the **Classification of 1855,** set up by wine brokers in Bordeaux to rank wines for something similar to a World's Fair held in Paris that year. Only wines from the Left Bank were chosen for this ranking, primarily from the appellation of Haut-Médoc and its communes. The sweet wines of Barsac and Sauternes were also categorized in a secondary classification. Estates were placed in five different categories based on their price at the time, and only sixty-one red wine châteaux were chosen. This has very little to do with the current state of Bordeaux winemaking, but it still affects the price of many wines, and only one change has been made since 1855—elevating the estate of Château Mouton-Rothschild to the top classification. Since so many estates and communes were left out of the Classification of 1855, many subsequent ranking systems have been developed. At the left is a list of the main classification systems of Bordeaux.

Burgundy: Obsessed with *Terroir*

Burgundy (***Bourgogne*** in French) is a long, thin collection of winegrowing districts located in central France, stretching about 200 miles from Chablis in the north to the city of Lyons in the south. The region covers more than 100,000 acres of vines, making it second only to Bordeaux in size and production amongst AOC regions. Grapes were first planted here around A.D. 200, and Burgundy has had a long and fabled history of wine production ever since, impacted by the Romans, the Catholic Church, the Crusades, and the French Revolution. Burgundy is considered by many to be one of the greatest wine regions on Earth, and its wines are some of the most expensive and sought after anywhere. The cool-continental climate in Burgundy is responsible for intense and complex wines made primarily from two noble grape varieties, Chardonnay and Pinot Noir.

The winemakers of Burgundy are obsessed with ***terroir*** and have divided the region into hundreds of recognized AOC appellations based on sometimes minor differences in climate, geology, and geography. For a region which only grows one white grape and one red grape, Burgundy can be very complicated to understand. The wines are classified by the particular region or vineyard in which the grapes are grown, following the French belief that the growing site of the grape determines the ultimate quality and individuality of the wine. Burgundy has more than 600 of these AOC regions! Add to that the fact that there are over 15,000 growers in Burgundy and you can begin to see why the region can get confusing. While there are many producers in Burgundy who grow all of their own grapes and make their own wines (typically referred to as a ***domaine*** or ***maison***), much of the wine produced in Burgundy is made and sold by firms that do not grow all of their own grapes.

Unlike those of many winemaking regions in France, Burgundy's vineyards are divided and fragmented into very small parcels, with the average grower's holding being less than 8 acres. This segmentation of vineyards in Burgundy is in large part a result of its history. In 1789, the French Revolution brought about a change to the inheritance laws of Burgundy. Estates had to be split up evenly amongst all heirs, and after several generations, some estates and vineyards have been split up so many times that some growers own only two rows of vines or less. Individual vineyards in Burgundy can have more than one hundred individual owners.

This being the case, many growers do not own enough acreage to produce their own wines, and therefore sell their grapes to ***négociant-éleveurs,*** wine brokerage firms that purchase grapes and wine from small producers, blend it together, and label it under their own *négociant* label. Almost 70 percent of the wine produced in Burgundy each year is sold by the more than 100 ***négociant*** firms in Burgundy.

The Facts on Burgundy

CLIMATE

Burgundy's inland location in east-central France is responsible for its cool-continental climate.

TOP WHITE GRAPE

- Chardonnay

TOP RED GRAPE

- Pinot Noir

TOP REGIONS

- Chablis
- Côte d'Or
  - Côte de Nuits
  - Côte de Beaune
- Côte Chalonnaise
- Mâconnais
- Beaujolais

IMPORTANT INFORMATION

- Burgundy is considered one of the top wine regions in the world, and the best wines are made from either 100 percent Chardonnay or 100 percent Pinot Noir.
- The region of Burgundy is a collection of different winemaking areas spread out over the course of 200 miles from north to south. Besides the region itself being fractured, many of the vineyards in Burgundy have also been fractured, with hundreds of owners splitting up a single vineyard in certain instances.
- Winemakers in Burgundy are completely obsessed with *terroir*, and the region is probably one of the most studied and surveyed pieces of land anywhere. The result is hundreds of small, individual AOC regions with sometimes only minor differences in soil and climate.
- A hierarchy of specific regions has been established in Burgundy, starting with a broad classification of wines made from grapes grown anywhere in Burgundy, all the way down to the top individual vineyard sites in the region. Quality arguably increases the more specific you get in Burgundy, but there is no argument that wines get more expensive.

REGIONAL HIERARCHY IN BURGUNDY

Burgundy is one of the most studied wine regions on Earth, and every corner has been mapped out and classified based on ***terroir***. As early as the tenth century, the Benedictine Order of monks began the first systematic mapping of the ***terroir*** zones of Burgundy, and several of the vineyards and regions they identified are still in use today.

There is a hierarchy of wine quality classifications in Burgundy that divides wines into categories of quality based upon the premise that the more specific the site the wine comes from, the more distinct and higher in quality that wine will tend to be. Therefore, a wine made from grapes grown in several vineyards throughout Burgundy is considered lesser in quality than a wine made from grapes grown in one specified (and highly regarded) vineyard. The classifications from least specific (lowest tier) to most specific (highest tier) are: **regional, commune/village, *premier cru* vineyard**, and ***grand cru* vineyard.**

Regional

The majority of the wine produced in Burgundy falls under the regional classification. These are mostly quality blends made from grapes sourced throughout the region. By far, these are the most simple and least expensive wines produced in Burgundy. An example of a regional classification wine would be "Appellation Bourgogne Contrôlée."

Commune/Village

This second tier of quality describes wines that are generally higher in quality than regional wines. They are produced from grapes grown in the vineyards surrounding one of Burgundy's important subregions (communes) or one of the many famous villages. Examples of this classification would be "Appellation Côte de Beaune Contrôlée" and "Appellation Pouilly-Fuissé Contrôlée."

Premier Cru Vineyard

Throughout Burgundy, hundreds of top-quality vineyard sites have been granted ***premier cru***, or "first growth" status. This is reserved only for those vineyards that have historically produced important and highly regarded wines. There are 562 *premier cru* vineyards located throughout Burgundy, ranging in quality level and price. *Premier cru* wines are labeled with the name of the village or commune they are grown in or around, the name of the *premier cru* vineyard itself, and the term *premier cru* or *1er Cru*. An example would be "Appellation Pommard Epenots Premier Cru Contrôlée."

These four bottles are examples of the four major regional classifications of Burgundy, from basic Bourgogne on the left to a *grand cru* vineyard on the right.

Grand Cru Vineyard

The highest designation a vineyard in Burgundy can be granted is *grand cru*, or "great growth." Wines labeled *grand cru* must be produced entirely from grapes grown in one of these famous vineyards. There are only thirty-four *grand cru* vineyards in Burgundy; one in Chablis and thirty-three in the Côte d'Or. These wines make up only 1 percent of Burgundy's total production, and are some of the most expensive produced on Earth, sometimes topping thousands of dollars for a single bottle. A bottle of wine from a *grand cru* vineyard will merely mention the name of the vineyard itself and the term *grand cru*, such as "Appellation Le Montrachet Grand Cru Contrôlée."

IMPORTANT GRAPES OF BURGUNDY

The winemakers of Burgundy produce almost all of their wines from just one red grape and one white grape that serve to exhibit the complexities of the region: Pinot Noir and Chardonnay. While these are the only two grapes used in the top-quality wines of Burgundy, there are also two other minor grapes that are grown in small quantities in the region, Aligoté and Gamay.

Chardonnay

Burgundy is the native home of the Chardonnay grape, and there is no better region on earth for the production of high-quality Chardonnay-based wines. In Burgundy, Chardonnay is predominantly grown in the cooler vineyards where red grapes will not ripen quickly enough. This is the only white grape allowed in the production of white wines from Burgundy's AOC subregions. The Chardonnays of Burgundy often exhibit a solid core of acidity and minerality. These white wines can be complex, intense, and extremely precise, and are some of the world's best food pairing wines.

Pinot Noir

Pinot Noir is the most important grape of Burgundy, and the producer of extremely complex red wines. Burgundy is the birthplace of Pinot Noir, and while it is grown today in several regions around the world, Pinot Noir is still at its best on native soil. This is the only grape allowed to be used in the top-quality red wines of Burgundy, where the Pinot Noir grape produces seductive and complex red wines that have a balance of velvety mouthfeel, intense aroma, pleasant acidity, red berries, savory earthiness, and spicy structure.

Other Notable Grapes

ALIGOTÉ A white grape that produces light, dry wines that typically lack complexity. The

The Town of Chardonnay

In the southern Burgundy commune of Mâconnais is the small town of Chardonnay. Its residents claim that the Chardonnay grape was actually first developed in the vineyards there and was named for the town, although this is widely disputed.

top region for the production of Aligoté is the village of Bouzeron in the Côte Chalonnaise.

GAMAY The main red grape of Beaujolais, Gamay is also grown in a few parts of Burgundy. This grape produces soft, fruity wines, and is mixed with Pinot Noir to produce a wine called passe-tout-grains.

TERROIR AND IMPORTANT REGIONS

Burgundy's location in central France has a continental effect on its weather that results in a cooler climate. Due to this climate, Burgundy tends to produce wines with higher acidity and lower alcohol, as grapes rarely ripen fully. The region itself is scattered over the course of 200 miles from northern extreme to southern extreme, and vineyards are usually planted only in areas with a high concentration of limestone in the soil.

About 160 million years ago, a shallow sea covered the region of Burgundy during the Jurassic period. Tiny shells and the remains of sea life formed a thick layer of sediment on the sea floor, which eventually compacted and solidified into rock. This unique soil profile was finally exposed when the region of Burgundy went through a major tectonic lift at the same time the Alps were being created, around 35 million years ago. This fossilized sea life is the basis for the unique Jurassic limestone soils of Burgundy that are found in all of its top vineyard sites.

The main communes or subregions of Burgundy from north to south are Chablis, the Côte d'Or (which is made up of the Côte de Nuits and the Côte de Beaune), the Côte Chalonnaise, and Mâconnais. The southernmost commune, Beaujolais, produces wines from a different grape and in a different style than the rest of Burgundy.

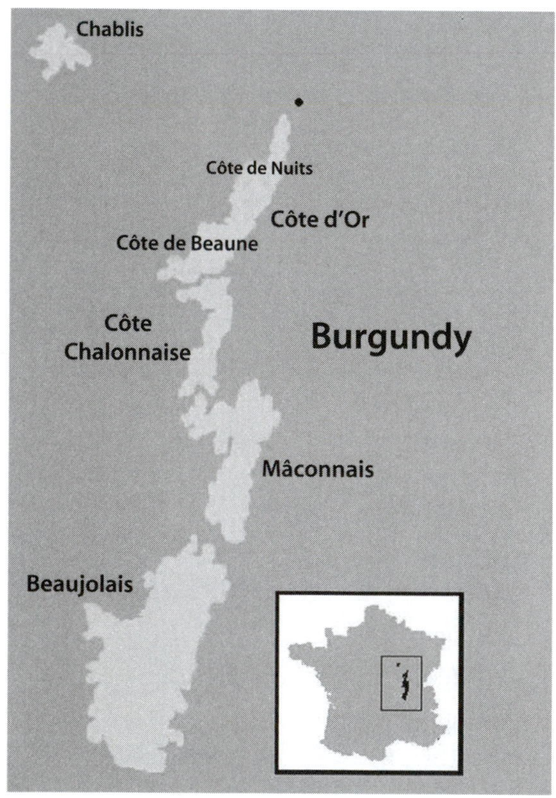

Burgundy and its major communes.

Chablis

The northernmost region of Burgundy, **Chablis** is located about 60 miles northwest of the Côte d'Or. As a result, it has a cooler climate than the rest of Burgundy. The region is also famous for its Kimmeridgian

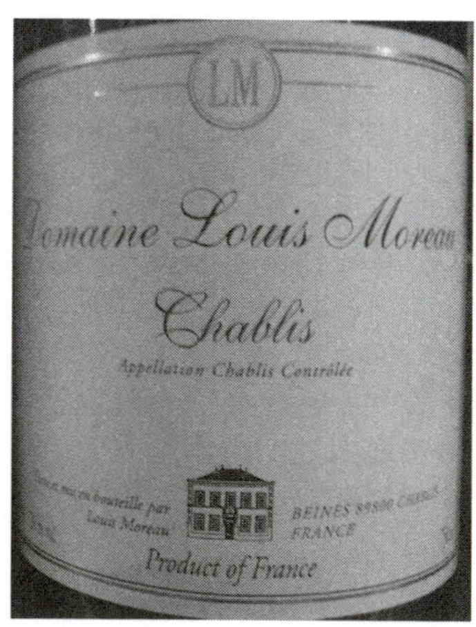

The white wines of Chablis are often lean and reminiscent of chalk and minerals.

limestone soil, made from the fossilized remains of millions of tiny, prehistoric oyster shells.

The region is completely devoted to growing Chardonnay, and produces some of the leanest, mineral-driven, and flinty whites in Burgundy. Most general-quality wines will receive a neutral oak aging regime, but higher-quality wines can pick up significant oak during the aging process. Chablis is home to forty ***premier cru*** vineyards and one ***grand cru*** vineyard. The *grand cru* is divided into seven ***climats*** or parcels.

The Seven Climats of Chablis *Grand Cru*

Blanchots	Grenouilles	Bougros	Les Clos
Les Preuses	Valmur	Vaudésir	

Côte d'Or

The **Côte d'Or** is the most famous region of Burgundy, and it is the source of its highest-quality whites and reds. Côte d'Or (French for "golden slope") is famous for its limestone soil and is on the eastern side of a 30-mile escarpment, perfectly oriented to the sun. The Côte d'Or is home to thirty-three *grand cru* vineyards and is generally divided into two major areas: the Côte de Nuits and the Côte de Beaune.

Côte de Nuits Planted almost entirely to Pinot Noir (approximately 99 percent of production), the **Côte de Nuits** is the northernmost of the two communes that make up the Côte d'Or. This commune stretches about 13 miles from north to south,

The Côte d'Or and its important villages.

Village		*Grands Crus*
Marsannay	●	-
Fixin	●	-
Gevrey-Chambertin	●	Chambertin Chambertin-Clos de Bèze Chapelle-Chambertin Charmes-Chambertin Griotte-Chambertin Latricierès-Chambertin Mazis-Chambertin Mazoyères-Chambertin Ruchottes-Chambertin
Morey-Saint-Denis	●	Clos Saint-Denis Clos de la Roche Clos des Lambrays Clos de Tart Bonnes Mares*
Chambolle-Musigny	○●	Bonnes Mares* Musigny
Vougeot	●	Clos de Vougeot
Flagey-Échezeaux	●	Échezeaux Grands-Échezeaux
Vosne-Romanée	●	La Grand Rue Richebourg La Romanée Romanée-Conti Romanée-Saint-Vivant La Tâche
Nuits-Saint-Georges	●	-

**Grand cru* vineyard shared by more than one village
○ Denotes a village producing white wines
● Denotes a village producing red wines

The major villages of the Côte de Nuits, types of wine they produce, and *grand cru* vineyards located there.

Village		*Grands Crus*
Ladoix-Serrigny	○●	Corton* Corton-Charlemagne*
Aloxe-Corton	○●	Charlemagne* Corton* Corton-Charlemagne*
Pernand-Vergelesses	○●	Charlemagne* Corton* Corton-Charlemagne*
Chorey-lès-Beaune	○●	-
Savigny-lès-Beaune	○●	-
Beaune	○●	-
Pommard	●	-
Volnay	●	-
Monthélie	○●	-
Auxey-Duresses	○●	-
Saint-Romain	○●	-
Meursault	○●	-
Puligny-Montrachet	○	Montrachet* Bâtard-Montrachet* Chevalier-Montrachet Bienvenues-Bâtard-Montrachet
Chassagne-Montrachet	○	Montrachet* Bâtard-Montrachet* Criots-Bâtard-Montrachet
Saint-Aubin	○●	-
Santenay	○●	-
Maranges	○●	-

**Grand cru* vineyard shared by more than one village
○ Denotes a village producing white wines
● Denotes a village producing red wines

The major villages of the Côte de Beaune, types of wine they produce, and *grand cru* vineyards located there.

and is named for the town of Nuits-Saint-Georges. The reds of the Côte de Nuits are some of the most structured, earthy, and complex in the region and tend to be quite expensive. The Côte de Nuits is home to 12 village designations, 140 *premier cru* vineyards, and 25 *grand cru* vineyards (the most *grand cru* vineyards of any commune in Burgundy). This is the most prime real estate in the world for Pinot Noir, and some of the most legendary wines of Burgundy are produced here.

Côte de Beaune The **Côte de Beaune** is located just to the south of the Côte de Nuits and makes up the second half of the fabled Côte d'Or. Stretching for 18 miles, the commune produces about twice as much wine as the Côte de Nuits. The Côte de Beaune is planted to both Pinot Noir and Chardonnay, although it is best known for its complex and long-lived Chardonnay-based wines. The Côte de Beaune is named for the largest town in Burgundy, Beaune, which serves as the commercial center for many of the region's top producers. The reds of the Côte de Beaune are extremely high in quality, although they are not as famous as their counterparts in the Côtes de Nuits. Their white wines, however, are considered to be the best in Burgundy; and seven of the eight *grand cru* vineyards in the commune grow nothing but Chardonnay. The Côte de Beaune is home to 17 village designations, 313 *premier cru* vineyards (the most *premier cru* vineyards of any commune in Burgundy), and 8 *grand cru* vineyards.

Côte Chalonnaise

Directly south of the Côte de Beaune, the **Côte Chalonnaise** is a collection of five communes located near the village of Chalon-sur-Saône. These five communes are Bouzeron, Rully, Mercurey, Givry, and Montagny. Côte Chalonnaise winemakers grow both red and white wines that are somewhat similar in style to the wines of the Côte d'Or, but lack complexity, intensity, and depth in comparison. Regardless, some of the best values in Burgundy can be found in the Côte Chalonnaise, and the wines tend to be more fruit-driven due to the more southern location and warmer climate. Besides the 5 commune designations that make up the Côte Chalonnaise, the area is home to 119 *premier cru* vineyards (and no *grand cru* vineyards).

Mâconnais

Mâconnais is a fairly large region in Burgundy, named for the largest village in the commune, Mâcon. This is the southernmost region of Burgundy that produces mostly Pinot Noir- and Chardonnay-based wines. It is just south of the Côte Chalonnaise and is home to mostly medium- to high-quality white wines and inexpensive reds. Of all the appellations found in Mâconnais, the best known is the commune of **Pouilly-Fuissé,** famous for its white wines made from 100 percent Chardonnay (not to be confused with Pouilly-Fumé, a 100 percent Sauvignon Blanc wine from the Loire Valley). Although most of the wines of the Mâconnais are bound for regional bottlings, there are forty village designations in the region. There are no *premier cru* vineyards, nor are there any *grand cru* vineyards in Mâconnais. This is the second highest producing region in Burgundy next to Beaujolais, with most of its production designated as regional wine labeled "Appellation Bourgogne Contrôlée."

Beaujolais

Beaujolais is the southernmost district of Burgundy and also the largest, responsible for almost half of the wines produced in the region. Its southern location actually places Beujolais in the same ***département*** or "state" as the Rhône Valley, and Beaujolais is by far the warmest part of Burgundy. Although technically products of Burgundy, the wines of Beaujolais are made in a very different style and with a different grape than the other wines of Burgundy.

Almost all of the wine produced in Beaujolais is red, although this does not mean Pinot Noir–based wines like in the rest of Burgundy. Conditions in Beaujolais are not ideal for that grape, and winemakers there abandoned the idea of growing Pinot Noir long ago. Instead, they grow a red grape called Gamay. Gamay is very different from Pinot Noir. Gamay is often fruity and simple, while Pinot Noir is earthy and complex. Gamay-based wines are intended for early consumption, while many other red Burgundy wines can be laid down for decades.

There are three basic classes of Beaujolais, set up in a similar manner to the wine classification system found in the rest of Burgundy. These classes are AOC Beaujolais, AOC Beaujolais-Villages, and finally Cru Beaujolais—wines from specific communes that are considered the best in the region. AOC Beaujolais wines make up about half of the production in Beaujolais. Most of the vineyards are found in the southern parts of Beaujolais and this classification is made up of mostly simple, forgettable wines. One-quarter of the wine produced in the region is AOC Beaujolais-Villages, wines produced in northern Beaujolais near roughly forty villages known for better quality. The best Beaujolais has to offer are the Cru Beaujolais, wines made from grapes grown in one of ten communes famous for their quality wines. These subregions are where you will find the best ***terroir*** for the Gamay grape, and only the name of the commune or village will appear on the label.

Charlemagne's Beard

Legend has it that Charlemagne was a great lover of the wines of Corton, today a *grand cru* vineyard near the village of Aloxe-Corton in the Côte de Beaune. He drank the red wines produced there with such abandon that wine would spill out of the glass, staining his beard. As his wife disapproved of this, he ordered white grapes to be planted in a vineyard nearby, which today is known as Corton-Charlemagne, a *grand cru* vineyard for white wines.

The Ten Cru Beaujolais Communes

Brouilly	Chénas	Chiroubles	Côte de Brouilly
Juliénas	Morgon	Moulin-à-Vent	Régnié
Fleurie	Saint-Amour		

Besides the normal production of Beaujolais wines in the region, there is one unique wine produced each year called AOC **Beaujolais Nouveau.** This wine is quickly produced over the course of seven to nine weeks after the grapes are picked and is used to celebrate the French wine harvest each year. It is always released on the third Thursday of November.

To produce such a wine so quickly, winemakers employ a special form of fermentation called **carbonic maceration.** Whole bunches of uncrushed grapes are put into vats filled with carbon dioxide, and fermentation ensues when the grapes at the bottom of the vat are crushed by the weight of the grapes above them. As more carbon dioxide is produced by this fermentation, it envelops all of the grapes in the vat and the fermentation continues *inside* the whole grapes at the top of the vat. Eventually the grapes burst, releasing more juice, until the fermentation of all grape sugars is complete and the wine is pressed. This type of fermentation extracts very little tannin from the grape skins and produces a soft red wine that is intended for easy and copious consumption (remember that this is a wine intended for celebration).

Beaujolais Nouveau is a style of wine produced to celebrate the French wine harvest each year.

AOC Beaujolais Nouveau wines are intended for immediate consumption and should not be aged.

The Rhône: The Original Classic Region

The ancient Greeks colonized the Mediterranean coastline of France almost 2,500 years ago, establishing the port city known today as Marseilles. They brought with them olive trees and grapevines, and eagerly introduced both to southern France. Following the Greeks, the Romans occupied the area, and winemaking continued to flourish. The most important wine region in southern France is known as the Rhône Valley, or simply the Rhône, and stretches almost 120 miles from north to south. Its northernmost appellations start just south of Lyons (where Burgundy ends), and it follows the course of the Rhône River as it flows south to the city of Avignon, eventually emptying into the Mediterranean Sea.

Although not as well known as either Burgundy or Bordeaux, the Rhône Valley is one of the top winemaking regions in France. It is home to some of the most important and famous wines in the world, like Hermitage, Côte-Rôtie, and Châteauneuf-du-Pape. The Rhône Valley is also where the French *Appellation d'Origin Contrôlée* laws were conceived and first ratified.

The Rhône Valley itself can be broken up into two major areas, the Northern Rhône and the Southern Rhône. Differences exist between the two in terms of geography and climate; however, the most important difference may be in winemaking philosophy. Winemakers in the Northern Rhône make wines from only a few different grapes. The only red grape legally allowed in the appellations that make up the Northern Rhône is Syrah, and the wines made from it are legendary. In the Southern Rhône, winemakers grow twenty-three different red and white varietals, and the bulk of the wines produced there are blends of several different grapes. The most important red wines in the Southern Rhône may have Syrah included as part of their overall blend, but the most significant red grape in these regions is Grenache.

The Facts on the Rhône Valley

CLIMATE

Separated from the Mediterranean Sea only by the region of Provence, the Rhône Valley has a predominantly warm-Mediterranean climate.

TOP WHITE GRAPE

- Viognier

TOP RED GRAPES

- Syrah
- Grenache

TOP REGIONS

Northern Rhône

- Côte-Rôtie
- Hermitage

Southern Rhône

- Côtes-du-Rhône
- Châteauneuf-du-Pape
- Tavel

IMPORTANT INFORMATION

- The Rhône Valley was one of the first areas of France to be planted to grapevines after the ancient Greeks established a port city in what is today known as Marseilles.
- Best known for powerful, earthy red wines, the Rhône is also home to some exotic white wines, sweet dessert wines, and some of the world's top rosés.
- The Rhône is separated into two distinct districts based on geography and winemaking philosophy. The Northern Rhône is very traditional, growing only a handful of grapes, with Syrah being the only red grape allowed. The Southern Rhône is very different, blending almost two dozen different grape varieties into wines, with the top red grape being Grenache.

IMPORTANT GRAPES OF THE RHÔNE

While the winemakers of the Northern Rhône use only one red grape and a handful of whites, the Southern Rhône is home to several famous blends, both white and red, using almost two dozen different varietals. White wines are not as common in the Rhône Valley as reds, but the majority of the whites from this region are made with grapes that have exotic, aromatic characteristics, most notably Viognier.

Syrah

The Syrah grape originated in southern France, and it is at its best in the Rhône Valley. Syrah is the only red grape grown in the Northern Rhône, where it produces dense, complex, age-worthy wines. The most notable of these Syrah-based wines in the Northern Rhône are made in the AOC regions of Côte-Rôtie and Hermitage. Syrah is also widely grown in the Southern Rhône, but almost always plays second fiddle to Grenache. It is used in lesser percentages as a blending grape to add density to the Grenache-based wines of these regions. Regardless of where it is grown in the Rhône Valley, Syrah tends to produce more earthy characteristics, reminiscent of smoke, peppercorns, and gamey aromas.

Grenache

The pigmented version of the Grenache varietal, also known as Grenache Noir, is the most important grape grown in the Southern Rhône. Grenache loves warm, arid conditions and thrives in the Southern Rhône, where most blended red wines contain at least two-thirds of the grape. The most famous of these Grenache-based blends are the wines of Châteauneuf-du-Pape. Rhône wines made from Grenache will be powerful and earthy, often with elevated levels of alcohol and spicy flavors, laced with strawberry jam. Besides red wines, Grenache is the most notable grape in the Rhône Valley used to produce rosés, especially in the appellation of Tavel.

Viognier

Many of the very best white wines produced in the Rhône Valley either are made from Viognier or at least almost always use it as a component in a blend. Viognier ripens fully in warm climates like that of the Rhône Valley, and when it does, the resulting wines are full-bodied, powerful, and bursting with stone fruit and exotic aromas. The top expressions of this grape would be the 100 percent Viognier wines produced in the Northern Rhône appellations of Condrieu and the miniscule Château-Grillet. Sometimes a percentage of Viognier will be blended into red wines to add aroma and complexity, especially in the Northern Rhône.

Other Notable Grapes

MARSANNE Typically a minor blending grape used in smaller percentages in both white and red wines. Marsanne does play a leading role in some of the lesser-known white wines of the Northern Rhône, where it is blended with Roussanne; often very aromatic.

ROUSSANNE A minor blending grape used in both white and red blends throughout the Rhône Valley. It often is added for its delicate nature to complement Marsanne in the Northern Rhône.

GRENACHE BLANC The white variety of the Grenache grape. Widely grown in the Southern Rhône, where it is used in both white and red blends.

MOURVÈDRE An important blending grape in the Southern Rhône, used to add color, gamey flavors, and tannins to red blends.

CARIGNAN An important and prolific blending grape used to add structure and spice to the red blends of the Southern Rhône.

CINSAUT/CINSAULT An important blending grape in the Southern Rhône, where it is used to add acidity and color to red blends.

TERROIR AND IMPORTANT REGIONS

The source of the Rhône River is found in the Swiss Alps, where it drops into Lake Geneva before flowing into France and south toward the Mediterranean. The wine regions of the Rhône Valley are found along both sides of the Rhône River starting about 20 miles south of the city of Lyons, stretching 120 miles south to the city of Avignon. The Rhône Valley can be broken up into two significant areas, the **Northern Rhône** and the **Southern Rhône.**

At less than 10 percent the size of the Southern Rhône, the wine regions of the Northern Rhône nevertheless produce wines of great stature. The northernmost point of the Northern Rhône is a mere 20 miles away from the southernmost region of Burgundy, and the two share a more continental influence on their climates. Overall, the Northern Rhône has a warm-continental climate due to its southern latitude, and the positioning of its vineyards maximizes sun exposure and aids in ripening grapes. The river banks of the Northern Rhône are often much steeper than those of the Southern Rhône, and vineyard sites are often terraced and must be worked by hand.

Closer to the Mediterranean Sea and just north of the sun-drenched region of Provence is the Southern Rhône. The temperatures in the Southern Rhône are considerably warmer than the northern appellations. In fact, the region would be too hot for growing premium grapes if it were not for a unique climate pattern that affects the Southern Rhône. This pattern is made up of a powerful wind, nicknamed *le mistral* or "the jester," that blows north from the Mediterranean where it is channeled up through the Southern Rhône (and the Northern Rhône to a lesser extent), cooling down the grapes during the heat of the day in the summer months. With this wind, the grapes of the Southern Rhône are kept from overripening, and slowly reach full ripeness.

Both the Northern and the Southern districts of the Rhône Valley typically have a well-draining sandy soil. The top vineyards will often be strewn with smooth river rocks called *galets*. These help to absorb energy from the sun during the day and then release it in the form of a gentle heat to the vines during the night, helping to achieve further ripeness in the grapes. In some vineyards, it appears as if the vines themselves are growing out of these rocks.

Northern Rhône

The Northern Rhône is very small in relation to the Southern Rhône, although it produces some

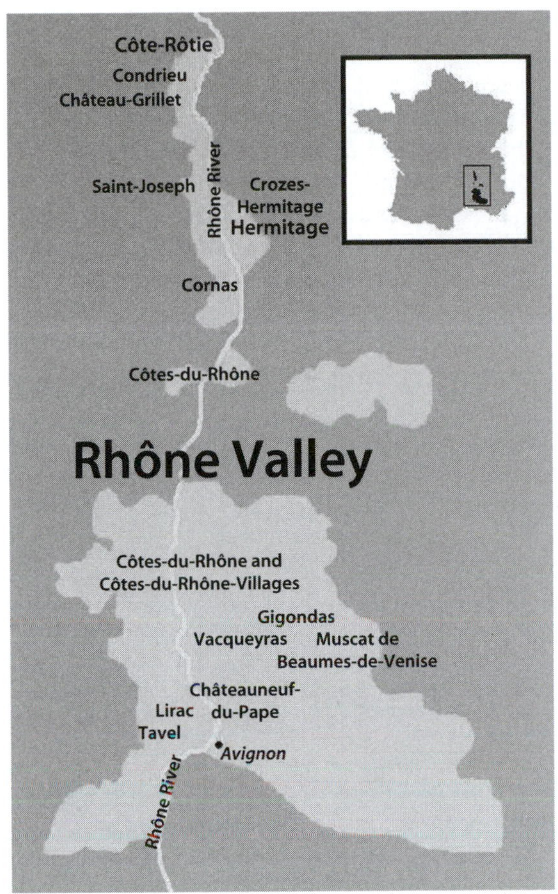

The Rhône Valley and its important appellations.

of the most storied wines in France. Syrah is the only red grape grown in the area and the world's greatest Syrahs are produced here, especially in the appellations of **Côte-Rôtie** and **Hermitage**. Significant amounts of white wines are also produced from Viognier, Marsanne, and Roussanne. Although cooler than the Southern Rhône, most of the top vineyard sites have a southern exposure that maximizes direct sunlight and ripeness.

Côte-Rôtie The term *Côte-Rôtie* literally translates to "roasted slope," and this region is so named because it is almost entirely made up of a steep hillside with a southern exposure that gets roasted by the sun. At less than 300 acres, Côte-Rôtie is small in size, but its wines are very large in stature. The region produces only red wines made from Syrah and up to 20 percent of the white grape varietal Viognier (although in practice this percentage is often much less). These wines are some of the most sought after in the Rhône Valley because of their intense flavors, complexity, and small production. They are especially noted for their spicy Syrah character and a perfumed quality which the Viognier adds to the blend. There are several well-known vineyard sections found in the Côte-Rôtie that will appear as subdesignations on labels, including Côte Blonde and Côte Brune.

Hermitage The AOC region of Hermitage, sometimes spelled Ermitage, produces some of the highest-quality red and white wines in the Rhône Valley. It is named in honor of Gaspard de Stérimberg, a knight who retired to the region in the 1200s to live in solitude as a hermit. Similar to Côte-Rôtie in topography, Hermitage is a steep, south-facing slope that rises up from the banks of the Rhône River and maximizes the vines' exposure to the sun to increase ripeness. The red wines of Hermitage are made with the red grape Syrah, with small amounts of Marsanne and Roussanne sometimes blended in for complexity. These reds are full-bodied and intense, capable of aging for decades. About a quarter of the production in Hermitage is white wine made from a blend of Marsanne and Roussanne, sometimes very powerful and aromatic in its own right.

Other Regions of Note in the Northern Rhône There are only a handful of AOC wine regions in the Northern Rhône, but even the lesser-known appellations are capable of top-quality wines (sometimes with a much smaller price tag). For Syrah-based red wines look to Saint-Joseph, Cornas, and Crozes-Hermitage, which borders the hillside appellation of Hermitage. Dedicated solely to the production of white wines made from 100 percent Viognier are Condrieu and its legendary subregion Château-Grillet, one of the smallest AOC regions in France at less than 10 acres.

Côtes-du-Rhône is the largest appellation in the Southern Rhône Valley in terms of both physical size and production.

Southern Rhône

The Southern Rhône is much larger than the Northern Rhône in terms of production and size, and is responsible for more than 90 percent of the wine produced in the Rhône Valley. Conditions are much warmer in the Southern Rhône due to its proximity to the Mediterranean, and ripeness levels can be extremely high. Focusing predominantly on dry, red wines, the most well-known and important appellations of the Southern Rhône are **Côtes-du-Rhône** and **Châteauneuf-du-Pape.** High-quality rosés are also produced in the AOC region of **Tavel.**

Côtes-Du-Rhône The Côtes-du-Rhône is the largest appellation in the Rhône Valley and easily produces the most wine—nearly half of the Rhône Valley's total production. Covering nearly 100,000 acres, the region is located almost wholly in the Southern Rhône, nestled in the hills and slopes that surround the Rhône River Valley. Primarily a red wine region (although whites and rosés are also produced here), Côtes-du-Rhône wines are often simple and straightforward and can be produced from any of the important red varietals grown in the Southern Rhône. Not surprisingly, they are usually Grenache-based blends. Located within the Côtes-du-Rhône appellation is the AOC subregion known as Côtes-du-Rhône-Villages. Made up of vineyard sites located near important winemaking villages in the Southern Rhône, standards for Côtes-du-Rhône-Villages wines are stricter and the quality is often better.

Châteauneuf-du-Pape The term *Châteauneuf-du-Pape* translates to "new house/castle of the pope." It refers to a palace built in the city of Avignon that served as the headquarters for the Catholic Church in the 1400s when a series of nine French popes decided to serve from there rather than the Vatican. This Papal influence can be seen throughout the region that surrounds the city of Avignon today, known still as Châteauneuf-du-Pape.

The wines of Châteauneuf-du-Pape are some of the most famous in the Rhône Valley and France, and by far the most important in the Southern Rhône. Châteauneuf-du-Pape is almost exclusively a red wine region, and Grenache almost always makes up two-thirds or more of the blends from this region. There are thirteen

Châteauneuf-du-Pape is the top quality wine region of the Southern Rhône Valley.

The Grapes of Châteauneuf-du-Pape

One of France's greatest wines, Châteauneuf-du-Pape is made from a blend of up to fourteen different approved grapes, both red and white.

Red grapes: Cinsaut, Counoise, Grenache, Mourvèdre, Muscardine, Syrah, Terret Noir, and Vaccarèse.

White grapes: Bourboulenc, Clairette, Grenache Blanc, Picardin, Picpoul, and Roussanne.

other approved grapes grown in the region as blending grapes, most notably Syrah and Mourvèdre. It is not uncommon to see white grapes used as components of red wines to soften their structure and add aroma. Châteauneuf-du-Pape is one of the southernmost and warmest areas of the Rhône Valley, and as high levels of ripeness are easily achieved here, it has the highest minimum alcohol level of any AOC wine in France.

Tavel The Southern Rhône produces some of France's best dry rosé wines, and the best of these are produced in the AOC region of Tavel. This appellation is located on the eastern bank of the Rhône, across from Châteauneuf-du-Pape and the city of Avignon. It is completely dedicated to rosé wines produced from mostly Grenache grapes, with Cinsaut often added. Tavel wines are often reminiscent of strawberries and cherries, and it is not unusual for them to have a detectable amount of tannins.

Other Regions of Note in the Southern Rhône The Southern Rhône's appellations produce a wide range of different styles. Besides the Grenache-based red blends of Côtes-du-Rhône and Châteauneuf-du-Pape, high-quality examples are produced in Gigondas and Vacqueyras. Lirac is an AOC region that produces rosés that rival the quality of Tavel. Sweet, fortified *vin doux naturel* wines are also produced in the appellation of Muscat de Beaumes-de-Venise from the Muscat grape. Recently, the AOC region of Costières de Nîmes was technically made a part of the Rhône region. Historically, this AOC has been part of Languedoc-Roussillon, but the quality of its Grenache- and Syrah-based wines and their similarity in style to Côtes-du-Rhône wines spurred this change.

Champagne: The Wine of Kings

The region of **Champagne** is dedicated to the production of top-quality sparkling wines. These wines are produced under strict AOC regulations, and true Champagne can come only from within this region. Many sparkling wines around the world call themselves Champagne, but real Champagne only comes from Champagne, France. Champagne produces the world's highest-quality, most famous, sought-after, and expensive sparkling wines. Its an interesting honor if you consider the early history of winemaking in Champagne during the 1500s and 1600s, when winemakers almost gave up on winemaking because they could not make a wine that did not have bubbles! Originally, winemakers wanted to make dry table wines like those produced in Burgundy from Chardonnay and Pinot Noir grapes. The cold climate of Champagne was the root of their problems. Fermentations were prematurely stopped when it got too cold for yeast activity. Since there was no real understanding of fermentation at the time, winemakers simply relied on tradition to produce their wines, and that basically meant that a wine was finished when it stopped producing bubbles (the carbon dioxide generated by yeast cells as they metabolize sugar).

Winemakers in Champagne would wait as far into the growing season as they possibly could before harvesting to attempt to maximize ripeness, but when they did harvest and begin fermenting wines, temperatures were getting quite cold. As the temperature of the wines being fermented began to drop, the yeast would eventually go dormant before consuming all of the sugar in the wine. Yeast activity ceases at around 50°F. Since carbon dioxide was no longer being generated, the bubbles produced during fermentation stopped and it was believed that the wine was completed. This wine would then be aged in bulk and eventually

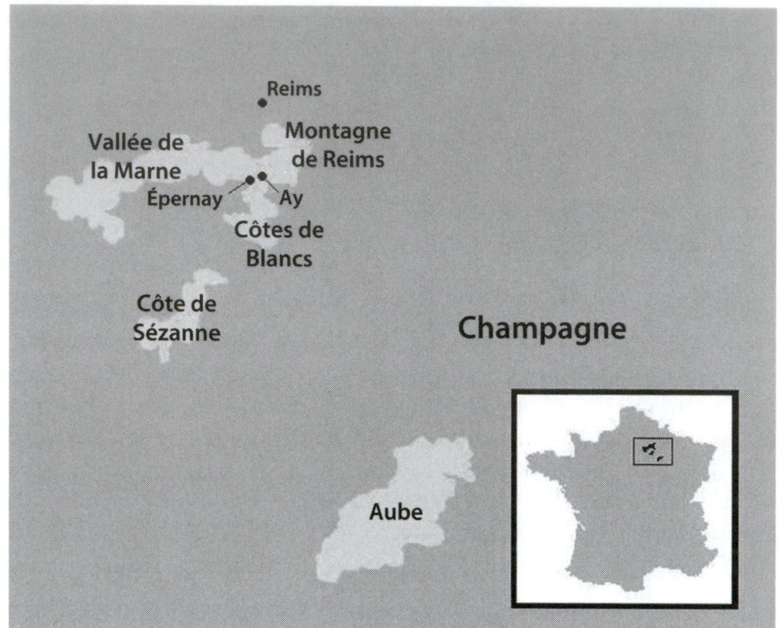

Champagne and its important districts.

bottled. As temperatures warmed up in the late spring and into summer, the yeast would eventually come out of dormancy and begin fermenting the sugar that remained in the wine. A small amount of alcohol would be produced, but a large volume of carbon dioxide would also be generated, building up pressure inside the bottle. This caused corks to pop out, bottles to explode, and fizzy to frothy wines to be revealed if the bottle survived the pressure. Cellar workers actually had to wear metal helmets to protect themselves from flying shards of glass!

Wines with bubbles simply could not be sold at the time, because they were considered flawed. The winemakers of Champagne had a choice to make: stop producing wine or attempt to control the bubbles. Luckily for fans of sparkling wines, they chose the latter, and began developing a means of producing sparkling wines they could control: *méthode champenoise*, or the "Champagne method." This process involves two separate fermentations: one in bulk to make a base wine and one in the bottle to create and trap carbonation (see Chapter 3 for a thorough discussion of *méthode champenoise*). To complete the first fermentation during the cold winter in Champagne, winemakers were forced to literally go underground.

Almost the entire region of Champagne is sitting on top of a rich deposit of chalk—a prized building material during Roman times. This chalk was formed millions of years ago when a shallow sea covered northern France. Countless fossilized oyster and bivalve shells were deposited on the ocean floor and eventually formed the chalk deposits of Champagne. In mining the chalk for hundreds of years, the Romans and others created a series of mines, caves, and excavations under Champagne that still remain. Winemaking operations were moved underground into these caves in the late 1600s and 1700s because the temperature was not greatly affected by the cold conditions on the surface. Fermentations could be fully completed and the double fermentation that makes up *méthode champenoise* was eventually perfected.

With the bubbles under control, the next task at hand was figuring out how to get the yeast out of the bottle while maintaining the carbonation in the wine. The processes of *remuage* (riddling) and *dégorgement* (disgorgement) were developed by the winemakers of Champagne to effectively force all of the yeast into the neck of the bottle and then remove it just prior to dosing and corking the bottle.

Due to the region's proximity to Paris, once the wines of Champagne gained popularity, they quickly became associated with the royal family. The French nobility drank Champagne to celebrate the coronation of monarchs and Champagne became known as the "wine of kings." As its fame spread into England and Russia, Champagne had truly arrived.

The Facts on Champagne

CLIMATE

Located 90 miles northeast of Paris, Champagne is the northernmost classic wine region of France. Without a large body of water nearby to help temper its climate, Champagne's weather conditions range from cool-continental to cold.

TOP WHITE GRAPE

- Chardonnay

TOP RED GRAPES

- Pinot Noir
- Pinot Meunier

IMPORTANT STYLES OF CHAMPAGNE

- Non-vintage Champagne
- Rosé Champagne
- Blanc de Blancs Champagne
- Blanc de Noirs Champagne
- Vintage Champagne
- Prestige Cuvée Champagne

TOP REGIONS

Champagne has no recognized AOC subregions, but there are five separate districts that make up Champagne: Aube, Côte de Blancs, Côte de Sézanne, Montagne de Reims, and Vallée de la Marne.

IMPORTANT INFORMATION

- The wines of Champagne are considered the greatest style of sparkling wine produced and one of the most classic wines in the world.
- The term *Champagne* has become synonymous with sparkling wines, but should be used only to describe the sparkling wines produced in the official region of Champagne.
- Winemakers nearly gave up on wine production early in the history of Champagne because of unplanned and inconsistent carbonation. It took several generations and thousands of winemakers to develop a production technique called *méthode champenoise* that could control carbonation in these wines.
- The vast majority of wines produced in Champagne are non-vintage blends. Most Champagne houses blend several different lots of wine from multiple vintages together to achieve a house style.

IMPORTANT GRAPES OF CHAMPAGNE

Although Champagne is generally considered a sparkling white wine, there is only one white-skinned grape varietal legally grown in the region, while there are two red wine grape varietals grown. Vineyard acreage in Champagne is heavily dominated by these red wine grapes. Due to the colder climate of Champagne, the grapes rarely reach full ripeness. The three grapes approved in the region are Chardonnay, Pinot Noir, and Pinot Meunier.

 Chardonnay

The often full-bodied, low-acidity version of this grape varietal produced in many regions around the world is not to be found in Champagne. Owing to the cold climate, Chardonnay never fully ripens in Champagne, providing an acidic, extremely light component to the wines of the region.

 Pinot Noir

Pinot Noir was originally planted in Champagne to produce red wines similar to those found in the cool region of Burgundy. Unfortunately, not even this fast-ripening red grape could ripen enough in Champagne to produce a quality red wine. Instead, Pinot Noir is used to produce sparkling white wines in the region, and contributes much of the body and fruit found in many Champagnes.

Did Dom Pérignon Invent Champagne?

While Dom Pérignon, a Franciscan monk, was very important in helping to develop the Champagne method of winemaking, he in no way individually invented Champagne. Pérignon was assigned as the head of winemaking at the Abbey at Hautvillers in Champagne in the late 1600s. He made several advancements in the production of the wines there, from sealing bottles with cork stoppers to mastering the art of blending different lots of wine together to achieve a consistent style. Today, a prestige cuvée Champagne produced by Moët & Chandon (who purchased the holdings where the Abbey at Hautvillers was located) bears his name.

 Pinot Meunier

This descendant of Pinot Noir serves as the unheralded workhorse grape of Champagne. Although Chardonnay and Pinot Noir get most of the attention in Champagne, Pinot Meunier is the most widely planted varietal in the region. This is due to the fact that it is heartier in the cooler conditions of Champagne and produces higher yields than the other varieties. Pinot Meunier contributes significant fruit and acidity to the wines of Champagne.

TERROIR AND IMPORTANT REGIONS

The style of wine produced in Champagne is dictated first and foremost by the cold-continental climate in the region. Located 90 miles northeast of Paris, Champagne is the northernmost classic wine region in France. This climate is marginal at best for growing wine grapes, as it significantly shortens the ripening season in Champagne. The result is grapes that are harvested when they are considerably underripe. These grapes produce a wine that is extremely acidic, light-bodied, and low in alcohol content—not ideal for dry table wine, but that combination is a perfect base for a sparkling wine.

Besides the climate of Champagne, the soil has the second most important impact on the characteristics of Champagne. Interestingly enough, the dirt in most of Champagne is white because it is made of chalk. There are two major benefits that this chalk provides for the winemakers of Champagne. First, its white color reflects sunlight to the vines, helping to further ripen grapes. Second, it gives the wines of Champagne a distinct, crisp, chalky flavor that is a great contrast to the acid and fruit in these wines.

Most of the region of Champagne is scattered around the three important towns of Reims, Ay, and Épernay, where many of the famous Champagne houses (producers) are headquartered. Unlike most of the other classic wine regions of France, Champagne has no subregions that have their own AOC status. All of the sparkling wines produced according to the strict regulations in the region are simply considered "Appellation Champagne Contrôlée" wines. This lack of AOC subregions does not mean that there are not recognized districts. Champagne can be divided into five major districts: Aube, Côte de Blancs, Côte de Sézanne, Montagne de Reims, and Vallée de la Marne. Each has its own individual *terroir,* grows different approved grapes, and gives its wines unique characteristics.

The villages and vineyards found throughout the region of Champagne have long been graded in terms of quality, with the highest designations being *premier cru* and *grand cru.* Top vineyard areas of grape quality are considered *grand cru* in status, and provide most of the grapes used for the highest-quality Champagnes, especially vintage and prestige cuvée/cuvée de prestige Champagnes. *Premier cru* communes are close in terms of quality to those with *grand cru* status, and are often used by better Champagne houses for both their vintage and non-vintage Champagnes.

IMPORTANT STYLES AND DESIGNATIONS

While there are no AOC subregions in Champagne, there are several different styles of Champagne produced and a number of different sweetness levels or designations that can be found on Champagne labels.

Sweetness Levels

One of the main designations found on Champagne labels refers to the level of sweetness in a particular wine. One of the final processes conducted on a bottle of Champagne during *dégorgement* is **dosage.** Dosage basically involves adding a liquid called ***liqueur d'expédition*** to the wine to top the bottle off. Champagne bottles are immediately corked after adding this liquid. The *liqueur d'expédition* is still wine that may or may not have sugar dissolved into it; the sweeter the *liqueur d'expédition*, the sweeter the resulting Champagne. Centuries ago, sweet Champagnes were the most common style produced. Eventually, tastes changed and today the majority of Champagne produced is made in a dry style. There are seven official sweetness levels found in Champagne, ranging from completely dry to dessert-wine sweet.

Sweetness Levels of Champagne

Brut Nature	No sugar at all is added; wines are bone dry.
Extra Brut	Only a minute amount of sugar is added; wines are very dry.
Brut	A minimal amount of sugar is added that is barely perceivable; wines are dry. This is the most popular style of Champagne produced.
Extra Dry or Extra Sec	Some sugar is added, making the wine off-dry. The second most popular style of Champagne.
Sec	The literal translation of the word sec is "dry," although Champagnes with this designation are semisweet.
Demi-Sec	Translates to "semidry," but Champagne labeled Demi-Sec will be quite sweet.
Doux	A heavy concentration of sugar is added. Doux Champagne is extremely sweet and is considered a dessert wine.

Champagne Styles

Although all Champagnes fall under the Appellation Champagne Contrôlée designation, there are a variety of different styles of Champagne produced. These vary in both quality and price, and some require unique winemaking practices.

Non-Vintage Champagne The most common style of Champagne produced is **non-vintage,** accounting for more than 80 percent of the wine produced there. These sparkling wines are a *cuvée,* or blend of several component base wines from a number of different vintages. Dozens of different wines from various vineyards and grape varieties are added to take advantage of their unique flavors and characteristics. The goal for most winemakers when producing non-vintage Champagnes is to replicate a **house style**—a flavor profile that is consistently the same for that producer.

Vintage Champagne In only the best of years, Champagne houses will produce vintage Champagne. There is no effort made to blend out the unique characteristics of that year's vintage, as that is what makes the wine special. Since vintage Champagnes are produced only two or three times every decade, there is a very limited supply of them, meaning they can be quite expensive.

Blanc de Blancs and Blanc de Noirs Champagne If a Champagne is produced solely from Chardonnay grapes, it will be labeled "Blanc de Blancs," which literally means "white from whites," a white wine made from white grapes. Champagnes made from Pinot Noir and/or Pinot Meunier grapes with no Chardonnay blended in will be designated "Blanc de Noirs." This means "white from blacks," a reference to a white wine made from black grapes, those with pigments in their skins. In general, **Blanc de Blancs Champagne** is very light and crisp, while **Blanc de Noirs Champagnes** are fuller and richer. Both Blanc de Blancs and Blanc de Noirs Champagnes can be vintage or non-vintage.

Rosé Champagne The vast majority of Champagnes will use at least some red-skinned grapes in their production, although the juice from those grapes will be pressed away from the skins quickly to protect against the extraction of pigments and tannins. Some winemakers will produce **rosé Champagnes** by either blending a small amount of red wine into their cuvée, or by allowing the skins to remain in contact with the juice of the grapes prior to or at the beginning of the initial fermentation. In general, rosé Champagnes are some of the highest-quality wines produced in

Champagnes like those pictured here are some of the most expensive and sought after sparkling wines in the world.

the region and will often be fairly expensive. Rosé Champagnes can be vintage or non-vintage.

Prestige Cuvée/Cuvée de Prestige Many Champagne houses will also produce a super-premium sparkling wine called a **prestige cuvée** (sometimes also referred to as a **cuvée de prestige** or cuvée speciale). This is typically the very best wine the maker produces, and is considered the show-piece of that Champagne house. These wines are typically very limited and very expensive. Two of the more famous *prestige cuvée* Champagnes are Dom Pérignon from Moët & Chandon and Cristal from Louis Roederer. Prestige cuvée Champagne is almost without exception a vintage product.

Champagne Bottle Sizes

Champagne is considered by many to be the ultimate celebration wine, and it has long been a custom for Champagne producers to bottle some of their wines in large- or small-format bottles. Typically, wine for these bottles will be fermented in standard bottles and then transferred into smaller or larger formats. Larger bottles are commonly named for biblical figures and kings. The chart above shows the major Champagne bottle sizes.

BOTTLE NAME	VOLUME	BOTTLE EQUIVALENT	NAME ORIGIN
Split	187ml	¼	
Demi/Half bottle	375ml	½	*Demi* is French for "half"
Imperial	750ml	1	Name sometimes used for a standard bottle
Magnum	1.5L	2	
Jeroboam/Double magnum	3L	4	Biblical king
Rehoboam	4.5L	6	Biblical king
Methuselah	6L	8	Oldest person mentioned in the Bible
Salmanazar	9L	12	Biblical king
Balthazar	12L	16	One of the Three Wise Men
Nebuchadnezzar	15L	20	Biblical king

The Loire Valley: Variety Is the Spice of Life

The Loire River is the longest river flowing through France. It begins in the south-central, mountainous region called the Massif Central. From its source, it flows north several hundred miles into the center of France near the city of Orleans before turning west and eventually emptying into the Atlantic Ocean. Before railroads began to crisscross the country, the Loire River was one of the main means of transportation of goods through France. Throughout the region known as the Loire Valley, the river banks and beyond are planted to a wide variety of different grape varietals. The climate of the Loire Valley gets cooler the further east one gets, away from the tempering effects of the Atlantic Ocean. Due to the fact that the climate can vary so widely in the Loire Valley, the four major zones of the region have very little in common. The

Loire Valley should not be thought of as just one continuous and consistent region, but rather a loose collection of different winemaking areas that happen to be located in the Loire River Valley.

These zones produce almost every style of wine possible. Red, white, and rosé table wines are widely produced as are sparkling wines, sweet wines, lush dessert wines, and even some fortified wines. Behind Bordeaux and Burgundy, the Loire Valley is the third largest classic French wine region in terms of vineyard acreage and production.

The Facts on the Loire Valley

CLIMATE

The climate of the Loire Valley ranges widely from temperate-maritime on the Atlantic coastline in the western portions of the region, to cool-continental in the eastern reaches.

TOP WHITE GRAPES

- Sauvignon Blanc
- Chenin Blanc

TOP RED GRAPE

- Cabernet Franc

TOP REGIONS

Pays Nantais

- Muscadet

Anjou-Saumur

- Savennières
- Coteaux du Layon

Touraine

- Vouvray
- Chinon

Upper Loire

- Sancerre
- Pouilly-Fumé

IMPORTANT INFORMATION

- The Loire Valley follows the course of the Loire River, the longest river in France, which flows west from central France and empties into the Atlantic.
- The Loire Valley is a 600-mile-long, narrow region that stretches from the temperate-maritime climate of the Atlantic coastline to the cool-continental climate of central France.
- Although the Loire Valley is the third largest wine region in France in terms of vineyard acreage and production, it is by no means one homogenous region of winemaking. The Loire Valley is more a collection of several unique AOC regions than one consistent region; several different white and red grapes are grown and almost every style of wine conceivable is produced there.

IMPORTANT GRAPES OF THE LOIRE VALLEY

For the most part, the Loire Valley is most famous for its food-friendly white wines made from two important varietals: Sauvignon Blanc and Chenin Blanc. The top red wines of the Loire Valley are mostly produced with the Cabernet Franc grape.

 Sauvignon Blanc

The origin of the Sauvignon Blanc grape is disputed between the Loire Valley and Bordeaux. Regardless of where this white grape varietal was first grown, it produces some of the most legendary white wines in the eastern Loire Valley. These wines are textbook examples of dry, Sauvignon Blanc–based wines with crisp acidity, light body, and pronounced grassy and herbal flavors and aromas. The two top AOC regions producing 100 percent Sauvignon Blanc wines are Sancerre and Pouilly-Fumé.

 Chenin Blanc

There is no dispute as to the origin of the Chenin Blanc grape—it was first developed in the central districts of the Loire Valley and named for Mount Chenin, a small mountain located in the Loire River

Valley. Chenin Blanc is responsible for some of the most stunning white wines produced in the Loire Valley, and can range in style from dry and highly acidic to rich and decadently sweet. Most of the white wine production in the central Loire Valley is dedicated to 100 percent Chenin Blanc wines. The very best dry examples are produced in the AOC region of Savennières. Vouvray is an AOC region that produces dry to sweet Chenin Blancs depending upon the warmth of the vintage. The top dessert wine in the Loire Valley is made from Chenin Blanc as well, in the AOC region of Coteaux du Layon and its subregions Bonnezeaux and Quartes de Chaume.

Cabernet Franc

Although the Loire Valley is probably best known for its white wines made from Sauvignon Blanc and Chenin Blanc, several top-quality red wines are produced in the central regions from the Cabernet Franc grape. A minor blending grape in its native region of Bordeaux, Cabernet Franc is used almost exclusively in the Loire Valley for red wines. With a body similar to its descendant Cabernet Sauvignon, Cabernet Franc has a much softer tannin structure and produces wines with ripe, dark fruit flavors as well as distinct herbal notes. The top AOC region for Cabernet Franc–based wines is Chinon.

Other Notable Grapes

MELON DE BOURGOGNE This white grape variety originated in Burgundy (hence the name) yet is no longer grown in that region. It produces light, dry white wines in the western AOC region of Muscadet. Sometimes the grape will actually be referred to as Muscadet.

CABERNET SAUVIGNON Grown in the red wine regions of the Loire Valley, Cabernet Sauvignon typically plays a minor role in red wines as a blending grape used to add structure to mostly Cabernet Franc–based wines.

GAMAY This minor grape grown in the Loire Valley is used as a single varietal or a component in blends of typically uninteresting red wines.

TERROIR AND IMPORTANT REGIONS

If not for the Atlantic, the Loire Valley would have a cool-continental climate similar to that found in its eastern regions throughout, due to its northern latitude. Instead, the western Loire has more of a temperate-maritime climate. Add to the wide range of climate zones found in the Loire Valley the fact that several different soil types and geological formations can be found throughout the region, and it is easy to see why so many different grapes and styles of wine are produced here. As with other winemaking

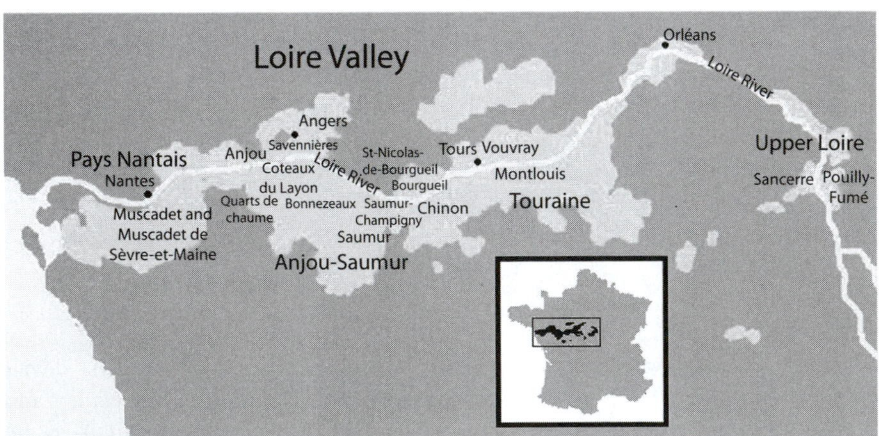

The Loire Valley and its major regions.

areas of France, winemakers in the Loire Valley have found the best combinations of grapes and styles to match the *terroir* of their individual regions.

The Loire Valley can be broken up into four major areas based on climate and other conditions. From west to east they are: **Pays Nantais, Anjou-Saumur, Touraine,** and the **Upper Loire.** These regions have very little in common except for the fact that they are all located along the banks of the Loire River.

Pays Nantais

Pays Nantais is the westernmost area of the Loire Valley, and its maritime climate is perfectly suited to the white Melon de Bougogne grape. Also known as Muscadet, this varietal is grown almost exclusively in Pays Nantais. The top AOC region for wines made from this varietal lends its name to the grape itself, Muscadet.

Muscadet The appellation of **Muscadet** is one of the largest individual regions in France, and mostly produces light, crisp white wines made from 100 percent Melon de Bourgogne grapes. This style of wine pairs perfectly with the seafood-rich cuisine of this coastal area. Basic-quality wines from the region will be labeled "Appellation Muscadet Contrôlée"; however, two more specific wines are produced there that are considered the highest quality in the western Loire.

Muscadet wines are an ideal accompaniment to many seafood dishes.

AOC Muscadet de Sèvre-et-Maine wines are made in a more specific and higher-quality subregion of Muscadet. Wines labeled "Appellation Muscadet Sur Lie Contrôlée" can come from anywhere within the Muscadet region, but must be produced using a special winemaking process. After fermentation, these wines are allowed to rest ***sur lie*** (on their lees), in contact with the dead yeast cells that will eventually settle to the bottom of a storage vessel after fermentation concludes. This results in wines with a richer body, deeper flavors, and sometimes even a slight carbonation.

Anjou-Saumur

The most important city in the area known as **Anjou-Saumur** is Angers. This area is in the west-central portion of the Loire Valley, and temperatures are slightly cooler than in Pays Nantais. Winemakers in Anjou-Saumur produce a wide range of different wines, including dry reds and rosés as well as dry, sweet, and sometimes sparkling whites.

Red wines and rosés in Anjou-Saumur are made predominantly from Cabernet Franc, although Cabernet Sauvignon and Gamay are also grown in the region. The most important reds produced here come from either of the AOC regions of Anjou or Saumur, and are mostly blends of Cabernet Franc and Cabernet Sauvignon. Saumur-Champigny is the best-known red wine appellation of Anjou-Saumur, and its delicate Cabernet Franc–based wines can rival the better-known red wines of Touraine.

By far the most prominent white grape grown in Anjou-Saumur is Chenin Blanc, and a handful of AOC subregions here produce classic examples of what this grape is capable of. Besides the well-known sparkling wine produced in the AOC region of Saumur Mousseux, Anjou-Saumur is famous for the dry wines of Savennières and the legendary sweet wines of Coteaux du Layon and its subregions Bonnezeaux and Quartes de Chaume.

Savennières Wines produced in the AOC region of **Savennières** must be made from 100 percent Chenin Blanc, and they are almost always made in a dry style. The cool climate found in Savennières leads to a piercing acidity in its wines. This is balanced by the fresh fruit characteristics Chenin Blanc is known for.

Coteaux du Layon Located right along the Layon River, a tributary that feeds into the Loire, is the sweet wine AOC region known as **Coteaux du Layon**. This appellation contains two AOC subregions that also produce sweet dessert wines from 100 percent Chenin Blanc grapes, **Bonnezeaux** and **Quarts de Chaume**. Conditions along the Layon River are ideal for the development of noble rot or botrytis. This mold attacks the superripe Chenin Blanc grapes in the vineyards of these regions and draws out moisture, concentrating sweetness. These wines, especially Quartes de Chaume, are considered the top examples of Chenin Blanc–based dessert wines.

Vouvray is considered one of the world's top Chenin Blanc wines.

Touraine

Just to the east of Anjou-Saumur is the picturesque district of Touraine, named for the city of Tours. There is a distinct difference in climate in Touraine compared to Anjou-Saumur, as almost all of the tempering effects of the Atlantic have faded this far inland. Touraine is the largest area of the Loire Valley, and is home to more than 150 AOC regions. Red wines, white wines, and rosés are all produced in Touraine with varying quality levels. Many of the top red wines of the Loire Valley are made in Touraine from the Cabernet Franc grape, including Bourgueil and Saint-Nicolas-de-Bourgueil. Arguably, the best red wine in the Loire Valley is also found in Touraine, produced in the AOC region of **Chinon.** For whites, Chenin Blanc is used almost exclusively. Touraine is home to spectacular white wines including those from the appellation of Montlouis. That said, the most famous Chenin Blanc wine in the world is produced in the AOC region of **Vouvray.**

Vouvray This district is named for the village of Vouvray, located across the river from Touraine's lesser-known white wine region, Montlouis. Vouvray is home to a staggering variety of styles of Chenin Blanc—all flavored intensely with the apple, melon, and tropical flavors typical of this varietal. The most common styles produced here range from dry whites with serious acidity produced in cooler years, to semisweet whites produced in warmer vintages when grapes more fully ripen. Sometimes, conditions in Vouvray are such that botrytis can begin to develop on the grapes, resulting in intensely sweet dessert wines. Even sparkling and slightly sparkling wines are produced in Vouvray using ***méthode tradition***. Fully carbonated wines here will be labeled "mousseux," while sparkling wines with more of a slightly fizzy carbonation are labeled "pétillant."

Chinon The greatest expression of the Cabernet Franc grape might be found in the appellation of Chinon. At their best, these wines are velvety smooth and have an aging potential of several years. Typically, these wines will be rich with raspberry and other red fruits, with just enough of the bell pepper character that Cabernet Franc is famous for.

Upper Loire

In the far eastern reaches of the Loire Valley, the coolest regions are found. The Upper Loire has a purely cool-continental climate similar to that in northern Burgundy. The area itself is made up of vineyards near the city of Orléans, located on the banks of the Loire River, where its course shifts from heading north to flowing westward toward the Atlantic. The wines of this region are sometimes referred to as *vins du Centre* because this region is almost squarely in the center of France. The same Kimmeridgian limestone found in Burgundy and Champagne can also be found throughout the Upper Loire, and it contributes the same chalky, mineral flavors to wines here. Very little red wine is produced in the Upper Loire; instead, the region focuses on white wines made from the Sauvignon Blanc grape. Two of the most famous regions in the world for Sauvignon Blanc are located in the Upper Loire, **Sancerre** and **Pouilly-Fumé.**

Sancerre Located south of Orléans, the village of Sancerre sits on the western banks of the Loire River, directly across from Pouilly-Fumé. The wines of Sancerre are almost all white, made from 100 percent Sauvignon Blanc grapes. Classic varietal characteristics of the Sauvignon Blanc grape, including grapefruit, grassiness, and musky hints of cat urine, are almost always intensely present in these wines. The better vineyards of Sancerre often contain a large presence of flint in the soil, which translates into slightly smoky flavors in finished wines.

Pouilly-Fumé Looking directly across the Loire River at Sancerre is the village of Pouilly-sur-Loire, located on the river's eastern bank and home to the Pouilly-Fumé appellation. Wines qualifying for Pouilly-Fumé AOC status are produced in the vineyards surrounding the village and are all 100 percent Sauvignon Blanc. The best are very similar to the wines found in Sancerre, although larger

Pouilly-Fumé and Sancerre produce some of the world's best Sauvignon Blanc.

percentages of flint in the soil in Pouilly-Fumé lead to smokier flavors. Pouilly-Fumé should not be confused with Pouilly-Fuissé, an AOC commune of southern Burgundy that produces 100 percent Chardonnay wines.

Alsace: The Exception

Located in northeastern France along the German border is the classic wine region of **Alsace.** The region itself is a narrow, north-south-running strip nestled in the eastern foothills of the Vosges Mountains along the banks of the Rhine River. There is a very strong German heritage and tradition in the region even though it is a part of France, because Alsace actually used to be part of Germany. Alsace has bounced back and forth from German control to French control throughout the centuries. This hotly contested region was officially deemed part of France in 1945 as one of the accords of the peace treaty that ended the European campaign of World War II.

As far as winemaking is concerned, the German heritage of Alsace runs deep. Wines are bottled in the tall, tapered bottles used by German winemakers. The vineyards and winemakers of Alsace have

German-sounding names. Differing greatly from the other classic French wine regions, Alsace grows mostly German grapes and makes German-style wines. The only major difference is that many German wines are sweetened and made from under-ripe grapes, whereas Alsatian wines are made from riper fruit and are almost always produced in a dry style.

Alsatian winemakers also label their wines like German winemakers do, by grape variety rather than by region. This makes them the exception to the rule of the AOC wine laws, as Alsace is the only AOC region to label by grape variety. "Appellation Alsace Contrôlée" will still appear on the label, but the name of the grape will be featured more prominently and the wine will be referred to by its grape name rather than regional name.

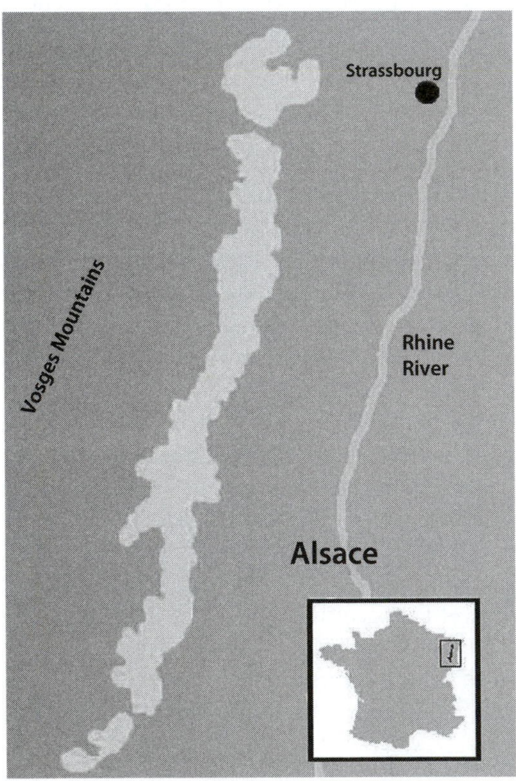

Alsace.

The Facts on Alsace

CLIMATE

Located along the German border in northeastern France, Alsace has a cool-continental climate that is usually spared severe weather and winter storms.

TOP WHITE GRAPES

- Riesling
- Gewürztraminer
- Pinot Gris

TOP STYLES

The vast majority of production in Alsace is dedicated to dry, white wines. Minimal amounts of red wines, sparkling wines, and sweet, late harvest or botrytised dessert wines are also produced.

TOP REGIONS

Alsace has no AOC subregions. Instead they have more than fifty *grand cru* vineyards designated throughout the region, which can be listed on the label in addition to "Appellation Alsace Contrôlée."

IMPORTANT INFORMATION

- Alsace is along the German border, and prior to World War II was a part of Germany—a fact that affects all aspects of life in Alsace, including winemaking.
- Alsatian winemakers produce wines and label their bottles not like other French winemakers, but rather like their German counterparts, making them the only AOC region in France to label by grape variety rather than region.
- Most of the wines produced in Alsace are made in a German style with predominantly German grape varietals, making Alsace the only region in France to grow the Riesling grape.

IMPORTANT GRAPES OF ALSACE

There are eight grape varieties legally allowed to be grown and individually bottled in the region of Alsace: Auxerrois, Chasselas, Gewürztraminer, Muscat, Pinot Gris, Pinot Noir, Riesling, and Sylvaner. Of these varietals, only Pinot Noir is a red-skinned grape varietal used to produce red wines; more than 90 percent of Alsatian production is white wine. For one of these varietals to be listed on a bottle of Alsatian wine, it

An Alsatian wine label. Alsace is the only AOC in France to label by grape variety rather than region due to its German heritage.

must contain 100 percent of the listed varietal. If an Alsatian wine is labeled "Edelzwicker," this means "noble wine" and refers to a blend of the allowed white grapes grown in the region.

Riesling

As in Germany, Riesling is the most important and famous grape varietal in Alsace, and is responsible for the top wines produced there. Losing Alsace to France was a major blow to the German wine industry, as many consider it to be the top region in the world for Riesling. Most of the Rieslings produced in Alsace are dry and made from fully ripened grapes. This gives these wines distinct fruity and citrusy notes, as well as higher alcohol content and fuller body than their German counterparts.

Gewürztraminer

Similar to Riesling, Gewürztraminer is an important grape varietal in Germany that is also prominent in Alsace. The exotic fruit and spicy flavors of Gewürztraminer are very pronounced when grown in Alsace. Interestingly, although the French language does employ the umlaut (the two dots above the "u" in the word Gewürztraminer; referred to as a ***trèma*** in French), Alsatian wines do not usually include the umlaut on the label, since the umlaut does not indicate the same pronunciation in French that it does in German.

Pinot Gris

Formerly known as (and sometimes still referred to as) *Tokay* or *Tokay d'Alsace,* Pinot Gris is the final of the three top grapes grown in Alsace. Unlike the Pinot Grigio produced in northeastern Italy, Alsatian Pinot Gris can be rich, full, and almost honeyed. Ripe citrus fruit and melon balance out the soft acidity found in these wines.

Other Notable Grapes

MUSCAT Although most Muscat around the world is sweet, Alsatian Muscat is almost always made in a dry style.

SYLVANER Another important German grape widely grown in Alsace.

PINOT NOIR The only red grape grown in Alsace, Pinot Noir produces red wines in warmer years but is usually underripe in cooler vintages and is vinified into rosé wines.

TERROIR AND IMPORTANT STYLES/REGIONS

There are two major factors that affect the climate of Alsace: the Vosges Mountains to the west, and the Rhine River to the east. The region itself runs roughly 60 miles from north to south and is nestled in the foothills of the Vosges. Its northern latitude and inland location dictate the cool-continental climate of Alsace, but the mountains to the west of Alsace protect the region from severe weather and winter storms. In fact, Alsace is one of the driest regions in France because it lies in the "rain shadow" of these mountains. This leads to sunny, dry conditions during the summer months as the grapes ripen, and explains why Alsatian wines are usually made from riper grapes than German wines are. There are several distinct soil types located throughout the region, which lead to differences in varietal selection and flavor profile in the various areas of wine production.

Alsace itself is dominated by small vineyards and a multitude of producers. The vast majority of vineyard acreage is made up of tiny holdings owned by more than five thousand independent growers. Larger producers tend to utilize fruit from their own vineyards as well as buy fruit from smaller growers to produce wines. Some Alsatian wine will be designated "Appellation Alsace *Grand Cru* Contrôlée," a reference to wines made from only a handful of important grapes grown in recognized premium vineyards. There are fifty-one ***grand cru*** vineyards located throughout Alsace. These vineyards have been historically recognized as the most important and highest-quality growing sites in Alsace. To receive the ***grand cru*** status, wines must be grown in one of these vineyards (whose name will appear as a subdesignation on the label), and can be made only from 100 percent of Riesling, Gewürztraminer, Pinot Gris, or Muscat grapes (actual regulations may differ slightly in certain ***grand cru*** vineyards). Less than 5 percent of the wines produced in Alsace receive this distinction.

Besides the predominant style of dry white wines produced in Alsace from individual grape varietals, other unique styles of wine are also produced in the region. **Crémant d'Alsace** is a sparkling wine made using the same winemaking techniques as Champagne. Rosé wines are often produced from Pinot Noir grapes, especially in cooler years when the red grapes do not fully ripen. Finally, two other important styles produced in Alsace that will appear as subdesignations printed on the label are ***Vendange Tardive*** and ***Sélection de Grains Nobles.***

Vendange Tardive is a term that applies to wines made from ultraripe, late harvest grapes that have very high sugar contents and fully developed flavors. This is the equivalent of the Auslese designation used in Germany. In Alsace, *Vendange Tardive* wines are almost always fermented completely dry, which gives them a high alcohol content and full flavors.

Sélection de Grains Nobles is the term used to describe sweet dessert wines made from fully ripened grapes infected with botrytis. This mold removes water from the grapes, leading to very concentrated sugar levels and honeylike flavors. Wines of this designation are produced only in certain years when the botrytis infection can occur naturally.

The Grand Cru Vineyards of Alsace

Starting in 1975, top vineyards throughout Alsace have been granted *grand cru* status, with the most recent edition being Kaefferkopf in 2007. Below is a list of the fifty-one official *grand cru* vineyards of Alsace.

Altenberg de Bergbieten
Altenberg de Bergheim
Altenberg de Wolxheim
Brand
Bruderthal
Eichberg
Engelberg
Florimont
Frankstein
Froehn
Furstentum
Geisberg
Gloeckelberg
Goldert
Hatschbourg
Hengst
Kaefferkopf
Kanzlerberg
Kastelberg
Kessler
Kirchberg de Barr
Kirchberg de Ribeauvillé
Kitterlé
Mambourg
Mandelberg
Marckrain
Moenchberg
Muenchberg
Ollwiller
Osterberg
Pfersigberg
Pfingstberg
Praelatenberg
Rangen
Rosacker
Saering
Schlossberg
Schoenenbourg
Sommerberg
Sonnenglanz
Spiegel
Sporen
Steinert
Steingrubler
Steinklotz
Vorbourg
Wiebelsberg
Wineck-Schlossberg
Winzenberg
Zinnkoepflé
Zotzenberg

Other French Regions of Note

Producing more than a billion gallons of wine each year, France is home to vineyards and wine regions all over the country. The classic regions of France may get all of the spotlight, but top-quality wines and exceptional values are often found in many of its other unique regions. This section will focus on some of the important but lesser-known wine-producing regions of France, including Languedoc-Roussillon, Provence, the Sud Ouest, Jura, Savoie, and Corsica.

LANGUEDOC-ROUSSILLON

Spanning the Mediterranean coastline of France from the Spanish border in the west to the banks of the Rhône River in the east is the immense area of **Languedoc-Roussillon,** France's largest wine region. In fact, Languedoc-Roussillon is the largest wine-producing region in the world, with almost 800,000 acres under vine, tens of thousands of growers, and an annual production rivaling that of the entire United States. Although the quantity of wine produced in the region is staggering, the quality of wines from Languedoc-Roussillon has historically been spotty. With recent modernization of facilities and techniques, financial investment by some of the top names in French winemaking and from abroad, and a new generation of winemakers in the region, however, the reputation of the wines of Languedoc-Roussillon has been rising steadily over the last few decades.

Running from the Pyrenees Mountains southeast to the coast, Languedoc-Roussillon covers such a large area that there are several unique climate zones and soil types found within the region. More than thirty different grape varietals are grown in vineyards throughout Languedoc-Roussillon, including the traditional red wine grapes Grenache, Syrah, Mourvèdre, Carignan, and Cinsaut; traditional white wine grapes like Mauzac and Muscat; and increasing amounts of international varieties like Cabernet Sauvignon, Merlot, Chardonnay, and Sauvignon Blanc. There is also a wide variety of wine styles produced throughout the region, with reds, whites, and rosés made in sweet, dry, fortified, and sparkling styles. Most of Languedoc-Roussillon enjoys a warm, sunny, Mediterranean climate, which allows for generous yields and easy ripening. In many ways, this region's *terroir* is more similar to what you would find in California than in most of France's classic wine regions.

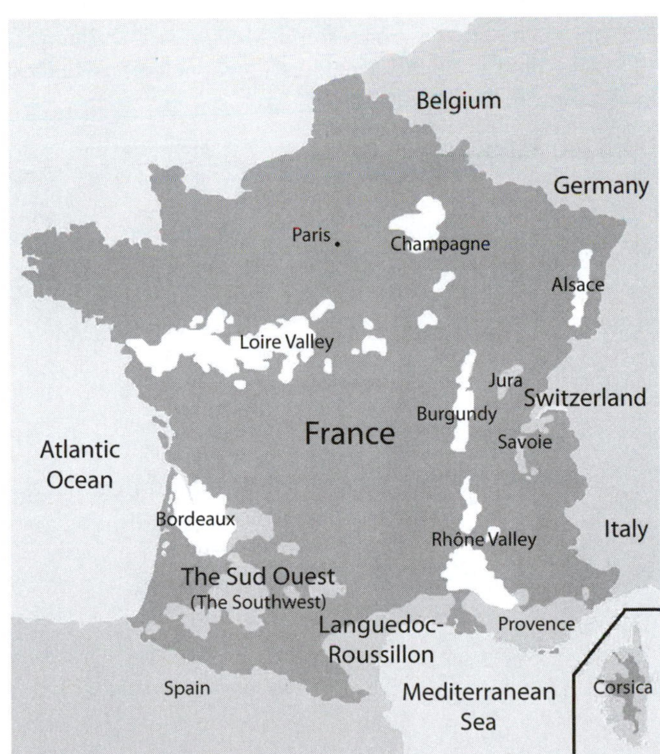

France's important wine regions.

Ideas on winemaking are also very different here from those in the rest of France. While there are several strictly regulated AOC regions found throughout Languedoc-Roussillon, the bulk of the production is dedicated to *vin de pays* wines, for which regulations are much looser and new winemaking traditions are being established. These *vin de pays* wines, usually labeled **"Vin de Pays d'Oc"** (d'Oc is short for "from Languedoc"), present some of the most approachable and value-driven wines in France and make up nearly 90 percent of the wines produced in the region.

For the AOC appellations of Languedoc-Roussillon that are dedicated to dry wines, most of the focus is on red wine production. This is because of the warmth of the climate, which is ideal for red wine varietals like Grenache, Syrah, Mourvèdre, and Carignan. Most of these red wines are hearty, rich, and spicy in character. The dry white wines and rosés produced in some appellations can range from uninspiring to surprisingly interesting, but they are almost completely overshadowed by the traditional red wines.

In far western Languedoc-Roussillon (the area known simply as Roussillon) just north of the Spanish border, much of the focus is on producing sweet dessert whites and reds. For dry wine production, the only AOC appellations of note are **Côtes du Roussillon** and the stricter northern subregion known as Côtes du Roussillon-Villages. Both produce mostly simple and fruit-driven red wines, and the predominant style is made from Carignan, Syrah, Mourvèdre, Grenache, and Cinsaut. With stricter regulations and tighter yields, Côtes du Roussillon-Villages wines are typically much more intense and enjoyable. Only limited amounts of dry white wine are produced in Côtes du Roussillon and none in Côtes du Roussillon-Villages.

The best known of the AOC appellations for dry wines in Languedoc-Roussillon is also one of the largest in the region, called **Corbières.** Located mostly in the foothills of the Pyrenees in western Languedoc-Roussillon, Corbières focuses on rustic red blends dominated by the Carignan grape. Similar styles of red wines made from blends of Carignan, Grenache, Syrah, Mourvèdre, and a handful of other approved grapes are produced in the AOC appellations of Fitou, located south of Corbières, and Minervois, Saint-Chinian, and Faugères, which arc north and east of Corbières in that order. Limited amounts of white wine and rosé are produced in Corbières and Minervois, but Fitou, Saint-Chinian, and Faugères are appellations dedicated solely to red wines.

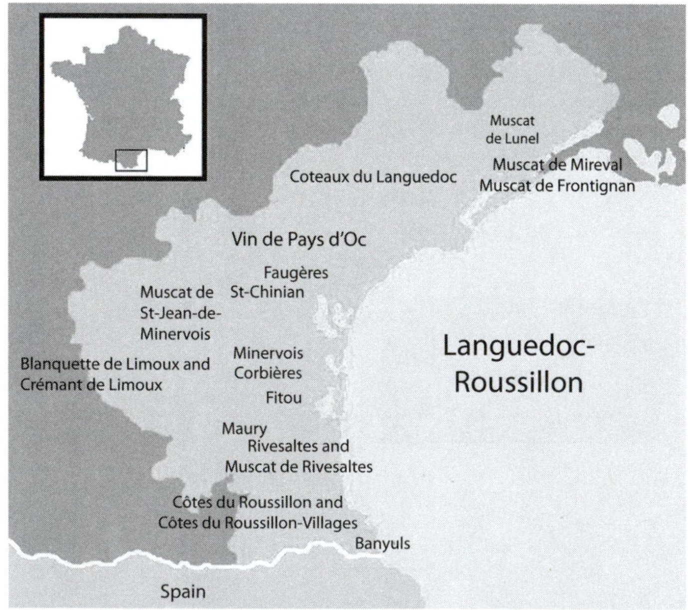

Languedoc-Roussillon and its important appellations.

To the east of these appellations is the rolling hillside that makes up the AOC called **Coteaux du Languedoc.** Home to several thousand acres of vineyards, Coteaux du Languedoc produces many unremarkable, dry reds made mostly from Grenache, Syrah, and Mourvèdre and a small amount of white wine. The best wines come from a number of small, recognized zones within the appellation that will be listed on the label. Most notable of these subdistricts are Le Clape, Montpeyroux, Pic Saint-Loup, and Picpoul de Pinet.

Some of the best-known AOC wines produced in Languedoc-Roussillon are sweet, fortified wines known as ***vin doux naturels***, or "naturally sweet wines." These wines are made from very ripe grapes, and to reserve natural sweetness, winemakers add neutral grape spirits to stop fermentation. Often quite sweet, these wines can also top 16 percent abv due to this fortification. Both white and red *vin doux naturels* are produced throughout Languedoc-Roussillon—the whites mostly from Muscat Blanc à Petits Grains and Muscat of Alexandria, and the reds from late harvest Grenache grapes.

The top white *vin doux naturels* appellations of Languedoc-Roussillon are Muscat de Rivesaltes and Rivesaltes in the far southwest, Muscat de Saint-Jean-de-Minervois in the center of the appellation, and Muscat de Frontignan, Muscat de Mireval, and Muscat de Lunel along the coast in the east. There are two AOC regions producing red *vin doux naturels* in far southwestern Languedoc-Roussillon: Maury and the far more well-known **Banyuls.**

Several sparkling wine appellations are found throughout Languedoc-Roussillon as well, and there is a long tradition of sparkling wines in the region. In fact, the Abbey at Saint-Hilaire found in western Languedoc-Roussillon has records showing the production of sparkling wines more than a century prior to the first sparkling wines of Champagne. Much of the production of these sparkling wines in the region is done in strict accordance to *méthode tradition* and is based on the local Mauzac grape (sometimes called Blanquette), although Chardonnay and Chenin Blanc are gaining popularity as blending components. The best-known AOC appellations for sparkling wine in Languedoc-Roussillon are the far western regions known as **Blanquette de Limoux** and **Crémant de Limoux**.

Blanquette de Limoux is a sparkling wine made in the traditional manner in western Languedoc-Roussillon. It actually predates Champagne by more than a century!

Vastly dominating production in Languedoc-Roussillon are the wines of the region classified as Vin de Pays d'Oc. The official category of *vin de pays* (see page 124) was added to the French wine laws in the 1970s, and no other area of France has utilized it as much as Languedoc-Roussillon. Production standards are much looser and practices are more relaxed for Vin de Pays d'Oc wines, and winemakers are not held to using traditionally approved grapes. Wines may also be labeled by grape variety in the manner of New World wine-producing countries if the vast majority of grapes used to produce the wine are the listed varietal. The most popular Vin de Pays d'Oc wines are indeed varietal wines, especially those made from Cabernet Sauvignon, Merlot, Syrah, Chardonnay, Sauvignon Blanc, and Viognier.

PROVENCE

The region of Provence is located in the southeastern corner of France, running along the Mediterranean coastline from the Rhône River in the west to the Italian border in the east. Many of the best-known appellations are found surrounding the largest city in

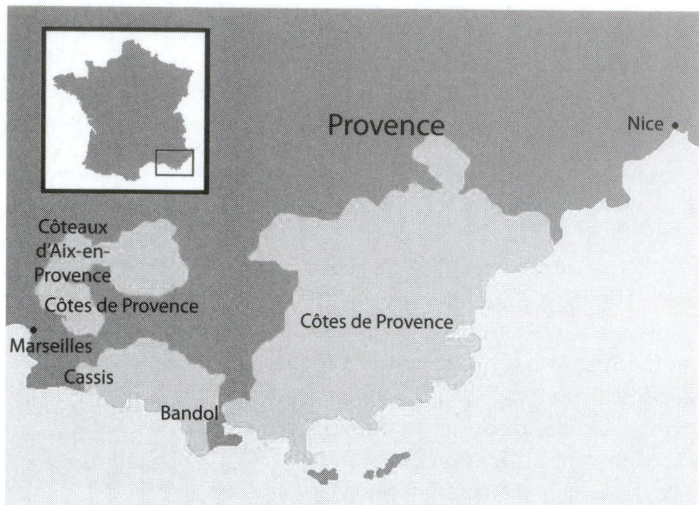

Provence and its important appellations.

the region, Marseilles. Located in western Provence, it is believed to have been the first area for wine production in France after it was settled and colonized by the ancient Greeks. Similar to that of Languedoc-Roussillon, the warm climate of Provence is dictated by the region's southern latitude and proximity to the Mediterranean Sea. Provençal winemaking is best known for and is dominated by the production of dry rosé wines, which can range from bland and simple to awe inspiring. That said, red wines have become increasingly important in Provence and their quality has been improving. Increasing quality standards and major investment in the region have led to a much higher profile for Provence in the last couple of decades.

Most Provençal wines are made from blends of different grapes. For rosés and red wines, the most important grapes are commonly grown in southern France—Carignan, Cinsaut, Grenache, Mourvèdre, and Syrah, although Cabernet Sauvignon is gaining in popularity. While not common, some white wine is produced in Provence, much of it lackluster in quality. The most widely grown white wine grapes in the region are Clairette, Grenache Blanc, Marsanne, and Ugni Blanc, with many winemakers experimenting with nontraditional grapes such as Chardonnay and Viognier.

The largest AOC appellation in Provence is Côtes de Provence, a collection of vineyard areas scattered throughout the region. Staying true to the region, much of the focus in Côtes de Provence is on the production of rosés, which can vary widely in quality due to the large size of the appellation (more than 40,000 acres of vineyards!). The best-quality and most renowned region of Provence is **Bandol,**

Provençal winemakers are most famous for their rosés.

located on the coastline just east of Marseilles, and home to several top dry rosés and Provence's best red wines, both of which are made from Mourvèdre-based blends. Interesting rosés and red wines (often made from Cabernet Sauvignon–based blends) are produced in the appellation of Côteaux d'Aix-en-Provence northwest of Marseilles, and the region's best white wines made from Clairette and Marsanne grapes are found in Cassis, just east of Marseilles.

THE SUD OUEST (SOUTHWEST)

The large area of southwestern France is known locally as the **Sud Ouest**. This region runs inland from the Atlantic coastline in the west and is bound by Bordeaux to the north and west and by the Spanish border and Languedoc-Roussillon to the south and east. The Sud Ouest is home to several isolated wine regions of note, many of which produce some of the most unique styles of wine in France, as well as the brandy-producing region of Armagnac. Despite varying geology and terrain, the climate of the Sud Ouest is fairly consistent, dominated by the influence of the Atlantic.

The Dordogne River flows west through the northern wine regions of the Sud Ouest, where wines similar to those found in the neighboring region of Bordeaux are produced, using many of the same grape varieties. Red wines center on blends of Cabernet Sauvignon, Merlot, and some Cabernet Franc, while white wines are made primarily from Sauvignon Blanc and Sémillon blends. The most notable AOC appellations producing these styles of wine are Buzet, Côtes de Duras, and **Bergerac,** best known for its Bordeaux-style reds and collection of subregions, especially Monbazillac and Saussignac, which produce sweet white wines from botrytised grapes in the style of Sauternes.

The best-known red wines of the Sud Ouest might come from the **Cahors** AOC, southeast of Bergerac. Cahors has been famous since medieval times for its "black wines," made mostly from the Malbec grape (locally called Auxerrois) in a rich, rustic style. The further one travels from Bordeaux in the Sud Ouest, the less the wines and grapes resemble those of Bordeaux. Southeast of Cahors is the appellation of Gaillac, where reds, whites, and rosés are produced from indigenous grape varieties like the white-skinned Len de L'elh and the black-skinned Braucol and Duras. Small amounts of sparkling wine are also produced in Gaillac.

Southern wine regions of the Sud Ouest are all quite unique in terms of grapes and styles. The best-known and top-quality appellation of the south is **Madiran,** which specializes in rich red wines

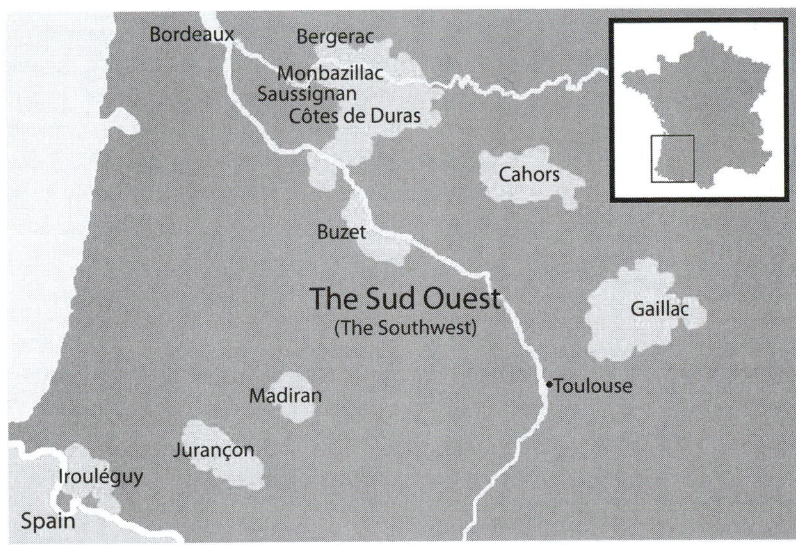

The Sud Ouest and its important appellations.

The obscure Tannat grape is used to produce the red wines of the Madiran AOC.

made from blends dominated by the Tannat grape. The rare Gros Manseng and Petite Manseng grapes are grown in the steeply sloped vineyards of the Jurançon AOC, which produces dry and sweet white wines. Bordering Spain's Basque country close to the Atlantic is the appellation of Irouléguy, where reds and rosés are often made from Tannat and whites from a grape called Courbu.

JURA

Tucked between Switzerland and Burgundy in eastern France is the wine-producing region of **Jura,** home to a handful of unique AOC appellations. The continental climate means that ripeness is at a premium in this region, and many of the top vineyards are planted on hillside vineyards to better maximize exposure to the sun. Much of the production of wine in Jura today is done in the manner and using the grapes of Burgundy, especially Chardonnay. That aside, the most interesting wines of the region are made in traditional ways from local grapes, including white wine grapes like Savagnin and red wine grapes such as Poulsard and Trousseau.

The top AOC appellation of Jura is **Arbois,** where white wines made from Chardonnay and reds and rosés from Trousseau and Pinot Noir dominate production. The appellations of L'Étoile to the south of Arbois and Côtes du Jura, a large appellation running parallel to Burgundy, focus primarily on white wines as well as some of the local specialties.

What truly makes Jura unique is the variety of specialty wine styles that have evolved in the area. The most famous of these is ***vin jaune,*** where late harvest Savagnin grapes are picked, fermented, and aged in large barrels for six years or more. During this time, they evaporate and develop a surface yeast (similar to some sherries, see page 215), ultimately producing intensely caramelized and nutty wines. This is the only style permitted in the AOC appellation of Château-Chalon, where it is their specialty, but it is produced in all of Jura's appellations. Other unique wine styles include sparkling wines labeled "Crémant de Jura," and ***vin de paille***, a wine made from grapes that have been dried into raisins before fermentation to concentrate flavors and boost alcohol content.

SAVOIE

The French Alps dominate the landscape of **Savoie** (sometimes spelled Savoy), and cause the winemaking regions of this area to be spread out and isolated. Located due east of Burgundy and southeast of Jura, Savoie is tucked against France's Swiss and Italian borders. The relative isolation of Savoie's wine regions, along with the cooler, continental climate and higher elevations found there, have led to the development of unique grape varieties and wine styles.

Most of the wine produced in Savoie is simply labeled with the AOC Vin de Savoie, and this appellation covers a lot of different grapes and styles. Within the designated area of Vin de Savoie, several important villages that are centers of wine production have their own local regulations and will add their names to the label along with Vin de Savoie. In the northern areas of Savoie, along the southern shores of Lake Geneva, the focus is primarily on white wines produced from Switzerland's favorite grape, Chasselas. Traveling south, more red wines and rosés are produced, but Savoie remains primarily a white wine region. Light, crisp whites are made in central and southern Savoie from Altesse, Jacquère, Molette, Roussanne, and Roussette grapes. The top red grape of the region is Mondeuse, which produces lighter, spicy wines.

CORSICA

Just a few miles north of the Italian island of Sardinia is **Corsica,** France's major island territory in the Mediterranean Sea. The most mountainous island in the Mediterranean, Corsica is home to a wide variety of vineyard conditions and elevations. With a mixture of French, Italian, and even Algerian heritage on the island, several grapes are grown here that are not found anywhere on the mainland of France. Though not famous for wine production today, the island is rich in winemaking history; it was one of the earliest regions of France to be planted to wine grapes by the ancient Greeks and Phoenicians and is also the birthplace of Napoleon Bonaparte, whose father was a winemaker.

Corsica is a crossroads of grape varieties. The one indigenous grape grown widely is Sciacarello, producing powerful reds and rich rosés. Other important grapes include those brought from Italy, such as the red grape Aleatico, the white Vermentino, and Nielluccio, a clone of Sangiovese. Some Rhône grapes such as Grenache are also grown, as well as various types of Muscat.

Much of the wine produced in Corsica today is at the ***vin de pays*** quality classification and is average at best, although the ***vin de pays*** appellation has one of the most captivating names, Vin de Pays l'Île de Beauté. Production mostly centers on rustic reds and dry rosés. However, quality is improving in Corsica today. The top AOC appellations of Corsica include Patrimonio and Ajaccio, regions on the west coast that mostly produce spicy reds, and the Vin de Corse appellations, a collection of wine regions encompassing much of the island's coastline. Many styles are produced throughout the Vin de Corse appellation (especially sweet, white ***vin doux naturels***), where specific subappellations will add their names to the Vin de Corse designation.

Summary

France is truly the greatest wine-producing nation on Earth. The scope of its winemaking is immense by any standard, and the French have been instrumental in raising quality standards for winemaking in their own country and the rest of the world. Six different classic wine regions located throughout France produce the majority of the country's top wines. These regions all grow very different grapes and produce unique styles of wine. The classic regions of France are Bordeaux, Burgundy, the Rhône Valley, Champagne, the Loire Valley, and Alsace.

Review Questions

1. France is the number one producer of wine in the world, responsible for roughly 50 percent of the world's premium wine.
   - A. True
   - B. False

Match the following classic grape-growing regions of France to the overall climate found there. Some answers may be used more than once, and some not at all.

2. Alsace	A. Cool-continental
3. Champagne	B. Temperate-maritime
4. The Rhône Valley	C. Warm-Mediterranean
5. Bordeaux	D. Hot-desert
6. Burgundy	

7. The wine laws of France are known by the acronym:
   - A. DOC
   - B. OAC
   - C. AOC
   - D. INAO

8. Which of the following wine regions is considered the most commercially successful in the world and produces around a quarter of France's premium wine?
   - A. Bordeaux
   - B. Burgundy
   - C. Champagne
   - D. The Loire

Match the following classic grape-growing regions of France to the subregions that are located within their boundaries, or the grapes that are grown there. Some answers may be used more than once, and some not at all.

9. Burgundy	A. Sancerre
10. Bordeaux	B. Chablis
11. The Loire Valley	C. Médoc
12. The Rhône Valley	D. Châteauneuf-du-Pape

13. The Rhône Valley	A. Chardonnay and Pinot Noir
14. Alsace	B. Riesling and Gewürztraminer
15. The Loire Valley	C. Syrah and Grenache
16. Burgundy	D. Chenin Blanc and Sauvignon Blanc

17. Alsace is the only top-quality region in France to label its wines by grape variety.
   A. True
   B. False

18. A Champagne labeled "Blanc de Blancs" is a sparkling wine produced with what types of grapes?
   A. Pinot Noir
   B. Pinot Meunier
   C. Merlot
   D. Chardonnay

19. The Loire Valley is a region of France that allows only one white grape and one red grape to be grown throughout the entire region.
   A. True
   B. False

20. Which of the following is *not* one of the most important grapes grown in Bordeaux?
   A. Cabernet Sauvignon
   B. Chardonnay
   C. Merlot
   D. Sauvignon Blanc

Key Terms

Appellation d'Origine Contrôlée (AOC)
vin de table
vin de pays
Vin Délimité de Qualité Supérieure (VDQS)
Institut Nationale des Appellations d'Origine (INAO)
Bordeaux
claret
château
Left Bank
Médoc
Haut-Médoc
Graves
Margaux
Pauillac
Saint-Estèphe
Saint-Julien
Pessac-Léognan
Right Bank
Pomerol
Saint-Émilion
Entre-Deux-Mers
Sauternes
Classification of 1855
Burgundy
Bourgogne
domaine
négociant-éleveurs
regional
commune/village
premier cru vineyard
grand cru vineyard
Chablis
climats
Côte d'Or
Côte de Nuits
Côte de Beaune
Côte Chalonnaise
Mâconnais
Pouilly-Fuissé
Beaujolais
Beaujolais Nouveau
carbonic maceration
Rhône Valley
Northern Rhône
Southern Rhône
Côte-Rôtie
Hermitage
Côtes-du-Rhône
Châteauneuf-du-Pape
Tavel
Champagne
non-vintage Champagne
house style
vintage Champagne
Blanc de Blancs Champagne
Blanc de Noirs Champagne
rosé Champagne
prestige cuvée/cuvée de prestige
Loire Valley
Pays Nantais
Anjou-Saumur
Touraine
Upper Loire
Muscadet
Savennières
Coteaux du Layon
Bonnezeaux
Quarts de Chaume
Vouvray
Chinon
Sancerre
Pouilly-Fumé
Alsace
Crémant d'Alsace
Vendange Tardive
Sélection de Grains Nobles
Languedoc-Roussillon
Vin de Pays d'Oc
Côtes du Roussillon
Corbières
Coteaux du Languedoc
vin doux naturels
Banyuls
Blanquette de Limoux
Crémant de Limoux
Provence
Bandol
Sud Ouest
Bergerac
Cahors
Madiran
Jura
Arbois
vin jaune
Savoie
Corsica

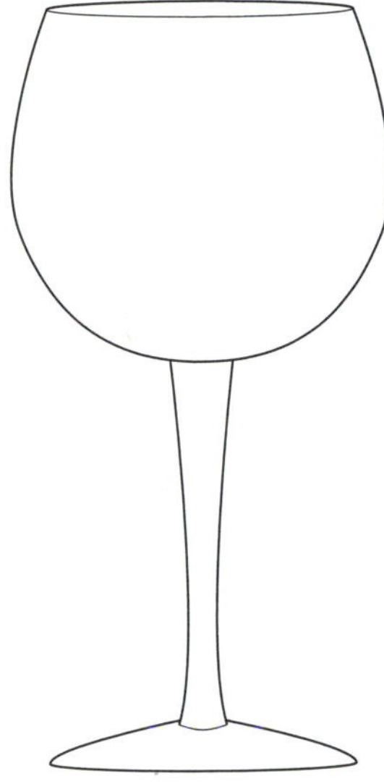

CHAPTER 10

The Wines of Italy

Old wine and friends improve with age.

—Italian proverb

Italy is one of the world's most important, historic, and prolific wine-producing countries. The country is one of the largest consumers of wine and one of the largest exporters. This chapter deals with the wine laws, wine labels, growing conditions, top grapes and wines, and the most important wine regions in Italy. The regions of Veneto, Piedmont, and Tuscany are covered in detail, and there is a brief look at other Italian regions of note.

The Facts on Italy

CLIMATE

A large peninsula jutting south from the continent of Europe into the Mediterranean Sea, Italy is home to several climate zones. Conditions can range widely, from alpine in the north to near desert conditions in the south.

TOP REGIONS

Classic Regions

- Piemonte (Piedmont)
- Toscano (Tuscany)
- Veneto

Important Regions

- Northwestern Italy
  - Emilia-Romagna
  - Liguria
  - Lombardia (Lombardy)
  - Valle d'Aosta
- Northeastern Italy
  - Friuli-Venezia Giulia (Friuli)
  - Trentino-Alto Adige
- Central Italy
  - Abruzzo
  - Lazio (Latium)
  - Marche (The Marches)
  - Molise
  - Umbria
- Southern Italy and the Islands
  - Puglia (Apulia)
  - Basilicata
  - Calabria
  - Campania
  - Sardegna (Sardinia)
  - Sicilia (Sicily)

IMPORTANT INFORMATION

- Italy is the number two producer of wine in the world, typically producing nearly 1.3 billion gallons of wine each year.
- Wine has been produced in Italy since long before the Romans, dating back some 4,000 years.
- Italians are some of the top consumers of wine in the world, and Italian winemakers produce some of the most food-friendly wines anywhere.
- The Italian wine laws, referred to as the DOC laws, are loosely based on the French AOC laws. These laws aim to establish areas of wine production throughout Italy and regulate how wines are produced in each of these areas. Due to local interpretations and deeply ingrained traditions throughout Italy, these laws can become confusing and illogical at times.
- The DOC laws break up Italian wines into four quality classifications. These classifications are, from strictest and highest quality to loosest and lowest quality: *Denominazione di Origine Controllata e Garantita* (DOCG), *Denominazione di Origine Controllata* (DOC), *Indicazione Geografica Tipica* (IGT), and *vino da tavola.*
- Top-quality wines in Italy can be labeled several different ways depending upon their region or state of origin. Some are labeled by region as in France, some by grape variety as in the United States, and some are labeled by a grape and region, or even a brand name.

The History and Importance of Italian Wine and Winemaking

Wine is an extremely important part of daily life in Italy. Italians are among the largest consumers of wine in the world, averaging more than 20 gallons of wine consumed a year per person. The Italians think of wine as food, part of every meal, and the wines produced in this country are some of the most food-friendly in the world.

Italy has a long tradition and history of winemaking dating back roughly four thousand years. The early Etruscans were already producing wine in southern Italy when the ancient Greeks first arrived there. Spreading their viticultural knowledge and prowess through several areas of southern Italy, the Greeks eventually came to call this region *Enotria,* meaning "land of wine." The wines produced in *Enotria* were some of the most highly prized in all of ancient Greece.

As the fledgling Roman Empire rose to power, wine was already an important beverage in Italy. Several temples were built throughout the empire dedicated to Bacchus, the Roman god of wine and revelry. The Romans expanded the area of Europe under vine immensely, taking wine and a wine culture with them as they eventually conquered most of the continent. As these provinces began producing more and better wine, Rome began to import more wine than it produced.

Major advancements in viticultural and vinicultural practices were developed by the Romans, and they bred many ancestors of today's top grapes. The quality of wine at the time was unmatched in ancient history, and it became firmly entrenched in European culture. Wine became the daily beverage of the continent and empire during Roman times, and in fact, still is in Italy and much of Europe today.

After the fall of the Roman Empire, the Catholic Church maintained a wine culture in Italy as it did for the rest of Europe. Winemaking flourished in Italy through the Middle Ages and Renaissance, as hundreds of new grape varieties were developed and the multiple climate zones and regions throughout the Italian peninsula were planted. With the introduction of more advanced winemaking science and new technologies like the cork to seal bottles, Italian wines became a major force in export markets in the early 1800s. Many of the top wine regions and styles in the country today began to rise to international prominence during this time, including Chianti, Marsala, Vin Santo, and Barolo.

The late 1800s and first half of the 1900s were a hard period for Italian winemakers. First, *phylloxera* and other vineyard pests and diseases ravaged much of Italy's wine regions. Grafting became a widespread practice around the turn of the twentieth century in Italian vineyards, but several indigenous grape varieties had been lost. Many vineyards and regions were replanted with heartier, although less distinct and quality-oriented, new varietals.

Two world wars and a worldwide depression era did further damage to Italy's once proud wine industry, and moving into the 1950s quantity of production became much more important than quality. Many high-yielding vines were planted throughout the country and winemaking practices turned more toward producing inexpensive, lower-quality, bulk wines. Heavily exported, these inexpensive but bland wines did serious damage to the reputation of Italian winemaking.

In the 1960s and 1970s, Italy went through a quality revolution, as many winemakers began lowering yields and focused on quality production. A strict system of wine laws was developed, similar to the French AOC laws, to control and regulate premium production within the hundreds of Italian wine regions. As quality standards increased, so too did the image of Italian wine around the world, and exports of more expensive, higher-quality wines rapidly increased. Today, Italy is considered one of the top wine-producing countries in the world in terms of both quantity and quality.

The sheer scope of Italian winemaking is amazing. Italy is the second leading wine-producing country in the world, just behind France. Each year Italian winemakers produce more than one and a quarter billion gallons of wine—an absolutely incredible statistic considering that Italy is only a few thousand square miles larger than the U.S. state of Arizona! To achieve these production levels, Italy is basically one giant vineyard, planted to vines from its northern Alpine regions to the hot southern tip of the country.

Italian wine can become quite confusing considering the immense diversity of grapes, styles, regions, and producers. There are more than 900,000 registered vineyards throughout the country and the majority of total production is made by thousands of small local producers. More than a quarter of the world's total number of different wines produced each year come from Italy. Hundreds of different grapes are grown throughout the country, which are often blended into an almost infinite number of possible combinations. Most of the grapes grown in Italy are indigenous and are not planted anywhere else in the world. Many of these have long histories and interesting names. Italian winemakers have also had much success in growing foreign grapes in their vineyards, adding to the total number of varietals grown.

The *terroir* of Italy is also extremely diverse. Measuring almost 800 miles from north to south, the Italian peninsula juts out of central Europe into the Mediterranean Sea. Along its length, climate zones range from alpine to desert, and innumerable different soil types are found throughout. Only about 20 percent of Italy is considered flat, with the bulk of the country made up of hills and mountains. This adds different elevation zones, which create new climate zones that are capable of producing unique styles of wine. The section of the Mediterranean located west of the Italian peninsula is known as the Tyrrhenian Sea, and to the east is the Adriatic Sea. These large bodies of water can have major impacts on the climates of coastal regions as well as the two large Italian islands located off the tip of the boot: Sicily and Sardinia.

In addition to all this, Italy is an extremely regional country made up of twenty distinct and unique political areas and cultures. It is sometimes best to think of Italy as twenty countries all rolled up into one rather than any sort of unified country. Different outlooks, tastes, and histories have shaped the wine industries found in all of these political areas, and each produces wines different from all others.

While there are far too many moving parts to ever completely understand Italian wine, a basic understanding is necessary for any wine lover or professional because Italian wine is important. Italy is one of the world's leading exporters of wine, and ranks first in terms of total wine exports to the United States. Americans drink more wine from Italy than from any other foreign producer. Italian wine is also designed to go with food. With the popularity of Italian regional cuisine in the United States and other countries around the world, Italian regional wines become that much more important.

The Secret to Italian Wine's Affinity for Food

One of the main reasons Italian wine is so versatile with food is because of higher acid levels. Many Italian grapes produce wines that seem thin and acidic on their own, but when paired with food, the wines bring out the best in the dish while coming alive themselves.

Italian Wine Laws

Throughout Italy's long history of wine production, few attempts were ever made to regulate the national wine industry. Regional laws and appellations were common, such as the drawing of specific boundaries for wine production in Tuscany in the early 1700s, but these had no unifying effects for any other part of Italy. Modern Italian wine law on a national scope was not established until the 1960s with the advent of the *Denominazione di Origine Controllata* laws.

The earliest version of these wine laws sought to break Italian wines into two categories: those from recognized, historical regions made using traditional methods, and simple table wines produced for everyday consumption. Although the Italian government worked quickly to classify hundreds of different wines using this system, it quickly became outdated in the 1970s and 1980s as Italian winemaking saw fundamental changes. Many winemakers began adopting new and modern techniques which did not fit into the current system of regulations. Top production regions were also upset that their wines were in the same category as many lesser wines. In the 1980s and 1990s, two new classifications of Italian wine were added, and the current system of wine regulations was born.

Italian wine law is still referred to as the ***Denominazione di Origine Controllata*** laws, or **DOC** laws for short. Similar to France's AOC laws, they are a system of controlled areas of origin for wine. In fact, the term *Denominazione di Origine Controllata* translates directly to *Appellation d'Origine Contrôlée* in French. The laws cover four classifications of Italian wine that get stricter and more specific the higher up the system an appellation goes.

In ascending order, the four official classifications are: ***vino da tavola***, ***Indicazione Geografica Tipica*** **(IGT)**, ***Denominazione di Origine Controllata*** **(DOC)**, and ***Denominazione di Origine Controllata e Garantita*** **(DOCG).** These classifications are not necessarily ranked in terms of quality; rather, they are simply classifications that control the origins and winemaking practices of individual wines. Some of the very best wines produced in Italy fall into the IGT category, and even some wines labeled DOCG are not always considered the best wines in their own areas. Labels will always list the appropriate designation.

The lowest classification of Italian wine is *vino da tavola*, which is Italian for "table wine." Filling the demand for daily consumption of wine by millions of Italians, this is the largest classification, responsible for more than half of Italy's total production. There are no legal restrictions of note on winemakers producing *vino da tavola* wines, which are rarely exported out of Italy. Often they are not even bottled, simply sold in bulk in local markets. In an effort to encourage winemakers to raise their wines into the next level, known as IGT, new regulations forbid *vino da tavola* wines from listing grape varieties, regions of origin, or even vintage dates.

Often a large step up in quality from the *vino da tavola* classification is *Indicazione Geografica Tipica* or IGT. This is a classification that is home to wines "typical of a region," and is very similar to the French *vin de pays* category, where winemakers make better-quality wines under fairly loose restrictions. The IGT designation was first established in the early 1990s, in an effort to properly classify higher-quality, critically acclaimed wines that did not fit into the stricter and more traditional DOC and DOCG classifications. Many of these new appellations that have been established in the IGT classification are traditional areas that also produce DOC- and DOCG-level wines.

Well over two hundred different wines produced using modern techniques or made from nontraditional grapes or blends qualify for IGT status. Many wines in the IGT are better known for their proprietary or brand name than by their

Denominazione di Origine Controllata e Garantita
Strictest and Top Quality Classification
Only a Select Few Appellations

Denominazione di Origine Controllata
Strict and High Quality Classification

Indicazione Geografica Tipica
Better-Quality Wines Made Under
Fairly Loose Restrictions

Vino da Tavola
Lower-Quality Wines Made with Very Few Restrictions
"Table Wines"

The Italian quality classifications for wine.

Many wines classified as *Indicazione Geografica Tipica* are labeled by grape variety.

official designation. The overall goal with the IGT classification is that a major shift will occur and that this will become the largest classification of production, growing from the roughly 15 percent of Italian wine it represents today to cover up to 40 percent of Italian wine.

Denominazione di Origine Controllata or DOC is the second highest classification and is far stricter than IGT or *vino da tavola* regulations. The term translates loosely to "area of controlled origin" and Italian wines from traditional winemaking regions that use traditional grapes and techniques make up the bulk of this classification. While this designation is used for approved appellations throughout Italy, it is often interpreted differently from region to region.

There are more than three hundred approved DOC appellations throughout the country, and combined with the DOCG category they represent approximately 20 percent of Italy's total production. While this classification is not perfect and is interpreted many different ways throughout Italy, it has certainly served the purpose of improving quality standards for traditional Italian wines across the board. DOC wines are often labeled by region (e.g., Soave DOC), or a grape and region (e.g., Barbera d'Alba DOC).

The top classification under the Italian wine laws is the only one that makes an attempt to guarantee quality, and is called *Denominazione di Origine Controllata e Garantita* or DOCG. This term translates to "area of controlled and guaranteed origin," and it is by far the most elite of the classifications. First established in 1980, DOCG wines must follow extremely strict production standards including severe restrictions on yield, approved grapes, and proper winemaking techniques. In addition, wines that follow the regulations must still go through an exhaustive battery of laboratory testing and pass a sensory analysis panel each vintage to qualify.

Wines that do qualify for DOCG status will place a distinct thin band stating their DOCG designation

DOCG wines are easy to spot with their distinctive pink or green band on the capsule.

Common Italian Label Terms

TERM	DEFINITION
Vino rosso	Red wine
Vino bianco	White wine
Vino rosato	Rosé wine
Spumante	Frothy/Carbonated
Secco	Dry
Dolce	Sweet
Passito	A type of dessert wine produced from grapes that have been dried out before crushing to concentrate their sugar content
Riserva	Aged for a specified period longer than the minimum regional standards
Classico	Typically a wine that comes from a traditional or more restrictive area inside a recognized region
Superiore	Can represent a higher level of alcohol, longer aging, or a more specific appellation depending on the region the wine comes from

Current DOCG Appellations by Region

REGION	DOCG APPELLATIONS	STYLE OF WINE
Abruzzo	Montepulciano d'Abruzzo Colline Teramane DOCG	Dry red
Campania	Fiano di Avellino DOCG	Dry white
	Greco di Tufo DOCG	Dry white
	Taurasi DOCG	Dry red
Emilia-Romagna	Albana di Romagna DOCG	Dry or sweet white
Friuli-Venezia Giulia (Friuli)	Ramandolo DOCG	Sweet white
	Colli Orientali del Friuli Picolit DOCG	Sweet white
Latium (Lazio)	Cesanese del Piglio DOCG	Dry red
Lombardy (Lombardia)	Franciacorta DOCG	Sparkling dry white and rosé
	Oltrepò Pavese Metodo Classico DOCG	Sparkling dry white and rosé
	Sforzato di Valtellina DOCG	Dry red
	Valtellina Superiore DOCG	Dry red
The Marches (Marche)	Conero Riserva DOCG	Dry red
	Vernaccia di Serrapetrona DOCG	Sweet or dry sparkling red
Piedmont (Piemonte)	Asti/Moscato d'Asti DOCG	Sweet sparkling white
	Barolo DOCG	Dry red
	Barbaresco DOCG	Dry red
	Brachetto d'Acqui DOCG	Sweet sparkling red
	Dolcetto di Dogliani DOCG	Dry red
	Dolcetto di Ovada DOCG	Dry red
	Gattinara DOCG	Dry red
	Gavi DOCG	Dry white
	Ghemme DOCG	Dry red
	Roero DOCG	Dry red
Sardinia (Sardegna)	Vermentino di Gallura DOCG	Dry white
Sicily (Sicilia)	Cerasuolo di Vittoria DOCG	Dry red
Tuscany (Toscano)	Brunello di Montalcino DOCG	Dry red
	Carmignano DOCG	Dry red
	Chianti DOCG (and all subregions)	Dry red
	Morellino di Scansano DOCG	Dry red
	Vernaccia di San Gimignano DOCG	Dry white
	Vino Nobile di Montepulciano DOCG	Dry red
Umbria	Sagrantino di Montefalco DOCG	Dry or sweet red
	Torgiano Rosso Riserva DOCG	Dry red
Veneto	Bardolino Superiore DOCG	Dry red
	Recioto di Soave DOCG	Sweet white
	Soave Superiore DOCG	Dry white

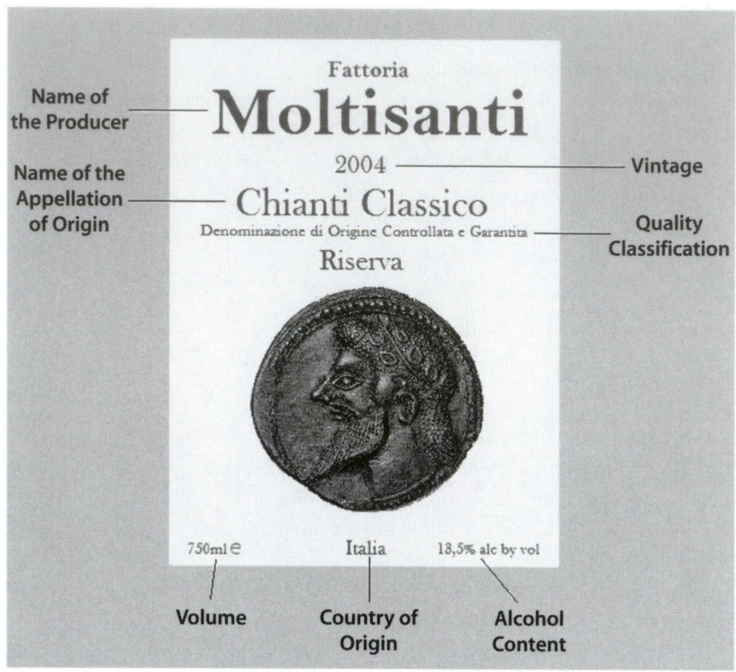

How to read an Italian wine label.

on the capsule of the bottle or over the cork. White wines are given a light green band and red wines will have a pink band. Qualifying for this classification is extremely difficult, and in more than twenty-five years, only a handful of different appellations have been elevated. To date, only thirty-seven appellations have been granted DOCG status, but more wines and appellations will fall into this category over time.

Zones of Italian Wine Production

The twenty Italian regions can be grouped together into four major zones of production. As a wide array of different styles is made throughout each zone and each region has its own winemaking personality, these groupings are based on geographical location rather than by style. The zones are:

Northwestern Italy	Emilia-Romagna Liguria Lombardia (Lombardy) Piemonte (Piedmont) Toscano (Tuscany) Valle d'Aosta
Northeastern Italy	Friuli-Venezia Giulia (Friuli) Trentino-Alto Adige Veneto
Central Italy	Abruzzo Lazio (Latium) Marche (The Marches) Molise Umbria
Southern Italy and the Islands	Puglia (Apulia) Basilicata Calabria Campania Sardegna (Sardinia) Sicilia (Sicily)

While significant amounts of wine are produced in all four of the zones and all twenty regions, there are three regions that produce the bulk of

The Italian regions broken into zones of wine production.

premium wine exported from Italy. These regions are known throughout the world for the quality of their wines, and many of their appellations are historic and famous. Two of these regions are found in Northwest Italy: Piemonte (Piedmont) and Toscano (Tuscany). The third is in Northeast Italy, the region of Veneto.

Piedmont: The Foot of the Mountain

The name **Piedmont** (Piemonte in Italian) means "foot of the mountain," a reference to the fact that the region is surrounded on three sides by large mountains, the Apennines to the south and the Alps to the west and north. Although Piedmont does not rank amongst the largest producing regions in Italy, more than 80 percent of its production is at the DOC level or higher. Piedmont is also home to more DOCG and DOC appellations than any other region in Italy. There are no IGT appellations in Piedmont, as the region is very traditional. Many wine experts consider Piedmont the top quality region in the country.

Piedmont has a long and colorful history beginning with its colonization by the Roman Empire around 200 B.C., when winemaking first began in the region. The main settlement and military base the Romans established there was destroyed during the Second Punic War around 26 B.C., when

The French Connection

With its proximity to the French border, Piedmont has a very strong French influence on not only its wines, but also its cuisine. Many dishes rely on ingredients like cream and butter rather than olive oil.

Hannibal crossed over the Alps into this area with thousands of troops and war elephants as he invaded the Roman Empire. The city was eventually rebuilt and is today known as Turin, the capital city of Piedmont.

After the fall of the Roman Empire, Piedmont was invaded continuously, changing hands from one European power to another. During the Italian Unification of the mid-1800s, Turin was declared the first official capital of Italy in 1861. Eventually the capital shifted to Florence and then, finally, to Rome.

Throughout its history, winemakers in Piedmont were influenced by several different cultures, none more so than the French. This is evidenced today by the fact that winemaking in Piedmont bears more resemblance to that of Burgundy than it does most other Italian regions. Very few blends are produced in Piedmont; instead winemakers focus on single-varietal wines that translate the unique *terroir* of small, classified regions.

The individual wines of Piedmont are considered some of the best in Italy if not in the entire winemaking world. Legendary, long-lived red wines that are produced from the indigenous Nebbiolo grape have been sought after for centuries. White wines run the gamut from sweet and sparkling to intense and dry. Other styles of red wine range from light and dry to sparkling and sweet.

The Facts on Piedmont

CLIMATE

The mountains that surround Piedmont create a true continental climate.

TOP WHITE GRAPE

- Moscato

TOP RED GRAPE

- Nebbiolo

TOP REGIONS/WINES

- Asti DOCG/Moscato d'Asti DOCG
- Dolcetto d'Alba DOC
- Barbera d'Alba DOC
- Barolo DOCG
- Barbaresco DOCG

IMPORTANT INFORMATION

- Piedmont is home to more DOC and DOCG appellations than any other region in Italy.
- The region produces a wide range of different wine styles, mostly produced as single-varietal wines.
- Much of the reputation of Piedmont is built on its sweet, sparkling white wines made in the Asti DOCG, and its tannic, powerful red wines made in the Barolo DOCG and Barbaresco DOCG.

IMPORTANT GRAPES OF PIEDMONT

Several different grape varieties are grown in Piedmont, resulting in a number of different styles of wine throughout the region. Most of the popular varietals are indigenous to either Piedmont or surrounding regions, but there is growing interest in experimental vineyards planted to international varieties. The most popular and well-known wines produced in Piedmont are the result of two important grapes: the white Moscato and the red Nebbiolo.

Moscato

Known as Muscat in the rest of the world, **Moscato** produces some of the most popular white wines in Piedmont. This varietal often has a limited yield, which concentrates its flavors and aromas. In Piedmont, Moscato produces the sweet, soft, sparkling wines of the Asti DOCG. These wines tend to burst with ripe tropical fruit and stone fruit flavors, and can also have a slight soapy scent. Moscato-based wines from Piedmont are often very low in alcohol because their fermentations are stopped early to retain natural residual sugar in the finished wine.

 Nebbiolo

Wines produced from Nebbiolo grapes in Piedmont are often extremely tannic, acidic, full-bodied, and high in alcohol. It produces very intensely flavored and complex wines with brooding dark fruit notes along with rich characteristics of wet earth, truffle oil, violets, and star anise. While several attempts have been made to plant this vine away from its native soil, quality production is almost exclusively limited to the vineyards of Piedmont and a few other pockets in Northwest Italy.

Other Notable Grapes

CORTESE This white grape produces light-bodied, acidic wines reminiscent of ripe citrus fruit. It is used exclusively in Piedmont's only dry white wine DOCG appellation known as Gavi DOCG, and is one of the most expensive white wines produced in Italy.

BARBERA Known as a red workhorse grape throughout much of Italy, Barbera is at its best in Piedmont. Here the grape produces rich, medium-bodied wines with dark fruit flavors, pleasant earthiness, and often a slight smoky characteristic. Several DOC appellations in Piedmont specialize in this grape.

DOLCETTO Meaning "little sweet one," Dolcetto produces high-quality, light red wines in Piedmont. Several DOC and two DOCG appellations located throughout Piedmont are exclusively dedicated to this varietal as well.

TERROIR AND IMPORTANT REGIONS

Piedmont is the second largest region in Italy, and one of the few to have four distinct seasons and a purely continental climate. Piedmont is completely landlocked, and is cut off from any Mediterranean influence by tall coastal mountains. Summers are warm and long in the region, slowly fading into temperate and foggy autumn months. Cold winters with significant snowfall are followed by a mild spring. It is bordered by France to the west, by the mountainous region of Liguria to the south, by the small Italian region of Valle d'Aosta and Switzerland to the north, and by Lombardy to the east.

The region is almost entirely ringed by tall mountain ranges, with the Apennine Mountains to the south and jutting into the interior of the region, and the Alps surrounding the western and northern districts. Starting in Piedmont, the Po River slowly cuts through the large basin created by the mountains, eventually flowing east toward the Adriatic Sea. While Turin is the capital and most important city, the centers for wine production in Piedmont are the towns of Asti and Alba, located in the south-central part of the region. Most vineyards are planted on hillsides that are often terraced, taking full advantage of maximum exposure to the sun.

There are more than forty DOC appellations in Piedmont, more than in any other region. In addition, it is home to ten DOCG appellations—almost 30 percent of the total number located throughout Italy. Many of these are world famous, and are the source for some of Piedmont's best wines. The most notable appellations of Piedmont are the Asti DOCG surrounding the town of Asti, the Barbera d'Alba DOC and Dolcetto d'Alba DOC surrounding the town of Alba, and finally the two most important appellations in the entire region: the Barolo DOCG and the Barbaresco DOCG found in the hills surrounding Alba.

Asti DOCG/Moscato d'Asti DOCG

Asti is a bustling market town in southern Piedmont, surrounded by vineyards. The Asti DOCG encompasses a large area around Asti and produces two important and widely exported styles of sweet, soft, sparkling white wines labeled either **Asti DOCG** or **Moscato d'Asti DOCG.** The ancient Moscato grape is the only varietal permitted in the appellation. Production levels in the region are extremely high to meet the demands for these wines. In fact, only the Chianti DOCG of Tuscany produces more DOCG-level wine than Asti.

Wines bearing the Asti (formerly known as Asti Spumante, which translates to "frothy Asti") and Moscato d'Asti designations are both made from 100 percent Moscato grapes and both come from the same area surrounding Asti. The differences between the two are stylistic: Asti is less sweet, higher in alcohol, and more carbonated than Moscato d'Asti. Because both styles rely heavily on their extremely fruity characteristics, they are best consumed when young.

The wines are made in a similar manner. Fermentation is conducted in a pressurized tank using a modified version of the Charmat method. Once the desired level of sweetness is achieved, the fermenting must is rapidly chilled, filtered under pressure, and bottled. Asti fermentations last longer than those of Moscato d'Asti, hence the additional carbonation and alcohol. Most Asti is bottled in traditional sparkling wine bottles with a large cork and cage, while Moscato d'Asti is bottled in normal wine bottles because it creates less pressure.

Barbera d'Alba DOC and Dolcetto d'Alba DOC

Located a little more than 20 miles southeast of Asti is the smaller town of Alba. Many of the best red

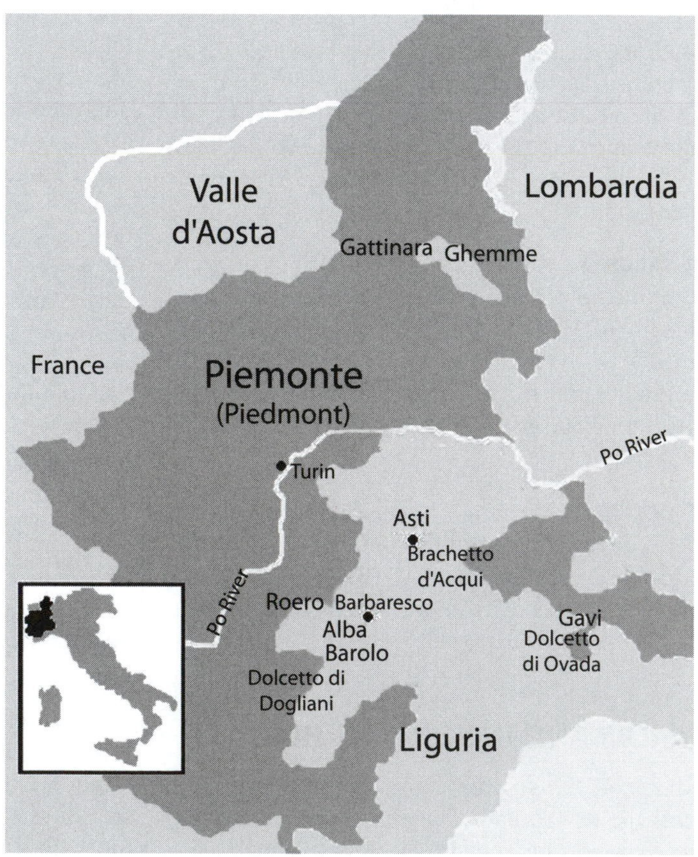

Piedmont and its important appellations.

wines produced in Piedmont come from appellations found in the hills that surround this town. Two of those appellations are **Barbera d'Alba DOC** and **Dolcetto d'Alba DOC.**

Barbera is the most widely grown grape in Piedmont, and produces some of the region's finest red wines. Several appellations around the region are solely dedicated to this varietal, but the best wines made from Barbera are generally found in the Barbera d'Alba DOC. These wines are often medium-bodied with a velvety tannin structure, solid core of acid, and ripe berry fruit flavors quite apparent in their youth. Many examples will age well, slowly developing complexity over time.

Another grape indigenous to Piedmont is Dolcetto. There are seven appellations located throughout Piedmont that focus on 100 percent Dolcetto wines, but none is as well known and widely regarded as the Dolcetto d'Alba DOC. Wines produced in the appellation are light-bodied and acidic, with bright red fruit flavors and often a touch of bitterness on the finish.

Barolo DOCG and Barbaresco DOCG

Much of the renown of Piedmont rests on the wines made from 100 percent Nebbiolo grapes that come from hillside vineyards surrounding the villages of Barolo and Barbaresco, both located near the town of Alba. When the DOCG classification was created in 1980, these were two of the first five appellations in Italy to be recognized. The two appellations are less than 15 miles apart and share many similarities; however, there are some very important distinctions.

The **Barolo DOCG** is located southwest of Alba in the hills of an area known as Langhe. Measuring only 7 miles long and 5 miles wide, this is a small appellation that produces big wines. Fully ripened Nebbiolo grapes produce amazingly powerful and structured red wines that can age for decades, earning the wines produced in the Barolo DOCG the nickname "Wine of Kings and King of Wines." Wines from this appellation must be aged a minimum of three years before being released, two of which must be in barrel. Extended bottle aging will be rewarded with a softer structure and breathtaking complexity.

The legendary red wines of Barolo can stand up to significant aging.

In the past few decades, many new wineries in the Barolo DOCG began utilizing modern techniques to produce their wines, including the use of small French oak barrels for aging. This has made many Barolo wines more approachable in their youth, but is a practice dismissed by more traditional producers. Soil types vary widely in the Barolo DOCG, and many winemakers are beginning to use vineyard designations on their wines as well as often listing the actual commune of Barolo where the grapes were grown.

Northwest of Barolo and Alba is the **Barbaresco DOCG.** The wines produced in this appellation are also made from 100 percent Nebbiolo, but the more temperate climate found here results in softer tannins, less structure, and more fruit than in the wines of the Barolo DOCG. Due to this, Barbaresco wines are often described as being more feminine in style and are certainly more approachable in their youth. The Barbaresco DOCG is even smaller than Barolo, producing a little less than half the quantity of the Barolo DOCG.

Other Wine Regions of Note

The most important dry, white wine produced in Piedmont comes from the Gavi DOCG in the southwest corner of Piedmont. These wines can be stunningly rich and complex when full ripeness is achieved

Although made from 100 percent Nebbiolo like Barolo, the wines produced in the Barbaresco DOCG are often quite a bit softer in structure.

in the Cortese grapes used solely in their production. Wines from the Gavi DOCG are some of the most expensive white wines produced in Italy. Another appellation for premium white wine production is the Roero Arneis DOC, which grows the Arneis grape.

Besides the Barolo DOCG and the Barbaresco DOCG, there are three additional DOCG regions in Piedmont dedicated to Nebbiolo. The Gattinara DOCG and the Ghemme DOCG are two small regions located in the foothills of the Alps in northwestern Piedmont. These wines are both powerfully structured, but are more rustic than those from Barolo and Barbaresco. Located near the village of Alba, the Ruero DOCG also produces Nebbiolo-based wines.

Two new DOCG appellations were recently established for Dolcetto wines: Dolcetto di Dogliani DOCG and Dolcetto di Ovada DOCG. Both are small appellations with limited production. The Dolcetto di Dogliani DOCG is located in a hilly area south of the village of Barolo, and the Dolcetto di Ovada DOCG is found about 40 miles east of Alba.

Finally, a sweet, sparkling red wine is also produced in Piedmont near the village of Acqui. The Brachetto d'Acqui DOCG is dedicated to the production of this style from the indigenous Brachetto grape. Often soft and fruity, these wines are frequently quite pleasant.

Tuscany: Tradition and Innovation

Tuscany (*Toscano* in Italian) is home to several of Italy's most recognizable and famous wines and appellations. The sun-drenched coastline of Tuscany runs up into gently sloped hills leading to the Apennine Mountains far into the interior. Premium wines are widely produced throughout Tuscany, and it is second only to Piedmont in total number of DOC and DOCG regions. Unlike the fiercely traditional winemakers of Piedmont, much of the Tuscan wine industry has led the charge for a new era of modern winemaking. The super Tuscan wines that began to emerge in the 1970s and 1980s challenged notions around the world about what Italian wine was capable of, and forced many changes to the DOC laws, including the implementation of the IGT category.

The region of Tuscany has a very long history of winemaking that even predates its absorption into the Roman Empire. Inhabited in the Bronze Age, Tuscany eventually became the center of the Etruscan civilization that flourished throughout Italy before the establishment of Rome. Winemaking dates back in Tuscany to almost 800 B.C. After it eventually became part of the Roman Empire in the first century B.C., several important cities were established in Tuscany including Siena, Pisa (home to the Leaning Tower), and most importantly, Florence.

During the Middle Ages, Florence became a wealthy trading center and Tuscany as a whole became regarded as one of the cultural centers of Italy, due to its draw of respected artists by the wealthy patrons living there. Florence is considered the birthplace of the Renaissance, and the city is rich with the artistic legacy the period left behind. Tuscany is the birthplace of Botticelli, Michelangelo, and Leonardo da Vinci.

With the wealth of Florence and ideal weather conditions, Tuscany also became a prime region for wine production in the Middle Ages and beyond. By the early 1600s the region of Chianti was well known for its wines, and in 1716 the Grand Duchy of Tuscany first laid out official boundaries for the production of premium Chianti wines. Along with the establishment of a legal formula of grapes to be used in the production of Chianti wines in the 1850s by Baron Bettino Ricasoli, who would eventually serve as prime minister of Italy, this laid the groundwork for the modern-day system of DOC appellations and regulation.

During the late 1800s, the wine industry in Tuscany was devastated as thousands of vineyards were destroyed by *phylloxera* and several vine diseases. This forced many winemakers to leave Tuscany, and a large number went to the Americas. Those that remained began to replant after the turn of the century, but this was widely disrupted by two world wars and the depression era that followed. Reemerging in the 1950s, most Tuscan producers began to stress quantity over quality, increasing yields and planting vigorously producing vines. Millions of gallons of cheap, diluted Chianti wines began to be exported across the globe in funny, basket-wrapped bottles.

The once proud winemaking reputation of Tuscany had been replaced with a bulk wine attitude and slipping quality levels. This direction changed in the latter decades of the 1900s, however, as the adoption of the DOC laws forced many winemakers to produce wine more strictly in the traditional way. Interest in quality winemaking was also reenergized in the region when top-quality wines that were like no others anyone had tasted from Tuscany began to appear in the 1970s. Eventually, these nontraditional wines would become known as the super Tuscans. Their success caused even very traditional winemakers to focus more on quality standards and modern techniques, ushering in a wine renaissance for this historic region.

The Facts on Tuscany

CLIMATE

Temperate to warm with a Mediterranean influence.

TOP RED GRAPES

- Sangiovese (Brunello)
- Cabernet Sauvignon

TOP REGIONS/WINES

- Chianti DOCG
- Chianti Classico DOCG
- Brunello di Montalcino DOCG
- Toscano IGT—the super Tuscans

IMPORTANT INFORMATION

- Tuscany is one of the top producers of DOC and DOCG appellation wines in Italy.
- Most Tuscan wine production is red, typically made from Sangiovese grapes.
- While several important traditional wines are produced throughout Tuscany, the super Tuscan style of wines made from unauthorized grapes or blends has been quite successful here.

IMPORTANT GRAPES OF TUSCANY

Tuscany is home to several grape varietals, many of which are indigenous to the region, although several surprising varietals have also been adopted by the Tuscan winemaking community, including Cabernet Sauvignon. More than 80 percent of Tuscan production is red wine, and the most important grapes are almost all red varietals. Almost every conversation about Tuscan wine will begin and end with the most important red grape grown in the region: **Sangiovese.**

Sangiovese

Sangiovese is the main grape varietal in almost every important red wine appellation in Tuscany, and is the most widely grown in all five of its red DOCG appellations. Sangiovese produces medium- to full-bodied red wines in Tuscany that are often quite earthy and complex. Notes of citrus, spice, and dried cherries often complement the powerful core of acidity always present with this varietal. There are hundreds of different Sangiovese clones grown throughout Tuscany, most derivatives of the two main clones, Sangiovese Grosso and Sangiovese Piccolo. In different regions, the grape is often called by the name of the specific clone used.

Appellation	Clonal Name for Sangiovese
Brunello di Montalcino DOCG	Brunello
Vino Nobile di Montepulciano DOCG	Prugnolo
Morellino di Scansano DOCG	Morellino

 Cabernet Sauvignon

First brought to Tuscany more than a century ago, the French varietal Cabernet Sauvignon has acclimated well to the region. It has been used as a staple blending grape for decades, especially in Chianti. When added in small percentages to Sangiovese-based wines, the grape adds power and tannins—a common practice for the red blends of the Chianti DOCG and its subregions. Until the 1970s and 1980s, Cabernet Sauvignon was thought of only as a blending grape, but its heavy use in super Tuscan wines has made it a favorite of modern winemakers in the region.

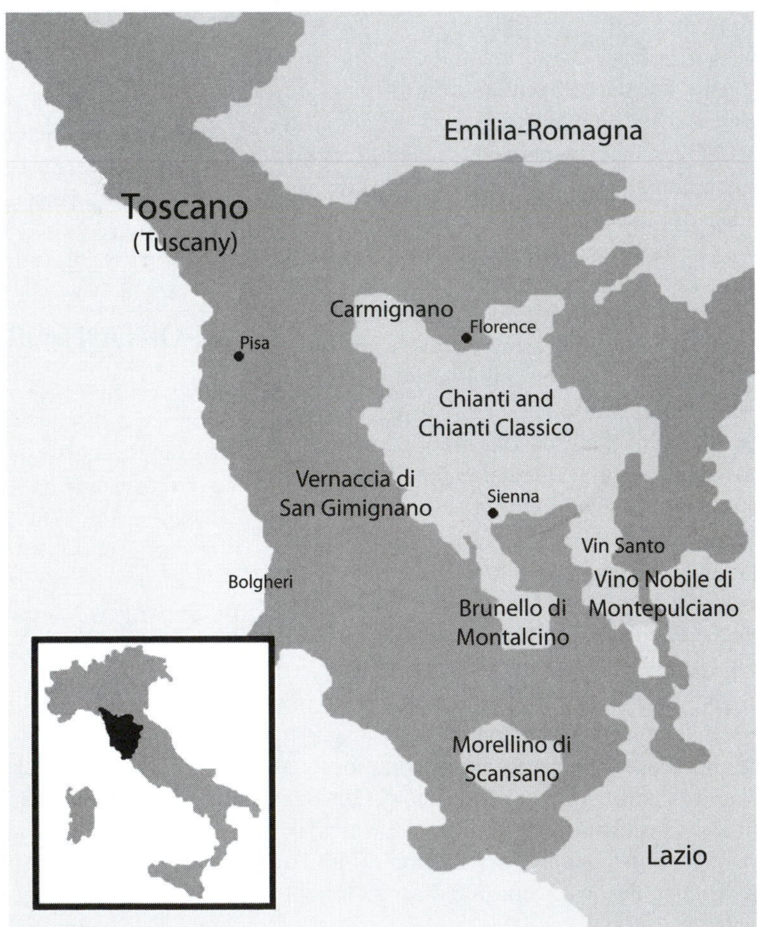

Tuscany and its important appellations.

Other Notable Grapes

VERNACCIA This white grape variety is used to produce the wines of the only DOCG appellation in Tuscany dedicated to white wines, the Vernaccia di San Gimignano DOCG. It produces medium-bodied, often acidic white wines that range from pale to gold in color.

CANAIOLO Besides Cabernet Sauvignon, Canaiolo is one of the main red grape varietals used to complement Sangiovese-based blends. Some super Tuscan producers have begun using the grape on its own and in larger percentages. It is noted for its tannins and slight bitterness.

MERLOT Owing to the success of Cabernet Sauvignon in Tuscany, Merlot is now being widely planted in the region for the production of super Tuscan wines. Most Tuscan Merlot is full-bodied and rich, with a firm structure and ripe berry flavors.

TERROIR AND IMPORTANT REGIONS

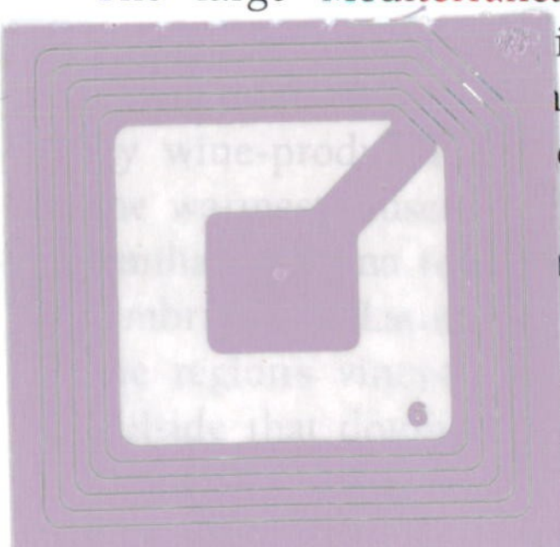

The large Mediterranean coastline of western [illegible] in influences on its warm, [illegible] ree most important qual- [illegible] ons of Italy, it is by far [illegible] bordered by Liguria and [illegible] north and northeast, and [illegible] the southeast. Most of [illegible] re planted in the rolling [illegible] he landscape of Tuscany. [illegible] ow steeper as they turn [illegible] tains in the eastern part of the region.

Tuscany is home to six DOCG and more than thirty DOC appellations. Several of the DOCG appellations of Tuscany have become world famous, most importantly the Chianti DOCG and its subregion the Chianti Classico DOCG, as well as the Brunello di Montalcino DOCG. IGT wines bearing the Toscano IGT are also widely present, as this is the designation used by super Tuscan producers.

Chianti DOCG and Chianti Classico DOCG

The region known as Chianti stretches more than 40 miles, from Florence south to the city of Siena. Hundreds of producers, both large and small, produce traditional, Sangiovese-based red wines throughout what is known as the **Chianti DOCG.** This appellation is made up of seven zones of production, all of which can be listed with the zone as the DOCG designated appellation on the label. If a wine is labeled simply Chianti DOCG without a zone listed, then the grapes were grown in two or more of the zones. Together, they represent the most widely produced DOCG wine in Italy.

For Chianti DOCG wines and its zones, Sangiovese must make up anywhere from 75 percent to 100 percent of the wine. Blending grapes include the red varietals Canaiolo and Cabernet Sauvignon, and the white varietals Trebbiano and Malvasia. Heavy use of the white varietals blended into the

The wines of Chianti Classico are some of the most famous in Italy.

The Seven Zones of Chianti Production

Chianti Colli Aretini
Chianti Colli Fiorentini
Chianti Colli Senesi
Chianti Colline Pisane
Chianti Montespertoli
Chianti Montalbano
Chianti Rufina

Sangiovese base can lead to a wine that seems acidic and diluted, and the practice is avoided by quality-conscious winemakers in the region. Using Cabernet Sauvignon and Canaiolo gives more power and tannins to the wines and is the preferred practice.

The **Chianti Classico DOCG** has its own unique DOCG designation and covers the central area of Chianti, encompassing the original borders first drawn up in 1716. Winemaking practices are more restrictive in this classic zone of production, often resulting in the most complex and intense wines produced in the entire appellation. Winemakers must use at least 85 percent Sangiovese to qualify for the Chianti Classico DOCG designation, and limited yields are mandated. Often, Chianti Classico wines will bear the distinctive *gallo negro*, or "black rooster" seal on the label, the symbol of the Chianti Classico growers association.

Brunello di Montalcino DOCG

Found in the hills south of Siena in southern Tuscany, the village of Montalcino is surrounded by world-class vineyards. This is where the most long-lived and powerful Sangiovese wines of Tuscany are produced in the **Brunello di Montalcino DOCG** appellation. Brunello means "little brown one" and is the local name for the Sangiovese clone grown here. It produces very structured wines with intense tannins and complex, earthy flavors. This is a much different version of a red wine made from Sangiovese than those of the Chianti DOCG appellation.

Brunello di Montalcino DOCG wines have some of the strictest regulations involving yield and aging requirements in Italy. These wines must be aged for at least four years before release, two of those in wood. The Rosso di Montalcino DOC appellation covers the same area and must also be made from 100 percent Brunello grapes. Aging restrictions are much looser, and the grapes not deemed suitable for Brunello di Montalcino DOCG standards are used in their production. Despite this, Rosso di Montalcino DOC wines can be quite intense and high in quality at a fraction of the price.

Toscano IGT: The Super Tuscans

The **super Tuscan** style of wine was first produced in the late 1960s and the early 1970s when several winemakers rebelled against the strict DOC regulations in place at the time. These forced winemakers in recognized appellations to use large percentages of inferior grapes in their wines to help stretch production. Deciding to focus on quality production, some producers made wines the way they wanted to, not following the DOC laws. They were forced to forgo the DOC status of their wines and instead these wines qualified only as *vino da tavola*.

While not common at first, two wines quickly brought this style into the international spotlight. In the early 1970s, a winemaker whose family had been producing wine in Tuscany for hundreds of years, Piero Antinori, released a *vino da tavola* wine called by its proprietary name, Tignanello. This was a Chianti-style wine that used Cabernet Sauvignon and Merlot as its main blending grapes into a Sangiovese base. He had been influenced by a 100 percent Cabernet Sauvignon wine made by relatives in the coastal area of Bolgheri called Sassicaia. Although both were technically part of the lowest classification of Italian winemaking, their intense flavors and complexity soon gained a cult following.

Soon, hundreds of wines produced in unclassified areas and/or made from unauthorized grapes and blends began appearing in Tuscany. While classified as *vino da tavola,* most were known by a proprietary or brand name. By the 1980s, these wines were some of the most expensive and sought after in Italy, quickly rising in price and stature above most traditional Tuscan wines. Dubbed the super Tuscans, these nontraditional wines are today a large part of the high-end wine market in Tuscany.

Their success forced a change to the Italian wine laws in 1992 when a new category called *Indicazione Geografica Tipica* (IGT) was created. Elevated from their *vino da tavola* status, most super Tuscan wines use the Toscano IGT appellation. Some of the best-known super Tuscan wines have even been granted their own DOC designations, such as the Bolgheri Sassicaia DOC.

While the quality of super Tuscan wines cannot be denied, a large debate still rages in both Tuscany and all of Italy about them. Traditional winemakers charge that these mostly modern-style wines are more similar to styles produced in France or California, and do not represent Italian winemaking. Many of the grapes used in the production of super Tuscans are French in origin, a fact that is hard to swallow for Italian traditionalists. Others believe that they point to the direction Italian winemaking should head to usher in a modern era. Regardless of which side Italian winemakers take, one positive benefit to come from these wines is the fact that traditional and modern winemakers alike have looked to increase quality standards and practices since they first were introduced.

Super Tuscan wines are labeled with a proprietary brand name.

Other Wine Regions of Note

Besides the Chianti DOCG and its zones of production and the Brunello di Montalcino DOCG, there are three other DOCG appellations in Tuscany dedicated to Sangiovese. The Vino Nobile di Montepulciano DOCG surrounds the city of Montepulciano (not to be confused with a red grape grown in the Italian region of Abruzzo in Central Italy). This area is just east of Montalcino and is planted to a Sangiovese clone known as Prugnolo. These wines are often blended with the same grapes used in Chianti.

The Carmignano DOCG and the Morellino di Scansano DOCG appellations are not as well known as the other producers of Sangiovese, but they both produce top-quality wines. Carmignano DOCG wines are produced in hilly vineyards to the west of Florence, and Morellino di Scansano DOCG is a coastal appellation in southern Tuscany.

White wines are not very common in Tuscany; however, there is one DOCG appellation dedicated to dry white wine production called Vernaccia di San Gimignano DOCG in central Tuscany, just west of Chianti. Another specialty white wine in Tuscany is Vin Santo, a style of white dessert wine made from

Inventive Names

Super Tuscan wines are labeled with a brand name, as they commonly cannot list a grape or specific appellation. Many of these names have interesting translations.

Sassicaia—place of stones
Dogojolo—it jumps out of the barrel
Ornellaia—place of ash trees
Solaia—sunny one

grapes that have been dried out to concentrate their sugar content and flavors.

Veneto: The Heart of the Northeast

Veneto is the top-producing wine region in Northeast Italy, and one of the largest producers in all of Italy. Here, along the warmer coastal appellations and cooler alpine appellations, winemakers produce more than 10 percent of Italy's total production—more than 12 million gallons a year! Much of this production is from classified appellations, and Veneto produces more DOC and DOCG wine than any other region in Italy, including Piedmont and Tuscany.

The region itself has been populated for more than four thousand years, and advanced cultures were there long before it was eventually made part of the Roman Empire. After the fall of Rome, Veneto saw constant invasions from Germanic tribes, which forced many Venetians to move to islands in lagoons off the coast, where large cities were eventually built over shallow waterways. The most important of these lagoon cities is known as Venice today.

By the ninth century A.D., Veneto had become its own autonomous republic, and acted as such for more than a thousand years. The growing wealth of Venice benefited winemakers who perfected their craft in the plains and foothills that surrounded the city. In the late 1700s, Veneto was finally conquered and came under foreign control. Both the French and Austrians occupied the region until the mid-1850s, when it became a part of the newly unified Italy.

Today, Veneto makes some of the best and most interesting wines in Italy. Known mostly for its Pinot Grigio wines that come from vineyards near Venice, the region also makes several exciting blends and top sparkling wines, and uses some of the most ingenious techniques in winemaking to produce stunning red wines. Veneto truly ranks among the best wine regions of Italy.

The Facts on Veneto

CLIMATE

Temperate to cool.

TOP WHITE GRAPE

- Pinot Grigio

TOP RED GRAPE

- Corvina

TOP REGIONS/WINES

- Soave DOC/Soave Superiore DOCG/Recioto di Soave DOCG
- Valpolicella DOC
- Amarone della Valpolicella DOC
- Prosecco de Valdobbiadene DOC/Prosecco di Conegliano DOC
- Pinot Grigio della Venezia DOC

IMPORTANT INFORMATION

- Veneto is one of the top wine-producing regions of Italy, and is home to a large number of DOC and DOCG appellations.
- Several different styles of wine are produced in Veneto, from sparkling whites to intense reds.
- The predominant grape grown in the region is Pinot Grigio, which represents the bulk of the region's production.

IMPORTANT GRAPES OF VENETO

Several of the top wines in the region are blends produced in cool climates using a laundry list of esoteric local grapes. Many of the top grapes grown in the Veneto region are indigenous to the area, such as the red Corvina grape. Modern success and international tastes have also thrust a grape developed outside the district into the forefront of Venetian winemaking: Pinot Grigio.

 Pinot Grigio

Pinot Grigio is the most widely grown grape varietal in Veneto, producing lean, acidic white wines with flavors reminiscent of green apples, citrus, and minerals. Winemakers in Veneto do not age their

Pinot Grigio in oak; rather, they prefer the fresh, bright characteristics of the grape when aged in stainless steel. The most widely produced wine made from Pinot Grigio in Veneto (and Italy) is from the Pinot Grigio della Venezia DOC appellation outside Venice.

Corvina

This cool-climate red grape varietal is grown in several areas of Veneto, where it produces light-bodied, acidic red wines. It is at its best in the Valpolicella and Bardolino areas, where it often shows concentrated red fruit and smoky characteristics. It is used to make very interesting styles of full-bodied reds in Valpolicella, where the grapes are often dried before fermentation to concentrate their flavors, sugar content, and tannins.

Other Notable Grapes

PROSECCO This ancient white grape varietal is used to produce some of Veneto's top sparkling wines, especially in the Prosecco de Valdobbiadene DOC and Prosecco di Conegliano DOC.

TERROIR AND IMPORTANT REGIONS/WINES

Veneto is a land of stunning landscapes and sights: with its city of canals and waterways in Venice, breathtaking architecture and Roman ruins in Verona, and the majestic Italian Alps. The mountains and the Adriatic Sea basically break Veneto up into two distinct climate zones. In the south, a flat plain is crisscrossed by rivers, especially the large Po River that starts in Piedmont and runs to the coastline of

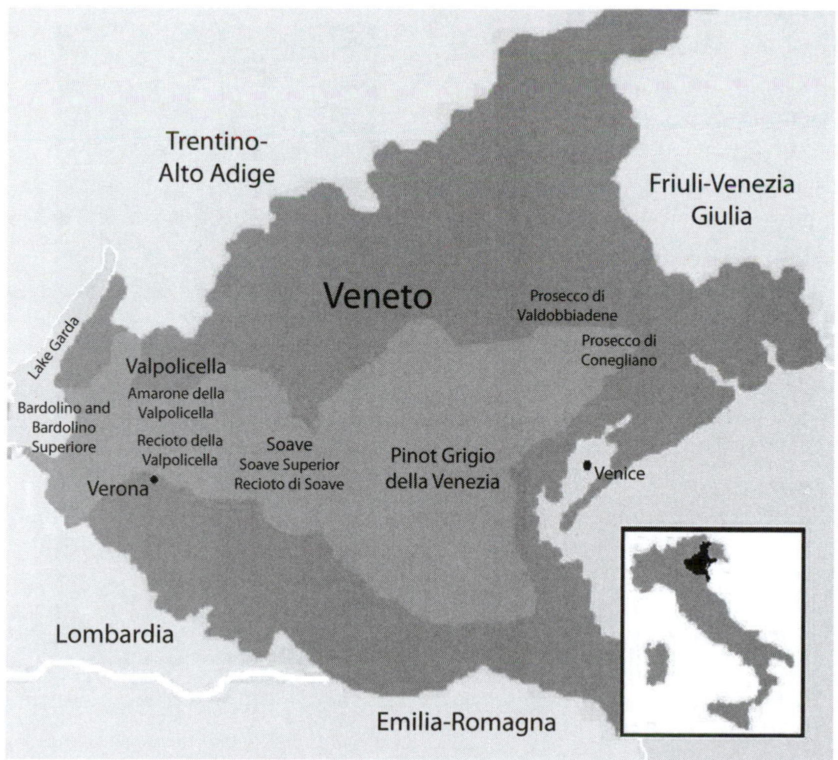

Veneto and its important appellations.

Veneto. Here, temperate climates are mitigated by the warming influence of the Adriatic. To the north lie the Alps, and cooler conditions are found in vineyards planted in the foothills.

Veneto is home to more than twenty DOC appellations and three DOCG appellations. Much of the top-quality white wines produced in Veneto, both sweet and dry, are made in the Soave DOC and in two subregions of Soave, Recioto di Soave DOCG and Soave Superiore DOCG. The Valpolicella DOC produces soft and light red wines of note, as well as a few powerful and unique reds in its other appellations. Prosecco di Valdobbiadene DOC and Prosecco di Conegliano DOC combine to make the most popular sparkling wine produced in Italy. Finally, exports are dominated by the simple white wines of the Pinot Grigio della Venezia DOC appellation, a large area outside of Venice.

Soave DOC, Soave Superiore DOCG, and Recioto di Soave DOCG

Soave is Italian for "suave," a fitting description for the often sleek and smooth white wines produced in the **Soave DOC.** Located in western Veneto near the city of Verona is the village of Soave. In the vineyards planted in the hilly surroundings, some of the most popular white wines in Italy and beyond are produced. The main grape used to produce the wines of this appellation is a little-known varietal called Garganega, which is blended with other white varietals, especially Trebbiano.

Wines labeled Soave DOC can be of good quality, but are often light and bland. The best dry wines of the appellation are made from only the best vineyard sites, with limited production and higher ripeness levels, and are called Soave Superiore DOCG. Sweet wines are also made in the area from grapes that have been allowed to dry out in temperature-controlled facilities, which concentrates their sugars and flavors before they are turned into wine. These qualify for the other DOCG designation in the region: Recioto di Soave DOCG.

Valpolicella DOC

Near the village of Soave and just north of Verona is the town of Valpolicella. The red wines produced in the wineries near Valpolicella are considered some of the best in Veneto, and production levels are quite high. Only the Chianti DOCG appellation of Tuscany produces more classified red wine than Valpolicella. There are several styles of red wine produced in the **Valpolicella DOC,** but all use the indigenous Corvina grape, along with Rondinella and Molinara, in their production.

Wines bearing the Valpolicella DOC are often light-bodied and acidic, typical of cool-climate red wines. The region makes two specialty wines that are considered better in quality, however. Wines labeled with the Recioto della Valpolicella DOC or **Amarone della Valpolicella DOC** appellations both begin unlike normal wines in the Valpolicella DOC. Grapes are harvested, but instead of immediately crushing

Valpolicella is one of the top red wine appellations of Veneto.

Sparkling wines made from Prosecco grapes are some of the most popular produced in Italy.

them and fermenting the must, the winemakers instead allow them to dry out. The grape bunches are stored in special climate-controlled rooms where they are allowed to slowly dry out into partial raisins for several weeks. Once they have lost much of their water content (in some cases up to 60 percent!), the grapes are then crushed and fermented. This is known as the ***recioto*** process. If the fermentation is stopped before it is completed, the resulting wine will be sweet and packed with rich fruit flavor. Wines made in this style are labeled Recioto della Valpolicella DOC and can sometimes even be bottled sparkling. If fermentation is carried out until the wine is dry, the wine will bear the Amarone della Valpolicella DOC appellation. These often massive wines are highly tannic and rich with dried dark fruit notes.

The Bellini

The Bellini is a classic sparkling wine cocktail that originated in the Veneto. It is traditionally a blend of Prosecco wine and white peach juice.

Prosecco di Valdobbiadene DOC and Prosecco di Conegliano DOC

The white Prosecco grape is used to produce still, fizzy, and sparkling wines throughout Veneto, but the sparkling versions are generally the best quality and very well known. Two appellations specialize in the production of mostly dry, light sparkling wines made from this grape variety in Veneto: the **Prosecco di Valdobbiadene DOC** and the **Prosecco di Conegliano DOC.** These adjacent appellations are both located near Friuli in north-central Veneto.

Distinctly different from Champagne or other sparkling wines produced in the same manner, these Prosecco-based sparkling wines are instead made using the Charmat method. This is a system of double fermentation similar to what is used for *méthode champenoise* wines; however, the second fermentation takes place inside large, pressurized tanks to create carbonation, rather than in the bottle. The results are clean, fruity sparkling wines that lack the yeasty notes of Champagne.

Pinot Grigio della Venezia DOC

The largest producing DOC in Veneto is the **Pinot Grigio della Venezia DOC** located east of Venice. Here, millions of gallons of Pinot Grigio wines are produced, most bound for the international and American markets. Italian Pinot Grigio is the number one selling style of foreign wine in the United States, and this appellation supplies a large percentage of that exported wine. While clean and crisp due to stainless-steel aging, these wines are often lacking in depth and character, although they can be pleasant.

Other Wine Regions of Note

Just to the east of Valpolicella, butting up against the shores of Lake Garda, is the region of Bardolino. The same red grapes grown in Valpolicella are also grown in Bardolino, and go into the production of Bardolino DOC wines. The best vineyards of the appellation can produce Bardolino Superiore DOCG wines if they ripen grapes further for a higher alcohol content and control yields.

Other Italian Regions of Note

NORTHWESTERN ITALY

Emilia-Romagna

Emilia-Romagna spans an area from the Adriatic Sea in the east almost all the way across northern Italy before it hits Liguria. It is a large region just north of Tuscany and south of Lombardy and Veneto. Famous for balsamic vinegar and the centrally located capital city of Bologna, this is also one of Italy's top-producing wine regions, accounting for almost 15 percent of total production. Most of this is produced in IGT and *vino da tavola* appellations, however.

The area east of Bologna is known as Romagna, and it is home to Italy's first DOCG region dedicated to white wine production: the Albana di Romagna DOCG. To the west of Bologna is Emilia, most famous for sweet or dry red sparkling wines made from the Lambrusco grape. Several other simple red and white wines are also made throughout this eastern section.

Liguria

Liguria is a thin, coastal region that wraps northwest around the border of Emilia-Romagna, across the southern boundary of Piedmont, and then finally ends when it hits the French region of Provence. This region is quite Mediterranean and makes up the Italian Riviera. In the center of Liguria is the most important city in the region, Genoa. The most important appellation is Cinque Terre DOC, which produces high-quality whites. Very limited winemaking takes place in Liguria, but they specialize in whites and rosés.

Lombardy (Lombardia)

Centrally located in the area of the Italian Alps is the region of Lombardy. To the south of Lombardy is Emilia-Romagna, to the west is Piedmont, to the east is Veneto and Trentino-Alto Adige, and to the north are Switzerland and the Alps. Lombardy is a small region in terms of production, but it produces some of Italy's top wines, notably sparkling wines. The region can be generally divided into three sections.

Along the southwestern border it shares with Piedmont is Oltrepò Pavese, known for high-quality sparkling wines and reds made from Pinot Nero (Pinot Noir). This area is home to several DOC appellations as well as the Oltrepò Pavese Metodo Classico DOCG, which produces top sparkling wines made using the same techniques employed in Champagne, known as *metodo classico* in Italy.

Near the city of Milan, the northern area of Valtellina is a large river valley in the foothills of the Alps that specializes in Nebbiolo, which is locally referred to as *Chiavennasca*. This is considered one of the few places in which the grape thrives, besides Piedmont. The most important appellation is Valtellina DOCG, which must be made from at least 70 percent Nebbiolo.

Perhaps the best sparkling wines in Italy come from the Franciacorta DOCG located in the eastern area of Brescia. These wines are made using *metodo classico,* and often spend extended time resting on their lees before disgorgement. Pinot Nero, Pinot Bianco (Pinot Blanc), and Chardonnay are used to produce the top sparkling wines of Brescia and also make dry, still wines in the area.

Northwestern Italy and its important wine regions.

Valle d'Aosta

The Valle d'Aosta is the smallest of Italy's twenty regions and produces the least wine, accounting for less than 1 percent of the country's total production. It is one of the most northern regions of Italy, bordered by Piedmont to the east and south, France to the west, and Switzerland to the north. The winemaking areas of Valle d'Aosta are mostly found in a central valley and up its slopes, surrounded by some of the tallest peaks of the Alps. These mountains protect the terraced vineyards of Valle d'Aosta from harsh winter weather. Several different grapes are grown throughout the region, both red and white, and most are adaptive to a cooler climate. There is only one DOC appellation in the region, the eponymous Valle d'Aosta DOC.

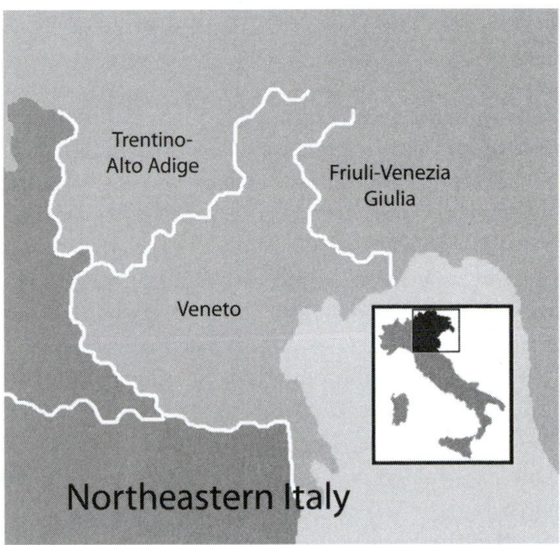

Northeastern Italy and its important wine regions.

NORTHEASTERN ITALY

Friuli-Venezia Giulia (Friuli)

Friuli-Venezia Giulia, often simply called Friuli, is a small region located northeast of Veneto, bordering Austria to the north and Slovenia to the east. This was one of the hardest-hit Italian regions during the *phylloxera* epidemic of the late 1800s, and following that period, many international grape varieties were planted here including Chardonnay, Riesling, and Pinot Nero (Pinot Noir). These are still widely planted today along with several indigenous varietals, especially Tocai.

With several DOC appellations in the region, much of the excitement in Friuli today revolves around modern-style white wines often made with international varietals. There are also two DOCG appellations in the eastern hills of Friuli: the Ramandolo DOCG that produces a variety of dry and sweet white wines, and the Colli Orientali del Friuli Picolit DOCG, famous for its sweet whites made from the Picolit varietal.

Trentino-Alto Adige

The northernmost region of Italy is Trentino-Alto Adige. It is bordered by Veneto to the south, Lombardy to the west, and Austria to the north. Most of the region is mountainous and has a cool to cold climate as the eastern stretches of the Italian Alps run through it. Many of the vineyards are planted on terraced slopes to maximize sun exposure. Trentino-Alto Adige is one of the three regions (Friuli and Veneto are the other two) that make up an area known as the Tres Venezie, or "Three Venices."

The region is divided into two very different sections: Trentino, the northern section, which has a strong German heritage; and Alto Adige, the southern area, with an Italian heritage. In Trentino, German-style wines and grapes are grown mostly in the coolest sections of the region. In Alto Adige, Pinot Grigio dominates much of the production, labeled Pinot Grigio Alto Adige DOC. There are no DOCG regions in Trentino-Alto Adige, but the majority of its production takes place in more than a dozen DOC appellations.

CENTRAL ITALY

Abruzzo

Abruzzo is a mountainous coastal region in central Italy bordered by Latium to the west, Molise to the south, Marche to the north, and the Adriatic Sea to the east. Many of the vineyards are planted on hillside slopes, as much of the western part of the region is home to the Apennine Mountains that gently drop in elevation through Abruzzo before disappearing into the Adriatic. It is a prolific winemaking region, accounting for more than 5 percent of Italy's total production, although much of this is destined for bulk *vino da tavola*.

The reputation of the two main DOC appellations of Abruzzo rests on two varietals: the white Trebbiano Abruzzo grape also known as Bombino Bianco, and the red Montepulciano grape. Trebbiano d'Abruzzo DOC wines are typically light and lean, but in the hands of some producers can be rich and complex. The Montepulciano d'Abruzzo DOC makes many basic red wines, although some examples are structured and packed with rich red fruit characteristics. The hilly Colline Teramane subregion of the Montepulciano d'Abruzzo DOC is home to the only DOCG appellation in the region. In the Montepulciano d'Abruzzo Colline Teramane DOCG, appellation yields are severely restricted, generally resulting in the best red wines in Abruzzo.

Central Italy and its important wine regions.

Latium (Lazio)

The region of Lazio is home to Italy's capital city, Rome. Located along the west coast of central Italy from Tuscany to Campania, vineyards spread throughout the region fanning out from Rome. Winemaking is dominated by white wine production in Lazio, using mostly Trebbiano and Malvasia grapes, although the vast majority of wines produced in the region are below the DOC level. There is only one DOCG appellation in Latium, called Cesanese del Piglio, which is a dry, sometimes spicy red wine made from the local clones of the Cesanese vine. Up to 10 percent white grapes are allowed to be blended into Cesanese del Piglio DOCG wines to add acidity and aromatics. The region also boasts several DOC regions. The most notable of these DOC appellations is the Est! Est!! Est!!! di Montefiascone DOC, more notable for its peculiar name than the quality of the lean white wines it produces.

The Marches (Marche)

The hilly and mountainous region known as Marche, or The Marches, runs along the Adriatic coastline bound by Abruzzo and Umbria to the south and west, and Emilia-Romagna to the north. Although a large amount of the region is covered with vineyards, more than 80 percent of the wine produced is below the DOC classification. Winemaking is centered around dry white wines made from Verdicchio, Malvasia, and Trebbiano, and soft reds made mostly from Sangiovese and Montepulciano grapes. One notable appellation in Marche for Montepulciano is the newly recognized Rosso Conero DOCG. The only other DOCG appellation in the region is the Vernaccia di Serrapetrona DOCG, which produces sweet or dry sparkling red wines, a local specialty.

Molise

Until the 1960s, Molise was an autonomous province of Abruzzo, the region with which it still shares its northwestern border. The youngest official region of Italy, Molise is just now beginning to recognize its winemaking potential. With warm Adriatic winds and the cooling effects of vineyards planted on

It Is!

The DOC appellation in Lazio known as Est! Est!! Est!!! di Montefiascone has one of the most interesting and unusual names for a wine or wine region. As legend has it, a German bishop was touring central Italy in the 1100s. He had dispatched a scout to travel in advance of his caravan to find the best wine of the region. This scout was supposed to mark any inns or taverns that poured exceptional wines with the term "Est," which means "it is" whenever he found any quality wines. Apparently the scout really enjoyed the wines of Montefiascone because he wrote a large "Est! Est!! Est!!!" on the door of a local tavern.

slopes in the southern Apennine Mountains, Molise has several regions with ideal conditions for growing grapes. Currently, the region produces only a small amount of wine equaling about 1 percent of Italy's total production, but major efforts are under way to expand vineyards and build modern winemaking facilities. Molise is definitely a region to watch.

Umbria

Umbria is located in almost the exact center of Italy. It is the only region south of Piedmont and Lombardy that is completely landlocked, and is surrounded by Tuscany, Marche, and Latium. Much of the production in Umbria is simple *vino da tavola,* although the region does boast one famous white wine DOC appellation and two lesser-known red wine DOCG appellations.

The expansive Orvieto DOC is located in the southwest corner of Umbria and produces white wines made from Trebbiano, Malvasia, and a handful of other indigenous varietals. While mostly dry and light, the Orvieto DOC does make some sweet wines, and in certain years these might even be from botrytised grapes. The two DOCG regions of Umbria are solely focused on red wine production. Sagrantino di Montefalco DOCG specializes in the Sagrantino grape, and Torgiano Rosso Riserva DOCG, the region's first DOCG appellation, grows mostly Sangiovese and Canaiolo, two of the top grapes also grown in the Chianti district of Tuscany.

SOUTHERN ITALY AND THE ISLANDS

Apulia (Puglia)

Known unofficially as the "heel of the boot," Apulia is a long, narrow region that runs more than 200 miles down the eastern coast of Southern Italy. The southeastern end of Apulia forms a long peninsula that stretches out into the Adriatic Sea. Molise, Campania, and Calabria make up the region's borders

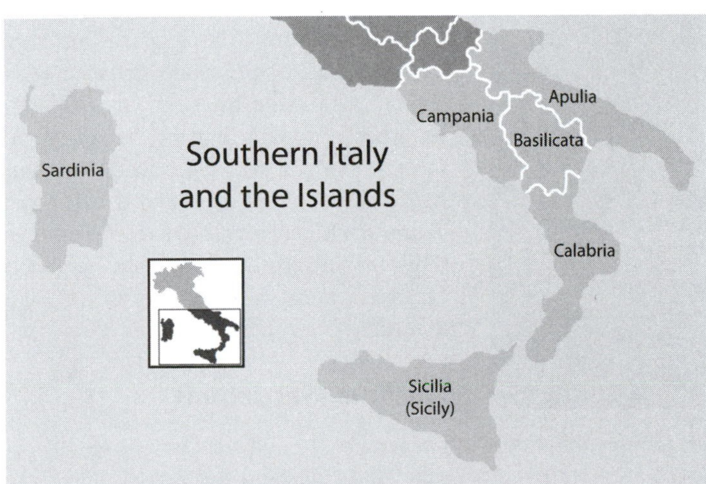

Important wine regions of southern Italy and the islands.

to the west and south. Hot conditions and long growing seasons are the norm in the region's vineyards, leading to high levels of ripeness and often enormous yields. Apulia is often the top-producing region in Italy.

Unfortunately, most of the millions of gallons of wine produced in Apulia each year are basic *vino da tavola,* as these high yields often preclude quality production. In fact, less than 2 percent of the wines produced in Apulia qualify for DOC status, and there are no DOCG appellations in the region. Warm-climate grapes obviously do best in Apulia, such as the red varietals Primitivo (a clone of Zinfandel), Uva di Troia, and Negroamaro, and more than four-fifths of the production in the region is red wine.

Basilicata

Basilicata is a predominantely red wine region in the center of southern Italy surrounded by Apulia to the north, Campania to the west, and Calabria to the south. It has only a small coastal area, and most of the region is quite mountainous as this is where the Apennine Mountain chain comes to an end. Basilicata produces very little wine, even though it is surrounded by many of Italy's top-producing regions. The only DOC appellation in the region is the Aglianico del Vulture DOC located on the slopes of Mt. Vulture, a dormant volcano. Made from the ancient Aglianico grape, these wines are a point of local pride and are considered some of the best in southern Italy.

The wines of the Aglianico del Vulture DOC are the pride of Basilicata.

Calabria

Making up the southernmost tip of mainland Italy and bordering only the region of Basilicata, Calabria is the toe of the boot. This peninsula is home to red wines almost exclusively, and vineyards cling to mountain slopes that rise up from the Mediterranean. Calabria does not produce a large amount of wine, but its most important DOC appellation, known as the Cirò DOC, has been producing wines since the time of the ancient Greeks.

Campania

The region of Campania is located to the west of Basilicata and south of Molise. Its northern provinces are mountainous, as the Apennine Mountains run through most of the region. Most of Campania is coastal, with Mediterranean winds tempering the warm climate. The region is a top tourist destination in Italy, as it is home to the cities of Naples and Salerno, as well as the ruins of Pompeii on the slopes of Mount Vesuvius.

Much of Campania's wine production is basic red and white *vino da tavola,* although it is home to several DOC regions and three DOCG appellations—more than any other region in southern Italy. Two of these DOCG appellations focus exclusively on white wine production and are found at higher elevations: the Fiano di Avellino DOCG producing aromatic whites from the indigenous Fiano grape, and the Greco di Tufo DOCG made from the Greco grape believed to have been brought here by the ancient Greeks. The most important wines produced in Campania (and many believe in all of southern Italy) come from the Taurasi DOCG. This red wine appellation, located in a hilly area just northeast of Naples, crafts intensely concentrated, tannic red wines from the Aglianico grape that can age for decades.

Sardinia (Sardegna)

Located in the Tyrrhenian Sea off the west coast of mainland Italy and just south of the French island of Corsica is the large island region of Sardinia. Conditions on the island are harsh for vines, as soils are relatively sparse and the climate is quite arid and windy. Sardinia produces a small amount of wine compared to Italy's other island region of Sicily, but a large percentage of Sardinian production qualifies for DOC status. Several styles of wine are produced on the island, with the most important local grapes being the red varietals Carignan and Cannonau (also known as Grenache) and the white varietals Vermentino, Moscato, and Malvasia. Powerfully built and full-bodied white wines are made from Vermentino grapes in the Vermentino di Gallura DOCG, the island's only DOCG appellation.

Sicily (Sicilia)

Sicily is a large island just off the tip of Calabria. This is the southernmost region of Italy, and conditions are often hot and arid. Ranking among the top producing regions in Italy, Sicily produces more than 10 million gallons of wine each year and has more vineyard acreage than any other region. Most of this production falls under the IGT or ***vino da tavola*** classifications, in large part because many winemakers in Sicily prefer the looser regulations and more generous yields for wines in these classifications. Using their own system of classifications, quality wines will often have the letter Q printed on the label or capsule.

Heat-loving grapes grow best on Sicily, and the island is home to several hearty red wines and fortified white dessert wines, including those from the Marsala DOC. While Marsala wines have lost much of their grandeur, a new generation of winemakers in the appellation is increasing quality standards to return it to its former stature, when it was comparable to the finest Ports, Sherries, and Madeiras. Red wine production is dominated by mostly local grape varieties like Nero d'Avola and Pignatello. Top white grapes include Catarratto, Trebbiano, Inzolia, and Grillo. Sicilian winemakers are also having success with newly planted nontraditional varietals like Sangiovese, Barbera, and a Zinfandel clone called Primitivo.

Sicily is home to the production of Marsala, one of the world's great fortified wines.

Summary

Italy is one of the most important and historic wine-producing countries in the world. It produces a staggering amount of wine for its small size, from hundreds of different grape varieties in almost every style that can be imagined. Fiercely regional, winemakers throughout Italy produce wines in very different ways from one another, resulting in the wide range of unique wine styles produced throughout Italy's twenty regions.

The country has worked hard to modernize since the 1960s and 1970s, not only in terms of equipment, facilities, and practices, but also in terms of how winemaking is regulated throughout the country. The DOC laws of Italy aim to identify and establish the top winemaking zones and styles produced, and to regulate approved practices and techniques for winemaking. This modernization and rededication of Italian winemakers have helped to show the world that Italy is one of the greatest and most prolific wine-producing countries in the world.

Review Questions

1. The red grape grown almost exclusively in Piedmont, Italy, that produces the red wines of Barolo and Barbaresco with extremely high tannins is called:
   A. Corvina
   B. Barbera
   C. Nebbiolo
   D. Sangiovese

2. Which Italian wine region is famous for the production of Sangiovese-based wines such as Chianti Classico?
   A. Tuscany
   B. Veneto
   C. Piedmont
   D. Sicily

3. Which of the following is used to produce sweet, sparkling wines in Asti, an appellation of Piedmont?
   A. Trebbiano
   B. Nebbiolo
   C. Pinot Grigio
   D. Moscato

For questions four through ten, match the classified appellations to the region in which they are produced. Some answers may be used more than once and some not at all.

4. Soave Superiore DOCG
5. Brunello di Montalcino DOCG
6. Barbera d'Alba DOC
7. Taurasi DOCG
8. Amarone della Valpolicella DOC
9. Chianti Colli Senesi DOCG
10. Ghemme DOCG

A. Piedmont
B. Tuscany
C. Veneto
D. None of the above

11. Italy is a major world producer of wine; however, the country is not very large in terms of landmass.
   A. True
   B. False

12. The Italian wine laws are known by what acronym?
   A. AVA
   B. AOC
   C. DOC
   D. BATF

13. Where does Italy rank in terms of wine exports to the United States?
   A. #1
   B. #2
   C. #3
   D. #4

14. A super Tuscan is a wine made in Tuscany using either nontraditional grapes or nontraditional blends; these wines are labeled with a brand name.
   A. True
   B. False

15. Italian Pinot Grigio is the number one–selling foreign style of wine in the United States.
   A. True
   B. False

Key Terms

Denominazione di Origine Controllata (DOC)
vino da tavola
Indicazione Geografica Tipica (IGT)
Denominazione di Origine Controllata e Garantita (DOCG)
vino rosso
vino bianco
vino rosato
spumante
secco
dolce
passito
riserva
classico
superiore
Piedmont
Asti DOCG
Moscato d'Asti DOCG
Barbera d'Alba DOC
Dolcetto d'Alba DOC
Barolo DOCG
Barbaresco DOCG
Tuscany
Chianti DOCG
Chianti Classico DOCG
Brunello di Montalcino DOCG
super Tuscan
Veneto
Soave DOC
Valpolicella DOC
Amarone della Valpolicella DOC
recioto
Prosecco di Valdobbiadene DOC
Prosecco di Conegliano DOC
Pinot Grigio della Venezia DOC

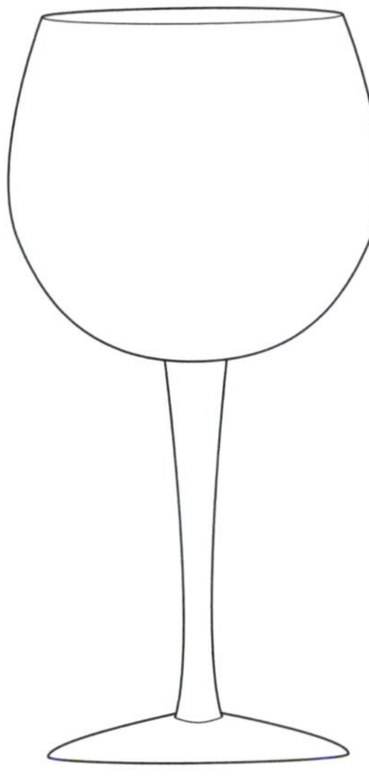

CHAPTER 11

The Wines of Spain

With wine and hope, anything is possible.

—Spanish proverb

Spain is a country of massive wine diversity. The Spanish produce some of the greatest red wines in the world. Some of their new, modern-style white wines are also receiving critical acclaim. Their top sparkling wines are second only to those of Champagne. And they produce one of the world's classic fortified wines. With all of that going for Spain, coupled with the fact that they are the third leading producer of wine in the world, it would be logical to assume that the wines of Spain were as well known as those of France, Italy, and California. Surprisingly, that is not the case. In this chapter, we discuss the history, grapes, laws, and wine regions of Spain.

TOP WHITE GRAPE

- Albariño

TOP RED GRAPES

- Tempranillo
- Garnacha

TOP REGIONS

Classic Regions

- Rioja DOCa
- Jerez DO (Sherry)

Important Regions

- Ribera del Duero DOCa
- Rías Baixas DO
- Priorato DOCa
- Cava DO

The Facts on Spain

CLIMATE

The wine regions of northern Spain are temperate to warm, but conditions get hotter quickly the further south you travel.

IMPORTANT INFORMATION

- Spain ranks third in the world in terms of total wine production, and has more vineyard acreage than any other country in the world.
- The Spanish are usually very traditional about their top red wines, focusing on their top varietal, Tempranillo.

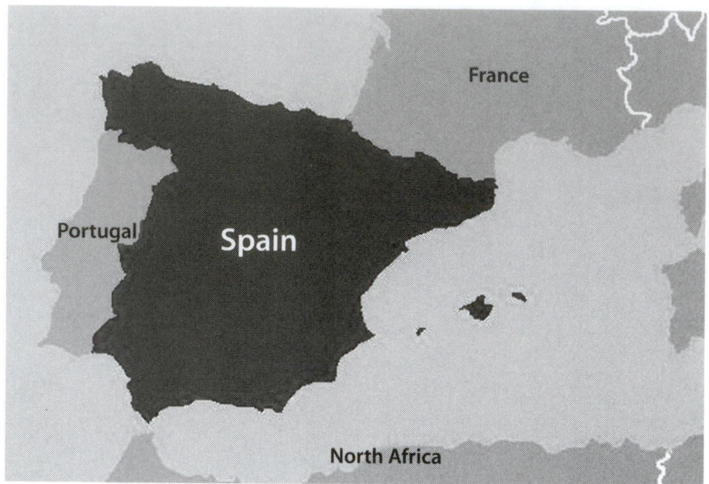

- White wines are not as prevalent, but a new breed of modern-style whites is on the rise.
- Spain has a system of wine laws known as the ***Denominaciones de Origen*** (DO) laws, which are based on the French AOC laws. Top-quality wines are typically labeled by the region from which they originate, and there are strict regulations regarding how wines are to be produced and what types of grapes can be used throughout these different regions.

Spain: Ancient Tradition and Modern Attitude

Spain is a massive producer of wine, despite the fact that its styles, grapes, and regions are not well known. The country ranks third in total worldwide wine production, trailing only the prolific nations of France and Italy. Huge expanses of land, especially in the interior of the country, are planted to grapevines in Spain. In fact, the traditional Spanish practice of planting vines sparsely throughout a vineyard results in the country having a larger area under vine than any other wine-producing nation in the world, more than 3 million acres! Wine has always been an integral part of life in Spain, and the Spanish are prodigious consumers.

Grapevines have been cultivated in Spain for thousands of years, long before early cultures brought ***Vitis vinifera*** vines to the region. Winemaking was brought by the Greeks and Phoenicians prior to 1000 B.C., as colonies and trading posts were founded along the Mediterranean coastline of the Iberian Peninsula. Spreading north from Africa, the civilization of Carthage colonized the region and introduced several advancements in winemaking, while at the same time increasing the number of vineyards.

After a series of wars between Carthage and the Roman Empire, the region was eventually conquered by Rome. The Romans increased the amount and quality of wines produced in the region they called ***Hispania,*** and soon these wines were being shipped throughout the Roman Empire. Many of the wine regions Spain is known for today were first established during this period of Roman rule.

When the Roman Empire eventually crumbled, barbarians from the north invaded and occupied parts of Spain during the Dark Ages. In the 700s, invaders from the south eventually took over and colonized the Spanish mainland. This was the time of the Moorish occupation of Spain, a powerful Muslim civilization from North Africa. Though their religious laws forbid the consumption of alcohol, winemaking in Spain continued for the non-Muslim population because it could be taxed. Exporting wine was a completely different story, so vineyard acreage and the amount of wine produced steeply declined.

By the 1200s, most of the Moorish occupiers were pushed out of Spain during a period called the *Reconquista,* and winemaking quickly flourished in the country once again. England became the top export market for Spain, which often supplied most of England's imports when the country was at war with France through various periods of the Middle Ages. Spain grew in influence and wealth during this period, becoming one of the major powers of Europe by the 1400s.

The discovery of the New World in 1492 by Columbus was a Spanish-sponsored expedition. Soon after, the strong Spanish navy and powerful armies were on their way to conquer and colonize the Americas. As the Spanish conquistadores conquered most of the New World, Spanish missionaries brought wine grapes and established several vineyards there. Winemaking and the wine grape were both brought to the Americas by the Spanish.

New World colonies and outposts initially provided a rich new market for Spanish winemakers and they began shipping their wines across the Atlantic. However, as these colonies started to grow, many of them began to develop their own wine industries—especially Mexico, Chile, and Argentina. At the same time, Spanish relations with their top European export country began to decline sharply as hostilities between Spain and England developed in the 1700s. With the defeat of the Spanish navy by the English fleet at the battle of Trafalgar in 1805, Spanish superiority on the seas ended. Trade with England was at a total halt, and many of Spain's colonies stopped buying wines produced in Spain as they now produced enough wine to supply themselves. In an effort to increase sales of Spanish wines, the royal government decreed that winemaking should cease in its colonies—an act that served to hamper the development of many emerging wine regions in North and South America.

Spanish winemakers went through lean times in the early 1800s. The English market was once again opened up to their production, but stiff international competition with France and other European countries hurt their sales. When many regions around Europe began modernizing winemaking facilities and techniques during the Industrial Revolution, the Spanish stuck to their traditional methods, resulting in wines that seemed much more rustic and plain. It was not until the mid- to late 1800s that bad news for most European winemakers turned into great fortune for the Spanish.

The *phylloxera* epidemic destroyed many of the vineyards and wine regions of France and then spread to the rest of Europe through the close of the nineteenth century. Due to isolation and natural barriers, Spain stayed mostly free of *phylloxera.* When it finally did arrive in full force from the 1890s through the early 1900s, the process of grafting had already been developed, sparing most Spanish wine regions. During the *phylloxera* era, Spanish winemaking flourished. While most of Europe was being devastated by the root aphid, Spanish winemakers were able to sell their wines with little or no competition and the export market boomed. Many French winemakers moved to Spain for work during the period, spreading their knowledge and practices to Spanish winemakers.

The future looked bright for Spanish wine at the turn of the twentieth century, but a bloody civil war and two world wars ravaged many wine regions and the industry fell into disarray. When the country finally stabilized in the 1950s and 1960s, a quality wine industry was not reestablished, as Spain was under the dictatorship of Francisco Franco and the country had severe economic woes. By the time democracy was established in Spain in the 1970s, much of the winemaking world had surpassed Spain in terms of modern techniques and technologies. The quality of Spanish wine did not measure up to the wines being produced in Europe and in the New World areas of the United States, Chile, or Australia. This resulted in meager success in international markets until Spain began to rapidly modernize in the 1980s and 1990s. As the country joined the European Union in 1986, their wine laws were revised and quality practices were promoted. International interest in Spanish wine once again led to millions of gallons of Spanish wine headed for export markets.

Today, Spain has a thriving but underrated wine industry. With the lower quality standards of Spanish wine several decades ago still fresh in the minds of many export markets, Spanish winemakers are fighting hard to spread the word about the quality of their wines. They are beginning to get their message out in large part because the Spanish do make some of the world's best wines today, and they offer some of the best values in the world.

Wine Laws of Spain

Spain has a system of wine regulations that is similar to the French AOC laws. Appellations of origin have been established throughout Spain that are classified in a hierarchy according to quality and strictness of production techniques. Because the Spanish laws are based on recognized areas of production with established borders, most high-quality wines are labeled by their region of origin.

The Spanish wine laws are generally referred to as the ***Denominaciónes de Origen* laws,** or DO laws for short. These laws are administered by a wing of the Spanish government that oversees regulatory councils in each official region called ***consejo reguladores.*** Each of these regional councils establishes, administrates, and regulates the official winemaking laws and regulations within their particular region.

Similar to most other European country's systems, the lowest classification is "table wine" or ***vino de mesa.*** This classification has very lax production standards and can be made from grapes grown anywhere in Spain. There is also a subclassification of the *vino de mesa* category called ***vino de la tierra*** or "country wine" in which restrictions are stricter and the grapes must be grown in one of a handful of large recognized areas. Similar to the IGT classification in Italy, the wine should show characteristics typical of its origin.

Spain's quality classifications for wine.

The next level of the Spanish wine laws is the ***Vino de Calidad con Indicación Geográfica*** classification. Wines with this designation must be produced from grapes grown within a specific, recognized region. The production laws are stricter in this category, with specific regulations regarding permissible grape varietals, yields, and winemaking practices. Labels for wines of this classification bear the designation "Vino de Calidad de" followed by the name of the specific region or origin.

Meaning "designation of origin," ***Denominación de Origen*** or **DO** is the next official classification. Similar to the AOC category in France, this classification covers select areas throughout Spain and the wines produced there have to be made following strict guidelines involving approved grapes, reduced yields, permissible winemaking practices, and aging minimums. This classification is responsible for more of Spain's production than any other, composing more than 50 percent of the total. Wines that qualify for this designation are labeled by their region of origin. There are nearly seventy DO regions located throughout Spain.

The top classification of Spanish winemaking is the **DOCa** classification, short for ***Denominación***

de Origen Calificada. This designation refers to "qualified designations of origin" and is only granted to regions that have had DO status for more than a decade along with a track record of historically top-quality wine. Restrictions on viticultural and vinicultural practices are the stiffest in this classification due to the reputation it affords a region. To date, only three Spanish appellations have been awarded this status: Priorato DOCa, Ribera del Duero DOCa, and Rioja DOCa—all primarily red wine regions.

Since 2003, for both the DO and DOCa classifications, specific wineries may earn the designation ***vino de pago***, which roughly translates to "estate bottled." This is supposed to be awarded only to single-estate wines that have a top-quality reputation. The wines must be made and bottled on the wineries' estates. Less than ten estate wines in Spain bear this designation. Spain's wine industry hopes that eventually this category will evolve into a collection of the top wine-producing estates or vineyards in the country, almost an equivalent of the French

Common Spanish Label Terms

TERM	DEFINITION
Vino tinto	Red wine
Vino blanco	White wine
Vino rosado	Rosé wine
Bodega	Winery or wine estate
Seco	Dry
Dulce	Sweet
Joven	A wine released young, usually with no oak aging
Crianza	Typically a wine aged for at least two years, several months of which must be in oak barrels; regulations differ in various appellations.
Reserva	Typically a wine aged for at least three years, one of which must be in oak; regulations differ in various appellations.
Gran reserva	Quite often a special wine, typically aged for at least five years, two of which must be in oak; regulations differ in various appellations.

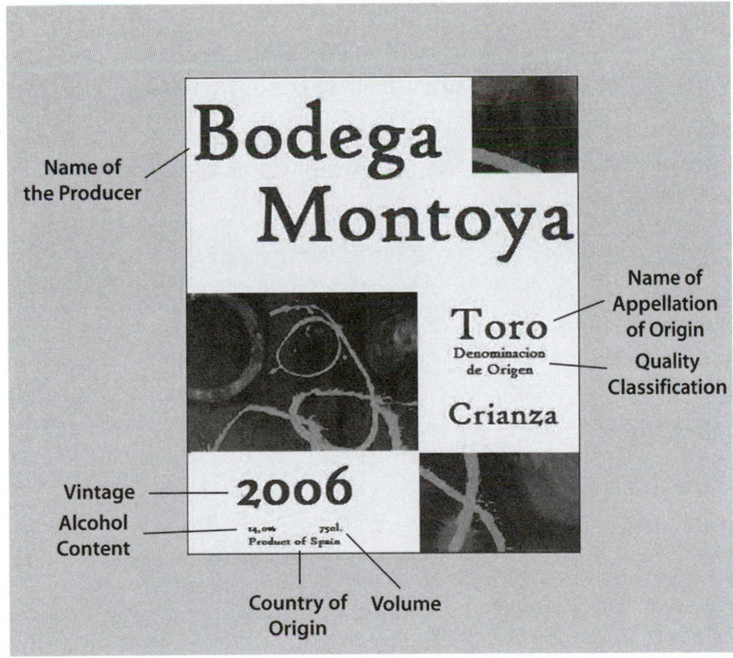

How to read a Spanish wine label.

grand cru system, but the jury is still out on how it will ultimately develop.

Important Grapes of Spain

Grapes have been cultivated in Spain for thousands of years, and over time, several hundred different indigenous wine grapes have been developed. Different grape varieties are associated with different regions throughout the country, but one varietal dominates premium red wine production and is used to produce Spain's best-known still wines: Tempranillo. For white wine production, the top grape is a relative newcomer that has come to receive commercial attention only in the last few decades, called Albariño. The red grape Garnacha, called Grenache in the rest of the world, is commonly grown throughout Spain and while it often only serves in a blending capacity, it can produce top-quality wines in specific regions.

 Albariño

Albariño has only recently become an important grape in Spain with the emergence of modern white wine making techniques. It is grown extensively throughout northwestern Spain, especially in the Rías Baixas DO. This grape produces light- to medium-bodied wines that have a zesty acidity and are often bursting with ripe fruit flavors such as peaches, citrus, melon, and kiwi fruit. Most Albariño-based wines produced in Spain will be aged in stainless steel to preserve the grape's fresh, fruity characteristics.

 Garnacha

The Garnacha grape is most famously grown in the Southern Rhône Valley of France, but it originated in Spanish soil. This heat-loving varietal often ripens fully in Spain's warm climates, yielding powerful wines with high alcohol content. Garnacha is almost always reminiscent of cooked red fruits and spice. Although this red grape is most commonly used in blends, single-varietal examples made from old vines are rising in popularity, especially in the northeastern appellation of Priorato DOCa.

 Tempranillo

Of all the grapes grown in Spain, Tempranillo is by far the most important. It is featured widely in many of the top red wines produced throughout Spain, including two of the country's most important appellations: the Rioja DOCa and the Ribera del Duero DOCa. This indigenous Spanish varietal produces medium- to full-bodied red wines with a powerful tannin structure. The flavors typical of wines made from the grape are reminiscent of ripe cherries and strawberries, spice, clay, and leather. Oak aging is often heavily utilized for Tempranillo-based wines and the flavors of oak complement the grape nicely.

Other Notable Grapes

 **AIRÉN** Although most of the wines made from this white-skinned varietal are not usually

A Grape by Any Other Name…

Tempranillo is known by several synonyms in different regions of Spain:

REGION	ALTERNATE NAME(S)
Cataluña	Ojo de Liebre and Ull de Lliebre
Ribera del Duero	Tinto del Pais and Tinto Fino
Rueda and Toro	Tinto de Toro
Valdepeñas and La Mancha	Cencibel

Major wine regions of Spain.

notable, the amount of Airén growing in Spain is. This is the most widely grown grape varietal in Spain, planted heavily in the hot, central plains of the country. It mostly produces ordinary white table wines.

MONASTRELL Known as Mourvèdre in France and most of the rest of the world, this red wine grape is commonly used as a component of blends in Spanish red wines, or on its own in powerful, earthy red wines. It is also used in the production of rosé wines.

VERDEJO The white wine grape Verdejo is used to produce some of Spain's top dry white wines. It can produce wines with intense fruit character and a pleasant acidity. It is also known as Godello in some Spanish regions.

VIURA Viura is an important white wine varietal in many regions throughout Spain, and the leading white grape from Rioja. Also known as Macabeo in some Spanish regions, this grape often produces pleasantly fruity white wines.

Terroir and Important Regions

Covering the entire Iberian Peninsula except for the southwestern corner where Portugal is found, Spain is a large European country. The southern latitude of Spain creates warm conditions that are often tempered in the west and to the north by the Atlantic. The Mediterranean warms the climate to the east and south. All locations throughout Spain are arid, and rainfall is scarce in all but a few coastal regions. Northern Spain is dominated by mountain ranges and river valleys that create several unique local climates. These mountains eventually drop into central Spain, which is dominated by an enormous plateau that covers almost half the country's landmass, known as the Meseta Central. Conditions are hot and dry throughout this area, and while several large wine regions are found here in the interior, they are often sparsely planted. To the south, Mediterranean conditions are found, down to the hot southern tip of the country.

There are almost seventy DO and DOCa regions located throughout Spain, many of them making premium red and white wines from local grapes and the Tempranillo varietal under one of its many synonyms. For dry white wine production, the most notable appellation to emerge in the modern era is Rías Baixas DO, located just north of Portugal in the northwest. Dry red wines are the primary style in Spain's two best-known still wine regions, the appellations of Rioja DOCa and Ribera del Duero DOCa.

Rioja DOCa.

Rioja: Spain's Most Famous Wine

The red wines of the **Rioja DOCa** are the most famous produced in Spain, and this was the first appellation to receive the exclusive DOCa designation. Wine production dates back thousands of years in the region, predating the Roman occupation of ***Hispania***. After coming under Roman rule, the lands that are now Rioja became some of the most important and prolific wine-producing regions in Western Europe. Wine production remained vital in Rioja through the Middle Ages, as it was a major stopping point along a popular religious pilgrimage route to the shrine of the apostle James in the western region of Galicia.

In the late 1700s, winemakers in Rioja began to adopt the use of oak barrels to age their wine, mimicking the practice of French winemakers in Bordeaux (and this would not be the last influence Bordeaux would have on Rioja). This process allowed the wines of Rioja to have a longer shelf life, opening up more international markets to these wines. The new boost in sales led to the founding of several new wine estates in Rioja, many of which are still top names in the region today. Oak aging brought the wines of Rioja into a modern era and is still a fundamental aspect of winemaking in the region. Heading into the mid-1800s, Rioja received another boost to its wine industry as trouble was brewing elsewhere.

As the *phylloxera* epidemic began to ravage many of Europe's classic wine-producing regions in the 1850s and 1860s, Rioja remained free of the pest. This caused sales of wines from the region to skyrocket, and thousands of new acres of vines were planted. With most of their own vine-yards wiped out, many winemakers from Bordeaux, which is less than 200 miles away, migrated to Rioja and established wineries, bringing many of their methods and winemaking philosophies with them. Their influence is still felt today in the winemaking of Rioja.

Phylloxera finally spread to Rioja around the turn of the century and destroyed many of the vineyards in the region. While Spanish winemakers began to replant their vines, France and the rest of Europe were also replanting, which closed off most of the region's newfound export markets. Turmoil and war

The Name Rioja

Flowing through the region of La Rioja is the Oja River, locally called the Rio Oja. The region's name is a contraction of Rio Oja: Rioja.

in both Spain and Europe further hurt winemaking in Rioja, and many wineries closed their doors and vineyards were replanted to other crops. Rioja was just a shadow of its former self in the first half of the twentieth century.

In the 1970s, a new age of winemaking in Rioja began. A string of successful vintages brought positive attention to the region's wines, and winemakers began to expand and modernize. Many new techniques and practices began to be utilized, and the emergence of other Spanish wine regions provided additional attention and some constructive competition for the winemakers of Rioja. Today, Rioja is one of the most popular wine regions in Spain and is enjoying international acclaim and interest. While traditions are still strong there, winemakers continue to experiment and refine their winemaking practices and wines.

Rioja is home to Spain's most famous red wines.

The Facts on Rioja

CLIMATE

Rioja is home to a dry, continental climate.

TOP RED GRAPE

- Tempranillo

IMPORTANT INFORMATION

- The red wines of Rioja are generally considered to be some of Spain's best and most popular.
- Most wines produced in Rioja are blends of different grapes, with their red wines focusing mostly on the Tempranillo varietal.
- Aging is quite important for many of the winemakers of Rioja, and extended time in barrel is quite common in the region.

TERROIR AND IMPORTANT STYLES/REGIONS

The Rioja appellation is located in the north-central part of Spain, in the Ebro River valley, just south of the Cantabrian Mountains. Most of the Rioja DOCa lies in the province of La Rioja, although parts of it extend into Navarra and Basque Country. The mountains to the north protect the appellation, shielding it from harsh winter storms. At more than 1,000 feet above sea level, the high elevation maintains a fairly dry, continental climate, unlike the scorching temperatures that can be found in parts of central and southern Spain.

Three zones of production make up the Rioja DOCa, each having its own personality. **Rioja Alta** in the west and **Rioja Alavesa** in the northern part of the appellation are the two coolest zones, located in the foothills and slopes of the mountains there. **Rioja Baja** is the largest and warmest of the three, covering the eastern reaches of the region.

More than 80 percent of the production in the appellation, and the wines the region is known for, are reds. These are often wines of great balance, elegance, and grace. Red wines from the Rioja DOCa will often go through an extended aging period before being released, during which they develop intense vanilla, toast, and spice notes, which complement their rich red fruit and wet earth characteristics.

As with the other DO and DOCa appellations of Spain, there are strict laws regarding the grapes that can be grown and used for the wines of this region. The vast majority of wines produced in Rioja are blends of different grapes, the most important of which is Tempranillo. This grape is used as the backbone for almost all of Rioja's red wines, usually accounting for well over half of the blend. While Tempranillo can be very hearty and robust in many regions of Spain, in Rioja it is often much softer and refined, producing earthy wines with finesse. To complement the main grape, winemakers blend it with other red grapes including Garnacha, Mazuelo (also known as Carignan in France), and Graciano. Tempranillo gives the wines of Rioja a complexity of flavor and richness, while the blending grapes are used to contribute additional flavor, aroma, acidity, and tannins.

Once these wines have been fermented and graded, long periods of oak aging typically ensue. Traditional winemakers of the region age their wines in American oak barrels to extract the stronger flavors they afford. Small, French oak barrels are also widely used, and produce the more modern style of Rioja that is gaining favor. Depending on their quality and characteristics, these wines can receive extensive periods of aging before release. There are three official age designations used on labels to signify the type and length of aging (see box above).

White wines are also produced in the Rioja DOCa, as well as some rosés. These were long held in much lower esteem than the reds of the region because they too were submitted to extensive periods of aging before release. This caused most of the wines to be oxidized and stripped of their fruit. Today, many winemakers have opted for a softer, brighter style of white that has been aged for shorter periods of time, utilizing the Viura grape, known as Macabeo in many other regions of Spain.

Official Aging Designations of the Rioja DOCa

DESIGNATION	AGING MINIMUM BEFORE RELEASE
Crianza	Two years, at least one of which must be in oak barrels.
Reserva	Three years, at least one of which must be in oak barrels.
Gran reserva	Five years, at least two of which must be in oak barrels. Only produced in the best vintages.

Other Spanish Regions of Note

RIBERA DEL DUERO DOCa

If Rioja is home to the most famous wine of Spain, then the **Ribera del Duero DOCa** is where you can find the country's most famous winery. Although this region has been planted to vines since the time of the Romans, it was not noteworthy for wine until the late 1800s, when a wine estate known as **Vega Sicilia** began to produce legendary wines. Vega Sicilia stood alone in the region until the 1970s, when several winemakers began planting vineyards here. The top wine of the Vega Sicilia estate is called *Unico,* which is Spanish for "unique," still one of the most expensive and highly prized wines produced in Spain today. Ribera del Duero is one of only three DOCa appellations in the country.

The Ribera del Duero DOCa is about 175 miles southwest of Rioja. Located on a large, elevated plateau, the area is home to hot, dry summers and cold, often harsh winters. Soils are sparse in the region and

The wines of Ribera del Duero are often heavier and more powerful than those of Rioja.

Cava is the most important sparkling wine produced in Spain, made using the same methods that winemakers use in Champagne, France.

yields limited, with gnarled vines stubbornly tolerating the harsh landscape. As its name suggests, the Duero River flows through the middle of the region, heading west until it crosses the Portuguese border and becomes the Douro River.

The wines of Ribera del Duero are almost completely red, and are known for their intense concentration, rich flavors of leather and dark fruit, and powerful structure. Tempranillo (locally called Tinto del Pais) is the primary varietal, but several others are planted in the region, including Garnacha and a handful of international varietals like Cabernet Sauvignon, Merlot, and Malbec. Blending is common, with Tempranillo typically used as the main base. The aging regime is often quite long for these full-bodied red wines, and many can be cellared for decades.

CAVA DO

Spain's most important and the world's most widely produced sparkling wine is Cava. These wines are produced using método tradicional (*méthode tradionale*)—a method borrowed from the winemakers of Champagne, whose wines inspired the first Cavas in the 1860s. In fact, Cava is actually the Catalan term for "cave," a reference to the extended aging period that these wines must spend in the bottle stored in caves or temperature-controlled cellars. While the winemaking techniques used to produce Cava might be the same as those in Champagne, that does not mean that Cava is simply a Spanish Champagne. The climate and soil of **Cava DO** and the grapes allowed in its production are quite different.

The Cava DO is a large region, covering much of northeastern Spain and overlapping several other DO appellations, most notably Penèdes. Conditions are often warm in Cava, as the Mediterranean has a large influence on the climate here. Grapes in the region ripen to levels that the winemakers of Champagne could only dream of, and the result is sparkling wines with more body, less acidity, and riper fruit and citrus flavors. Most of the grapes used to produce Cava are indigenous to the region, with the three most important being the white-skinned varietals Macabeo, Parellada, and Xarel-lo; although Chardonnay is now allowed in the region and is gaining in popularity.

Like Champagne, many Cavas are non-vintage blends with winemakers attempting to achieve a standard style or flavor profile. In better years, vintage Cavas are also produced and commonly receive more aging and more attention than the more widely produced non-vintage style. Cava can also range in sweetness level based on the Champagne model, although most Cava is produced in a drier style. With mammoth production levels (over four times more Cava than Champagne is produced each year), much Cava is simple and mass-produced by large winemaking cooperatives and companies. Top-quality examples are readily available, however, from producers both large and small, and continuing strides are being made to improve quality in the region.

Wines made from 100 percent Albariño grapes in Rías Baixas can be labeled by grape variety.

RÍAS BAIXAS DO

In a country known for its red wines, the **Rías Baixas DO** stands out for its impressive whites. Located along the Atlantic coastline in northwestern Spain, this appellation is in the region of Galicia just north of the Portuguese border. The cooler maritime climate found in Rías Baixas is very different from the arid conditions found just a few hundred miles away in Spain's interior, and this is one of the wettest parts of the country. The landscape is made up of a network of steeply carved river valleys that run to the sea.

Once known more as a fishing region than for wine, Rías Baixas did not begin to receive critical acclaim for its wines until the 1970s. The main grape grown in the rocky, sloped vineyards of the appellation is Albariño. A grape known for its elegant, ripe fruit aromas, historically it had been hidden in blends or stripped of its fruit and masked with oak. Employing modern techniques such as cool fermentations and stainless-steel aging, the winemakers of Rías Baixas developed a crisp, fresh style of white wine unlike any other whites in Spain.

Quickly, the Spanish and the international wine markets took notice, and today, 100 percent Albariño wines from the Rías Baixas DO are some of the most expensive white wines produced in the country. Wines made in the region from 100 percent Albariño are authorized to list the varietal on the label.

PRIORATO DOCa

Northeastern Spain is home to the country's only DOCa that does not focus on Tempranillo production, the **Priorato DOCa.** Sometimes known as Priorat, the Catalan term, this region has reinvented itself over the last couple of decades. In the 1990s, this poor, isolated, and mountainous region was barely known for wine. This all changed when enterprising winemakers began to craft intensely powerful

Monastic Ties in Priorat

The name *Priorat* is actually the Spanish term for a priory, a religious building housing monks and led by a prior (one step down from an abbot). A monastery known as *Scala Dei*, or "God's Stairway," is located in the modern region of Priorat, although it is abandoned today.

red wines from old-vine Garnacha and Cariñena (known as Carignan in France). Modern winemaking techniques were utilized and many wines were aged in small French oak barrels. These wines quickly garnered international attention and soared in both popularity and price.

Since then, outside investment has been growing in Priorato, especially from large wineries found in surrounding areas like Penedès and Rioja. New plantings in the sparse, dark soils of the region have included international varietals like Syrah, Merlot, and Cabernet Sauvignon, along with the traditional Garnacha and Cariñena grapes. These modern-style, dense, dry red wines produced in Priorato are truly ushering in a new era of Spanish winemaking.

OTHER IMPORTANT WINE REGIONS

Vineyards are planted throughout the country of Spain, and with almost seventy DO appellations, there is a wide variety of different styles produced. Warm conditions found in much of the country favor the production of red wines. Many of these are hearty red wines often made from the widely grown Tempranillo varietal, although many interesting and high-quality white wines, sparkling wines, and fortified dessert wines are also produced.

Until recently, the wines of Priorato were almost unknown.

In the northwestern Spanish provinces of Galicia and Castilla y León, the well-known regions of Ribera del Duero and Rías Baixas often overshadow top wines made in the regions of **Toro DO, Bierzo DO,** and **Rueda DO.** These regions are beginning to share in the limelight, however, as quality seems to increase in every vintage. Tinto de Toro is the local name for the Tempranillo grape in the Toro DO, where it is used to make many rich, concentrated red wines. Bierzo is an appellation that is gaining more prominence, especially for its softer red wines produced from the indigenous Mencía grape. The Rueda DO is completely dedicated to white wine production, mostly growing the soft and aromatic Verdejo grape, although the recent introduction of Sauvignon Blanc (often used as a blending component with Verdejo) has proven very successful.

In northeastern Spain, the provinces of Aragón and Cataluña are home to the famous wines of Rioja, Cava, and Priorato, but other important wine regions are found throughout. The region of **Navarra DO,** just north across the Ebro River from Rioja, makes intense red wines from the Garnacha varietal, as do winemakers in the **Cariñena DO** and **Calatayud DO.** The coastal regions of **Penedès DO** and **Tarragona DO** produce dry, still white wines from the same grapes used to make the sparkling wines of the Cava DO that overlaps both regions, as well as top-quality white and red wines from indigenous grapes and, increasingly, international varietals like Chardonnay and Cabernet Sauvignon.

Central Spain is home to the province of Castilla-La Mancha and the Meseta Central, an expansive central plateau with hot, arid conditions. Here you will find the largest classified appellation in Spain, called the **La Mancha DO.** The most common grape is the often bland white grape called Airén, which is the most widely planted wine grape in Spain, mostly due to its extensive vineyards located in La Mancha. The **Valdepeñas DO** is a southern subregion of La Mancha that makes some very good red wines from Tempranillo, known in this region by the synonym Cencibel.

The most important wines produced in southern Spain are the fortified wines produced in the province of Andalucía, but the table wines of the province of Extremadura in the southwest and Murcia and Valencia in the southeast are gaining interest. Extremadura is dominated by the large region of **Ribera del Guadiana DO,** where the best wines are Tempranillo-based reds. Murcia and Valencia are located on the Mediterranean coastline, and the wine regions there focus mostly on red wines made from Tempranillo, Monastrell, and, increasingly, international varietals like Syrah. Most of these regions are unknown to most of the world, but in time that will most likely change. Some of the emerging appellations here include Valencia DO, Almansa DO, Yecla DO, Jumilla DO, and Bullas DO.

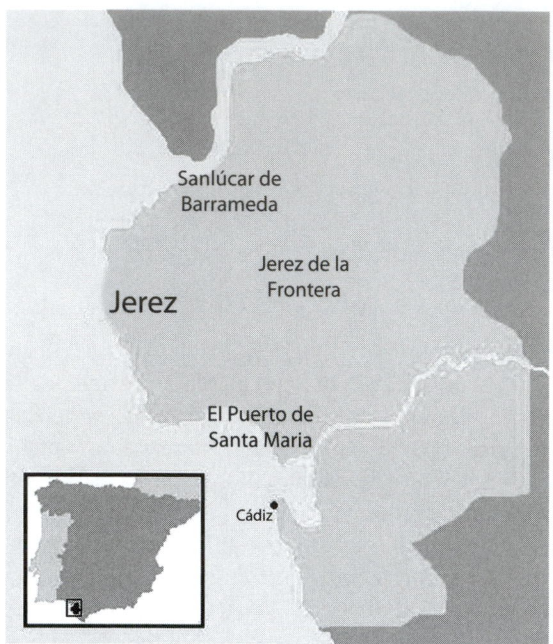

Jerez DO.

Sherry: The World's Greatest Wine Value

Fortified wine produced in the appellation of Jerez, commonly referred to by its English name, **Sherry,** is quite possibly the greatest wine for the money in the world. Sherry's pedigree is long and storied, its production complicated and labor intensive, and its quality—in the hands of a top producer—is unquestionable. Once considered one of the world's greatest wines, as well as one of the most sought after, Sherry has fallen on hard times in recent history as consumers have lost touch with these treasures of southern Spain.

The Facts on Jerez

CLIMATE

Jerez is located along the Atlantic coastline of southern Spain and can have a fiercely hot climate which is tempered only by ocean influences.

TOP WHITE GRAPE

- Palomino

IMPORTANT STYLES OF SHERRY

Fino-Style Sherries

- Fino Sherry
- Manzanilla Sherry
- Amontillado Sherry

Oloroso-Style Sherries

- Oloroso Sherry
- Cream Sherry
- Pedro Ximénez (PX) Sherry

IMPORTANT INFORMATION

- "Sherry" is the English term for Jerez, and the name most commonly used to describe the wines of this region, which are considered to be some of the world's most classic fortified wines.
- Sherry is produced using unique techniques and practices that result in a wide range of styles, from bone dry to syrupy sweet, and light and crisp to intense and heavy.
- Many Sherries rely heavily for their flavor profile on the solera system, a system of fractional blending in which wines from many different vintages are slowly mixed and aged for extended periods of time. This leads to heavy oxidation and unique caramel and dried fruit–rich flavors.

Jerez is located on the Atlantic side of the southern tip of Spain, almost guarding the entrance to the Mediterranean Sea from the vast ocean, and has been populated for millennia. Phoenician traders first planted wine grapes in the region before 1000 B.C., and the vineyards of Jerez continued to flourish when it became part of the Roman Empire. In the early 700s, Jerez and the rest of southern Spain came under control of the Moors. Despite the fact that these Muslim conquerors forbade the consumption of alcohol, wine production still continued for over five hundred years of Moorish occupation. In fact, the Moors introduced Jerez to the process of distillation, and the brandies produced from this process were eventually used to fortify wines in the region. The fortification of Jerez's wines helped to preserve them and they were commonly stocked aboard ships bound for long voyages. In fact, Christopher Columbus set sail on his legendary voyage to the New World in 1492 from Sanlúcar de Barrameda, located in Jerez, loaded with fortified wines from the region. The true rise to prominence for the wines of Jerez began in the late 1500s, however, as they were discovered by the English.

After English trading posts in southern Spain were kicked out of the country by the Spanish king, the English king responded by dispatching a naval fleet under the command of Sir Francis Drake. In 1587 the English fleet attacked and destroyed a fleet of Spanish ships docked in the port of Cádiz, still the most important city in Jerez. After their victory, the English hauled off more than 400,000 gallons of wine from Jerez and took it back with them to England. This began the English love affair with Sherry. In fact, to this day, many of the wineries of Jerez are owned and operated by English companies, and certain styles of Sherry were developed specifically for the English market.

From the 1600s to the early 1800s, Sherry was considered one of the world's greatest wines. Owing to its extended shelf life, it was traded extensively throughout Europe and the American colonies. With the growing wine industry in Jerez came unsustainable growth, however, and quality levels began to drop significantly. After *phylloxera* hit the region in the late 1800s, winemakers were quite slow in replanting on resistant rootstock once it became available. By the time Jerez got back on its feet, its market and fame were fading quickly.

Today, Sherry is a very misunderstood wine. Most believe it to be a cooking wine or a simple dessert wine, but true Sherry is neither. Diligent winemakers in the region have refocused their talents on quality production, but the prices for the top Sherries are amazingly low. With the range of styles and the complex and interesting flavor profiles produced in Jerez, these wines still rank among some of the best in the world.

This southern region is quite hot, and the blazing sun is tempered only by ocean breezes that come off of the Atlantic. Throughout the region, much of the soil is a bright white clay called *albariza* which contains significant amounts of chalk and is ideally suited to the grape varieties of the region. The winemaking appellation of **Jerez DO** is located within the triangle created by the three most important production areas in the region. **Sanlúcar de Barrameda** is found along the Atlantic coastline in the northernmost area, **Jerez de la Frontera,** which is centrally located and the furthest inland, and **El Puerto de Santa Maria,** the southernmost point along the port of Cádiz.

There are only three grapes legally grown in the Jerez DO: Palomino, Pedro Ximénez, and Moscatel. By far, the most important of these three to the region is Palomino, which represents more than 90 percent of the vineyard plantings. Palomino is prized for producing Sherry for what at first seems an odd reason: it produces bland wines. This bland character would be bad for a dry table wine, but provides a clean slate or a blank canvas on which the winemakers of Jerez can practice their skills. Sherry does not derive its flavor profile from the grapes used in its production, but rather from the production itself.

Pedro Ximénez grapes are sometimes used to produce sweet Sherries on their own, but are more commonly used as sweeteners for Palomino-based Sherries. The ultraripe grapes are usually dried in the sun for a few days so they can raisin and their sugars can be concentrated before they are crushed and pressed. The resulting extremely sweet juice is called *vino dulce*, which is added just prior to bottling to

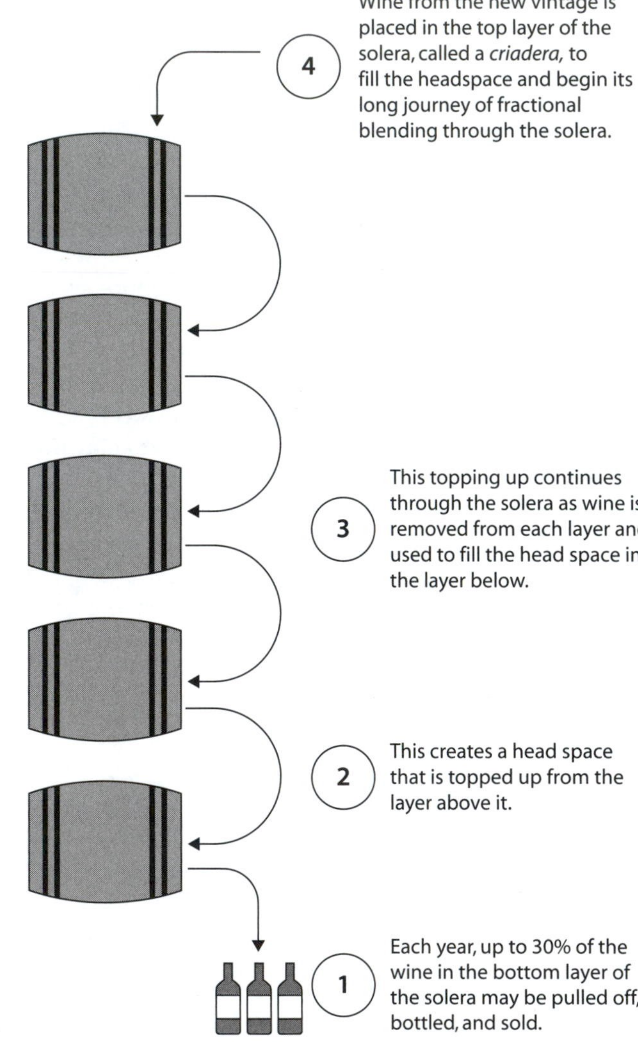

A solera system.

produce sweet styles of Sherry. Moscatel vineyards are becoming exceedingly scarce in Jerez, but this grape—known as Muscat of Alexandria in other parts of the world—is still used, like Pedro Ximénez, as a base for a sweetener, or more commonly as a means to color Sherries. The must of Moscatel grapes is cooked for more than a day, intensely darkening its color to produce what is known as *vino de color,* which is added to a Sherry just prior to bottling, giving it a darker color.

The winemaking techniques used to produce Sherry are quite different from those used to produce most wines. After being fermented completely dry, the wines are then fortified with grape spirits. Once fortified, they are graded (see below) and are then placed in a system of barrels filled with blends of multiple vintages of wine, called a **solera.** One of the unique aspects of winemaking in Jerez is the use of the solera system, a labor-intensive process of aging and blending.

A solera is basically made up of a number of different layers of large American oak barrels called butts. There may be as few as four or as many as fourteen layers in a solera, sometimes stacked on top of one another or stored in different parts of an aging facility. The bottom layer of a solera contains the oldest wine in the solera, and each year up to 30 percent of the wine in this bottom layer is drawn out and bottled. This creates a headspace in the barrels that make up the bottom layer, which is then filled up with wine pulled out of the next oldest layer above it. The barrels used to fill the bottom layer are then topped off by the layer above them, and this process continues up the layers in a solera until the youngest layer, sometimes called the *criadera* or nursery, has partially emptied barrels. The new wine from that year's vintage is then placed in the criadera and begins its journey through the solera.

The consistent flavor profile of a house style is the goal of this process in the solera, as all of its different parts are blended together. This slow but dynamic process of blending different vintages allows each new vintage to become absorbed by the solera. It also allows for significant exposure to oxidation over time, unless something occurs in the wine that protects it from oxygen. The final product of Sherry that is pulled out of the bottom layer in a solera is therefore a multivintage blend made up of components of possibly dozens of different vintages—complex and consistent, year after year.

There are two basic types of Sherry: **fino** style and **oloroso** style. Much of the difference between the two is what happens to them as they spend time in the solera. After fermentation, wines in Jerez are tasted, graded, and classified into one or the other of these two types, with the more pale, aromatic, and lightest wines usually classified as fino-style Sherries. Once designated, the two styles begin to be treated in very different ways.

It is typical for fino-style Sherries to be only minimally fortified with grape spirits after fermentation to an alcoholic strength of roughly 15 percent alcohol by volume. The wines are then placed in used barrels which are not filled completely, usually only about 75 percent full. At this point, the hope is that a special type of yeast found only in Jerez will form naturally on the surface of the aging wine within a month or two. This yeast, called **flor,** then forms a thick blanket floating on the surface of the immature fino-style Sherry. The flor serves two major purposes that make fino-style Sherries unique. First, it protects the wine from oxidation—even though component wines might spend several years in a solera before being bottled, they typically emerge light in color and delicate in nature, lacking heavy oxidation flavors like caramel and dried fruit. Second, this strain of wild yeast slowly consumes acids in the wine, making fino-style Sherries some of the least acidic wines in the world. This biological aging process is unique to Jerez, and much time and effort is utilized to allow its development. When pulled out of a solera to be bottled, fino-style Sherries are light, dry, and often reminiscent of bread dough and toasted nuts.

Important Styles of Fino-Style Sherries

Fino Sherry The most classic and widely produced fino-style Sherry, Fino Sherries are light, crisp, and dry. Fino Sherries are some of the least acidic wines in the world because of the acid-consuming action of the flor yeast that protects the wine from oxidation during aging. Delicate by nature, these wines are often reminiscent of toasted almonds and should be consumed within a day or two after opening before they lose their freshness.

Manzanilla Sherry Produced only in the seaside district of Sanlúcar de Barrameda, this is one of the palest, lightest, and most delicate of the fino-style Sherries. Ocean breezes impart an almost briny or salty character to these aromatic wines. Manzanilla Sherries are light and dry, and should be consumed as fresh as possible. They will only last a day or two after the bottle is opened, so most winemakers use smaller, 500-milliliter bottles.

Amontillado Sherry An Amontillado Sherry is a fino-style Sherry that receives significantly more aging than a fino or manzanilla, much of it without the presence of flor yeast. This additional aging and exposure to oxidation produce a rich, dry, dark, nutty-flavored style of Sherry.

Oloroso-style Sherries, on the other hand, are often fortified to 18 percent alcohol by volume or higher. At this level of alcohol, it would be impossible for flor to survive on an oloroso-style Sherry. Following fortification, these wines are often put through an extended aging period in soleras with multiple layers. During this time, the wines become extremely oxidized, becoming darker in color, richer in flavor, and often fuller in body.

Important Styles of Oloroso-Style Sherries

Oloroso Sherry Oloroso Sherries are often dark, rich, and full-bodied—exposed to significant amounts of oxidation while in the solera and then sweetened to varying degrees by the addition of sweeteners, usually from concentrated Pedro Ximénez grape juice. These wines are often heavily fortified to 18 percent abv or more, and as such will stay flavorful for weeks after opening.

Cream Sherry These specialty oloroso-style cream Sherries were first produced for export to the English market. They are usually quite heavily fortified and intensely sweetened with concentrated Pedro Ximénez grape juice. While some top-quality examples exist today, most are mass-produced, simple, and oversweetened.

Pedro Ximénez (PX) Sherry Unlike most Sherries, which are produced from the juice of Palomino grapes, PX Sherries take their name from the Pedro Ximénez grape, which is usually reserved for sweetening wines, not making them. These grapes result in ultrarich, almost black-colored Sherries rich with dried fruit and burnt sugar characteristics.

Besides the major styles of Sherry produced in Jerez, there are several lesser-known styles. One unique and rarely produced style is palo cortado Sherry, which is an amontillado Sherry that has been aged an unusually long time to the point when its body and palate begin to take on the characteristics of a dry oloroso Sherry. A sweetened fino-style Sherry is called pale cream Sherry, made sweet with the addition of pure sugar so as not to affect the light color and delicate aromas. East India Sherry is made to resemble Sherries of old that were shipped around the world in the holds of ships. Constant churning from the waves and intensely hot conditions would cause these Sherries to oxidize and age quickly, leading to a dark brown color and almost maderized or cooked flavors. Another sweet style of Sherry is rayas Sherry. These are oloroso-style Sherries that are allowed to age exposed to the sun for a year or two. This hastens oxidation and concentrates the wine through evaporation.

OTHER SPANISH FORTIFIED WINES

The scorching conditions found in the province of Andalucía in southern Spain are home to the country's top fortified wines. Andalucía is best known for the Sherry produced in Jerez, but there are two other distinctive fortified DO regions located just north. Both **Montilla-Moriles DO** and **Málaga DO** specialize in sweet, dark, oxidized white wines that are often reminiscent of burnt sugar, olives, and dried fruits. Pedro Ximénez is the most common grape in both appellations, although some Moscatel is used, especially in Málaga.

Summary

Spain is a land of long traditions and new beginnings. After a period of struggle and modernization in the many famous regions of the country, Spain has emerged once again as a leading producer of wine. Famous for its many traditional regions and wines, such as the red wines of Rioja and Ribera del Duero, sparkling wines of Cava, and fortified wines of Jerez, Spain has also introduced many new regions to the world in the past few years that are making exciting and distinctive wines. Expect new innovations and old traditions to continue producing some of the best wines in the world here on the Iberian Peninsula.

Review Questions

1. Spain ranks ________ in the world in terms of wine production.
   - A. first
   - B. second
   - C. third
   - D. fourth

2. Overall, the climate in Spain gets much warmer the further south one travels.
   - A. True
   - B. False

3. The most important red grape grown in Spain is ________.
   - A. Garnacha
   - B. Tempranillo
   - C. Abariño
   - D. Monastrell

4. The wine laws of Spain are known as the ________ laws.
   - A. AOC
   - B. DOC
   - C. DOCa
   - D. DO

5. The highest quality classification for appellations in Spain accounts for roughly 50 percent of the country's total production.
   - A. True
   - B. False

Match the following winemaking regions of Spain to the predominant style of wine produced there. Some answers may be used more than once, and some not at all.

6. Rioja DOCa	A. Dry white wines
7. Ribera del Duero DOCa	B. Sparkling wines
8. Rías Baixas DO	C. Dry red wines
9. Cava DO	D. Fortified wines
10. Priorato DOCa	
11. Jerez DO	

12. Which of the following is *not* one of the approved grapes used in the production of Rioja?
    - A. Tempranillo
    - B. Verdejo
    - C. Garnacha
    - D. Mazuelo

13. Although most top-quality wines produced in Spain are labeled by region, wines produced in Rías Baixas DO from 100 percent Albariño grapes may be labeled by grape variety.
    - A. True
    - B. False

14. Which of the following is *not* a major difference between the wines of Cava and Champagne?
    - A. Approved grape varieties
    - B. Climate in region of origin
    - C. Winemaking techniques
    - D. All of the above are major differences

15. What is the name of the unique system used to age Sherry?
    - A. Solera
    - B. Flor
    - C. Oloroso
    - D. Manzanilla

Key Terms

- *Denominaciónes de Origen* laws
- *consejo reguladore*
- *vino de mesa*
- *vino de la tierra*
- *Vino de Calidad con Indicación Geográfica*
- *Denominación de Origen* (DO)
- *Denominación de Origen Calificada* (DOCa)
- *vino de pago*
- *Vinto tinto*
- *Vino blanco*
- *Vino rosado*
- *Bodega*
- *Seco*
- *Dulce*
- *Joven*
- *crianza*
- *reserva*
- *gran reserva*
- Rioja DOCa
- Rioja Alta
- Rioja Alavesa
- Rioja Baja
- Ribera del Duero DOCa
- Vega Sicilia
- *método tradicional*
- Cava DO
- Rías Baixas DO
- Priorato DOCa
- Toro DO
- Bierzo DO
- Rueda DO
- Navarra DO
- Cariñena DO
- Calatayud DO
- Penedès DO
- Tarragona DO
- La Mancha DO
- Valdepeñas DO
- Ribera del Guadiana DO
- Sherry
- Jerez DO
- Sanlúcar de Barrameda
- Jerez de la Frontera
- El Puerto de Santa Maria
- solera
- fino Sherry
- oloroso Sherry
- flor
- manzanilla Sherry
- amontillado Sherry
- cream Sherry
- Pedro Ximénez Sherry
- Montilla-Moriles DO
- Málaga DO

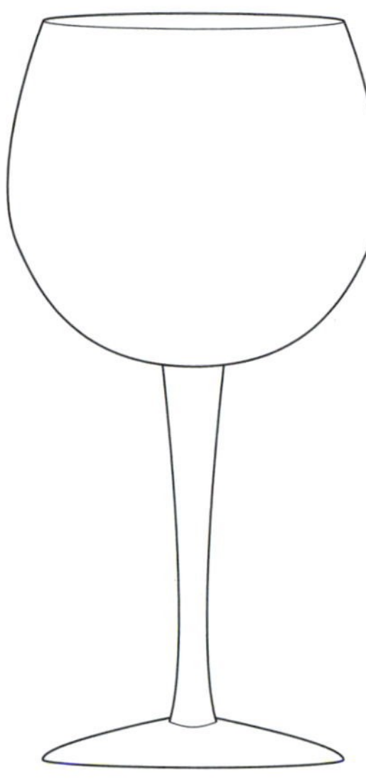

CHAPTER 12

The Wines of Germany

Drink wine, and you will sleep well. Sleep, and you will not sin. Avoid sin, and you will be saved. Ergo, drink wine and be saved.

—Medieval German saying

Germany has a wine industry unique in Europe. While most of the wine-producing countries in Europe model their wine laws and regulations after the French system, Germany has its own way of doing things. This chapter discusses the wines of Germany: the grapes they grow, the wines they produce, their unique wine laws and classification system, and their top regions.

The Facts on Germany

CLIMATE

Germany is home to the northernmost premium vineyards in the world, where grapes grow in a cool to cold climate.

TOP WHITE GRAPES

- Riesling
- Gewürztraminer
- Müller-Thurgau

TOP RED GRAPE

- Spätburgunder (Pinot Noir)

TOP REGIONS

- Mosel (Mosel-Saar-Ruwer)
- Pfalz (Rheinpfalz)
- Rheinhessen
- Rheingau

IMPORTANT INFORMATION

- Germany ranks ninth in the world for wine production.
- Ripeness is quite often the main concern for winemakers in Germany, as their wine laws and quality classifications are all built around the sugar content of grapes at harvest.
- Germany produces a wide range of wine styles from sweet to dry, growing mostly white grapes like the famous Riesling, but also producing significant amounts of red wine.
- The main wine regions of Germany are almost all located near the Rhine River, in the warmer southwestern part of the country.

Germany: The Battle for Ripeness

Germany is first and foremost a beer-drinking country. Of all the major European wine-producing countries, Germany ranks as one of the lowest in per capita wine consumption. Regardless, they have developed a unique, top-quality wine industry that produces some of the best cool-climate wines in the world. Germany is home to piercing dry wines and lush dessert wines, and is the origin of one of the most acclaimed white wine grape varietals grown anywhere: Riesling.

Similar to many other European countries, Germany was introduced to winemaking by the ancient Romans. The first records for wine production date back to the first century A.D., after Roman legions first invaded the Germanic lands. Subsequent centuries and the spread of Christianity saw winemaking expand, and wine became a more popular beverage throughout Germany.

From the Middle Ages until the 1800s winemaking in Germany was almost exclusively controlled by the Catholic Church. Monastic wineries and vineyards produced the largest quantity and highest quality of wine in the country. Winemaking most likely reached its peak in Germany sometime around the 1500s, after thousands of vineyards and wine regions had been established along the Rhine River and throughout the warmer southern areas. The popularity of beer and centuries of warfare slowly led to a decline of winemaking in Germany and to a shrinking amount of wine produced.

Germany is quite famous for its late harvest dessert wines, and many unique styles of sweet wines are produced there today. The myth surrounding the beginnings of these sweet styles is based on an event that took place in 1775. The top wine region in Germany at the time was Rheingau, and one of its best vineyard parcels dedicated to Riesling vines is Schloss Johannisberg. A courier on his way to this region with documents that granted permission for the vineyard workers to begin harvesting was delayed for two weeks. During this time, the grapes were infected with botrytis, which concentrated their sugar content dramatically. Normally these mold-covered grapes would have been discarded, but with an official decree to pick the grapes, they were harvested anyway. Surprising everyone with their quality and rich sweetness, the resulting wines became a model for late harvested dessert wines produced throughout Germany. This marked the beginnings of the development of Germany's unique system of quality classifications based on ripeness.

The early 1900s was a time of limited wine production and decreases in quality as Germany fought and lost two world wars. As a result, one of their top wine regions was stripped from the country as the disputed district of Alsace was ceded to France in the late 1940s. Many German wine regions had been destroyed by the ravages of warfare, and the wines that were produced typically ended up in semisweet, low-grade bulk blends. This style is still associated with German winemaking, even though the country has rebuilt its wine regions and regained much of its former glory.

Today, Germany is considered one of the top wine-producing countries of Europe. It ranks ninth in the world in terms of wine production, behind only France, Italy, and Spain for European producers. Well-known for its sweet white wines, Germany is home to a variety of different styles, and most of its production is actually geared toward dry wine production. Germany has seen a steady increase in the amount of red wine produced in the country in recent years, and a steady increase in plantings of Riesling, showing the country's commitment to quality. Germany even makes copious amounts of a sparkling wine called **Sekt,** producing twice as much annually as the French region of Champagne.

Due to the cold conditions in Germany, ripeness is one of the most important considerations when making wine. Fully ripened grapes produce wines that qualify for Germany's top quality classifications, and this often dictates the value of a wine. German winemakers go to great extremes to maximize ripeness in their grapes, from planting on steep slopes to maximize sun exposure to the development of quick-ripening hybrids and crosses. Ripeness is everything to a German winemaker, and each year they diligently battle to ripen their grapes to the highest degree possible.

The Steepest Vineyard in the World

Planting vines on slopes to maximize their exposure to the sun has long been practiced in Germany, but it can be taken to the extreme in some German growing sites. The steepest vineyard in the world is along the banks of the Mosel River. Called Calmont, the vines there seem to have been planted on the side of a cliff, as the slope can be up to a 76-degree grade.

Wine Laws of Germany

Germany has developed one of the most unique systems of regulations and quality classifications for wine in the world. In most wine-producing countries, laws center on specified, official regions and styles. German winemaking laws are based on a completely different premise—the one thing always on the minds of German winemakers—ripeness.

Unlike most premium European wines, German wines are most often labeled by grape variety rather than region or appellation. This stems from a long history of developing and breeding different grape varietals suited to the unique conditions found in the country's varied wine regions. If a grape is not listed on the label of a German wine, this indicates that the wine was made from a blend of different grapes. These wines will list the quality classification of the wine, which is what the wine should be called.

Sometimes, wines will be labeled by a unique style instead of by a grape variety. The most famous of these is **Liebfraumilch,** a typically mass-produced, semisweet, soft white wine. These styles are usually lower in quality, and should not be confused with the more important varietal wines of Germany.

Most of Germany's top wines are labeled by grape variety, unlike most European countries' that are labeled by region.

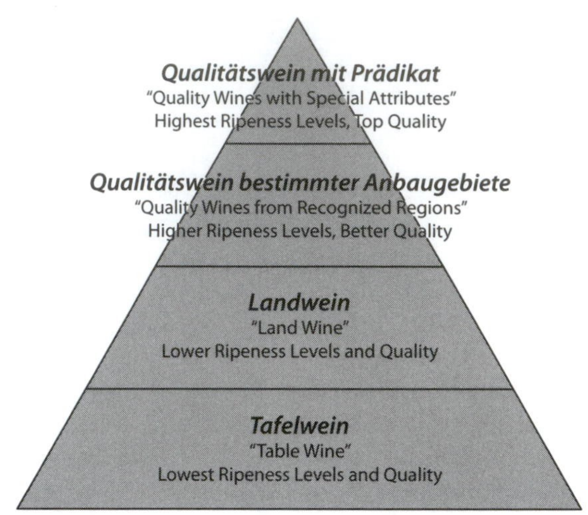

The four major German wine quality classifications.

Wines are strictly regulated, and individual wines are judged each vintage based on their unique characteristics from that harvest. Strict quality testing is done using both laboratory equipment and sensory analysis conducted by a panel of experts. Each wine that passes at least minimum quality control standards is awarded an official test number, called an **Amtliche Prüfungsnummer** or **A.P.Nr.** Under this system, individual wines are judged each year on their own merits. A wine made by the same winemakers from the same vineyards may qualify for a different quality classification each year. In this way, the German wine laws can be helpful because they are specific to each individual wine.

The ripeness level and resulting sugar content of grapes are what defines and classifies wines in Germany. Sugar content of grape juice or must at harvest is determined by density, using a unit of measurement called degrees **Oechsle.** This measure can be used to estimate the potential alcohol content in a wine once fermented, and is used to classify wines into a hierarchy of quality. Wines are divided into four major categories based on the degrees Oechsle of the grapes used to produce them: ***Tafelwein, Landwein, Qualitätswein bestimmter Anbaugebiete*** **(QbA)**, and ***Qualitätswein mit Prädikat*** **(QmP)** in ascending order.

For all but the highest classification, *Qualitätswein mit Prädikat,* ripeness is at such a low level in the grapes that a wine cannot be made without the addition of sugar during fermentation. The process of adding sugar, usually in the form of beet sugar or cane sugar, to fermenting wines is called **chaptalization.** This is done to raise the alcohol content of a wine by as much as 3.5 percent, and chaptalized wines must be completely fermented until dry by law.

While this helps the winemaker achieve minimum alcohol levels, it will throw off the balance of many wines. High acid levels, the result of unripe grapes, often have to be masked by the addition of ***Süssreserve*** (sweet, unfermented grape juice) just prior to bottling. There are some quality wines produced in Germany that are chaptalized, but higher natural ripeness in grapes is always preferred. Chaptalization is also common in Austria and the colder regions of France, where the practice originated.

The two lowest quality classifications, made from the least ripe grapes harvested each year, are *Tafelwein* and *Landwein. Tafelwein* is the lowest quality classification, and the term translates to "table wine"—the same designation used for the lowest-quality wines in almost every European country. *Landwein* translates to "land wine," and is made from grapes that are just slightly riper. The grape juice used to produce these wines will often only have enough natural sugar to achieve a few percentage points of alcohol content. Chaptalization is heavily used to increase fermentable sugars. *Tafelwein* and *Landwein* make up only a small percentage of the wines produced in Germany, and are very rarely exported. If a *Tafelwein* or *Landwein* is made from 100 percent German-grown grapes, it will be labeled "Deutscher Tafelwein" or "Deutscher Landwein."

A "quality wine" or *Qualitätswein* in Germany is made from riper grapes that range from just under-ripe to overripe. These represent the best wines produced in Germany, and account for roughly 95 percent of the country's production. The flavor and sweetness of these wines can vary widely, and many different sweetness designations are used on wine labels. Quality wines are broken up into two major categories: *Qualitätswein bestimmter Anbaugebiete* (QbA) and *Qualitätswein mit Prädikat* (QmP).

QbA wines will be labeled with the designation "Qualitätswein." This classification is for wines made from grapes that just miss the amount of degrees Oechsle necessary to be produced without chaptalization. *Qualitätswein bestimmter Anbaugebiete* translates to "quality wine from a recognized region" and these must be made from approved grapes grown in the thirteen official winemaking regions of Germany. The region will be listed on the label. Wines in the QbA classification are often sweetened with *Süssreserve* to help balance their naturally higher levels of acidity just prior to bottling. They are often solid wines that are reasonably priced.

Wines made from grapes that have achieved at least minimum levels of natural ripeness so that chaptalization is unnecessary fall into the top quality classification of German wine, QmP. The term *Qualitätswein mit Prädikat* means "quality wine with special attributes" and represents the best dry, semisweet, and dessert wines produced in Germany. Like QbA wines, they must be made from approved grapes that have naturally ripened in one of the thirteen official German wine regions. The category is further divided into six different style designations which will be listed on the label and identify the wines as being in the QmP classification. These styles from least to most ripe are ***Kabinett, Spätlese, Auslese, Beerenauslese* (BA), *Eiswein*,** and ***Trockenbeerenauslese* (TBA).**

THE STYLES OF QMP

Kabinett

The style designation known as *Kabinett* applies to wines made from grapes that just qualify for minimum QmP ripeness levels, generally considered a normal harvest in Germany. This is the lightest of the QmP styles in both body and alcohol, usually bottled at 7 percent to 10 percent abv. Wines in this style tend to be intensely high in acidity, and though they can be produced dry, it is more likely to find them off dry or semisweet. While the grapes used to make these wines are technically considered ripe, they would be considered unripe in most wine

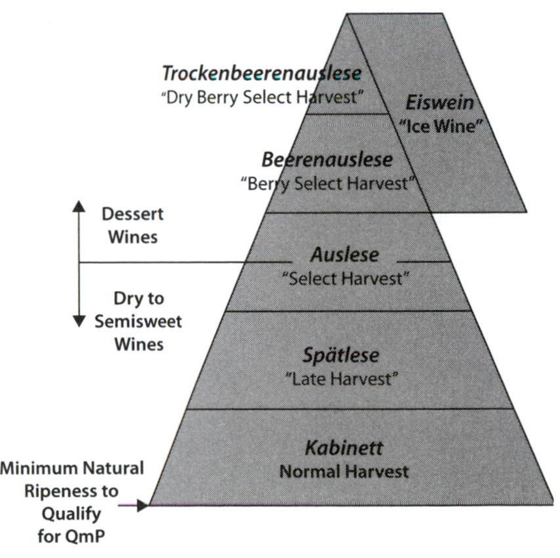

The six styles of QmP.

regions. *Kabinett* literally translates to "cabinet," an old reference to premium wines that were put away or stored.

Spätlese

Spätlese is the German term for "late harvest," a style of wines made from grapes harvested a couple of weeks after the *Kabinett* harvest. This extra time on the vine allows the grapes to ripen more fully, meaning more body and alcohol. Wines of this style designation will usually have more concentrated flavors than lower designations. *Spätlese* wines will range from dry to sweet depending upon the characteristics of the individual wine, the vintage, and the winemaker's preference.

Auslese

The term *Auslese* means "select harvest," referring to the practice of harvesting only very ripe bunches of grapes by hand. These are often full-bodied white wines with intense flavors and aromas. *Auslese*-style wines can be produced only in warmer years, when grapes have enough time on the vine to achieve peak ripeness. Grapes for these wines are typically harvested in late November to early December. While predominantly a style produced into semisweet or dessert wines, *Auslese* wines can also be made in a dry style. Dry *Auslese* wines are among the highest-alcohol wines produced in Germany due to their significant sugar levels at harvest, sometimes achieving 14 percent abv or more.

Beerenauslese (BA)

Meaning "berries select harvest," *Beerenauslese* or BA style wines are some of the sweetest, richest, and rarest wines produced in Germany. *Beerenauslese* wines are made from overripe *Auslese* grapes that have almost always been naturally infected with botrytis, known as ***edelfäule*** (meaning "noble rot") in German. Certain fast-ripening, but lower-quality, grape varieties can sometimes achieve the concentration of sugar to qualify, but they are often not highly regarded.

Botrytis must form on the grape bunches naturally, and only certain vineyards in the various regions of Germany are affected. *Beerenauslese* wines are always intensely sweet and syrupy because of heightened sugar levels, and fermentation is never allowed to fully progress. These high sugar levels also mean that this style of wine can have amazing longevity, maturing in the bottle for decades. Due to its naturally high acidity, Riesling almost always produces the top *Beerenauslese* wines. This acidity helps to balance out the sugary sweetness.

Trockenbeerenauslese (TBA)

Trockenbeerenauslese, also known as TBA, is the style designation for wines made from grapes with the highest sugar concentration at harvest in Germany. Producers are lucky to make them once or twice a decade because near perfect conditions are necessary for the grapes to reach this point. ***Trocken*** is the German word for "dry," but in this connotation the term dry does not describe the sweetness level of the wine; TBA wines are some of the sweetest wines produced on Earth. *Trockenbeerenauslese*

The grapes used to produce *Eiswein* are hand harvested when they are partially frozen on the vine.

translates to "dry berries select harvest" with the "dry" reference being to the berries (grapes)—in other words, this is a wine made from grapes that have begun to turn into raisins!

If *Beerenauslese*-level grapes, already some of the sweetest in the world, are allowed to sit on the vine for extended periods they will begin to dry out on the vine. As these botrytis-infected, ultraripe grapes start to shrivel as more moisture is drawn out of them, sugar concentrates to its highest levels. As a result, *Trockenbeerenauslese* wines are some of the sweetest, most intense, richest, and thickest dessert wines produced in the world.

Eiswein

The cold conditions found in German wine regions can make grape growing very difficult, but winemakers there have adapted to the climate and learned to use it to their advantage. One way they do this is by allowing the weather itself to help them concentrate sugar levels in grapes for a style designation known as *Eiswein*. German for "ice wine," *Eiswein* refers to wines produced from partially frozen grapes.

If grapes freeze completely solid, their skins will split open and their juice is often degraded—a disaster for normal wine production. On the other hand, partially frozen grapes harvested at 12°F to 17°F contain ice crystals, providing an opportunity to produce world-class dessert wines. In Germany, *Eiswein* is made from grapes with *Beerenauslese*-level ripeness to start with that must reach the partially frozen stage naturally on the vine. Often picked at night, the partially frozen grapes are taken to a special wine crusher and press located outdoors so that it will not thaw the grape juice while initially processing it. As the juice is pressed away from the grape solids, water crystals are removed, further concentrating sugar levels and flavor in these decadent, ultrasweet dessert wines.

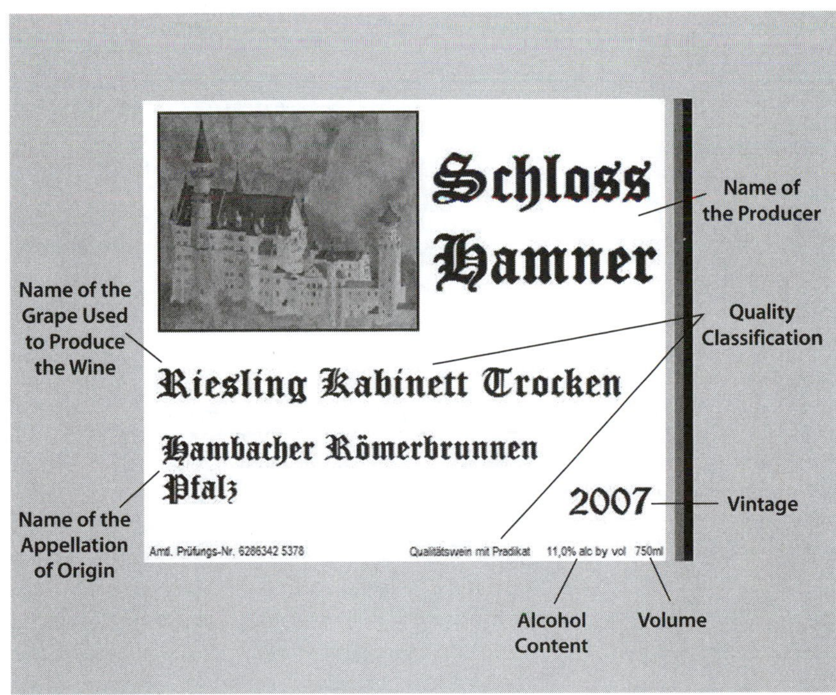

How to read a German wine label.

German Label Terms

Author Kingsley Amis once wrote, "A German wine label is one of the things life's too short for," and there is much truth in that. German winemakers have established very intricate laws with several qualifications, styles, regional terms, and special designations. Below are some label terms you might find on German wine labels.

TERM	DEFINITION
Rotwein	Red wine
Weisswein	White wine
Weissherbst	Rosé wine
Trocken	Dry or containing very little residual sugar
Halbtrocken	Off dry, containing some residual sugar; if this term or *Trocken* does not appear on the label, then the wine in question is most likely made in a sweet style.
Classic	Along with "Selection," this term was adopted in 2000 in an attempt to simplify German wine labels for consumers. Classic wines must come from one of Germany's thirteen recognized wine regions, or *Anbaugebiete*, made from a grape varietal traditional to that region. The wine must be produced in a drier style, with a slight amount of sweetness at most (balanced with the wine's acidity), and be produced from ripe grapes having an alcohol content of at least 12% by volume (11.5% in Mosel).
Selection	Selection wines are similar to Classic in that they are produced in a drier style and must be made from ripe grapes (in this case, at least *Auslese*-level ripeness must be achieved) traditional to a recognized region, but they must also meet stricter additional qualifications. For a wine to qualify for Selection status it must come from a recognized, individual vineyard site (known as an *Einzellage*) and be made from hand-harvested grapes, and yields in the vineyard are severely restricted.
Weingut	A wine estate
Gutsabfüllung/ Erzeugerabfüllung	Translates roughly to "estate bottled." The wine has to be made and bottled by the winemaker, and produced from grapes grown in vineyards the winemaker owns.
VDP	Acronym for the ***Verband Deutscher Prädikatsweingüter***, a private association of top-quality winemakers found throughout most of Germany's recognized regions that established an official designation system for top wine estates and promotes the wine they produce. Member estates use the terms *Erste Lage* and *Grosses Gewächs* on their labels and use a distinctive capsule on the bottle displaying an eagle with a cluster of grapes.
Erste Lage	Classified estate recognized by the VDP, similar to a "first growth" estate in France. To utilize this term, the recognized estate must produce a wine from grapes that have been hand harvested, meet minimum ripeness levels, and enforce strict limits on yield; called an ***erstes Gewächs*** in the region of Rheingau.
Grosses Gewächs	Similar to an *erste Lage* except that the estate must be dedicated to the production of dry wines.

Important Grapes of Germany

Only select grape varietals can survive the cool climate and northern extremes of Germany, and wines are produced from only a little more than one hundred different grape varietals in the country today. Several grapes have been adapted to these conditions through a process of selection lasting centuries, but many additional crosses and hybrids have been developed by grape growers and horticulturalists over time. Many of these engineered grapes are widely grown throughout Germany because of their fast ripening times and large yields.

White wine production has always far outweighed red production because white grapes do not take as long as most red grapes to ripen. The number of red wines has increased in recent years, however, along with the planting of traditional grapes rather than crosses. Some of the more important grapes grown in Germany today include white varieties like Gewürztraminer and Müller-Thurgau, as well as red varieties such as Spätburgunder and Dornfelder, but none comes close in either importance or quality to Germany's best-known native grape variety: Riesling.

Riesling

The grape most associated with Germany, producing its most famous and highest-quality wines, is Riesling. This international varietal has spread far around the world from its native homeland, but most consider it best when grown in the vineyards of Germany. Riesling is the most widely planted grape varietal in Germany today and makes a wide variety of different styles, from racy, dry wines all the way to some of the sweetest dessert wines in the world—all featuring the grape's hallmark acidity.

This aromatic grape variety does not produce the highest yields and is a slow ripener in comparison with other German grapes, but its cold heartiness and quality more than make up for this. Riesling produces elegant and balanced wines in Germany, whether sweet or dry. Often floral in its youth, German Riesling will have very different flavor characteristics depending upon where it is grown.

Gewürztraminer

Gewürztraminer is one of the most distinctly flavored white wine grapes of Germany, with its unique combination of lychee, rose petals, perfume, and spice.

Gewürztraminer produces white wines with often exotic aromas in Germany.

Though not as widely grown as the other important grape varieties of Germany, Gewürztraminer is still considered one of the top-quality grapes grown in the country. Gewürztraminer is vinified into both dry and sweet styles, but only rarely is it made into a dessert wine.

Müller-Thurgau

Due to its ability to ripen extremely quickly and yield considerable amounts of fruit even in cooler vintages, Müller-Thurgau was until recently the most widely grown grape in Germany. Still today, roughly 20 percent of Germany's vineyards are planted to the grape. In an industry that has generated hundreds of different grape varieties through genetic crosses, Müller-Thurgau (a Riesling cross) is by far the most commercially successful. Although it does ripen much quicker and yield far more than Riesling, it is often severely lacking in acidity and character. Most of the production of Müller-Thurgau in Germany is intended for use in lower-quality, sweetened blends like Liebfraumilch.

Dry versions of Müller-Thurgau are sometimes labeled with another name for the grape, Rivaner.

 Spätburgunder

Spätburgunder, known as Pinot Noir in the rest of the world, literally translates to "late Burgundy," referencing the late-ripening grape of Burgundy. This is the most widely grown red grape varietal in Germany, and produces most of its top red wines. Due to the climate in these northern regions, German Spätburgunder tends to be lean and acidic with tart, red fruit flavors. The quality of German Spätburgunder can range widely, from thin, diluted styles, to rich, oak-aged styles with fuller body and tannin structure. This grape, along with most other red varietals, is almost exclusively grown in the warmest, southern regions of Germany.

Other Notable Grapes

SILVANER Silvaner is a fast-ripening but fairly neutral white wine grape that produces fair-quality dry and semisweet wines. Up until the 1960s, this was the most widely planted grape in Germany, but it has long since been surpassed by Riesling, Müller-Thurgau, and others.

SCHEUREBE A genetic cross of Silvaner and Riesling, Scheurebe produces average dry white wines but some rather good sweet, late harvest wines.

DORNFELDER The second most widely planted red grape in Germany is Dornfelder, which ripens quickly and produces deeply colored red wines that are often fuller-bodied and more tannic than other German reds.

Terroir and Important Regions

Germany is home to some of the northernmost and coldest wine regions in the world. Wine production is mostly limited to the southwestern area of the country, although some regions are clearly above the 50th parallel of latitude, which is the typical limit for viticulture. To put this into perspective, consider that the bulk of the border between Canada and the United States is the 49th parallel! If not for the warming influence of the Gulf Stream on southwestern Germany, winemaking would not be possible. Regardless, ripening periods and warm seasons are short in Germany and only certain grape varieties can thrive there.

Soil types throughout German wine regions can vary greatly, but many of the top vineyards are planted in rocky soil often made of a dark type of rock called slate. This can give wines a strong mineral or flinty characteristic, but it is more important for its ability to absorb energy from the sun, rereleasing it in the form of heat to the vines. German grape growers utilize many different techniques to help maximize the level of ripeness they can achieve in their grapes, with the most common and effective

Many of Germany's top vineyards are planted on steep slopes to maximize sun exposure and ripeness levels.

being maximizing exposure to sunlight by planting on steep, south-facing slopes.

Rivers crisscross the German countryside, and are often responsible for digging deep gorges and river valleys. The most important river flowing through Germany is the Rhine River, and the majority of recognized wine regions are found along this large river or its tributaries. These river valleys give winemakers steep slopes to plant vineyards, allowing vines to catch the full impact of direct sunlight. The best of these sloped vineyards face south toward the sun, translating to full exposure to sunlight, and are often quite steep: grades of 70 degrees or more are not uncommon.

German wine law breaks the wine-producing areas of the country into a large number of geographical units. Lower-quality wines made from very underripe grapes will be labeled with one of the many *Tafelwein* or *Landwein* regions, many of which overlap and cover the top-quality appellations of Germany. Higher-quality wines, where full ripeness is often achieved, are labeled with very specific regions that are broken down into a strict hierarchy based on size.

There are thirteen officially recognized, large winemaking districts located in Germany, referred to as ***Anbaugebiete.*** Each *Anbaugebiet* has distinct boundaries, and *Qualitätswein*-level wines must be made from grapes completely grown in one of these regions. The specific *Anbaugebiet* a wine comes from will be listed on the label.

The *Anbaugebiete* are further broken down into appellations called ***Bereiche.*** A *Bereich* is similar to a large subregion or district, often formed and

Official Geographic Areas

NAME	DESCRIPTION	NUMBER
Anbaugebiet	Large winemaking district	13
Bereich	Specific winemaking area within an *anbaugebiet*	39
Grosslage	Collection of adjoining vineyards within a *bereich*	160+
Einzellage	Individual vineyard site within a *grosslage*	2,600+

The Thirteen Official *Anbaugebiete* of Germany

Ahr	Baden	Franken	Hessische Bergstrasse
Mittelrhein	Mosel	Nahe	
Pfalz	Rheingau	Rheinhessen	Saale-Unstrut
Sachsen	Württemberg		

recognized to signify a high quality of winemaking. There are thirty-nine *Bereiche* found in the thirteen *Anbaugebiete* regions, with some containing only one *bereich* and others as many as nine.

From there, *Bereiche* are divided into ***Grosslagen.*** The term *Grosslage* translates to "large site," and an individual *Grosslage* is made up of a collection of different individual vineyard sites. These *Grosslagen* are intended to represent individual growing communes similar to the specific subregions of Burgundy or Bordeaux that are supposed to highlight superior and unique wine production. In practice, their boundaries just serve the purpose of grouping adjoining vineyards together. There are more than 160 *Grosslagen* in Germany.

The smallest recognized geographic areas in Germany are single vineyards called ***Einzellagen,*** which means "individual sites." There are more than 2,600 official *Einzellagen* in Germany. Each *Einzellage* is found within the boundaries of a *Grosslage,* which must be within a *Bereich* that is located inside an *Anbaugebiet.* As you can see, this system can get quite confusing, and limited production of many wines is the norm in Germany.

Several different label designations are used to indicate the exact origin of each wine. In general, the more specific the listed appellation, the higher in quality a wine will be considered. The *Anbaugebiet* will always be listed on the label before any other geographic designation. For wines made from grapes grown completely within one of the smaller geographic areas found within the thirteen *Anbaugebiete,* this specific region will be listed on the label as well.

For a wine that comes from an individual *Bereich,* the name of that *Bereich* will appear after

German wine label showing an *Anbaugebiet* (Mosel), Village (Piesport), and *Einzellage* (Goldtröpfchen).

the *Anbaugebiet*. The smaller and more specific designations, *grosslage* and *Einzellage*, will also appear on the label preceded by a village name. A *Grosslage* will be listed after the most famous village in the area, and an *Einzellage* will come after the nearest village to the vineyard site.

Of the thirteen *Anbaugebiete*, most are located along the Rhine River or one of its tributaries. Due to the fact that climatic conditions and soil types differ from region to region, each will have its own varietal profiles and classic wine styles. Typically, cooler areas focus on white wine production, growing significant amounts of Riesling. Warmer areas will usually grow a majority of white grapes, but more winemaking focus is dedicated to red wine production. The most famous of the *Anbaugebiete* are Mosel, Pfalz, Rheinhessen, and Rheingau.

MOSEL

Until recently, the **Mosel** *Anbaugebiet* was known as Mosel-Saar-Ruwer. The area is made up of vineyards planted on the steep slopes of the Mosel River and

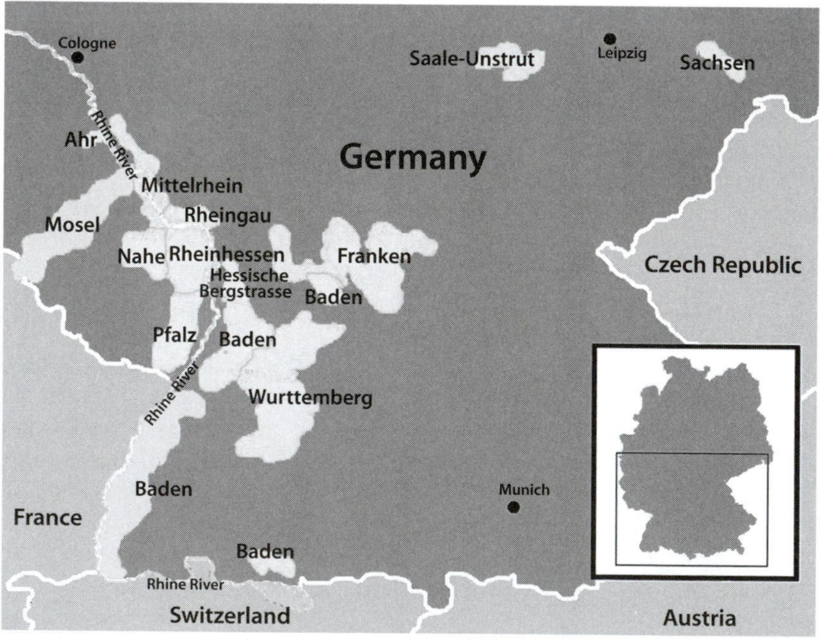

Germany's *Anbaugebiete*, large recognized wine regions.

two tributaries that feed it called the Saar and Ruwer Rivers. It is the westernmost wine region in Germany, as its western tip borders Luxembourg near France. As the Mosel snakes its way northeast, eventually feeding into the Rhine River, it cuts very steep gorges and valleys. Many of the steep slopes that rise from the banks of the river are planted to vines and are often covered with valuable slate. Mosel is the third largest wine-producing region in Germany, and probably the most acclaimed and well known today.

Riesling dominates production in Mosel, with more than half the vineyards in the region dedicated to the varietal. This is one of the more northern *Anbaugebiete* of Germany, and therefore ripeness is often at a premium. Typically wines are relatively low in alcohol and have a piercing zip of acidity that is almost always softened with a touch of sweetness. Traditionally wines from this region are bottled in tall, slender "Rhine" bottles made of green glass. Mosel is home to six *Bereiche*, nineteen *Grosslagen*, and more than five hundred *Einzellagen*. The most famous *Bereiche* are Zell and especially Bernkastel, home to the famous *Grosslage* of Michelsberg near the village of Piesport.

PFALZ

The warmest *Anbaugebiet* of Germany is the **Pfalz** region, formerly known as Rheinpfalz and sometimes called Palatinate. Bordering the Rhine River to the east and France to the south, the southern tip of Pfalz is not far from the northern vineyards of Alsace. Pfalz is one of the most important agricultural regions of Germany in addition to being a top wine region, as the warmer conditions welcome a whole host of different crops, from lemons to figs.

Pfalz is the second largest *Anbaugebiet* in terms of vineyard acreage, but often is the leading production area, yielding more wine than any other. Winemaking varies widely throughout Pfalz, with dry Rieslings of intense power mostly produced in northern areas and whites and reds produced in the south. Many new Dornfelder vineyards have been planted in the Pfalz, producing rich, fruity red wines with aging potential. Pfalz is home to two *Bereiche*, more than twenty *Grosslagen*, and well over three hundred *Einzellagen*.

RHEINHESSEN

Germany's largest recognized wine region in terms of acreage and second leading wine producer is **Rheinhessen.** This region is bordered by Nahe to the west, Pfalz to the south, and the Rhine River to the north and east. The landscape is mostly rolling hills that run along a large plateau, surrounded by thick forests that protect the area from harsh weather. Fertile soils and ample sunshine make Rheinhessen a leading wine region as well as an area covered with farms and orchards.

Varied soil conditions found throughout Rheinhessen allow winemakers there to grow a wide variety of grapes, both white and red. Many of the genetic crosses developed for Germany's cooler climate were bred in this region and still are heavily grown. Aromatic and soft wines are the hallmark of the region, where the most widely planted grape varietals are Müller-Thurgau and Silvaner for white wine production and Dornfelder for reds. Rheinhessen was the birthplace of the style of wine known as Liebfraumilch. There are three *Bereiche* in Rheinhessen, twenty-four *Grosslagen*, and more than four hundred *Einzellagen*.

RHEINGAU

Rheingau is located on the north banks of the Rhine River directly across from Rheinhessen. The region itself is made up of a large hillside that rises from the river's bank, getting progressively steeper the further west you go. A warmer climate is found in Rheingau, as the region is ringed by forests which protect it from cold, northern weather conditions. Almost all of the vineyards planted in Rheingau have a southern orientation, maximizing their exposure to sunlight and ripeness. Mists that rise off the Rhine River can lead to the development of botrytis during the harvest season, and Rheingau produces every style of QmP. In fact, many of the different QmP styles were pioneered and evolved in Rheingau.

Charta Riesling

In 1983, a group of Rheingau winemakers established an association called Charta that was dedicated to increasing the quality and promoting the style of fully ripened, drier Rieslings in the region. Official vineyard sites were recognized, strict regulations and standards were developed, and minimum ripeness levels were determined. In addition, every wine attempting to qualify to become a **Charta Riesling** must be tasted and approved by a special panel judging these prospective wines on their quality and flavor. Today, Charta Rieslings represent some of the best wines produced in Rheingau, and are bottled in tall, tapered brown bottles with the distinctive double Romanesque arch, the symbol of the Charta association.

Historically the most important wine region of Germany, Rheingau has been overtaken in terms of quality and popularity by other regions in recent decades. Winemakers in the region are looking to regain their former glory as they concentrate on planting only the best and most traditional varietals and limiting yields. The most important white grape planted in Rheingau is Riesling, which produces everything from dry, crisp white wines to decadent, botrytised dessert wines. Red wine production is focused on Spätburgunder, which produces rich, velvety wines. There is only one *Bereich* in Rheingau, the famous district of Johannisberg. In addition, there are ten *Grosslagen* and more than one hundred *Einzellagen*.

THE REMAINING ANBAUGEBIETE

Nahe is just to the west of Rheinhessen, and named for the Nahe River, which flows through the region, bound to join up with the Rhine. The region is famous for its various soils, which allow winemakers to grow a wide variety of grapes and produce several different styles. Riesling, Müller-Thurgau, and Dornfelder are the most widely planted varietals. Wines from the Nahe region are traditionally bottled in tall slender bottles made of blue glass.

Located across the river from one another, Mittelrhein and Ahr are the northernmost *Anbaugebiete* located along the banks of the Rhine River. Despite this northern latitude, Ahr (the smallest *Anbaugebiet*) is best known for its red wines made from Spätburgunder and Portugieser grapes. Just to the east, Mittelrhein focuses almost exclusively on Riesling, often planted on steep, slate-covered slopes.

On the eastern banks of the Rhine River in southern Germany, you will find two *Anbaugebiete*: Hessische Bergstrasse and Baden. Both focus on light, fruity white wines, and Müller-Thurgau is the most widely planted grape. Baden is the largest *Anbaugebiet* in terms of size, but vineyards are only sporadically planted throughout the region.

To the east of Baden is Württemberg, Germany's largest red wine–producing region. Württemberg grows many grape varieties that are not found anywhere else in Germany, including Trollinger, Schwarzriesling, and Lemberger. These traditional grapes are still widely grown in Württemberg, but new vineyards have been increasingly planted to Spätburgunder and Dornfelder, Germany's top-quality red varietals.

Franken is a large winemaking district located to the northeast of the Rhine River in Bavaria. Due to its shorter growing season, winemakers in Franken rely on grape varietals that ripen quickly, such as Müller-Thurgau and Silvaner. Many lesser-known genetic crosses are also planted throughout the region, especially Bacchus. Dry white wines are the most common style produced in Franken, and their wines are traditionally bottled in squat, round flagons made of green or brown glass, known as *bocksbeutels*.

There are only two *Anbaugebiete* located in the former East Germany: Saale-Unstrut and Sachsen. Further east and well north of the other wine-producing districts of Germany, they are both relatively small regions with very cold climates. It is uncommon to find QmP-level wines produced in either region, and fast-ripening grapes such as Müller-Thurgau, Weissburgunder (also known as Pinot Blanc), and Silvaner are the most widely planted.

Summary

Germany is a remarkable wine-producing country, adapting to conditions that would probably not even be considered for vineyards in other parts of the world. Through centuries of experimentation and perseverance, Germany has become famous for its distinct and unique styles of wine. The struggle to maximize ripeness in grapes is what defines the country's wines, determining everything from wine styles to official quality classifications, and even the price that can be demanded by a wine at market.

Review Questions

1. German wine laws are based upon what?
   A. Grape variety
   B. Ripeness
   C. Region/*terroir*
   D. French wine laws

2. Which of the following is *not* a top wine region in Germany?
   A. Rheingau
   B. Rheinhessen
   C. Rheinoceros
   D. Rheinpfalz

For the following questions, match the QmP style designation to the correct description. Some answers may be used more than once and some not at all.

3. *Kabinett*
4. *Trockenbeerenauslese* (TBA)
5. *Eiswein*
6. *Beerenauslese* (BA)

A. Highest sugar content; made from raisins
B. Second highest sugar content; botrytised
C. Wine made from partially frozen grapes
D. Lowest sugar content; normal harvest

7. German wines are always sweet.
   A. True
   B. False

8. Chaptalization is a process in which sugar is added to fermenting wine to:
   A. boost alcohol content
   B. add sweetness
   C. discourage bacterial growth
   D. add a fruity flavor

9. The German grape Spätburgunder is known as what in the rest of the world?
   A. Pinot Noir
   B. Riesling
   C. Chardonnay
   D. Syrah

10. The largest designation for a top wine-producing region in Germany is a *Bereich*.
    A. True
    B. False

11. An officially recognized, individual vineyard site in Germany is known as:
    A. an *Anbaugebiet*
    B. a *Bereich*
    C. a *Grosslage*
    D. an *Einzellage*

12. The most widely planted grape in Germany is Riesling.
    A. True
    B. False

Key Terms

Sekt
Liebfraumilch
Amtliche Prüfungsnummer (A.P.Nr.)
Oechsle
Tafelwein
Landwein
Qualitätswein bestimmter Anbaugebiete (QbA)
Qualitätswein mit Prädikat (QmP)
chaptalization
Süssreserve
Qualitätswein
Kabinett
Spätlese
Auslese
Beerenauslese (BA)
Eiswein
Trockenbeerenauslese (TBA)
edelfäule
trocken
halbtrocken
rotwein
weisswein
weissherbst
Classic
Selection
weingut
Gutsabfüllung
Erzeugerabfüllung
Verband Deutscher Prädikatsweingüter (VDP)
erste Lage
erste Gewächs
grosses Gewächs
Spätburgunder
Anbaugebiet
Bereich
Grosslage
Einzellage
Mosel
Pfalz
Rheinhessen
Rheingau
Charta Riesling

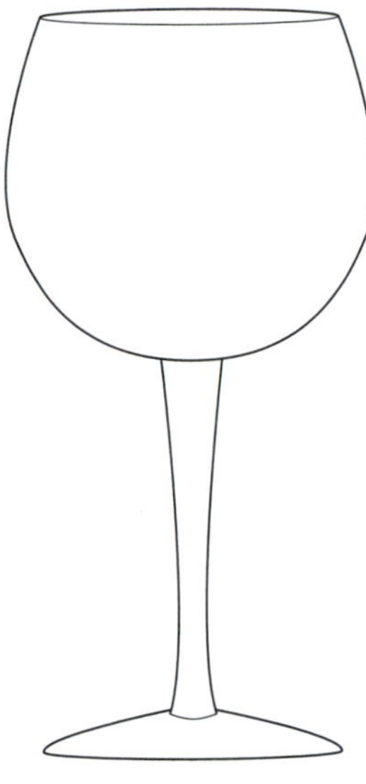

CHAPTER 13

The Wines of Portugal

He pours a radiant nectar, two score and ten years old, that blushes in the glass to find itself so famous, and fills the whole room with the fragrance of southern grapes.

—**CHARLES DICKENS** writing about Port, *Bleak House*

While not generally considered alongside the great wine-producing countries of Europe, Portugal produces a wide array of quality wines and some of the most classical dessert and fortified wines produced in the world. Once passed over, the table wines of Portugal today are garnering much attention, and a newfound commitment to quality is beginning to take hold in this country. Through a long history of wine production that spans thousands of years, Portugal is finally gaining respect.

The Facts on Portugal

CLIMATE

Mostly warm to hot.

TOP WHITE GRAPE

- Alvarinho

TOP RED GRAPES

- Touriga Nacional
- Baga

TOP REGIONS/WINES

Table Wines

- Douro
- Dão
- Bairrada
- Vinho Verde

Fortified/Dessert Wines

- Port
- Madeira

IMPORTANT INFORMATION

- Portugal ranks eleventh in the world in terms of total wine production.
- The most famous wines produced in Portugal are both fortified dessert wines: Port and Madeira.
- Portugal is becoming better known for its dry table wines, and possibly produces the best value wines in Europe.

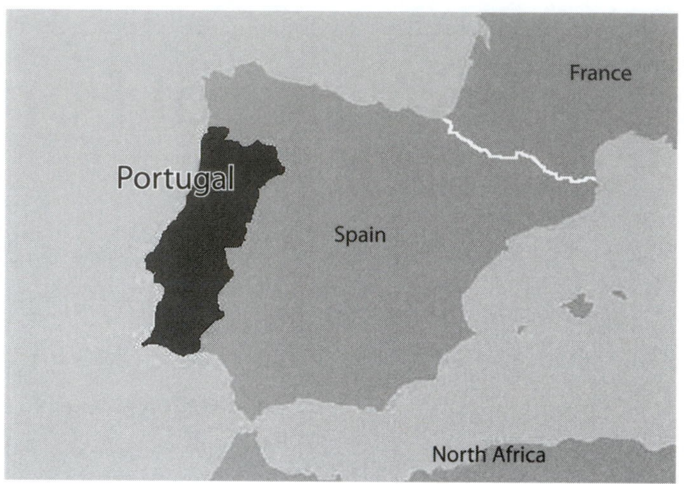

Portugal: Ancient Tradition and Bright Future

Portugal is one of the new stars of European winemaking, although they have been producing wines there for thousands of years. Vineyards and wine production in Portugal are believed to date back almost four thousand years, with vineyards possibly planted by the Phoenicians or the Greeks. Winemaking was significantly developed while Portugal was a Roman outpost, and the wines of Portugal were known throughout the Empire.

Located along the western coastline of the Iberian Peninsula, Portugal borders the Atlantic Ocean to the west and south, and Spain to the east and north. With its rugged terrain and far southwestern location, the country is one of the most isolated areas of Europe. This has meant that Portuguese winemakers have developed traditional methods and styles that can differ greatly from the other European wine regions. It also has led to the breeding of several hundred unique and distinct grape varietals in Portugal. Even today, Portuguese winemakers stick to their unique traditions, avoiding the acceptance of international grape varieties and styles so common in other parts of the world.

As early as the 1100s, Portugal became an important supplier of wine to England, an association that remains strong to this day. With the English and French sporadically fighting wars with one another from the Middle Ages through the colonial era, England was constantly being cut off from supplies of French wine. English efforts to find new supplies of wine eventually led them to northern Portugal. The fortified style of wine from the Douro region of Portugal known as Port was first produced as English shippers added brandy to wine barrels to preserve the wine's quality during the long ocean voyage to England. This sweet, high-alcohol wine quickly became a huge success throughout the British Empire. Many of the top producers of Port wines today are still English companies.

Due to the fact that Portugal is a very agricultural country, it has always been slow in adapting to modern technologies and industry. With several scientific advancements in winemaking techniques and vine growing taking place during the late 1800s and throughout the 1900s around the world, Portuguese winemakers were very slow to catch on. This caused their table wine industry to fall behind the rest of Europe in terms of quality and popularity, with only Port wines enjoying success in export markets.

With a successful marketing campaign and a knack for determining popular taste, the Portuguese wine industry was reintroduced to the world in the 1970s with the emergence of its immensely successful blush wines. The two most famous brands were Lancer's and Mateus, selling millions of cases. These slightly sweet and fizzy rosés took the international markets by storm, and an influx of capital and interest helped begin the modernization of the domestic wine industry.

The next major step that helped bring Portuguese wines into the modern era was when the country joined the European Union (EU) in the late 1980s. In doing so, they had to adapt their wine laws and regulations to the French model. New quality classifications and official wine regions were established, and higher quality standards were soon enforced in an effort to increase export sales throughout Europe and abroad.

Today, Portugal is a wine-producing nation that is poised for the future. Their industry enjoys the benefits of healthy domestic sales—the Portuguese rank only behind the French and Italians in terms of wine consumption per person. International interest and excitement about Portuguese wines are also making the investment in modernization well worth the effort. The fortified wines of Portugal, especially Port and Madeira, may always be the most famous wines produced there, but with quality production and exceptional value, Portuguese table wines are now taking their rightful place amongst the quality wines of the world.

Wine Laws of Portugal

Although the French lay claim to the oldest regional wine laws in the world, Portugal actually established recognized wine regions almost two hundred years before France did. A traditional set of wine laws in Portugal was replaced in 1986, when the country joined the European Union and had to change their wine laws to more closely resemble the other regulations used throughout Europe. The new laws are modeled on the French AOC system, where areas of wine production are established and, depending on quality and the strictness of production methods, placed into a quality classification. Due to this fact, most of the top-quality wines produced in Portugal are labeled by region.

The wine laws of Portugal are generally referred to as the ***Denominação de Origem Controlada*** laws or **DOC** laws, named for the highest quality classification of Portuguese wine. The system is made up of four quality classifications based on the French system. Although these laws were intended to promote quality production and important regions, they have sometimes been applied in a confusing manner because they do not always fit with how wine has traditionally been produced in many Portuguese regions.

There are almost two dozen recognized regions in Portugal that have qualified for the highest classification of *Denominação de Origem Controlada* or DOC. When loosely translated into English, this term means "controlled area of origin." Official boundaries, winemaking practices, approved grapes, and grape-growing techniques are strictly regulated and enforced. This classification is very similar to the French *Appellation d'Origine Contrôleée* or AOC category of quality.

Wine regions that are attempting to improve quality and be granted DOC status fall under the **IPR** or ***Indicação de Proveniencia Regulamentada***

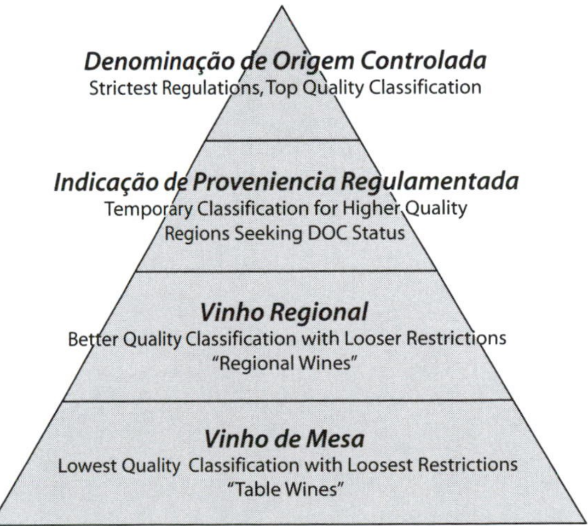

Portugal's quality classifications for wine.

Common Portuguese Label Terms

TERM	DEFINITION
Vinho tinto	Red wine
Vino branco	White wine
Vino rosado	Rosé wine
Maduro	Old
Seco	Dry
Doce	Sweet
Colheita	Vintage
Garrafeira	Wine of very high quality; aged for a specified period longer than the minimum regional standards.
Quinta	Winery/Estate

classification. Similar to the French VDQS quality classification, IPR regions are strictly monitored for a set period of time to see if they can stick to tougher regulations and maintain quality of production. After that period, the regions will either be granted DOC status or relegated back into the lower categories.

Looser restrictions and production standards are found in the two lowest quality classifications: ***vinho regional*** and ***vinho de mesa***. While most *vinho regional* (or "regional wine," based on the French *vin de pays* category) is simple and intended only for local consumption, many quality examples exist. These come mostly from winemakers who choose to adopt nontraditional grapes and techniques for wines produced in otherwise traditional regions. *Vinho de mesa* or "table wine" is the lowest quality classification, made with the fewest restrictions. It is meant only for local consumption and is not exported as a general rule.

Important Grapes of Portugal

Portugal is home to roughly five hundred indigenous grape varietals. Many of these are rustic and simple on their own, but most Portuguese winemaking is

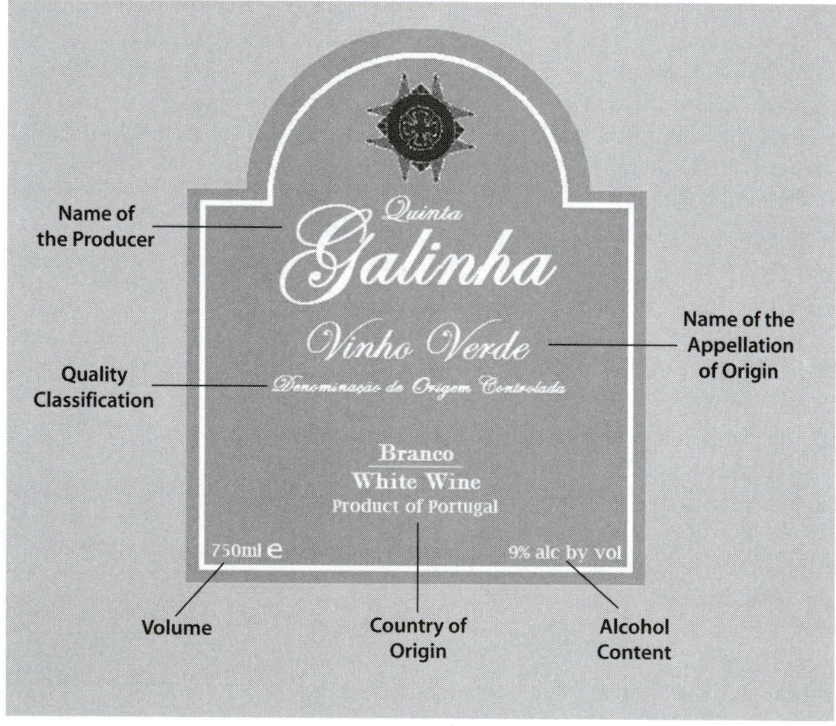

How to read a Portuguese wine label.

about blending grapes together, not making single-varietal wines. Many winemakers there feel that blending several ingredients is the best way to gain complexity in a wine.

Today there are a handful of Portuguese grapes that have risen to prominence either on their own, or as the main component of a blend. Because of its warmer climate, many of the grapes and wines of Portugal are hearty reds, although significant amounts of top-quality white wines are produced as well. The most important grapes for table wine production in Portugal are the red-skinned varietals **Touriga Nacional** and **Baga**, and the white-skinned varietal Alvarinho.

Unique Grape Names

Portugal is home to hundreds of indigenous grape varieties, many with very colorful names. Here are three of the most interesting, if not eye-opening examples.

GRAPE NAME	WHAT THE NAME MEANS
Esgana Cão	"Dog strangler"
Rabigato	"Ewe's tail"
Borrado das Moscas	"Fly droppings"

Touriga Nacional

The most important red grape of Portugal, Touriga Nacional is commonly the preeminent variety used when blending grapes to produce top-quality Ports. In recent years, the grape has also begun to be respected when used to produce dry red wines. Hearty and rustic, Touriga Nacional delivers full-bodied, fruit-rich, tannic wines of power and structure. For dry wine production, the grape is grown throughout Portugal, but is at its best in the regions of Douro and Dão, where it is heavily grown. Most production is bound for blends with traditional DOC designations, but many wine makers are forgoing this higher quality classification to bottle 100 percent Touriga Nacional labeled by grape variety.

Baga

Baga is the most widely grown grape variety in Portugal, and is heavily relied upon for the production of red table wines in all of the northern Portuguese regions. It is grown heavily in Dão, Douro, and Minho, but is probably best known in the region of Bairrada. In fact, the grape is also known as Tinta Bairrada. In Bairrada, Baga is by far the most important grape, responsible for the vast majority of wines produced there. Baga produces powerful wines that can often have a biting astringency from high tannins and flavors of clay and ripe dark fruit.

Alvarinho

The most important white grape grown in northern Portugal, Alvarinho is often the main grape used in the production of the white wines of Minho and especially Vinho Verde. This varietal is also widely grown in Spain, where it is known as Albariño. In Portugal, Alvarinho is often harvested early to retain natural acidity and to keep the grapes from overripening. Alvarinho typically produces lighter-bodied wines with a moderate acidity and alcohol. This grape is all about fruit flavors and aromas—commonly peaches, citrus, kiwi fruit, and melon—and the wines it produces are best when served young.

Terroir and Important Regions

Surrounded by Spain and the Atlantic, Portugal is a rugged country that clings to the southwestern corner of the Iberian Peninsula. A little over 350 miles long and almost 120 miles wide, the country has a climate that is impacted by its southern latitude and ocean influences. Rivers and valleys cut across the mountainous terrain that runs the length of the country from north to south, reaching toward the coast.

The northern regions of Portugal are where the majority of quality wine production takes place. Along the coastline, conditions are temperate to warm, and generous rainfall makes the landscape very lush and green. Heading into the interior of northern Portugal, temperatures rise and the lands are more arid. Ripening periods are long and hot, sometimes forcing grape growers to harvest early so that their grapes do not overripen. Many of the vineyards are planted on steep slopes with sparse soils formed by mountain ranges or deep river valleys.

Southern Portugal is not as mountainous or rugged, but conditions are much warmer. On a latitude equal to that of North Africa, a more hot-Mediterranean climate exists there. Important wine-making regions and DOCs fan out from the capital of Lisbon, the most populous city in Portugal. Most wine production in the south is geared toward rustic red table wines and sweet fortified wines.

Portugal's top wine regions.

DOURO

The Douro River flows westward through Spain, passing through the Spanish wine region Ribera del Duero and crossing the Portuguese border, where it is known as the Rio Douro. From there, the Douro cuts west across northern Portugal before emptying into the Atlantic. The **Douro DOC** is limited to the warmer, inland stretches of the river valley created by the Douro River. This valley is home to many vineyards that cling to steep, terraced slopes that can climb almost 1,000 feet from the valley floor. *Rio Douro* translates to "river of gold," and the DOC region of Douro is home to the highest-quality dry red wines produced in the country. The region is also covered by the Porto DOC, home to Portugal's most famous wine: Port.

Although a small amount of white wine is produced in the Douro DOC, the region is predominantly dedicated to the production of full-bodied reds. Touriga Nacional is the most important grape grown in the region, producing the top dry red wines and making up the backbone of the best Port wines. Vineyards are extremely difficult to work in Douro, as many vineyards cling to the steep slopes of the region and summer temperatures can rise well above 100°F.

DÃO

Named for the Dão River, the **Dão DOC** region is located in the interior of northern Portugal, east of Bairrada and just south of the Douro Valley. Dão is one of the oldest recognized wine regions in Portugal, and its winemakers began taking measures to protect the name of their region and the wines named for it as far back as the 1300s. Dão is a mountainous region, where elevation tempers the warm climate, and the mountains can protect vineyards from extremes of heat and cold.

Several grapes are grown in the Dão DOC, and both dry whites and reds are produced. Most of the serious production centers around well-aged red wines made from blends dominated by Touriga Nacional. Once dominated by large cooperative wineries, Dão is seeing an exciting trend of smaller, quality-minded wineries opening their doors.

BAIRRADA

The name *Bairrada* comes from the Portuguese word *barros,* which means "clay," due to the rich clay soil in the area. The DOC region of **Bairrada** is found on the Atlantic coastline of northern Portugal, a little south of Minho. Although white wine is produced in this sun-drenched region, their specialty is dry red wines. These are often long-aging, tannic reds most commonly produced from the Baga grape, which is ideally suited to the clay soils and warm sunshine.

VINHO VERDE

Vinho Verde is the largest of all the DOC regions of Portugal, located in the northwestern province of Minho. The region's name literally translates to "green wine," but this is not a reference to the actual color of the wine. Rather it is a reference to the fact that these wines should be consumed in their youth, when their fruity flavors are at their peak. There is actually more red wine produced in the region than white, but very little red Vinho Verde is exported, so white Vinho Verde wines are far more well-known around the world.

White wines produced in Vinho Verde are often made from grapes harvested a little early, retaining some of their natural acidity and a lower alcohol content. The Alvarinho grape is widely used as a base for blending, producing crisp whites that are often quite fruity with a slight spritz of carbonation. Most are of medium quality but are affordably priced.

OTHER WINE REGIONS OF NOTE

The most important wine regions of Portugal are located in the northern portions of the country, but central and southern areas of the country also produce quality wines. Central wine regions fan out from the capital of Lisbon, and most fall under the ***vinho regional*** designation. Whites, reds, and fortified wines are all produced in these regions, but most are of average quality.

Southern Portugal is home to many rustic red wines and a few notable whites, but the most important wines made in the south are the fortified white wines of the DOC region of Setúbal. Made from a handful of different Moscatel (Muscat) grape varieties, these wines are fortified with grape-based spirits during active fermentation, which retains natural sweetness. Often aged for extended periods, they frequently show rich caramel and dried fruit flavors. If the wine is made from 85 percent or more Moscatel grapes, it will be labeled "Moscatel de Setúbal"; otherwise it is simply labeled "Setúbal."

The largest wine-producing region in all of Portugal is Alentejo, which covers almost the entire southeastern portion of the country. Most wine produced in Alentejo is hearty and red, made from local and obscure grapes. The region is probably better known

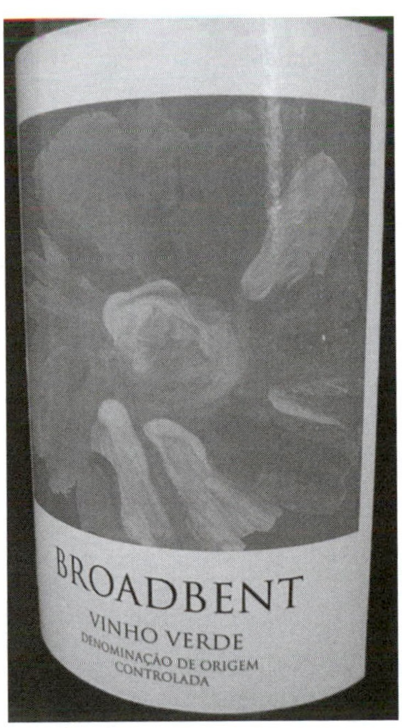

Vinho Verde is Portugal's most famous white wine.

for supplying a majority of the world's cork than it is for wine. Very little quality wine is produced in this region today, although significant investment is currently being made throughout the area.

Port: The World's Most Classic Dessert Wine

The most famous and collectible dessert wine produced in the world comes from northern Portugal's Douro region. Sometimes called **Porto** or **Oporto**, Port is named for the city of Oporto located at the mouth of the Douro River, which is home to the headquarters of many of the top producers. Port is a fortified dessert wine with a long and storied past, but its origins stem from desperation and necessity. The Douro has long been a wine region, but the style of fortified dessert wine known as Port was not produced there until the late 1600s. England was once again at war with France, and as hostilities escalated the English were cut off from their supply of French wine. Enterprising English shippers began scouring other regions of Europe for a ready supply of wine and stumbled upon the rustic reds of Douro.

The problem was that when they shipped barrels of this wine to England, it rarely survived the ocean voyage. Dry wines would turn bad while sweet wines would often begin refermenting, leading to pressure building up and, in some cases, barrels exploding. To solve this problem, high-proof brandy was added to the wine before shipping to help stabilize the wines. After a little experimentation, the production method that is still used to produce Port today was perfected, and Port was born.

The Facts on Port

REGION OF PRODUCTION AND CLIMATE

Port is produced in the Douro Valley, home to a warm to hot climate.

TOP RED GRAPES

- Touriga Nacional
- Touriga Francesa (also known as Touriga Franca)
- Tinta Roriz
- Tinta Barroca
- Tinto Cão

IMPORTANT STYLES OF PORT

Bottle-Aged Ports

- Vintage Port

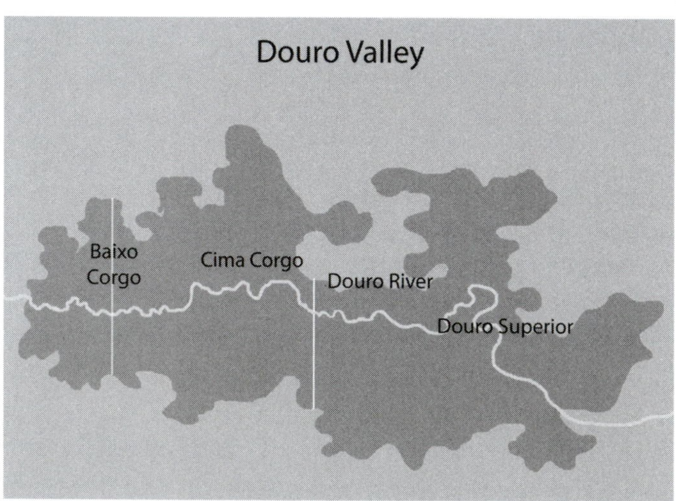

The Douro Valley and major Port-producing areas.

Wood-Aged Ports

- Ruby Port
- Tawny Port
- Aged tawny Port
- Late-bottled vintage (LBV) Port

IMPORTANT INFORMATION

- Port, also known as Porto or Oporto, is considered by many to be the world's greatest dessert wine. This is a surprising fact considering that the vast majority of dessert wines are white wines, and most Port is red.
- During fermentation, Port is fortified with high-proof brandy. This spikes the alcohol content up to 20 percent or higher, killing the yeast and retaining the residual sugar of the grapes.
- There are two major styles: bottle-aged Ports and wood-aged Ports.

Port is a wine that is almost always sweet because it is fortified during fermentation. A few days into the fermentation process, the fermenting wine will be spiked with one part 154-proof brandy (called *aguardente*) to roughly four parts wine. This will raise the alcohol content of the wine to approximately 20 percent abv, effectively killing off the yeast. Natural sugars from the grapes are left in the wine, resulting in a fortified wine that is both strong and sweet. Port houses (the term used to describe a Port producer) will develop a house style that governs how sweet they make their Ports.

Due to the fortification process used to produce Port, these wines are often quite powerful and intense on the palate. Sweetness levels vary from producer to producer, but most styles are quite rich and sweet. Depending upon how a Port is aged, it might be a deep red color and reminiscent of cooked dark fruit and berries, or it may be amber or tawny in color with flavors of caramelized sugar, dried fruit, and spice.

There are a multitude of different grapes grown in the Douro, and all Port wines will be blends of several grapes. In fact, Port producers are legally allowed to blend more than eighty different grape varieties in the **Porto DOC**. This is done because many of the grapes grown there are simple and rustic. By blending multiple varieties, characteristics from each grape are utilized and complex wines are produced. Today, most Port houses limit their blends to the five most important grapes grown in the Douro for Port production: Touriga Nacional, Touriga Francesa/Franca, Tinta Barroca, Tinta Roriz (known as Tempranillo in Spain), and Tinto Cão. Each contributes a different characteristic such as aroma, color, fruit flavors, sugar content, or softness. Touriga Nacional makes up the backbone of most top-quality Ports, although Touriga Francesa is the most widely grown varietal.

Port's English Connection

England has always maintained close ties with Port since its beginnings, and the English are still some of the top consumers of Port in the world. In fact, many of the top Port producers are English companies and have names that will never be confused as being Portuguese, such as Graham's, Dow's, Taylor-Fladgate, Warre, and Cockburn.

Port production is limited to the three important subregions of the Douro: Baixo Corgo, Cima Corgo, and Douro Superior. Baixo Corgo encompasses the western Douro where the river valley's slopes flatten out, and is home to a warm climate and fertile soils. Most production here is limited to basic styles of Port. Cima Corgo is home to the steep, terraced slopes of the central valley, and this area is considered the heart of Port production. Warmer conditions and nutrient-deprived soils combine to make this the top-quality subregion where the best aged tawny and vintage Ports are produced. Douro Superior is the warmest part of the Douro Valley, far inland from Atlantic influences, near the Spanish border. A wide range of different Port styles and quality come from Douro Superior.

There are two basic types of Port, based on how they are aged. Once fortified, the wines will be graded according to their characteristics and sorted into the two categories. Ports that receive a majority of their aging in the bottle are referred to as **bottle-aged Ports**, and those that receive the majority of their aging in barrels are called **wood-aged Ports.**

The major difference between these types is exposure to oxygen during the aging period, which is minimal for bottle-aged Ports and often extreme for wood-aged styles.

Bottle-aged Ports are aged for only a year or two in barrels, at which point they might age for decades in the bottle while oxygen slowly interacts with the wine, mellowing and maturing it. Wood-aged Ports, on the other hand, will be aged in barrels until they have matured and are ready to be consumed. At that point, they are bottled and sold. Since barrel aging exposes a wine to massive amounts of oxidation over time, wood-aged Ports will appear amber in color and have flavors associated with oxidation: dried fruit and caramelized sugar. Bottle-aged Ports will instead have a deeper red color and exhibit flavors of ripe fruit. The most important styles of wood-aged Ports are **ruby Port, tawny Port, aged tawny Port,** and **late-bottled vintage (LBV) Port.** There are not as many styles of bottle-aged Ports, but the one known as **vintage Port** is widely considered the top style produced.

Important Styles of Wood-Aged Port

Ruby Port The most widely produced style of Port, ruby Port is often simple and of basic quality. Named for their vibrant red color, ruby Ports are blends of different vintages that have been aged for two to three years in large casks before bottling. Ruby Ports usually have ripe berry and jam flavors. They are ready to drink upon release.

Tawny Port If there is no reference to age on a bottle of tawny Port, it will be of similar quality to a basic ruby Port. They are often bottled after only three years of barrel aging, and have an amber or tawny color and caramel flavors. Sometimes, a small amount of white Port is added to these wines to lighten up the color and flavors. Tawny Ports often have pleasant caramelized flavors. These non-vintage blends are ready to drink when bottled.

Aged tawny Port The best tawny Ports will be aged for long periods in barrel and labeled by the average age of their components in multiples of ten years. From ten-year-old tawny Port all the way to forty-year-old tawny Port and beyond, these non-vintage wines are richly flavored and complex. The best are considered the equal of vintage Port in terms of quality, and do not require additional bottle aging when released.

Late-bottled vintage (LBV) Port Although made from a single vintage, late-bottled vintage or LBV Ports should not be confused with higher-quality vintage Ports. Made in good but not great years, LBV Ports receive longer barrel aging (usually four to six years) than regular vintage Ports, which matures them more quickly, and they are ready to be consumed when bottled.

Great Port Vintages

Vintage Port is a style produced only in the best years. Some of the best vintages since 1970 include: 1970, 1975, 1977, 1980, 1983, 1985, 1991, 1992, 1994, 1997, 2000, and 2003.

Important Style of Bottle-Aged Port

Vintage Port In the very best years in the Douro (often only two or three years every decade), conditions are ideal and a Port house will declare its intentions to produce a vintage Port. These will be made only from the best grapes sourced from top vineyards, and after a short period of barrel aging the wines will mature for decades in bottle before hitting their peak. This is considered the highest-quality style of Port, and the reputation of a Port house is often tied to the quality of their vintage Ports.

Besides the major styles of Port produced in the Douro, there are several other lesser-known styles. While Port is generally red, white Ports are also produced from white-skinned grape varietals. These wines are made in a similar manner to other basic wood-aged Port styles, but are often much drier and intended as aperitifs. Another style of wood-aged

Port is colheita Port. These are tawny Ports from a single vintage and are rather uncommon. Single-quinta Ports are bottle-aged Ports from a single year, produced only when a vintage has not been declared. They are produced in a similar manner to vintage Port, but are made from grapes grown in only one vineyard or farm, known as a *quinta*.

Madeira: Cooked Wine

About 350 miles west of Morocco in the Atlantic Ocean is **Madeira,** an island home to large volcanic mountains that steeply rise thousands of feet above sea level. An important stop on shipping routes during the Age of Discovery and the colonial era, Madeira produced fortified wines that were routinely purchased by ships bound for destinations around the world. They were popular because of their ability to survive conditions that would quickly spoil most wines. Madeira wine was especially popular in the New England colonies, and was even used to toast the signing of the Declaration of Independence in 1776.

As the casks of Madeira wine slowly rocked in the hulls of these wooden ships, oxidation accelerated, darkening and flavoring the wine. Most of the trade routes of the time passed near the equator, where tropical temperatures would actually cook the wine, leading to rich nutty and burnt-caramel flavors. While these conditions would completely destroy most wines, winemakers in Madeira marveled at how their wines improved greatly when casks sometimes returned from long ocean voyages. Many winemakers actually paid to have their wines placed on ships as ballast, selling it when the ships returned after months at sea.

The Facts on Madeira

REGION OF PRODUCTION AND CLIMATE

The island of Madeira has a southern latitude, which leads to an extremely warm to hot climate.

TOP WHITE GRAPES

- Bual
- Malvasia
- Verdelho
- Sercial

IMPORTANT INFORMATION

- Madeira wine is produced on the island of Madeira in the Atlantic Ocean, about 350 miles west of North Africa.
- Madeira is a wine that is both fortified and maderized or cooked. It ranges in style from dry to sweet, and due to the production methods used, it is one of the most age-worthy wines produced in the world.

Today, the DOC region of Madeira makes wines produced under tortuous conditions meant to simulate those long, hot ocean voyages. A fortified white wine, Madeira is often heavily oxidized and high in alcohol, but what makes it unique is the fact that it is **maderized** or cooked during production. Lesser-quality, bulk Madeira is heated to over 120°F in large vats for several months before being fortified and possibly sweetened.

Top-quality Madeira, on the other hand, will be fortified during fermentation if it is meant to be sweet or after fermentation for dry styles. Large casks of wine will then be placed in attics or storage facilities with no temperature control, where they are left to age and bake for years or even decades. With the island's hot summers, the wines slowly maderize and develop intense, complex flavors. This unique process creates wines that are capable of maturing for centuries in some cases, and that can last for months once opened.

There are four basic styles of Madeira, named for the classic variety of Madeira grape that makes up at least 85 percent of the wine. These four varietals are **Sercial,** Verdelho, **Bual,** and Malvasia (called **Malmsey** on Madeira). Each produces very different wines that range from light and dry to dark and sweet. Besides these classic varieties, a lesser-quality grape called Tinta Negra Mole is widely grown and heavily used in basic, bulk Madeiras. Any of these different styles can be aged for just a couple of years or for decades or more, depending upon their quality and characteristics.

Styles of Madeira

Sercial Grown at the highest elevations on the terraced slopes of Madeira, Sercial grapes are used to produce this pale, dry, acidic style of Madeira noted for its nutty flavors.

Verdelho Verdelho grapes are grown at higher elevations, and produce semisweet wines that are amber in color and often showcase smoky aromas.

Bual Sweet wines reminiscent of dates and raisins are produced from Bual grapes grown closer to sea level in warmer vineyard conditions.

Malmsey Malmsey Madeira is the sweetest style produced on the island. Made from Malvasia grapes grown at lower elevations, this style can often be considered a dessert wine, although its high acidity balances a lot of its sweetness. These wines are often very dark with intense burnt caramel and dried fruit characteristics.

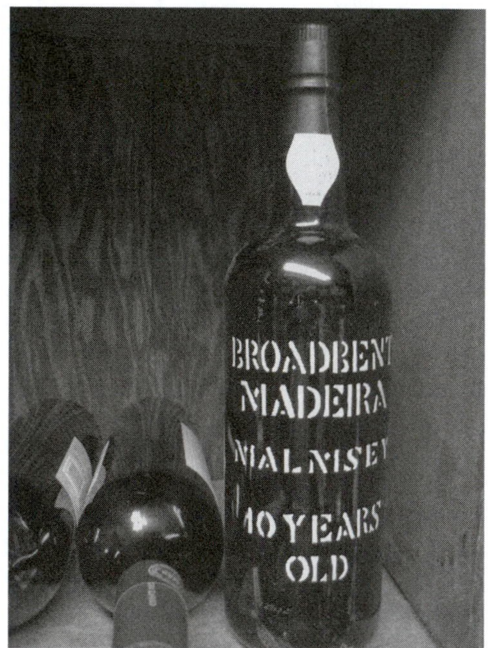

Because of the unique process of cooking used to produce them, Madeiras are some of the longest-lived wines produced in the world.

Bulletproof Wine

Due to the fortification, extreme oxidation, and cooking that Madeira goes through, the wines that result are almost indestructible. They will not be affected like other wines when exposed to heat or oxygen. An open bottle can last months, if not years, without degrading in quality.

Summary

Portugal has produced very distinct wines from unique grape varieties for thousands of years. Although best known for its fortified wines like Port and Madeira, the country is gaining more international acceptance for its table wines. There is no limit to the potential of Portuguese winemaking as the industry continues to modernize and increase quality production.

Review Questions

1. The most famous wines of Portugal are dry, red table wines.
   - A. True
   - B. False

2. The most important red grape grown in Portugal is:
   - A. Tempranillo
   - B. Vinho Verde
   - C. Alvarinho
   - D. Touriga Nacional

3. The Portuguese wine laws are based upon the French AOC system, and the term used to describe the highest quality classification with the most important wine regions and strictest standards is:
   - A. *Denominação de Origem Controlada*
   - B. *Indicação de Proveniencia Regulamentada*
   - C. *Vinho regional*
   - D. *Vinho de mesa*

4. A dry, highly tannic red wine made from Baga grapes would most likely come from the _________ region of Portugal.
   A. Douro
   B. Dão
   C. Bairrada
   D. Madeira

5. The most famous wine regions of Portugal are found in _________, home to Port and top-quality red wines.
   A. the south
   B. the Douro River Valley
   C. the province of Minho
   D. the areas surrounding the capital city of Lisbon

6. Portuguese fortified wines are made stronger by:
   A. the use of grapes affected by *phylloxera*
   B. the addition of sugar to fermenting wine
   C. the addition of high-proof brandy
   D. the addition of extra yeast to fermenting wine

7. A light, acidic white wine made mostly from Alvarinho grapes would most likely be from which Portuguese region?
   A. Douro
   B. Dão
   C. Bairrada
   D. Vinho Verde

8. Vintage Port, the highest-quality style produced, receives a majority of its aging in large, wooden casks.
   A. True
   B. False

9. Port wines are fortified _________ fermentation to retain natural sweetness.
   A. before
   B. during
   C. after
   D. instead of going through

10. Madeira is a unique type of fortified wine that goes through the process of maderization, during which it will be _________.
   A. sweetened
   B. diluted with high-proof brandy
   C. cooked
   D. blended

Key Terms

Denominação de Origem Controlada (DOC)
Indicação de Proveniencia Regulamentada (IPR)
vinho regional
vinho de mesa
Baga
Douro DOC
Dão DOC
Bairrada DOC
Vinho Verde DOC
Porto
Oporto
Porto DOC
bottle-aged Ports
wood-aged Ports
ruby Port
tawny Port
aged tawny Port
late-bottled vintage (LBV) Port
vintage Port
Madeira DOC
maderized
Sercial
Bual
Malmsey

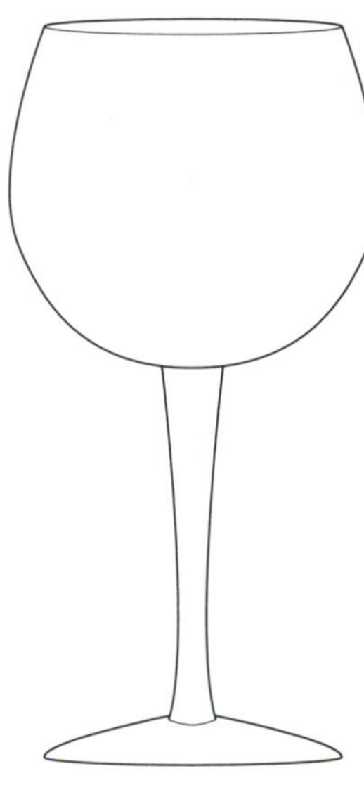

CHAPTER 14

The Wines of Austria, Hungary, Greece, and Other European Regions

No thing more excellent nor more valuable than wine was ever granted mankind by god.

—**PLATO,** Greek philosopher

This chapter rounds out the wines of Europe by offering a snapshot of three lesser-known wine-producing regions—Austria, Hungary, and Greece—as well as a few additional European regions of note. These countries are not covered in the same detail as the more prolific wine-producing countries in the previous chapters, but their most important wines are discussed.

Austria

Wine has been produced in Austria for thousands of years, with some archaeological evidence suggesting that it could date as far back as 2000 B.C. Production certainly increased under the control of the Roman Empire, and through the Dark Ages and Middle Ages viniculture in Austria was the domain of the Catholic Church. In the 1400s, Austria became a major production center for wine, and it remained so until the *phylloxera* epidemic of the 1800s. After surviving *phylloxera* and two world wars, Austria was a country that focused on high-yield, mass-produced wines. These were often sold in bulk to Germany to be used as components in generic blends. This all came to an end in 1985, when a winemaking scandal almost destroyed the Austrian wine industry completely.

To help give wines more sweetness and body, a handful of Austrian wine brokers began adulterating them with small amounts of diethylene glycol, an ingredient in antifreeze. No one was hurt, but when word of this practice got out, the reputation of Austrian wine was ruined and exports dropped to nothing. This forced the Austrian wine industry and government to administer some of the strictest wine regulations in the world and refocus on quality grapes and production. After almost two decades in exile, Austria has reestablished its reputation as a top-quality wine country. The new system of regulations and focus on quality have made this country's wine industry proud once again. Today, Austria produces some of Europe's best and most exciting wines, with the uniquely Austrian Grüner Veltliner grape leading the way.

WINE LAWS

Austria has some of the most confusing wine laws in Europe because more than one system is used throughout the different wine regions. The main system used is similar to Germany's, with quality classifications linked to ripeness. Wines are ranked in a hierarchy based on the sugar content in their grapes at harvest. The two top classifications are ***Qualitätswein*** for wines made from fairly ripe grapes, and ***Prädikatswein*** for wines made from late harvest grapes and beyond. As in Germany, the bottom classifications are ***Landwein*** and ***Tafelwein,*** which contain wines made from underripe grapes that have to be chaptalized.

Besides this common system utilized in Austria, one ancient system is used in a single region while another modern system is being attempted in a few regions. Wachau, a wine region in northeastern Austria, has a unique classification system that only they use. There are three classifications based on alcohol content of dry wines: *Steinfeder* (the lowest), *Federspiel,* and *Smaragd* (the highest).

A new classification system is being given a trial run in a few select regions located throughout Austria. The regulations for this system are called the **DAC** laws, which stands for ***Districtus Austriae Controllatus,*** Latin for "controlled district of Austria." This is a system of geographical appellations and designations, similar to the AOC laws of France.

Lizards in the Vineyard

The term *Smaragd,* an official wine quality designation used to denote the wines from Wachau with the highest alcohol content, means "emerald." The reference here is not to the green-colored foliage of the vines nor the rolling green hills that cover much of the region. It actually refers to the nickname of small green lizards that inhabit the vineyards of Wachau. They are often found, like the grapes that produce *Smaragd* wines, basking in the warm summer sun.

IMPORTANT GRAPES

Compared to most European countries, Austria does not grow many different grape varietals: there are slightly fewer than forty varietals officially sanctioned for wine production. Many of these grapes are either foreign transplants like Riesling and Chardonnay, or genetic crosses developed in Austria for their unique growing conditions.

Much of the country's winemaking is dedicated to white grape varieties such as **Welschriesling**, which is used to produce dry whites and sweet, botrytised wines; as well as a smattering of German varietals like Riesling and Müller-Thurgau. The unique red wines of Austria are also beginning to gather international attention, especially those made from the spicy **Zweigelt** and the richly flavored Blaufränkisch grapes. Regardless, much of the recent success in Austrian winemaking is due to the country's most widely planted varietal, Grüner Veltliner, which is considered their national grape.

 Grüner Veltliner

Rarely grown outside the country's borders, Grüner Veltliner is the most important grape of Austria. More than a third of the country's vineyard acreage is planted to the Grüner Veltliner grape. Considered a point of national pride, wines made from this white varietal are typically light, dry, and crisp. These wines are intended to showcase their intense flavors, reminiscent of citrus, herbs, tropical fruit, and spicy white pepper.

TOP REGIONS AND WINES

Most of Austria's wine regions are found on the eastern side of the country, in the foothills of the Alps, down into rolling plains that run to the border. Although similar to Germany's in many ways, the climate of Austria is warmer, allowing grapes to more

Grüner Veltliner is considered the national wine of Austria.

The Art of the Wineglass

The most famous and renowned wineglass company in the world is called Riedel. This Austrian company is renowned for the quality and design of its crystal glassware, and designs glasses that aim to maximize the most pleasure and flavor from different grape varietals and wine styles.

fully ripen. This is largely due to its more southern location—most of the vineyards and wine regions of Austria lie at the same latitude as Burgundy, France. Austria is home to four major wine-growing areas: **Niederösterreich, Burgenland, Steiermark,** and **Wien.** These are further divided into sixteen recognized wine regions.

Niederösterreich, known as Lower Austria, is a political district in the northeastern corner of Austria, and home to some of the country's largest and best-quality regions. The most important of these wine regions are Kamptal, Wachau, and Weinviertel. Kamptal is located in north-central Niederösterreich, and is well known for its Grüner Veltliner and Riesling wines that possess lean, mineral flavors. A long, narrow valley with steep, terraced slopes makes up the region of Wachau, known mostly for its quality whites made from Riesling and Grüner Veltliner. Wachau is unique in Austria because it has its own system of wine classifications (see "Wine Laws," page 250). The largest wine region in Austria is Weinviertel, where they specialize in softer, fruitier Grüner Veltliner wines and a handful of red varietals.

To the south and east of Lower Austria is Burgenland, a narrow province that runs along the eastern section of the country bordering the Czech Republic and Hungary. Slightly warmer than the other major regions of Austria, Burgenland produces top white wines and significant amounts of red wines from a variety of different grapes. Their most important wines, however, are late harvest and botrytised dessert wines produced from the wine regions of

Austria and its wine regions.

Neusiedlersee and Neusiedlersee-Hügelland, located along the shores of Lake Neusiedl. The most famous of these sweet dessert wines are those falling in the ***Pradikätswein*** classification ***Ausbruch,*** produced by mixing late harvest and botrytised grapes together prior to fermentation.

South of Lower Austria and west of Burgenland is the district of Steiermark, sometimes called Styria. Much less Grüner Veltliner is produced here than in the other major regions of Austria. Instead the focus is on other varietals such as Sauvignon Blanc, Zweigelt, and even Chardonnay (locally called Morillon). The most well-known wine region in Steiermark is Südsteiermark, located in the southern part of the district.

Unique amongst all the capital cities of Europe, Wien (the Austrian name for Vienna) is an officially recognized, active wine region. The city and region are embedded within the district of Lower Austria. Wine grapes are grown on the outskirts of the city and good-quality whites and reds are produced from the more traditional Austrian varietals, especially Grüner Veltliner.

Hungary

As with many wine-producing countries in Europe, the ancient Romans introduced grape growing and winemaking to Hungary. The Roman occupation of this region would not be the last, though, as Hungary has been an occupied nation for much of its history. As different cultures and civilizations battled over control of this region, new grapes and wine styles were introduced.

Influenced by the Slavic nations to the east and Germanic nations to the west, Hungary has developed a unique winemaking culture and tradition. From the 1600s through the early 1900s, Hungary was a famous winemaking region, due mostly to its two most important wines of both the past and present—the red wine **Egri Bikavér** and the sweet white wines called Tokaji. This fame was destroyed after World War II, however, when Hungary became a Communist bloc country. Under communism, the quality of Hungarian wine dropped severely as privately owned wineries were taken over by the state. Several traditional grapes were torn up from vineyards and high-yielding varietals planted in their place. Hungary's once rich and thriving wine industry was replaced by a high-volume, bulk-quantity mindset.

Since the fall of communism in Hungary, traditional methods, grapes, and styles of wine have slowly returned. Foreign investment in top regions, especially Tokaj, has spawned new interest in international markets. Hungary is once again the most important wine nation in Eastern Europe.

WINE LAWS

Hungary only recently adopted a modern system of wine regulations, quality classifications, and official winemaking regions. This system is loosely based on the French AOC laws. These laws were first enacted a couple of years after the fall of communism in Hungary, and their goal is to improve quality production and preserve traditional grapes and wine styles. The first official controlled region of origin in Hungary was for Egri Bikavér, the most famous red wine produced in the country.

IMPORTANT GRAPES

There are only a handful of quality grape varieties believed to be indigenous to Hungary. Most of their more popular wines are produced from grapes that have been brought to the country from different invading and occupying cultures. The most important grape used to produce the dry and legendary sweet white wines of Tokaji is Furmint, thought to be of Italian origin. **Kadarka** probably came from Serbia and Kékfrankos (better known as Blaufränkisch) from Germanic lands. Both are used in the hearty red blend Egri Bikavér.

Hungary and its wine regions.

TOP REGIONS AND WINES

There are wine regions located throughout the Hungarian countryside: in the foothills of the Carpathian Mountains to the north, in the hilly lands to the west, and in the grassy plains to the east that roll to the Romanian border. Hungary is home to a primarily cool-continental climate, with a few warm grape-growing areas to the south. While a wide variety of rustic red and white blends are produced throughout Hungary, its two most important wines, Egri Bikavér and the sweet botrytised wines of Tokaj, are both produced in northern regions.

One of the most important wine regions in Hungary is Eger, located in the northeastern corner of the country about 70 miles east of Budapest. The most famous red wine produced in Hungary comes from this region and is called Egri Bikavér, which means "Bull's Blood of Eger." Made from a blend of several red grapes, especially Kadarka and Kékfrankos, Egri Bikavér can range widely from simple and hearty to elegant and complex.

The northern region of Tokaj is located near the Carpathian Mountains along the border shared with the Czech Republic, and is home to the most legendary wine produced in Hungary, Tokaji, meaning "of Tokaj." While the majority of wines produced there are basic, dry white wines, the region is best known for its ultrasweet wines made mostly from Furmint grapes infected with noble rot. When the climate is just right, warm conditions leading up to a late harvest and moisture in the air create the perfect conditions for botrytis, called ***Aszú*** in Hungarian. These conditions only happen two to three times every decade, and the wines produced are very sweet, lush, and decadent.

Dessert wines produced from botrytised grapes in Tokaj date back hundreds of years to the Turkish occupation of Hungary. Legend tells of winemakers forced from their vineyards by the threat of conflict in the region just before the harvest, only to return weeks later to find that a mold had grown on their grapes. Attempting to salvage the harvest, they made wine from these shriveled grapes, and to the surprise of everyone, these wines were thick, complex, and reminiscent of honey.

After the fall of communism in Hungary, foreign investors quickly moved into the Tokaj region to reestablish these historically notable wines that had once been prized by monarchs throughout Europe. In fact, Louis XIV of France famously christened Tokaji wine "*Vinum Regnum, Rex Vinorum*" or "Wine of Kings, King of Wines." There are several styles of sweet and dry Tokaji wine produced, but the most famous are **Tokaji Aszú** and Tokaji Aszú Essencia.

The Other Mold Used to Make Tokaji Wines

While the mold *Botrytis cinerea* is fundamental to concentrating sugar in the grapes used to produce the decadent, sweet wines of Tokaj, it is not the only beneficial mold at work. There are hundreds of underground cellars in the Tokaj region that are used to slowly age Tokaji Aszú wines to perfection. Many of these are covered from floor to ceiling with a thick, black mold that helps to regulate temperature and humidity.

Tokaji Aszú is made with late harvest grapes that have been infected with botrytis. These grapes are then crushed into a paste, traditionally through foot treading. Grapes unaffected by botrytis are crushed, and their juice is then added to this paste in large vats for a day or two. This mixture is then sent to barrels, where it will slowly complete fermentation and mature. For the sweetest Tokaji Aszú wines, this fermentation can last a year or longer.

The sweetness level of Tokaji Aszú is measured in terms of ***puttonyos,*** from 3 *puttonyos* all the way to 6 *puttonyos*. This is in reference to the number of traditional baskets (called *puttonyos*) of botrytised paste added to roughly 36 gallons of grape juice. The more *puttonyos* added, the sweeter and richer the wine becomes. Wines with sugar content in excess of the 6 *puttonyos* style of Tokaji Aszú are designated **Essencia**. At over 70 percent residual sugar in some cases, Essencia is one of the world's sweetest wines.

Greece

Greece is the original wine-producing country in Europe, and one of the oldest wine-producing regions in the world, first producing wine more than six thousand years ago. Wine was an everyday beverage in ancient Greece, enjoyed year round by almost all levels of society. The ancient Greeks spread wine and a wine culture to several regions of Europe as their civilization grew, including Italy, Portugal, Spain, and southern France.

Greek wines were enjoyed and praised through the times of the Roman Empire all the way through the Middle Ages. Some of the often sweet, strong wines of the Greek islands became legendary. Through wars and centuries, Greece remained a top producer of sought-after wines in Europe, but as the world's winemakers modernized in the late 1800s and especially in the early to mid-1900s, Greece lagged behind. As the rest of the winemaking world adopted modern technologies and techniques, Greece was slow to act. Economic problems, civil conflicts, and an industry ruled by large, bulk-wine producers effectively served to keep quality levels low. In the 1960s and 1970s, **retsina** wines became popular in Greece. These are white wines aged in pine barrels lined with pine resin, often low-grade and with bitingly bitter flavors. As international wine markets began to open up for most European wine industries, Greece was linked to these lower-quality retsina wines, further marginalizing their export sales and reputation.

In the 1980s, Greek winemakers began a quality revolution in their industry. New modern methods were practiced, wineries and equipment were updated, and a new generation of winemakers—many of whom studied winemaking in top regions throughout Europe—began to focus on quality production. International grape varietals were introduced and indigenous grapes explored as Greece began to regain its place as one of the top wine regions in the world.

There are many challenges that Greek winemakers still face even today. Most of their grapes and regions are unfamiliar to international customers, and many new competitive wine regions have emerged around the world. Regardless, the Greek wine industry strives to educate wine drinkers about their unique wines, and has found more acceptance as consumers continue to experiment. The glory of ancient Greece may never return, but Greek winemakers still have thousands of years of tradition to lean on as they attempt to usher in a new era of wine greatness.

WINE LAWS

Greece established a modern set of wine laws in the 1970s, loosely modeled after the French AOC system of classified appellations. One of the major goals for these laws was to attempt to preserve traditional grapes, winemaking techniques, and classic wine regions. With limits on production levels and approved techniques, Greek wine certainly improved in quality. This official system also allowed for an easy transition for Greek winemakers when the country joined the European Union.

There are four quality classifications in the Greek wine laws, which mirror the Italian DOC laws to a degree. Quality wines from traditional grapes fall in the top two categories: ***Onomasía Proeléfseos Anotéras Piótitos*** **(OPAP)**, which is the highest designation with the strictest regulations and is used primarily for dry reds and whites, and ***Onomasía Proeléfseos Eleghoméni*** **(OPE)** just below it, which is primarily for sweet wines. ***Topikos Inos*** is a classification similar to the Italian *Indicazione Geografica Tipica* (IGT), with winemakers producing wines "typical of the region." Looser regulations allow these wines to be made from all manner of grapes and using several techniques. The lowest classification, as in most European countries, is "table wine" or *Epitrapezios Inos*.

IMPORTANT GRAPES

Many of the top-quality wines of Greece are made from hundreds of indigenous grapes grown nowhere else in the world. These grapes have limited exports of Greek wines to a certain degree, because many customers are unfamiliar with them. While some winemakers have switched to international grape varietals allowed in the lower quality classifications, most of the traditional winemakers still use the indigenous grapes and continue to try to educate the public about their unique flavors and characteristics.

Greece's Mediterranean climate lends itself more to red wine grapes, but some very interesting and unique white grape varietals are also grown there. The high-acid **Assyrtiko** grape is grown throughout many of the Greek islands and has pleasant floral and citrus flavors. **Moschofilero** is one of the more high-profile white grape varietals, with some major wineries using it to produce lean, perfumed wines in the Peloponnese regions. Grown throughout central Greece, the **Rhoditis** grape produces light, fragrant white wines. **Savatiano** and **Athiri** are both grapes widely used in white wines in Attica and on some of the Greek islands.

Several red wine grape varieties are grown throughout Greece, producing everything from soft, fruity reds to dense, tannic wines, and even fortified dessert wines. Xinómavro, meaning "sour black," is an acidic and tannic grape varietal grown throughout central and northern Greece producing rich, age-worthy, dry red wines. One of the top grapes used to produce sweet red wines is Mavrodaphne, which typically shows plum, raisin, and chocolate characteristics. Used widely throughout the Greek islands, especially Crete and Rhodes, **Mandilaria** grapes produce powerful reds. **Agiorgitiko** produces softer, fruit-laden red wines throughout southern Greece.

TOP REGIONS AND WINES

Greece is a land of mountains and islands. The climate is very Mediterranean, most suitable to heat-tolerant grape varieties. While the surrounding sea can temper the heat of the Greek sun, ripeness is rarely a problem in this country, which can be divided into five major zones of wine production. **Macedonia** makes up the northern Greek mainland while central Greece covers the southern portion. The large peninsula of **Peloponnese** juts out into the Mediterranean to the south of central Greece. The islands in the Aegean Sea to the east of Greece and the islands in the Ionian Sea to the west make up the final two areas of production.

The northernmost area of mainland Greece is called Macedonia (sometimes spelled *Makedonia*),

Greece and its wine regions.

and is one of the oldest wine-producing regions in this historic country. Far more temperate than other regions of Greece, Macedonia enjoys a continental influence on its climate. It is home to some of the most distinct traditional wines produced in Greece from varietals such as Xinómavro, as well as some of its most modern, including Bordeaux-style blends. Some of the most important wines in Greece are produced in the famous wine subregion of **Náoussa.**

Central Greece is one of the most populous and travelled areas of the country, home to Mount Olympus and the capital city of Athens. It is made up of the regions of **Attica, Thessaly,** and **Epirus.** Attica is the region that surrounds Athens, and is largely an area for bulk-wine production and large cooperative producers specializing in retsina. The most important wine-producing region of central Greece is Thessaly, divided in half by the mountain range that includes Mount Olympus. Most of the quality production in Thessaly takes place at higher elevations in the foothills of those mountains where top red, white, and sweet wines are produced. To the west of Attica is Epirus, the most isolated and mountainous of the Greek wine regions and home to some of the country's best red wines made from indigenous grapes unique to the area.

The peninsula that makes up Peloponnese extends out from central Greece south toward the sea. This area is home to some of the most important classified regions of Greece and some of the top export producers. **Neméa** is considered the top region for production in Peloponnese, where

Phylloxera-Resistant Greek Vine

The white Assyrtiko grape variety is indigenous to the Greek island of Santorini and is one of the few varietals of *Vitis vinifera* that is resistant to the dread *phylloxera*. While this insect was wreaking havoc throughout Greece and the rest of the winemaking world, vineyards planted with Assyrtiko were amazingly spared. Scientists are not entirely sure why Assyrtiko shows this resistant trait, but this is one varietal that does not need to be grafted on different rootstock to survive in *phylloxera*-infested vineyards. Some of the oldest vineyards in Greece are planted with Assyrtiko, some dating back more than 150 years.

many grapes are grown but the fruity red wines made from Agiorgitiko are considered legendary. South of Neméa is Achaïa, where some of Greece's best-known wineries produce sweet wines made from Mavrodaphne and other varietals.

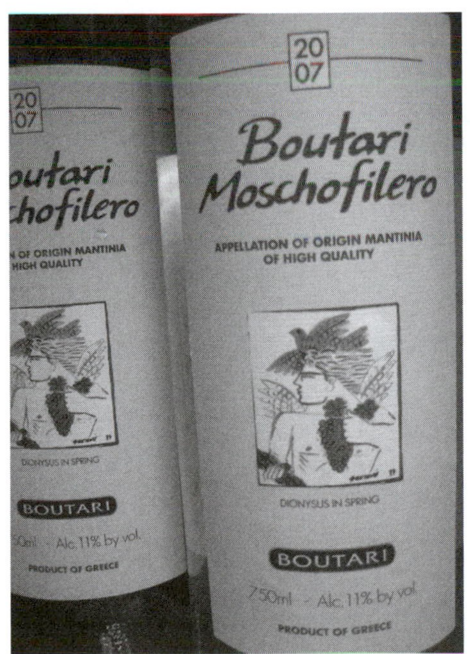

Greece produces a staggering number of interesting wines from indigenous grapes.

To the east of mainland Greece is the Aegean Sea, home to thousands of picturesque and important islands. The largest island in the Aegean is Crete, an important wine producer although modernization has not moved quickly there. To the north of Crete is the volcanic island known as **Santorini.** Rugged conditions and sparse soils produce some of Greece's top dry and sweet white wines on Santorini, mostly from Assyrtiko grapes. Several other important wines are produced throughout the Aegean Islands, especially Lemnos, Páros, Rhodes, and Samos.

The Ionian Sea is located to the west of mainland Greece toward Italy, and a strong Italian influence is found on the Greek islands there. Unique varieties and styles are grown and produced on the Ionian Islands, which are fewer in number than the Aegean islands and more sparsely populated. Focusing primarily on light, dry white wines, important wineries and regions are found on the islands of Cephalonia, Lefkada, and Zákinthos.

Other European Regions of Note

Aside from the Scandinavian countries, Ireland, and Scotland, every country in Europe produces wine. Many of the smaller countries of Western Europe produce only small amounts of wine in comparison to some of their larger neighbors, but there are hidden wine gems produced in most. And after decades of communist control, the once proud wine industries of many Eastern European countries lay in ruin, but foreign investment, capitalism, and modernization have all helped to reestablish quality winemaking in many of these countries.

SWITZERLAND

It is surprising that Switzerland does not produce more wine, given its neighbors. The country shares borders with France, Italy, Germany, and Austria—all major producers and exporters of wine. Much of the

Other European wine-producing countries of note.

cause of the lack of production has to do with the geography of Switzerland: the high elevations and Alpine conditions are simply inhospitable to wine grapes in most of the country. That said, vineyards are planted on almost every site that is capable of supporting vines, many of them planted on steep slopes to maximize exposure to the sun. Although they are not as common as some of the international varietals grown throughout Switzerland today, the country is home to interesting and sometimes outstanding indigenous grapes such as the white wine grapes Chasselas and **Petite Arvine** and the red wine varietal **Cornalin.**

Western Switzerland has a strong French heritage and is the center for most of the country's top wines as well as the bulk of its production. The **canton** (region) of **Vaud** hugs the northern shores of Lake Geneva and focuses much of its production on the white Chasselas grape, which is capable of producing nicely acidic, citrus- and mineral-flavored wines. To the east of Vaud is the canton of **Valais,** which straddles the Rhône River very near its source. Chasselas is grown here as well (locally called Fendant), but much of the excitement in the region is for red wine varietals such as Pinot Noir (sometimes called Blauburgunder) and Gamay, which are often blended together to produce a wine called **Dôle.** The canton of **Neuchâtel** is north of Vaud and makes Chasselas-based wines.

Southern Switzerland borders Alpine Italy, just north of Lombardy, Piedmont, and Trentino-Alto Adige. Italian-style wines dominate production in the area, but the most sought after are top red wines made from Merlot produced in the canton of **Ticino.** Northern Switzerland borders Germany and shares a strong viticultural influence with its neighbor. Müller-Thurgau, Sylvaner, and Pinot Blanc are some of the top white wine grapes for production, although more red wines—made mostly from Blauburgunder—are gaining popularity.

ENGLAND AND WALES

Great Britain is known for many beverages—tea, gin, ales, and scotch, to name a few—but has never been considered a top region for wine. Regardless, the English are major consumers of imported wines and there is a growing interest in developing more of a domestic wine industry in the country. The cool, often damp climate found in most of the British Isles is the biggest challenge to growing grapes and getting them to an adequate level of ripeness, which makes Wales and southern England the only two areas capable of producing quality wines. English winemakers focus mostly on early ripening grape varietals ideally suited to their cooler climates, such as German varietals like Müller-Thurgau and Bacchus, French varietals like Chardonnay and Pinot Noir, and some hybrids like Seyval Blanc.

CYPRUS

The island of Cyprus is located in the far eastern waters of the Mediterranean Sea, just south of Turkey. Although wine production has taken place in Cyprus since before the times of the ancient Greeks, recent history has not been kind to its winemakers. Occupation, civil war, communism, and severe economic hardships have all taken their toll on the wine industry of Cyprus, but there is a renewed interest of late, and quality producers are beginning to reestablish the wine fame of old.

Many producers are looking to revitalize traditional styles and wines in Cyprus, focusing on ancient grapes like the red wine varietal **Mavron** and the white Muscat of Alexandria. The wine the island was best known for through history, called **Commandaria,** is also making a comeback. Commandaria is an ultrasweet dessert wine (several times sweeter than most Port wines) produced from grapes that have been allowed to raisin in the warm sun. Besides these traditional styles, new plantings have mostly been export-friendly red wine varietals like Grenache and even Cabernet Sauvignon.

RUSSIA AND THE FORMER SOVIET REPUBLICS

The areas surrounding the Black Sea and Caspian Sea in the southwestern stretches of the former Soviet Union have long been planted to wine grapes, with archaeological evidence pointing to wine production several thousand years ago. Wine was considered a beverage of tolerance in Soviet times (compared to vodka), and massive winemaking undertakings were conducted by the communist government. Hundreds of thousands of vineyards were planted in the southwestern Soviet Union from the 1950s through the 1970s, producing an ocean of mass-produced, bland wines. Many of these wine operations were forced to shut their doors in the late 1980s, however, as the Gorbachev regime pushed an anti-alcohol agenda. With the breakup of the Soviet Union in the 1990s and the resulting independence of its former republics, winemaking is once again flourishing in the region, although many winemakers are beginning to focus on quality production with an eye on the international export market.

By far the most important viticultural region of the former Soviet Union and the top-producing country still today is Moldova. The warmest and furthest west of the former Soviet republics, Moldova is covered with vineyards, with nearly 10 percent of its total landmass planted to wine grapes. The Black Sea to the south keeps temperatures mild in the summer months and protects wine regions from harsh winters, allowing many grape varietals to thrive in its dozens of river valleys. While the region is best known for simple, pleasant red wines, many new wineries are attempting to produce distinguished wines using grape varietals old and new. The most notable are Cabernet Sauvignon–based wines, often blended with lesser-known, locally grown grapes like **Saperavi.**

To the east of Moldova along the Black Sea coastline is Ukraine, another important wine-producing region in its own right. Although the country has an often extreme climate featuring hot summers and cold winters, Ukrainian growers have succeeded in establishing hearty vineyards that produce a host of different wine styles. Dry table wines are a new concept for many winemakers, as the region is historically known for dessert wines, often fortified. The most exciting region of production in Ukraine is the southern peninsula of Crimea, which juts out into the Black Sea and is home to the country's warmest vineyard sites.

Western Russia lies to the south of Ukraine, with a large coastal area on the shores of the Black Sea to the west and the Caspian Sea to the east. Russia was never considered a major supplier of wine in the Soviet Union, which relied far more on western republics and satellite communist countries like Romania and Bulgaria for wine than on domestic production. Nevertheless, enterprising winemakers have recently begun planting vineyards and starting winemaking operations throughout western Russia, focusing much of their energy on the production of simple sparkling wines and sweeter whites. By far the most important grape grown in Russia, along with many of the former Soviet republics, is **Rkatsiteli,** a hearty white wine grape varietal that produces often average, light-bodied wines that range from dry to semisweet.

Georgia is the former Soviet republic found on the Black Sea south of Russia's top wine regions. Located south of the Caucasus Mountains, Georgia is believed to be part of the original birthplace of the *Vitis vinifera* vine. Today Georgia is home to hundreds of indigenous grape varietals and often produces unique, rustic wines. The most important of these would be the white grape Rkatsiteli—which shows far more character here than in most of the surrounding regions—and the red wine grape Saperavi. Most of the production in Georgia takes place in the easternmost inland reaches of the country, with vineyards planted in the shadow of the Caucasus.

ROMANIA

Lying at the same latitude as France, but with a cooler, continental climate, Romania's wine industry shows great promise. As with other Communist bloc countries, quality of vineyards and wines was replaced with quantity, but winemakers there today have their vision firmly set on becoming an important wine-exporting region. The country is dominated by the Carpathian Mountains, which run right through the middle of Romania and help protect many of the top wine regions from cold winter storms that would otherwise blow through from the north. Proximity to the Black Sea also helps to keep the continental climate mild. Vineyards are located throughout Romania, with the most important regions being Romania's portion of Moldova in the northwest, the high plains of central **Transylvania, Muntenia** in the south which borders Bulgaria, and the coastal region of **Dobrogea** in the southeast along the Black Sea.

Most of Romania's production today is dry, white wine made from local grape varieties such as **Fetească Regală** and **Fetească Albă,** although nontraditional white wine grapes are growing in popularity, especially Welschriesling, Muscat, and even some Chardonnay. Botrytised dessert wines are also a specialty in many regions, with the most famous being a fragrantly sweet wine reminiscent of Hungary's Tokaji, called **Cotnari,** which is produced in the northeastern province of Moldova. Red wine grapes are grown in areas warm enough for them to ripen, with notable red wines made from the native **Babeasca,** as well as Merlot and Cabernet Sauvignon.

BULGARIA

After shedding the shackles of communism, Bulgaria is a country firmly set on becoming a major exporter of wines. Unlike many Eastern European countries whose production is mostly intended for domestic consumption, Bulgaria currently exports more than half of its wines. With government incentives and international investment, Bulgaria is increasing its production year after year.

Bulgaria is sandwiched between Romania to the north and Greece and Turkey to the south, and winemaking in the country dates back to the ancient Greeks. The climate of the region is warm and dry, impacted by the Black Sea to the east and the Aegean to the south. This allows for long ripening periods and full-bodied, often pleasantly fruity red wines in most of the country. These are the specialties of the southern regions of the **West** and **East Thracian Valleys.** White wines are not as common as reds, but the best are from the cooler, eastern region of **Sofiya.**

Much of the wine produced in Bulgaria today is made using internationally recognizable grape varieties like Cabernet Sauvignon, Merlot, and Chardonnay, which are easy to market and sell in England and in other European countries. Native grapes have been slowly losing vineyard acreage, but some older producers still make interesting red wines from the local **Mavrud** and **Melnik** grapes.

SLOVENIA, CROATIA, AND THE BALKANS

The former Yugoslavia is home to a variety of different cultures, lands, and winemaking traditions. Located across the Adriatic Sea from Italy, this part of the world is surrounded by other wine-producing countries, including Greece, Bulgaria, Romania, Hungary, and Austria, all of which have had influences on wines here. Most of the countries that resulted from the breakup of Yugoslavia produce significant amounts of wine, most notably Slovenia and Croatia.

Slovenia is the northernmost country in the region, and is considered by many to be the best wine producer. It grows dozens of different indigenous and obscure grape varieties, but is increasing plantings of foreign grapes, mostly French and Italian. The eastern wine regions of Slovenia border northeastern Italy, and their wines are often very similar: light-bodied, dry whites. Northwestern Slovenia is best known for decadent dessert wines similar to those found across the border in Austria.

Croatia is just to the south of Slovenia, and is a combination of a large inland area that reaches east to Hungary and a large stretch of Adriatic coastline and islands that stretch south along the Adriatic. This country is home to a variety of unique regional wines, many of which evolved without foreign influence. One of the most important grapes grown in the region is **Plavac Mali,** once mistakenly believed to be identical to the Zinfandel grape. Much of the best production is found along the coastline, with the focus on spicy, powerful reds and aromatic whites.

Several other areas of the former Yugoslavia have unique and interesting winemaking traditions, and producers are beginning to develop export-quality wines. Serbia produces several different white wine styles, but its southern neighbor Kosovo is more famous for sweet, red wines. East of Kosovo is Montenegro, and to the south is Macedonia, both producers of hearty red wines. Albania is the warmest and southernmost of any of these regions, but thus far remains mostly undeveloped for wine production.

The Mysterious Origins of Zinfandel

There has been much debate over the past several decades as to the exact origins of one of California's most important and widely planted grape varieties, Zinfandel. There were several different theories on the origin of this grape, but the leading argument was that Zinfandel was actually a popular Croatian grape variety called Plavac Mali, grown widely along the Dalmation Coast of that country. In the late 1990s, DNA testing revealed that Zinfandel was not the same as Plavac Mali, but the two were related. It turned out that Zinfandel was actually one of the parents of Plavac Mali, along with another obscure Croatian grape called Dobricic.

While these findings disproved the most widely believed theory about Zinfandel's origins, they did confirm that the grape was most likely indigenous to Croatia. Many samples from sparsely planted, sometimes forgotten grape vines planted throughout Croatia's western shores finally yielded a match. Zinfandel turned out to be genetically identical to a local varietal called Crljenak, an unassuming blending grape, unimportant at the time. Since the match, plantings of this grape are increasing significantly in many of Croatia's vineyards, and single-varietal wines are being produced there.

Summary

Europe is a continent of wine-producing nations: every country in Europe that can produce wine does so. While the most famous and important European regions receive most of the attention in the international and American markets, many wine drinkers are beginning to take notice of several lesser-known wine-producing nations. Of these, the most important are Austria, Hungary, and Greece. Each has a rich history of wine production and fame that was lost along the way for many reasons, including scandal, war, and failure to modernize. Today, the winemaking traditions in these countries and many others have been revitalized as they attempt to regain the quality and status their wines enjoyed in the past.

Review Questions

1. The most widely grown and important grape of Austria is ______________.
   - A. Chardonnay
   - B. Riesling
   - C. Grüner Veltliner
   - D. Furmint

2. The Austrian wine industry has some of the strictest wine laws in the world today as a result of:
   - A. a strong French influence in the country.
   - B. a scandal in the 1980s involving adulterated wine.
   - C. rebuilding after World War II.
   - D. tradition.

3. Austrian wines are classified by ripeness, similar to the system used in Germany.
   - A. True
   - B. False

4. *Ausbruch* is an Austrian ________________.
   - A. style of dessert wine
   - B. wine region
   - C. grape variety
   - D. style of red wine

5. Which of the following is the name for the top red wine produced in Hungary, whose name translates to "Bull's Blood of Eger"?
   - A. Tokaji Aszú
   - B. Eger Blodva
   - C. Egri Bikavér
   - D. Kadarka Eger

6. The most important grape variety used in the production of sweet Tokaji wines is ______________.
   - A. Furmint
   - B. Kékfrankos
   - C. Essencia
   - D. Riesling

7. What is the Hungarian term for botrytis, a mold that attacks grapes and concentrates their sugar content for the production of sweet wines?
   - A. Puttonyos
   - B. Aszú
   - C. Furmint
   - D. Essencia

8. Greece is considered the first European region to produce wine.
   - A. True
   - B. False

9. Which of the following is *not* a difficulty faced by Greek winemakers trying to sell their wines on the international market?
   - A. They grow many unfamiliar, indigenous grapes
   - B. They lack an organized system of wine laws
   - C. Their wines are often associated with low-grade retsinas
   - D. Failure to modernize caused their industry to fall behind other regions

10. The Greek grape Xinómavro translates to ______________.
    - A. "sweet one"
    - B. "little fog"
    - C. "lion heart"
    - D. "sour black"

Key Terms

Prädikatswein
Districtus Austriae Controllatus (DAC)
Welschriesling
Zweigelt
Niederösterreich
Burgenland
Steiermark
Wien
Ausbruch
Egri Bikavér
Kadarka
Aszú
Tokaji Aszú
puttonyos
Essencia
retsina
Onomasía Proeléfseos Anotéras Piótitos (OPAP)
Onomasía Proeléfseos Eleghoméni (OPE)
Assyrtiko
Moschofilero
Rhoditis
Savatiano
Athiri
Mandilaria
Agiorgitiko
Macedonia
Peloponnese
Náoussa
Attica
Thessaly
Epirus
Neméa
Santorini
Petite Arvine
Cornalin
canton
Vaud
Valais
Dôle
Neuchâtel
Ticino
Mavron
Commandaria
Saperavi
Rkatsiteli
Transylvania
Muntenia
Dobrogea
Fetească Regală
Fetească Albă
Cotnari
Babeasca
West Thracian Valley
East Thracian Valley
Sofiya
Mavrud
Melnik
Plavac Mali

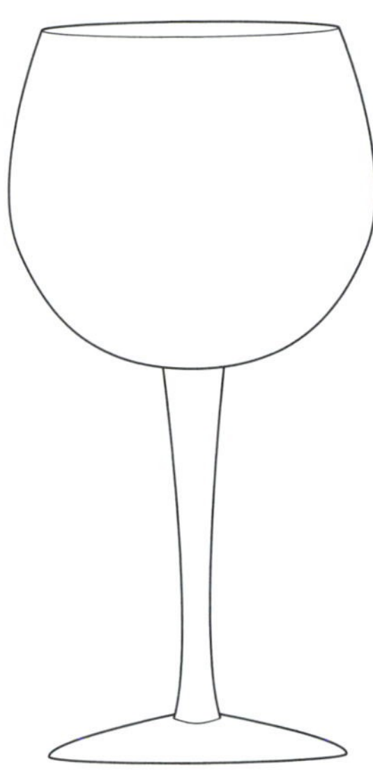

CHAPTER 15

The Old World and the New World of Wine

Following the light of the sun, we left the Old World.

—CHRISTOPHER COLUMBUS

One of the most important ways that wines and wine regions around the world are categorized is in terms of Old World or New World. It is a division in both winemaking style and philosophy. Generally speaking, "Old World" describes wines from Europe or produced in a traditional European style. "New World" refers to wines produced outside of Europe, or according to modern winemaking styles. This chapter reviews the previous section covering European wines and introduces the next section dedicated to winemaking regions in the New World. It summarizes the winemaking styles, laws, and philosophies of both the Old World and the New World, including the major differences between the two.

Old World versus New World

Important wine grapes and wine styles have been developed and established in Europe over the course of thousands of years. With the discovery of new continents over the sea and the resulting expansion of colonial empires, European nations spread to the Americas, Africa, and Australia. In establishing colonies in these new lands, early settlers and Catholic monks looked to quickly establish vineyards, planting them to the grapes of Europe. Wine and other fermented beverages were important staples in these colonies.

Conditions were different from Europe in most of these new vineyards and wine regions, and grape growers and winemakers had to adapt. As **New World** wine regions experimented with different grapes and styles, their wines never approached the quality of those back in Europe. It would take technology and science to help the New World create wines that rivaled the traditional wines of the **Old World.**

Winemaking in the New World during the latter half of the last century began to focus on the production of premium wines using modern, scientific techniques rather than traditional practices. These winemakers started producing their own unique interpretations of many of Europe's classic styles and grapes. This new style contrasted with traditional European winemaking in many different ways.

Important Wine Countries of the Old World and New World

OLD WORLD COUNTRIES	NEW WORLD COUNTRIES
France	United States
Italy	Australia
Spain	New Zealand
Germany	South Africa
Portugal	Chile
Austria	Argentina
Greece	Canada
Hungary	Mexico
Romania	Uruguay

Today, the term "New World" is used in the wine industry to describe wines that are made using technical innovation, experimentation, and manipulation. "Old World" techniques in the vineyard and cellar rely more on tradition and less on science. The notion of ***terroir*** is an important and well-established one. In the Old World, the characteristics of the regions create the wine, not the winemaking regime.

While Old World refers to most European wines, and New World refers to wines produced outside of Europe, these are just generalities. There are winemakers in the New World who use very Old World methods to produce their wines, while many European winemakers have adopted modern practices of winemaking. In this way, we can also use the terminology to describe a style, not just a geographical origin. Nevertheless, the differences between Old World and New World wines are primarily defined by climate and conditions, as well as winemaking philosophies and regulations.

CLIMATE AND CONDITIONS

One of the fundamental differences between wine-producing countries in the Old World and those in the New World is climate. Overall, the wine regions of Europe are cooler than those found outside of Europe. The top production regions of the New World—California, Australia, Chile, South Africa, and Argentina—are all considered warmer than average as viticultural areas. This climate difference can have a huge effect on how grapes ripen, and that can fundamentally alter the characteristics of a finished wine. Grapes tend to achieve much higher levels of ripeness in warmer climates because the growing seasons are longer. The ripeness found in a grape will directly affect three of the most important characteristics of any wine: acidity, alcohol, and body. In the Old World, where conditions are cooler, grapes rarely achieve high levels of ripeness. The resulting wines will be acidic in nature, contain average to low levels of alcohol, and have lighter body than their New World counterparts.

The overall power of a wine is also related to ripeness and climate. New World wines tend to focus much more on brute force and power than those produced in Europe. Ripe fruit flavors, full body, and potent alcohol content are all aspects that contribute to the power of a wine. In the Old World, brute force is replaced by finesse and elegance. European wines tend to be more restrained and subtle.

Maybe the most important difference between Old World and New World wines, caused by the climate and growing conditions in their winemaking regions, is their distinct flavor profiles. Because New World wines are mostly produced from grapes that ripen more than they do in Europe, fruit flavors

Although this Australian Shiraz is made with the same grapes as this Rhône Valley wine, the climates the grapes were grown in will make the two wines taste very different.

develop in these wines to a much more significant degree. Instead of trying to suppress this **fruit-forward** style of wine, the winemakers in the New World have instead embraced it.

In cooler Old World countries, fruit flavors are much more subtle and refined. Most European wines focus on other flavors instead, especially those from the earth. These wines are considered ***terroir*-driven,** and feature wet earth and mineral flavors rather than the ultraripe, jammy fruit of New World wines.

Old World Wines	New World Wines
Higher acidity	Lower acidity
Lighter body	Fuller body
Lower alcohol	Higher alcohol
Restrained and elegant	Powerful
Terroir-driven	Fruit-forward

WINEMAKING PHILOSOPHIES AND REGULATIONS

Not only are growing conditions different in the New World and the Old World; so too are the philosophies on how wine should be produced. With thousands of years of grape-growing trial and error, Europeans certainly have the advantage over New World winemakers in knowing their land. This close link to their vineyards has allowed them to systematically determine which grapes grow best and what style of wine should be produced based on where their vineyards are located.

Most European wines are "made in the vineyard." Not literally, of course, but the Old World style of winemaking dictates that the vineyard itself, having been matched to the proper grapes and style, should determine the flavors and characteristics of the wine. Viticulture is more important than viniculture. It is the job of the winemakers to stay out of the way of the vineyard when they make the wine, simply showing off what that vineyard produced. In fact, there is not even a word in the French language for "winemaker." Instead they use the term ***vigneron,*** which means "grape grower," to describe someone who actually makes wine.

New World winemakers do not have the same luxury of historical production. While most European countries have been producing wine for thousands of years, most New World countries have only been at it for hundreds. This lack of tradition is made up for in science and technology, and that has helped to establish a fundamental difference in philosophy. If Old World wines are "made in the vineyard," then New World wines are undoubtedly "made in the winery." Winemakers practice much heavier manipulation of wines to gain control over them, and have developed many winemaking techniques to change the characteristics of wines. In this case, viniculture is more important than viticulture. This is a necessity in many cases, because the right grape might not be matched to a particular region. Winemaking has to cover up any problems or shortfalls in the vineyard.

This focus on manipulation is evidenced in the aging and conditioning processes used to finish wines. New World wines tend to be much more aggressively oaked than those from the Old World. Oak can actually drive the flavor profile of a New World wine, while it only plays a supporting role in most European wines. Due to the power and stronger flavors of New World wines, this only makes sense. More intensely flavored wines can stand up to stronger oak flavors. The more subtle flavors found in Old World wines would be dominated by such heavy use of oak aging.

Other winemaking techniques like the use of ***sur lie*** aging or malolactic fermentation (see Chapter 4) are limited or outright forbidden in several parts of Europe, but New World winemakers have no such restrictions. They readily use these techniques and others to add complexity and flavors to their wines.

Besides philosophy and winemaking, the tradition of Europe and the lack of tradition outside Europe have also had a major impact upon the winemaking laws and regulations of the Old and New Worlds. With thousands of years to experiment in its wine regions, Europe has had enough time to figure out what they do best. Since Europeans have determined which grape varieties grow best in various regions and how wines should be produced from them, their wine laws can be set up in a way that is much stricter and more rigid than those in the New World.

Europe's wine laws are filled with strict regulations governing approved grapes, styles, and winemaking techniques that can be used in a particular region. These laws usually require all the winemakers of a region to follow the same criteria when producing a wine. This is completely acceptable to those winemakers, because they know that these laws will guide them in producing the very best type of wine suited to their vineyards. This is why most of the European wine laws are regionally based—the region determines everything. As an extension of the laws, wine labels in the Old World do not bear the names of the grapes from which they were produced; rather, they list the region in which those grapes were grown.

In New World regions and vineyards, there is very little historical data, and even less tradition, compared to Europe. Winemakers simply have not had enough time there to figure out what it is they do best. This means that winemakers and grape growers in the New World are constantly experimenting, trying new grape varieties in different vineyards, and exploring new wine regions.

The wine laws of the New World mirror this experimental focus. In countries outside of Europe, wine laws are not excessively strict; rather, they are purposely loose and full of exceptions. Without tradition to fall back on, the wine laws of the New World are written to allow those winemakers the opportunity to experiment. This allows them to try new grapes and techniques, and to constantly refine the knowledge they have about their vineyards. That is why wines in the New World are not labeled by region as they are in Europe; instead, winemakers label wines by the predominant grape used to produce them.

Old World wines are usually labeled by the specific region in which the grapes were grown rather than the name of the grape.

Old World Wines	New World Wines
"Made in the vineyard"	"Made in the winery"
Viticulture-dominant	Viniculture-dominant
Little manipulation of wines	Heavy manipulation of wines
Subtle oak flavors	Powerful oak flavors
Tradition	Science and technology
Strict laws	Loose laws
Label by region	Label by grape

Summary

This chapter is intended to transition the reader from wines and winemaking in traditional European countries to the different philosophies and styles of the New World. There are major differences in winemaking, grape growing, and style between these two areas of winemaking and arenas of thought. Understanding these differences is key to having a better appreciation for the wines produced in both the Old World and the New World, and allows one to better describe and explain these distinct styles.

Review Questions

1. Which of the following is considered a New World wine country?
   - A. France
   - B. Australia
   - C. Italy
   - D. Germany

2. An Old World–style wine cannot be produced in California.
   A. True
   B. False

3. On average, New World countries are warmer than Old World countries.
   A. True
   B. False

4. If tasting a powerful, fruit-forward wine, it is best to describe that wine as being ___________ in style.
   A. Old World
   B. New World

5. The wine laws found in Old World countries are far stricter than those of New World countries.
   A. True
   B. False

6. Winemakers rely more on technology and science in the:
   A. Old World
   B. New World

7. Winemakers are more reserved about the use of heavy oak aging and other manipulations of wine in the:
   A. Old World
   B. New World

8. It is common for winemakers in the ___________ to label their wines by the main grape variety used to produce the wine.
   A. Old World
   B. New World

Key Terms

New World
Old World
fruit-forward
terroir-driven
vigneron

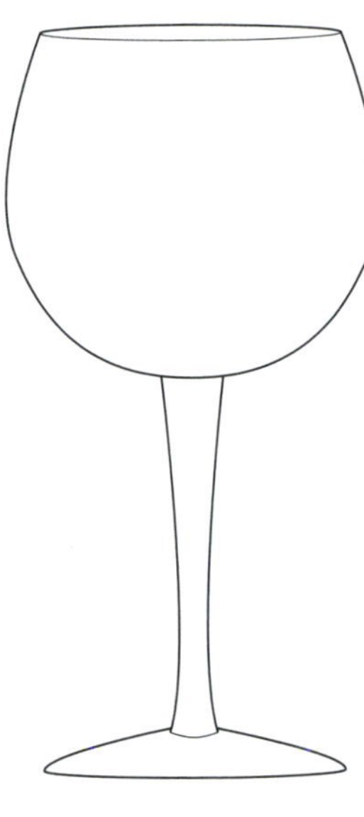

CHAPTER 16

The Wines of the United States

Wine to me is passion. It's family and friends. It's warmth of heart and generosity of spirit. Wine is art. It's culture. It's the essence of civilization and the art of living.

—**ROBERT MONDAVI**, American winemaker and legendary proponent of California wines

The United States is the top wine-production area outside of Europe, and all of the other New World wine countries model their wine laws and industries after the United States. This chapter covers the wine laws, wine labels, growing conditions, top grapes and wines, and most important wine regions within the United States—including California, Oregon, and Washington, as well as a brief snapshot of other states of note.

The Facts on the United States

CLIMATE

Located almost entirely between the 30th and 50th parallels of latitude, the continental United States is home to a temperate climate overall.

TOP REGIONS

- California
- Oregon
- Washington

IMPORTANT INFORMATION

- The United States is the fourth leading producer of wine in the world, and the top-producing country outside of Europe.
- With a little over four hundred years of grape growing and wine production, the United States has a very short history of winemaking when compared to the major wine-producing countries of Europe.
- The American wine laws are much looser than their European counterparts, mostly in an effort to allow American winemakers an opportunity to experiment and try new things in the vineyard.
- A system of officially recognized wine regions has been established throughout the United States, called American Viticultural Areas (AVAs). These are areas that have shown unique winemaking conditions and have specific boundaries.
- Most American wine is labeled by grape variety, as long as the vast majority of the grapes used to produce the wine are the listed varietal.

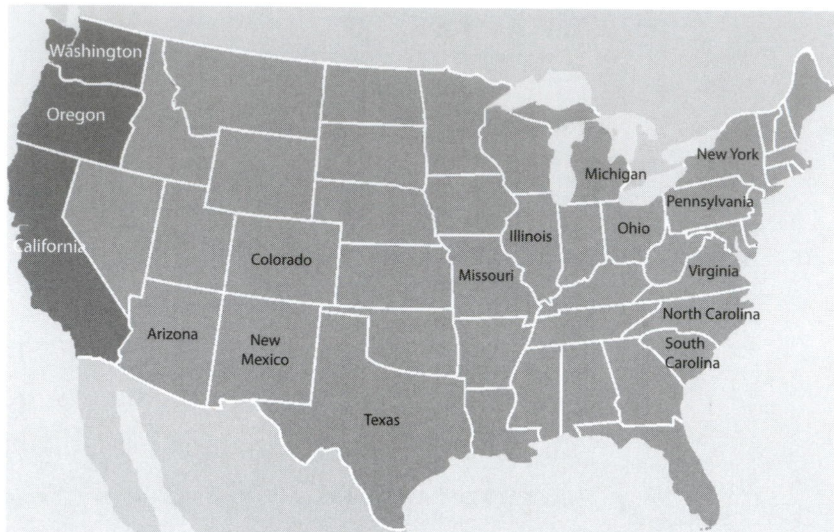

Important wine producing states in the United States, including the three top quality regions of California, Oregon, and Washington.

The United States: Land of Potential

The United States of America is the top winemaking country in the New World, ranking fourth in worldwide wine production behind the European powerhouses of France, Italy, and Spain. Although the country has a very short history of wine production when compared to the classical powers of Europe, it has come a long way in rapid fashion. The potential for winemaking in the United States will take generations to be fully realized, as the industry is truly in its infancy.

Winemaking and wine grapes were first brought to the United States by Spanish missionaries and European settlers in the late 1500s and the early 1600s. Many early settlements made it a point to establish winemaking operations, and although severe setbacks occurred, attempts continued to be made. Through the colonial era, European vines were planted up and down the East Coast, although these attempts failed miserably because ***phylloxera*** infested the soils.

After the Revolutionary War, several of the Founding Fathers including Washington and Jefferson repeatedly tried to start vineyards planted to wine grape vines. Although the European vines never survived, several hybrids were developed and native grape species were commonly used. These wines were not equal to those produced in Europe, but a local supply fed the demand for thirsty Americans.

As the United States began to spread west, so too did winemaking. New vineyards were established and successful wineries opened their doors in areas of the Ohio River Valley, especially in Missouri and Ohio. Leading up to the early 1800s, winemaking started to grow substantially in the United States. This was just a taste of things to come, though, as the United States was about to expand all the way to the Pacific Ocean and important events were about to unfold in the 1840s and 1850s.

When the United States defeated Mexico during the Mexican American War, it gained the most important area for wine production in the country today, California. Mild weather conditions and fertile soils were ideal for growing grapes, and even pure ***Vitis vinifera*** vines could thrive with the lack of vineyard pests and diseases. The only problem was that there was not a large enough population in the state to fill local demand or establish winemaking operations—at least not until someone discovered gold in California.

Thomas Jefferson: America's First Wine Connoisseur

Besides being a proponent of establishing vineyards in America and developing a domestic wine industry, Thomas Jefferson was also an avid collector of wine, especially French wine, after spending time in that country. There are two wine cellars at Monticello, Jefferson's Virginia estate, and records show that while he was president he spent the bulk of his budget for food and beverage on French wine. (He felt that five hundred bottles of Champagne should be in stock at all times!) After his term as president was over, he served as the unofficial wine advisor to presidents Madison and Monroe. The most expensive bottle of wine ever sold was a 1787 vintage of Château Lafite from Bordeaux believed to be from Jefferson's private collection. It fetched more than $150,000 at a London auction in 1985.

The gold rush era began in California in 1849 and lasted nearly twenty years. During that time, California saw an extreme increase of its population as hundreds of thousands of settlers made their way there to strike it rich. Several enterprising farmers began to plant grapes in northern California, establishing many of the first wineries in Napa Valley and Sonoma County. By the turn of the century (and after a brief bout with the dreaded *phylloxera* that was accidentally spread there), California was poised to challenge the powers of American winemaking that were then found in the Midwest.

Despite successes in California and other U.S. states in producing wine, the early history of wine production in the United States was about to come to an end as Prohibition was enacted in 1920. During the thirteen-year period of Prohibition, thousands of American wineries closed and millions of vines were dug up and replaced with other crops. After Prohibition was repealed in 1933, the U.S. wine industry was nearly gone. It would take several decades for forces of change to rebuild U.S. winemaking.

During the depression era of the 1930s, California witnessed its second major population boom as millions of unemployed Americans continued to move west to find work. This demographic shift allowed California to rebuild its wine industry faster than other areas of the United States, and the state has never looked back since. After first experimenting with quality winemaking in the 1960s and winning a world-changing wine tasting competition in the 1970s, California was finally a serious wine-producing region respected around the world.

Following California's model, winemakers in Washington and Oregon also began experimenting with different methods, grapes, and regions, and quietly established their own premium wine industries in the 1960s through the 1980s. Other states around the country also began or started to rebuild winemaking industries with quality production in mind. The passage of modern winemaking laws in 1978 paved the way for officially establishing premium wine-labeling regulations and recognizing distinct areas of wine production throughout the country.

Today, wine has become a multibillion-dollar industry for the United States, with thousands of wineries across the country. As most of the continental United States is located between the 30th and 50th parallels of latitude, temperate conditions are found throughout the country. California currently dominates wine production in the United States, but several other states are beginning to build their wine industries. Relative newcomers such as Oregon and Washington show great promise, and make up in quality what they lack in quantity.

Due to the temperate climate zones found throughout most of the United States and an increased interest in wine production, new wineries have been opening across the United States at an amazing rate. Believe it or not, all fifty U.S. states produce wine today, and are home to at least one commercial winery! This means that they do make wine in places like Alaska, Arizona, Hawaii, North Dakota, Rhode Island, Louisiana, Maine, and Tennessee. That said, the four top-producing states are:

1. California
2. Washington
3. New York
4. Oregon

Among these four states, more than 97 percent of America's total wine is produced, with California accounting for a whopping 90 percent of the national total.

The United States is poised to become a world power in wine production. Domestic consumption levels and the popularity of wine have not been as high as they are today since well before Prohibition. Established wine-producing states and regions continue to grow, evolve, and perfect their craft. The rest of the world has finally taken notice of the important wine produced in the United States, and export sales are increasing. U.S. winemakers do not make as much premium wine as some countries, but wine for wine, the quality of this country's best wines will stack up to anyone's. It is time to turn potential into reality.

WINE LAWS OF THE UNITED STATES

The wine laws of the United States are much looser and more lenient than those of Europe, in an effort to allow winemakers an opportunity to experiment with different practices, grape varieties, and wine styles. There are no strict regulations on winemaking, nor are there official quality classifications based on appellation. In large part, this is due to the fact that American winemakers do not have the same tradition found in most European countries that have been practicing winemaking for thousands of years.

Used as the model for most other New World countries, the wine laws of the United States deal primarily with the producer, grapes or styles produced, and the wine's origin. Overseeing the American wine laws is a wing of the Federal Treasury Department known as the **Alcohol and Tobacco Tax and Trade Bureau**, or **TTB.** It has established regulations for winemakers across the country that do not focus on the establishment of strict quality standards, but rather serve to collect tax revenues and protect consumers from fraudulent labeling practices and against health concerns. It is the labeling regulations that make up the most important part of these laws. In this section, only premium wines will be discussed in detail.

Producers and Brand Names

A brand name is often displayed on a U.S. wine label, as it is used to identify, market, and promote the wine. Regulations are quite loose in regard to brand names, as only profane or misleading terms are prohibited. Misleading terms include any reference to a recognized region from which the wine did not originate (e.g., a wine could not use the brand name "Sonoma Heights" if it was not made from grapes grown in the Sonoma County or one of its official subregions).

The brand name of a wine may or may not be the actual name of the winery, bottler, or producer. The name of the winery, bottler, or producer does need to appear on the label, however, along with a reference to their role in the wine's production and a physical address made up of a town and state. Several different terms can appear to relate the role of the company or bottler selling the wine. The main terms are detailed in the box at right.

Grape Variety/Style

Most premium American wines are labeled by the grape variety most used in their production, instead of the European standard of labeling a wine by its place of origin. With no legal restrictions on which grapes can be grown in any American winemaking area, labeling by region would make no sense and would quickly confuse consumers.

If an American wine is labeled by grape variety, then by U.S. law it must contain at least 75 percent of the listed varietal and must also state the name of the area of origin. This 75 percent figure was negotiated between the wine industry and the federal government to allow winemakers the opportunity to practice the common technique of blending different grapes together and still be able to call their wines by a specific varietal name. Although it often appears somewhere on the label, there is no regulation that winemakers have to list any other grapes used in the production of a wine except the main varietal. States are allowed to make their specific wine regulations stricter than these federal guidelines, but thus far

Common Terms Regarding the Role of the Bottler/Producer

TERM	DEFINITION
Bottled by	This term usually means that the stated producer had very little to do with the wine's production. The minimum involvement only relates to bottling the wine, as it is often purchased from a third party that actually produced and bulk aged the wine.
Cellared by	Term used by wineries that typically buy their wine from another source and then bottle it and age it on their premises. There are no legal restrictions for the length of aging.
Estate bottled	The strictest term governed on a wine label. It guarantees that the producer grew 100% of the grapes for the wine in vineyards it owns or controls through long-term leases. The wine must be fermented, aged, and bottled on the premises of the producer in the same winemaking region where the grapes were grown.
Grown, produced and bottled by	To use this term, the producer must grow the grapes used in the wine in vineyards they own or control, and then produce at least 75% of the wine on their premises before bottling it; similar to "Estate bottled," but not as strict.
Made and bottled by	This term is used when a producer ferments at least 10% of the wine and then bottles it on their premises; the other 90% comes from a third-party source.
Produced and bottled by	To use this term, the stated producer must have crushed and fermented at least 75% of the wine and bottled and aged it on their premises.
Vinted by	This term simply means the wine was purchased already bottled, and was aged on the premises of the listed producer.

only Oregon has done so, raising its minimum to 90 percent for most varietals.

If no grape used to produce a wine makes up more than 75 percent, the wine will commonly be labeled by color and/or style—for instance, red wine, white wine, rosé wine, table wine, sparkling wine, or dessert wine. In most cases, winemakers will also label their wines by a proprietary or brand name. These are usually trademarked brand names, and they are sometimes fiercely guarded and marketed. In a few cases, winemakers might label a wine by a proprietary name even when one of the grapes used to produce it does cross over the 75 percent threshold, although this is rare.

Appellation of Origin

Besides listing a grape variety, style, and/or proprietary name on the label of a premium U.S. wine, winemakers must also list an appellation of origin. There are several levels of origins, from the national level down through states, counties, and specific winemaking regions called American Viticultural Areas (AVAs). Each has different minimum standards for the percentage of grapes that must be grown within the appellation of origin to list it on a label.

Origin Listed on Label	Minimum Percentage of Grape's Origin
United States/American	100%
Any state (except CA or WA)	75%
California or Washington	100%
County	75%
American Viticultural Area	85%

An **American Viticultural Area (AVA)** is a specific, official winemaking region recognized and registered by the TTB. There are currently almost two hundred AVA regions located throughout the United States, with more than half found in California. American Viticultural Areas range in size from less than 500 acres to well over 15 million acres. To qualify for AVA status the region in question must have specific boundaries and either distinct historical or viticultural reasons for being created. This is often based on one or more geographical or *terroir*-based characteristics, such as soil type, climate, elevation, or, most commonly, a geographic feature such as a valley, basin, mountain, and so on.

In theory, an AVA region should be more specific than a state or county appellation. Its purpose is to provide specific information to a consumer about the origin of a wine, which should have a major impact on the wine's characteristics. The listed AVA is supposed to have some viticultural aspect or feature that distinguishes it from other areas. Simply being produced in an American Viticultural Area is not a guarantee of quality or strict winemaking practices as it is with most European appellations. It is simply a listed region from which the wine originated.

While the AVA system can get confusing quickly, rest assured that most producers will use the smallest appellation possible to label their wines. This is because the smaller the appellation, the less the supply and thus the higher the prices. But consider this example: A wine made from grapes grown in the Mount Veeder AVA could list the appellation as Mount Veeder, Napa Valley (the larger AVA that Mount Veeder is within), or North Coast (the regional-sized AVA that Napa Valley is a part of). In addition, winemakers could actually label the wine with an appellation of Napa County, California, or even the United States. This one wine technically qualifies for six different appellations of origin that could be put on the label!

The Evolution of the AVA System

As the AVA system of recognized regions across the United States has developed, several peculiarities have evolved:

- There are no size restrictions on AVA regions, so they can range greatly in size. Several AVA regions are much larger than most counties or states, even though they are supposed to be more specific wine-growing regions, in theory.
- AVA regions can be found within other AVA regions, either as a subregion completely contained within the larger AVA, or even simply overlapping another AVA.
- The boundaries of AVA regions are not designed to fit neatly within states, counties, or other political borders, and several encompass more than one county or state.
- Several states have developed a hierarchy of AVA regions. Enormous AVAs are established to group together a number of large AVAs. In turn these large AVAs contain smaller subregions with AVA status.

This wine label lists the American Viticultural Area of Napa Valley, where at least 85 percent of the grapes used to produce it must have been grown.

Other Label Terms and Laws

Besides the basics mentioned above, many other terms appear on American wine labels. Some of these terms are strictly regulated by the federal government, while others legally mean nothing. At right is a chart listing some of these common terms.

TERM	DEFINITION
Name of a vineyard	If a vineyard is listed on a label in addition to an area of origin, this means that at least 95% of the grapes used to produce the wine must have been grown in the listed vineyard.
Vintage	If a vintage appears on a bottle of U.S. wine, then at least 95% of the grapes used to produce the wine must have been harvested in that vintage.
Reserve	There is no legal definition for the term "Reserve" or any of its many forms ("Winemaker's Reserve," "Special Reserve," etc.). It is a term that is defined by the producer of the wine, and can mean many different things to different producers. The one exception is in Washington State, where Reserve means that the wine is 10% or less of the winery's total production and is of a higher quality than normal wines the winery produces.
Contains Sulfites	Appears on any bottle of wine that contains 10 parts per million or more of sulfites. These come in the form of naturally occurring compounds formed during fermentation or the use of sulfur dioxide, an antimicrobial agent, during the winemaking process. For the vast majority of the population, sulfites are harmless.
Old Vines	There is no legal minimum for the age of vines used to produce a wine. This definition is determined solely by the producer, although it usually refers to vines that are at least thirty to forty years old or more.

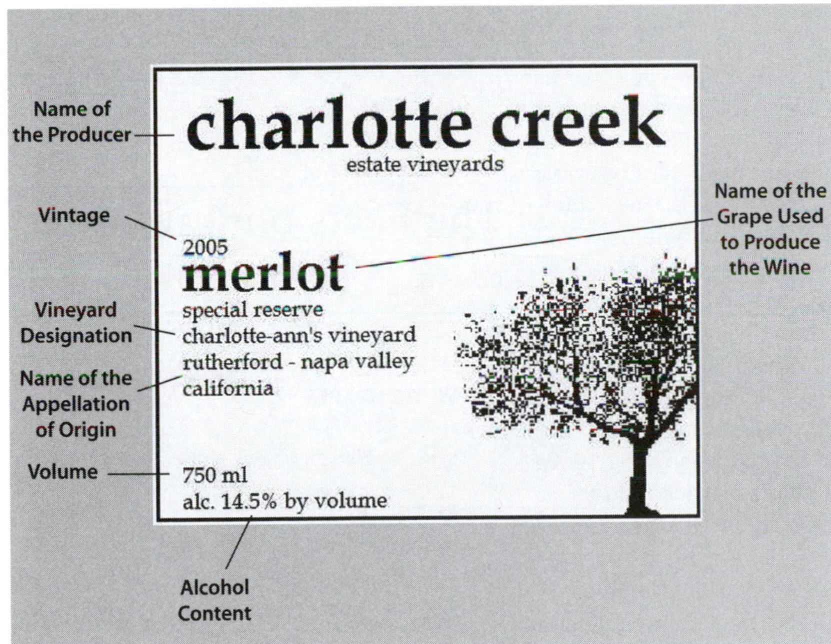

How to read an American wine label.

California: The Golden State

California is by far the most important area of wine production in the United States, if not the most important region outside of Europe. California accounts for roughly 90 percent of U.S. wine, and if the state was its own country, it would still rank fourth in the world in terms of wine production. Winemaking has become a multibillion-dollar industry in California, but this current success came from difficult beginnings.

Wine was first produced in California by Spanish missionaries who established a chain of missions starting in the early 1600s, from San Diego in the south several hundred miles north along the California coast. In order to provide wine for the sacrament, these missions planted grapes and produced wines. The predominant varietal was known as the Mission grape, a hearty red grape of high yields and low quality (known as Criolla in Argentina and Pais in Chile, where it was widely planted by Spanish monks for the same reasons). Mission grapes were still important to winemaking and widely planted in California until the early 1900s.

Throughout the early 1800s, wine production was limited throughout the state, and many of the best-known wine regions in the state today did not have a single grapevine planted within their borders. After the first commercial plantings of wine grapes during the gold rush era of the mid-1800s, areas like Napa Valley and Sonoma County were rapidly planted. While these plantings certainly showed promise, California's wine industry faced several major challenges over the course of the next hundred years, including *phylloxera*, Prohibition, and the Great Depression.

When the California wine industry eventually landed back on its feet, it did so by producing generic bulk wines and sweet fortified wines throughout the 1950s. California at long last surpassed all other states in the United States for total wine production, but none of this was quality production. The 1960s ushered in a new era for California's wine industry, as new producers began to experiment with higher-quality French grapes and techniques, setting the stage for a wine quality revolution in the state. The Spurrier Tasting of 1976 ushered in that new era as California announced its importance in the wine world and turned the international wine industry on its ear. Following their victory against France, California winemakers began replanting vineyards throughout the state with top-quality grape varietals, and the focus shifted to quality over quantity of production.

Strings of successful vintages and savvy marketing continued to build the reputation of California's wines. State college and university degree programs in winemaking and grape growing have produced a new generation of trained winemakers and viticulturalists, especially at the revered University of California at Davis. A country of citizens who continue to drink more wine per person year after year has also added fuel to the state's wine industry. Today, California is far and away the top state in the United States for wine production in terms of both quantity and quality, and its wineries are some of the most modern, state-of-the-art winemaking facilities in the world.

Thus far, premium production has revolved around only a handful of grapes and a few select regions. As traditional regions perfect styles, new areas are established, and different varietals are planted, there is no telling how far this state can go as one of the world's top winemaking regions. California is truly the Golden State for wine in the United States.

The Facts on California

CLIMATE

Overall, California has a warm climate that is often tempered in regions by the Pacific Ocean.

TOP WHITE GRAPES

- Chardonnay
- Sauvignon Blanc (Fumé Blanc)

TOP RED GRAPES

- Cabernet Sauvignon
- Merlot
- Pinot Noir
- Syrah
- Zinfandel

TOP REGIONS

Sierra Foothills AVA

Central Coast AVA

North Coast AVA

- Napa Valley AVA
- Sonoma County

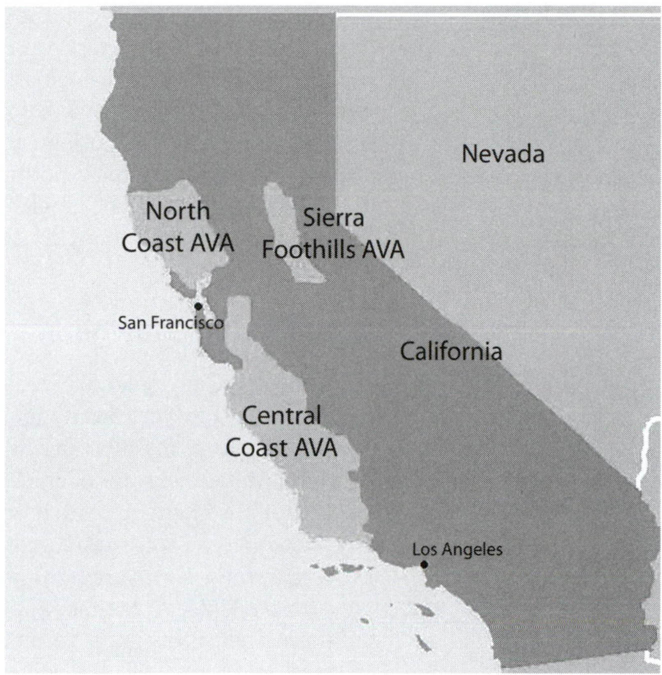

California and its three most important regionally sized AVA areas.

IMPORTANT INFORMATION

- California is the top wine-producing state in the United States, producing roughly 90 percent of U.S. wine.
- A short but colorful wine history combined with varying climate and soil conditions throughout the state account for the wide array of grape varietals and wine styles produced throughout California.
- While the largest quantity of wine produced in California comes from the fertile Central Valley, premium wine production is mostly limited to three regionally sized winemaking areas: the North Coast AVA, Sierra Foothills AVA, and the Central Coast AVA.

IMPORTANT GRAPES OF CALIFORNIA

With no legal restrictions governing the type of grapes that can be grown in California and a wide variety of different climate zones and soil types, the state grows an amazing diversity of grape varietals. Winemakers in California are always willing to experiment, and while French grapes dominate production and vineyard acreage, significant amounts of Italian, Spanish, Portuguese, and even German grape varietals have been planted throughout the state. Due to the warmer climate, a bulk of the wine production is from red grapes, the most important of which are Cabernet Sauvignon and Zinfandel. Not far behind, white wine production is fairly dominated by the most widely planted grape in the state, Chardonnay. Other important grape varieties grown in the state include Merlot, Pinot Noir, Syrah, and Sauvignon Blanc.

Chardonnay

The most planted grape varietal in California and the top-selling white wine style in the United States is Chardonnay. This grape variety has adapted well to its new home and very rarely shows the lean, mineral-driven characteristics of its native Burgundy. Instead, with much riper grapes in California, the wines can

Robert Mondavi: California Wine Legend

California has always had pioneering winemakers who were willing to take chances and try new grapes and methods, and who constantly lobbied for the state's wine industry. Robert Mondavi was possibly the most notable of these winemakers. He was a tireless advocate for California winemaking and wines. His family's vineyards were some of the first to adopt modern methods, plant premium grape varieties, and produce world-class wines. The Mondavi winemaking empire of the 1980s and 1990s was the result. In constantly marketing and promoting California wine, he gained quite a reputation. Eric Wente of Wente Vineyards said of Mondavi: "He was able to prove to the public what the people within the industry already knew—that California could produce world-class wines." Mondavi passed away in 2008 at the age of 94. The Robert Mondavi Institute for Food and Wine Science located on the campus of the University of California at Davis was named in his honor later that year.

seem to burst with ripe pineapple, pear, and apple flavors. Winemakers tend to have a heavier hand with Chardonnay wines in California, using a variety of winemaking techniques in their production including barrel fermentation, heavy oak aging, malolactic fermentation, and *sur lie* aging. This results in often rich, full-bodied white wines with toasted oak and buttery notes that complement the fruit. Although still in the minority, a handful of winemakers are beginning to turn away from this style, making leaner wines with minimal manipulation and often without any oak aging. These wines are often labeled "unoaked" or "unwooded."

Sauvignon Blanc/Fumé Blanc

A distant second behind Chardonnay for white grape plantings, Sauvignon Blanc nonetheless produces some of California's most delicious and least expensive wines. The ripeness achieved by most Sauvignon Blanc vineyards brings out the tropical fruit and grapefruit notes of the grape variety, with only hints of its herbaceous side. Winemakers will sometimes put Sauvignon Blanc wines through similar winemaking practices to Chardonnay, making them far richer and creamier than normal. Some wineries call the grape Fumé Blanc, a reference to the famous French Sauvignon Blanc region, Pouilly-Fumé.

Cabernet Sauvignon

The most widely planted red grape variety in California is Cabernet Sauvignon. It is also responsible for some of the most legendary and expensive wines the state has to offer. California Cabernet Sauvignon is often quite rich, dense, and tannic. Very ripe berry fruits and currants predominate in younger wines, slowly aging to a complex bouquet of earth and spice over time. The warmer climate of California takes this grape to much higher levels of ripeness and higher alcohol content than you would find in its native Bordeaux.

Cabernet Sauvignon is often used as a base for Bordeaux-style blends that are usually given proprietary names instead of listing the grape itself. Some of these wines will be labeled **Meritage** (rhymes with "heritage"), a term used to describe a wine made from only the classic Bordeaux varietals, especially Cabernet Sauvignon. If one region in California is considered optimal for this noble grape, it is the Napa Valley, where some of the best wines in the world are produced from Cabernet Sauvignon.

Merlot

Largely planted throughout California, Merlot produces wines with a wide range of qualities and styles. Often, it is used to make medium-bodied, berry-flavored wines of average quality, meant to be consumed in their youth. Higher-quality versions see the grape treated much like Cabernet Sauvignon, with lower yields, richer flavors, and intense structure. This grape is often blended in proportions large and small with Cabernet Sauvignon.

California's "Cult" Cabernets

A current trend in California, especially in Napa Valley, is super-expensive, very limited Cabernet Sauvignons produced in small vineyard sites. Definitely a lesson in supply and demand, these wineries often have waiting lists of customers ready to spend hundreds of dollars on single bottles of wine. Some of the best known "cult" Cabernets of California include Screaming Eagle, Colgin, Bryant Family, Harlan Estate, and Grace Family.

Zinfandel is considered "California's grape."

 Pinot Noir

Planted throughout the cool-climate areas of the North Coast and Central Coast of California, Pinot Noir is responsible for some of the most important red wines and sparkling white wines in the state. Often fruit-forward in style, California Pinot Noir is typically richer and softer than examples from Oregon or Burgundy.

 Syrah

Many of the new plantings in California over the last decade have been Rhône varietals, chiefly the Syrah grape. Thriving in the state's varied conditions, Syrah produces mostly powerful, fruity red wines in warmer vineyard sites, and more brooding, earthy, and gamey versions in cooler areas.

 Zinfandel

Zinfandel is known as "California's grape," as the state is the only area in the world with large plantings of this varietal. Until the 1990s, Zinfandel was the most widely planted grape variety in California. Unlike the other widely planted grapes of California that are mostly of French origin, Zinfandel actually calls Croatia home.

Although many wine drinkers associate Zinfandel with lower-quality, semisweet blush wines called White Zinfandel, truly this is a grape that produces powerful and rich red wines. Frequently heavily aged in American oak barrels, Zinfandel is often reminiscent of blackberry jam, black peppercorns, spice, and toasted coconut. The grape loves the warmest vineyard sites found in the state, and it is not uncommon to see extremely high alcohol content of 15 percent and higher in these often full-bodied wines.

Other Notable Grapes

CHENIN BLANC Prior to the 1980s, Chenin Blanc was the most widely grown white grape varietal in California. Although much of its production is bound for generic blends, some producers severely restrict yields and produce distinct, complex white wines from the grape.

VIOGNIER Although it is a relative newcomer to California winemaking, this white Rhône varietal has taken well to its adopted home. Viognier does best in warmer regions of California where it is capable of producing rich, high-alcohol, extremely aromatic wines reminiscent of stone fruits and honeysuckle.

PETITE SIRAH Considered almost a cult classic by many proponents, Petite Sirah is a red grape that produces dense, deeply colored wines. Not related to the Syrah grape, Petite Sirah is known as Durif in its native southern France.

TERROIR AND IMPORTANT REGIONS

Although the California wine industry is based around mostly French grape varietals, the climate is much warmer than that found in France. In fact, if you were to superimpose the west coast of the United States onto the west coast of Europe, California would be mostly located in Spain and Portugal. Due to the warmer conditions in the state, most premium wine production takes place in the more temperate northern and central areas. In many of these areas, grape-growing conditions are almost ideal from harvest to harvest. There is ample sunshine to ripen grapes during the summer and deep into the fall, and rainfall is concentrated in the winter and early spring. The tempering effect of the Pacific Ocean keeps temperatures from dipping too low in winter months, and spring frosts are rare. As for negative conditions, the only real concern is the threat of extreme heat during the summer months, which will cause grapes to ripen too quickly. Soil conditions vary widely throughout California's winemaking regions, allowing winemakers to grow a multitude of different grape varieties and produce a number of different styles.

Most of the wine regions of California are found in valleys located near the coastline and in the central parts of the state. The leading grape-growing region in the state is the Central Valley, home to most of California's agricultural production and a majority of the plain, bulk wines produced. Fertile conditions and plenty of summer warmth combine to yield enormous numbers of grapes, but a lack of stress in vineyards leads to average quality in the resulting wines. Many of these wines will simply list California as their appellation of origin, as few AVAs are found in the area. One notable exception is the Lodi AVA found in the northern part of the Central Valley, where bulk-wine producers have begun focusing on single-varietal, premium wines, especially warm-climate varietals like Zinfandel and Syrah.

The most notable areas for premium production are fairly limited to areas east or west of the large Central Valley, with the exception of a few small outposts in far northern California and the limited production areas of the South Coast AVA and its inland AVA subregion called Temecula, located in Riverside County between Los Angeles and San Diego. The major premium wine-producing areas of California are covered by three regional-sized AVAs: **North Coast AVA, Sierra Foothills AVA,** and the **Central Coast AVA.** Most of California's famous and top-quality winemaking districts are found within these regions.

North Coast AVA

The large North Coast AVA stretches from the San Francisco Bay north along the coastline for roughly 120 miles. It covers more than 50 miles inland from the Pacific coastline and encompasses several of the most important wine regions found in the state. While significant quality production takes place in the northern part of the AVA, especially in Lake County and southern Mendocino County, it is the southern districts located in Napa County and Sonoma County that get most of the attention. Napa County is home to the famed **Napa Valley AVA** and its AVA subregions, while the larger **Sonoma County** is home to a number of important AVA regions.

Napa Valley The Napa Valley is the premier wine region of the United States, and is generally considered the most important viticultural area outside of Europe. Formed by ancient shifts in tectonic plates and the Napa River, this north-south running valley is separated from Sonoma County to the west by the Mayacamas Mountains and from Solano County to the east by a rugged chain of hills. The word Napa comes from the language of the native American *Wappo* tribe that once inhabited this region, and means "land of plenty."

Although quite famous, Napa Valley is not a large wine region, producing only around 4 percent of California's total production. The consistent quality of the wines produced here is what led to the region's fame, not massive amounts of production. Only a little over 30 miles long and less than 5 miles wide, Napa Valley has a surprising number of different climate zones and soil types. Cooler conditions exist in higher elevations and the southern

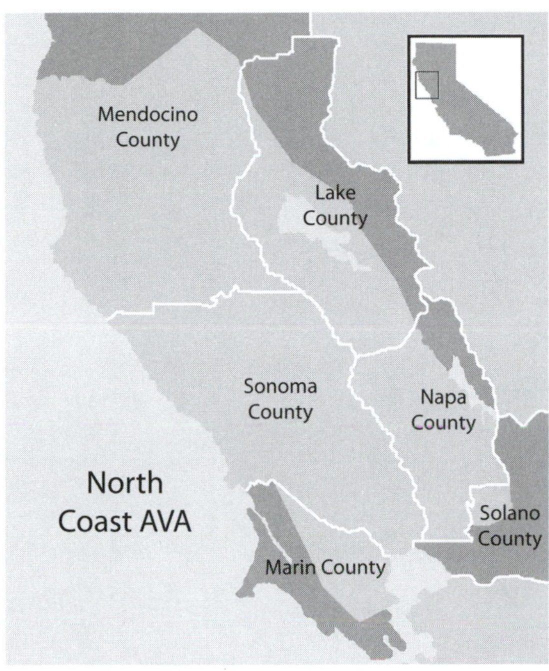

The North Coast AVA and its important wine regions.

Cabernet Sauvignon is Napa Valley's most important grape varietal.

regions of the Napa Valley due to cold marine air that is channeled north up from the San Pablo Bay. Warmer conditions and more vineyard acreage are found in northern Napa Valley, mostly along the valley floor.

Is Sparkling Wine the Future for Napa Valley?

Napa Valley will never be mistaken for Champagne, but more and more sparkling wineries are opening in the region. While Napa is still known for dry red wines, many European sparkling wine producers have invested in the Napa Valley and are producing top-quality sparkling wines there. Here are some examples:

- Moët & Chandon, a top Champagne house, owns Domaine Chandon in Napa Valley.
- Mumm, another Champagne house, operates the sparkling winery called Mumm Cuvee Napa.
- One of the top Cava wineries, called Codorníu, runs Codorníu Napa.

Depending on soil conditions and local climate, a staggering number of different grapes grow throughout the Napa Valley. Cool-climate areas like the Napa Valley overlap of the **Carneros AVA** and the higher-elevation regions located in the mountainous AVAs focus on grapes like Chardonnay and Pinot Noir. In warmer areas in the north and along much of the valley floor, grapes like Cabernet Sauvignon and Merlot dominate winemaking and produce full-bodied, massively structured, fruit-forward red wines. Although Cabernet Sauvignons and Merlots are often bottled as single varietals, a lot of Bordeaux-style blends based on these two grape varieties and known by proprietary names or as Meritages are produced in Napa Valley as well. The reputation of Napa Valley was built upon Cabernet Sauvignon more than any other grape variety.

Napa Valley is home to thirteen AVA subregions located entirely within the Napa Valley AVA, and also overlaps the Carneros AVA to the south. Even if one of these subregions is the origin for a wine, the label will still list Napa Valley in addition to the name of the specific AVA.

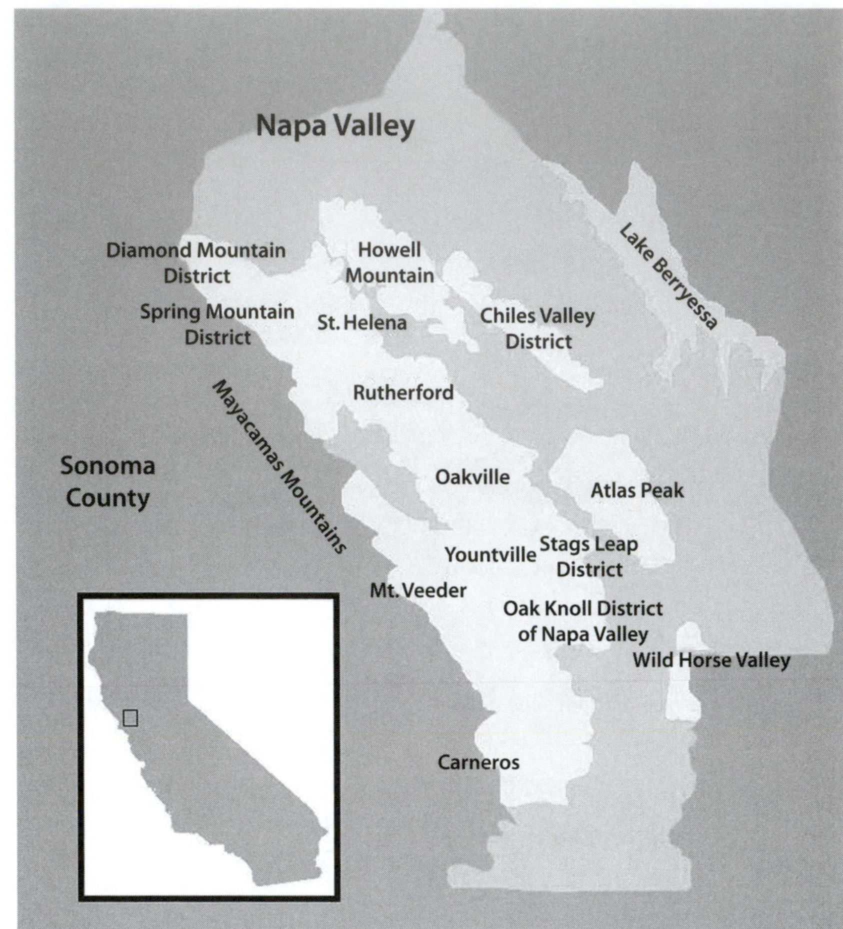

Napa Valley and its appellations.

The AVA Subregions of the Napa Valley AVA

Central AVAs on the Valley Floor	
Carneros AVA (partial overlap)	Stags Leap District AVA
Oak Knoll District of Napa Valley AVA	Saint Helena AVA
Oakville AVA	Wild Horse Valley AVA
Rutherford AVA	Yountville AVA
Western Mountain AVAs	**Eastern Mountain AVAs**
Diamond Mountain District AVA	Atlas Peak AVA
Mount Veeder AVA	Chiles Valley District AVA
Spring Mountain District AVA	Howell Mountain AVA

Sonoma County Almost twice as large as Napa County, Sonoma County lies to the west of Napa, sandwiched between the Mayacamas Mountains to the east and the Pacific Ocean to the west. Sonoma County is generally credited as the first northern California wine-producing region, as grapes were planted near a Catholic mission established here in the early 1800s. Since that time, a number of different grape varieties have been established in vineyards covering the different subclimates and soil structures of Sonoma County.

A series of coastal mountain ranges control the various climates of Sonoma County. These mountainous areas act to either trap the cool ocean air from the Pacific Ocean or to block its flow, leading to warm, Mediterranean-type conditions. Most of the southern vineyards and AVAs of Sonoma County have cooler climates and concentrate on producing stunning wines from Chardonnay and Pinot Noir. To the north, mountains stop the ocean influence and full-bodied reds made from Cabernet Sauvignon, Syrah, and Merlot, as well as quality Sauvignon Blanc dominate winemaking. In the hottest areas of wine production in far northern Sonoma County, the heat-loving Zinfandel grape is widely planted.

Many wines of varying quality produced in Sonoma County are made from grapes that were not grown within an AVA region, and the label will simply list the name of the county as the appellation. Sonoma County is home to twelve subregions with AVA status located completely within the county, and one overlapping AVA called Carneros that it shares with the Napa Valley.

The AVA Subregions of Sonoma County

Alexander Valley AVA	Knights Valley AVA
Bennett Valley AVA	Northern Sonoma AVA
Carneros AVA (partial overlap)	Rockpile AVA
Chalk Hill AVA	Russian River Valley AVA
Dry Creek Valley AVA	Sonoma Coast AVA
Green Valley of Russian River Valley AVA	Sonoma Mountain AVA
	Sonoma Valley AVA

Other North Coast AVA Regions of Note The Carneros AVA is located roughly 30 miles north of San Francisco, and it is where the southern areas of both the Napa Valley AVA and Sonoma County end. Portions of Carneros are found in both Napa and Sonoma counties. Due to the geographic shape of this region, Carneros almost acts like the head of a giant vacuum cleaner, sucking cold, moist ocean air from the nearby San Pablo Bay and pumping it north into Napa and Sonoma. This is why the coolest vineyards in these regions are in the south, rather than the north. Carneros is one of the top cool-climate

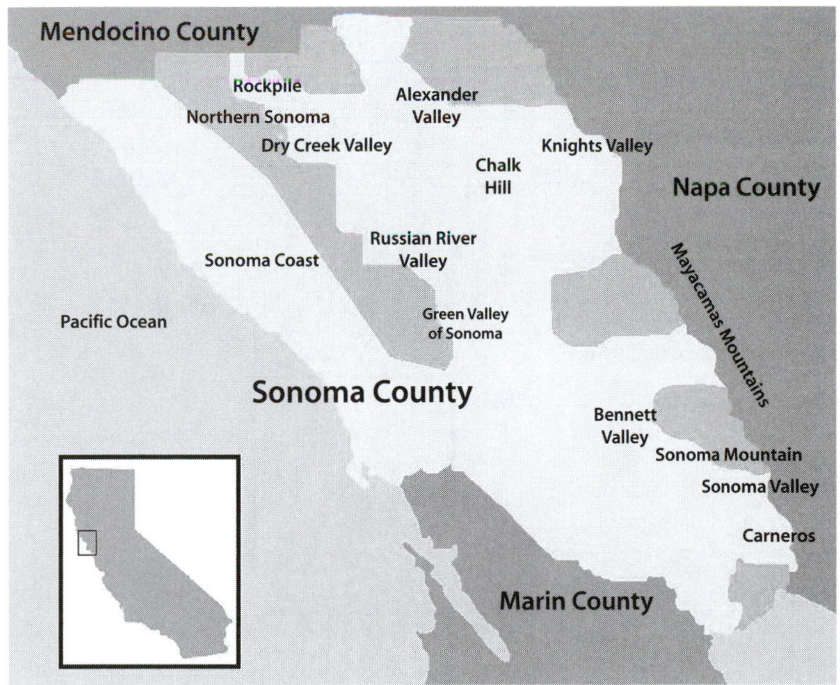

Sonoma County and its appellations.

regions in California, specializing in grapes like Chardonnay and Pinot Noir and producing some of the best sparkling wines in the state.

North of Sonoma County, along the Pacific coast, is Mendocino County. The North Coast AVA covers much of the southern portion of Mendocino County, and pockets of both warm and cool climates are found within these borders. This county is known primarily for cool-climate wines, both still and sparkling, most of which are produced in the south. Like Napa and Sonoma Counties, Mendocino County is often warmer the further north you travel, focusing more on full-bodied red varietals. There are ten AVA subregions found within Mendocino County, the most famous of which is the cool-climate Anderson Valley AVA.

The AVA Subregions of Mendocino County	
Anderson Valley AVA	Mendocino Valley AVA
Cole Ranch AVA	Mendocino Ridge AVA
Covelo AVA	Potter Valley AVA
Dos Rios AVA	Redwood Valley AVA
McDowell Valley AVA	Yorkville Highlands AVA

To the east of Mendocino County and immediately north of Napa County is the warmer region of Lake County. Sparsely planted, Lake County is home to five AVA regions known mostly for elegant red wines made from classic Bordeaux and Rhône varietals.

The AVA Subregions of Lake County	
Benmore Valley AVA	High Valley AVA
Clear Lake AVA	Red Hills Lake County AVA
Guenoc Valley AVA	

"Islands in the Sky"

The Mendocino Ridge AVA in Mendocino County is known by the nickname "islands in the sky" because of its unique disposition. Instead of being one general area, it is actually made up of several different vineyard sites that are all at 1,500 feet in elevation or higher.

Sierra Foothills AVA

East of the large Central Valley of California, at roughly the same latitude as the North Coast AVA, you will find the regional-sized Sierra Foothills AVA. Within its boundaries is a collection of scattered wine regions and vineyards, most of which are located at higher elevations on the western slopes of the Sierra Nevada Mountains. The area encompasses parts of eight counties; listed from north to south the counties include Yuba, Nevada, Placer, El Dorado, Amador, Calaveras, Tuolumne, and Mariposa. Of these, Amador County and El Dorado County are the most important areas for wine production. A booming wine industry once

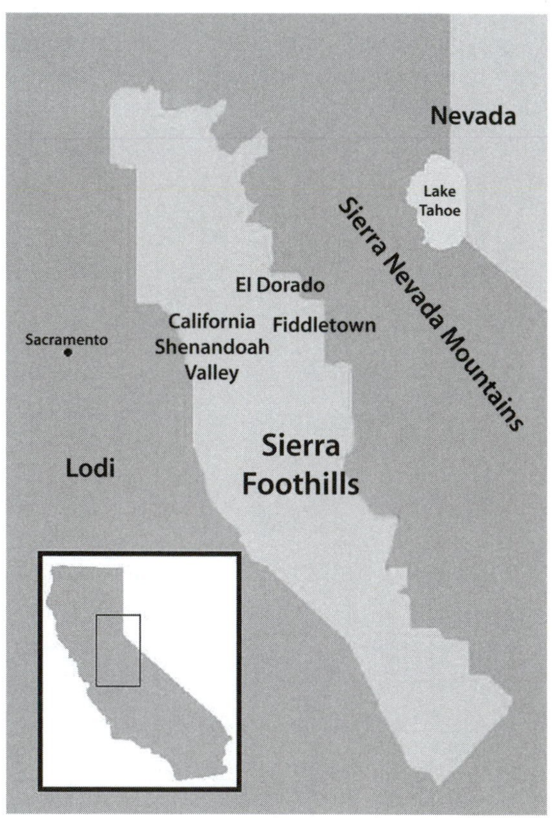

The Sierra Foothills AVA and its appellations.

thrived in the Sierra Foothills during the height of the gold rush, but most vineyards were quickly abandoned as boomtowns disappeared and many settlers left. Today the region is undergoing a second boom, and more than one hundred wineries are in operation. Inexpensive land and favorable climate conditions are attracting many new wine producers to the area.

The most important grape grown in the Sierra Foothills AVA and its AVA subregions is Zinfandel. These reds tend to be more elegant than aggressive as a result of cooler conditions. Large plantings of Syrah, Cabernet Sauvignon, and Chardonnay can also be found.

There are five subregions with AVA status that are located completely within the boundaries of the Sierra Foothills AVA.

The AVA Subregions of the Sierra Foothills AVA

California Shenandoah Valley AVA	Fair Play AVA
El Dorado AVA	Fiddletown AVA
	North Yuba AVA

Central Coast AVA

The regional area known as the Central Coast AVA is the third and final major premium winemaking district in California. Its climate conditions and resulting important grapes and wine styles are defined by its proximity to the Pacific Ocean. The tempering effects of the ocean and the cooling currents that flow just offshore create cool, foggy wine regions along the coast, and conditions are much warmer as you travel inland over a coastal mountain range where these marine influences are not felt.

Covering nearly 400 miles of coastline from just east of Oakland in the north to the city of Santa Barbara in the south, this is the second largest regional winemaking district in California behind the Central Valley. It encompasses or cuts into parts of nine counties, and can be roughly broken into three major sections. The northern includes the large San Francisco Bay AVA and covers portions of the counties of Alameda, Contra Costa, San Francisco, Santa Clara, and Santa Cruz. The central area of the Central Coast AVA is made up of Monterey and San Benito Counties. Finally, San Luis Obispo County and Santa Barbara County cover the southernmost district.

The northern district of the Central Coast AVA is almost completely overlapped by the large San Francisco Bay AVA. This area is home to mostly temperate to cool conditions dictated by the Pacific Ocean. Several grapes are grown throughout the San Francisco Bay AVA and the counties and AVA subregions it covers, and top-quality wines are especially made from Merlot, Chardonnay, and Petite Sirah. There are two major AVA subregions within the San Francisco Bay AVA: Livermore Valley AVA and Santa Clara Valley AVA. Many wineries large and small are located in these regions, and are responsible for much of the best wine from the area.

To the south of the San Francisco Bay AVA are the counties of Monterey and San Benito. These counties make up the central winemaking areas of the Central Coast AVA. Monterey County runs along the coastline for almost 100 miles, while San Benito County is inland, just to the east. Ocean fog and cooling ocean breezes maintain a cooler temperature throughout much of these two counties, and Chardonnay is the grape that seems to have adapted to the conditions best, although several other vines have been planted, notably Pinot Noir. Monterey County is where the majority of wine production takes place and is home to the most well-known AVA subregions. Despite the fact that there are several AVA regions in San Benito County, many are only sparsely planted to grapevines. The southern district of the Central Coast AVA is made up of San Luis Obispo County, which borders Monterey County to the north, and Santa Barbara County, home to the southernmost vineyards. Several east-west valleys run the length of these two counties, helping to funnel cooling ocean air to inland wine regions. Cooler climate regions

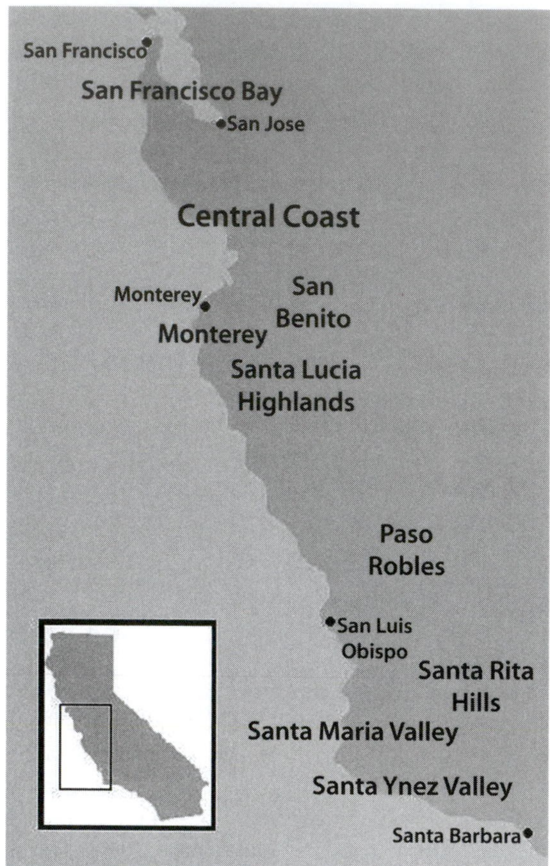

The Central Coast AVA and its important appellations.

dominate the western areas of both counties. Their top-quality wines, especially made from Pinot Noir, gained international exposure after many wineries located there were featured in the movie *Sideways*. Most notable of these cool-climate AVA subregions are the Santa Lucia Highlands AVA, Santa Maria Valley AVA, and Santa Rita Hills AVA (which, due to legal issues, will be listed as Sta. Rita Hills on wine labels). Further east, covering much of the northeast corner of San Luis Obispo County, is the largest AVA in the region, Paso Robles. The Paso Robles AVA is far inland, away from the Pacific's effects, and as a result has a warm climate that is especially suited to Zinfandel and superripe Cabernet Sauvignon. Another important wine region is the warmer Santa Ynez Valley AVA, which focuses primarily on Rhône varietals.

The AVA Subregions of the Central Coast AVA

NORTHERN AREAS	CENTRAL AREAS	SOUTHERN AREAS
Livermore Valley AVA	Arroyo Seco AVA	Arroyo Grande Valley AVA
San Francisco Bay AVA	Carmel Valley AVA	Edna Valley AVA
Santa Clara Valley AVA	Chalone AVA	Paso Robles AVA
San Ysidro District AVA	Cienega Valley AVA	Santa Lucia Highlands AVA
Pacheco Pass AVA	Hames Valley AVA	Santa Maria Valley AVA
	Lime Kiln Valley AVA	Santa (Sta.) Rita Hills AVA
	Monterey AVA	Santa Ynez Valley AVA
	Mount Harlan AVA	York Mountain AVA
	Paicines AVA	
	San Antonio AVA	
	San Benito AVA	
	San Bernabe AVA	
	San Lucas AVA	

Oregon: America's Top Cool-Climate Region

Although Oregon is just north of California, it is a relative newcomer to winemaking. Wines were produced in the state as early as the 1800s, but it was not until the 1960s and 1970s that premium production of wines made from grapes ideally suited to the state's climate conditions began being produced. The cool conditions of Oregon had long been thought a detriment to grape growing, and as a result little serious winemaking was practiced in the state until a few pioneering winemakers changed several minds.

Instead of fighting the cooler conditions in an effort to produce full-bodied whites and reds like those produced in much of California, winemakers instead looked for inspiration in some of the cooler wine

The Oregon wine industry is most famous for Pinot Noir.

regions of Europe. Grapes like Pinot Noir, Riesling, Pinot Gris, and Chardonnay were planted, and new winemaking and grape-growing techniques were experimented with. Within a few decades, Oregon wines began to gain international attention, and a new era of wine production began in earnest.

Today, Oregon is considered one of the most important winemaking areas of the United States and is easily the best cool-climate region. While the state ranks fourth in terms of wine production in the United States, it actually ranks second in terms of the number of wineries in operation, behind only California. The vast majority of Oregon wine is made by small, independent producers, and large winemaking companies are next to nonexistent.

The most important grape grown in Oregon is Pinot Noir, and the state is becoming synonymous with this grape when it comes to winemaking. Their success with this varietal as well as the cooler conditions found in the state's wine regions have led to several comparisons between Oregon and the French wine region of Burgundy. The comparison is only strengthened by the fact that several Burgundian winemakers have purchased land in Oregon and have begun to produce wines there, too.

The future of Oregon is bright as winemakers continue to improve their winemaking and grape-growing methods. Sales have never been higher for the state, and many of their highly regarded Pinot Noir wines fetch as much as or more than

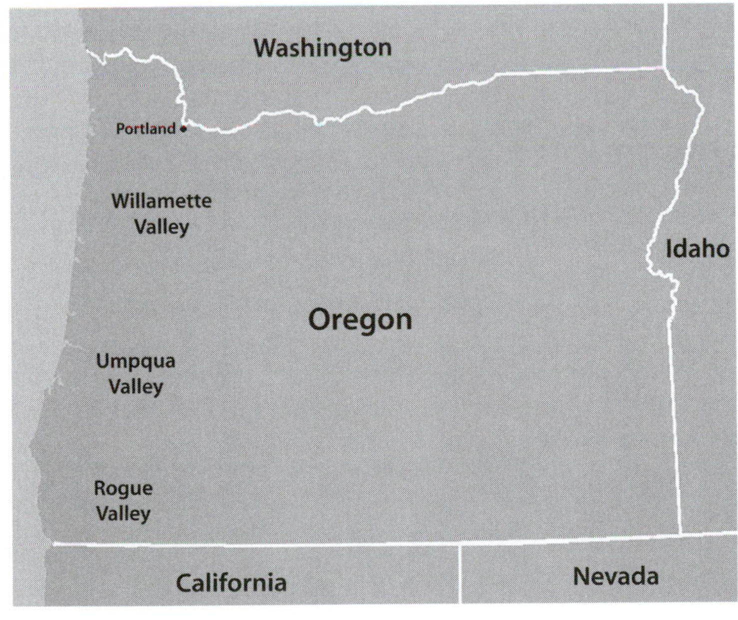

Oregon and its important wine regions.

top California examples. The pioneering spirit and independent tradition of Oregon's winemakers continue to serve them well.

The Facts on Oregon

CLIMATE

Temperate to cool and typically moist due to the Pacific Ocean and Cascade Mountains.

TOP WHITE GRAPE

- Pinot Gris

TOP RED GRAPE

- Pinot Noir

TOP REGION

- Willamette Valley

IMPORTANT INFORMATION

- Oregon ranks fourth among wine-producing states in the United States.
- Winemaking laws are stricter in Oregon than in other parts of the United States, as wines listing a grape variety must contain at least 90 percent of the listed varietal in most cases.
- Due to the cooler climate found in Oregon, most of their top wines are made from grapes that thrive in cooler conditions, like Chardonnay, Pinot Gris, and especially Pinot Noir.

IMPORTANT GRAPES OF OREGON

Blending different grapes to make a wine is uncommon in Oregon, as most are produced with only a single varietal. Due to this fact, the state's winemakers petitioned for the Oregon laws regarding labeling to become stricter than federal guidelines. Oregon wines listing a grape variety must be made from at least 90 percent of the listed varietal, unlike the case in the rest of the country where the minimum is only 75 percent. This was in an effort to protect the reputation of Oregon's wines, made mostly from grapes that should not be blended with other varieties. The only exceptions to this law are little-produced Cabernet Sauvignon–based wines, which only have to follow the 75 percent limit due to the grape's propensity for blending.

Oregon grows a large number of different grapes, but those that do better in cool climates produce the top wines there. High-quality white wines are common throughout Oregon's western wine regions, especially from Pinot Gris. The state is best known, however, for their stunning and complex red wines made from Pinot Noir grapes.

Pinot Noir

Oregon Pinot Noir is considered by many to be the top example of this varietal outside of its native homeland of Burgundy, France. In the state, it is the most widely grown and top-selling varietal. The cool climate of Oregon keeps the grape from ripening too quickly, resulting in wines that have higher acidity and a balanced alcohol content. Often bursting with red fruits like cranberries and cherries, Oregon Pinot Noir also shows the earthy and spiced characteristics this grape is known for.

Pinot Gris

Pinot Gris is quickly becoming the most important white grape variety in Oregon, and it produces many of the state's best white wines. Oregon has more acreage dedicated to this descendent of Pinot Noir than any other state in the United States. Often packed with apple, citrus, and honey notes, Pinot Gris wines in Oregon are most often aged in oak to pick up toasted notes and slight hints of spice.

Other Notable Grapes

CHARDONNAY Another Burgundian transplant to the vineyards of Oregon, Chardonnay produces much leaner styles of oak-aged white wine here than in California.

RIESLING The most widely planted white grape varietal in Oregon is Riesling, which produces average- to higher-quality wines that range from dry to sweet.

TERROIR AND IMPORTANT REGIONS

Logically, one might assume that Oregon has a warmer climate than its northern neighbor of Washington because it is further south. In practice, this is not the case, as Washington's main wine regions are far warmer than those of Oregon. The cause of this difference in climate is based on the fact that weather in the Pacific Northwest is not chiefly governed by typical factors such as latitude. Rather, the climate of both states is determined by their physical location in relation to the **Cascade Mountains**.

The climate of Oregon is largely defined by the Pacific Ocean and by the Cascade Mountains, which run north to south through the middle of the state. All of the important winemaking regions and vineyards of Oregon are found on the western or Pacific side of the Cascades. As cold, moist ocean air batters the Oregon coastline, it is forced inland until it hits the solid barrier of the Cascades. As more weather systems blow into the state from the Pacific, this air is forced up so that it can eventually crest the mountains. The increase in elevation and resulting drop in temperature squeezes these weather cells of their moisture, causing precipitation. For this reason, western Oregon has a cool, moist climate. Washington's main wine regions are on the eastern side of the Cascades, and therefore home to more temperate, dry conditions in the rain shadow of the steep mountain range.

Most of the top wine regions in Oregon are located in the large system of valleys that run from north to south between the Cascade Mountains and a series of coastal mountain ranges that protect vineyards from the worst of the weather in winter months. Soil types can vary widely throughout Oregon, but most vineyards do best when planted in well-draining soils because of the significant amount of rainfall. Luckily, the majority of precipitation falls during the winter months when the vines most need it, with a relatively dry summer and fall.

With the exception of four lesser-planted areas of wine production in eastern Oregon, three of which are simply overlaps of Washington AVA regions and one AVA shared with Idaho, premium winemaking is limited to western Oregon. This region can be divided into two major areas of wine production, the north and south. Northern Oregon is cooler than the southern regions, and production is mostly concentrated in the Willamette Valley. The climate slowly warms the further south you travel toward California, allowing

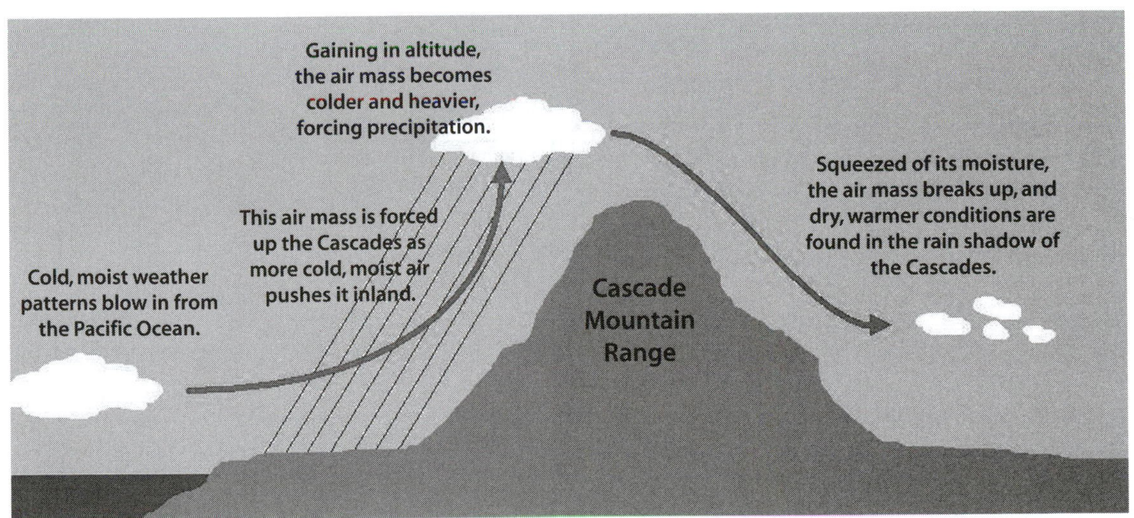

This diagram shows how the Cascade Mountains dictate the climate of the western and eastern Pacific Northwest.

grape growers in the southern areas like the Umpqua Valley and the Rogue Valley to grow many more varietals. Although not as well known, the AVA regions in southern Oregon continue to be expanded. There are currently sixteen AVA regions located throughout Oregon, with its largest and most famous being the **Willamette Valley AVA**.

Willamette Valley AVA

Flowing north toward the Columbia River and the city of Portland, the Willamette River slowly cuts through the valley named for it. The Willamette Valley AVA is the largest and most famous appellation in Oregon. Most premium wine production takes place in the northwest portion of the valley. Pinot Noir is the most widely planted grape, and is what the region is most famous for, although Chardonnay, Riesling, and Pinot Gris also have several large plantings. The maritime influence of the Pacific dictates the cooler weather found in the region, although a coastal mountain range on the western side of the valley protects the Willamette from the harshest weather.

Willamette Valley's Other Vines

Besides being known for top-quality wine grapes, Oregon's Willamette Valley is also known for growing another vine crop: hops. One of the main ingredients used in the production of beer, hops are the green flower buds of the hop vine. One of the most important varieties of hops growing in the Willamette Valley is the Cascade hop, named for the Cascade Mountains that dominate the landscape of the Pacific Northwest.

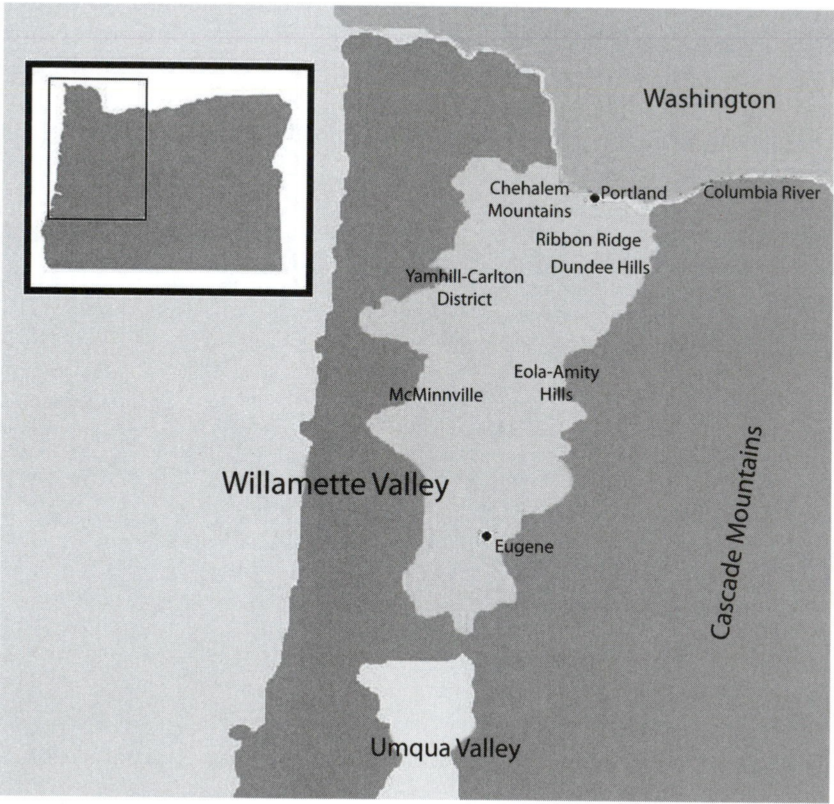

The Willamette Valley AVA and its appellations.

The mostly volcanic soils of the Willamette Valley AVA are home to the majority of the state's producers, many of which are only tiny operations that make limited amounts of wine. The northwestern part of the Willamette Valley AVA is also home to six additional subregions with AVA status. These are typically areas noted for superior quality and wines with distinct characteristics.

The AVA Subregions of the Willamette Valley

Chehalem Mountains AVA	McMinnville AVA
Dundee Hills AVA	Ribbon Ridge AVA
Eola-Amity Hills AVA	Yamhill-Carlton District AVA

Other Wine Regions of Note

The large, regional Southern Oregon AVA covers most of the remainder of the state's winemaking districts, and is basically comprised of the Rogue Valley AVA and the Umpqua Valley AVA. Both are warmer and drier than the Willamette Valley and grow grapes such as Cabernet Sauvignon, Merlot, and Sauvignon Blanc in addition to Oregon's most famous grape varieties.

In the eastern portion of the state, there are four AVA regions that cross over the border into Oregon from other states. Areas of Washington's Columbia Valley, Columbia Gorge, and Walla Walla Valley AVAs overlap slightly into Oregon, as does the Snake River Valley AVA of Idaho. Production on the Oregon side of the border is very limited in all four of these regions.

Washington: New Kid on the Block

If any state in the United States can speak to the potential of quality winemaking in this country, it is Washington. Although grapes were first planted in the state with the arrival of many European immigrants in the early 1800s, no major wineries were established in the state until much later. The first bonded winery opened after the repeal of Prohibition in the 1930s, followed by several others, all in western Washington.

In the 1950s, irrigation systems were developed in eastern Washington, and the once dry, barren landscape there was transformed. This quickly became the leading agricultural section of the state. Two wineries were established there in the late 1950s and early 1960s that would go on to become large commercial winemaking operations, called the Columbia Winery and Chateau Ste. Michelle. These wineries are still the largest in the state, and have paved the way for hundreds of smaller wineries that were subsequently established in eastern Washington. Over the last few years, new wineries have been opening at an amazing rate.

With most of the population and large cities located on the western side of the state, most of Washington's wineries are also located there. The vineyards are located on the eastern side of the state, however. This means that for most wineries, grapes are trucked across the Cascade Mountains to be produced into wine!

Unknown for wine just a few decades ago, today Washington is the second leading producer among U.S. states, and produces some of the country's best wines. Currently, red wines dominate production, but several white grape varieties thrive

Where Reserve Does Mean Something

The term **"Reserve,"** when listed on a label of U.S. wine, has no legal definition except in the state of Washington. While most winemakers around the country are allowed to use the term at their discretion, in Washington only certain wines qualify. The Washington Wine Quality Alliance established the regulations for the use of the term "Reserve" on Washington wines as being higher in quality than other wines from the winery and making up no more than 10 percent of the winery's total production.

in Washington vineyards as well. Ideal growing conditions and the strong winemaking community found in eastern Washington have combined to make this a premium wine region undergoing rapid growth.

The Facts on Washington

CLIMATE

Temperate and dry due to the rain-shadow effect of the Cascade Mountains.

TOP WHITE GRAPE

- Chardonnay

TOP RED GRAPES

- Cabernet Sauvignon
- Merlot

TOP REGION

- Columbia Valley

IMPORTANT INFORMATION

- Washington ranks second among wine-producing states in the United States.
- Washington has a very short history of large-scale wine production, as the first serious commercial wineries did not open in the state until the 1950s and 1960s.
- Due to its late start and relative isolation, Washington has avoided many different vineyard pests and diseases, including *phylloxera*.
- Temperate and extremely dry conditions are the norm in the wine-producing regions of eastern Washington, most of which are located near the Columbia River.

IMPORTANT GRAPES OF WASHINGTON

Washington has only recently begun to concentrate on a few high-quality grape varieties. Along the way, dozens of different *Vitis vinifera* vines and a surprising number of hybrids have been planted in vineyards throughout the state. Dry weather conditions, sandy soils, and relative isolation have helped winemakers avoid most vineyard diseases and pests, such as *phylloxera*, throughout eastern Washington. Most vines are planted on their original rootstock, and chemical spraying of vineyards is minimal. The most important grapes now grown

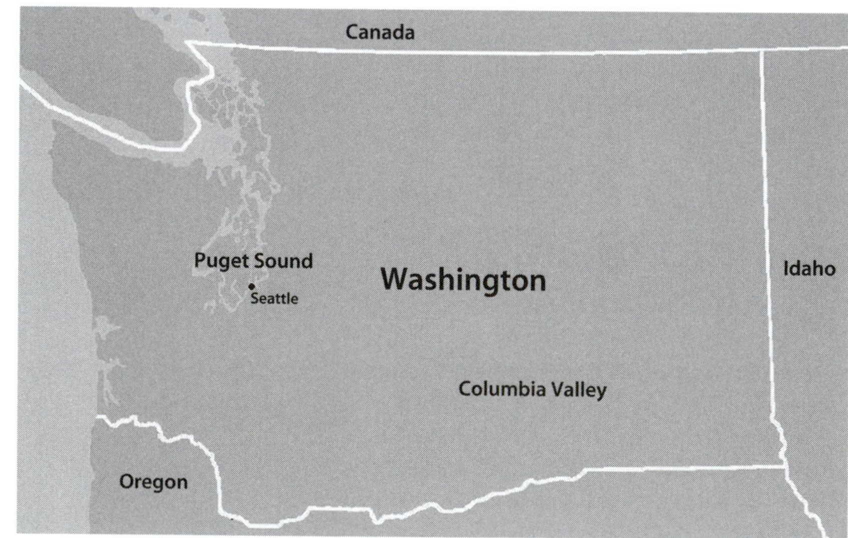

Washington and its important wine regions.

in Washington are French varietals. Of these, the grape varieties the state is best known for today are Chardonnay, Merlot, and especially Cabernet Sauvignon.

Chardonnay

Chardonnay is the most widely planted white grape varietal in Washington, and top-quality examples are produced in the state. Washington Chardonnay tends to be less ripe than California's versions, and winemakers do not often manipulate their wines as much. This leads to white wines that have a central core of acidity, along with citrus and apple notes and a touch of oak and butter.

Cabernet Sauvignon

The most expensive, highly regarded, and critically acclaimed wines of Washington are made with Cabernet Sauvignon grapes. This grape achieves full ripeness in many of eastern Washington's AVA regions, producing intensely concentrated wines packed with dark fruit flavors, earthy notes, and spice. Often not as alcoholic and fruit-forward as many California Cabernets, Washington styles frequently display more acidity and a softer tannin structure. Sometimes this grape is used as a key component in traditional Bordeaux-style blends.

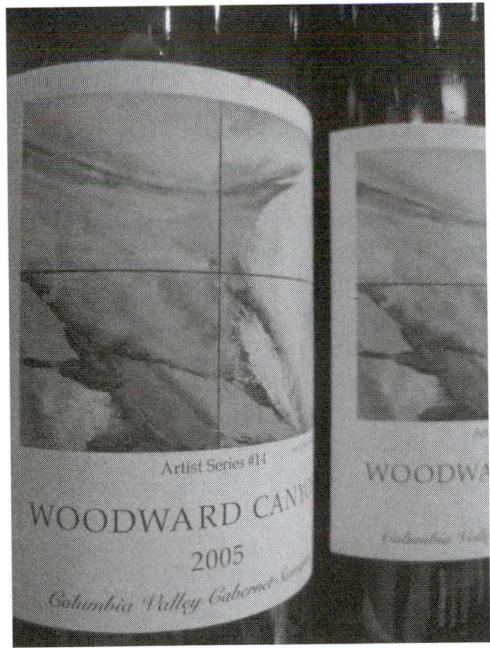

Cabernet Sauvignon is responsible for some of Washington's best wines.

Merlot

Soft and spicy, Washington State Merlot is often grown to be blended in small percentages into Cabernet Sauvignon–based red wines, or bottled on its own. Rich fruit flavors develop in Merlot grapes during the long days of the summer months, creating full-bodied wines reminiscent of blueberries, black cherries, and currants.

Other Notable Grapes

SAUVIGNON BLANC Adapting to Washington in a similar fashion to other Bordeaux varieties, Sauvignon Blanc produces crisp, lean white wines and is gaining more favor with the state's winemakers.

RIESLING The second most widely planted white grape variety behind Chardonnay is Riesling. Riesling is often planted in cooler vineyard areas, and the resulting wines can range from dry to softly sweet.

SYRAH Warmer vineyards throughout eastern Washington have been successful in planting the Syrah varietal, producing especially spicy and peppery red wines from the grape.

TERROIR AND IMPORTANT REGIONS

With the exception of a few small wineries in the Puget Sound AVA, the vast majority of vineyard land in Washington is found east of the Cascade Mountains. Unlike Oregon's cool wine regions on the western side of the Cascades, Washington's wine country is temperate and very dry as it sits in the rain shadow of the mountains. Rainfall averages roughly 6 to 8 inches a year in most places, so almost all of the vineyards planted in eastern Washington have to be irrigated.

During the summer months, days are quite long and there are few clouds, allowing for maximum sun exposure. In fact, the location gets almost two more hours of sunshine a day than California in the growing season because of the tilt of the earth's axis and Washington's relative latitude. The downside to this is that winters are bitterly cold in eastern Washington, and it is not uncommon for freezes to wipe out entire vineyards.

Most of the predominant wine-growing areas of eastern Washington are found around the 46th parallel up to the 47th parallel of latitude. This is roughly equivalent to the latitudes of central France, just north of Bordeaux. Because of this northern location and the temperate summer climates found in eastern Washington, comparisons are often drawn between the state and Bordeaux. Many of the top grapes grown in the state originated in Bordeaux, and their red wines are often more similar in structure to the red blends of the famous French region than to those produced in California.

Glaciers once covered most of Washington State, and as they receded thousands of years ago they reshaped the terrain and soil structure. Most areas are covered with a thick layer of sand and gravel that can cause vines to struggle, as most moisture quickly drains away. While this has caused winemakers to rely on irrigation water from the Columbia River and snowmelt from the Cascades, it has meant a lack of vineyard pests such as ***phylloxera*** and better-quality production from vines under stress. Washington is home to nine AVA regions, most of which are located within the large appellation of the **Columbia Valley AVA** in the eastern part of the state.

Columbia Valley AVA

The Columbia River flows west through the Pacific Northwest, forming a large, sometimes steep river valley as it makes its way across the Cascades to the coast. Serving as the majority of the border between Washington and Oregon, this river defines most of eastern Washington's wine country. The Columbia Valley AVA is immense, covering more than a quarter of the entire state and spilling across the border into Oregon. It stretches from the Idaho border all the way across southeastern Washington to the Cascade Mountains, and stretches north nearly 200 miles from the Oregon border.

Along with its important subregions, the Columbia Valley AVA is home to more than 90 percent of Washington's vineyard acreage. Most wine production takes place in the southern areas, near the river; however, many winemakers are beginning to explore further north. The state's top red wines, especially Cabernet Sauvignons and Cabernet-based blends, are produced in the region. Several important winemaking areas within the Columbia Valley have been granted their own AVA status. These smaller appellations have more specific regional characteristics, and often higher-quality production. Currently there are seven AVA's that are covered by the much larger Columbia Valley AVA.

The AVA Subregions of the Columbia Valley AVA

Columbia Gorge AVA	Wahluke Slope AVA
Horse Heaven Hills AVA	Walla Walla Valley AVA
Rattlesnake Hills AVA	Yakima Valley AVA
Red Mountain AVA	

Other Wine Regions of Note

While most of the attention on Washington's wine production is focused on the Columbia Valley, small amounts of wine are produced in other parts of the state. The only AVA in western Washington is Puget Sound, which covers an area stretching from the Canadian border south along the coastline to Olympia, encompassing all of the waterways and islands found in and around the Puget Sound. The cool, often damp climate of Puget Sound causes most growers to focus on cool-climate grape varietals such as the almost unknown Madeleine Angevine and Müller-Thurgau.

As different areas of *terroir* are explored in Washington, new areas of wine production will undoubtedly be identified. Several new wine-producing regions are currently being planted in

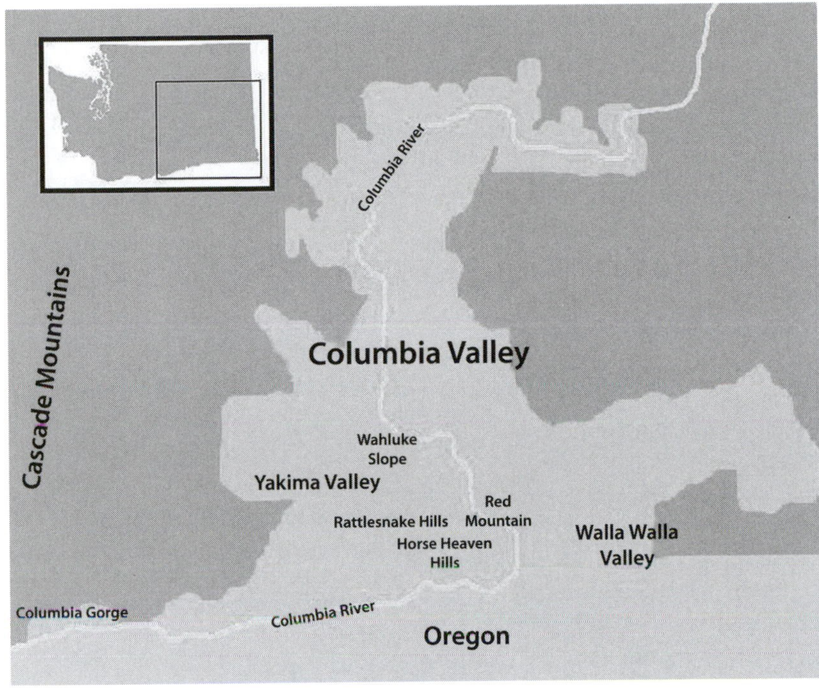

The Columbia Valley AVA and its appellations.

Washington, and some have even filed for AVA status. Of these new regions, Cold Creek and Columbia Basin/Snake River, both found in the Columbia River Valley, as well as the north-central area of Lake Chelan, show the most promise.

Other Important Wine States

New York ranks third among wine-producing states, although much of the production there is dedicated to native American grape species and varietals, especially Concord grape wines. Premium production is based in three primary areas of the state: the Hudson River Valley, the Finger Lakes, and Long Island. Much of the production in the upstate regions along the Hudson River and in the Finger Lakes is similar in style to German winemaking. Riesling is the most important grape variety, and high-acid wines that often contain residual sugar are the norm. Although relatively new to premium, commercial wine production, Long Island has begun producing many exciting wines from grapes such as Chardonnay, Merlot, and Cabernet Sauvignon.

Difficult conditions found in the eastern United States limit wine production to a few notable regions. In fact, New York is the only state that produces significant amounts of wine from *Vitis vinifera* grapes in the entire region. Nevertheless, small pockets of quality production can be found in Pennsylvania, Virginia, and the Carolinas.

In the Midwest and Great Lakes regions, winemaking was once a major industry, with states like Ohio and Missouri dominating national wine production. Following the repeal of Prohibition, many of these states were unable to rebuild their wineries and replant their vineyards. New interest and exciting wines have recently returned to several states in this area of the country, including Missouri, Michigan, Ohio, and Illinois.

The Southwest and Rocky Mountain states have also seen a rise in winemaking, and new wineries open their doors in these areas every year. In fact, several new AVA regions have been established throughout both areas in recent years. Winemaking shows great promise in these states, especially Arizona, Colorado, New Mexico, and Texas.

Summary

The wine industry of the United States has proven itself in the international wine world to a definite degree, but with a short history of wine production and large areas of temperate climate zones, the full potential of American wine has not yet been realized. As the fourth largest wine-producing country in the world and the top area of production outside of Europe, the United States leads the way among New World wine-producing countries in quantity, industry regulations, and quality.

California is the most important wine-producing region of the United States, responsible for nearly 90 percent of the country's wine and certainly its most famous wineries. Oregon and Washington have also been thrust into the limelight, setting the stage for a number of other states to possibly rise in prominence for wine production. Only time will tell the limits of America's wine potential.

Review Questions

1. California grows a red grape that has no other large plantings anywhere else in the world. The grape produces jammy, high-alcohol wines, with hints of black pepper. What is the name of this grape?
   - A. Sémillon
   - B. Gamay
   - C. Cabernet Sauvignon
   - D. Zinfandel

2. Pinot Noir is the primary red grape grown in the state of ____________.
   - A. Oregon
   - B. California
   - C. Washington
   - D. Arizona

3. For a bottle of American wine labeled Sauvignon Blanc, what is the minimum percentage of Sauvignon Blanc grapes that needed to be used in the production of the wine?
   - A. 65%
   - B. 75%
   - C. 85%
   - D. 100%

4. If a label states an American Viticultural Area, what is the minimum percentage of the grapes that must have been grown in that AVA region?
   - A. 65%
   - B. 75%
   - C. 85%
   - D. 100%

5. In terms of worldwide wine production, which of the following lists is correctly ordered, from most to least wine production?
   - A. Italy, Spain, United States, France
   - B. France, Italy, Spain, United States
   - C. Italy, France, Spain, United States
   - D. France, United States, Italy, Spain

For the following questions, match the region or regions to the state they are completely or primarily located within. Some answers may be used more than once and some not at all.

6. Napa Valley	A. California
7. Willamette Valley	B. Washington
8. Carneros	C. Oregon
9. Columbia Valley	D. New York
10. Hudson Valley	
11. North Coast	
12. Rogue Valley	

13. Select the answer that correctly ranks U.S. states according to wine production, from most to least.
   - A. California, Washington, Oregon, New York
   - B. California, New York, Oregon, Washington
   - C. California, Oregon, Washington, New York
   - D. California, Washington, New York, Oregon

14. California is the most important wine region in the United States, responsible for around ____________ of American wine production.
   - A. 30%
   - B. 50%
   - C. 70%
   - D. 90%

15. There are several states in the United States that do not produce wine.
   A. True
   B. False

16. Napa Valley is most famous for its ____________ wines.
   A. Cabernet Sauvignon
   B. Pinot Noir
   C. Shiraz
   D. Sangiovese

Key Terms

Alcohol and Tobacco Tax and Trade Bureau (TTB)
bottled by
cellared by
estate bottled
grown, produced and bottled by
made and bottled by
produced and bottled by
vinted by
American Viticultural Area (AVA)
meritage
North Coast AVA
Sierra Foothills AVA
Central Coast AVA
Napa Valley AVA
Sonoma County
Carneros AVA
Cascade Mountains
Willamette Valley AVA
reserve
Columbia Valley AVA

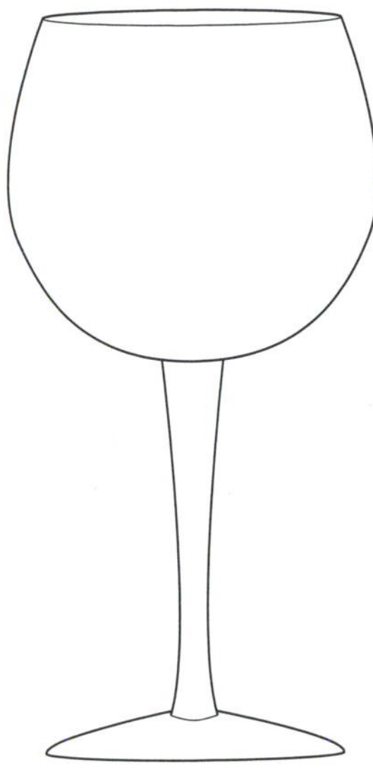

CHAPTER 17

The Wines of Australia

You have only so many bottles in your life, never drink a bad one.

—**LEN EVANS,** Australian wine columnist and author

Australia does not have a long tradition of winemaking, but its wine industry has seen rapid growth and international acceptance and praise. Wine is produced throughout the southern, more temperate regions of this large island nation, and exports continue to increase. Large wineries dominate the landscape of Australian winemaking, but hundreds of small wineries continue to explore new areas of production and experiment with new grape varieties and styles. This chapter details the history of winemaking in Australia, the current state of its wine industry, the wine laws of the country, and its most important grapes and wine regions.

The Facts on Australia

CLIMATE

Most of Australia is too hot for grape growing, with nearly 90 percent of the country being either desert or tropical. The southern portions of the country are mostly warm to hot with temperate and sometimes even cool pockets.

TOP WHITE GRAPE

- Chardonnay

TOP RED GRAPES

- Shiraz
- Cabernet Sauvignon

TOP REGIONS

Western Australia

- Margaret River

South Australia

- Barossa Valley
- Clare Valley
- McLaren Vale
- Coonawarra

Victoria

New South Wales

- Hunter Valley

IMPORTANT INFORMATION

- Australia ranks sixth in the world in terms of total wine production.
- This nontraditional wine-producing country is today the second leading exporter of wine to the United States, and exports continue to increase.

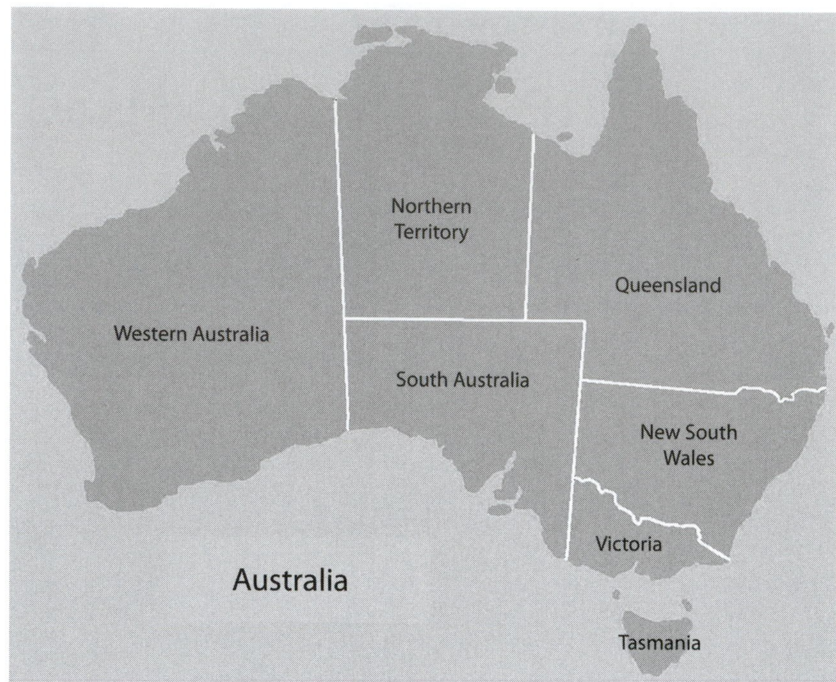

Australia's states and territories.

- Much of Australia's fame is based around the Shiraz grape, known as Syrah in France.
- Roughly one hundred recognized wine regions are located throughout the southern states of Australia, with a wide range of grapes and styles produced throughout.

Australia: The Land Down Under

The fact that Australia is one of the leading producers of wine in the world is surprising to say the least. The continent has no indigenous grapevines, and the barren landscape found throughout most of Australia is quite inhospitable to agriculture. Even the native Aboriginal people of Australia never produced fermented beverages, making them one of the few cultures in the history of the world not to do so. Regardless, winemaking thrives in the country today and the future looks quite bright for the Australian wine industry.

Wine first arrived in Australia when grapevine cuttings purchased in Cape Town, South Africa, were planted in Sydney in 1788. At the time, Australia was a penal colony of England, and many of its first settlers were sent there involuntarily. These first colonists made several attempts to establish wine making and plant vineyards throughout the original state of New South Wales surrounding the settlement of Sydney, but harsh conditions and a lack of winemaking experience led to difficult beginnings.

As the colonial area of Australia grew, a small amount of winemaking was spread to new regions. Vines were planted on the island of Tasmania and in areas of current-day South Australia with the establishment of the city of Adelaide in the early 1800s. When gold was discovered in the state of Victoria in the 1850s, Australia experienced a gold rush similar

Aboriginal Names

Many of the names found on Australian wine labels are actually Aboriginal words. The Aborigines of Australia have their own unique language developed in almost complete isolation from other cultures. Some wine regions have Aboriginal names like Mudgee ("nest in the hills") and Coonawarra ("honeysuckle"), and some wineries even use Aboriginal terms for their names, like Killibinbin ("to shine") and Yalumba ("the earth all around").

to that of California. As boomtowns were established in once unpopulated areas and settlers arrived by the thousands to strike it rich, new vineyards were planted throughout the country and winemaking in Australia became a much larger industry.

Phylloxera arrived in the country in the late 1800s, and ravaged the vineyards in Victoria, which was the top-producing region at the time. The epidemic was contained to just Victoria and a small section of New South Wales, allowing other states to emerge as winemaking centers, especially South Australia. At the turn of the century, Australian winemakers produced mostly sweet fortified wines that were popular domestically and in the English market.

With the emergence of quality production in California and other regions outside of Europe in the 1960s and 1970s, Australian winemakers followed suit and began to concentrate on dry, varietal wines. Shiraz immediately became successful, as it is ideally suited to many of the country's warmer vineyard sites, and it is still the most important grape grown in Australia. Several top-quality Australian wines began to garner critical acclaim in the 1970s and 1980s, chief among them Penfolds Grange Shiraz, an ultrapremium Shiraz wine sourced from some of the best vineyard sites in the country.

As irrigation projects helped to expand vineyard acreage, several large wine operations rose to power, and still dominate much of Australian winemaking today. Hundreds of small, family-owned wineries were also established, and Australia became home to well over one thousand wineries. Official wine laws, similar to those found in the United States, were established throughout the latter parts of the twentieth century, and a modern wine industry was born.

Australia is an enormous country. The total landmass of Australia is roughly equal to that of the continental United States—about 3,000 miles across and nearly 2,000 miles from north to south. Being in the Southern Hemisphere, the country gets cooler the further South one goes, and wine production is limited to the cooler, southern areas of the country.

The geographic size is not matched by its population, however, as this huge country only has a total population equivalent to that of New York State! This small but proud population consumes more wine per person than that in any other major English-speaking country. Wine is much more a part of life in Australia than in the United States, yet they import very little wine, with far more domestic production than consumption.

With this vast surplus of wine and a small domestic population, exporting has become the focus for Australia's wine industry. They plan to eventually become the leading exporter of wine in the world, and they have a track record that makes this goal realistic. Although Australia is not traditionally known as a wine-producing country, it ranks sixth in the world in terms of total wine production and already exports more wine than most European countries.

Australian winemakers often use off-the-wall labels for their wines.

In the United States market, the largest wine import market in the world, Australia is the second leading exporter of wine behind Italy. It surpassed France in export sales to the United States in 2003, surprising many industry experts. Its success in exporting wine to the United States is due to a combination of several different factors, although the three most important are:

1. Their wines are inexpensive because of international currency exchange. The Australian dollar is worth less than the American dollar, meaning Australian wines can provide incredible value. At the same time, European imports cost more because of the value of the Euro.
2. The wines of Australia are easy to understand. English is their official language and their system of wine laws is very similar to American regulations, meaning that they label wines by grape variety. Irreverent and humorous brands and labels are often used to make Australian wine less stuffy and more approachable.
3. They make wines specifically for the American market. After decades of American consumer research, the Australian wine industry focuses on producing wines targeted to American preferences. Many of the brands that they export to the United States are not even sold in Australia because they are not intended for that market.

Australia is a vast and exciting wine nation, constantly striving to produce better-quality wines and increase international sales. Although much of its success has centered on large, industrial wineries growing just a handful of grapes, hundreds of small, boutique wineries are emerging as quality producers of a surprising number of grapes and styles. Australian wine is one of the most important segments of the retail wine industry in the United States and many other countries, and that trend should continue.

WINE LAWS OF AUSTRALIA

Australia's wine laws are very similar to those of the United States and the rest of the other New World countries. Regulations are purposely loose to grant winemakers maximum freedom to experiment, and there are no legal restrictions on winemaking methods or which grape varieties can be planted. Most premium Australian wine is labeled by grape variety.

If a grape is listed on a label of Australian wine, then at least 85 percent of the grapes used to make the wine must be the listed grape. If two or more grapes were used in its production, and none meet the 85 percent minimum, then the grapes will be listed in descending order of content, often accompanied by relative percentages. As for regional labeling laws, if a recognized wine region is listed, then at least 85 percent of the grapes must have been grown in the listed region.

A system of recognized appellations of origin, similar to the U.S. American Viticultural Areas, was first established in Australia in 1993. These official wine-producing areas are known as **Geographic Indications,** abbreviated as **GI.** A hierarchy of size has been established for the GI system, often based more on physical location than on viticultural reasons. The largest official Geographic Indication of South Eastern Australia is the only region that is larger than a single state, covering all or part of every state in southern and eastern Australia. Below that, each state that produces wine is considered its own GI and can be designated on a wine label. Large GI winemaking zones located in specific areas of each state hold one or more GI regions established for distinct grape-growing reasons. These regions are often home to several subregions that produce specific styles of wine or share unique climate or geographical conditions.

IMPORTANT GRAPES OF AUSTRALIA

There are no native species of grapevines found in Australia, so all of the grapes grown in the country have foreign origins. With no legal restrictions on grape growing in Australia, the country has planted and experimented with many different grapes. Currently, more than one hundred different varietals are planted in vineyards around the country, although a select

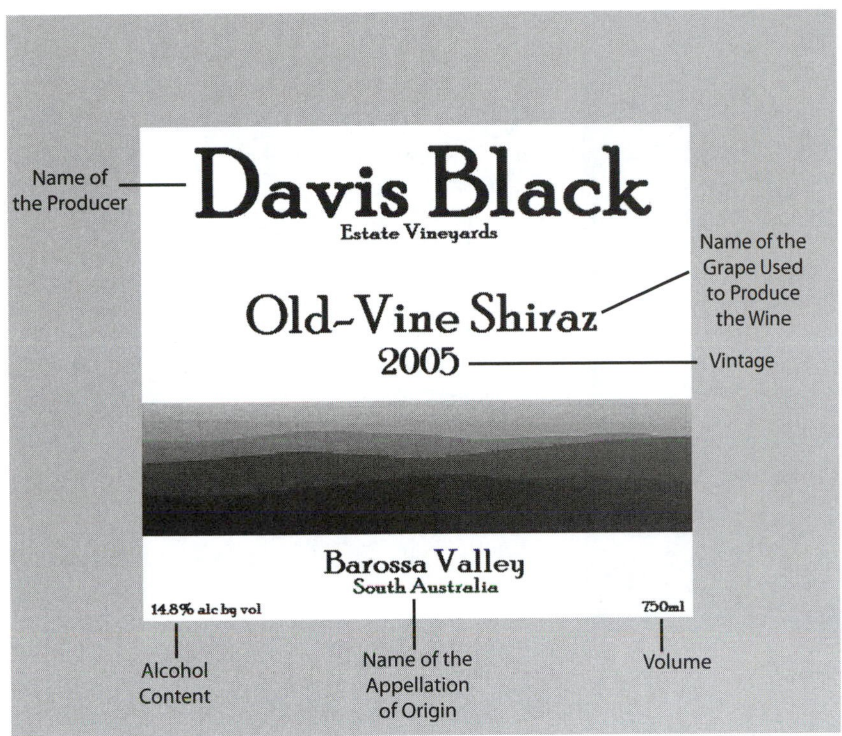

How to read an Australian wine label.

handful of grapes dominate most wine production. Due to the warm to hot conditions found in Australia, heat-loving grapes tend to do best in its winemaking regions. The most important, well-known, and widely planted grape variety is Shiraz, but several other grapes have adapted well to the conditions here, especially Chardonnay and Cabernet Sauvignon.

Chardonnay

In recent years, vineyard acreage dedicated to Chardonnay has steadily increased, almost challenging Shiraz as the most widely planted grape. Much of Chardonnay's popularity with Australian winemakers has to do with its ability to sell in export markets, especially the United States. Regardless, quality-conscious grape growers have found several regions throughout Australia that produce marvelous and complex Chardonnay wines, rivaling the quality and critical scores of California Chardonnay and even white Burgundies.

Australian Chardonnay can range widely in style and quality. Depending upon the winemaker and characteristics of the wine, it can be heavily manipulated, with buttery and oaky flavors dominating the flavor profile. Cooler-climate regions will produce more reserved and acidic Chardonnay wines, and the practice of bottling these unwooded, or without any oak aging, is gaining popularity.

Shiraz

Australia's most important grape is Shiraz. Ideally suited to the warm conditions and infertile soils of Australia's winemaking regions, this grape is the most popular, widely planted varietal in the country. Named after the Dutch term for the Syrah grape (initial cuttings

Shiraz is Australia's most important and widely planted grape varietal.

"Cult" Shiraz?

Most Australian Shiraz is reasonably priced, fruity, and abundant. That said, the emergence of super-premium, limited-production, very expensive Shiraz began with the release of Penfolds Grange Hermitage (now simply called Grange) in 1951. Today, there are several super-premium Shirazes produced in Australia that garner enviable press and huge price tags. Below is a list of a few.

- Penfolds Grange
- Henschke's "Hill of Grace"
- Jim Barry "The Armagh"
- Gemtree "Obsidian"
- Torbreck "Run Rig"
- Hentley Farm "The Beast"
- Amon Ra
- Glaetzer "Godolphin"
- Yalumba "Octavius"
- Mollydooker "Carnival of Love"
- d'Arenberg "Dead Arm"
- Jasper Hill "Emily's Paddock"

were sourced in South Africa, a Dutch colony at the time), this Rhône Valley transplant has simply found a second home in Australia. Many of the intensely concentrated and complex Shiraz-based wines produced from the best vineyard sites in Australia rank with the top-quality styles in the world.

Australian Shiraz is often bursting with ripe and cooked berry fruit. Full ripeness is almost always achieved, and this means a rich, almost chewy body and significant levels of alcohol. Not far behind Italian Pinot Grigio, Australian Shiraz is the second most popular style of foreign wine sold in the United States.

Cabernet Sauvignon

Recently, Australia has begun to produce some very exciting wines made with Cabernet Sauvignon grapes. By matching this grape with vineyards and wine regions ideally suited to the varietal, Australia has developed its own style of Cabernet-based wines. These tend to be powerful and rich, with dark fruit flavors and a noticeably soft tannin structure.

Other Notable Grapes

MUSCAT The ancient Muscat grape is grown around the world to produce sweet wine, and Australia is no exception. Most Muscat wines are fortified and intensely sweet, a style of wine the Australians call "**stickies.**"

SÉMILLON While Chardonnay dominates white wine exports, the Sémillon grape is often the choice for white wines in the domestic market. Australia is one of only a few production areas in the world for 100 percent varietal Sémillon, and Australian versions are often rich, round, and have pronounced honey flavors. Sémillon is sometimes called **Hunter Valley Riesling.**

RIESLING Although the success of this almost exclusively cool-climate grape seems completely illogical in the warm conditions of Australia, winemakers here take advantage of elevation and cooler pockets of vineyards to grow Riesling. Due to full ripeness, most Australian Riesling is bottled dry and often shows characteristics of white pepper and lime zest.

VIOGNIER This white Rhône varietal has shown great success with experimental plantings throughout South Australia. Warm conditions bring out the rich stone fruit and floral aromas of the grape, along with higher alcohol and a rich mouth-feel. Many producers add a small percentage of Viognier to their Shiraz wines, a traditional practice in the Rhône Valley region of Côte-Rôtie.

GRENACHE The most important red grape in France's southern Rhône Valley was a logical choice for winemaking in Australia following the country's success with Syrah. Bottled individually or in blends (most commonly **Grenache/Shiraz/Mourvèdre** or **GSM** for short), this grape brings power and red fruit flavors to the glass.

MERLOT The Merlot grape is planted throughout Australia, and produces mostly soft, fruity red wines, often intended solely for the export market.

MOURVÈDRE This lesser-known red Rhône varietal is not commonly bottled on its own, but rather is used in blends with other grapes, especially Grenache and Shiraz. Mourvèdre is sometimes called Mataro.

TERROIR AND IMPORTANT REGIONS

Located in the Southern Hemisphere, Australia is basically the world's largest desert island. Almost 90 percent of the country is classified as either desert or tropical rain forest—conditions far too hot for grape growing. The southern 10 percent of the country is below the 30th parallel of latitude, and home to most of the country's population and almost all of its vineyard acreage. Temperate conditions are found only in this part of Australia.

Even in the southern areas, conditions are still quite warm and extremely arid, as this is the driest inhabited continent in the world. Irrigation is a widely practiced necessity in almost all Australian wine regions because of extremely scarce rainfall. A complex system of rivers and canals connects most Australian wine regions to the precious supply of irrigation water. The warm climate leads to full to extreme ripeness in grapes, and warm-climate varietals are best suited to most of Australia's wine regions.

The country is very flat, with only a few coastal mountain ranges of note. Proximity to the ocean and elevation often combine to temper the climate in most of the top regions. In certain wine regions, cooler climates can be found, but this is the exception to the rule.

Soil types found in Australia are unique, as this landscape is home to the oldest and least-fertile soils in the world. Centuries of erosion and weathering have leached most of the top soils of nutrients and minerals. The soil is often acidic and very high in salinity, a poor combination for agricultural crops. When grapevines can survive, the soil often limits yields—although this can be a blessing, as limited yields and stress often translate to higher quality in wines.

The country of Australia is broken up into six states and two territories. Australian states include New South Wales, Queensland, South Australia, Tasmania, Victoria, and Western Australia. The territories are the sparsely populated Northern Territory located in the heart of the Outback, and the tiny Australian Capital Territory surrounding the country's official capital of Canberra.

Significant amounts of wine are produced in five of these states, with the exception of Queensland, where northern latitudes and hot climates limit grape growing. Neither of the two territories is home to any commercial vineyards of note. The largest and top-producing region in Australia is the **South Eastern Australia GI**, which covers all of the wine-producing states except Western Australia. Most bulk wines produced in Australia will bear this appellation. Traveling from west to east along Australia's southern coastline, the wine-producing states of the country are **Western Australia**, **South Australia**, **Victoria**, and **New**

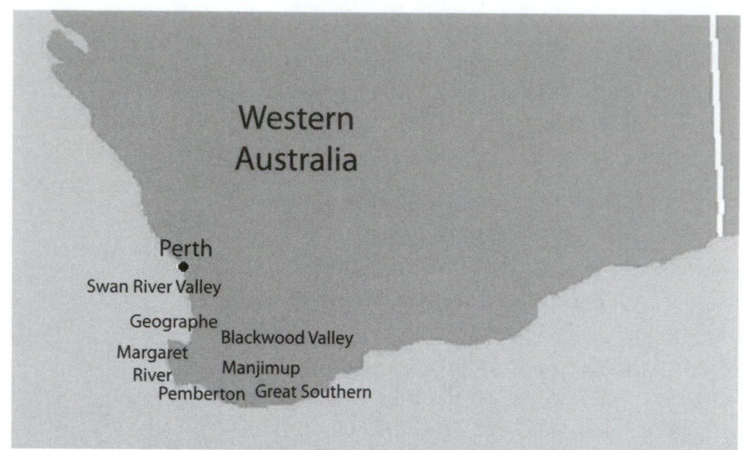

Western Australia and its important wine regions.

South Wales. Tasmania is a wine-producing island off the southern coast of Victoria.

Western Australia

Western Australia is the largest Australian state, covering the western third of the country, but it has one of the smallest amounts of vineyard acreage for a state. Wine regions are located almost exclusively in coastal areas south of the state capital and most important city in the region, Perth. Due to the isolation of Western Australia from the rest of the populated areas of the country, much of its production is geared toward international exports rather than domestic markets.

The southwestern tip of Western Australia is where the Indian Ocean and the Southern Ocean converge. Maritime influences play a major role in the climate of Western Australia and its wine regions. Localized temperate climate zones are where the top production in the state takes place, especially in the most famous GI of Western Australia, **Margaret River.**

Margaret River Margaret River is named for the river that flows through the center of this region, and it is made up of a large area of land that juts out into the ocean. The region is more than 150 miles south of the city of Perth. Just offshore is the area where the Indian Ocean meets the Southern Ocean, and together their marine influence creates a temperate climate in the region. This is one of the largest individual GI regions of Australia, covering almost 75 miles from north to south, and extending nearly 20 miles inland to its eastern border.

The region is fairly new to winemaking, as the first commercial winery did not start operations until the late 1960s. Since that time, Margaret River has been rapidly planted and almost one hundred wineries are found there today. Dry red wines are the most important style produced in Margaret River, especially Shiraz and Cabernet Sauvignon. The region is also home to ideal growing conditions for Chardonnay, and some of these complex white wines have received international and critical fame.

Other Regions of Note in Western Australia Just south of Perth is the warmest wine region in Western Australia, called the Swan River Valley GI. The extreme heat and lack of rainfall here make producing premium wine difficult. Fortified wines and simple jug wines dominate production.

Surrounding the Margaret River region are several GIs that share its temperate-maritime climate. Most are dedicated to red wine production, and Shiraz is the most widely planted grape variety. The GI of Geographe is just north of Margaret River, and the GIs of Blackwood Valley, Great Southern, Manjimup, and Pemberton are to the south and east.

South Australia

The state of South Australia is the most important wine-producing region in the country. Several factors played a role in South Australia's rising production and importance beginning in the 1800s, not the least of which are its ideal conditions for producing high-quality, dry table wines.

Today, South Australia is responsible for roughly half of the country's total wine production and is

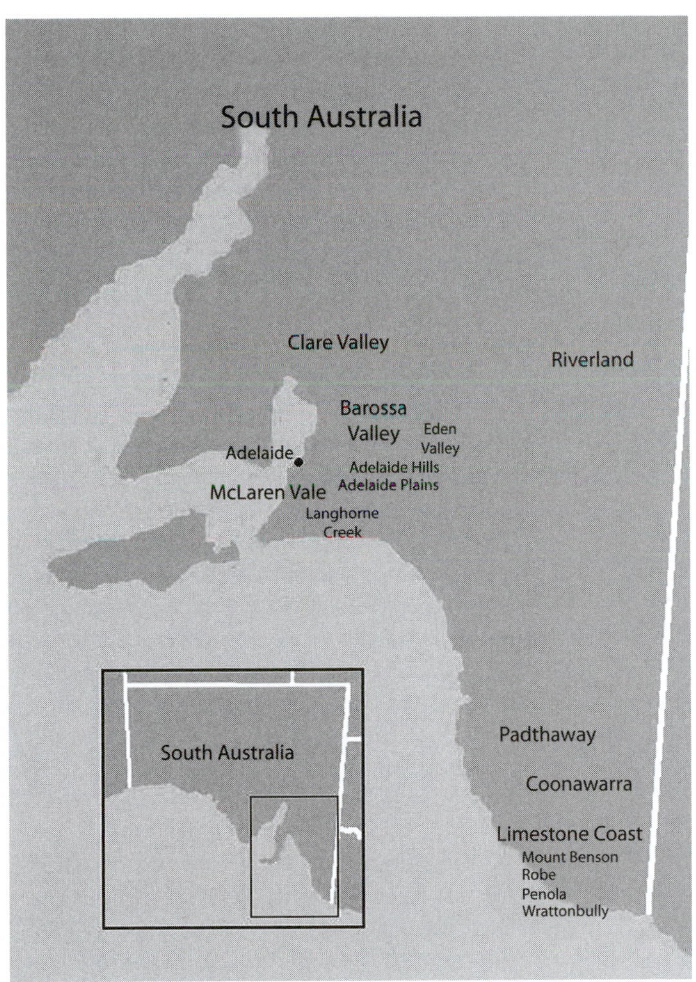

South Australia and its important wine regions.

home to many of its top-quality wines. Dozens of important wine regions spread to the north and the south of the state's capital and most populous city of Adelaide. These recognized vineyard areas include the GI regions of the **Barossa Valley, McLaren Vale, Clare Valley,** and **Coonawarra.**

Barossa Valley Located about 40 miles northeast of Adelaide is the Barossa Valley, one of the most important Australian wine regions and the heart of Australian winemaking. Here you will find the headquarters for many of the largest and most important Australian wineries, side by side with some of the smallest and most renowned boutique wineries in the country. The Barossa Valley has a long tradition of winemaking dating back to the 1840s, and old-vine blocks of Shiraz and Grenache found in the region can sometimes date almost as far back.

Shiraz is the most important grape grown in the region, and it ripens fully in the warm, dry climate of the Barossa Valley. Often dry farmed with no irrigation, Barossa Valley vineyards also produce high-quality Grenache and Cabernet Sauvignon. To the east lies a series of steep hills that rise up from the valley floor, home to the subregional GI of Eden Valley. Cooler climates in higher elevations in Eden Valley produce high-quality dry Riesling, and at lower elevations, some of the most legendary Shiraz wines in Australia are made.

Clare Valley About 25 miles northwest of the Barossa Valley is the town of Clare and the surrounding GI wine region known as the Clare Valley. Temperate to cool climates and long, sunny days combine to make this one of the top appellations for dry Rieslings and full-bodied complex Cabernet Sauvignon and Shiraz.

Barossa's German Heritage

Many of the first settlers and winemakers in the Barossa Valley were German immigrants. They helped to establish some of the top wineries in the Barossa and are one of the reasons that Riesling is such a popular grape in the cooler, high-altitude vineyards of South Australia.

McLaren Vale McLaren Vale is a coastal region, home to a warm climate that is often impacted by cooling ocean breezes. A little over 20 miles south of Adelaide, McLaren Vale is one of the most highly regarded wine regions in Australia. The region specializes in powerful, long-lived red wines made from Shiraz, Grenache, and Bordeaux varieties. Exciting white wines made from Chardonnay and other varietals are also widely produced.

Coonawarra The southernmost winemaking zone of South Australia is known as the **Limestone Coast**, named for the limestone-rich subsoils that are covered with a mixture of red clay and sand known as *terra rossa* soil. These geological conditions are ideal for Cabernet Sauvignon, the specialty of the Coonawarra GI located in the heart of the Limestone Coast. Coonawarra means "honeysuckle" in the native Aboriginal language, and this wine region feels the cooling influences of the ocean even though it is almost 60 miles inland.

Slow ripening and the special soils found in Coonawarra combine to produce structured, intense Cabernet Sauvignon wines. Other red grapes and a smattering of whites are also grown in Coonawarra, but most new production has been geared toward its most important grape. The Limestone Coast GI that encompasses Coonawarra is more than 200 miles south of Adelaide. It also covers the important GI region of Padthaway, just north of Coonawarra, as well as the newly established GI regions of Mount Benson, Penola, Robe, and Wrattonbully. All of these surrounding regions focus on Cabernet Sauvignon production.

Other Regions of Note in South Australia The largest specific appellation in South Australia is Riverland, a large region that is planted well inland along the Murray River. This is the top wine region in Australia for production, supplying almost half of the wine made in South Australia and nearly a quarter of the country's total. Most of the wines are of basic quality, and will be labeled either South Australia or South Eastern Australia if blended with wines from other regions or states.

Closer to the city of Adelaide are three regions of note: Adelaide Hills and Adelaide Plains, which are in the same Mount Lofty Ranges GI zone as the Clare Valley, and Langhorne Creek, part of the Fleurieu GI zone along with McLaren Vale. Most of the vineyards planted in the Adelaide Hills are at higher elevations, above 1,500 feet, so cool-climate grapes and styles predominate. The Adelaide Plains GI is much warmer, and the focus there is big, full-bodied reds. About 40 miles southeast of the state's capital is Langhorne Creek, an area dedicated to red wines made from Cabernet Sauvignon and Shiraz. Several large wineries own land in Langhorne Creek, but a new generation of small, boutique wineries have begun opening their doors.

Victoria

Victoria is home to the southernmost wine regions of mainland Australia, and is bordered to the west by South Australia and to the north and east by New South Wales. Its southernmost point is about 150 miles north of the island state of Tasmania, the only state smaller than Victoria. Significant amounts of wine are produced in Victoria for its smaller size, and it ranks third amongst Australian states.

Serious winemaking first began in Victoria in the 1850s, after a gold rush in the state brought thousands of settlers who planted vineyards in areas far and wide around the state's capital and Australia's second largest city, Melbourne. Despite their late start, winemaking rapidly expanded in Victoria, and by the 1890s the state produced almost half of Australia's wine. Unfortunately, ***phylloxera*** finally reached Australia around the same time and Victoria was one of the few places it hit. After ***phylloxera*** destroyed most of the vineyards in the state, Victoria's wine industry was in a shambles, and it did not really reemerge until the 1970s and 1980s, when a new generation of winemakers reclaimed the state's historic vineyard land and wine regions.

Today, Victoria is home to an amazing array of different grape varietals and wine styles. The state has several different climate zones, allowing winemakers to make top-quality cool-climate wines in some areas and riper styles and sweet fortified wines, called stickies, in others. There are six major GI

Victoria and its important wine regions.

Stickies

Most of Australia's wine production prior to the 1960s was sweet, fortified wines from grapes like Muscat and Tokay (also called Muscadelle). Of all the regions of Australia, Victoria still holds to this tradition the strongest, producing wonderful examples of these wines that are commonly referred to as stickies because of their extreme sugar content.

zones in Victoria, which cover almost twenty different recognized GI regions.

The Port Phillip zone is located along the coast mostly south of Melbourne. It is noted for its cool-climate wine regions, and some of the best Chardonnay and surprisingly good Pinot Noir are produced here. The most well-known wine region in the Port Phillip zone is the **Yarra Valley,** but Mornington Peninsula, Geelong, and the Macedon Range are also regions to watch. To the north of Melbourne is the Central Victoria zone, a much warmer district than the Port Phillip zone and home to mostly elegant red wines, especially the Shiraz of the Heathcote and Bendigo GIs.

To the west of Melbourne you will find two important production zones, Western Victoria and North West Victoria. Western Victoria borders South Australia and is the cooler of the two, producing some of the best sparkling wines in the country, especially in the Pyrenees GI and Grampians GI. North West Victoria shares its northern border with New South Wales, with some of its larger GIs straddling that border. This part of Victoria is hot and dry, where the Murray Darling and Swan Hill appellations produce large amounts of bulk wine often destined for a South Eastern Australia designation.

East of Melbourne, along the border with New South Wales, you will find the South East Victoria and North East Victoria GI zones. North East Victoria has a much warmer, more continental climate and produces everything from dense, full-bodied red wines to sweet fortified wines made from the Muscat grape. Rutherglen is the best-known GI region in this zone, although the King Valley appellation is growing rapidly as well. South East Victoria is dominated by the giant Gippsland GI region. As large in size as it is, Gippsland is sparsely planted.

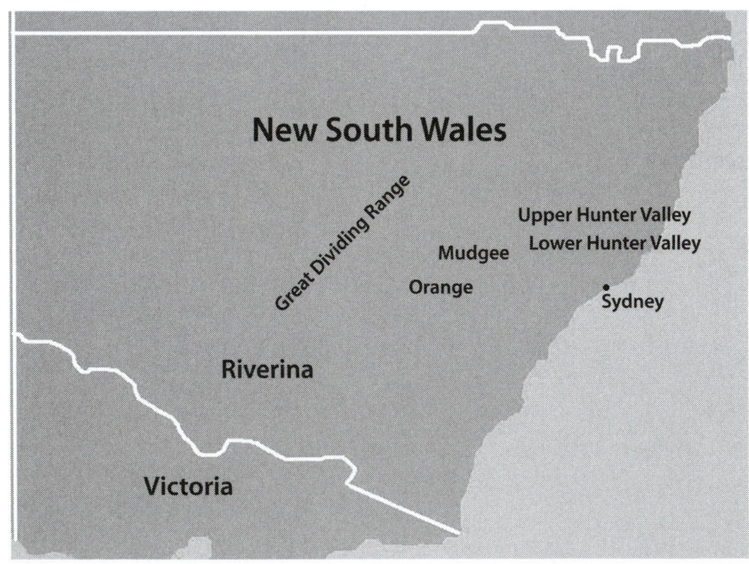

New South Wales and its important wine regions.

New South Wales

Home to Sydney, the largest city in Australia, New South Wales was the site of the original colonial settlements in the country and was the first place wine grapes were planted. Much of the wine produced in this state is consumed domestically by the large population base in both Sydney and Canberra, the nation's capital. New South Wales is north of Victoria and shares a border to the west with South Australia. Its northern location means that most of the wine regions are warm and often muggy.

New South Wales is home to several historic wine regions and is second only to South Australia for wine production among states. As early settlers spread out from the original settlement of Sydney, they took grapevine cuttings with them and established some remarkable regions. Irrigation projects and harnessed rivers spread agriculture far into the Outback of New South Wales, where new wine regions were established. Of all the areas of winemaking in the state, the most famous region by far is the **Hunter Valley.**

The Hunter Valley Second only to the Barossa Valley in name recognition among Australian wine regions, the Hunter Valley is one of the oldest areas of winemaking in the country. About 100 miles north of Sydney, this region's subtropical climate and often barren soil can make grape growing difficult. The Hunter Valley GI can be broken up into two major winemaking areas: the Upper Hunter Valley is the northern area and the Lower Hunter Valley makes up the southern part of the region. The Lower Hunter Valley is the area where vineyards were first planted, and is mostly dedicated to Shiraz and the white Sémillon grape, a local favorite sometimes called Hunter Valley Riesling. The Upper Hunter Valley is primarily a white wine region with large plantings of Chardonnay.

Other Regions of Note in New South Wales Most of the remaining GI regions of New South Wales are located further inland. Warm to hot conditions are the norm in most of these regions, except for those planted on the slopes of the Great Dividing Range, a long chain of mountains that cuts through New South Wales heading north to Queensland and south to Victoria. The warmest region is Riverina, and this heavily irrigated region produces large quantities of bulk wines, although it is also known for fortified wines and famous for its sweet Sémillon wines made from botrytis-infected grapes. Closer to the Great Dividing Range, several regions have both warm conditions at the foot of the mountains and cooler conditions at higher elevations along the western slopes. Mudgee and Orange are two of the most well-known GI appellations in this interior section of New South Wales.

Tasmania

Although Tasmania was the second state planted to vines in Australia after New South Wales, a large wine industry has never been established on this large island. Tasmanian production is only a very small part of the nation's total, but the wines of the region are often high in quality and unique. With the coolest climate of any Australian state, the region specializes in cool-climate varietals like Pinot Noir and Chardonnay, and is home to some stunning sparkling wines. Expect continued growth of winemaking in Tasmania, as many new wineries have been established recently.

Summary

Australia is an unlikely part of the world for a large, modern wine industry. Industrious grape growers and enterprising winemakers have diligently tamed the country's harsh landscape and developed a model for exporting wine countries today. Through a wide range of states and regions, vineyards in southern areas of Australia produce an array of different styles and grow several different grapes, chief among them the famous Shiraz. The future looks bright for the Australian wine industry as it continues to expand, improve quality standards, and develop into one of the major players in the international export market.

Review Questions

1. Australia ranks _________ in terms of worldwide wine production.
   A. second
   B. fourth
   C. sixth
   D. eighth

2. The most important red grape varietal in Australia, and the country's most widely grown grape, is ____________.
   A. Grenache
   B. Shiraz
   C. Cabernet Sauvignon
   D. Merlot

3. Australia's wine regions are limited to the cooler, northern areas of the country.
   A. True
   B. False

4. The first grapevines planted in Australia were in the region now known as:
   A. New South Wales
   B. Victoria
   C. South Australia
   D. Western Australia

5. Sweet fortified wines produced in Australia are locally referred to as "stickies."
   A. True
   B. False

6. The leading state for wine production in Australia today is ______________.
   A. New South Wales
   B. Victoria
   C. South Australia
   D. Western Australia

7. An officially recognized wine region in Australia is called a GI, which stands for ______________________.
   A. Geographic Index
   B. Geological Index
   C. Geographic Indication
   D. Geological Indication

8. If a label on an Australian bottle of wine lists a grape variety, the wine must contain at least _________ of the listed grape.
   A. 75%
   B. 85%
   C. 95%
   D. 100%

For the following questions, match the important GI region to the state in which it is found. Some answers may be used more than once, and some not at all.

9. Barossa Valley	A. Western Australia
10. Hunter Valley	B. South Australia
11. Margaret River	C. Victoria
12. McLaren Vale	D. New South Wales

Key Terms

Geographic Indication (GI)
stickies
Hunter Valley Riesling
Grenache/Shiraz/Mourvèdre (GSM)
South Eastern Australia
Western Australia
South Australia
Victoria
New South Wales
Tasmania
Margaret River
Barossa Valley
McLaren Vale
Clare Valley
Coonawarra
Limestone Coast
Yarra Valley
Hunter Valley

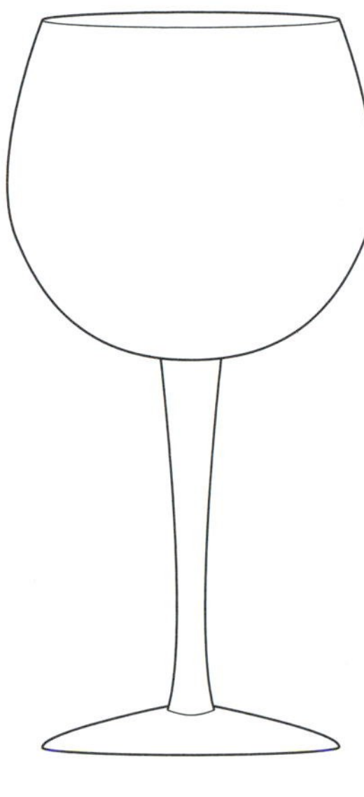

CHAPTER 18

The Wines of New Zealand

No previous wine had shocked, thrilled, entranced the world before with such brash, unexpected flavours of gooseberries, passionfruit and lime, or crunchy green asparagus spears . . . an entirely new, brilliantly successful wine style that the rest of the world has been attempting to copy ever since.

—**OZ CLARKE**, English wine writer, speaking on New Zealand Sauvignon Blanc

Although New Zealand has only recently become known for its winemaking, the quality inherent in its wines has won them serious critical acclaim. The bright and shining star of this island nation is the Sauvignon Blanc grape, while Chardonnay and Pinot Noir are rapidly gaining in quality. In this chapter we discuss the wines, winemaking, and top regions of New Zealand.

The Facts on New Zealand

CLIMATE

Mostly temperate to cool.

TOP WHITE GRAPES

- Sauvignon Blanc
- Chardonnay

TOP RED GRAPE

- Pinot Noir

TOP REGIONS

North Island

- Gisborne
- Hawke's Bay
- Wairarapa/Wellington

South Island

- Marlborough
- Central Otago

IMPORTANT INFORMATION

- New Zealand is not a large producer of wine; however, the wine it does produce is considered high in quality.
- New Zealand is home to the southernmost vineyards in the world; however, the oceans that surround it maintain a temperate to cool climate.

New Zealand: An Island Nation

New Zealand is home to the southernmost and easternmost vineyards in the world. Long known for its breathtaking scenery (it has been the backdrop for many movies, including the *Lord of the Rings* trilogy), New Zealand is a land of diverse geography, including

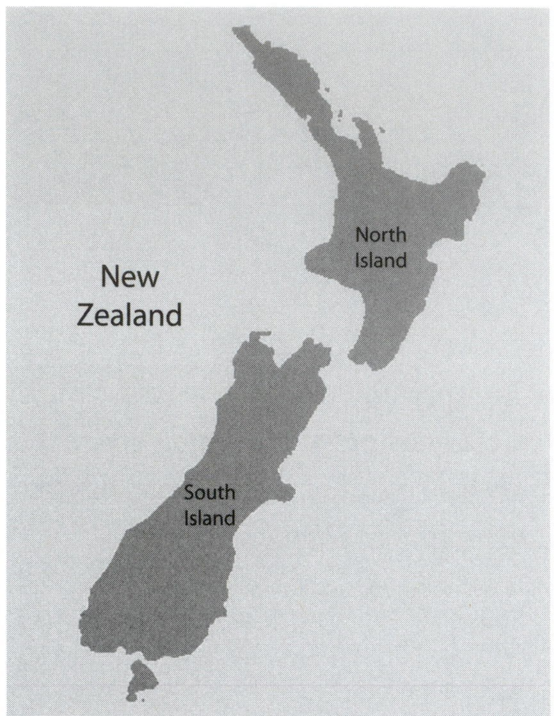

Strict Prohibition

Many of the obstacles to the emergence of the modern New Zealand wine industry were self-induced, as this country adopted prohibition laws that were much stricter than those in the United States, and that lasted far longer. From the early 1800s to the mid-1900s, wine sales in New Zealand were either forbidden or extremely restricted. As an example, selling wine in a restaurant was not legal until the 1960s!

dense forests, steep mountains, and a rugged coastline. Located about 1,200 miles east of Australia, the country is made up of two very different, large islands: the **North Island** and the **South Island.**

While wine grapes were first planted in New Zealand in 1819, the modern wine industry did not truly begin until the 1970s. The most important changes that marked the modernization of the New Zealand wine industry were the introduction of refrigerated, stainless-steel fermentation tanks, which allowed winemakers to produce the clean, crisp whites they have become famous for; and the **Stelvin closure** or **screw cap.** New Zealand is today the world's leader in the use of Stelvin closures to seal their wines.

New Zealand is a minor wine-producing country in terms of quantity—it ranks twenty-first in the world in terms of total wine production. However, the wines New Zealand does produce are world class in terms of quality. Modern winemaking techniques and a commitment to international grape varieties have thrust New Zealand onto the world winemaking scene.

WINE LAWS OF NEW ZEALAND

Similar to other New World countries, New Zealand has a loose set of wine laws to allow freedom for winemakers. There are no restrictions as to which grape varieties can be planted or which winemaking methods can be used. The wines of New Zealand are labeled by grape variety. If a grape or region is listed on a wine labeled for export, then at least 85 percent of the grapes used to make the wine must be the listed grape, and at least 85 percent of the grapes must have been grown in the listed region.

IMPORTANT GRAPES OF NEW ZEALAND

The vast majority of grapes grown in the vineyards of New Zealand are international varieties of French origin. Several grape varieties are grown in New Zealand, but white-skinned grapes dominate and are responsible for around 70 percent of total production. The most important grape grown in New Zealand is Sauvignon Blanc, although Chardonnay and Pinot Noir are both gaining in terms of popularity.

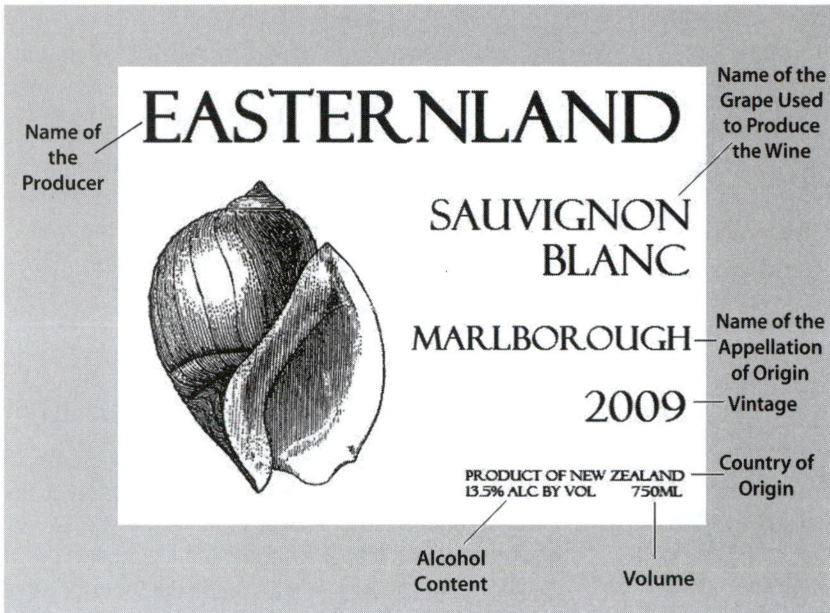

How to read a New Zealand wine label.

 Sauvignon Blanc

Although not planted in New Zealand until the 1970s, Sauvignon Blanc has become the country's claim to fame in the international wine market. Today, Sauvignon Blanc is the most widely grown grape variety in New Zealand, accounting for more than a third of the country's vineyard acreage.

The secret to the success of New Zealand Sauvignon Blanc is the fact that it is so unique when compared with wines made from the same grape elsewhere. While most Sauvignon Blanc tends to be very grassy and herbal, in New Zealand it takes on more of a grapefruit, gooseberry, and tropical fruit profile. With this grape's zesty acidity, these wines pair well with a wide range of foods and can be extremely bright and refreshing. Most of the Sauvignon Blanc produced in New Zealand is aged in stainless steel rather than oak to preserve the freshness and fruitiness of this varietal. The highest-quality Sauvignon Blancs from New Zealand tend to come from the large region of Marlborough (located on the South Island), where more than two-thirds of the country's vineyard acreage of this grape is planted.

Chardonnay

The second most widely planted grape variety behind Sauvignon Blanc, Chardonnay is another New Zealand specialty. Although this grape variety was first planted in New Zealand in the 1800s, it was never grown in large quantities until the emergence of the premium wine industry there in the 1970s. Chardonnay styles in New Zealand can vary greatly, from buttery and heavily oaked examples to vibrant, crisp sparkling wines. While Chardonnay is grown in all ten of New Zealand's wine regions, the best examples come from the relatively warm climates of Marlborough and the regions of the North Island.

Sauvignon Blanc is New Zealand's most important grape variety.

Pinot Noir

Notoriously difficult to grow, Pinot Noir has thrived in its newly adopted home of New Zealand. The most widely planted red grape in New Zealand, Pinot Noir was first grown in the country for the production of sparkling wines in the 1970s, but very quickly began to be made in a dry, red style as well. New Zealand Pinot Noir tends to be New World in style with bright fruit characteristics dominating its subtle earthiness. The top regions for Pinot Noir in New Zealand include the districts of Central Otago, Marlborough, Nelson, and Hawke's Bay.

Other Important Grapes

CABERNET SAUVIGNON Often simple and lighter in body and structure than most New World Cabernet Sauvignon, versions from New Zealand come primarily from the warmer North Island and are commonly blended with Merlot in the style of Bordeaux.

MERLOT Increasingly important in New Zealand, Merlot can often ripen more quickly than Cabernet Sauvignon, making it a better fit for the cooler conditions of New Zealand. Most of this Merlot comes from the North Island, like Cabernet Sauvignon, and at its best it can be very fruity and aromatic.

TERROIR AND IMPORTANT REGIONS

Even though New Zealand is the southernmost wine region in the world (it is roughly at the same latitude as Tasmania), the overall climate in New Zealand's winegrowing regions ranges from temperate to cool due to the maritime effects of the ocean that surrounds this island nation. No matter where you are in New Zealand, the ocean is always less than 100 miles away! The warmest regions of New Zealand are found on the North Island, and cooler temperatures tend to be found on the South Island. Most of the vineyards and wine regions in New Zealand are on the eastern side of the two islands, sheltered from strong winds that blow across the Pacific from the west by large mountain chains.

The North Island

In general, the wine regions located on the North Island of New Zealand are warmer and more humid than the regions to the south. This climate makes conditions on the North Island more suitable for growing red grapes such as Cabernet Sauvignon and Merlot. The North Island is home to six of the ten wine regions in New Zealand, although these regions make up less than 40 percent of the country's total vineyard acreage. The top regions located on the North Island include **Gisborne, Hawke's Bay,** and **Wairarapa/Wellington.**

Gisborne Located on the eastern tip of New Zealand, Gisborne is the second largest wine region

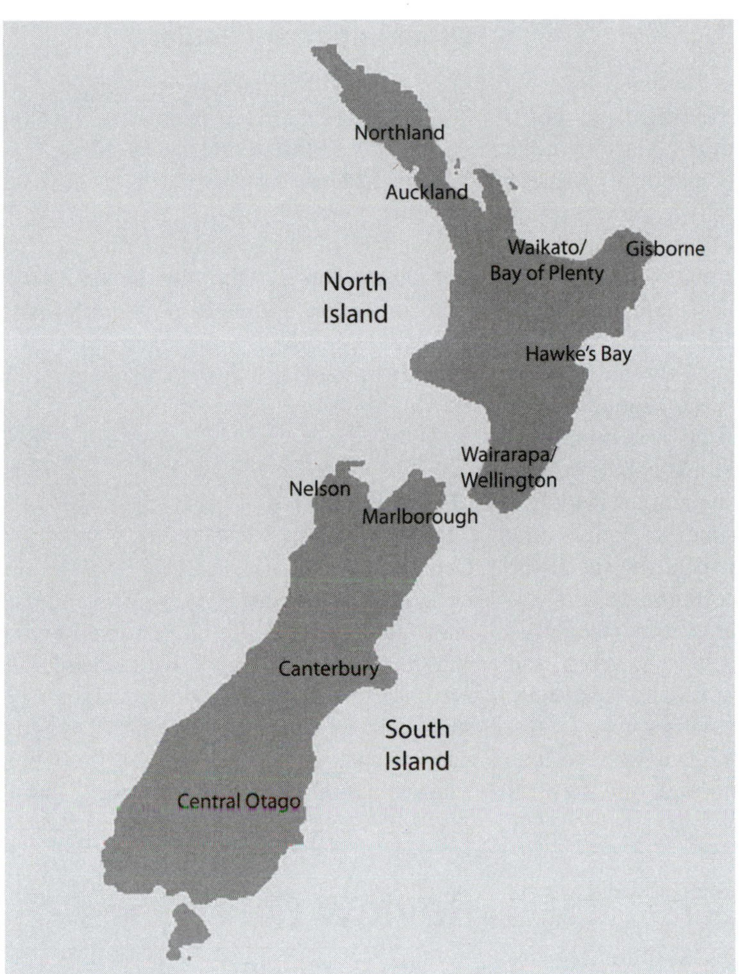

The wine regions of New Zealand.

on the North Island. With its temperate to cool maritime climate, the region focuses on white wines as well as sparkling wines, with more than half of its vineyard acreage planted to Chardonnay.

Hawke's Bay Widely considered to be the top quality wine region on the North Island, Hawke's Bay produces significant amounts of both still and sparkling wine. Winemaking began here over one hundred years ago; and as New Zealand's second largest region behind Marlborough, it is home to more than sixty wineries. Chardonnay dominates production, although the region also grows significant amounts of Cabernet Sauvignon and Merlot.

Wairarapa/Wellington On the southern tip of the North Island, Wairarapa (sometimes referred to as Wellington) and its famous subdistrict, Martinborough, share climate conditions much more similar to those found on the South Island. The specialties of this small, high-quality region are Pinot Noir and Sauvignon Blanc.

The South Island

The southernmost wine regions in the world are located on the South Island of New Zealand, which is home to a much cooler and drier climate than the North Island's. This cool, mostly maritime climate is more suitable for fast-ripening grape varieties such as Sauvignon Blanc and Pinot Noir, its two most widely grown grapes. The South Island is home to the Southern Alps, the tallest mountain range in the Southern Hemisphere, with several peaks near or above 10,000 feet in elevation. This causes a rain shadow effect for many of the wine regions located on the eastern side of the island by protecting them from the majority of the weather that comes in from the west. Although cool due to its southern latitude, many regions of the South Island get long sunny days in the summertime, because of the tilt of the Earth's axis, that help to fully ripen grapes.

The South Island is home to four recognized wine regions, including the country's largest and most well-known winemaking area, and as a result, more than 60 percent of the country's wine is produced here. The two most important wine regions of the South Island are **Marlborough** and **Central Otago.**

Marlborough The largest and most popular wine region in New Zealand, Marlborough produces almost half of the country's wine. Marlborough's rise to the top has been rapid; in fact, the first vines were not planted there until 1973. A combination of a cool climate and abundant sunshine make conditions there perfect for producing intensely flavored Sauvignon Blanc and Pinot Noir. The country's largest winery, Montana, is also based in Marlborough.

Central Otago Central Otago is a relatively new wine region in New Zealand, and is home to the world's most southern vineyards. The region has a uniquely continental climate, as it is the only one in New Zealand not located near the coastline. Central Otago shows serious potential for high-quality Pinot Noir.

Other Important Regions

There are only ten recognized wine regions in New Zealand. The other wine regions on the North Island are **Northland**, **Auckland**, and **Waikato** (also known as **Bay of Plenty**). The major focus in these warmer viticultural areas is Chardonnay, along with smaller productions of Merlot and Cabernet Sauvignon.

On the South Island, the remaining two regions are **Canterbury** and **Nelson.** As with Marlborough, the most important wine region in New Zealand, these areas focus primarily on Sauvignon Blanc.

Summary

New Zealand's wine industry focuses on quality rather than quantity. This tiny island nation has made an impact on the international wine industry with its exciting Sauvignon Blanc-based wines; however, it also shows serious promise for other grapes such as Pinot Noir and Chardonnay. There is much international excitement indeed for the modern wines and wineries in New Zealand.

Review Questions

1. The most widely grown and famous grape of New Zealand is ______________.
   - A. Cabernet Sauvignon
   - B. Pinot Noir
   - C. Sauvignon Blanc
   - D. Chardonnay

2. New Zealand is home to the southernmost vineyards in the world.
   - A. True
   - B. False

3. The country of New Zealand is made up of two major islands, the North Island and the South Island, but wine grapes are grown only on the North Island.
   - A. True
   - B. False

4. The vast majority of wines produced in New Zealand are ______________.
   - A. red
   - B. white
   - C. sparkling
   - D. fortified

5. Overall, New Zealand is home to a ______________ climate due to the effects of the ocean that surrounds it.
   - A. cool-cold
   - B. warm-hot
   - C. temperate-warm
   - D. temperate-cool

6. Late-ripening red grape varieties such as Cabernet Sauvignon and Merlot are mostly grown on the ______________ because of the relatively warmer conditions found there.
   - A. North Island
   - B. South Island

7. For New Zealand wine labeled Chardonnay, what percentage of the grapes used to produce the wine must be Chardonnay by law?
   - A. 75%
   - B. 85%
   - C. 95%
   - D. 100%

8. The most widely grown red grape variety of New Zealand is ______________.
   - A. Cabernet Sauvignon
   - B. Merlot
   - C. Shiraz
   - D. Pinot Noir

9. While wine grapes were first planted in New Zealand in 1819, the country's modern wine industry did not begin until the ______________.
   - A. 1950s
   - B. 1960s
   - C. 1970s
   - D. 1980s

10. Which of the following regions is best known for Pinot Noir?
   - A. Hawke's Bay
   - B. Auckland
   - C. Central Otago
   - D. Marlborough

Key Terms

North Island
South Island
Stelvin closure
screw cap
Gisborne
Hawke's Bay
Wairarapa/Wellington
Marlborough
Central Otago
Northland
Auckland
Waikato/Bay of Plenty
Canterbury
Nelson

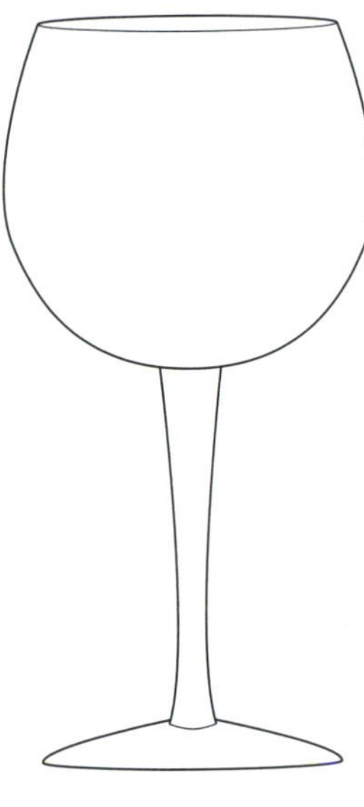

CHAPTER 19

The Wines of South Africa

Landmark developments in the Cape Wine industry have led to the beginning of a renaissance evidencing the region's potential to produce New World caliber wines offering fine quality and good value.

—*The Wine Journal*

South Africa is a New World wine-producing country that has deep Old World roots. Wines have been produced there since it was first a Dutch colony in the 1600s, and South African winemakers enjoyed solid trade with Europe during the colonial period. With such a long history of wine production, it would seem that South African wines would be relatively well known. That is not the case, however; due to decades of trade embargoes resulting from Apartheid, their wines are practically an afterthought.

The repeal of Apartheid in the early 1990s has changed the outlook for the wine industry in South Africa. Since that time, the country has attempted to reinvent itself and capture some of its past glory. This makes for some outstanding values and interesting wine styles. In this chapter, we discuss the history, grapes, laws, and wine regions of South Africa.

The Facts on South Africa

CLIMATE

Temperate to hot.

TOP WHITE GRAPES

- Chenin Blanc (called Steen)
- Muscat

TOP RED GRAPES

- Pinotage
- Shiraz
- Cabernet Sauvignon

TOP REGIONS

- Stellenbosch
- Paarl
- Constantia

IMPORTANT INFORMATION

- South Africa ranks eighth in the world in terms of total wine production.
- The country has a long history of wine production, but due to trade embargoes in place because of Apartheid, their wines are practically unknown today.
- South Africa has a Dutch colonial heritage, which is evidenced in their names for many grapes.
- Today, South Africa's wine industry is attempting to reestablish itself by adopting modern techniques and focusing on international grape varieties as well as its own unique grape, Pinotage.

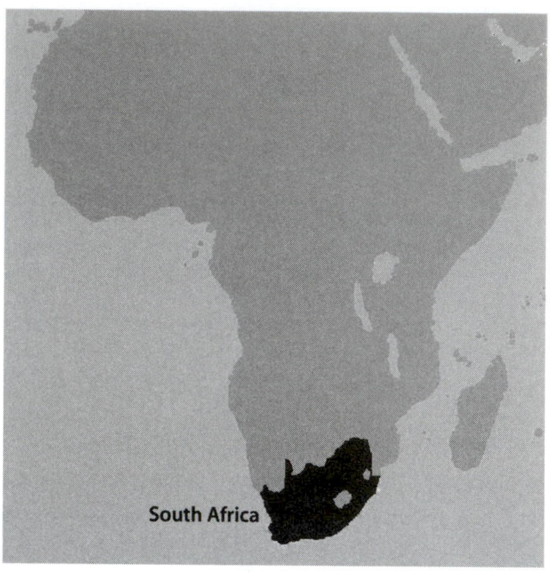

South Africa: A Region Reborn

In 1659 the first South African wine was produced by Jan van Riebeeck, an administrator for the Dutch East India Company. The temperate conditions found in the areas surrounding Cape Town proved ideal for grape growing. South Africa was a colony of the Dutch, and several facets of South African life today, including its wine industry, reflect this colonial heritage.

The country rose to wine prominence in the late 1600s due to a sweet, Muscat-based wine called **Constantia,** named after the region in which it was produced. This wine was a favorite for several European monarchs, from Napoleon to Frederick the Great. Its popularity helped to secure a place for South African wine imports into Europe, which is one of the main reasons South Africans consider themselves to be an Old World wine-producing country. All this came to an end when ***phylloxera*** wiped out most of the country's wine regions in the late 1800s. This epidemic devastated the South African wine industry, and it was never the same afterward.

When vineyards throughout the country were replanted on resistant rootstock around the turn of the last century, winemakers began to focus more on quantity than quality. Several massive winemaking cooperatives were formed to ostensibly help farmers sell their wines. Unfortunately, these cooperatives began to cannibalize the industry, and the results were mass-produced table wines lacking varietal or regional identity. This system began to dominate wine production in South Africa, just as the industry was headed for very difficult times. The system of government that evolved in South Africa, descended from its colonial past, was called **Apartheid.** Following World War II, a national party in South Africa controlled by minority elites established a system of legalized racial segregation. To pressure this government into changing, most of the countries of the western world placed trade embargoes against South Africa, boycotting products that were produced there. This was bad news for the country's winemakers.

While South Africa was at least relevant on the international wine market before these embargoes went into effect, it was unrecognizable when they were finally lifted. Decades went by while the rest of the winemaking world was modernizing and turning toward premium wine production. South Africa, on the other hand, was reduced to producing jug wines for its domestic market, as the large cooperatives eventually gobbled up most of the remaining independent vineyards and wineries.

When the trade embargoes were lifted after the fall of Apartheid in the early 1990s, the South African wine industry raced to re-enter the international wine market and fell flat on its face. Years of neglect and a focus on mass production meant that the wines of South Africa simply could no longer compete with wines from the rest of the world. Fortunately, this is rapidly changing.

South Africa revamped its wine laws in the mid-1990s and began to refocus on premium wine production from important grape varieties. Hundreds of small, often family-owned wineries have opened, further pushing a quality revolution in the country. Modern techniques and technologies have been adopted and this industry has truly been reborn. One of the best things about South African wine today is that the country is again focused on quality, but it is also trying to reestablish itself. This means that South African wines present a terrific value as they become more and more popular.

WINE LAWS OF SOUTH AFRICA

South Africa modernized its wine laws in the 1990s after the fall of Apartheid. The laws are known as the **Wine of Origin (WO)** system. It is basically made up of several tiers of recognized regions and subregions called geographical units, regions, districts, and wards, in order of declining size. Similar to other New World countries, the wine laws are unrestrictive and relaxed to allow freedom for winemakers. There are more than seventy different official grape varieties that can be grown in South Africa, and there are minimal laws governing which winemaking methods can be used.

Although the label laws of South Africa are similar to those in the United States, they are somewhat stricter. Most premium wines are labeled by grape variety, although there are some important blends that are labeled by proprietary or brand names. If a recognized WO region is listed on a wine label, then 100 percent of the grapes used to make the wine must be grown in that region. Wines that are labeled by grape variety must contain at least 85 percent of the listed grape.

IMPORTANT GRAPES OF SOUTH AFRICA

Although there are more than seventy different grape varieties that can be legally grown in South Africa, important production is limited to just a handful

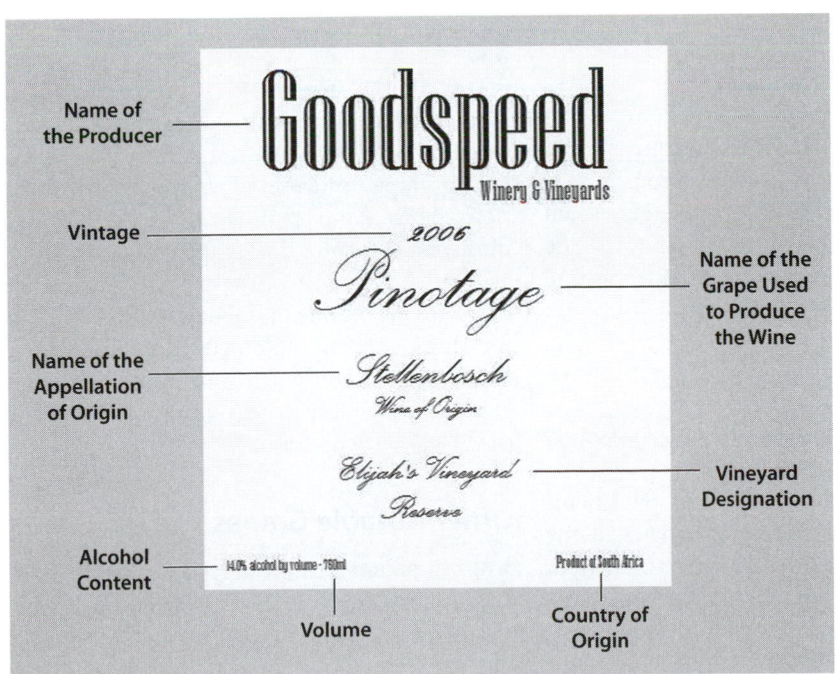

How to read a South African wine label.

of quality varietals. The country has traditionally been known more for its white wines than its reds, although this is slowly changing and only a little more than half its vineyard acreage is dedicated to white grape varietals today. Most of the grapes grown in South Africa are French in origin, first planted and established when the country was a Dutch colony. The only true standout is a grape that is uniquely South African, a red grape variety called **Pinotage.**

Chenin Blanc

South Africa has more acres dedicated to Chenin Blanc than any other country in the world. The grape accounts for more than 50 percent of the white wine produced in the country. In South Africa, the grape is referred to as **Steen,** although it is uncommon to see that term on a label of wine intended for the international market. South African Chenin Blanc runs the gamut of styles that this grape is capable of, from top-quality to inferior, sweet to dry. Most production focuses on simple, pleasant, dry white wines that can be extremely refreshing.

Muscat

The first wines that brought attention to South Africa were very sweet, sometimes fortified dessert wines. Many of these wines were made from various clones of Muscat. Today, this style is emerging again with Muscat still being heavily used. The best are lush, concentrated, and packed with ripe tropical fruits.

Pinotage

Pinotage is a grape unique to South Africa, and it is not grown in large quantities anywhere else in the world. It was developed in the 1920s by viticulturalists attempting to breed a grape that had the characteristics of Pinot Noir yet was able to thrive in the country's hot climate. Pinotage is a genetic cross between Pinot Noir and a red grape variety native to the Rhône Valley that is called Hermitage in South Africa (it is called Cinsaut in the rest of the world). Although it was not popularized until the 1960s, Pinotage has grown to become one of South Africa's most important and interesting varieties. Pinotage tends to be lighter in body with soft tannins and can range from simple, fruity table wines to intense and complex. The grape usually produces wines reminiscent of red fruits, but that can be extremely earthy and smoky. Pinotage plays a key role in the production of a style of wine called a **Cape Blend.** This is a wine made from a blend of different red grapes grown in South Africa, where Pinotage must make up at least 30 percent of the blend.

Cabernet Sauvignon

Cabernet Sauvignon has historically produced the most important red wines in South Africa, and is still the source for its most serious reds. The warmer climate maximizes the grape's dark fruit characteristics and helps to soften tannins. Cabernet Sauvignon is the most widely planted red grape variety in South Africa today.

Shiraz

Shiraz is the second most widely planted red grape variety in South Africa behind Cabernet Sauvignon. The climate is ideal for this heat-loving grape, and the wines made from it can be rich, dense, and peppery. The Australian wine industry also calls this grape Shiraz (it is known as Syrah in the rest of the world). This is because Cape Town was one of the final provisioning points for ships carrying colonists from England to the island nation, and when they purchased grapevine cuttings to establish new vineyards they adopted the South African term.

Other Notable Grapes

COLOMBARD A white grape variety that produces simple, everyday drinking wines, it is also used as a minor component in some white blends.

A Pinotage bottle.

SAUVIGNON BLANC Produces fruity, aromatic white wines in South Africa, although the grape can sometimes overripen in warmer climates leading to a lack of acidity.

CHARDONNAY Produces mostly full-bodied white wines that range from heavily oaked and manipulated to light, fresh, and unoaked.

MERLOT Mostly produces simple, fruity, full-flavored red wines with softer tannin structures. Often used as a blending grape with Cabernet Sauvignon or as a component of Cape Blends.

TERROIR AND IMPORTANT REGIONS

The wine regions of South Africa fan out from the southern capital of Cape Town, growing warmer and more arid the further north they are located. Wine grapes can be farmed only in the southern one-third of the country, as conditions grow far too hot in the northern regions. The area nestled near the **Cape of Good Hope** would actually be too hot for quality viticulture itself if not for two moderating influences: proximity to the ocean and elevation. Winds from the ocean cool most of the southern coastal regions. The Cape of Good Hope is actually where the Atlantic Ocean and the Indian Ocean meet. This conjunction, combined with a cooling ocean current that flows north toward South Africa from Antarctica, tempers the heat of the day during the summer months.

As one heads north and further inland, this tempering effect grows much weaker, and it is elevation that contributes to a suitable climate. Several older parcels and many of the new vineyards being planted are found in the foothills of inland mountain ranges. This keeps vines off the much warmer valley floors, although conditions can still be extreme. Many of these regions are quite arid, and irrigation water is needed to allow most vineyards to survive.

Stellenbosch

Stellenbosch is located in the center of South Africa's most important region, the **Coastal Region**, about 30 miles from Cape Town. It is one of the best-known and respected appellations in the country, and home to a world-class viticulture department at the University of Stellenbosch, where the Pinotage grape was developed. Although much of the production in South Africa focuses on white wines, Stellenbosch is primarily a red wine region. Its best-known wines are Cabernet Sauvignon and Cabernet-based Bordeaux blends, although it also

The Cape Doctor

The strong, southeasterly wind that blows across the southern Cape of Good Hope through the summer months is called the Cape Doctor. It earned that name in colonial times because of the supposed effects it had in blowing pollution and disease out of the Cape. For winemakers, the Cape Doctor is usually a welcome guest, as its dry gusts can keep the vines in often humid vineyards from being damaged by mildew or rot.

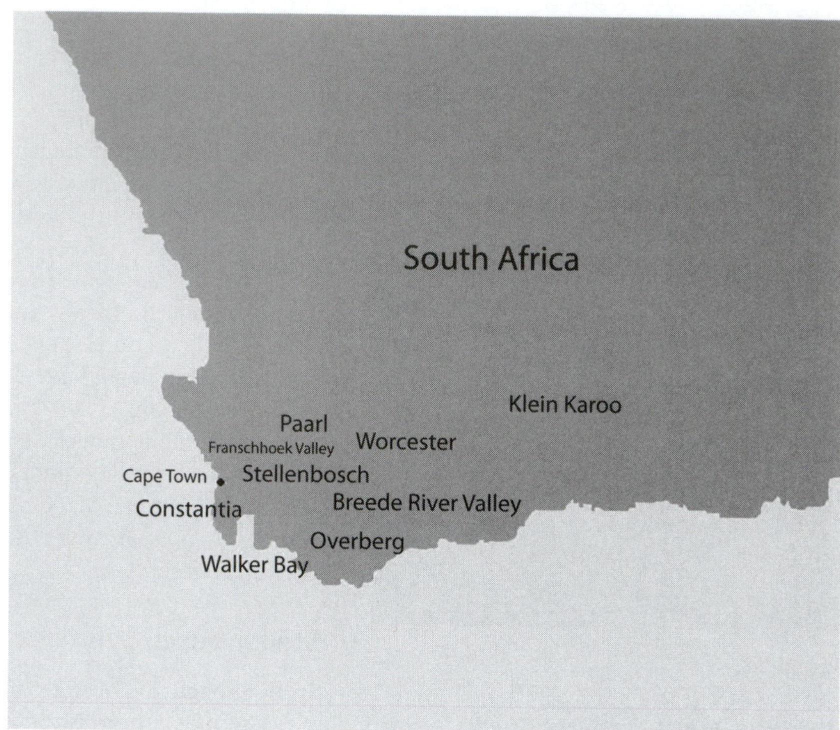

Major wine regions of South Africa.

produces top-quality Pinotage. Stellenbosch is a large region of various geology and soil types, and is home to many small, family-owned estates at the forefront of the quality wine revolution in South Africa.

Paarl

The region of **Paarl** is dominated by the massive wine-growing cooperative called **KWV** (Kooperatieve Wijnbouwers Vereniging), and produces copious amounts of medium-quality table wines and fortified wines. It is also home to several small wine estates that are gaining international attention for their top-notch warm-climate reds such as Shiraz and Pinotage. Located about 30 miles east of Cape Town, it is home to several well-known subregions or districts including the **Franschhoek Valley** and **Wellington.**

Constantia

Constantia is located just south of Cape Town and is home to the most historically important wine of South Africa, which bears the region's name. A dessert wine made from Muscat grapes, Constantia was all the rage in Europe in the 1700s and 1800s. *Phylloxera* destroyed the vineyards of Constantia in the late 1800s, however, and the style was not produced again until the 1990s.

Other Wine Regions of Note

Except for the **Western Cape** (home to Stellenbosch, Paarl, and Constantia), many of South Africa's recognized wine regions are too hot for premium wine production. Most instead produce simple table wines or the base wines for distillation into brandy.

Where ocean breezes or elevation can temper the climate, premium wines can be produced.

In the large geographical unit of the Western Cape, quality production is found in several regions both large and small. **Overberg** and **Walker Bay** are both noted for producing cooler-climate varietals such as Sauvignon Blanc, Chardonnay, and even some Pinot Noir. The **Breede River Valley** and **Worcester** both produce a wide range of wines, both white and red. **Klein Karoo,** like Constantia, focuses production on sweet dessert wines that are often fortified.

Summary

South Africa is a country trying to reinvent itself in today's wine world and recapture its past glory. Once considered the crown jewel for wine production in the New World, South Africa's wine industry was devastated by decades of trade embargoes against the country. Today, South Africa is quickly modernizing its laws, vineyards, and winemaking facilities to catch up with the rest of the world in terms of quality, and can often represent incredible value. While the country is still dominated by large wine-growing cooperatives, most of the excitement in the wine industry is created by small, family-owned estates. They are leading the charge by producing premium wines made from the country's unique Pinotage grape as well as from classic French varietals.

Review Questions

1. Although wine has been produced for hundreds of years in South Africa, their wines are relatively unknown on the international market because of:
   A. low-quality production
   B. the *phylloxera* epidemic
   C. trade embargoes
   D. high tax rates

2. Most of South Africa's top wine regions are in the cooler, northern portions of the country.
   A. True
   B. False

3. Which of the following is *not* an important wine region in South Africa?
   A. Paarl
   B. Canterbury
   C. Constantia
   D. Stellenbosch

4. The South African wine laws are known as:
   A. the Wine of Origin (WO) laws
   B. the South African Viticultural Area (SAVA) laws
   C. the Region of Origin (RO) laws
   D. South Africa does not have an official system of wine laws

5. South Africa is a former ______________ colony.
   A. French
   B. German
   C. Dutch
   D. Spanish

6. The white grape variety Chenin Blanc is known as ______________ in South Africa.
   A. Pinot de Loire
   B. Chenin Vert
   C. Steen
   D. Pinotage

7. If a recognized wine region is listed on a bottle of South African wine, then at least ______________ of the grapes used to produce the wine must have been grown in that region.
   A. 75%
   B. 85%
   C. 95%
   D. 100%

8. If a wine from South Africa lists a grape variety on its label, then at least ______________ of the grapes used to produce that wine must be the listed grape varietal.
   A. 75%
   B. 85%
   C. 95%
   D. 100%

9. The most widely grown white grape varietal in South Africa is ________________, making up more than half of the country's white wines.

A. Chardonnay
B. Chenin Blanc
C. Muscat
D. Sauvignon Blanc

10. Pinotage was a grape variety developed for South Africa's wine industry by crossing which two grape varietals?

A. Pinot Noir and Cinsaut
B. Pinot Noir and Grenache
C. Pinot Noir and Shiraz
D. Pinot Gris and Shiraz

11. The most widely planted red grape variety in South Africa is ________________.

A. Pinotage
B. Steen
C. Shiraz
D. Cabernet Sauvignon

Key Terms

Constantia	Cape Blend	KWV	Walker Bay
Apartheid	Cape of Good Hope	Franschhoek Valley	Breede River Valley
Wine of Origin (WO)	Stellenbosch	Wellington	Worcester
Pinotage	Coastal Region	Western Cape	Klein Karoo
Steen	Paarl	Overberg	

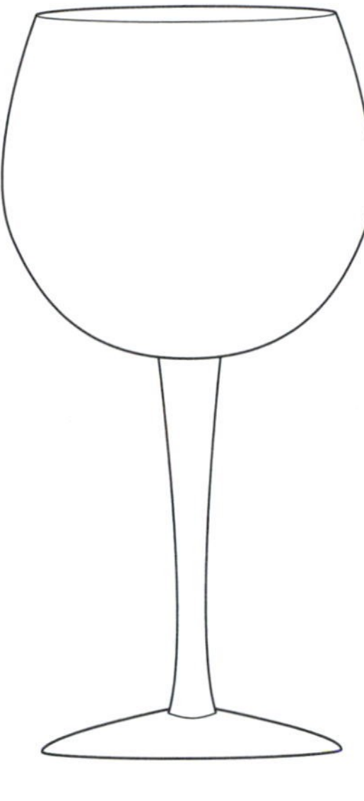

CHAPTER 20

The Wines of Chile

Wine stirs the spring, happiness
bursts through the earth like a plant,
walls crumble, and rocky cliffs,
chasms close, as song is born

—**PABLO NERUDA,** Chilean poet

Although European wine grapes were first planted in South America in the 1500s, it is only in the past few decades that the wines of Chile have come to international prominence. Chile is home to the most consistent wines in Latin America, and is the tenth largest producer of wine in the world. Its history has significantly shaped the Chilean wine industry, and in recent years Chilean winemakers have made sweeping changes in the way they produce their premium wines and have gained serious attention in the international and U.S. wine markets. In this chapter, we discuss the history, grapes, laws, and wine regions of Chile.

The Facts on Chile

CLIMATE

Mostly temperate to warm in the winemaking regions.

TOP WHITE GRAPE

- Chardonnay

TOP RED GRAPES

- Cabernet Sauvignon
- Carmenère

TOP REGIONS

The subregions of the Central Valley (Valle Central):

- Maipo Valley
- Rapel Valley
- Curicó Valley
- Maule Valley

IMPORTANT INFORMATION

- Chile ranks tenth in the world in terms of total wine production.
- Chile produces the most consistent wines in Latin America.
- Chile is a very isolated country, which has spared Chilean winemakers from viticultural problems such as *phylloxera*.
- Despite its Spanish heritage, Chile had a large French influence on its wine industry.

Chile: Land of Isolation

Chile is one of the most isolated countries in the world, bordered by ocean, mountains, desert, and ice. The country runs down the Pacific coast of southern South America, from Peru in the north to the Straits of Magellan in the south. While the country is indeed long, almost 3,000 miles from north to south, it is extremely narrow, averaging only a little over 100 miles wide. The two main geographic features in the country are the Pacific coastline to the west and the Andes Mountains to the east. Most of the population of the country resides in the central valleys of Chile, away from the desert conditions to the north and the Antarctic islands to the south.

Wine arrived in Chile during the Spanish conquest of the Americas in the sixteenth century. The first wine grapes were planted in Chile by Spanish monks in the 1500s as they established missions throughout the country. Still widely grown today, these first vines were probably of the **Pais** variety, a simple and rustic red grape known as Criolla in Argentina and the Mission grape in California and Mexico.

The isolation of Chile, along with strict quarantine laws, makes the country unique in viticultural terms. It is one of the few wine regions in the world that has never had to deal with vineyard pests and diseases such as *phylloxera* and powdery mildew. Chile is also home to some of the purest vine stock in the world, as the European grape varieties planted here were spared the serious outbreaks that raged throughout Europe in the 1800s, destroying vines and vineyards. Unlike most wine regions around the

Carmenère: The Lost Grape of Bordeaux

An interesting twist in the wine history of Chile involves the grape variety Carmenère, nicknamed the "Lost Grape" of Bordeaux. Carmenère used to be widely grown in Bordeaux prior to the onset of *phylloxera* there. Unfortunately, this grape had very little resistance to disease and pests and so was quickly wiped out or removed as the root louse spread through Bordeaux. After grafting *vinifera* vines onto resistant rootstock proved a way around the *phylloxera* scourge, vines were replanted in Bordeaux—except for Carmenère.

For over one hundred years, the grape variety was considered practically extinct. In 1995, at the request of a small group of Chilean winemakers, grapes that were believed to be Merlot growing in Chile were tested for their DNA by researchers at the University of California at Davis. This testing proved that these "Merlot" vines were indeed mislabeled and were in fact Carmenère vines—the Lost Grape of Bordeaux had been found. Recently, Carmenère vine cuttings have been sent from Chile to Bordeaux, as French winemakers attempt to reestablish the variety there.

world where vines have to be grafted, most of Chile's vines are planted on their own roots.

Despite the fact that Chile is a former Spanish colony, the wine industry has a major French influence. Premium grape varieties, especially Bordeaux varietals, were planted in the early 1800s as the beginnings of a modern wine industry took shape there. Wealthy land owners in Santiago began to establish wine estates to the south of the city in the **Central Valley**, hiring mostly French winemakers, specifically those from Bordeaux. These winemakers brought with them their grape varieties, wine styles, and ideas on how to set up a wine estate. Bordeaux varietals are still prominent in Chile, and are responsible for its most renowned wines.

Today, most of Chile's production is geared toward medium-quality value wines intended for the American and international markets; but due to major changes in winemaking and grape techniques and technology, the country is currently undergoing a quality revolution. More care is being taken to ensure grape quality and the winemaking industry is quickly modernizing, not in small part because of international investment in the country.

WINE LAWS OF CHILE

Chile adopted a modern set of wine laws, similar to those found in the United States, in the 1990s. As in other New World countries, the wine laws in Chile are unrestrictive and relaxed to allow freedom for winemakers. There are no restrictions as to which grape varieties can be planted or which winemaking methods can be used.

Most premium wines are labeled by grape variety, although it is becoming more common to see

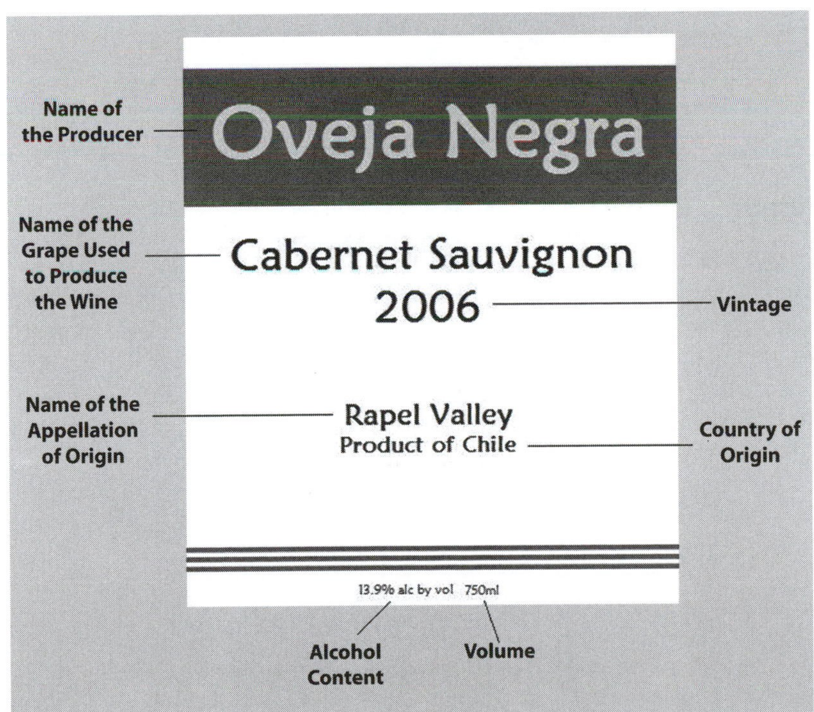

How to read a Chilean wine label.

proprietary names assigned to top-quality blends. Chile's label laws are different depending upon whether the wine is intended for domestic sales or bound for international markets. If the wine is being exported from Chile, the laws become stricter. If a grape, region, or vintage is listed on a wine label, then at least 85 percent of the grapes used to make the wine must be the listed grape, at least 85 percent of the grapes must have been grown in the listed region, and at least 85 percent of the grapes must have been harvested in that vintage. If sold domestically, Chilean winemakers must follow what is known as the "law of 75%," where anything listed on the label with regard to grape type, region, or vintage must be true for a minimum of 75 percent of the grapes used.

Carmenère is becoming more important in Chile.

IMPORTANT GRAPES OF CHILE

Several grape varieties are grown in Chile, with the most widely grown variety being the humble, red Pais grape (20 percent of production), which produces simple jug wines or is distilled into brandy. For premium wines, there are three important varieties, all of French origin, the most important being Cabernet Sauvignon.

Cabernet Sauvignon

The most important red grape of Chile, this grape was brought to the country by Bordeaux's winemakers in the 1800s during the *phylloxera* epidemic. Chilean Cabernet Sauvignon tends to be of good quality, fruity, tannic, and nicely structured; but, as Chilean winemakers begin to modernize both vinicultural and viticultural practices, stunning wines of intense focus are beginning to emerge. It is not uncommon to see Merlot and Carmenère blended into Cabernet Sauvignon, in the classic Bordeaux style.

Carmenère

This grape was historically (and unintentionally) mislabeled Merlot in Chile and is sometimes referred to as the "lost grape" of Bordeaux. Chilean Carmenère produces a wide range of red wines from simple, full-bodied, fruity reds to red wines of extreme complexity and intense dark fruit flavors.

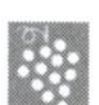

Chardonnay

Chardonnay is the most important white grape grown in Chile, with sales in the U.S. market fueling increases in production. Most Chilean Chardonnays are soft, of medium quality, and produced in the New World tradition with heavy oak and malolactic fermentation. As Chilean winemakers begin to explore this grape varietal, some producers are focusing on a leaner and more fruit-driven style, mostly sourced from the cooler regions.

Other Notable Grapes

SAUVIGNON BLANC Gaining in popularity, this grape produces light- to medium-bodied white wines that are usually aged in stainless steel and possess clean, often citrus and herbal flavors. Most plantings are found in the Central Valley. Recent research has shown that many of the vines that were believed to be Sauvignon Blanc growing in Chile are actually Sauvignon Vert, a lower quality clone of the grape.

MERLOT Often used as a softening component in the Bordeaux-style blends of Chile, Merlot is frequently pleasant and rich with berry fruit here. It is not certain how many of the Merlot vineyards planted throughout Chile are actually planted to Carmenère vines.

SYRAH Although serious vineyard acreage of Syrah in Chile is a recent development, this heat-loving varietal thrives in the country's warmer regions, mostly producing very ripe, fruit-forward red wines.

PAIS The Pais grape (known as Criolla in Argentina and Mission in California) was the first wine grape brought to and planted in Chile, and to this day it is still the most widely planted there. It mostly produces simple jug wines not intended for international export.

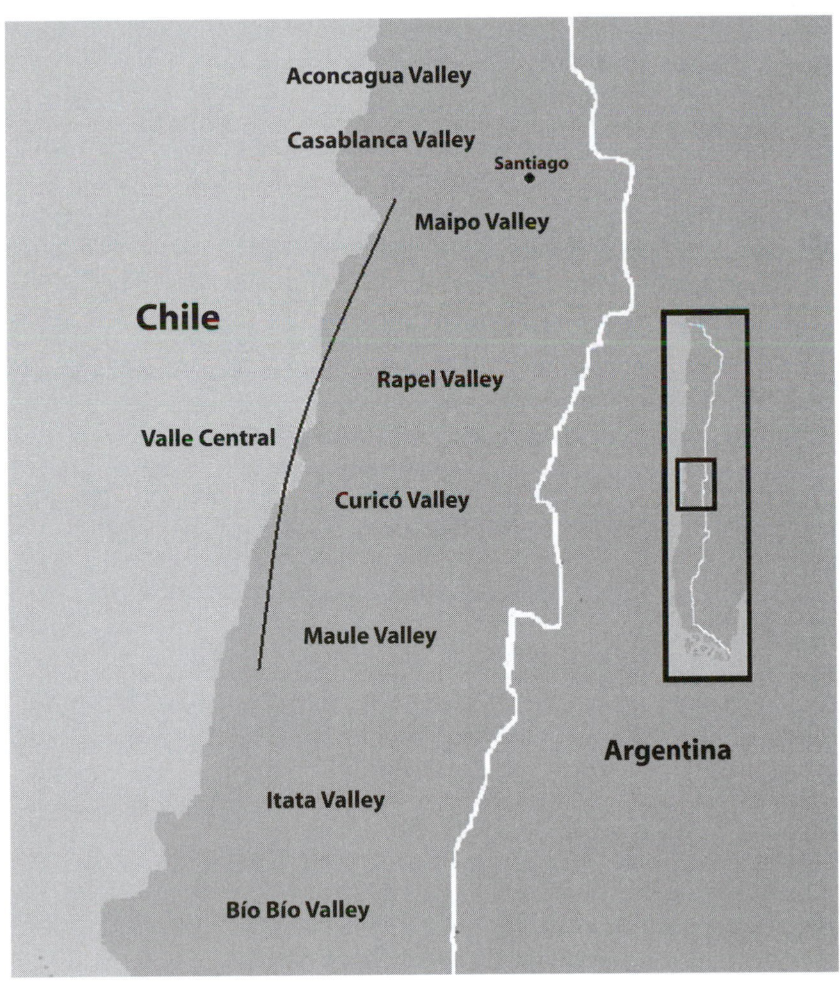

Major wine regions of Chile.

TERROIR AND IMPORTANT REGIONS

The most important wine regions of Chile are located along river valleys nestled between coastal mountain ranges on the Pacific coast and the Andes Mountains. The climate in the central regions is strongly influenced by the proximity to the Pacific and a powerful, cold current which runs along the coast. This maintains a temperate, almost Mediterranean climate in central Chile, and conditions typically get warmer as you move to the north and cooler as you move to the south.

The coastal mountain ranges that run parallel to the Andes on the Pacific coast protect the region from most storms, but leave the area somewhat dry. Most of the rainfall that does occur in Chile's wine regions comes during the winter months, but irrigation is possible year-round from the rivers that flow through most of its wine regions, fed with snow melt from the Andes.

Central Valley (Valle Central)

The largest and most important wine region in Chile is the Central Valley, which is comprised of four distinct river valleys: the **Maipo Valley, Rapel Valley, Curicó Valley,** and **Maule Valley.** Spreading south from the capital of Santiago, these regions were the first to be planted to vines in colonial Chile.

Maipo Valley The region closest to the population center and capital city of Santiago is the Maipo Valley. One of the first viticultural areas of Chile, the Maipo was first planted to grapevines in the 1500s. A major change occurred there when wealthy landowners began growing premium French varieties in the 1800s, mostly as an attempt to show off their wealth and status, with wine estates modeled after the châteaux of Bordeaux.

The Maipo has a fairly dry, warm climate, and irrigation is common. While the valley is home to many different soil types and vineyards at varying elevations, it is predominantely a red wine region, boasting some of the top Cabernet Sauvignon and Carmenère in the country. Many of the best-known wineries in Chile and much of the international wine investment occurring in the country claim the Maipo Valley as home.

Rapel Valley The Rapel Valley, located just south of the Maipo Valley, has experienced tremendous growth in the last couple of years, mostly with high-quality red wines. The coastal range that separates the Rapel from the Pacific is lower in elevation than elsewhere in the Central Valley, and this allows more of a marine influence in the valley, yielding a cooler, moister climate. Cabernet Sauvignon, Carmenère, and Sauvignon Blanc are the most important grapes grown in the Rapel today, although the winemakers in the region are also experimenting with other grape varieties, with Syrah showing the most promise. The Rapel Valley is home to the famous subregion of the **Colchagua Valley.**

Curicó and Maule Valleys While it is further south than the Rapel Valley, a lack of ocean influence on the Curicó Valley means that the climate is warmer here. The Curicó is a very wide, fertile region specializing in aromatic Sauvignon Blanc, and more of that grape is planted here than anywhere else in Chile.

The most widely planted region in Chile is the Maule Valley region, with over 40,000 acres planted to wine grapes. This region accounts for more than 25 percent of Chile's vines. Most of the Pais traditionally planted here is being replaced, due to the cooler climate, with the top white grapes of Chile: Chardonnay and Sauvignon Blanc.

Other Wine Regions of Note

Surprisingly, the two northernmost wine regions of Chile include both the warmest premium region, the **Aconcagua Valley,** and the coolest premium region, the **Casablanca Valley.** The Aconcagua Valley is best known for rustic red wines, made mostly from Pais, while a quarter of Chile's Chardonnay is grown in Casablanca Valley.

In the south, the two most important regions are the **Itata Valley** and the **Bío Bío Valley.** Most of the production in these two regions is limited to simple table wines or the base for brandies.

Summary

Chile has a long and unique history of wine production, affected by its isolation, Spanish conquest, French winemakers, and the international wine market. Most of Chile's production is centered around French grape varieties grown in the temperate central valleys throughout the country. While most of Chile's production today focuses on medium-quality value wines, the future of premium wines and international investment in Chile's wine industry is full of promise.

Review Questions

1. The most important red grape variety grown in Chile is ________________.
   A. Cabernet Sauvignon
   B. Pinot Noir
   C. Syrah
   D. Pais

2. Chile is one of the most isolated countries in the world.
   A. True
   B. False

3. Chile is one of the world's smallest wine-producing countries.
   A. True
   B. False

4. The first wine grape planted in Chile in the 1500s and the most widely planted still today is:
   A. Cabernet Sauvignon
   B. Pinot Noir
   C. Syrah
   D. Pais

5. The European country that has had the largest influence on Chilean winemaking is Spain, as Chile used to be a Spanish colony.
   A. True
   B. False

6. Which important Chilean grape variety is called the "Lost Grape of Bordeaux"?
   A. Cabernet Sauvignon
   B. Merlot
   C. Carmenère
   D. Pais

7. If a label of Chilean wine listed Sauvignon Blanc as the grape used in its production, what percentage of the grapes used to produce this wine must be the listed varietal by Chilean law (assuming that the wine is intended for export)?
   A. 75%
   B. 85%
   C. 95%
   D. 100%

8. The wine regions of Chile are located in the river valleys nestled between coastal mountain ranges and:
   A. the Pacific Ocean
   B. the Atacama Desert
   C. the Andes Mountains
   D. the Amazon River

9. *Phylloxera* and powdery mildew wiped out many of the vineyards of Chile in the mid- to late 1800s, causing the winemakers there to replant higher-quality grape varieties.
   A. True
   B. False

10. Which of the following wine regions is *not* located in the Central Valley of Chile?
   A. Maipo Valley
   B. Curicó Valley
   C. Aconcagua Valley
   D. Maule Valley

Key Terms

Pais
Central Valley (Valle Central)
Maipo Valley
Rapel Valley
Curicó Valley
Maule Valley
Colchagua Valley
Aconcagua Valley
Casablanca Valley
Itata Valley
Bío Bío Valley

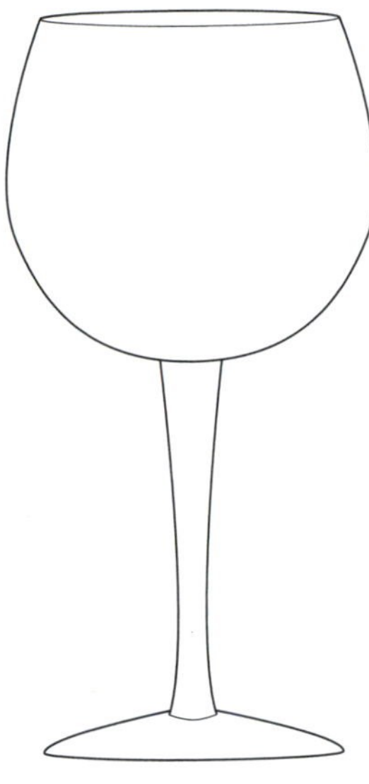

CHAPTER 21

The Wines of Argentina

By the year 2015, the greatness of Argentinean wines made from the Malbec grape will be understood as a given.

—**ROBERT PARKER JR.,** American wine critic and author

Looking to duplicate the success of Chilean winemakers across the Andes Mountains, Argentina is finally trying to make its mark on the international wine world. Long a prolific producer ofwine, Argentina today is the fifth largest producer of wine in the world—second only to the United States in the New World. Much of that production has been historically intended solely for domestic markets, as Argentines have a strongly European heritage. In just the past few decades, winemakers in Argentina have been shifting from a focus on quantity toward quality, with most placing their bets on the success and appeal of exciting red wines made from the Malbec grape. In this chapter, we discuss the history, grapes, laws, and wine regions of Argentina.

The Facts on Argentina

CLIMATE

Mostly temperate to warm.

TOP WHITE GRAPE

- Torrontés

TOP RED GRAPES

- Malbec
- Cabernet Sauvignon

TOP REGION

- Mendoza

IMPORTANT INFORMATION

- Argentina ranks fifth in the world in terms of total wine production.
- Argentina has historically had a very large domestic consumption due to a population with a European heritage.
- Most of Argentina's quality wine production takes place in the foothills of the Andes Mountains, where elevation tempers an arid, high-desert climate.
- Argentines eat more beef per person than the people of any other country, and many of their wines are made to pair with beef dishes.

Argentina: The Sleeping Giant

Argentina is one of the most intriguing wine-producing countries in the world. On one hand, it is a powerhouse of wine production—the fifth largest producer in the world behind Italy, France, Spain, and the United States. On the other hand, its wines are practically unknown in the world today because exporting wine was all but an afterthought for Argentine winemakers until the 1990s.

Mirroring the history of the Chilean wine industry in many ways, wine arrived in Argentina in the 1500s during the Spanish conquest. The first wine grapes planted in Argentina were probably **Criolla** (known as Pais in Chile and Mission in California), a varietal spread throughout the Americas by Spanish monks. While the missionary vineyards of Argentina were a humble beginning, the changing population of Argentina in the 1800s would cause an explosion of vine planting and winemaking.

The population of Argentina is unique in Latin America, with more than 95 percent of its citizens having some European heritage. This is a result of the mass emigration of Europeans (mostly Italians) to the country in the 1800s and early 1900s, mirroring the same type of immigrations that occurred in the United States at the same time. Although wine was produced in Argentina prior to their arrival, these immigrants brought with them an interesting mix of different grapevine varietals, the knowledge of how to make wine, and a large thirst for it.

This European heritage explains the historically high levels of domestic production and consumption. Until recently, Argentine winemakers did not have to export because they had such a robust domestic market. Times are changing, though: wine consumption is steadily declining in Argentina as generations are getting further and further away from their original European origins and as the country has faced economic hardships. This leaves winemakers in Argentina at a crossroads: either they try to increase overall quality and compete on the international market, or they plow under their vines and grow other crops. Luckily, most winemakers have chosen the former, and the sleeping giant of Argentina is waking up!

WINE LAWS OF ARGENTINA

As with almost all other New World countries, Argentina's wine laws are loosely based on the wine laws of the United States. They are intended to be unrestrictive and relaxed to allow freedom for winemakers. There are no restrictions as to which grape varieties can be planted or which winemaking methods can be used.

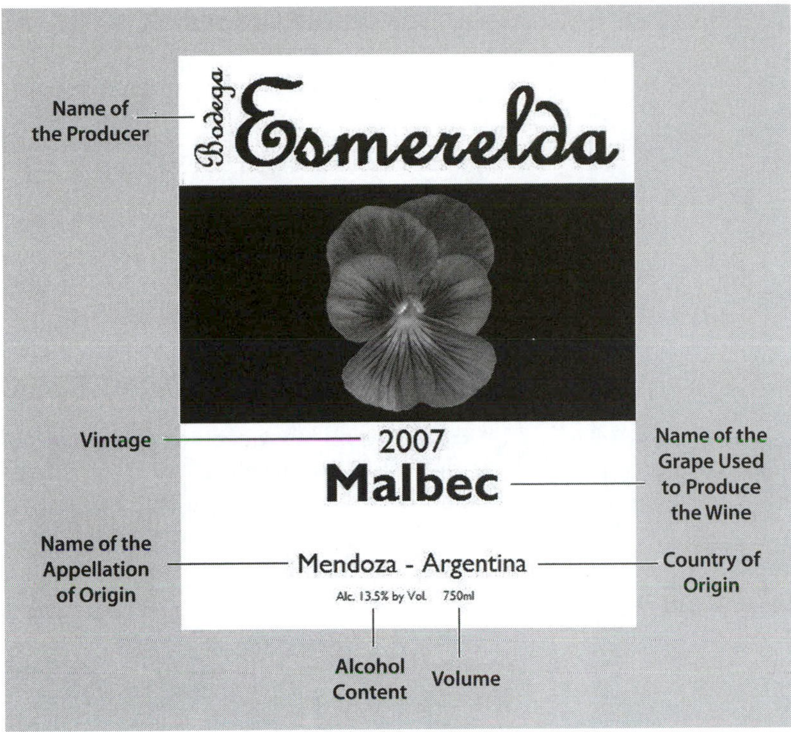

How to read an Argentine wine label.

Most premium wines are labeled by grape variety, and if this is the case, then at least 80 percent of the grapes used to make the wine must be the listed grape. Similar restrictions are in place for listing a recognized wine region, where at least 85 percent of the grapes must have been grown in the listed region.

IMPORTANT GRAPES OF ARGENTINA

Argentine winemakers grow several grape varieties, most of either French or Spanish origin. Much of the country's vineyard acreage is dedicated to the production of simple table wines intended for the domestic market; however, most new plantings are of Malbec and international varieties producing wines intended for export. In established regions, old vines are common, often producing some of the richest and best-quality wines in the country. The top wines produced in Argentina today, and the ones that the country is gaining fame for, are from the red grape Malbec.

 Malbec

Although it is considered a minor blending grape in its homeland of Bordeaux, France, Malbec is elevated to star status in Argentina, where growing conditions for this varietal are ideal. Often bottled and released young, Argentine Malbecs tend to have a rich purple color and deliver concentrated, spicy dark fruit flavors. Malbec has a rich, almost velvety body similar to Cabernet Sauvignon or Merlot, but it often has a softer tannin structure.

Malbec is Argentina's most important grape variety.

Cabernet Sauvignon

Not as refined as Chilean Cabernet Sauvignon, the grape produces full-bodied, spicy, somewhat rustic wines in Argentina. Plantings are on the rise in Argentina due to the grape's name recognition and the country's new focus on the international export market.

 Torrontés

Torrontés is the most exciting white grape grown in Argentina today. A relative of the Malvasia grape family, Torrontés produces light-bodied, aromatic white wines. Torrontés is typically aged in stainless steel rather than oak to maximize its fresh stone fruit and citrus characteristics.

Other Notable Grapes

 **BONARDA** This widely planted red grape produces rustic wines.

 **CRIOLLA** A rugged red wine grape with a long history in Argentina, Criolla is known as Pais in Chile and Mission in California.

 **SYRAH** This is an international red variety that shows promise in Argentina.

TERROIR AND IMPORTANT REGIONS

Most of Argentina's winegrowing regions are located in the isolated western reaches of the country, away from the populated Atlantic coastline and often nestled in the shadows of the **Andes Mountains.** While most of this countryside is too hot and dry for

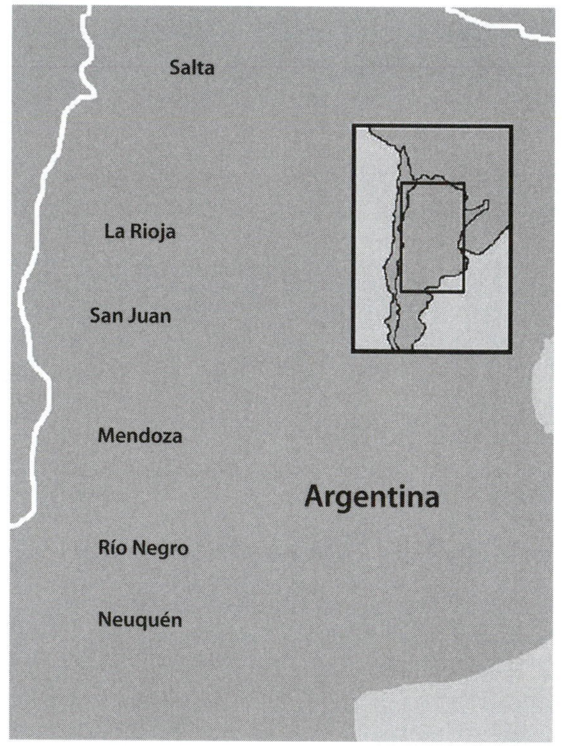

Major wine regions of Argentina.

premium wine production, the actual growing areas resemble oases in the middle of arid, high-desert conditions. Irrigation has always been a problem for Argentine winemakers as most of the country is dry. This is due to the rain shadow effect caused by the Andes, which shield Argentine vineyards from precipitation. Snow melt from the mountains is the typical source of irrigation water.

Ideal locations for growing grapes in Argentina are usually linked to elevation. Top vineyard sites are located in the foothills of the Andes, ranging from 2,000 to 4,500 feet in elevation, including some of the world's most extreme vineyards located well above 7,000 feet! At these high elevations, temperatures drop at night enough that grapes do not overripen, and they are able to develop deep, rich flavors. Viticulture is not without challenges at these high elevations, however, as winter conditions can drop dangerously low for even hearty vines, and storms and frost present danger for newly forming grapes in the spring.

Ancient Irrigation System

Since Mendoza averages less than 8 inches of rain a year, it would be difficult to grow much of anything there without irrigation. This problem was solved hundreds of years before any winemaker arrived in the region. When the Spanish first arrived in Mendoza, it was inhabited by the Huarpes Indians, a peaceful, agricultural tribe that had large planted fields and orchards throughout Mendoza. To provide irrigation water for their crops, they had developed a labyrinth of canals that were fed from glaciers high up in the Andes more than 100 miles away. When the Spanish colonized the region, they further developed this canal system, and it still provides irrigation water to the farmers of Mendoza, including grape growers, today.

Mendoza

Clearly the most important wine region of Argentina is **Mendoza,** located in the foothills of the Andes Mountains. Mendoza is responsible for nearly 70 percent of Argentina's total wine production, and is home to its top-quality production. Mendoza itself is a large, mostly sparse area. Dry, arid conditions are tempered by elevation and most of the water for irrigation is supplied by an ancient canal system.

Much of the production of Mendoza is dedicated to the Malbec grape, with several vineyards planted to very old vines. The high-elevation conditions of Mendoza allow Malbec to ripen slowly, developing intense and concentrated flavors. With the size and scope of Mendoza so important to wine production in Argentina, the country's wine future is clearly in the hands of the producers in this region.

Other Wine Regions of Note

Wine is produced in several other recognized regions located throughout Argentina. Most of these viticultural areas are located in the foothills of the Andes to the north and south of Mendoza. Just to the north of Mendoza are the notable regions of **San Juan** and **La Rioja.** While both have proven capable of producing exciting wines made from Malbec, Torrontés, and a few other varieties, most of their production is geared toward simple table wines meant for domestic consumption.

The country's best Torrontés might actually come from the northernmost premium region, called **Salta,** which is also responsible for some of the best Cabernet Sauvignon. The most exciting regions for the future in Argentina, however, may be those located south of Mendoza. **Neuquén** and **Río Negro** are on the fringes of the Patagonian wilderness, and their southern latitude produces a cool climate ideal for growing Chardonnay and Sauvignon Blanc and for producing sparkling wines.

Summary

Although Argentina is a major world producer of wine, their wines are relative newcomers to the international market. Historically, winemakers in the country have always relied on a large amount of domestic consumption to create the demand for their products. Consumption levels there are dropping, however, and this means that the country will have to compete on the international market to succeed.

Much of the success of Argentine wine hinges on the Malbec grape variety, a minor blending grape from France that rises to new heights in the vineyards of Argentina. Most of the quality production of Malbec takes place in the region of Mendoza, a prodigious wine region located in the foothills of the Andes Mountains. This region is leading the way for the rest of the country in terms of modern winemaking technologies, updated vineyard techniques, and foreign investment, attempting to copy the success enjoyed in the neighboring country of Chile.

Review Questions

1. Argentina ranks ________ in the world in terms of overall wine production.
   A. third
   B. fourth
   C. fifth
   D. sixth

2. ______________________ are believed to have been the first to plant wine grapes in Argentina in the late 1500s.
   A. Conquistadores
   B. Spanish monks
   C. Italian settlers
   D. French winemakers

3. Argentina has a unique population for South America, with the vast majority of its population having some European heritage.
   A. True
   B. False

4. If a region is listed on a bottle of Argentine wine, then at least _____ of the grapes used to produce that wine must have been grown in that region.
   A. 75%
   B. 80%
   C. 85%
   D. 100%

5. Argentine winemakers label most of their wines by grape variety.
   A. True
   B. False

6. The most important grape grown in Argentina is __________.
   A. Cabernet Sauvignon
   B. Torrontés
   C. Merlot
   D. Malbec

7. Torrontés is one of the most important _________ grapes of Argentina.
   A. white
   B. red

8. The vast majority of Argentina's wine is produced in __________________.
   A. the cooler southern regions of the country
   B. the warmer northern regions of the country
   C. the temperate foothills of the Andes Mountains
   D. the temperate coastal regions near the Atlantic Ocean

9. The most important wine region of Argentina, where more than 70% of the country's total wine production takes place, is ____________________.
   A. Mendoza
   B. San Juan
   C. Salta
   D. La Rioja

10. Overall, Argentina's wine regions are relatively dry and arid—a result of being located in the rain shadow of the Andes Mountains.
   A. True
   B. False

Key Terms

Criolla	Mendoza	La Rioja	Neuquén
Andes Mountains	San Juan	Salta	Río Negro

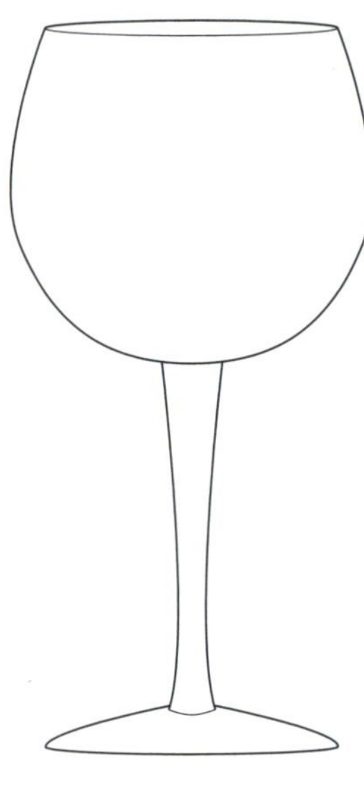

CHAPTER 22

Emerging Wine Regions Around the World

There exist limitless opportunities in every industry. Where there is an open mind, there will always be a frontier.

—**CHARLES KETTERING,** American inventor

There are several other regions and countries around the world producing wine—some with thousands of years of tradition and others with just a few decades—and many are beginning to emerge onto the international wine market. This chapter rounds out the discussion of New World countries by offering a profile of three lesser-known New World wine regions on the rise—Canada, Mexico, and Uruguay—as well as a snapshot of other emerging wine-producing countries around the world.

Canada

The Viking Leif Eriksson is believed to have been the first European to see the continent of North America, landing in what is today the country of **Canada.** He was so impressed with the abundance of wild grapevines he found upon his arrival that he named the land "Vine Land." The French colonists that eventually settled in Canada began producing small amounts of wine from these Native American grapes, but quickly imported European vines in an effort to make better wine.

With strong French heritage, it is only natural that Canada's temperate regions would be planted to grapevines. The country has a high domestic rate of consumption, as it is one of the few wine-producing nations of note that imports more wine than it produces. Canada's wine industry is currently in a state of growth. Although the country has been producing wine for more than two hundred years, it is only now becoming known as a quality producer, mostly due to its recent success with ice wine.

The Vintners Quality Alliance (VQA)

The Vintners Quality Alliance, or VQA, is the official body that regulates the Canadian wine industry. It began as a voluntary organization in Ontario in the 1980s made up of winemakers, wine writers, and government officials whose goal it was to establish a system of official winemaking appellations throughout Canada. In the late 1990s, the VQA spread to most of Canada, and its member wineries now produce almost half of the wines in that country. Winemakers in VQA must follow strict regulations governing how they produce and label their wines.

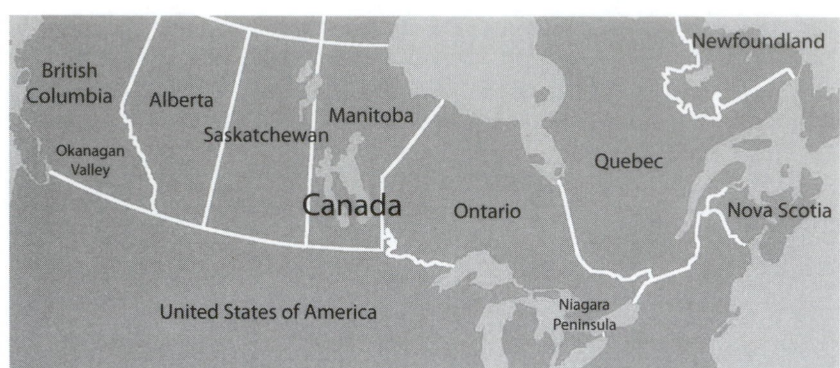

Canada and its important wine regions.

TOP REGIONS AND WINES

Most of Canada is too cold for growing wine grapes, and production is limited to the southern portions of the country where the climate is more temperate. While the landlocked interior of Canada prohibits viticulture, conditions are tempered along the Atlantic and Pacific coasts of the country as well as near the Great Lakes. The two best-known provinces for wine production in Canada are Ontario and British Columbia.

Ontario is the one of the oldest regions in Canada for viticulture, and arguably its best. While the province does not have a long ocean coastline, the climate of Ontario is very much tempered by large bodies of water as it is bordered to the south by the Great Lakes. This has the effect of maintaining a climate temperate enough to grow grapes for wine production. There are several wine regions in Ontario, including the country's most important and largest viticultural area: the **Niagara Peninsula.**

While several styles of wine are produced in the Niagara Peninsula from dozens of different grape varieties, the shining star of the region is ice wine. This rich dessert wine, produced from the juice of partially frozen grapes, is Canada's most important wine export. The Great Lakes provide a long period for ripening grapes and prevent temperatures from growing too cold in the wintertime, so that grapes do not freeze solid. Ice wine is in large part why the world is taking notice of Canadian wines, as examples continue to win awards and critical praise in the international wine community.

British Columbia is Canada's most western province, with hundreds of miles of coastline on the Pacific Ocean. It is a very large area, the majority of which is, like most of Canada, too cold for winemaking; however, certain areas of southern British Columbia are ideal. The oldest and most important wine region of the province is the **Okanagan Valley,** an enormous valley in central British Columbia running from the U.S. border north more than 150 miles.

At roughly the same latitude as Champagne or central Germany, this region actually enjoys a temperate climate due to the lack of precipitation, caused by its high-desert conditions, and is very similar in climate to Washington State's wine country just south of the border. The Okanagan is known as the "Land of Orchards" due to the amazing amount of farming that takes place there; however, in recent years it has been gaining more of a reputation for wine than anything else. Winemaking is mostly centered around international grape varieties with a focus on Chardonnay, Pinot Gris, Merlot, Cabernet Sauvignon, and Pinot Noir.

Mexico

Mexico was home to the first vineyards in the Americas, as Spanish missionaries arrived in the wake of the conquest of the Aztecs, bringing with them grape seeds to grow vines for sacramental wines.

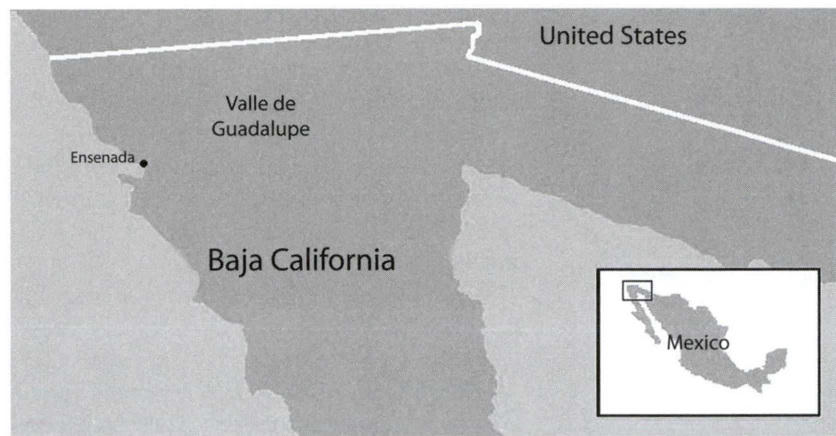

Mexico and its important wine regions.

Upon assuming the governance of Mexico in the late 1500s, the first Spanish ruler, Hernando Cortez, decreed that wine grape vines had to be planted by the thousands by all newly arriving Spaniards being given holdings of land. Wine production promptly ensued, and eventually the wine was of such a high level of quality and was so abundant that the Spanish crown outlawed its production to protect Spanish winemakers.

Through independence and revolution, winemaking continued in Mexico, although much of this production was intended for distillation into the country's very popular brandies, not into wines. Modern winemaking and a focus on quality began in the 1970s, as a new breed of winemaker and many small, independent wineries ushered in a new era. Today, much of Mexico's production is still of lesser quality and is intended for bulk consumption or distillation, but the country's premium wineries are surprising wine lovers and critics alike with their exciting, New World–style wines.

TOP REGIONS AND WINES

Wine production takes place throughout northern Mexico, although much of this production is of inferior quality or intended for distillation. The vast majority of Mexico's premium wine production and the country's top-quality wineries are located in the **Valle de Guadalupe.** This temperate, fertile valley is located a half hour's drive from the tourist city of Ensenada, in Baja California. Valle de Guadalupe is home to vineyards owned by some of Mexico's largest corporate wineries; however, the real stars in this basin are small, independent wineries focused on producing quality-oriented varietal wines. Although much further south than California's top-quality wine regions, this pocket of land is home to a Mediterranean-type climate because of cooling ocean winds from the Pacific.

Many of the top wines produced in Mexico bear resemblance to the wines of its neighbor to the north, California. Chardonnay and Sauvignon Blanc produce the best white wines, mostly medium- to full-bodied whites aged in oak and showing tropical notes. The wines with the most promise, however, are the reds produced in the Valle de Guadalupe. The specialties of the region tend to be Bordeaux-style red blends along with single varietal wines made from Cabernet Sauvignon, Merlot, and Zinfandel. These reds show the same ripe fruit characteristics and full-bodied power of the top reds of California.

These wines are from the Valle de Guadalupe, Mexico's top-quality wine region.

Uruguay

Between Argentina and Brazil, on the Atlantic coast of South America, lies the small country of **Uruguay.** Grapevines thrive throughout most of Uruguay's countryside due to largely temperate weather conditions. Although the country is not historically known for winemaking, it is today home to some very intriguing wines which are on the verge of international discovery.

The first vines were planted in Uruguay some 250 years ago as a wave of Spanish and other European immigrants began to arrive in the country. This European heritage, similar to what is found in Argentina, helped to fuel the beginnings of winemaking in the country, and is what drives Uruguay's high levels of domestic consumption. While there are over three hundred wineries in Uruguay, most do not export their wines yet.

TOP REGIONS AND WINES

There are no mountains in Uruguay like the Andes in Argentina and Chile—just fertile, rolling hills. Uruguay is located between 30 and 35 degrees latitude, the same latitudes that are home to the top wine regions of Australia, Chile, and Argentina. This location and the tempering effects of the Atlantic Ocean make viticulture ideal in Uruguay.

While wine is produced throughout Uruguay, the vast majority is grown in vineyards near the capital city of Montevideo, where temperate conditions allow for premium wine production. In recent years, more development and planting has taken place in the interior of the country, where a handful of important wineries have opened their doors. For the most part, Uruguayan wine production is concentrated on producing single varietal, dry wines

from grape varieties such as Chardonnay, Merlot, Cabernet Sauvignon, and Tannat.

The most important grape grown in Uruguay is Tannat, and it produces the nation's top-quality red wines. Much as Argentina's wine industry is centered on an obscure French grape (Malbec) that has flourished in Argentine vineyards, the wine industry of Uruguay is placing its bets on the Tannat grape. Tannat is considered an important grape only in the few regions of southern France where it is grown, but in the unique conditions of Uruguay, Tannat has thrived away from its native soil. Uruguayan Tannat tends to produce full-bodied red wines with intense structure, strong tannins, and an almost smoky fruitiness.

Other Emerging Regions

There are more than sixty countries producing significant amounts of wine around the world. Some of these countries have been growing grapes for wine production for quite some time, while others are relative newcomers to wine. In this section, we will take a quick glimpse at some of the world's lesser-known wine-producing countries to keep an eye on as they attempt to enter the international market.

SOUTH AMERICA

Chile, Argentina, and Uruguay are not the only wine-producing regions found in South America. Spanish and Portuguese colonists and missionaries planted wine grapes in several areas of South America in the 1500s and 1600s in an attempt to establish local supplies of wine. European immigrants brought winemaking skills and a demand for consumption with them as millions immigrated to South American countries in the 1800s and early 1900s. Besides the three main South American countries known for wine today, quality-minded winemakers and investors are also modernizing and increasing production levels in **Brazil** and **Peru.**

A former Portuguese colony, Brazil has a long history of wine production dating back to the colonial era. Although Brazil is the largest country in South America, its wine-producing regions are severely limited to the southernmost portions of the country. The equator runs through northern Brazil and conditions are far too warm for wine production there. Although the humidity and isolation present severe challenges for serious wine production in southern Brazil, new grape varietals including some hybrids are beginning to show promise.

Pisco: National Drink of Peru

Pisco is a type of grape brandy that originated in Peru but has since spread to Bolivia and Chile. Named for the Peruvian city of Pisco, these brandies can be smooth, aged, and refined at their best, but are usually fiery and young.

Despite the high elevations found in most of this mountainous country, Peru boasts vineyards and wine regions along its coastal valleys, some of which were first planted in the 1500s. Most of the production in Peru is focused around **pisco,** a distilled brandy that is considered a national drink. Investment and modernization have helped to improve the quality of table wines in this country, with much of the attention on dry reds and whites made from a variety of French grapes including Cabernet Sauvignon and Chardonnay.

THE MIDDLE EAST AND NORTH AFRICA

It should come as no surprise that wine grapes can be grown in the Mediterranean countries of the Middle East, as this is where they originated. The first wines were produced in Mesopotamia, which is modern-day Iran and Iraq, before production and viticulture spread into Europe and North Africa. Today, wine production is severely limited or nonexistent in most Middle Eastern countries, as consuming alcoholic beverages is forbidden by Muslim religious law. Nevertheless, winemaking does still take place in a select number of Middle

Eastern countries, with the three most important being **Turkey, Lebanon,** and **Israel.**

The land that is now Turkey was part of the area that was home to some of the world's first wines. Modern Turkey is still an important wine-producing nation, growing many of its own indigenous grape varieties. Winemaking varies widely in Turkey, as wineries grow several different local grape varietals as well as a growing number of international grapes. Climate conditions in most of the country's wine regions are strongly affected by the Mediterranean Sea, and more than half of Turkey's wine is produced in coastal areas.

The warm Mediterranean climate of Lebanon is ideal for growing wine grapes, and this country has historically been known for wine production. Civil conflicts and a large Muslim population (for whom it is against religious law to consume alcoholic beverages) have limited modern wine production, but some top-quality wines are still produced here. Most of these wineries grow French grape varietals including Cabernet Sauvignon, Merlot, Grenache, and Chardonnay, and they even use the French term Château in the names of many wineries.

Wine has been produced in what is today Israel since before biblical times. The climate in this country is quite warm and dry, presenting challenges to aspiring winemakers, although modern irrigation systems are helping to expand winemaking regions. The most important region, ideally located at a higher and cooler elevation, is **Galilee.** Here, as in most of the rest of Israel's wine-producing regions, the focus is on French grape varieties, especially those from Bordeaux.

North Africa was once a major wine-producing region when France occupied several colonies there. This French presence is felt today in the few areas that still produce wine in North Africa. Independence and the establishment of Muslim governments in most of North Africa effectively ended much of the winemaking that once took place, but small amounts of wine are still produced in **Morocco** and **Algeria.** Most of these are powerful, earthy reds made from many of the same grapes grown in the Rhône Valley of France.

ASIA

Wines made from grapes have not been traditionally produced in Asia, but this began to change in the 1980s and 1990s as Asian consumers began to discover wines. While this caused imports of European, American, and Australian wines to skyrocket throughout many Asian countries, it also created an interest in domestic production. The use of Western consultants along with significant international investment in winemaking have resulted in an explosion of new vineyards and wineries throughout Asia. The Asian countries looking to move to the forefront of this domestic winemaking boom include Japan and India, but the country making the largest strides in the continent thus far is **China.**

Fermented beverages have been produced in China for thousands of years. Sake originated in the country before it migrated to Japan, beverages made from a variety of grains and fruits were produced in China through the dynastic period, and there is even some disputed archaeological evidence that winemaking in China predates that in Mesopotamia by hundreds of years. Fine wines made from wine grapes and produced in the European tradition, however, have not been produced in the country until recently.

With the help of Western consultants, science, and viticultural techniques, China is racing to supply wine for the exploding domestic demand and enter the international wine market. Much of this activity has been spurred on by the success China has seen with the wine industries in countries such as Australia and Chile, where wine is a multibillion-dollar export industry. Most of the development of Chinese wine regions has taken place in the fertile, temperate farmlands near Beijing. Here, several French and American companies are partnering with Chinese wineries to develop the burgeoning fine wine industry. The most important wines being produced are from well-known varieties like Chardonnay, Merlot, and Cabernet Sauvignon. Expect to begin seeing the fruits of this labor in the next five to ten years as Chinese wines begin to hit wine store shelves.

Summary

Wine is produced in several surprising corners around the world, and a region unknown for their wines today could become a serious wine region in just a short amount of time. The frontiers of wine production continue to expand throughout the world. Countries like Canada, Mexico, Uruguay, and China may not be the best known for wine, but the continuing focus of their winemakers and wine industries will continue to increase the quality and widespread interest in their top wines.

Review Questions

1. Canada is one of the few wine-producing countries in the world where they import more wine than they produce.
   - A. True
   - B. False
2. The most important style of wine produced in Canada is ______________.
   - A. dry red wine
   - B. dry white wine
   - C. ice wine
   - D. late harvest dessert wine
3. The top Canadian region for table wines, __________, is located directly north of Washington State's wine country.
   - A. Niagara Peninsula
   - B. Ottawa
   - C. Columbia Gorge
   - D. Okanagan Valley
4. The vast majority of wines produced in Mexico end up being distilled into Brandy.
   - A. True
   - B. False
5. Mexico's top wine region is ______________.
   - A. Valle de Luna
   - B. Valle de Ensenada
   - C. Valle de Guadalupe
   - D. Valle de Baja
6. The most important style of wine produced in Mexico is ____________.
   - A. dry red wine
   - B. dry white wine
   - C. ice wine
   - D. late harvest dessert wine
7. Uruguay is a South American country located along the Atlantic coastline, just north of Argentina.
   - A. True
   - B. False
8. The most important grape variety grown in Uruguay is ______________.
   - A. Malbec
   - B. Cabernet Sauvignon
   - C. Tempranillo
   - D. Tannat
9. The population of Uruguay has a large European heritage similar to that found in Argentina, explaining in large part why wine production is so important there.
   - A. True
   - B. False
10. Although the country has not historically produced wine made from grapes, China has made serious investments in developing a modern wine industry.
    - A. True
    - B. False

Key Terms

Canada	Valle de Guadalupe	pisco	Galilee
Niagara Peninsula	Uruguay	Turkey	Morocco
Okanagan Valley	Brazil	Lebanon	Algeria
Mexico	Peru	Israel	China

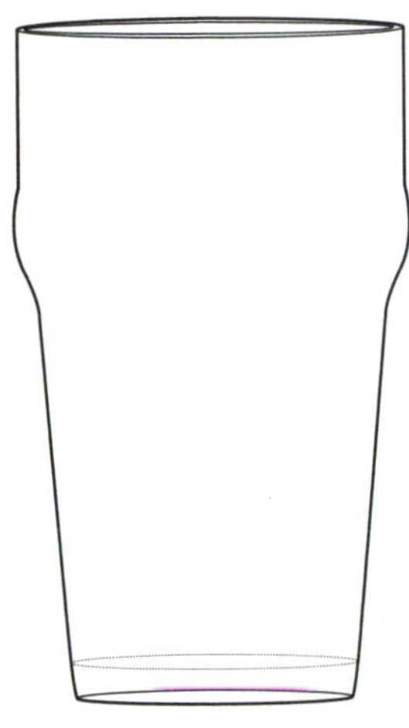

CHAPTER 23

Beer and the Brewing Process

Without question, the greatest invention in the history of mankind is beer. Oh, I grant you that the wheel was also a fine invention, but the wheel does not go nearly as well with pizza.

—**DAVE BARRY,** *Dave Barry's Bad Habits*

Beer is the world's other great fermented beverage. A part of the human diet for thousands of years, beer has evolved into hundreds of styles all produced from the same basic ingredients. In this chapter, we define beer and discuss its history, the raw ingredients used to make it, and the basic brewing process.

Beer: Importance and Introduction

> **Beer** A fermented beverage produced by fermenting a mixture of water and cereal grains, usually malted barley.

Beer has been a part of the human diet for at least seven thousand years, if not longer. It is considered by some historians to be the oldest form of alcoholic beverage. In fact, some consider beer to be the reason Western civilization began. Nomadic hunter-gatherers began to settle down to farm in ancient Mesopotamia, and the first domesticated crops were grains, grown especially to produce beer. Agriculture allowed these early people an opportunity to develop new technologies, and they began to settle and establish small outposts. These outposts eventually grew to become cities. Different cities in Mesopotamia banded together to form the first organized society, and civilization was born. If nothing else, it is an interesting theory to ponder over a pint of your favorite beer.

Regardless, beer has been produced widely around the world, and almost every civilization or society has produced some form of fermented grain beverage. Many of the famous styles of beer were developed in Europe over the centuries, but this brewing tradition was definitely adopted throughout the New World during the colonial era.

The United States also has a proud brewing history, even with the dark days of Prohibition and the hurdles that followed. Although American brewing has in the past been dominated by mass-production breweries and American consumers are accustomed to their lightly flavored, simple styles of beer, the market is beginning to change. Over the past twenty-five years a beer renaissance has taken place in the form of small breweries and **brewpubs** across the United States that are hand crafting distinctive beer styles. Once-forgotten European breweries and beers have been rediscovered. Today is truly the golden age of the beer drinker!

A SHORT HISTORY OF BEER AND BREWING

No one is quite sure when the first beer was actually produced because it happened long before the development of the written word. Most likely, it was accidentally discovered in Mesopotamia, in a manner similar to the way the first wines were created well over seven thousand years ago. Rainwater could have leaked into a clay pot storing a surplus of cereal grains. Wild yeast could have settled into this mixture of grain and water and fermented it into a crude beer. Not wanting to throw these grains out, hunter-gatherers would have had to at least try these "spoiled" grains, which would not have tasted good but would have brought on a sensation of euphoria and intoxication—a magic potion was born.

To early civilizations like the Mesopotamians and Egyptians, beer was the most important beverage they produced. Cereal grains were available year round, and that meant that beer could be produced at any time of year. Unlike wine, which was produced only for royalty and religious figures because of its scarcity and tendency to spoil quickly, beer was a drink enjoyed by all levels of society. As the Greeks discovered how to age and store wines, allowing wine to become more prevalent, beer fell out of favor. The ancient Greeks and Romans certainly enjoyed beers, but wine became the most revered and important beverage of the time in these Mediterranean regions. The Romans did, however, introduce beer to the cooler-climate regions of Europe, where it was difficult or impossible to grow grapes, especially Germany and the English isles.

With the fall of the Roman Empire, Europe stumbled into the Dark Ages. Catholic monasteries, in an effort to remain self-sufficient and to provide healthy and safe beverages for Europe, took over the production of beer throughout the continent. Beer was a welcome refreshment in this time of polluted water supplies and poor nutrition, and some of these monastic orders still produce beer today.

As Europe colonized the Americas, beer went along for the ride. It quickly became a favorite beverage in the New England colonies because wine grapes were almost impossible to grow, while cereal grains took quickly to these new lands. One of the first orders of business in any new settlement was to establish a brewery and tavern. When the United States declared its independence from England, beer was so popular and important that there was talk of establishing a national brewery and even creating a Secretary of Beer position in the President's cabinet.

The Story Behind the Story of Thanksgiving

Everyone knows that the Pilgrims sailed across the Atlantic on the *Mayflower* and landed at Plymouth Rock, but did you know why they landed there? The *Mayflower* was a boat that the Pilgrims had chartered to get from England to the colonies, but Plymouth Rock was not their intended destination. On the voyage, the *Mayflower* encountered rough weather and was blown off course, setting the voyage back by several weeks. The sailors forced the captain of the *Mayflower* to leave the Pilgrims at Plymouth Rock, fearful that they might run out of their beer provisions on the return voyage.

The Industrial Revolution in Europe and the United States brought several technological and scientific advances to the production of beer in the 1800s. Louis Pasteur's discovery of the role yeast plays in fermentation in the late 1850s ushered in a new era of brewing science. This led to the viable production of a new family of beers called **lagers**, which quickly became the leading style of beer sold in the world as they were adopted by traditional powers like Germany and Czechoslovakia. Around the turn of the century, the American brewing industry was in its prime. Beer was the drink of the United States, which boasted more breweries than any other country in the world. Regional beer styles were developed and traditional European styles were adopted. It seemed that nothing could stop the growth of America's brewers—until 1920, when everything came to a screeching halt.

Prohibition began in the United States in January of 1920, and well over two thousand breweries had to shut their doors. For thirteen years, the production of beer was outlawed and the once proud brewing tradition in the country was decimated. The first day after the repeal of Prohibition in 1933, Americans consumed nearly one million gallons of beer. The United States was a country of thirsty people, but only a handful of commercial breweries made it through Prohibition. While Prohibition itself was repealed, much of the bureaucracy and red tape remained and state laws further confused the situation. While the demand for beer was high, the supply was closely controlled by just a few regional and national breweries that gained a virtual monopoly on American beer sales. Even as late as the 1970s there were only around forty breweries legally brewing beer in the United States, and options of different styles were limited.

This all changed in 1971, when the federal government loosened regulations on establishing breweries. In that year, the Anchor Brewery in San Francisco, which had been closed for over ninety years, was purchased, reopened, and began to produce a traditional-style beer. Many believe that this marked the beginning of the American **microbrewery** movement.

Today, there are once again more breweries in the United States than in any other country. While the large, corporate breweries here still dominate the vast amount of beer sales, consumers once again have a choice when it comes to beer. This beer renaissance has been led by microbreweries and brewpubs, smaller breweries focusing on hand crafting distinctive styles of beer. The term microbrewery refers to a small- to medium-sized brewery producing beer for the retail market, while a brewpub is a small brewery attached to a restaurant, producing beer for that restaurant. With the success of these smaller breweries, America now boasts more than two thousand breweries.

American beer drinkers have more choices than ever, and have also begun to rediscover Europe's classical beers. The combination of a thirsty public and the availability of top-quality brewing ingredients and equipment have allowed small, local breweries an opportunity to become part of the community once again. Fueled by the search of beer drinkers for more styles, choices, and flavors, brewpubs and microbreweries continue to gain popularity.

Raw Ingredients for Beer

There are hundreds of different styles of beer produced around the world, ranging greatly in color, flavor, and characteristics. This variety is amazing considering that the vast majority of these styles are produced from just a few basic ingredients. In fact, the majority of the world's beer styles actually contain only four ingredients: **malted barley,** water, **hops,** and yeast.

MALTED BARLEY

Barley is a member of the grass family and is closely related to wheat. For thousands of years barley has been cultivated for use in flour, bread, and most importantly, the production of beer. In its raw form, barley has no real fermentable material, and has to go through a special process called **malting** to become the sugar source for beer. The barley kernels that are harvested to produce beer are actually the seeds of the barley plant. Malting is the process of causing these barley kernels to begin germination by placing them into a warm, dark, moist environment. Once germination begins, enzymatic changes inside the seed create a starch reservoir as an energy source for the plant during the period of its early development.

The starch is the product that is needed during the brewing process. During the **mashing** phase of the brewing process, this starch is converted into sugar. When yeast is introduced, this sugar will be converted into alcohol and carbon dioxide during fermentation. Once the barley kernel creates this starch reservoir, the newly sprouted plant needs to be killed off before it consumes the starch as an energy source. This is done by putting the kernels into a kiln—think of it as a modified oven—and heating the kernels until the seedlings die. It is during this kilning process that malted barley can gain its color: pale, amber, or dark malts. The color of this barley (or more likely the blend of differently colored barleys) is the sole source of color for most beers.

Several different colors and grades of malted barley can be produced depending on how it is kilned.

Malted Barley Gives Beer
Color
Sugar to create alcohol and carbonation
Flavor
Body and mouthfeel

WATER

The water used to extract the color, flavor, and sugar from malted barley during the brewing process plays a large role in the finished beer, especially since beer is approximately 95 percent water. The hardness and mineral contents found in local water supplies have dictated the styles of beer that different regions have brewed. It is no accident that Ireland is the home of stouts, because the hard water there enhances the color of beer, or that pilsners come from the Czech Republic, whose soft water brings out the delicate flavor of hops.

Water Gives Beer
The basis for what style of beer is brewed
Extraction of the sugar, color, and flavor from malted barley

HOPS

The green flower buds of the plant known as the hop vine have been added to beer for hundreds of years as a flavoring and aroma agent, as well as a natural preservative. These hop flowers contain acids, resins, flavoring agents, and essential oils that give a beer its bitterness and spicy, floral aromas. This bitterness helps to balance the malty sweetness that malted barley gives beer.

Hops are small green flower buds harvested from the hop vine.

Hops Give Beer
A balancing bitterness
Aroma
Flavor

Skunky Beer

Without naming any names, there are several European imports that can taste and smell a little skunky. A beer that has this type of aroma or flavor is most likely lightstruck; that is, damaged by exposure to light. Ultraviolet light rays can actually break down certain compounds extracted from hops into a beer. The byproduct that is created is what causes that skunky characteristic. This is why most premium beers come in dark, amber-colored glass bottles that better block out these UV waves. Green or clear glass allows more of these waves into the beer. Regardless of the type of glass used, it is always best to store bottles of beer in a dark environment.

YEAST

As in all alcoholic fermentations, yeast, a single-celled fungus, is the agent that acts upon sugars to produce alcohol and carbon dioxide in beer brewing. Brewer's yeasts are specialized yeast strains that have been developed and refined over hundreds of years. These yeasts used to ferment beers can be broken up into two main categories—**ale** or **top-fermenting yeast** and lager or **bottom-fermenting yeast**—and the type of yeast used determines which family of beer is produced: an ale or a lager.

Yeast can have a large effect on the flavors, aroma, and body of a beer, and in some styles is the main flavoring component, such as in German-style hefeweizens. Individual yeast strains, although members of the same species, can have vastly different characteristics. Breweries develop and protect their individual yeast strains and use them to help achieve a house style.

Yeast Gives Beer
Fermentation of sugars into alcohol and carbon dioxide
Flavor
Aroma
Mouthfeel

OTHER INGREDIENTS

In addition to the malted barley, water, hops, and yeast used to produce a beer, there are several other ingredients that a brewer has at his or her disposal to affect the characteristics and flavors of a finished beer. These ingredients can be used to add flavors and aromas or additional fermentable sugars. The two major categories of other ingredients are flavoring agents and **adjuncts.**

Flavoring Agents

Throughout most of the history of brewing, beers have been flavored with all manner of ingredients. Originally, this was to cover spoilage flavors resulting from a lack of proper sanitation and understanding of fermentation science. Popular flavoring agents have included a wide variety of sweeteners, fruits, spices, herbs, and seeds. There are medieval recipes that call for everything from tree sap to powdered crab claw to flavor beer. Today, since modern brewing techniques and technologies have eliminated most of the off flavors of old, ingredients are added to beers simply to enhance their flavors and characteristics. Common examples of flavored beers would include fruit beers, Belgian white beers that have coriander and orange peel added, and several spiced beers produced for the winter holiday months.

Adjuncts

Adjuncts include any fermentable sugar source that is added to beer besides those from malted barley. These adjuncts can be used in two main ways when producing beer. Sometimes they are added as an inexpensive source of sugar that does not contribute significant amounts of color or flavor, almost as a filler. Grains like corn and rice are fairly neutral examples of this type of adjunct, and are often added to mass-produced beers. Adjuncts can also be used by a brewer to enhance the flavor, character, or complexity of a beer. Examples of these types of adjuncts include the wheat that makes a hefeweizen crisp, the oats that add grainy flavors and a rich texture and mouthfeel to oatmeal stout, or even the rock candy sugar that adds a winelike complexity to Trappist ales.

The Brewing Process

For each brewery in the world, there is a unique process used to produce beer. Despite all of the differences from one brewery to the next, almost every beer produced goes through the same four basic stages:

- **Mashing**—Converting starch into sugar
- **Boiling**—Sanitizing the wort and adding hops
- **Fermenting**—Converting sugar into alcohol and carbon dioxide
- **Conditioning**—Preparing the beer for service

MASHING

Mashing is the stage during which the starch in malted barley is converted into fermentable sugar. The malted barley is first run through a malt mill, which cracks the kernels open, exposing their starch reservoirs created through the malting process. **Grist** is the term used for cracked barley kernels.

Once cracked, the grist is mixed with hot water in a vessel called a **mash tun.** Hot water activates enzymes in the husks of the barley kernels, which convert the starch inside into fermentable sugars. The water also extracts color, flavors, aroma, and body from the malted barley. Once this has taken place, the brewer separates the liquid produced, called **wort,** from the spent grains and prepares it to be boiled.

BOILING

Once this wort has been produced, it is pumped into a vessel called a brew kettle, in which it can be heated to a boil. This boil is done for several reasons, the two most important being sanitation and hop addition. The brewer wants to sanitize the wort and kill all of the microorganisms that might be found in it, so that the brewer's yeast added during fermentation is

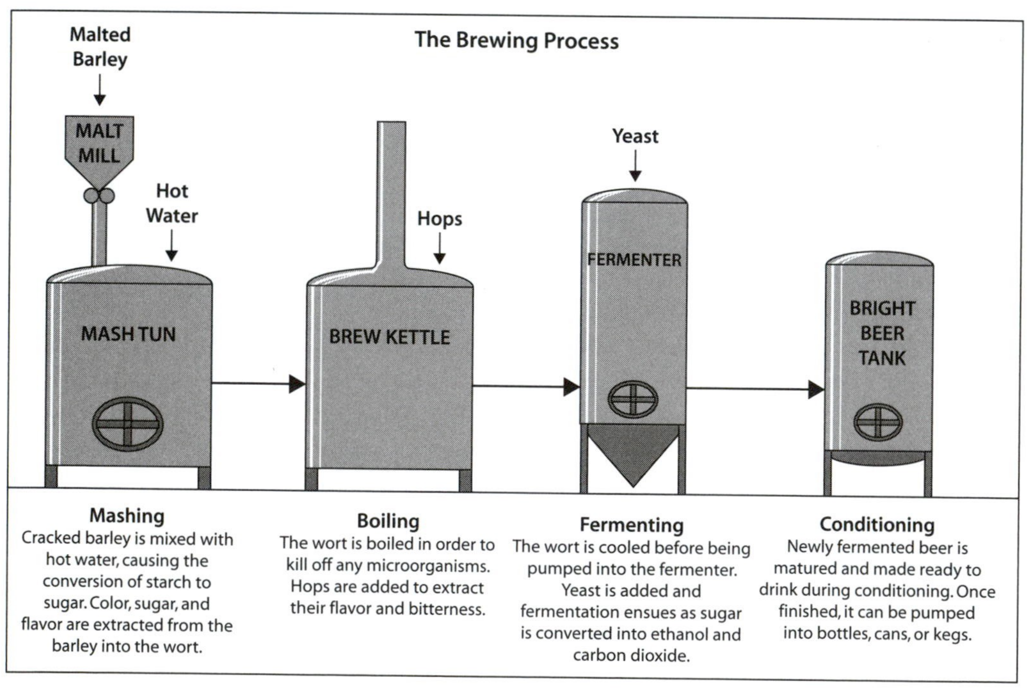

A typical small-scale brewery.

the only microorganism acting upon the wort. Hops are added to the boiling wort because the only way to extract their bitterness and flavor is to place them in a boiling solution. Hops used to add aroma to a beer are added after boiling has commenced.

FERMENTATION

Once the wort has been boiled, it is cooled down to the temperature at which its respective yeast ferments, and is then added to the yeast in a fermentation vessel (or fermenter). The yeast begins eating the sugars and producing alcohol and carbon dioxide. At this point, the wort has been transformed into beer.

CONDITIONING

Once fermentation has ended, the beer is conditioned, or made ready to serve. The temperature of the beer is dropped almost to the freezing point, causing all of the yeast and other suspended particles to sink to the bottom of the fermentation vessel. This yeast sediment will be either removed and discarded, or added to the next batch of beer during its fermentation. (Brewer's yeast can sometimes be used up to eight or nine times before a new culture is needed.)

After this period of settling, the beer can be filtered depending on the style of beer being produced. Beer is filtered to make it clear or **bright.** After filtration (or instead of filtration, depending upon the style), the beer is pumped into a storage vessel (often known as a bright beer tank). The beer will then be either served directly to a bar or pumped into bottles, cans, or kegs.

Green Beer

The phrase "green beer" brings up visions of light beers dyed green for St. Patrick's Day, but the term means something very different for a professional brewer. While going through the conditioning phase, when the beer is not yet matured, it is referred to as green beer. Once conditioning is over, the beer is ready to drink.

Summary

Beer is one of the world's oldest and most important beverages. Throughout history, several cultures have shaped beer and the brewing process into what it is today. While beer can be an extremely complex beverage, its production and ingredients are often quite simple.

Despite the wide array of beer styles produced throughout the world, most are made from only four basic ingredients: malted barley, water, hops, and yeast. These four ingredients are combined and beer is produced through four basic stages: mashing converts the starch in malted barley into sugar, boiling sanitizes the unfermented beer and extracts hop flavor, fermenting converts sugar into alcohol and carbon dioxide, and finally, conditioning makes the beer ready to drink.

Review Questions

1. Beer is technically a fermented beverage produced from a mixture of water and cereal grains.
   - A. True
   - B. False

2. Beer is believed to have been first produced in ________________.
   - A. Mesopotamia
   - B. Egypt
   - C. Sumeria
   - D. Germany

3. The country that is home to the most breweries in the world is ________________.
   - A. Germany
   - B. England
   - C. the United States
   - D. the Czech Republic

4. Which of the following is *not* one of the four main ingredients used to produce beer?
   - A. Malted barley
   - B. Water
   - C. Hops
   - D. Corn

5. The process of malting changes raw barley into malted barley, creating sugar inside the kernel which can later be converted into alcohol.
   A. True
   B. False

6. The number one ingredient in beer by volume is ____________.
   A. malted barley
   B. water
   C. hops
   D. corn

7. Hops provide a sweet flavor and aroma to beer.
   A. True
   B. False

8. Fermentable sugar sources other than malted barley used in the production of beer are called ____________.
   A. adjuncts
   B. fillers
   C. malts
   D. worts

9. Which of the following answers puts the four major phases of the brewing process into the proper order?
   A. Boiling, mashing, conditioning, fermenting
   B. Mashing, boiling, fermenting, conditioning
   C. Fermenting, mashing, conditioning, boiling
   D. Conditioning, mashing, boiling, fermenting

10. The primary function of the mashing phase of the brewing process is to convert starch into fermentable sugar.
   A. True
   B. False

11. Unfermented beer is referred to as ____________.
   A. grist
   B. adjunct
   C. wort
   D. must

12. Which of the following is *not* one of the reasons for boiling as part of the brewing process?
   A. To sanitize the unfermented beer
   B. To carbonate the beer
   C. To extract flavor from the hops
   D. All of the above are reasons to boil

Key Terms

beer
brewpub
lagers
microbrewery
malted barley
hops
malting
mashing
ale
top-fermenting yeast
bottom-fermenting yeast
adjuncts
boiling
fermenting
conditioning
grist
mash tun
wort
bright

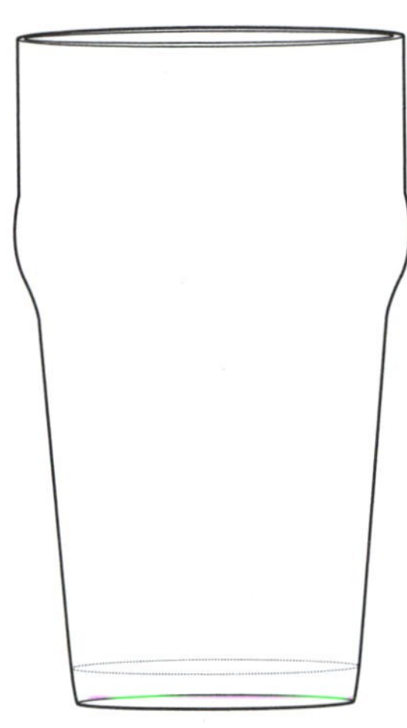

CHAPTER 24

Ales, Lagers, and Beer Styles

A quart of ale is a dish for a king.

—**WILLIAM SHAKESPEARE,** *A Winter's Tale*

While there are hundreds of different beer styles, there are only two major types of beer: ales and lagers. This chapter explores these families of beer, discussing the major differences between the two. Each is produced in a unique manner, and that results in very different flavor characteristics. Further, the major styles of both ales and lagers are discussed, introducing you to the breadth of beers commercially available today.

The Families of Beer: Ales and Lagers

All beers can be categorized into two main families, ales and lagers. Each of these families is brewed in a similar manner—it is not until fermentation that we see major differences. The fundamental difference between the two is the yeast used during fermentation. Ales are fermented with a different species of yeast than lagers are. Since these two species of yeast prefer distinct conditions while carrying out fermentation, the result is many differences in characteristics and flavor between the finished beers.

ALES

Ales were the original type of beers brewed back in ancient Mesopotamia somewhere between seven thousand and nine thousand years ago. They are produced with a species of yeast called *Saccharomyces cerevisiae,* commonly referred to as either ale yeast or top-fermenting yeast. This is the same yeast used in the winemaking industry and for baking bread. *Top-fermenting* refers to this yeast's behavior of floating on the surface of the liquid going through fermentation when all of the sugar has been consumed. Beers produced with ale yeast have specific characteristics due to the conditions under which the yeast works best. Ale yeast prefers fermenting in warmer temperatures, typically between 55°F and 75°F. In this temperature range, the yeast cells quickly metabolize sugar molecules—ale fermentations take approximately a week, a relatively short period of time.

This rapid fermentation causes the yeast to form large amounts of biochemical flavor compounds while it is breaking sugar down into ethanol and carbon dioxide. Because of this, ales tend to have stronger, fuller flavors than lagers. One of the most common compounds formed are **esters,** responsible for the often fruity flavors found in ales (esters are also found in large concentrations in many fruits and vegetables).

Besides using top-fermenting yeast and its resulting strong flavors, ales also differ from lagers in terms of where they are produced. Over the last 150 years, beer-producing countries and regions around the world have evolved into either ale brewers or lager brewers. There can be exceptions, but ales are the predominant style of beer brewed in Ireland, England, and Belgium, and by American microbreweries and brewpubs.

LAGERS

Lagers are a relatively new family of beers, and have been commercially brewed on a large scale only since the 1800s. Various forms of lagers had been produced for a couple of hundred years prior, but they had to be produced under difficult and often less than ideal conditions. It was not until the Industrial Revolution brought refrigeration technology and advances in the understanding of yeast and fermentation science that widespread lager brewing became possible.

Derived from the German word for "storage," lager refers to a family of beers that spend an extended time going through fermentation followed by a subsequent period of cold storage. Lagers are fermented with ***Saccharomyces uvarum,*** a species of yeast known also as lager yeast or bottom-fermenting yeast. Unlike ale yeast, lager yeast has a propensity to sink to the bottom of a liquid once it has finished fermenting sugars, hence the term *bottom-fermenting*.

While ale yeast prefers warm conditions and works rapidly, lager yeast does the exact opposite. In its early history, lager beer could be brewed only in cooler regions over the cold months, where a steady cold temperature could be maintained during fermentation and storage. Lager yeast thrives in cold temperatures, commonly fermenting at around 40°F. Instead of the yeast fermenting sugars quickly, it moves much more slowly, often taking a month or more to complete fermentation. This almost sluggish fermentation causes the yeast to methodically reproduce and break down sugars, so very few flavor compounds are created by the yeast during fermentation. This is why ales tend to have stronger flavors and are much fruitier. Lager yeast simply does not produce the same esters and flavors in beer; instead, lager beers tend to be very clean and smooth.

It is because of this smoothness that many large, corporate breweries will go to the added expense of producing lagers rather than ales. This seems most apparent with the large American breweries, who also use large amounts of adjuncts to further soften their products' flavors. In these ways, beer can be made in a very neutral fashion in order to avoid strong flavors that might offend some consumers.

Fortunately, there are several lagers produced that do have distinct flavors from malted barley and hops, and often exhibit unique regional character. Lagers are the predominant style of beer brewed in both Germany and the Czech Republic, the traditional areas where the lager family was first produced. Most Latin American and Asian countries have become lager-brewing nations because they used German brewmasters to help them establish their brewing industries as they industrialized.

COMMON MISCONCEPTIONS

While there are several distinct differences between ales and lagers, there are also some widely held misconceptions about the characteristics of these two beer families. The two most important misconceptions involve color and alcoholic strength.

The use of ale yeast or lager yeast will not affect the color of a beer: both ales and lagers can range from light straw to dark black in color. This belief probably exists because the most popular styles of beer sold in the world are extremely pale-colored lagers. The color of a beer is extracted from malted barley before fermentation even takes place. A wort made from light or dark grains will result in the same color of beer regardless of which type of yeast is used for fermentation.

Another common misconception about ales and lagers involves alcoholic strength, and neither ales nor lagers are generally stronger than one another. Like color, alcoholic strength in a beer depends upon the malted barley and other fermentable sugars used in its production, not the yeast used for its fermentation. Whether fermented quickly with ale yeast or slowly with lager yeast, all of the sugars in a wort will be fermented into alcohol. If more barley is used, more sugar will be extracted during brewing and higher alcohol levels will result. Both the ale and lager families have examples of low-alcohol and high-alcohol styles.

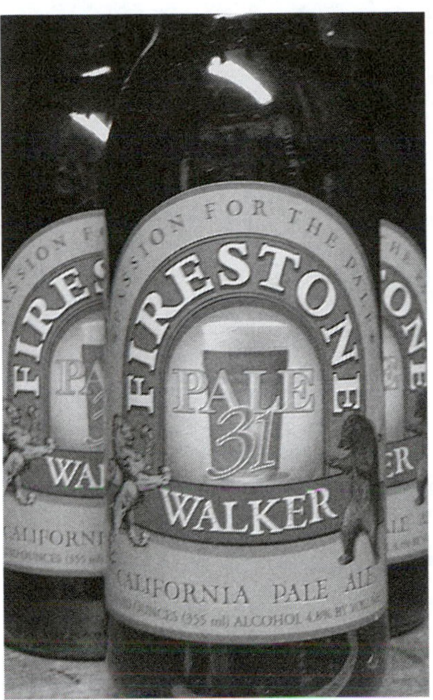

Pale ales are some of the most popular styles of ales produced.

Popular Styles of Ales

A wide range of ale styles are brewed today, showcasing a variety of different colors, bodies, flavors, and characteristics. Many of these styles originated long ago, as ales are the original family of beer brewed. Over time, these styles were shaped (mostly in Europe) by adapting to the differing water and ingredients found in brewing regions throughout Europe and beyond.

PALE ALE

Pale ale is so named because it is light or pale in color. Most will range in color from straw to deep amber. There are many different substyles of pale ale (including India pale ale, discussed next) which can emphasize different ingredients used in the brewing process. Most American versions emphasize hoppy and sometimes bitter flavors, while British versions emphasize a rich, malty sweetness.

INDIA PALE ALE (IPA)

India pale ale or **IPA** is a style of beer that was developed out of necessity. During the English colonization of India, thousands of English soldiers and citizens lived there. The country was too hot to grow quality barley or hops, so beer had to be shipped all the way from England. Since this involved long shipments at sea, where the beer had to travel through various climates, the beers invariably spoiled. To prevent this, brewers in England concocted a new style of beer by increasing the amount of ingredients that contained natural preservatives. This meant more hops and more alcohol. Today, India pale ales are typically stronger than pale ales and are often much more bitter and aromatic because they are heavily hopped.

BITTER AND EXTRA SPECIAL BITTER (ESB)

These styles of ale were both developed in England and are still popular there today. Although they are called **bitters**, they are surprisingly malty rather than bitter. Both are copper colored and are very similar to British-style pale ales.

AMBER ALE

Named for their rich amber hue, **amber ales** are produced with a variety of different caramel-colored (and flavored) grades of malted barley. These beers typically have a smooth, toffeelike maltiness from the use of these specialty malts.

BROWN ALE AND NUT BROWN ALE

Named for their deep brown color, **brown ales** tend to have a nutty, malty character. Like amber ales, their distinct color and flavors come from the use of darker malts that have been kilned longer during the malting process.

WHEAT BEER AND HEFEWEIZEN

The German Beer Purity Law of 1516, called the ***Reinheitsgebot,*** allowed for only one source of fermentable sugar other than malted barley: wheat. **Wheat beers** are made from a blend of malted barley and wheat, which causes them to be very crisp and light-bodied. They are usually light gold in color and very refreshing.

A special style of wheat beer developed in Germany is called **hefeweizen.** The term translates to "yeast-wheat" and refers to wheat beers fermented with a special strain of yeast that gives them unique flavors of banana and cloves. While most wheat beers are crystal clear, hefeweizen is almost always cloudy because this flavorful yeast is not filtered out of these beers after fermentation.

BELGIAN WHITE AND WIT

Belgium has one of the longest and proudest brewing traditions in Europe, but its brewers have always used a variety of flavorful and sometimes exotic ingredients to produce their beers. **Belgian white** or **wit** beer is similar to hefeweizen in that they are both unfiltered wheat beers, except the yeast used to produce Belgian whites is not nearly as flavorful. They are flavored instead with coriander and orange peel, giving them a spicy, citrus flavor. Most authentic examples are brewed in Belgium, although it is a style gaining more popularity in the United States.

Hefeweizens are unfiltered and cloudy.

PORTER

Another ale style that originated in England is **porter,** named for nineteenth-century railroad porters whose job it was to load and unload trains. It was thirsty work, even if it did not pay very well. To attract their business, creative pub owners created a beer called "porter" by mixing old, stale beer with dark and light ales to produce a beer that could be attractively priced. This dark-colored beer eventually evolved into the porter of today. Porters are dark and often chocolaty because they are brewed with specialty dark-kilned malts. The resulting beers are rich and medium-bodied with a slight roasted flavor.

STOUT

Like porters, **stouts** are dark-colored ales. They differ in that stouts are brewed with fully roasted barley, produced similarly to roasting espresso beans. This roasting degrades all of the malted barley's starch, but results in an intensely dark beer with strong, roasted flavors and usually a rich, full body.

Stouts are the darkest ales, brewed with roasted barley.

The Six Trappist Breweries

Trappist ales can be produced only at six Trappist monasteries, each of which makes its own brand of beer.

BRAND	MONASTERY	LOCATION
Chimay	Abbaye de Notre-Dame de Scourmont	Belgium
Orval	Abbaye de Villers-devant-Orval	Belgium
Rochefort	Abbaye Notre-Dame de Saint Rémy	Belgium
St. Sixtus	Abbaye de Saint-Sixte	Belgium
Westmalle	Abbaye de Notre-Dame du Sacré-Cœur	Belgium
La Trappe	Abbey of Our Lady of Koningshoeven	The Netherlands

Stouts come in many different styles. The most popular version, called **Irish dry stout,** is clean and dry and often carbonated with a blend of nitrogen and carbon dioxide that gives it a creamy texture. Other styles include **imperial stout,** which is very strong and sweet; **outmeal stout,** which has oats added to it to help provide a rich full body; **milk stout,** which has lactose or milk sugars added during fermentation to give it rich, sweet notes; and even **oyster stout,** which has crushed oyster shells added to the brewing water, which results in an extremely dry style.

TRAPPIST ALE AND ABBEY ALE

Trappist ales are some of the rarest beers produced in the world today. While monasteries throughout Europe have brewed beer for centuries, very few commercially available examples still exist except for Trappist ales. These are beers that are brewed by Trappist monks in Trappist monasteries, and only six still produce beer today (five in Belgium and one in Holland).

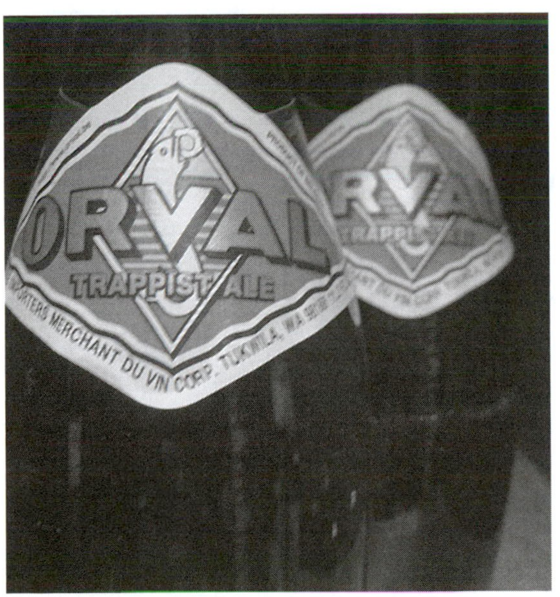

Trappist ales are some of the rarest and most unique beers produced in the world.

These unique ales are often brewed using rock candy sugar as an adjunct, giving them a winelike flavor. Special yeast strains and multiple fermentations also add to the layers of flavor found in these complex, high-alcohol brews. Although similar in style, **abbey ales** are not brewed by monks, but rather by commercial breweries found throughout Belgium and even a few in the United States.

Barleywines are the strongest style of ales.

STRONG ALE AND OLD ALE

Strong ales (sometimes called **old ales**) can range very widely in both color and flavor. What they have in common is that extra malt is used during the brewing process, making them stronger than typical ales. These styles are most commonly brewed in England.

BARLEYWINE

Barleywine is the strongest style of ale produced. It is named for the fact that its alcohol content is more similar to wine than to beer. Made by fermenting the sugar-rich first runnings created during the mashing phase of brewing, they are malty sweet and often quite heavily hopped. Deeply colored, barleywines are usually brewed for special occasions or in winter months and can be as strong as 12 percent to 13 percent alcohol by volume.

Lambics often have intense fruit flavors and a natural acidity from a wild yeast fermentation.

LAMBIC

Oddities in the brewing world, **lambics** are a throwback to the ancient days of beer. They are brewed in a few areas in Belgium by allowing the wort to be spontaneously fermented with wild yeast that is floating around in the air. Since wild yeast (and bacteria) are used during fermentation, the resulting beers have an intense, sour flavor.

This sour flavor is commonly masked by adding macerated fruit to the beer that gives it sweetness, fruit flavors, and vibrant colors. Several different fruits can be used, but the most common flavors are raspberry (called ***framboise***), cherry (called ***kriek***), and peach (called ***pêche***). Fruit lambics are considered the world's greatest fruit beers.

Popular Styles of Lagers

Although relative newcomers to the world of beer, several distinct styles of lagers have been developed. Many of these styles were first brewed in the important lager-producing nations of Germany and the Czech Republic. These styles have added a number of new flavor profiles enjoyed by beer drinkers everywhere.

LIGHT LAGER

Light lager is a category of light-colored and softly flavored beers produced from 100 percent malted barley—these beers do not use adjuncts like the dominant light lagers made in America. This style is very popular in Europe, Asia, and Latin America. Typically it will show characteristics that are marked by smooth, malty flavors and soft, crisp hops.

AMERICAN LIGHT LAGER

American light lager is the top-selling style of beer in the United States, and the favored style brewed by large corporate breweries. The "light" in the name does not refer to light in calories, but rather to light in color, body, and flavor. This style is different from other light lagers due to the use of large percentages of neutral adjuncts along with malted barley as the sugar source. The most common adjuncts used are rice and corn, which contribute alcohol with little flavor or color.

PILSNER AND PILS

The style of **pilsner** is named for the Czech city of Pilsen where it was first produced, and it is considered the world's first golden-colored beer. While the appearance of this style is similar to that of other light lagers, the flavor profile is distinctly different. Pilsner (sometimes called **pils** in Germany) is marked by its extremely pale color and crisp, hoppy aromas and flavors.

Pilsners originated in the city of Pilsen in the Czech Republic, and are considered the world's first golden-colored beer.

DUNKEL AND SCHWARZBIER

Dunkel means "dark" in German, while ***schwarzbier*** means "black beer." Both styles are medium- to full-bodied lagers that have specialty malts added to give them clean, roasted flavors and colors ranging from brown to black.

MÄRZEN AND VIENNA LAGER

Märzens and **Vienna lagers** are similar in style to one another; they are just from different origins. The style known as Märzen was developed in Germany. *Märzen* is the German word for the month of March, and these beers were traditionally brewed near the end of spring for the hot summer months ahead. Vienna lager is a style that originated in Austria. Both styles are medium-bodied, copper-hued lagers with a pleasant malty flavor and generous hop bite.

OKTOBERFEST

Oktoberfest beers are brewed in honor of, and to be served at, Germany's Oktoberfest celebrations. These copper- to deep-amber-colored beers were traditionally brewed to contain less alcohol than other beers (so that you could drink liter after liter at the holiday celebrations). They typically feature a rich, malty flavor and a pleasant, dry finish. At the Oktoberfest held in Munich (Germany's most important), there are only six breweries that are legally allowed to brew this style of beer for the celebrations.

Munich's Oktoberfest: The Party that Started It All

Each year, the largest and original Oktoberfest celebration takes place in Munich, Germany. It is a larger-than-life event that needs to be witnessed to be believed. Here are some interesting facts about Munich's Oktoberfest.

- Most of the Oktoberfest celebration takes place in September; the official end to the Oktoberfest is the first Sunday in October.
- The party lasts for sixteen days and nights.
- This is the original Oktoberfest celebration, which began as the wedding festivities of a Bavarian prince and princess in 1810.
- Each year, it is estimated that more than five million liters of beer are consumed!

BOCK AND DOPPELBOCK

Bock is the German word for goat (**doppelbock** literally translates to "double goat") and the reference here is that if you drink too much of these higher-alcohol beers, the next day you will feel like you got kicked in the head by a goat! These styles can range in color from light gold to deep brown and have rich, malty characteristics. Bocks are relatively high in alcohol, while doppelbocks can be extremely high in alcohol—sometimes up to 13 percent to 14 percent alcohol by volume.

Summary

All beer can be placed into one of two categories based on what type of yeast is used for fermentation: ales and lagers. Ales are produced with ale yeast during relatively warm, quick fermentations that produce heavily flavored beers. Lagers are fermented with lager yeast, and these fermentations take much longer and are much cooler than those used for ales. This slow fermentation produces a more softly flavored, smoother style. Both ales and lagers can be made in a wide array of styles, which vary greatly in color, flavor, and characteristics.

Review Questions

1. The primary difference between ales and lagers is the species of yeast used for each during fermentation.
   A. True
   B. False

For questions two through eight, determine whether the following statements describe ales or lagers, or if they are a common misconception and not really a difference between the two.

A. Ales
B. Lagers
C. Not a difference

2. These beers are fermented with top-fermenting yeast.
3. These beers ferment for a relatively long period of time.
4. These beers ferment at a relatively cool temperature.
5. These beers are darker in color.
6. These beers tend to have stronger, fruity flavors.
7. These beers are relatively higher in alcohol content.
8. These are the original style of beer produced, dating back thousands of years.

9. The German term *lager* means ______________.
   A. cold filtered
   B. storage
   C. cold brewed
   D. lumberjack

Determine whether the following styles of beer are ales or lagers.

A. Ale
B. Lager

10. IPA
11. Marzen
12. Oktoberfest
13. Hefeweizen
14. Lambic
15. Extra special bitter (ESB)
16. Pilsner

Key Terms

esters
Saccharomyces uvarum
pale ale
India pale ale (IPA)
bitter
amber ale
brown ale
Reinheitsgebot
wheat beer
hefeweizen
Belgian white
wit
porter
stout
Irish dry stout
imperial stout
oatmeal stout
milk stout
oyster stout
Trappist ale
abbey ale
strong ale
old ale
barleywine
lambic
light lager
American light lager
pilsner
pils
dunkel
schwarzbier
Marzen
Vienna lager
Oktoberfest
bock
doppelbock

CHAPTER 25

Saké, Mead, and Cider

Mankind: The animal that fears the future and desires fermented beverages.

—**ANTHELME BRILLAT-SAVARIN,** French author

Wine and beer are the world's most important and common fermented beverages, but there are a wide variety of other alcoholic beverages produced through fermentation. This chapter serves as an introduction to three of these beverages: saké, mead, and cider. Production techniques, raw ingredients, flavor profiles, important production areas, styles, and specific vocabulary are discussed for each. As these beverages are becoming more popular, it is important to have a basic understanding of them.

Saké

Saké is the most important alcoholic beverage produced in Japan, where it is considered a point of national pride and a drink of religious significance. Although it is mistakenly referred to as "rice wine," saké is not a wine at all, nor a form of beer. Due to the ingredients and methods used to produce saké, it falls into its own unique class of fermented beverages. Although hugely popular in Japan and Asia for centuries, saké is finally coming into its own as an important beverage in the United States and throughout the Western world.

HISTORY OF SAKÉ

The exact origins of fermented beverages produced from rice are unclear, but most believe that the first were produced in China around the second century A.D. As with other early Chinese influences, eventually this crude form of saké made its way to Japan. These early sakés are often referred to as ***kuchikami no saké***, which means "mouth-chewed saké," because they would have been produced by villagers (usually young female virgins because they were considered pure) chewing on rice and grains and spitting them into a communal vat, where fermentation would occur. Enzymes in the saliva would have converted the starches found in the rice into sugar, which would then be fermented into alcohol.

By the seventh century, a version of saké emerged in Japan that is similar to the modern versions produced today, and it quickly became Japan's most important beverage. It was made with water, rice, yeast, and ***koji***—a mold that would break starches into sugars (replacing saliva, to the relief of all!). Over the next few centuries, saké production was controlled first by the imperial government of Japan, then by the monks of the Shinto church. The production of saké was a closely protected industry.

In the late 1800s, the production of saké was eventually opened up to anyone in Japan, and thousands of saké breweries sprang up overnight. As taxes were raised and competition stiffened, most of these producers were soon forced out of business, but saké was now a private, commercial enterprise in Japan. Major scientific advancements in the techniques and technology of saké production in the early 1900s ushered in a new era of high-quality saké.

This all came to an end during World War II, when many saké breweries were forced to close and rice shortages severely hampered those producers that remained. During this period, saké brewers began to experiment with the use of distilled spirits mixed with saké to increase yield and boost alcohol while using less rice. The majority of Japanese saké is still produced in a similar fashion, with distilled alcohol being added to lower-grade saké.

Since World War II, the premium saké industry in Japan has continued to improve its quality standards and new export markets have begun opening up. Because freshness is often paramount to top-quality saké, many saké breweries have been built around the world, often under the supervision of Japanese saké brewers. The popularity of saké has never been as high in the United States as it is today, and consumption (especially of the higher-grade sakés) continues to steadily grow.

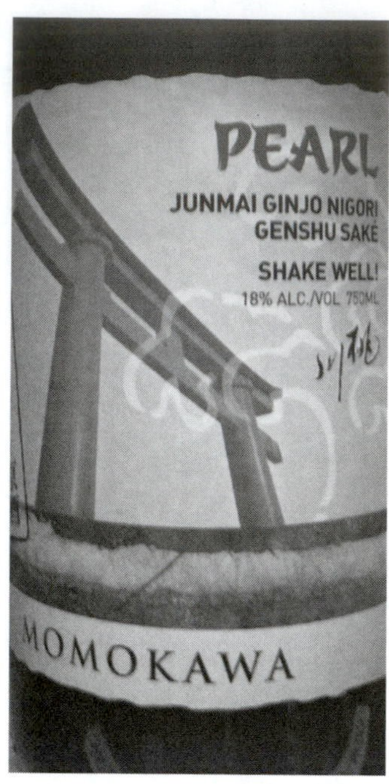

Saké is a fermented beverage made from rice.

INGREDIENTS AND PRODUCTION

Most saké is produced with just four basic ingredients: saké rice, water, yeast, and ***koji*** mold, although several styles of saké also have distilled alcohol added for additional strength and yield. As with beer, the water and the yeast can play a significant role in the final style, characteristics, and flavor of finished saké. What makes saké unique, however, is the type and handling of the rice that serves as its eventual sugar source, and the use of a species of mold called ***koji*** in its production.

Saké rice is a unique type of rice that differs from ordinary rice that is eaten. In this variety, the majority of the starch is found in the center of the grain, with the surface made up mostly of proteins and other compounds. Saké rice is milled to remove some or all of this outer layer, which concentrates the starch content that will eventually be converted into sugar and finally into alcohol. In general, the more the rice is milled, the higher the quality of saké it will produce. The highest-quality grades of saké are made with rice that has 50 percent or more of its total weight milled away.

When brewing beer, enzymes found in the husks of malted barley kernels serve to convert the starch of the kernel into sugar. Saké rice contains significant amounts of starch, but unlike in malted barley there is nothing in the grains that can convert this starch into sugar. To cause this conversion to take place, saké brewers inoculate their rice with a specific species of mold called ***koji***. This mold feeds on the starch from the rice, converting it into fermentable sugar. *Koji* mold is also used to turn soybeans into soy sauce and miso.

Saké is produced using a unique production technique called **parallel fermentation.** After being milled, the rice is washed, soaked in water, and eventually boiled or steamed. Once processed, this rice mash is then cooled to fermentation temperature before a small portion of ***koji***-infected rice is added. The ***koji*** will then begin to inoculate the rice mash, converting starches into sugar. As this conversion begins, yeast is introduced to the mash, which begins fermenting sugars into alcohol.

This process is referred to as a parallel fermentation because the ***koji*** and the yeast are working at the same time. As ***koji*** converts starch into sugar, yeast ferments the sugar into alcohol. Over the course of several days, more steamed rice is added daily and the parallel fermentation continues until the final volume of rice mash is achieved.

After this parallel fermentation is completed and all of the starch in the mash has been converted into sugar, the yeast completes its fermentation over the course of up to several weeks. Once fully fermented, the saké is then pressed to separate it from the solids of the mash. For several styles of saké, distilled alcohol is added just prior to pressing to either increase yield in lower-grade saké or, in small percentages, to help extract flavors from the solids of the mash.

Following pressing, the saké is often filtered and pasteurized, depending on style. Water can also be added to dilute the alcohol to lower, more approachable levels. A few styles of saké will go through a period of bulk aging at this point, but most will be immediately bottled.

MAJOR QUALITY CLASSIFICATIONS AND STYLES

Saké can be divided into two major categories: ***futsuu-shu*** or "normal saké" and ***tokutei meishoshu,*** which translates to "special designation saké." Roughly 80 percent of the saké produced in Japan is considered ***futsuu-shu,*** often mass-produced with considerable amounts of distilled alcohol added to increase yield. Much of this is basic and crude, although some better-quality examples are produced.

Although it is a far smaller portion of the total production of saké, ***tokutei meishoshu*** constitutes the vast majority of premium saké. This "special designation saké" is further divided into several categories depending upon quality, the degree to which the rice is milled, and production methods. Small quantities of distilled alcohol are added to many of these styles of saké, but only to help extract extra flavor and aroma, not to increase yield as in lower-grade saké. If a high-grade saké is made without distilled alcohol, it will use the term ***junmai*** in its name.

Classifications of "Special Designation Saké"

Daiginjo	Also known as *daiginjo-shu* (the suffix -shu is simply another way to say saké), this is the highest quality classification of saké produced. To qualify, the rice used must be milled by half or more to expose its purity. *Daiginjo* saké can be dry to slightly semisweet with elegant and complex characteristics. If a *daiginjo* is made without distilled alcohol, it will be labeled *junmai-daiginjo.*
Ginjo	Also called ginjo-shu, this classification is a close second to *daiginjo* saké. The rice must be milled at least 40% for a saké to be considered *ginjo* quality. If a *ginjo* saké is made without distilled alcohol, it will be labeled as *junmai-ginjo.*
Junmai	This classification of saké is also referred to as *junmai-shu*. This is a quality saké that is made with just rice, water, yeast, and *koji*. No distilled alcohol may be added. These sakés come in a wide range of styles and flavors and are made with rice that must be milled at least 30%.
Honjozo	Also known as *honjozo-shu*, this is a classification of quality sakés that have a small amount of distilled alcohol added just before pressing to help extract more flavor from the solids. There is a world of difference between *honjozo* saké and lower-grade saké, where distilled alcohol is added to increase yield.

Saké comes in a dazzling array of styles. They can range from bone dry to surprisingly sweet, and vary in color from clear to milky white to amber. Higher-quality saké will have all of the complexity and intensity of a fine wine, and can display fruity, floral, earthy, spicy, and honeyed flavors.

All of the different styles of saké can fall under most or all of the different quality classifications, depending upon how they are produced. The basic style of saké, which is pasteurized, filtered, and diluted, will often just list the quality classification on the label. Special styles of saké will have both the style and the quality classification listed on the bottle.

Special Styles of Saké

Namazake	Unpasteurized saké that requires refrigeration.
Nigori	Unfiltered or cloudy saké that is often sweet. After fermentation, *nigori* saké is not pressed, but rather passed through a mesh screen that allows rice particles to pass through. These particles are bottled along with the saké, and when agitated, cause the saké to turn milky white and opaque; also called *nigorizake*.
Genshu	Undiluted saké that has no water added before bottling to dilute alcohol content. These sakés will often be 18% abv or higher.
Koshu	Saké that is aged for extended periods. This will cause it to darken in color and develop complex and rich flavors.

SERVING AND STORING SAKÉ

There are several ways to serve saké depending on the quality of the saké, the season, and the occasion for which it might be consumed. Saké can be served hot or at room temperature, although most premium-grade saké should be served chilled. Saké is far more perishable than wine, and only certain styles will age well—most saké should be stored in a cool, dark place and should be consumed as fresh as possible. After opening a bottle, saké should be consumed within 24 hours, as it is prone to oxidizing quickly.

Oregon Saké?

Several Japanese saké companies as well as a few domestic startups have begun to produce top-quality sakés in the United States. This allows them to supply fresh saké to Americans, who are drinking more and more saké each year. Many of the top saké breweries located in the United States are found in the state of Oregon.

Mead

Mead is one of the oldest fermented beverages, possibly even predating wines and beers. An alcoholic drink sometimes called "honey wine," it is made by fermenting a mixture of water and honey. Mead was a favorite beverage of the ancient Greeks, Vikings, barbarians, medieval knights, poets, and monarchs. It was mentioned in *Beowulf,* featured in ancient Hindu scripts, and even written about by Aristotle. While its popularity has risen and fallen over the centuries, there are still plenty of fans of this ancient drink.

The exact origins of mead are unknown because it was first produced well before the beginnings of civilization, probably during the Neolithic period. Mead in some form has been independently developed in Europe, Asia, Africa, and the Middle East. It was an important beverage to many of the first cultures from Chinese dynasties to the Roman Empire. As the development of beekeeping advanced, so too did the production of mead. During the Middle Ages, it was widely produced in the cooler northern areas of Europe where grapevines could not be

Mead and the Honeymoon

The term *honeymoon* has its origins in sixteenth-century England, where a tradition arose around weddings. The in-laws of the happy couple would provide them with enough mead for their first month of marriage. In other words, enough honey for a full cycle of the phases of the moon.

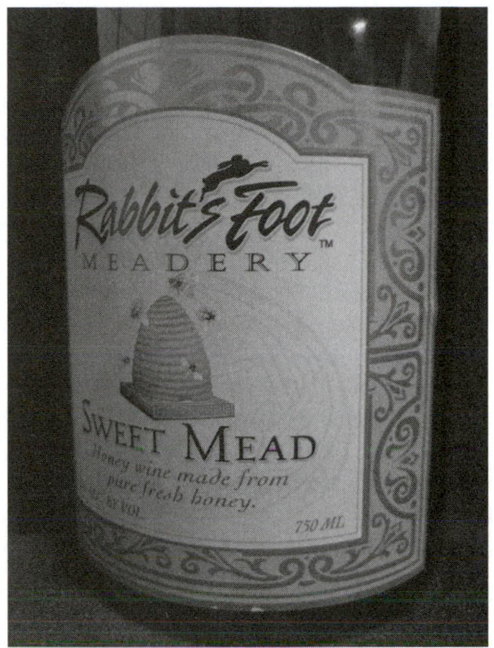

Mead is fermented honey and water.

established, especially in Germany and the British isles. Today, commercial mead producers are not common, but the beverage has seen resurging interest in the United States and beyond.

Basic mead is produced by mixing honey and water together and adding yeast to begin a fermentation. Mead has many varieties and variations. It can range from bone dry to extremely sweet, similar to a late harvest dessert wine, depending upon the degree to which it is fermented. Some meads are aged and some are meant for immediate consumption. Sparkling meads are produced in a similar fashion to *méthode traditionale* sparkling wines. Mead can even be distilled into a spirit resembling brandy.

The actual flavor profile of mead is determined by the quality and source of honey used, as well by the addition of several different kinds of adjuncts and flavor compounds. There are multiple styles of mead, which are determined by the type of additives used. From malted barley and hops to spices, fruits, and herbs, the variations of mead are seemingly endless.

Styles of Mead

Mead	Simply fermented honey and water. Meads will range widely in sweetness level and flavor.
Braggot	Mead made with the addition of malted barley as an adjunct and/or hops, which contribute a balancing bitterness.
Cyser	Mead produced with apple juice added as an adjunct prior to fermentation; basically a hybrid of mead and cider.
Melomel	Mead produced with fruit added as an adjunct. All sorts of berries and fruits are used to give these meads unique flavors. Technically, cyser and pyment are both melomels.
Metheglin	A basic mead that has different herbs and/or spices steeped in it after fermentation. Common flavorings include vanilla, ginger, cloves, cinnamon, coriander, lavender, orange peels, oregano, and basil.
Pyment	Mead made with either red or white grape juice added as an adjunct; basically a hybrid of mead and wine.

Cider

Cider, sometimes referred to as **hard cider,** is a fermented beverage made from the juice of apples. In many colder regions of Europe and the rest of the world, cider production takes the place of wine production because apple trees thrive in these marginal climates. Today, cider producers have enjoyed a renewed interest in their products, and the number of brands and styles of cider on the market have increased significantly.

Cider production has long been a staple on the English isles and in northern France, especially near the region of Normandy. The cooler climate found in these areas was well suited to planting apple orchards, but too far north for wine grape vineyards. Hundreds of different cultivars of cider apples have been developed in these regions, similar to the different varietals of wine grapes. In colonial New England, cider was one of the most important beverages produced. With attempts to grow wine grapes a failure, enterprising farmers turned to apple trees to produce alcoholic drinks. Many of the top cider producers in the United States are still located in the New England states.

Cider is technically a wine, as it is the product of fermented fruit juice. To produce ciders, apples are crushed and pressed to extract their juices. The juice of cider apples is often as sweet as that of eating apples, but typically far more acidic. Yeast is then introduced to the apple juice and fermentation ensues. For most styles, the cider will be racked into new, pressurized containers near the end of fermentation to remove it from the yeast lees and to allow it to develop carbonation. Unfermented apple juice and sweeteners may also be added after fermentation to give the cider a sweet flavor.

There are several different cider styles, many of them tied to regional tradition. Almost all ciders will have strong apple characteristics, with a complexity of other flavors ranging from tropical to earthy. Cider can range in sweetness from dry and tart to surprisingly sweet. Color and appearance can range from dark and cloudy to light straw and clear. While most cider is carbonated, some still versions are also produced. Most cider will have an alcohol content similar to that of beer, ranging from roughly 3 percent to 8 percent abv or more.

Johnny Appleseed

Although the story of Johnny Appleseed traveling the American frontier in the 1700s and planting apple seeds is considered a tale for children today, that version of the story leaves out the most important part. Johnny Appleseed's real name was John Chapman, and he was not just aimlessly wandering about growing apple trees because he thought they were pretty or he really liked apples. He grew apple orchards in advance of settlers moving west so that he could sell those apples for the production of hard cider in new settlements—and he grew very wealthy from the practice.

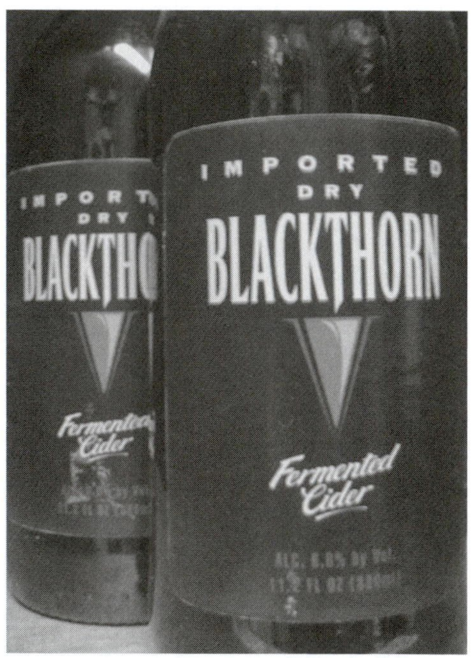

Cider is technically a wine made from apples.

Major Cider-Producing Regions and Styles

English Ciders	The British Isles are by far the world's leading producers and consumers of cider. Wales and western provinces of England constitute the main production areas. Many large, commercial cider producers in England both sell their products domestically and export them. There are a range of different styles and sweetness levels, although most English cider is pasteurized, light-colored, and carbonated. "Farm ciders" can also be found, mostly in the more rural areas. These ciders tend to be produced on a much smaller scale, and they are unpasteurized, often darker in color, richer in flavor, and typically still.
French Ciders	The northern French regions of Normandy and Brittany have long been known for their ciders, which in French are known as *cidre*. Directly across the English Channel from England, conditions in these areas never supported wine grapes like the areas of central and southern France. French ciders are typically carbonated, and range in sweetness from dry (*sec*) to sweet (*doux*). Most French cider is sold in corked bottles similar to those used for Champagne. In Normandy, cider is distilled into top-quality brandy called calvados.
American Ciders	The term *cider* is often used in the United States to describe a rustic form of unfermented apple juice. Most fermented cider is called "hard cider." A traditional beverage in the colonies, cider has seen a rebirth in the United States with New England and California emerging as the top-producing regions. Most American cider is light-colored, carbonated, and pasteurized, and is often far sweeter than European versions.
Canadian Ciders	With the French and English colonial heritage of Canada, it seems only natural that they would produce cider. Many traditional styles of cider are produced in Canada, but much of the excitement about Canadian cider today revolves around **ice ciders.** An homage to the ice wines for which Canada has grown famous, ice ciders are made by harvesting superripe apples and, after crushing them, allowing their juices to partially freeze. Ice crystals that form from freezing water in the apple juice are skimmed away, concentrating sugars and flavors. Ice ciders are often only partially fermented, retaining the rich sweetness of the concentrated sugar.

Another fermented fruit juice beverage known as **perry** is related to cider, and is quite often considered a subclassification. Sometimes called "pear cider," it is a fermented beverage produced from pears rather than apples. Perry has traditionally been produced in European regions known for growing pears, including England and France.

The most prolific and important cider-producing regions of the world include the northern French regions of Brittany and Normandy, as well as England and Wales. In the New World, significant amounts of cider are produced in New England, California, and Canada. The new growth of cider sales in the United States can be explained as a function of the success of the microbrewery movement.

Summary

Fermented beverages have been produced since the beginnings of civilization. Although wine and beer are the most common fermented beverages, there are a wide variety of sugar sources that can be fermented. Three of the most important fermented beverages after wine and beer are made from rice, honey, and apples—saké, mead, and cider respectively.

Review Questions

1. *Koji* is:
   - A. a special grade of rice
   - B. a style of unfiltered saké
   - C. a mold that converts starch in rice into sugar
   - D. the Japanese term for a saké serving cup

2. Saké is produced using a unique production technique called __________ fermentation.
   - A. hybrid
   - B. parallel
   - C. pressure
   - D. *koshu*

3. All saké that has distilled alcohol added to it falls into the lowest quality classification.
   - A. True
   - B. False

4. *Junmai-daiginjo* is one of the highest quality classifications of saké and must be produced without distilled alcohol.
   - A. True
   - B. False

5. Basic mead is produced by mixing ______ and water together and adding yeast to begin a fermentation.
   - A. pear juice
   - B. grape juice
   - C. wild berries
   - D. honey

6. Cider is a fermented beverage made from the juice of apples.
   - A. True
   - B. False

7. Cider is technically a ________.
   - A. beer
   - B. wine
   - C. distilled spirit
   - D. mead

8. Which of the following regions is not a major producer of cider?
   - A. Southern Italy
   - B. Northern France
   - C. England
   - D. Canada

Key Terms

saké	*daiginjo*	*koshu*	pyment
koji	*ginjo*	mead	cider
parallel fermentation	*honjozo*	braggot	hard cider
futsuu-shu	*namazake*	cyser	perry
tokutei meishoshu	*nigori*	melomel	ice cider
junmai	*genshu*	metheglin	

CHAPTER 26

Spirits and Distillation

No animal ever invented anything so bad as drunkenness—or so good as drink.

—**G.K. CHESTERTON,** English poet and playwright

This chapter serves as an introduction to spirits and how they are produced: the process of distillation. The basics of alcoholic distillation, alcoholic strength measurement, the equipment used for distillation, and how the finished flavor of a spirit is manipulated are covered in detail. Readers will also learn about the impact of the sugar source on the end product, and how this sugar source divides spirits into distinct categories.

Distilled Spirits: History and Importance

Distillation is a process that was first perfected by Arab scientists and doctors attempting to concentrate different compounds out of substances to create medicine. This practice was first used on fermented beverages during the Moorish occupation of Spain in the early 700s, as wines were distilled to extract medicinal properties. In fact, the word ***alcohol*** comes from the Arabic word *al-koh'l,* meaning the "essence of wine."

Spirits are alcoholic beverages, often with high levels of alcohol, that are produced by the process of distillation. Before being distilled, all base alcoholic beverages must first go through the process of fermentation, which creates the alcohol.

Distillation then separates alcohol from other substances (namely water). It does not create any alcohol itself.

Distillation of fermented beverages into spirits meant for consumption would not occur until the 1100s, as Celtic monks in Ireland turned an abundance of barley into a crude spirit they called *uisge beatha,* meaning "water of life." The practice of distilling spirits was further refined in the 1600s with the invention of the **pot still.** These are still used today to produce most spirits, including some whiskies, rums, brandies, and tequilas. In the 1830s, during the height of the Industrial Revolution, the **continuous** or **column still** (also called a **Coffey still)** was invented. Much more efficient than a pot still, it allowed distillers to produce spirits of extremely high alcoholic content (up to 95 percent). Continuous stills are still used today to produce many spirits, including **neutral spirits.**

Until Prohibition officially began in the United States in 1920, beer and wine were the most common alcoholic beverages consumed. When purchasing alcohol became illegal, most people switched to spirits because they packed more of a punch. Since then, a large portion of our population has been consuming cocktails and spirits. Today, luxury spirits (such as aged rum, single-malt scotch, single-batch bourbon, cognac, armagnac, 100 percent blue agave tequila, and ultra-distilled vodka) are becoming a major force in the beverage industry, and can be found in many restaurants and bars.

PROOF: MEASURING THE STRENGTH OF SPIRITS

The two units of measurement for the alcoholic strength of distilled spirits are alcohol by volume (abv) and **proof.** Alcohol by volume refers to how much of the volume of a spirit is alcohol. If the chemical breakdown of a bottle of vodka shows us that 40 percent of the liquid in the bottle is ethanol, then that spirit is considered 40 percent alcohol by volume.

Proof, on the other hand, is a number equal to double the percentage of alcohol by volume in a beverage. Therefore, a spirit that is 100 proof will contain 50 percent alcohol by volume. Most spirits are sold at or around 40 percent abv, or 80 proof.

Why "Proof"?

The origin of the term *proof* to describe alcoholic strength comes from centuries ago. Before there was scientific equipment to measure the amount of alcohol in a spirit, traders used a much simpler approach. They would soak gunpowder in a spirit and then attempt to set it on fire. If it did not light, then the spirit was certainly watered down, but if it did light, that was "proof" that it was a high-strength spirit and was worthy of purchase.

DISTILLATION

The highest alcohol content that can be produced in an alcoholic beverage through the process of fermentation is roughly 20 percent. How then are spirits, which can be as strong as 95 percent alcohol, made? The answer is distillation, the process of separating substances through the use of controlled heat. Distillation is used not only in the production of spirits, but also to produce perfumes, petroleum-based fuels, and distilled water, as well as having many scientific and industrial applications.

When producing alcoholic spirits, distillation basically separates and captures the ethanol (alcohol) in an alcoholic beverage from the water and other compounds in the solution. The ethanol captured is very concentrated, and can reach an extremely high alcoholic strength. Distillation can occur because ethanol and water have different **vaporization points** (the temperatures at which they are converted into steam):

Ethanol begins to vaporize at 173°F.

Water begins to vaporize at 212°F.

Therefore, distillation of alcoholic spirits takes place in a temperature range of 173 to 211°F. The fermented liquid is heated to a temperature within this range, and the ethanol is captured as it begins to vaporize.

Pot Still versus Continuous Still: Selecting the Right Tool for the Job

The equipment used to produce a distilled spirit is known as a **still.** There are two distinct types of stills used in the spirit industry: the pot still and the continuous or column still. The basic principles of how they work are similar: they both separate ethanol from other components in a fermented beverage through the use of controlled heat. But the two types of stills are used specifically for different types of spirits.

Distillation of fermented beverages into spirits was first conducted in crude pot stills, and the basics of how this piece of equipment works have not changed in the hundreds of years that it has been used. Due to

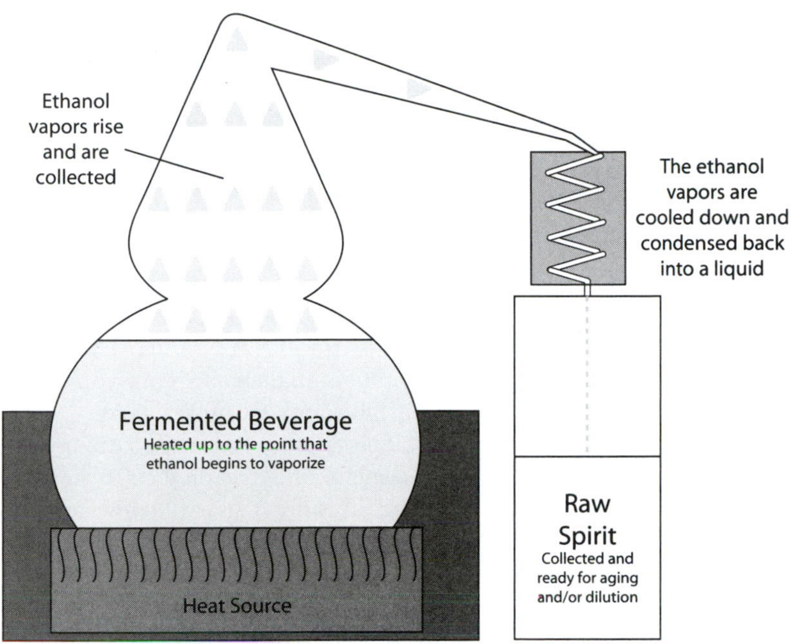

A pot still.

the fact that a pot still is relatively inefficient (it only distills to roughly 140 proof), more flavor from the fermented beverage is retained in the final product.

The continuous, Coffey, or column still, which was invented in the 1830s, is much more efficient than a pot still. It allows distillers to produce spirits of extremely high alcoholic content (up to 95 percent). At that high a concentration, it is difficult or impossible to detect flavors from the original sugar source or fermented beverage, rendering a spirit neutral. Continuous stills are used today to produce many spirits, especially two neutral spirits: vodka and gin. They can also be used to produce other spirits by setting the still to be less efficient.

FINISHING SPIRITS

Once distillation has occurred, the resulting spirit is typically:

- Finished at 120 to 190 proof
- Colorless
- Very harsh, with fiery characteristics

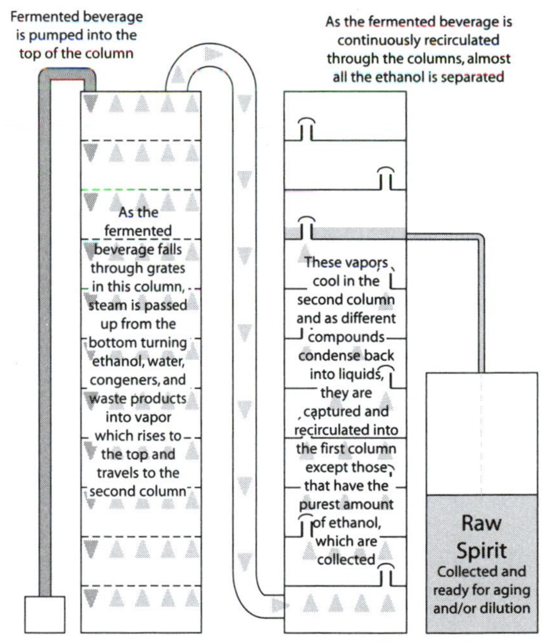

Column or continuous stills perform very efficient distillations.

These products are tamed or mellowed using several techniques:

Multiple distillations—The more times a spirit is distilled, the smoother it will be, as more and more impurities are separated from the spirit and discarded. Multiple distillations, however, will also result in a spirit with less character and flavor.

Flavor addition—Flavoring agents (fruits, herbs, spices, etc.) can be added to a spirit to mask the harsh flavors, producing spirits known as **cordials** or **liqueurs.**

Dilution with water—Prior to being bottled and sold, most spirits are diluted with water to lower their alcohol content. In fact, most bottles of vodka available commercially contain more than half water. Depending on the makeup and flavor of the water, it can have a huge impact on the final flavor of the product.

Aging—Spirits are most often aged in oak barrels because of their unique properties. They are commonly aged to leach flavor, color, aroma, and body from the barrels in which they are held. Oxidation also impacts a spirit the longer it is aged, darkening the color and mellowing the flavors and aromas.

RAW MATERIALS AND THE FAMILIES OF SPIRITS

Almost any sugar source can be used to produce a fermented beverage that can in turn be distilled, and the sugar source used is typically one of the main contributors to the flavor of a spirit. The sugar source itself will contain several different compounds that give it a unique flavor and aroma, called **congeners.** Many of these congeners will not be separated during distillation but will carry through to the finished spirit, causing it to have flavor compounds from the original sugar source. Hence, a spirit made from malted barley will contain different congeners and taste different from a spirit made from molasses. When spirits are produced using pot stills, this is almost always the case.

Since pot stills are relatively inefficient, not only is ethanol separated and collected during distillation, but so too are essential oils, aromatics, flavor compounds, and other characteristics from the original sugar source. Column or continuous stills can also be set up to be purposely inefficient in order to produce spirits with similar characteristics. If this did not occur, then all spirits would taste exactly the same: like pure ethanol.

Spirits produced in a continuous still at its full efficiency do not rely on their sugar source for flavor. In fact, it is impossible to tell what the sugar source is in a spirit that is produced at 190 proof. Any spirit distilled to that high an alcoholic content will taste the same, whether the sugar source was corn or fruit or potatoes. These types of spirits are referred to as neutral because they lack distinguishing characteristics, and include vodka and gin.

Based upon their sugar sources, two other families of spirits can be distinguished: **grain-based spirits,** which include whiskies, and **fruit- and plant-based spirits,** which include rum, tequila, and brandy. Spirits from all of the above categories that have had flavors, and sometimes sugar, added to them make up the last family of spirits; they are referred to as liqueurs or cordials.

Summary

Spirits are high-alcohol beverages produced through the process of distillation. This process concentrates the alcohol of a fermented beverage by separating it from the water and some of the extracts in the base fermented beverage. The importance of spirits can be seen in their widespread popularity around the world.

Review Questions

1. Distillation is the process that creates ethanol in a spirit.
    A. True
    B. False

2. A spirit distilled to 150 proof would contain ______ alcohol by volume.
    A. 150%
    B. 50%
    C. 75%
    D. 15%

3. The maximum temperature to apply to a spirit distillation would be _______ degrees Fahrenheit.
    A. 164
    B. 173
    C. 211
    D. 212

4. Which of the following is *not* one of the characteristics found in most raw spirits?
    A. full-bodied and viscous
    B. high in alcohol, usually 120 to 190 proof
    C. colorless
    D. harsh and fiery

5. Which of the following is *not* a way to finish/soften a spirit?
    A. Multiple distillations
    B. Dilution
    C. Heat exchange
    D. Flavor addition

6. Most amber-colored spirits, such as whiskies, get their color from extended aging in oak barrels.
    A. True
    B. False

7. Any fermentable sugar can be used as the base for producing a distilled spirit.
    A. True
    B. False

Match the following spirits to the family they belong to.

8. Vodka
9. Rum
10. Peppermint schnapps
11. Irish whiskey
12. Tequila
13. Gin
14. Tennessee whiskey
15. Brandy

A. Neutral spirits
B. Grain-based spirits
C. Fruit- and plant-based spirits
D. Liqueurs and cordials

Key Terms

spirit
distillation
pot still
continuous still
column still
Coffey still
neutral spirit
proof
vaporization point
still
cordial
liqueur
congener
grain-based spirit
fruit- and plant-based spirit

CHAPTER 27

Important Styles of Spirits

When the liquor was gone the fun was gone.

—Irish proverb

This chapter discusses the major styles of spirits produced in the world today, organizing them according to the major families of spirits discussed in Chapter 26. These four families include neural spirits, grain-based spirits, fruit- and plant-based spirits, and flavored spirits (liqueurs and cordials). Each family is broken down into its respective styles, and for each style the raw materials, production methods, flavor profiles, and important areas of production are covered.

Neutral Spirits

Neutral spirits are some of the most common spirits used in the bar, and are the base ingredient for a wide variety of cocktails. They are considered neutral because they are produced through such an efficient distillation that very little of the aroma and flavor compounds of the original sugar source remain. They are typically distilled in continuous stills to upwards of 190 proof, effectively concentrating ethanol to such a point that there is only a minimal amount of water and extract in the finished product. In most cases it is extremely difficult, if not impossible, to determine the original sugar source by tasting.

While there are only two major styles of neutral spirits produced today—**vodka** and **gin**—these styles are represented by a multitude of brands. Vodka is the most classic neutral spirit, and if properly made it should show no distinct characteristics other than that of pure ethanol. Gin is classified as a neutral spirit even though it does have a distinct flavor. This is because it is first distilled as a spirit very similarly to vodka, then is flavored with botanical compounds during a subsequent distillation.

VODKA

Sugar source: Any source of sugar that can be fermented may serve as a base for vodka. Typically cereal grains are used, or less commonly, potatoes.

Appearance: Clear

Flavor profile: Vodka should have no distinct flavors or aromas other than pure ethanol. High-quality vodka should be produced in such a way that it is almost flavorless, so that it is perceived as clean and crisp, rather than hot and reminiscent of rubbing alcohol. This lack of distinct flavor makes it an ideal spirit for cocktails and mixed drinks, because it will not mask the mixers used to produce the drink.

Areas of production: Vodka is produced widely around the world, including in Sweden, Poland, Russia, Holland, France, and the United States.

Although the term *vodka* comes from the Polish word *voda* (meaning "little water"), the origins of vodka are much disputed. Sweden, Poland, and Russia all claim to have produced a form of it first. Regardless of where it originated, vodka is one of the most important and top-selling spirits in the world today. Quality vodka is all about one thing—smoothness—and producers go to great lengths to produce the smoothest vodkas possible. They often rely on multiple distillations (in some cases five or more) and charcoal filtration with activated carbon to achieve these results. To compare vodkas to one another, the best way is to taste them at room temperature side by side. At room temperature it is usually easy to determine which vodka is the smoothest because harsh impurities and higher alcohol levels are accentuated.

The original sugar source used to produce vodka plays a very small role in the flavor profile of the finished product. Vodkas are distilled to such a degree that very little of the aroma and flavor compounds (congeners) from the original sugar source will remain. Because of this, most producers will simply use the least expensive sugar source available to them. Far more important to the flavor profile of a particular vodka are the production methods used, as discussed above, and the water used to dilute it to its bottle strength.

While most vodka is distilled to around 190 proof, it is most commonly diluted with water prior to bottling to 80 proof. Since more than half of an average bottle of vodka is water, the water used for dilution is one of the main components that can determine a vodka's character. Often, distillers will tout their pure water supplies, such as water from artesian wells or melted icebergs.

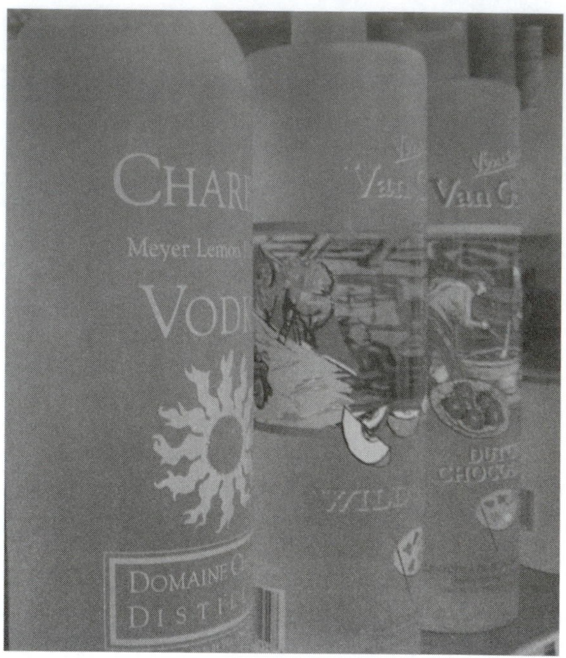

Flavored vodkas are a growing trend in the spirits industry.

Vodka is a dominant spirit in terms of sales today, and one of the growing trends in the spirit industry is to produce flavored vodkas. Flavored vodka begins like all other vodkas: as a neutral spirit. The flavoring agents are added after the vodka has been distilled. A wide range of ingredients are used in flavored vodkas, and new flavors seem to emerge at a constant pace. Common flavors used include berries, citrus fruits, spices and peppers, and vanilla beans.

GIN

Sugar source: Gin is typically grain-based, especially corn or malted barley.

Appearance: Clear (although some unique styles will be golden or amber).

Flavor profile: Gin is a neutral spirit flavored with juniper berries and other herbs, spices, and botanicals. Juniper is the main flavor found in gin and lends it characteristics of evergreen and pine resin.

Areas of production: The most popular style and top-selling brands are produced in England, but gin is also commonly made in the United States and Holland.

Gin originated in Holland, where it was first produced as a medicinal tonic believed to prevent the bubonic plague. Many medicines at the time were made by extracting botanical compounds from plants, herbs, nuts, spices, and seeds using ethanol rather than water, because it is a much better solvent. In the case of **juniper berries,** it was believed that they contained compounds that fought off the plague, so they were commonly used in medications. The name ***gin*** actually comes from the Dutch word *genever,* which means juniper.

While gin was originally considered a medicine in Holland, it was popularized by the English as an alcoholic beverage. The English began widely drinking and making gin in the 1600s. Today, most of the top brands of gin are still produced in England, where they produce a distinct style called **London dry gin.**

Most gin is produced using a two-step process. First, a base neutral spirit is produced using a column or continuous still. This base is then split up into two parts, with the majority being distilled to a high degree a second time. The other portion is actually put into a pot still, to which the juniper berries and other botanicals are added. When distilled in this inefficient manner, not only is alcohol distilled during the process, but so too are aroma and flavor compounds from the juniper berries and other ingredients. These two parts are blended back together, diluted with water, and bottled.

Juniper berries may be the source for the dominant flavor found in gin and the characteristic for which it is best known, but they are by no means the only botanical compounds used in its production. A wide variety of spices, roots, and seeds are used as ingredients in gin, from caraway to iris root. The complexity of top-quality gin is often determined by the variety and quality of these botanical compounds.

Juniper berries provide the main recognizable flavor in gin.

A selection of brands of London dry gin.

Origin of the Gin and Tonic

The main flavoring in tonic water, a common cocktail mixer, is quinine. The original purpose for quinine was as a medication used to ease the symptoms of malaria. How does a malaria drug end up as a major ingredient is several cocktails? A couple of Englishmen got malaria, of course. Working on a construction project in India, several English workers contracted malaria. To make the bitter-tasting medicine they were given more interesting, they added gin, squeezed in some lime, and the gin and tonic was born!

Grain-Based Spirits

Grain-based spirits are believed to be the oldest form of spirits, first produced by Celtic monks in Ireland from a surplus of cereal grains. The monks called them ***uisge beatha,*** meaning "water of life." Today, these often fiery spirits are called whiskies.

Whiskey production begins by fermenting a mixture of water and cereal grains into a crude "beer" called a **mash.** This mash is then distilled, most often in a pot still, anywhere from one to three times depending on the desired style. Whiskies are not distilled to the same degree as neutral spirits, and are finished at roughly 120 to 170 proof. As a result of this inefficient distillation, distinctive flavor and aroma compounds from the mash will appear in the finished spirit. Once the raw spirit for a whiskey has been produced, it will be graded, sorted, and aged. Much of the complexity and color of whiskies are achieved during a period of extended aging in oak barrels that can last up to several years. Oak is used to age spirits for many of the same reasons that it is used for wine, including the fact that it contributes pleasant cedar, spice, vanilla, and toasted characteristics. As whiskies age, they are slowly impacted by oxidation, which causes their harsh flavors to soften as they mellow and mature over time. A whiskey's color is achieved during aging as it leaches color out of the toasted insides of the barrel and as it oxidizes (in the same way that a cut apple changes color over time).

Once the aging period is completed, whiskies are prepared for possible blending, diluted with water to roughly 80 proof, and bottled. The decision to blend or not is an important one, and it depends upon the quality and style of whiskey being produced. Most of the premium whiskies produced in the world are unblended or **straight.** Once a batch has been distilled and aged, it is not mixed with any other batches—it stands alone. Unblended whiskies tend to have intense and unique characteristics and are generally higher in quality and considered superior to blended whiskies, although high-quality examples of blended whiskey do exist. Blended whiskies tend to be more neutral than straight whiskies, because they are purposely blended to be mellow and smooth in flavor.

While there are whiskies produced in several regions around the world, the most important come from Ireland, Scotland, the United States, and Canada. These four countries all make their whiskies differently and produce a variety of styles. They even spell the word differently: Whisky is the common spelling in Scotland and Canada, while it is spelled whiskey in Ireland and the United States.

IRISH WHISKEY

Sugar source: Typically a unique blend of malted and raw barley.

Appearance: Pale gold to deep amber.

Flavor profile: While most of the world's whiskies are distilled only twice, most Irish whiskey is distilled three times and tends to be smoother as a result. Irish whiskey is often marked by flavors and aromas of citrus, earth, and caramel.

Areas of production: Irish whiskey can be produced only in Ireland. The distilleries are scattered across the country.

Legend has it that whiskey and distillation were first brought to Ireland by Saint Patrick. **Irish whiskey** is considered to be the oldest form of grain-based spirit, dating back to Celtic monks producing a rough spirit from an abundance of cereal grains in the 1100s. Since then, Ireland has become a country synonymous with whiskey. Several styles of whiskey are produced in Ireland today, using a variety of grains and blends. The most important and well-known style calls for the use of malted and unmalted barley to produce a mash. Raw barley contains no fermentable sugars, and therefore is simply added for flavor.

Historically, Ireland dominated whiskey production in the world and there used to be a multitude of distilleries located there. With the country's unpredictable economy and centuries of competition with Scottish distillers and conflict with England, time has taken its toll on the Irish whiskey industry. Today, there are only a handful of distilleries left in Ireland, each of which produces a variety of brands. Regardless of the current scope of the country's whiskey production, Irish whiskies can have all of the complexity, flavor, and breed found in the finest whiskies in the world.

Irish whiskey is often quite smooth because most are distilled three times.

AMERICAN WHISKEY

Americans have been producing whiskey since the establishment of the thirteen original colonies. As large groups of Scottish and Irish immigrants began to settle in the areas of Kentucky and Tennessee in the 1700s and 1800s, these areas became the center for whiskey production in the United States. These immigrants brought from their homelands not only a thirst for whiskey, but also the technical knowledge of how to produce it.

The major adaption they had to make was using a different cereal grain to produce these fiery spirits. While malted barley is the base ingredient for whiskies in both Ireland and Scotland, corn was much more prevalent and inexpensive in their new home. Over time, several different styles of whiskey emerged in the United States. The predominant styles of whiskey produced there today are **bourbon, Tennessee whiskey,** and **blended American whiskey.**

America's distilling industry was deeply impacted in the early part of the twentieth century by Prohibition. When it became illegal to manufacture, sell, or produce intoxicating beverages in the United States, many distilleries simply closed their doors forever. Without having to contend with Prohibition, producers in countries like Canada and Scotland were able to ramp up production as they bootlegged their products into the United States. Several American distilleries struggled to make it through that period and took decades to fully recover.

Bootlegger's Legacy

During Prohibition, moonshiners throughout the Southeast produced a steady supply of homemade spirits with interesting names like "white lightning" and "mountain dew." This moonshine had to be delivered to thirsty customers, but to avoid run-ins with the law, many moonshiners began to modify their automobiles to outrun the cops. Pretty soon these moonshiners began racing each other with these fast cars and eventually a new American sport and institution were born: stock car racing and NASCAR.

The only legal loophole that allowed any whiskey distilleries in the United States to operate during Prohibition involved the fact that whiskey could be used as a medicine prescribed by doctors. (Prescriptions, not surprisingly, skyrocketed during this time!) The only hitch was that these whiskies had to be bottled at exactly 100 proof, and they had to be aged and bottled in a government-bonded warehouse. Today, American whiskies can be labeled with terms that are holdovers from that time—"Bonded" or "Bottled in Bond"—if they are bottled at this higher alcoholic strength.

Even with a different base ingredient, most American whiskies are produced in a manner similar to that of Irish or Scottish whiskies. Double distillation in pot stills is the norm, producing spirits of high alcohol content that retain some of the natural flavors from the mash that is used as a base. The only major difference is that American whiskies use a special production method when fermenting this base, called the **sour mash process.**

Bourbon

Sugar source: At least 51 percent corn.
Appearance: Pale gold to deep amber.

The Sour Mash Process

The sour mash process is a means of maintaining consistency in whiskies from batch to batch, and it adds a subtle sour flavor to American whiskies. After a mash of grains and water is fermented, only 75 percent of it is sent to the distillery. The other 25 percent is left to grow sour, similar to a sour dough starter in baking. When the next mash is brewed, it is dumped into the residual sour mash from the last batch. The yeast from the last batch then ferments the sugars from the new batch. This means that every batch of whiskey distilled is made up of at least 25 percent of the prior batch, allowing the distiller to lessen the variance between batches, since each new batch of the spirit contains a major component of the last batch.

Flavor profile: Bourbons maintain much of their fiery character or heat, even with extended aging. They exhibit characteristics of smoke, corn, burnt sugar, and spice.
Areas of production: Bourbon must be produced in the United States, and most is produced in the state of Kentucky.

Bourbon is the most famous style of whiskey produced in the United States, and many would argue that it is the highest-quality example of American whiskey. It is named after Bourbon County, Kentucky, the area where this style of whiskey was first produced and still one of the most important sources for bourbon today. Besides being America's most prevalent and recognizable spirit, bourbon is also one of this country's most regulated beverages.

Unlike the wine laws of the United States, which are purposely loose and allow maximum flexibility, the laws regarding the production of bourbon are very strict. In 1964, several top bourbon producers petitioned the U.S. Congress to pass these regulations in an effort to protect the term "bourbon" from being used for inferior-grade whiskies. As a result, a resolution was passed establishing exactly where bourbon could be produced and how it could be made.

Congress stipulated that bourbon had to be produced in the United States, protecting the name

Bourbon is the most important style of whiskey produced in the United States.

bourbon in a similar fashion to the way the wine regions of Europe have protected their names. No whiskey produced outside of this country can be called bourbon and still be sold here.

The rest of the resolution laid out exactly how bourbon could be produced, establishing strict regulations about the ingredients used to produce it (at least 51 percent corn) and how it was to be aged. By law, bourbon must be aged for at least two years in brand-new American white oak barrels that have been heavily charred on the insides. The aging time must be listed on the label unless the period exceeds four years (which is most commonly the case). Much of bourbon's unique character and flavor results from the strong flavors a new barrel imparts and the heavy char on the inside of the barrel. The trend in bourbon today is **single batch** or **single barrel.** These are individually aged batches of bourbon judged to be of exemplary quality and flavor, and sometimes bottled undiluted at cask strength. Many of these bourbons will receive extended aging well above the minimums, making them softer and more complex.

Tennessee Whiskey

Sugar source: At least 51 percent corn.
Appearance: Pale gold to deep amber.
Flavor profile: Tennessee whiskey is similar in style to bourbon, but tends to be slightly smoother and has a hint of sweetness.
Areas of production: Tennessee whiskey must be produced in the state of Tennessee.

Tennessee whiskey is identical to bourbon, except for two major differences:

1. It must be made in Tennessee
2. It must be filtered through a bed of Tennessee sugar maple charcoal.

The use of sugar maple charcoal is not to be confused with the process of charcoal filtration, which utilizes activated carbon to strip neutral spirits of impurities. Tennessee whiskey distillers instead use hardwood charcoal, which is intended to make the whiskey smoother and to add a touch of sweetness.

Jack Was a Nickname

The iconic figure Jack Daniels was actually born Jasper Daniels. Jack was just his preferred nickname. A rather colorful figure in the history of Tennessee whiskey, Jack owned his first distillery as a young teenager, when his uncle sold it to him for a dollar to avoid tax collectors.

With the exception of one major brand, Tennessee whiskey has mostly fallen out of fashion. Today, there are only two producers of Tennessee whiskey left: Jack Daniels and George Dickel. The reason that this style of whiskey is still considered important is the commercial success of the former, one of the top-selling distilled spirits in both the United States and international markets.

Blended American Whiskey

Sugar source: Several cereal grains are used, especially corn.
Appearance: Pale gold to light amber.
Flavor profile: Blended to be soft and smooth, these spirits can be reminiscent of caramel and cooked cereal grains.
Areas of production: Must be produced in the United States.

While these spirits can be blends of several straight whiskies, that is not very common. By law, blended American whiskies must contain a minimum of only 20 percent straight whiskey. Up to 80 percent can be neutral spirits, which drastically softens this type of whiskey's flavor and power. All too often, the result is a whiskey that lacks much character, and of the three major styles of whiskey produced in the United States, this is considered the lowest in quality.

CANADIAN WHISKY

Sugar source: Corn, malted barley, rye, and wheat are all used in the production of Canadian whisky, although no one sugar source may be responsible for more than 50 percent of the blend.

Appearance: Pale gold to light amber.

Flavor profile: Canadian whiskies are always blended, and are made to be smooth and palatable.

Areas of production: Must be produced in Canada.

Canadian Whisky must be made from a blend of different whiskies made from various cereal grains. Most often the result is a lightly flavored whisky that is simple but approachable. Canadian Whisky must be aged for a minimum of at least two years prior to bottling, and most producers age their products in used oak barrels because they contribute a softer flavor.

Much of the fortune of Canadian distilleries and the popularity of their product is owed to America's Prohibition years. Millions of gallons of Canadian Whisky were smuggled into the United States during that thirteen-year period, as American whiskey distilleries sat idle and Canadian distilleries ramped up production to meet demand. Today, Canadian Whisky still has a presence in the United States because it became so ingrained in American culture during that time.

Canadian Whiskies are blended to be smooth.

SCOTTISH WHISKY

Whisky was brought from Ireland to Scotland centuries ago, and since has been refined and improved to the point that **Scottish whisky** (or simply **scotch**) is considered by many to be the best whisky produced in the world. There are two major styles of Scottish whisky—**blended scotch** and **single-malt scotch**—the former blended for smoothness and the latter noted for its complexity and intense flavors. Regardless of style, what makes scotch unique is the production process used, which imparts smoky and peaty characteristics. **Peat** is the fossilized remains of decomposed plant matter (mostly grasses), which builds up in thick layers on the surface of the soil throughout Scotland. This precursor to coal has been used for ages in Scotland as a fuel source because of its ready availability and because it burns slowly. It is also used in the malting process of barley as the fuel that kilns the barley kernels. During this process, the malted barley kernels are infused with the large quantities of smoke that the peat generates as it burns, giving the resultant whiskies their unique character.

Blended Scotch Whisky

Sugar source: Blended scotch is mostly blended from malted barley–based whiskies, and whiskies made from corn and other cereal grains are added in smaller quantities to soften the finished product.

Appearance: Light gold to deep amber.

Flavor profile: Blended scotch whisky tends to be smoother and have less character than unblended or single-malt scotch whisky. It exhibits flavors and aromas of spice, light smoke, peat, and citrus.

Areas of production: Must be produced in Scotland. There are several distilleries located throughout the country, with the largest concentration near the city of Speyside.

These products are mostly blended to be smooth and easy to drink, often lacking the intense smoke and peat flavors found in most single malts.

Most producers will make a blend of several different component whiskies, most made with malted barley. Lesser percentages of other grain whiskies are then added to lighten up the finished product.

Like single-malt scotch, blended scotch whiskies benefit from extended aging, as they slowly gain complexity over time. They are almost always blended after the component whiskies are barrel aged individually, unique amongst other blended whiskies from around the world. This allows the distiller to fully assess the qualities and characteristics of the components before putting them together into a blend. Most blended scotch is considered inferior to single-malt scotch, because it lacks the same depth and character. There is a growing category of blends that do show these characteristics, however, called **vatted scotch whiskies.** Vatted scotch is a blend, but the only components used are various single-malt scotch whiskies.

Single-Malt Scotch

Sugar source: 100 percent malted barley (hence, "single malt").

Appearance: Light gold to deep amber.

Flavor profile: Single-malt scotch whiskies typically have distinctive and complex flavors of smoke, peat, citrus, honey, and ocean brine. The main flavor components will differ greatly depending on where in Scotland the whisky was produced. As single-malt scotch matures, it softens in character and gains more depth.

Areas of production: Single-malt scotch must be produced in Scotland, and there are various recognized regions throughout the country whose names will appear on the label.

Single-malt scotch is considered by most aficionados to be the best whisky produced in the world. It is very complex and deep in flavor, often exhibiting strong smoky and peaty characteristics. Much care and pride is taken in the crafting of these spirits, which can show astonishing regional differences based on where in Scotland they are produced.

Although single-malt scotch whiskies only need to be aged in oak barrels for a minimum of three years by law, most are aged for much longer periods, from eight to thirty years. This age will be listed on the label, and the longer it has been aged, the smoother and softer the resulting scotch should be. The type of barrels used to age single-malt scotches add much to their flavor and charm. Most other whiskies are aged in brand-new, heavily charred oak barrels. Single-malt scotch is typically aged in used barrels that have previously held a variety of other beverages. The most common barrels used are those that once aged bourbon, Sherry, Madeira, or Port. The type of barrel used contributes to the complexity and character of the scotch it ages, adding flavors reminiscent of the past beverage without contributing the sometimes harsh flavors of a new barrel.

Single-malt scotch can vary greatly depending on where in Scotland it is produced. Differences in peat and water create these unique regional

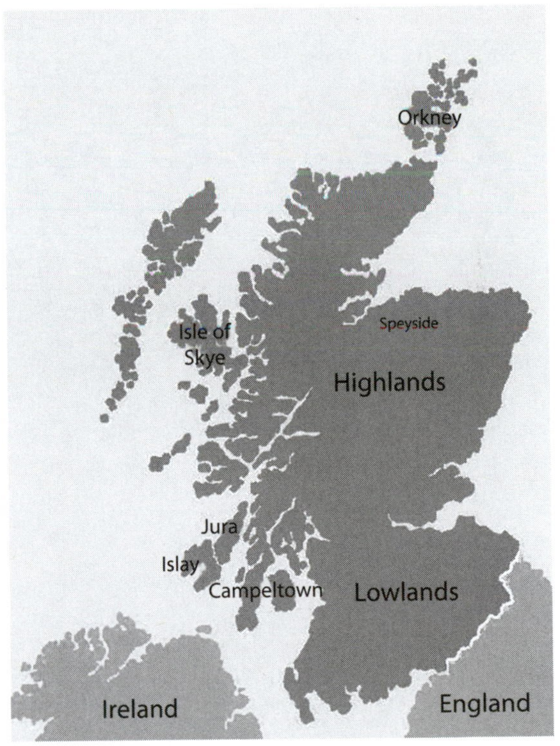

Scotland and its single-malt scotch districts.

characteristics, and the specific region a single malt comes from is almost always listed on the label. The most important districts of production are the **Highlands**, the **Lowlands**, **Islay**, and **Campeltown**, as well as a selection of islands located off the coast of Scotland.

A selection of single-malt scotches.

Regional Differences Among Single-Malt Scotches

The Highlands

Highland malts are the most popular and widely produced style of single-malt scotch. The Highland region covers approximately the northern two-thirds of Scotland and is named for the numerous hills and mountains found throughout. Highland scotch is considered to be light and refined, slightly smoky with a touch of spice, and full-flavored. Most distilleries in the region are found in the unofficial capital of Scottish whisky, the coastal city of Speyside.

The Lowlands

Most whiskies made in the Lowland regions of Scotland are used to make blended scotch. The single-malt scotch from this area is typically light-bodied and mellow, with hints of smoke and peat.

Islay

Islay whisky comes from an island of the same name, and is considered the strongest-flavored and most distinctive of all single-malt scotches. It has very sharp flavors and aromas of smoke, peat, iodine, and briny seaweed, which comes from the salty air from the North Sea to which the barrels of aging whisky are exposed.

Campeltown

Besides the various individual islands that produce single malts, Campeltown is one of the smallest of Scotland's producing regions. It is located on a peninsula that extends from the Lowland region on the country's west coast. The single malts from there have a rich body and distinct peatiness.

The Islands

There are several islands off the coast of Scotland that produce very distinct styles of single-malt scotch. Most of these tend to be quite aggressive, with strong flavors of peat and smoke. The best-known islands for single-malt production are Jura, the Isle of Skye, and Orkney.

Fruit- and Plant-Based Spirits

As distillation spread throughout Europe and on to the rest of the world, people began distilling several different indigenous sugar sources into spirits. Cereal grains were the first major ingredient used to produce spirits, but several new spirits later emerged that were produced from fruit juice or from the sap of certain sugar-bearing plants. These new spirits showcased unique flavors contributed by the sometimes exotic plant materials being fermented and distilled. There are three major styles of spirits produced from fruits and sugar-bearing plants:

1. Sugarcane-based spirits called rums
2. Agave-based spirits such as tequila and mezcal

3. Fruit-based spirits called brandies, including cognac, armagnac, California brandy, grappa or marc, slivovitz, and calvados.

RUM

Sugar source: Mostly molasses, although sometimes pure sugarcane sap is used.

Appearance: Clear to deep amber.

Flavor profile: Rum exhibits sugar and caramel flavors as well as a slight sweetness. Young rums tend to be fairly simple, but with age, rum can achieve serious depth and complexity, reminiscent of caramelized sugar, dried fruits, and spices.

Areas of production: Rum is produced in most sugarcane-producing regions around the world, including the Caribbean, Central and South America, Australia, French Polynesia, and even the U.S. states of Hawaii and Louisiana.

Rum was first produced during colonial times in the Caribbean, which at that time was the center for sugar production in the world. To refine the sap of the sugarcane plant used to make all this sugar, it had to be boiled to create sugar crystals. This also created a byproduct: a thick, dark, slightly sweet syrup called molasses. Considered a waste product, molasses was either discarded or used as animal feed, making sugar production quite inefficient. Not wanting to waste anything that still contained so much sugar, British colonists on the island of Barbados decided to mix molasses with water, ferment it, and then distill it. Rum was born. Throughout the evolution of rum, it has been known by many other names, including rhum, rumbullion, and even kill-devil. The drink of pirates and sailors, rum eventually became one of the most important drinks in the American colonies. Rum is still produced today from molasses (and, to a much lesser degree, from pure sugarcane sap).

Rum is produced in almost every country that grows sugarcane, a plant that needs a tropical climate to thrive. Puerto Rico is the number one producer of rum in the world, but it is also produced in large quantities throughout the rest of the Caribbean, Latin America, and even in Hawaii and Louisiana. The island of Jamaica in particular is well known for the quality and variety of its rums. Most rum can be placed into one of two categories: **light rum** and **dark rum.** Light rum is typically produced in a continuous still, similar to vodka and other neutral spirits. This is done to remove impurities and produce a style of rum that is light in color and flavor. These rums are sometimes aged in oak to pick up color and some complexity, although caramel can also be added to darken the spirit. These rums are best suited for blending into cocktails and mixed drinks.

Dark rums tend to have much more character than light rums because they are produced in a pot still. This inefficient means of distillation results in a raw spirit of lesser alcohol content, but with much more character and flavor. Dark rums are often aged for several years before being released, gaining a complexity of flavors and aromas. This style of rum is far superior in quality to light rum, and can be sipped on its own like a fine brandy or whiskey.

In recent years, **flavored** and **spiced rums** have been gaining in popularity. Many of them are used like liqueurs in a variety of cocktails, and a few are meant to be consumed on their own. These spirits can be flavored with anything from coconut to vanilla and cinnamon.

Rum comes in several different styles.

Nelson's Blood

One of the most interesting nicknames for rum is "Nelson's blood." The reference is to Admiral Horatio Nelson, one of the greatest heroes of the English navy, who led the English to victory over Napoleon's navy. Nelson died in battle in 1805, and his body was taken back to England for a state funeral. To preserve his body while at sea, his remains were placed in a barrel that was filled with rum. Upon arriving in England, the barrel was opened, but surprisingly, the rum was all gone. Apparently hard up for something to drink, the ship's crew had secretly drilled a hole in the barrel and drained it of the rum inside.

A blue agave plant used in the production of tequila.

TEQUILA

Sugar source: The sap of the blue agave, a succulent plant native to central and northern Mexico as well as the southwestern United States.

Appearance: Clear to deep amber.

Flavor profile: Tequila tends to be very floral, with characteristics of black pepper, light smoke, citrus, and what can only be described as agave flavors.

Areas of production: Tequila can be produced only from blue agave grown in officially recognized regions near the city of Tequila in central Mexico.

When Spanish conquistadores arrived in Mexico in the 1500s, they were introduced to an Aztec drink called *pulque*. This was a milk-colored beverage produced by fermenting a mixture of water and the sap of an agave plant. Because the drink was not to their liking, the Spanish brought stills to the region and began distilling *pulque* into a spirit called mezcal wine.

The very best of these spirits were produced from blue agave plants grown on the slopes of a dormant volcano that stood over the city of Tequila in the west-central state of Jalisco. Blue agave–based spirits from this region were soon referred to by the name of that city. Today, by Mexican law **tequila** must be produced from plants grown in the area surrounding the city of Tequila.

Contrary to popular belief, the blue agave is not a cactus but rather a succulent related to the aloe plant. It can grow quite large, its core weighing up to 200 pounds when fully matured. When used for tequila production, the spikes of the plant are removed to reveal this core or heart called the *piña* (the Spanish word for pineapple, which the core resembles). The *piña* is then baked and crushed, and the sap is mixed with water. This base is then fermented into *pulque*. In turn, the *pulque* is double distilled in a pot still, retaining much of its original character.

Tequila can be divided into two main categories of differing quality: **mixto** and **100 percent blue agave.** Mixto tequila is made from a blend of at least 51 percent blue agave, with the remaining sugar typically made up of molasses. Since the blue agave is diluted and blended, the result is a lower grade of tequila. The 100 percent blue agave tequila is more expensive and is not as popular as mixto in terms of sales, but it tends to be much better in terms of quality and purity of flavor.

100 percent blue agave tequila has surged in popularity (and price) in recent years.

To tell the difference between these two styles, look for the term "100% Blue Agave" or "100% de Agave" on the label. If you can find that term, then it is a tequila made from pure blue agave. If that term is not on a label, the tequila is a mixto.

Both styles of tequila can also be categorized by age. There are four different categories, depending on how long the spirit has been aged in oak barrels. In order from youngest to oldest, these official age grades are **blanco/white/silver, oro/gold, reposado,** and **añejo.** Due to the warm climate, aging is quite rapid for tequila. As it ages, it will become more complex, darken in color, and soften in harshness.

Although similar to tequila, **mezcal** is definitely different. Mezcal is produced using a different agave plant that is roasted before distillation, giving it a distinctly smoky characteristic. It is usually unaged and only goes through a single distillation, making it much more rustic than tequila. Mezcal is made throughout Mexico, especially in the southern state of Oaxaca.

Age Categories of Tequila

AGE CATEGORY	AGING REGIME
Blanco/White or Plato/Silver	Receive little if any aging.
Oro/Gold	Receive little if any aging (mostly darkened with caramel).
Reposado	Spanish for "rested"; aged from two months to a year in oak barrels.
Añejo	Spanish for "aged"; aged for at least one year in oak barrels.

What's the Deal with the Worm?

Mezcal is often bottled with a unique guest inside the bottle: the worm. In reality, it is not a worm, but a moth caterpillar that lives on the agaves used to produce mezcal. Despite many myths, consuming this "worm" will not lead to psychotropic effects or sexual prowess, nor is it an indicator of a mezcal's quality. It is simply a marketing gimmick that caught on.

BRANDY

Brandy is simply distilled wine. The term brandy comes from the Dutch word *brandewijn* or "burnt wine." This name was given to brandy because the wine was burnt or cooked during distillation. Like wine, brandy can be produced from the juice of any fruit. Several different fruits are used around the world to produce brandies, including apples, cherries, strawberries, plums, and pears. That said, the most common fruit source for brandy is the wine grape, and many of the world's top wine regions are also centers for the production of brandy.

Most brandies depend heavily on aging in oak barrels to soften the unusually harsh flavors created during distillation. As a result, most aged brandies exhibit a pleasant warmth as well as flavors associated with age, such as vanilla and spice. The most important style of brandy available is **cognac,** although other high-quality examples of brandy include armagnac, California brandy, grappa or marc, slivovitz, and calvados.

Cognac

Sugar source: Mostly Ugni Blanc grapes (a variety of wine grape).

Appearance: Light gold to deep amber.

Flavor profile: Although fiery when young, as cognacs age they become extremely smooth, soft, and delicate, with citrus, honey, fruit, smoky, earthy, vanilla, spice, and oak flavors lending complexity.

Areas of production: Cognac may be produced only from grapes grown in the Cognac region of France.

Located on the Atlantic coast of France just north of Bordeaux is a region called Cognac. Like its neighbor to the south, Cognac is a wine region, although its wines have historically had a terrible reputation. These wines were always lean and low in alcohol compared with the wines of Bordeaux. This makes for an inferior wine, but is great as a base for brandy.

Cognac is the name for brandy that is produced under strict regulations in the region of Cognac. These brandies are the most famous style produced in the world, and are also generally considered the pinnacle of quality. To produce these spirits, a wine from the lowly Ugni Blanc grape is double distilled into what is known as an *eau-de-vie* and aged in French oak barrels.

Common Age Categories for Cognac

V.S. (Very Special) or * (Three Star)**

The youngest *eau-de-vie* in the blend must be aged at least 2½ years, although the average age of the *eaux-de-vie* used is around 8–10 years.

V.S.O.P. (Very Superior Old Pale) or V.O. (Very Old)

The youngest *eau-de-vie* in the blend must be aged at least 4½ years, although the average age of the *eaux-de-vie* used is 12–15 years.

X.O. (Extra Old) or Napoleon

The youngest *eau-de-vie* in the blend must be aged at least 6½ years, but the average age of the *eaux-de-vie* used is more than 20 years, and up to 60 years. This is typically the oldest and finest cognac a producer makes.

These brandies can be aged for very long periods of time, picking up complexities and mellowing slowly. Differently aged *eaux-de-vie* are blended together before bottling, as the producer attempts to achieve a consistent style over time. Based on how old these component *eaux-de-vie* are, Cognac is divided into different age categories.

The region of Cognac can be divided into six distinct subregions, each of which produces brandies of differing characteristics and styles. If a cognac comes from grapes grown in only one of the subregions, that subregion's name will appear on the label. The two most important subregions, producing what is considered to be the highest quality cognac, are **Grande Champagne** and **Petite Champagne** (these have absolutely nothing to do with the sparkling wine of the same name). If cognac is made from a blend of components from both regions, it can be labeled **Fine Champagne,** as long as a majority of grapes from Grande Champagne are used.

Cognac is considered the top brandy produced in the world.

Other Important Brandies

Armagnac **Armagnac** is the name of a top-quality French brandy that is produced in the southwestern region of Armagnac, along the Spanish border.

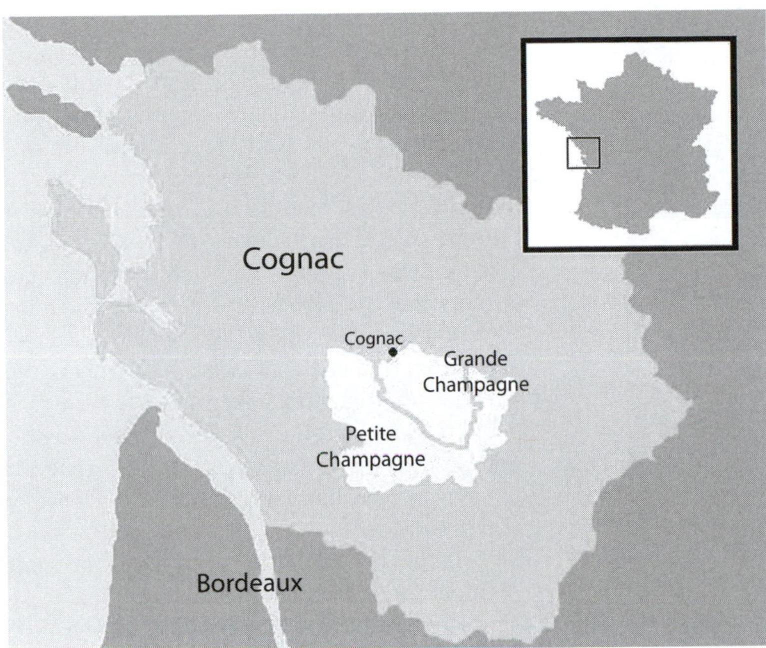

Cognac and its important subregions.

Although it is similar to cognac in many ways, there are some striking differences between the two. Both are distilled from wines made with the same grape variety (Ugni Blanc), and both are the recipients of extended oak aging. That, however, is where the similarities end. Most armagnac is bottled from a single vintage, while cognac is made from a blend of different vintages. There is a rustic character found in armagnac that is not present in cognac, along with heartier flavors of oak and spice. This is a result of the different production methods used. Cognacs are double distilled, while armagnac is only distilled once. While white oak barrels are used to age cognac, armagnac is aged in barrels made from black oak—a species of oak that imparts stronger, more distinct flavors. Regardless, the finest armagnacs can be ranked at the same level of quality as top cognacs.

California Brandy Although much of the brandy produced in California is inexpensive and lacking in character, there are some small distillers producing high-quality, small-batch spirits from wine. **Alambic brandy** is the name often used to describe premium grape spirits. The term alambic refers to the specific type of pot still traditionally used to produce both cognac and armagnac. Alambic brandies in California are typically produced using the traditional methods of French distillers, and are aged for extended periods in French oak barrels.

Grappa or Marc Tracing its roots back to its peasant beginnings, **grappa** is a unique type of brandy distilled from **pomace** in Italy (the French name is **marc**). Pomace is the name for the leftovers from a (usually red) wine fermentation, made up of the skins, seeds, and pulp of the grapes that have been pressed away from the wine. A residual amount of wine will always be found in pomace, which can be mixed with water and distilled into a brandy. Because most grappa is not aged it has a clear appearance, and can tend to be fiery and rustic. The best can be refined and perfumed with alcoholic-fruity flavors.

Calvados is a style of French brandy made from apples.

Slivovitz The most popular style of brandy produced in Eastern Europe is **slivovitz.** Produced from plums rather than grapes, it often retains some fruity characteristics when distilled. Most slivovitz is bottled unaged, and is clear in color with strong alcohol aromas.

Calvados **Calvados** is a brandy produced in the Normandy region of northern France from the juice of apples. These brandies do not take as long as grape-based brandies to age, and exhibit complex and distinct apple characteristics. They are generally considered to be the top-quality style of brandy made from a fruit other than grapes.

Liqueurs and Cordials

Since the invention of distillation, producers have been using a wide variety of sweeteners and flavoring agents to mask the harsh flavors of distilled base spirits. Today, many spirits have flavors (and usually sugar) added to create a unique spirit referred to as a liqueur or cordial. Although most liqueurs and cordials are neutral spirits that have been flavored, any type of base spirit can be used, from scotch whisky to cognac. Almost every flavor imaginable has been used to produce these spirits, from garlic and artichokes to honey and pasteurized cream, although the most common flavoring agents are fruits, herbs, spices, nuts, and seeds. These flavored spirits were originally used as either **aperitifs,** intended to whet the appetite before a meal, or **digestifs,** taken after a meal to aid in digestion. Although many are still produced for this purpose, new styles of cordials have been created for mixing into cocktails, not meant to be consumed on their own.

Liqueurs and cordials can be divided into two distinct categories: generic and proprietary. Generic liqueurs are flavored spirits that can be produced by several different companies—e.g., triple sec or peppermint schnapps. Brand-name liqueurs, which can only be produced by one company, are considered proprietary—e.g., Grand Marnier or Kahlúa. The recipes for most proprietary liqueurs are strictly guarded so that imitations cannot be produced.

An amazing number of different liqueurs and cordials are produced around the world.

Common Liqueurs and Cordials

Below is a table showing some of the most common liqueurs and cordials, what their base spirit is, what they are flavored with, and where they are produced.

SPIRIT	ORIGIN	BASE	MAIN FLAVORING
Amaretto di Saronno	Italy	Neutral spirit	Almonds
Anisette*	France	Neutral spirit	Star anise/black licorice
Bailey's Irish Cream	Ireland	Irish whiskey	Vanilla and pasteurized cream
Benedictine	France	Brandy	Various herbs
Chambord	France	Neutral spirit	Wild black raspberries
Chartreuse	France	Neutral spirit	Various herbal extracts
Cointreau	France	Neutral spirit	Orange peel
Drambuie	Scotland	Scottish whisky	Honey and herbs
Frangelico	Italy	Neutral spirit	Hazelnuts
Galliano	Italy	Neutral spirit	Vanilla, anise, and herbs
Grand Marnier	France	Cognac	Orange peel
Jägermeister	Germany	Neutral spirit	Various herbs, spices, and roots
Kahlúa	Mexico	Neutral spirit	Coffee
Midori	Japan	Neutral spirit	Melon
Ouzo*	Greece	Neutral spirit	Anise
Sambuca*	Italy	Neutral spirit	Anise
Southern Comfort	United States	Bourbon	Peaches
Triple Sec*	Various countries	Neutral spirit	Orange peel
Tuaca	Italy	Neutral spirit	Citrus and vanilla

*Generic liqueurs that can be produced by multiple distillers

FLAVORING SPIRITS

There are four main processes used to flavor spirits:

Infusion: This is the process of steeping the flavoring agent in the water used to dilute the distilled spirit. It is used for strong flavors that are easy to extract, like fruit juices and most herbs.

Maceration: This is the process of steeping the flavoring agent in the distilled spirit before water is added to dilute it. It is used to extract subtle flavors from flavoring agents such as citrus peels and some spices.

Percolation: This is the process of extracting flavor and aroma by repeatedly passing the heated spirit over a basket containing the flavoring agents, similar to making coffee in a percolator. Percolation is used for flavoring agents like nuts, spices, and roots.

Distillation: Some spirits are flavored through the process of distillation. In essence, the spirit goes through a secondary distillation along with the flavoring agents. This type of distillation is usually conducted in an inefficient pot still, so that the essential oils, flavor compounds, and aromatics are carried through to the resultant finished spirit. This is often done for flavoring agents that need extensive extraction, such as seeds.

Summary

There are a wide variety of spirit styles produced around the world, each with its own unique ingredients, production techniques, and flavor profiles. The most important neutral spirits are vodka and gin—both the result of intense distillation, which strips them of any flavor from their original sugar source. Grain-based spirits are called whiskies, and top examples are produced in Ireland, the United States, Canada, and Scotland, which is the home of single-malt scotch, the highest-quality whisky produced in the world. Unique among spirits are those made from fruit and plants, such as the rums and tequilas that emerged in the western hemisphere and the top brandies of Europe. The final family of spirits, liqueurs and cordials, are base spirits that can be flavored with unlimited variety.

Review Questions

1. Vodka and tequila are both considered neutral spirits.
   A. True
   B. False

2. The main flavoring compound of gin is:
   A. pine needles
   B. corn, its sugar source
   C. vermouth
   D. juniper berries

3. The most popular style of gin is made in England.
   A. True
   B. False

4. The oldest/original style of whiskey comes from:
   A. Scotland
   B. Ireland
   C. Bourbon County, Kentucky
   D. France

5. The sour mash process is used to make American whiskies with the main purpose of:
   A. maintaining consistency
   B. adding a sour taste to a spirit
   C. masking its harsh flavors
   D. diluting the finished spirit

6. The main sugar source used to make both bourbon and Tennessee whiskey is:
   A. malted barley
   B. Gummi Bears
   C. corn
   D. grapes

7. The main sugar source used to make single-malt scotch whisky is:
   A. malted barley
   B. sugar packets
   C. corn
   D. grapes

8. The best way to judge the quality of a particular vodka is by looking at the raw ingredients/sugar source from which it is produced.
   A. True
   B. False

9. Which style of whisky/ey is considered by most experts to be the greatest style produced?
   A. Bourbon
   B. Single-malt scotch
   C. Irish whiskey
   D. Canadian whisky

10. The region of the world that produces the most rum is:
    A. Jamaica
    B. Hawaii
    C. Puerto Rico
    D. New York State

11. Rum can be produced with either sugar cane syrup or molasses.
    A. True
    B. False

12. Which of the following is not a major American whiskey?
    A. Bourbon
    B. Tennessee whiskey
    C. Kentucky whiskey
    D. Blended American whiskey

13. The main sugar source used to make tequila is the sap of the blue agave, a plant native to central and northern Mexico, as well as the U.S. Southwest.
    A. True
    B. False

14. Which of the following terms describes the oldest tequila?
    A. Silver/Blanco
    B. Reposada
    C. Añejo
    D. Mixto

15. Which of the following terms describes the oldest cognac?
    A. V.S.
    B. V.O.C.
    C. X.O.
    D. V.S.O.P.

16. The main sugar source for cognac is malted barley.
    A. True
    B. False

17. Cognac is a brandy that is made in the region of Cognac, France.
    A. True
    B. False

Key Terms

vodka
gin
juniper berries
London dry gin
uisge beatha
mash
straight
Irish whiskey
bourbon
Tennessee whiskey
blended American whiskey
sour mash process
single batch
single barrel
Canadian whisky
Scottish whisky
scotch
blended scotch
single-malt scotch
peat
vatted scotch whisky
Highland
Lowland
Islay
Campeltown
rum
light rum
dark rum
flavored rum
spiced rum
tequila
mixto
100% blue agave
blanco/white/silver
oro/gold
reposado
añejo
mezcal
brandy
cognac
V.S.
Three Star
V.S.O.P.
V.O.
X.O.
Napoleon
Grande Champagne
Petite Champagne
Fine Champagne
armagnac
alambic brandy
grappa
pomace
marc
slivovitz
calvados
aperitif
digestif
infusion
maceration
percolation

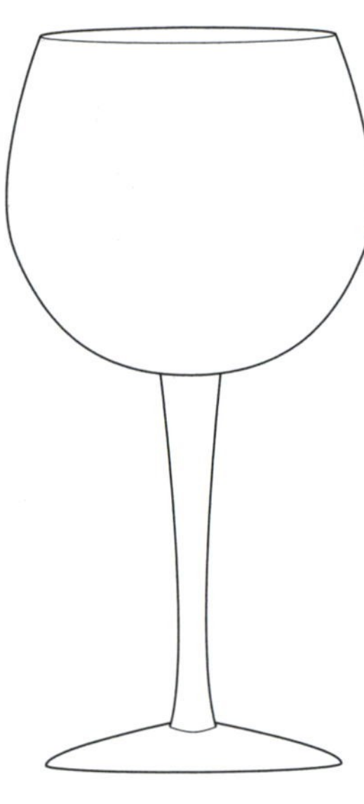

CHAPTER 28

Beverage Service and Storage

Wine is a living liquid containing no preservatives. Its life cycle comprises youth, maturity, old age, and death. When not treated with reasonable respect it will sicken and die.

—**JULIA CHILD,** chef and author

Proper service, storage, and handling seem like a forgotten art in many parts of the wine, beverage, and service industry today. Fortunately, it only takes following a few simple instructions and using a little common sense to master these procedures. In this chapter, we discuss the proper tableside service of table wines, sparkling wines, beers, and spirits. The decanting of wine, both young and vintage, is also covered, along with the long-term and short-term storage and handling of wine and other beverages.

Proper Service of Table Wines

Proper **wine service** should be simple and seamless, with a lack of fanfare and flourishes. A good sommelier or server will be able to interact with the guests while opening and serving a bottle—whether that be discussing the wine itself, menu selections, or other topics of conversation. Snobbery or arrogance should be avoided completely, as this can be insulting to guests and only exposes the server's own ignorance. Remember that wine and wine knowledge are meant to be enjoyed, appreciated, and shared. The actual details involved in proper wine service, including the steps and level of formality, will differ greatly from establishment to establishment. The following instructions serve as a basic guide to wine service, and are easily adaptable to different styles and management preferences.

WINE SELECTION AND SERVICE PREPARATION

Many guests need help selecting wine from a wine list. This may come in several different forms, including assistance with pairing particular foods with the right wine, information about vintages, producers, grapes, or regions, or simply assistance navigating the list. It is the responsibility of the sommelier or server to know the restaurant's wine list well and to be able to answer questions about the wines found on it and offer advice.

The host should be whichever guest actually orders the wine. Many of the subsequent steps of wine service revolve around this host. If you are serving a large party, it is wise to advise the host that normal wine bottles hold only approximately four to five full glasses. Suggest a second bottle or warn the host that his or her guests will not receive full glasses.

Once selected by the host, the wine should be located and secured and the table prepared for wine service. If wineglasses are not part of the normal table setting, the appropriate number and type should be brought to the table. Wineglasses should be clean, polished, and free of any residue. Glasses should be taken to a table on a tray and always handled by their stems. Typical placement of wine glasses is on the right-hand side of the guest's table setting, above the silverware.

If your establishment uses ice buckets to hold white wines and sparkling wines at cold temperatures, these should be filled about two-thirds full with ice and water and then brought to the table. Ice buckets should be accessible to the guest and within reach. A serviette or heavy linen napkin should be hung from the ice bucket so that water can be wiped from the bottle before the wine is served. Once dirty or excessively wet, this serviette should be replaced.

If a coaster will be used for a partial bottle to be set on the table, it should initially be placed above the host's table setting. A small saucer or plate should also be placed to the right of the host's setting so that the cork can be placed on it once removed. This will keep the bottle and the cork from staining the table or tablecloth.

PRESENTING THE WINE BOTTLE

When everything at the table is set, the bottle of wine and all equipment necessary to open and serve it should be retrieved. To successfully serve wine, a sommelier or server will need at minimum a **wine key** and a serviette. The most common type of wine key used is the **waiter's friend** style, which can easily open a bottle held in the server's hand. This style has a knife that can be opened and closed, a worm or screw that folds up against the body of the wine key, and a lever on a hinge to pull the cork from the bottle.

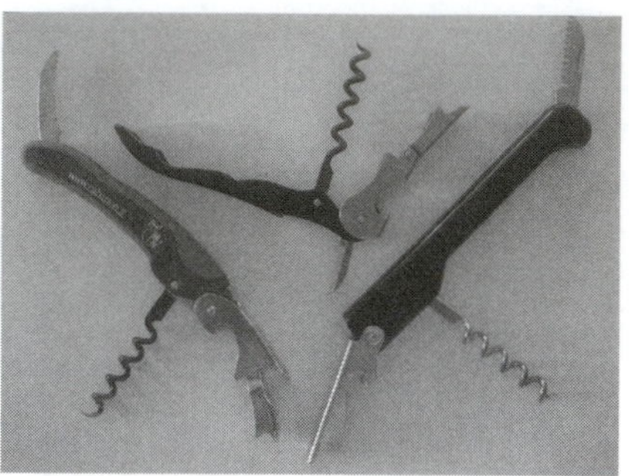

A selection of waiter's friend–style wine keys.

Before approaching the table, the wine's label should be reviewed to ensure that it is what the host ordered and the bottle is checked for proper temperature. Serving a wine at the wrong temperature can have a dramatic impact on its qualities and flavors. Wines should always be stored at their proper serving temperatures so that they can quickly be brought to the table and served.

Once the wine and its temperature have been confirmed, hold the bottle of wine by the neck with your non-dominant hand, with the main label facing directly forward. Your hand or fingers should not obscure or cover the label. Avoid excessive shaking or movement of the wine bottle so as not to disturb any sediment that might be in it. The wine key should be placed in a pocket of your apron or pants that is easy to get to with your free hand. Draped over your forearm above the hand holding the bottle, your serviette will be easy to retrieve and use during the different steps of wine service.

Proper Service Temperatures for Table Wines

Sweet white wines	45° to 50°F
Dry white wines and rosés	50° to 60°F
Lighter-bodied red wines	55° to 65°F
Fuller-bodied red wines	60° to 65°F

Approach the table and, whenever possible, position yourself on the right side of the host. The wine should always be presented to the host with the label clearly visible. At this time, you should recite the important information about the wine to the host, including the vintage, name of the producer, and grape variety or appellation by which the wine is labeled. Once the wine is acknowledged as being what the host ordered, you may begin opening the bottle. If there is a discrepancy, the bottle should be replaced or opened, depending upon the host's wishes.

REMOVING THE CAPSULE AND CORK

The first step in opening a wine bottle is to cut the top of the **capsule** off, revealing the cork. The capsule is the thin piece of plastic or metal that is wrapped around the top of the bottle. It is both decorative and functional, as it holds the cork in the bottle and protects it from exposure. Every effort should be made to maintain the integrity of the capsule.

Using the knife of the wine key, the top of the capsule should be cleanly cut below the raised lip near the mouth of the bottle. This lip can be used as a guide for making straight cuts. It is important to move the knife around the neck, never twisting or shaking the bottle. Resist the temptation to use a pull tab if there is one on the neck of the bottle, as it is considered proper to cut the capsule.

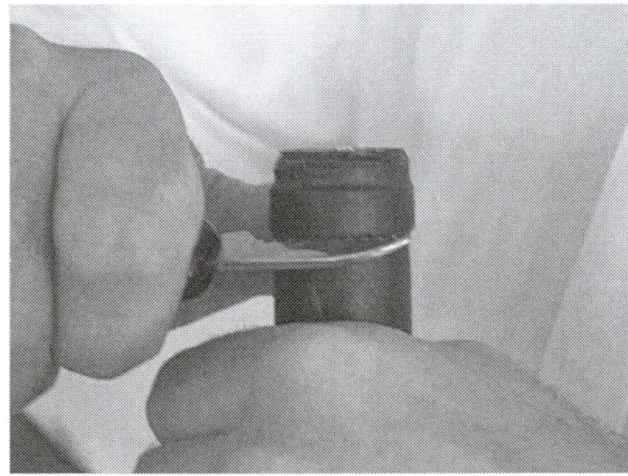

Where to cut the capsule.

Cutting the capsule can be accomplished using two cuts. First, reach around the front of the bottle's neck and place the knife at an angle securely against the raised lip. Bring the blade toward your body, holding it securely against the lip, to make the first cut. Pull the blade away from the bottle, flip the wine key in your hand, and reach around the back of the neck, with your thumb controlling the blade, to the point at which the first cut was started. Bring the blade around the neck in the opposite direction of the first cut until the two cuts meet. Next use the blade to pry the top of the capsule slowly from the neck of the bottle until it pulls off cleanly. This piece of the capsule is trash and should be placed in your pants pocket or the pocket of an apron so it can be discarded.

At this point, the mouth of the bottle and the top of the cork should be exposed. Your wine key should temporarily be put away and you should

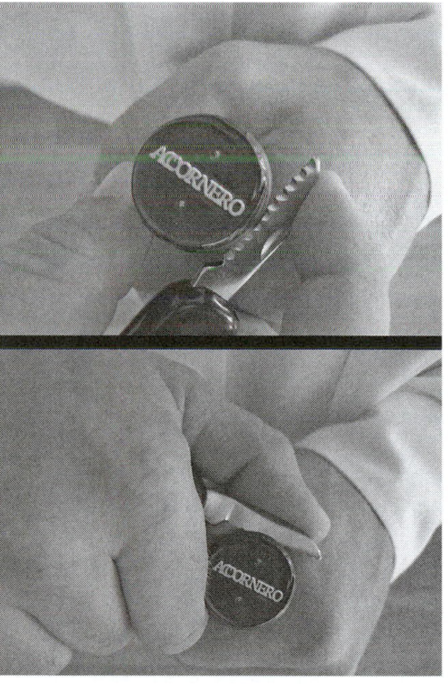

Properly cutting the capsule can be accomplished using two cuts. Note how the server's index finger is on the back of the knife for the first cut, and his thumb is on it for the second cut.

inspect the condition of the mouth and cork. Many times there will be sediment or residue around the mouth of the bottle or on top of the cork, and this should be removed with your serviette. Be careful throughout this process not to move or agitate the bottle.

Next, retrieve your wine key, open the lever, and place the worm or screw in a perpendicular position to the body of the wine key. This is often best accomplished by placing the body of the wine key in the fingers of the hand holding the bottle, then using your dominant hand to open things up. If a wine key is well broken in, you might be able to open it with just one hand, but make sure this can be done using little effort and seamless motions. Once the wine key has been opened, place it in your dominant hand.

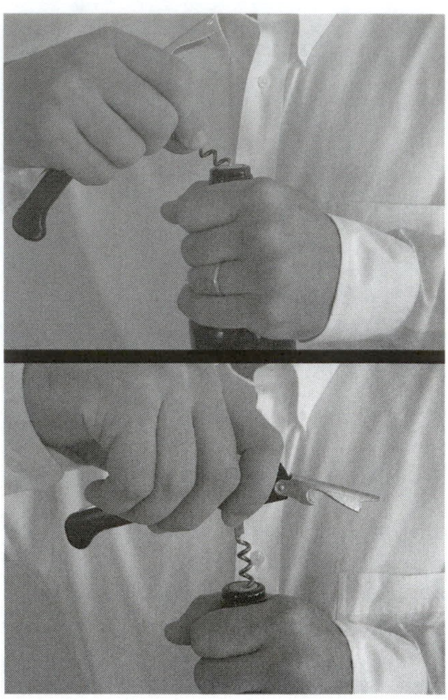

Screwing the worm into the cork. Note how the worm of the wine key starts at an angle, but is upright once it has been screwed into the cork.

When first piercing the cork near its center with the tip of the worm, the wine key should be at an angle so that the tip goes directly into the cork. Once the cork has been pierced, you should slowly twist the body of the wine key in as you bring the worm back into an upright position. You should screw the spiral of the worm into the cork completely before attempting to remove it. If you do not screw it in all the way, you risk breaking the cork, and if the worm goes in too deeply, you can break pieces of the cork off into the wine.

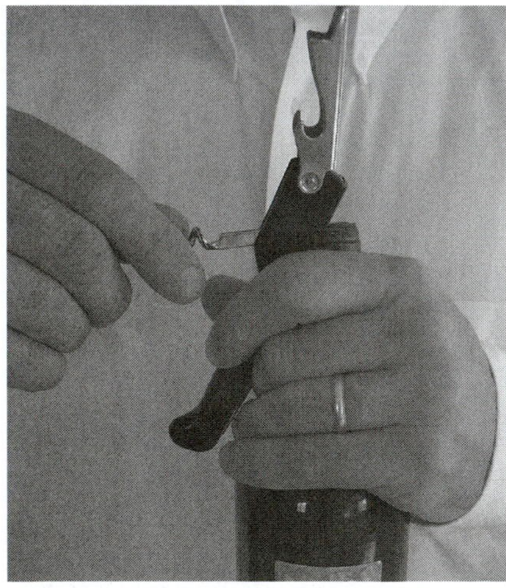

Opening the lever and screw of the wine key while holding it in the nondominant hand.

The wine key should then be tilted down by the end opposite the lever, so it may be placed on the rim of the bottle's mouth. Ensure that the lever is securely positioned against the rim, and holding it tight with the thumb or forefinger of your bottle hand, slowly tilt the body of the wine key back up, letting leverage do the work, and pull the cork almost completely out of the bottle. Remove your hand from the wine key and grasp the cork itself, gently rocking it completely out of the bottle so that no wine is spilled and no sound is made; a pop heard when the cork is finally removed is considered bad form.

For corks that are difficult to remove, it is acceptable to gently place the bottle on the table or some other flat surface for extra leverage. If you simply lack hand strength to remove most corks, a

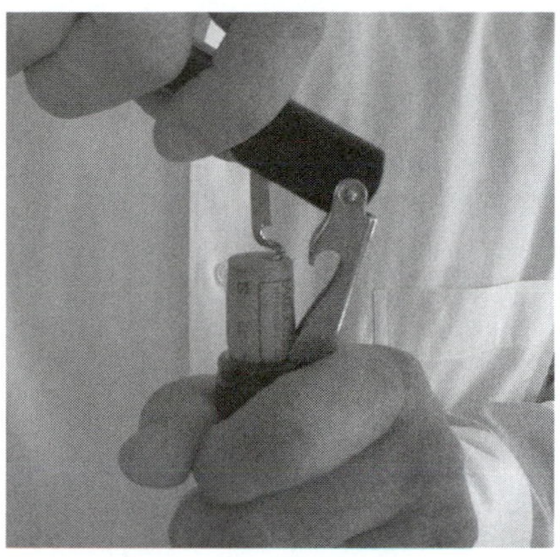

Removing the cork. Be sure to let the lever do most of the work—that is what it was designed for!

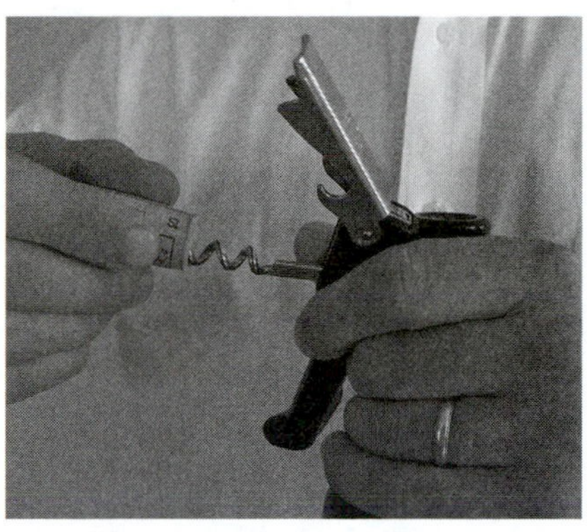

Remove the cork from the worm of the wine key before presenting it to the host.

double-hinged wine key will give you much better leverage and will make most bottles easy to open. Extra care should be taken with older wines, because the cork can be quite fragile and can easily break. In any situation when a cork does break, an attempt should be made to carefully remove the remaining section from the neck of the bottle.

Once the cork has been successfully removed from the bottle, it should slowly be removed from the worm of the wine key and presented to the host. If a saucer is used for this purpose, the cork should be carefully placed on the saucer; otherwise, place it on the table to the right of the host. Traditionally, corks were presented so that the guest could verify that the cork matched the bottle and was in good condition. Although commonly practiced, smelling the cork will not tell you much about the wine. A quick glance at it will often suffice, since the host is about to be served a sample of the wine anyway.

The process of opening a bottle sealed with a Stelvin closure or screw cap is far quicker and easier. After the bottle is presented to the host, the Stelvin should be twisted smoothly off the bottle and the cap placed in a pocket for disposal. Once opened, bottles sealed with Stelvins and corks will both be poured in the same manner.

SERVING THE WINE

After you have put your wine key away and presented the cork to the host, the wine is ready to serve. Make sure that there are no pieces of cork or sediment in the opening of the bottle, and if there are, simply use your serviette to wipe them out so they do not end up in the guest's glass. Gently transfer the bottle to your dominant hand, firmly grasping the body of the bottle with your palm covering the

If you are holding the bottle correctly when pouring—with your palm on the back label—the front label should always be facing the guest you are serving.

Properly pouring wine for a guest.

back label. In this way, all the guests will be able to see the front label when you pour their wine. The host is always served first, but he or she should be poured only a one- to two-ounce sample, not a full glass.

Whenever you pour wine into glasses, the mouth of the bottle should be held roughly two inches above the top of the glass and centered over the glass. Using a smooth motion, tilt the bottle for the wine to flow into the glass, and then quickly cut off the flow when the appropriate amount has been poured. When bringing the bottle up, you should give it a slight twist inward to slow the formation of any drips. Using the serviette in your other hand, wipe the mouth of the bottle to catch any drips that might have formed.

Once the host has been served, wait until he or she approves or disapproves the wine before doing anything else. If a wine is refused, it is important to apologize and find out what prompted the guest to disapprove. It is proper etiquette to politely accept this disapproval, and not charge the guests for the wine. The wine should not be discarded, however; but rather tasted by a sommelier or other trained employee to detect whether there really is a problem. Wines that have obvious faults should be given to a manager so they can be returned to the purveyor for a discount. In the situation where a guest simply does not like what he ordered, help him make another selection. Bring the host a new glass, and open the new bottle using the steps detailed above. Refusal of wine is not common, but when it occurs it should be dealt with professionally and without confrontation.

With the host's approval of a wine, it is time to serve the rest of the guests. Their glasses should be poured first before you return to fill the host's glass. Positioning yourself to the right of each guest in turn, fill each glass one-third to one-half of the

Be sure to use a slight twist inward when stopping the flow of the wine into a glass. This will help you catch any drips that might form.

Common Wine Faults

There are faults that can occur in wine as the result of improper storage, poor winemaking, or even the stopper used to seal the bottle. Although guests will commonly refer to a wine as being corked or off when refusing a bottle of wine, the problem may be any one of a number of faults. While this wine should obviously not be served, it can often be returned to the purveyor who sold it for a refund. Before returning it, however, it is often educational to allow servers to smell and in some cases taste the faulty wine so that they can detect the fault in the future. At right is a list of common wine faults.

Corked wine	If a wine is truly corked or suffering from cork taint, then it contains perceptible levels of an organic compound called 2,4,6 Trichloroanisole or TCA. This compound has a pronounced unpleasant moldy or musty aroma that can dominate the other flavors in a wine. TCA occurs in a wine when chemical precursors, often picked up during the sterilization of corks or simply found in the corks themselves (although there are several places in a winery where this can develop), come in contact with the wine.
Maderized or cooked wine	Strong toffee and wet cardboard aromas and a browning of color can signal a wine that is maderized. This occurs when a wine is subjected to excessive heat during production or storage.
Oxidized wine	If a wine bottle's cork dries out or begins to leak, excessive amounts of oxygen can then damage the wine. Oxidized wines will appear and smell similar to maderized ones.
Fizzy wine	Secondary fermentations can sometimes occur in a bottle of wine. If bubbles or a slight spritz are detected when pouring what you know is a still wine, the wine should be removed from the table and a new bottle returned in its place.
Hazy wine	All wines should be free of haze and suspended particles, so if you pour a wine that appears hazy, it should be removed from the table and a new bottle returned in its place.
Acetic wine	If a wine has strong, acrid aromas reminiscent of vinegar, it is spoiled and should be removed. This is often caused by faulty corks that allow air into a bottle and/or by bacterial infections.

way full. Try to ensure that all of the glasses at the table are filled to the same approximate level. While pleasant conversation is an important part of service, you do not need to wait for the guests to approve of the wine.

The order in which you serve the guests depends widely upon your establishment's policies and physical setup. Traditionally wine is served to ladies first, and then gentlemen, always moving clockwise around the table. Once all the guests' glasses have been filled, return to the right side of the host. Before placing the wine bottle on the table in front of the host with the label facing him or her, fill the host's glass to the same level as the rest of the guests' glasses.

Proper table service involves constantly being aware of the situation at your tables. Check the level of wine in glasses and bottles so that you may quickly top off guests' glasses with more wine or help the host select an additional bottle. When a new bottle of wine is brought to a table, new glassware should be brought to all the guests, and the wine should be presented, opened, and poured again following the same steps used for the first bottle.

Once all guests and the host have been served, place the bottle in front of the host with the label facing the host.

Proper Service of Sparkling Wines

Sparkling wine service is very similar to table wine service. The steps of presenting the bottle and pouring the wine are the same, and the only major differences are the type of glassware used and the way the bottle is opened. Extra care should always be taken with bottles of sparkling wine because they contain such intense amounts of pressure. There is often up to 115 psi of pressure inside a bottle of sparkling wine, and corks have been clocked at speeds of 100 mph leaving bottles!

When a sparkling wine is selected by a host, the table should first be set with appropriate glassware. Flutes are best because they help to maintain the carbonation in the wine. Extra care should be taken to ensure that the glasses are completely free of any film or residue, as this can quickly deaden the bubbles and flatten the carbonation. It is extremely important to make sure that the wine is at a proper serving temperature of 40°F to 45°F, as warmer temperatures will cause the carbon dioxide to rapidly escape from the solution, lessening your control when opening the bottle.

After presenting the selected sparkling wine to the host, the top of the capsule should be cut off with the blade of your wine key and completely removed. While opening the bottle, always make sure that the cork and opening of the bottle are not pointed at anyone or anything. Hold the neck of the bottle with your nondominant hand, and place the thumb of that same hand on top of the cork. With your other hand, unscrew the wire cage that holds the cork in the bottle. Once it has been completely loosened and unscrewed, do not remove this cage. If you were to remove it, the cork might actually pop out of the bottle on its own when you take pressure off it. Remove your thumb from the top of the cork, still holding the neck of the bottle with your nondominant hand, and immediately grasp the cork and loosened cage with your dominant hand. Throughout the removal of the cork you want to exert pressure on the cork down into the bottle. You do not need to remove the cork yourself; you simply allow the pressure in the bottle to do it in a controlled manner.

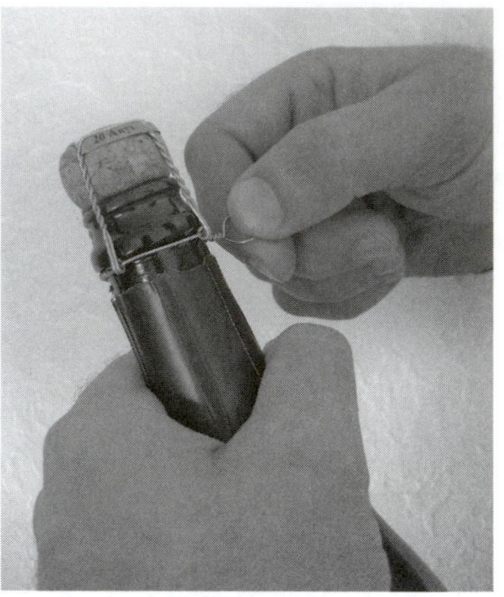

Once the capsule has been cut to expose the cork and cage, untwist the cage to loosen it.

It is often best to hold the bottle at an angle while removing the cork. Slowly twist the bottle, not the cork, to unseat it. Once you feel it begin to pull out of the bottle, continue pushing against the pressure until the cork is completely removed. Unless you just won the world championship in a major league sport, you do not want to hear a huge popping sound and watch wine spill out of the bottle. If done properly, only a slight hiss should be heard as the cork is removed.

The sparkling wine should now be served like a table wine: pour a sample for the host, and then fill the rest of the guests' glasses in the proper order before again returning to the host. Place the bottle in an ice bucket once the wine has been served to keep it cold. If available, attach a stopper specially designed for sparkling wine bottles to the mouth of the bottle to help keep in the carbonation.

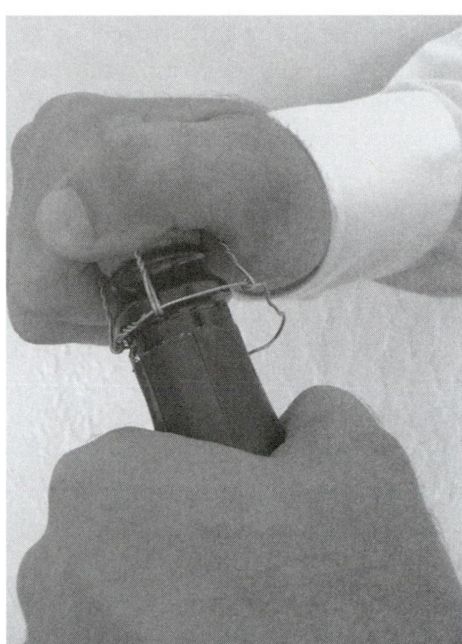

Grasp the cork and loosened cage with your hand and twist the bottle to loosen the cork and allow the pressure inside the bottle to push the cork out.

Decanting Wine

Decanting wine may seem like an archaic tradition only practiced in times past, but it should be used in the course of proper wine service for certain wines. Younger red wines will benefit from decanting, as it allows them to **breathe** and allows their characteristics to soften and develop. Older wines should be decanted to allow volatile off aromas to dissipate and so that the wine can be removed from any sediment it has thrown. Decanting is an easy process, and the types of containers used can range from hand-blown, lead crystal decanters to simple glass juice carafes.

DECANTING YOUNGER RED WINES

Young red wines are often bottled when they are still quite tannic and rough. Allowing these wines to breathe will allow the harsh edge to these wines to soften as oxygen is dissolved into the wine, mimicking the mellowing effects of aging. Many consider the act of opening a bottle and simply allowing it to sit that way for a period of time to be breathing. In reality, this will do little to nothing for a wine—to properly "breathe" it must be decanted.

Rapidly pouring the wine into the decanter once it has been opened will cause the maximum amount of oxygen to incorporate itself into the wine. You want the wine to splash as much as possible in the decanter, and some decanters actually have a device that does this for you, called an aerator. By dissolving air and oxygen into the wine, tannins will be softened and pleasant fruity and earthy flavors will be revealed. Once the wine has been decanted, it can be served to the guests as if it were the original bottle, with a sample poured for the host and then glasses poured for the rest of the guests. Policies differ amongst establishments, but the most common etiquette is to decant the wine at the table in front of the guests. This step is simply placed in the normal flow of wine service between the removal of the cork and the pouring of the sample to the host.

DECANTING VINTAGE WINES

Wines that have received extended periods of cellaring or bottle aging should also be decanted, but for a different reason and using a different method. Over time, off flavors may form in an older wine during bottle aging. These are often quite volatile, and decanting will allow them to quickly blow off. The other reason to decant vintage wines is to separate the wine in the bottle from sediment that it has thrown over time.

The formation of sediment is a natural occurrence for most older vintages of wine and should not be cause for alarm. Usually made up of tartrate crystals that are created slowly from tartaric acid in the wine, or particulate matter formed when different compounds in the wine eventually combine, sediment should have no impact on the flavor of a wine. Regardless, it is aesthetically unpleasing and often feels unpleasant when consumed.

What to Do When Facing Common Wine Service Challenges

Even the most experienced server or sommelier will run into problems when serving wine to guests. Regardless of the situation, you should always keep your cool and maintain decorum. Two of the most common problems you might run into while serving wine are breaking a cork when removing it and spilling wine.

If a cork breaks as you are removing it from the neck of a bottle but no cork falls into the wine, remove the portion of the cork on the worm of your wine key, rescrew it into the remainder of the cork lodged into the neck of the bottle, and continue opening. If cork pieces do fall into the wine, apologize to the guest and remove the bottle before bringing another. The wine that has cork pieces floating in it can later be decanted to remove the cork, and then poured by the glass.

If wine spills or drips as you are serving it, immediately use your linen to wipe it up if possible. If the linen gets more than a little soiled or comes in contact with a dirty surface like the floor, you should replace it before continuing wine service. In the case of any amount of wine being accidentally spilled on a guest, a manager should be informed and it is proper to offer to pay for the guest's dry-cleaning bill.

When decanting an older vintage bottle, great care should be taken not to over-aerate the wine. Practices used for a young wine like rapidly pouring and splashing will cause an older wine to lose its delicate aromas and flavors and will cause sediment to be churned up. Often, vintage bottles are placed in a decanting basket, which gently holds the bottle stable so as not to cause excessive agitation. If stored properly, the bottle should have been laid down on its side as it aged to keep the cork moist. When preparing to decant, the bottle should be kept face up in the same orientation in which it was aged. Maintaining this orientation will help to avoid agitating the sediment inside the bottle. Before decanting, the entire capsule should be removed from the bottle to completely expose the neck. The cork should then be removed without disturbing the bottle. Then the neck of the bottle should be held over a light source, such as a candle, as the wine is poured slowly into a decanter with a minimal amount of splashing.

By watching the wine moving through the neck of the bottle, you can see the bulk of the sediment begin to eventually move toward the opening of the bottle when most of its contents have been poured. Just before this sediment gets to the mouth of the bottle, the flow of liquid into the decanter should be stopped. A small amount of very fine sediment is acceptable, as this will not have the same negative effects as the larger pieces do. For very old vintages, it is common to have up to a cup of wine that is thick with sediment remain in the bottle. After decanting, the wine will be served from the decanter as if it were the original bottle. As with younger wines, older wines should be decanted tableside if room and protocol allow.

Wine Storage

Most wines that are stored in a restaurant or service environment are intended to be served not long after they are purchased and received. Short-term aging should be done at the proper serving temperature for each particular type of wine. This will allow quick service of the wines after they are ordered. Very little must be done to ensure proper aging in this case, because the wine is intended for immediate consumption without a period of maturation.

Storing wine for longer periods, allowing it to slowly bottle age, mature, and mellow, can be far more challenging in any environment. To lay wines down and properly age them, several factors must be addressed. The most important of these are temperature, humidity, exposure to light and movement, and bottle positioning.

TEMPERATURE

Storage temperature may be the most important concern when bottle aging wines. Normal room temperatures are far too warm for wine storage and will cause a wine to degrade rapidly, oxidize, and break down. The ideal temperature range for storing most wines during aging is 50°F to 55°F. This is similar to the temperature found in most underground cellars and storage rooms used by the winemakers themselves before releasing their wines. When held in this cooler temperature range, wines will slowly mature, developing the maximum amount of complexity. If the temperature is much warmer, the process will be accelerated too quickly, while cooler temperatures will slow down the aging process.

While storing a wine at an ideal temperature is important, maintaining a constant temperature is just as vital. Rapid increases and decreases in the temperature of the storage area can quickly ruin wines. Fluctuating temperatures can cause air inside the **ullage** of the bottle (the head space below the cork and above the wine when a bottle is standing upright) to expand and contract. This can cause the seal of the cork to weaken over time, ultimately breaking down and allowing spoilage, oxidation, and/or seepage. To protect against fluctuating temperatures, a thermometer that can trigger an alarm if the temperature becomes too warm or too cold is ideal.

HUMIDITY

Not only should the temperature of the space used to age wines be controlled, but so too should the humidity. A moderately damp cellar is ideal for long-term storage. A humidity range of 50 percent to 70 percent is best, as this will keep corks moist and properly sealed in the bottles. If the humidity is too low, the corks may dry out, allowing air to enter the bottles. Too high a level of humidity will encourage the growth of mold in the cellar and might cause labels to loosen from the bottles.

AVOIDING EXPOSURE TO LIGHT AND MOVEMENT

Even if it is stored at the right temperature and humidity, direct exposure to light can quickly ruin a wine. Direct sunlight or exposure to ultraviolet light is especially to be avoided as UV rays can penetrate the glass and cause a wine to develop off flavors and aromas. Wines impacted by this are described as being **light struck.** Complete darkness is ideal when cellaring wine, but that is not always possible. If an aging area must be lighted some or even most of the time, it should be done with incandescent lighting. Leaving bottles in the cardboard cases or wooden boxes in which they are sold or simply covering the bottles with a cloth can help to reduce the effects of light on the wine.

Exposure to movements and even vibrations can also negatively affect wine that is being stored. Movement can cause sediment to be churned up in the wine and oxidation to be expedited. Care should be taken in selecting an area isolated from possible movement and excessive vibrations.

BOTTLE POSITIONING

Wine bottles sealed with a traditional cork should be stored on their sides or at an angle during the aging process. This will allow wine to stay in contact with the cork, keeping it from drying out and helping to maintain a tight seal. It is ideal to store the bottles with their labels facing up, so that when the wine is eventually decanted, the sediment will not be stirred up when the label is presented to the host. This will also keep labels from being scuffed or scratched on the racks on which they are stored. Bottles sealed with Stelvin closures can be aged standing up, since there is no concern about the stopper drying out.

Proper Service of Beer and Spirits

The service of beers and spirits is not as labor intensive as that of wine, nor as full of ritual. This does not mean, however, that certain steps and procedures should not be taken to properly serve these beverages. Remember that a lot of time and care went into their production, and it would be inappropriate to serve them in a manner that is disrespectful to the product you are serving or the guest to whom it is being served.

BEER SERVICE

The days when the only drinks a restaurant would serve were ice-cold domestic lagers in chilled mugs are gone for many establishments, as they attempt to offer an increasingly diverse selection of beer styles to their guests. Just as not every wine should be served the same way, not every beer should be served in the same manner. When done correctly, proper beer service will enhance the flavors and characteristics of a beer.

Depending upon the style of beer being served, appropriate glassware can differ widely. Just as wine calls for a specially designed glass, so too do different styles of beer. **Beer mugs** are fine for American light lagers, but other styles call for different glasses. Most ales are best served in **pint glasses,** which are commonly designed with a wide base that tapers outward toward the top. Wheat beers and hefeweizens are traditionally served in very tall, thin glasses that very slightly taper up to a tulip-shaped opening that helps concentrate their aromas. Pilsners should be served in **pilsner glasses,** which are tall and thin with a slight taper from base to opening. Many Trappist ales, barleywines, strong ales, and even doppelbocks should be served in stemmed **goblets** or even **snifters** to aid in the enjoyment of their complex aromas. Beer glasses should always be clean and without residue, which can adversely affect the **head** on the beer and carbonation. If a subsequent beer is ordered by a guest, he or she should be given a new glass.

Speaking of a beer's head, it should always be present to help bring out the most flavor in a beer. The head on a beer should be at least half an inch to an inch thick, although for some styles of beers like hefeweizens and Trappist ales it might be much thicker. When a head is formed, the aroma compounds found in the beer are allowed to escape, maximizing the flavor. Beer glasses should be designed to hold not only the contents of a bottle or draft pour, but also the head. Filling a glass completely to the rim with beer and no head will mute its full flavor potential.

Beer should also be served at the proper temperature, which, despite marketing and personal beliefs to the contrary, should never be ice cold, unless your intention is to cool down and dull the taste of the beer. Thus, it is inappropriate to chill most beer glasses. Ice-cold temperatures will actually shock your taste buds, almost killing a beer's flavor. As with wine, there are different service temperatures for different styles of beer.

Proper Service Temperatures for Common Beer Styles

LAGERS	
Pilsners and light lagers	45° to 50°F
Marzens, Vienna lagers, and Oktoberfest beers	50° to 55°F
Bocks and doppelbocks	55° to 60°F
ALES	
Pale ales, amber ales, and brown ales	50° to 55°F
Hefeweizens and wheat beers	45° to 50°F
Porters, stouts, and dark lagers	50° to 55°F
Barleywines, Trappist ales, and strong ales	55° to 60°F

As with wine service and every other aspect of an establishment, the server or sommelier should be educated about every product the establishment offers. Guests may need assistance when ordering beers or guidance on what type of beer would best pair with a particular dish. The server should be able to answer most questions about the beers on the menu, including origin, flavor profile, and style. Once a beer has been selected by a guest, the next step of proper beer service begins.

Tableside beer service is uncommon, but even if a beer is being poured in a service area away from guests, the same procedures should be followed. If serving a beer in a bottle (or even a can) that is to be poured into a glass, the bottle should be held in the dominant hand after it has been opened. Holding the glass starting at almost a 90-degree angle to the bottle, the lip of the bottle should be placed over the edge of the glass. As you begin to raise the bottle up to begin pouring it into the glass, slowly decrease the angle of the glass to about 45 degrees when it is half full, and eventually to an upright position as you finish pouring the contents into the glass. Take care not to pour the beer too quickly, as this will agitate the beer and will cause the carbonation to escape and create foaming. Pouring too slowly, on the other hand, will result in a beer without head, which mutes the aroma. A steady pace without any chugging is best. Once the glass has been filled, place it to the right side of the guest's place setting if possible, taking care not to place your hand or fingers near the opening of the glass.

Pouring a **draft beer** is similar, except the tap is stationary. Again, it is best to hold the glass in your nondominant hand to give you maximum control of the tap. Tilt the glass to just a little less than a 90-degree angle with the edge of the glass just beneath, but not touching, the tap's spigot. Pull the tap fully open throughout the entire pouring process. Beer taps are designed to operate this way—partially opening the tap will cause the carbonation of a beer to be released too rapidly, causing excessive foaming. If the flow out of a tap is slow or excessively foamy when fully opened, have a draft technician or trained employee check and adjust the pressure lines flowing into the keg that push the beer out. As the glass begins to fill, slowly decrease the angle just as you would with a bottled beer until the glass is full and completely upright. The beer should then be taken to the guest quickly and served.

SPIRIT SERVICE

Most spirits are simply poured into a glass or mixed into a cocktail at a bar, and then delivered to the guest. If this is the case, simply follow the procedures of your establishment when delivering and serving the drink to the guest. Tableside spirit service takes place in only a select number of fine-dining establishments that are usually equipped with a rolling cart stocked with cognacs, brandies, fine whiskies, and cordials. This will typically be wheeled by a table as the guests are finishing their entrees to offer an after-dinner drink.

When serving spirits to guests tableside or at a bar, the first step is to aid the guest if necessary in making a decision on what spirit they would like. As mentioned in the sections on both wine and beer service, it is the responsibility of every server and sommelier to know the products that they sell. Once the spirit has been ordered, the proper glassware must be selected.

If a cocktail is being served, then it should be poured into the appropriate glass—a martini in a martini glass, and so on. If the spirit is being served on its own, then the two main glasses used are **rocks glasses,** alternately called highballs, old-fashioned glasses or buckets, and snifters. Rocks glasses are squat, heavy glasses that resemble a cylinder with a thick base. They are appropriate for serving fine whiskies, like single-malt scotch or bourbon, ordered **neat** (simply poured into the glass with no ice), or spirits that are ordered **on the rocks** (poured over ice). For other often aromatic spirits that are commonly served neat, such as cognacs, most brandies, and even well-aged rums and tequilas, the traditional and appropriate choice is a snifter. A snifter is a round-shaped glass with an opening that is narrower than the insides of the glass. This helps to concentrate the aromas into the opening, so even the most subtle of nuances can be detected. The short leg and foot cause the guest to hold the snifter by the bowl of the glass, allowing the heat from the hand to slowly warm the contents, releasing more aroma.

Once the proper glass has been selected, it should be placed to the right side of the guest's place setting, if possible. The bottle can be presented to the guest prior to pouring, but this is more a courtesy to the guest than a formality. Depending upon the policies of your establishment, the proper amount of the spirit—usually somewhere between one and two ounces—should then be poured into the glass. If serving a drink on the rocks it is best to pour the spirit first, then use ice tongs to gently drop ice cubes into the spirit until the guest signals that they have the appropriate amount of ice, or when the glass is roughly half full. If subsequent drinks are ordered, always replace guests' used glasses with new.

Storage of Beer and Spirits

Like wine, beer and spirits should be stored properly so that they will taste their best. Beer is generally intended only for short-term storage, as the flavor of most beer is optimal when it is as fresh as possible. Consideration must be paid to how and where beer will be stored in an establishment, depending upon whether the beer comes in bottles, cans, or kegs. Spirits have very few requirements to be stored properly, but they too can spoil or break down if exposed to the wrong conditions.

BOTTLED AND CANNED BEER STORAGE

Most mass-produced beers are **pasteurized** after being poured into bottles or cans. This helps to prolong their shelf life and allows them to be stored—at least in the short term—unrefrigerated, but never much warmer than around 70°F. As long as they are kept at a fairly stable temperature that does not fluctuate much and are kept out of direct light and especially sunlight, which can cause them to become light struck and create off flavors (often referred to as skunky flavors), they should easily last up to three months without losing character. If beer is to be stored in a refrigerator, it is important to ensure that it is kept above freezing.

Most microbrewed beer and many imported specialty beers are not pasteurized, however, as the pasteurization process, which quickly heats up and then cools down the full bottles or cans, can have the effect of degrading some of a beer's flavor. While this might protect flavors, it also means that unpasteurized beer in bottles (these types of beers are rarely canned) is more perishable and susceptible to spoiling or getting stale. Unpasteurized beer bottles should always be refrigerated, should never be allowed to freeze, and like all bottled beer, should be kept out of direct light.

Although uncommon, there are actually a few styles of beers that will benefit from long-term storage and cellaring. As with some wines, the flavors in these beers will develop in the bottle as a controlled oxidation slowly takes place. The best candidates for aging are typically beers with either higher alcohol contents, like barleywines, many Trappist and abbey ales, strong ales, old ales, and doppelbocks; or high levels of acidity that are often acquired by wild yeast fermentations, like lambics. The same general rules and care you would utilize for a wine also apply to aging beer.

DRAFT BEER STORAGE

Draft beer served out of kegs is unpasteurized, unlike many bottled beers and almost all canned beer. This contributes to much of the rich flavor and character of draft beer. Unpasteurized beer has to be kept cold at all times, because it can quickly spoil or grow stale otherwise. Beer kegs should always be kept refrigerated, whether they are attached to a draft-dispense system or kept in a storage area. Also remember that there is beer in the lines that run from the keg to the tap as well, so they too should be refrigerated, carefully maintained, and cleaned regularly.

As with all beer, freshness is also a major factor for draft beer, which is more perishable than most bottled or canned beers. Most breweries stamp or mark kegs with a date when they are filled, so it is important to learn how your products are dated. Most distributors and breweries will gladly explain how their products are marked and give suggestions as to how long the beers can be served before quality begins to degrade. Several weeks would be reasonable for most draft beer, but the faster your turnover, the better. Always monitor your kegs and how old they are to ensure the freshest and best-tasting beer for your customers.

SPIRIT STORAGE

Ethanol is a natural preservative, and due to their high alcohol content, spirits do not need much special attention for storage. Direct sunlight or other

Do Spirits Age in the Bottle?

By aging a bottle of ten-year-old scotch for ten years, you will not turn it into a twenty-year-old scotch. Spirits do indeed age once bottled and flavors can mellow and develop, but it is a very long process. The high alcohol content in most spirits acts as a natural preservative, so major changes in the spirit will occur only after decades in the bottle for most products. A ten-year-old scotch turns into a twenty-year-old scotch after ten additional years of barrel aging. In the barrel, spirits are exposed to massive amounts of oxygen in comparison with in the bottle, as well as being exposed to the wood of the barrel itself, from which flavors and color can be drawn out. So if you were to age that ten-year-old scotch for ten more years, all you would have when you were done is a ten-year-old bottle of ten-year-old scotch.

light sources should be kept to a minimum, as long-term exposure can hurt the flavor of a spirit as it does with wines and beers. Major fluctuations in temperature can also have an adverse effect on spirits, but most can simply be stored at room temperature even after the bottle has been opened. The exceptions are certain styles of spirits, such as Irish creams, that actually contain pasteurized cream, which are best kept refrigerated once the bottle is opened.

Even though most spirit bottles are opened and then poured over the course of time, oxidation or microbial spoilage is not normally a major issue as long as they are poured within a year, or in the case of sweetened spirits like many liqueurs and cordials, within a couple of months. If the bottles are fitted with pour spouts, these should be cleaned nightly to discourage bacterial or microbial buildup that could end up spreading into the bottle or poured into your customer's glass. When not in use the bottles should be sealed up, either with the original cap or with some other covering, so that smoke, debris, or even small flying insects cannot accidentally get into the bottle.

Summary

The actual tasks involved in properly serving and storing wines, beers, and spirits are quite simple. While individual establishments and situations may call for adapting these tasks, the basics remain the same. With a little care, knowledge, and skill, every beverage can be treated properly and enjoyed by your guests.

Review Questions

1. The guest who is considered the host for wine service is:
   - A. The oldest male at the table
   - B. Whoever ordered the wine
   - C. Whoever is paying for the meal and wine
   - D. Whoever made the reservation

2. The ideal style of wine key used for tableside service is called a butler's friend.
   - A. True
   - B. False

Match each of the following styles of wine to its proper serving temperature range.

3. Full-bodied red wines	A. 50° to 60°F
4. Light-bodied red wines	B. 60° to 65°F
5. Dry white wines and rosés	C. 45° to 50°F
6. Sweet white wines	D. 55° to 65°F

7. When opening a bottle of sparkling wine, the cage should remain on the cork after it has been unscrewed.
   - A. True
   - B. False

For the following statements concerning decanting wine, indicate whether each is a reason for decanting an older wine or a younger wine.

8. To remove sediment	A. Reason to decant a young wine
9. To allow the wine to breathe	B. Reason to decant a vintage wine
10. To allow volatile off aromas to dissipate	
11. To dissolve as much oxygen as possible into a wine	

12. Beer should be served as cold as possible.
   A. True
   B. False

13. Draft beer kegs should always be kept __________.
   A. in a dark room
   B. in the freezer
   C. in a refrigerated area
   D. at room temperature

14. Cognac is properly served without ice in a snifter.
   A. True
   B. False

Key Terms

wine service
wine key
waiter's friend
capsule
corked wine
maderized wine
cooked wine
oxidized wine
fizzy wine
hazy wine
acetic wine
decanting
breathe
ullage
light struck
beer mug
pint glass
pilsner glass
goblet
snifter
head
draft beer
rocks glass
neat
on the rocks
pasteurized

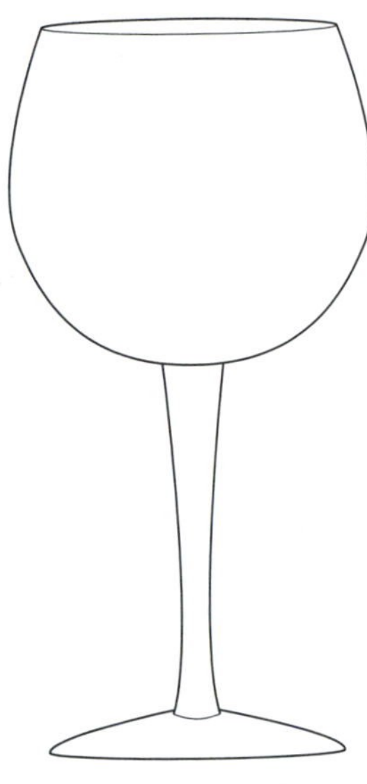

CHAPTER 29

Beverage Sales and Wine Lists

A wine list is praised and given awards for reasons that have little to do with its real purpose, as if it existed only to be admired passively, like a stamp collection. A wine list is good only when it functions well in tandem with a menu.

—**GERALD ASHER,** wine editor for *Gourmet* magazine

Alcoholic beverages are offered in a restaurant setting for several reasons: customers enjoy them, properly matched wine and other beverages can pair to the menu, and many patrons expect it. The main reason restaurants sell wine, beer, and spirits, though, is to generate sales and profit. Developing wine and beverage programs and writing and formatting wine lists are some of the main responsibilities of a sommelier or restaurant manager.

Building Beverage Sales

Selling wine, beer, and spirits is not rocket science. The basics are simple, but the number of restaurants, resorts, wine bars, and other establishments who do a poor job of selling alcoholic beverages is both sad and surprising. A successful wine and beverage program is something that needs to be built, developed, and maintained over time. Several important decisions will need to be made concerning the training of your staff, your establishment's focus on wine, promotions geared to build sales, and how to price the products you sell.

AN EDUCATED STAFF

The most powerful tool any establishment has to sell alcoholic beverages is its staff. Regardless of how knowledgeable the managers, wine buyer, or sommelier of an establishment are, the staff are the people who come face to face with customers and actually sell them products. If a sales staff know the wines on their wine list and feel comfortable discussing wine with customers, they will sell more wine. A solid understanding of the beers and spirits offered will lead to more sales of beer and spirits. An intensive knowledge of wine and other alcoholic beverages is not necessary—all that is needed is an intensive knowledge of your particular wine list and beverage offerings. This can only be developed through achieving comfort and familiarity with both.

Educating your sales staff begins when they are first hired. New servers should be made aware of the wine list, beers and spirits offered, wine and beverage promotions, and the standards of beverage service. Just handing them the wine list or listing the beers and spirits you sell is not enough; they will need to be able to describe and suggest products.

Have them train with a knowledgeable and experienced peer, or provide study materials and tests.

Ongoing education is also important. Regular server training and tasting can teach your staff about new products or remind them of existing products you offer. Allowing servers to taste different wines, beers, and spirits can definitely help them with descriptions and get them more excited about the products they enjoy. Teach the staff about more than just the wine: the story behind the winemaker, vineyard, or region can sometimes be more effective and easy to remember. Sharing this type of information can also prove just as helpful for the beers and spirits you sell. Have your beverage purveyors come in and give seminars on their products—they should be happy for the opportunity. Try to make your staff enthusiastic about your wines, beers, and spirits; passion is often more important than technical knowledge.

Beverage service should also be part of training. Proper techniques should be regularly demonstrated and practiced. If decanting wine is common in your establishment, your servers should know how to do it and feel comfortable with its performance. Servers who are intimidated and feel awkward opening wine bottles and pouring wine will be less likely to suggest wines and will hurt sales. Improperly poured beers and sloppy cocktails will leave guests unsatisfied. Regular restaurant customers and serious beverage aficionados appreciate proper service.

FOCUS ON WINE

By making a concerted effort to focus on wine in your establishment, you will generate more sales. This can be something as simple as always setting tables with wine glasses as part of the setting. Doing this sends an unspoken message to your customers that "we normally sell wine here."

If you have a wine list, it should always be given to your guests as they are seated, along with their menus. Servers should always suggest wines that pair with menu items that are ordered. Champagne and sparkling wines should naturally be offered when guests are dining out to celebrate a special occasion, which is often the case. You can even decorate your restaurant with large-format and signed wine bottles or with wooden wine boxes.

A focus on offering and selling wine is easy to lose in the course of busy days and filled schedules. This loss will translate into lost sales if you are not careful. Be conscious about decisions you make and messages your restaurant sends to both staff and customers—it can make the difference between an average wine program and an exceptional one. The devil is in the details.

FOCUS ON BEER

With the dazzling variety of new beers available on the market today, both domestic and imported, customers are demanding more and better choices. Offering a wide variety of beers is one thing, but if that is not supported by a beer sales program, do not expect the beer to sell itself. As with a successful wine program, you must make a concerted effort to alert your customers about the beers you sell.

Beer lists are becoming more accepted in restaurants, especially those that have a wide offering. Suggestive selling works for beer in the same way it does for wine. Offer suggestions to your customers about the beers you sell, or spotlight a particularly interesting new offering or an old favorite. Display beer bottles behind the bar if possible, so customers can recognize a favorite brand or be intrigued by a label that is new to them. Use traditional and authentic glassware, much of which can be quite striking in design, to pique customers' interest.

FOCUS ON SPIRITS

Most restaurateurs, sommeliers, and servers act like their customers should automatically know what is found in their spirit selection. While many establishments offer similar spirits for sale, most are likely to stock at least a couple of interesting or unique products that probably need to be hand sold. Quite often, customers simply order what they usually do because no one makes an effort to sell them anything different. It is absolutely fine if a customer dismisses a suggestion and sticks with his or her old standby, but sometimes you might turn someone on to something new.

After-dinner drinks should always be suggested by a server or sommelier if such choices are offered. Many times these are impulse buys, but they can significantly increase check averages while at the same time enhancing a customer's positive experience. Spirit and cocktail lists can also be produced. These serve as a kind of cheat sheet for customers to look through your products and know all of their options. **Up-sell** customers to more prestigious brands or styles of what they normally drink. It is not difficult to do if you can explain why they are considered superior or higher in quality. Most guests in an establishment are there to celebrate and often to try something new—help them!

PROMOTIONS

Another way to build interest and generate profits from wine and other beverages is to offer promotions. These do not need to be complicated and difficult. They should fit into your natural flow of business and match your environment and atmosphere. Some basic promotions include server incentives, wine events or dinners, by-the-glass wine lists, and featured beverages. A motivated server is a powerful sales tool. Offering different incentives for servers to sell more alcoholic beverages in general, or more of a specific brand, can greatly influence their approach to selling. Competitions will help many servers get enthusiastic to sell, and they often cost little to set up in terms of money and time. You can work with your purveyors to offer prizes (where legal) for the server who sells the most of a particular product they offer. Remember, those purveyors only benefit from your servers selling more of their products, so it is in their vested interest to participate.

There are also several different events your establishment can host to foster more beverage sales. Wine dinners are a great way to show off the talents of your staff and introduce your customers to different wines that you sell. Throughout the year, many winemakers and winery representatives travel to different markets to help support their brands. Find out when they will be in your area and schedule a wine dinner featuring them presenting their products. Schedule wine tastings or specific time periods when wine prices are discounted on slower business days to bring new and existing customers into your establishment to try something new. With increasing consumer interest in microbreweries and high-quality beers, many establishments are also beginning to host beer tastings and beer dinners to highlight beer-and-food pairings, and these are another great way to increase beverage sales and get your customers to try a new product.

Utilizing a list of wines served **by the glass** can also create new sales. If you offer wines only by the bottle, many customers will not want to order because it might be too expensive or be too much wine. If you have a customer dining alone, or a party with only one person who wants to drink wine, a by-the-glass list will allow them to order wine. Many customers would rather have one top-quality glass of wine to savor than a lesser bottle. You can also use a list like this to introduce customers to new products you offer. In the same way, half bottles (375 ml) and splits (187 ml) are a great alternative.

Featuring a particular wine, beer, spirit, or cocktail is another way to generate more sales. This can be done by printing it on the menu or using menu inserts, or simply by including it as part of a server's script when their guests are greeted. Many establishments will also offer special pricing on their featured beverage or beverages, although that is not always necessary. Allow your staff to participate in selecting the featured beverage so that they feel some ownership of that offering. They will always select a product they think they can sell, and will feel like their opinions matter.

PRICING WINE

The prices at which you decide to sell your wines can be one of the best and easiest ways to impact sales. Most restaurants and service establishments mark prices up 300 percent to 500 percent. While this may work for many establishments and the profits are high for every bottle sold, it may also cause wine sales to become sluggish.

It may sound illogical at first, but sometimes you need to sell wines for less to earn more. High prices can keep many customers from selecting a bottle or glass of wine during their visit. Depending on your situation, selling a large volume of moderately priced wine might generate more actual profit than selling far fewer bottles at higher prices. If you offer wines that are commonly sold in the retail market, many of your customers may know what a bottle normally costs. A large price tag might make them feel as if you are gouging them and overcharging. If you are known for good wines offered at great value, it can drive more business through your doors. Like any business decision, though, the decision to lower prices in order to increase volume should involve a careful cost-benefit analysis, as it may not be right for every establishment.

There are many different ways to determine pricing besides simply marking your wines up by a given percentage. Many wine programs are moving toward adding a certain dollar figure to the cost of every bottle of wine rather than a percentage. Imagine if you priced wine simply by adding $20 to the cost instead of determining the price by multiplying it by a percentage factor. For a bottle of wine that cost you $50 wholesale, you would charge $70, while a competitor with a 300 percent **markup** would sell it for $150! Talk about getting noticed and providing value. Would this increase the volume of sales you could make? Which restaurant would you want to dine at?

Pricing your wines that are served by the glass rather than by the bottle is done a little differently. The price you set should be attractive enough to customers that you sell the wine quickly, well before it has a chance to spoil. At the same time, it should be high enough that you can cover the cost of the bottle if only one glass of wine is served from it. Most establishments set up their pricing so that one glass is roughly equal to the cost of the bottle. Many purveyors will actually offer special pricing for wines sold for the purpose of being poured by the glass because they will typically turn over much more quickly. Use this to your advantage when planning your by-the-glass wine list.

Pouring wines by the glass requires establishing the standard amount that goes into each glass. Too much, and a new bottle will have to be opened to top off the last glass poured from an open bottle. Customers can feel cheated if too little is poured. You should always determine an exact number of servings found in a standard, 750-ml/25.4-ounce bottle of wine. Most establishments pour either four glasses (6.4 ounces), five glasses (5.1 ounces), or six glasses (4.2 ounces) per bottle. To ensure consistency, mark one of the wine

How Long Will an Open Bottle of Wine Last?

Once opened, a bottle of wine is exposed to a great deal of oxygen that it has been purposely kept away from during aging and/or storage. This oxygen will rather quickly begin to degrade a wine's flavor, and eventually the wine will spoil. The amount of time a wine will stay fresh and flavorful depends upon several factors, including style, origin, grape varietals used, and more, but the vast majority of wines will only be good for two to three days at most after opening. Due to this, informed decisions should be made in determining the number of wines sold by the glass and the types of wines chosen.

There are several contraptions and products sold to extend the shelf life of opened bottles of wine, including vacuum pumps that remove air from the bottle and gas blends that can be sprayed into the bottle to displace air and create a barrier to it. These can definitely help prolong the life of a wine, but only to a certain degree. One of the best methods for prolonging the freshness of open bottles is easy and absolutely free. When not serving them, partial bottles should always be stored sealed and refrigerated, including red wines. Oxygen works more slowly at colder temperature, so refrigeration will slow (but not stop) the degradation of your wines. When preparing for service, the white wines can remain chilled and the red wines can be removed and brought to their proper service temperature.

glasses you use for glass service with a line at the appropriate fill level with a permanent marker. When pouring glasses of wine at the service bar, a new clean glass can be placed beside your marked glass when being filled to hit the proper mark. With practice and repetition, you or your staff should be able to consistently pour the proper amount.

How to handle pricing is an important decision that every establishment must make individually. Many different factors must be taken into account including the establishment's financial situation, the current level of wine sales, what your competitors charge, and what the market will bear. If almost all your sales are in your lower price categories, or you do not sell very much wine, it might benefit your wine program greatly to reconsider your pricing.

PRICING BEER

Setting pricing for beer is often more straightforward than pricing wine. Most bottled and canned beers are sold by the case, which typically holds twelve or twenty-four beers. Most establishments will determine the cost per serving and then mark it up by a given percentage from 200 percent to 600 percent. Be sure to round the price so that it does not seem awkward, or establish pricing tiers and place different products within each.

It is important to pay attention to the prices charged by your direct competition, and price your beer accordingly. This will help you to understand what prices the market will bear. Setting your prices too high will cause sales to be sluggish, while underpricing will mean you are losing out on potential income and profit.

For draft beer, you should determine the amount a keg will yield. Common keg sizes are 5 gallons, 7¾ gallons (often called a **pony keg**), and 15½ gallons (referred to as a **half-barrel**). This amount should then be divided by the serving size to determine the number of units found in the keg. Because of the way beer is dispensed in a draft system, there will be some loss, usually around 10 percent. This is caused by spillage and foaming that will occur in the natural course of dispense, and should be factored in when determining the number of servings a keg contains. Once the number of servings has been determined, divide the cost of the keg by servings to determine the cost per serving. A price based on a percentage can then be determined in similar fashion to pricing bottled or canned beer.

How Many Beers Are in a Keg?

This question has been pondered at scores of fraternity parties and backyard barbecues, but should be taken seriously in a service establishment, as miscalculation can cost you money. Below is an example of how to determine the number of beers in a typical half-barrel keg.

keg volume = 15.5 gallons = 1,984 fluid ounces
loss factor = 10% of total volume = 198.4 fluid ounces
1,984 fluid ounces – 198.4 fluid ounces = 1,785.6 fluid ounces to be sold

SERVING SIZE	NUMBER OF SERVINGS PER KEG
12 ounces	148.8
14 ounces	127.6
16 ounces	111.6
18 ounces	99.2
20 ounces	89.3
22 ounces	81.2

PRICING SPIRITS AND COCKTAILS

Spirits and cocktails can serve as a great profit generator for an establishment that serves and prices them correctly. Establishing the correct amount to serve and the number of servings per bottle is fundamental to maximizing profits and customer satisfaction. With a lack of control or sloppy service, however, even the best-planned spirit program can quickly spiral into chaos.

The first thing to do when determining the cost of a spirit or cocktail is to establish the **standard pour** that your establishment will use. A standard pour is the amount of alcohol served in the vast majority of drinks or cocktails. Some specialty drinks like martinis and tropical cocktails might use a different measurement, but they should be priced independently. Most bars and restaurants will use a standard pour of anywhere between one and two ounces per drink. Your bartenders and servers should be well trained to hit this standard pour every time they make a drink, and should be tested on their ability to consistently pour the proper amount.

Once you have a standard pour, you can then determine the number of servings in a bottle. Most spirits will be sold in either a 750-ml/25.4-ounce bottle (sometime called a **fifth**) or in a 1-liter/33.8-ounce bottle. Simply divide the volume of the bottle by the amount of your standard pour to determine the number of servings. Once you know the number of servings in a bottle, you can divide it into the bottle's cost to determine your cost per serving.

Because the ice, mixers, and garnishes that are added to the spirit to produce a cocktail are not free, they too should be figured into the cost per serving. Many establishments determine an average cost of these components per drink, and add it to the cost per serving of the spirit. This total cost per serving amount will then serve as the basis for determining the price you will charge a customer for a drink made with that product.

Since most properly stocked bars will carry several dozen brands of spirits, it could quickly become confusing for servers and bartenders if each and every brand had its own individual price. To alleviate any confusion, most bars and restaurants will develop a multitier system for the brands they offer, where spirits are grouped by similar costs per serving and then priced as a group.

Once your costs have been determined and the spirits you offer have been placed in their appropriate **price tiers**, you must determine the price you will charge for each price tier. As with other alcoholic beverages, this is often a 300 percent markup or more. Investigating what the market will bear and knowing what your direct competition charges will further help you to adjust your pricing accordingly. At this point, if controls are maintained and quality service is consistent, profits and happy customers should be the result.

Spirit Price Tiers

Below are the names of some common price tiers, although not every bar needs to have all of these categories, nor should a bar or restaurant feel limited to only these four.

Well	The least expensive cost category of spirit brands, although this does not always denote inferior quality. These are the spirits that will be served if a brand is not indicated when the drink is ordered (e.g., "vodka and tonic" rather than "Absolut vodka and tonic"). Sometimes referred to as a "house brand."
Call	More expensive category of spirit brands, usually made up of premium brands that are commonly ordered.
Premium	Even more expensive category of spirit brands, usually made up of premium brands that are commonly ordered.
Top shelf	The most expensive category of spirit brands, often priced individually. These are usually the top-quality brands served.

Wine Lists

Your establishment might offer an incredible selection of quality wines at a good value, but you will never realize your sales potential if you cannot adequately get that message to customers. The main tool you will have to communicate the wines you offer is a **wine list.** Whether it has ten selections or a thousand, thought needs to go into how to format and write your wine list. This should begin long before the initial list is ever written, in the decisions you make about which products to sell.

SELECTIONS AND BALANCE

One of the most enjoyable yet overwhelming tasks when writing a new wine list is choosing what you will offer. Every selection should be made purposefully and thoughtfully. A good wine list is balanced and offers many choices. It should reflect your atmosphere and especially your menu. You should have your target market in mind when putting a wine list together. After determining the size of your wine list based on your target market, storage space, and concept, you should choose broad categories before selecting individual wines. This will help focus your list and ensure that it will not become too heavy in one area. Once you have selected the different styles, classifications, and price points that will make up your list, you can then begin selecting individual wines. Throughout the process, it is important to keep in mind that you are writing this list for your customers and to maximize sales. Do not simply fill the list with wines you like, as your tastes and biases may be quite different from those of your customers.

There are no rules as to which wines to select or how long a list should be. You just want the list to match your theme and menu at all times. An Italian restaurant should have a list made up of mostly Italian wines. A restaurant that sells entrees for an average of $10 a plate should not have a wine list that averages $70 a bottle. Extensive menu selections should be matched to wine lists with several choices. Small, commonsense decisions will always help you write your list. Keep in mind that this list is not about reds and whites to your establishment, it is about green.

PROPER MAINTENANCE

Wine lists will change over time. New vintages will be released, wines will come and go from your offerings, and prices can fluctuate. Keeping up with these changes is incredibly important and should be done on a regular basis. You can upset or confuse customers and staff if there are mistakes or discrepancies on your wine list. Maintaining a list involves constant review and, commonly, frequent reprinting. Ensuring that your wine list is accurate and reviewing your listings can also be a great way to determine where there might be holes in your list that are causing you to miss sales opportunities. Always make sure that the following information is accurate, if listed: pricing, vintage, and availability.

Categories to Consider for a Balanced Wine List

Old World and New World wines
Whites, reds, rosés, sparkling wines, and dessert wines
Fruitier styles and earthier styles
Inexpensive, mid-range, and expensive wines
Large, respected producers and smaller, boutique producers
Well-known brands and undiscovered producers
Well-known varietals and styles and lesser-known, quality varietals and styles

WINE LIST FORMATS

Once you have selected and priced your wine offerings it is time to format and write your wine list. There are several different formats that can be used for a successful wine list. Two of the most important factors to consider when formatting your list are what information you plan to include about each wine, and how it will be organized for ease of use.

How much information to include in the description for each wine you offer depends upon the competence of your staff, the number of choices you offer, and the sophistication of your customers. For some wine lists it is completely acceptable to include written descriptions for each wine. This would benefit an inexperienced sales staff and help to answer questions a guest might have. Due to lack of space or the length of your list, this may not be an option. Some wine lists simply include the name of the producer, type of wine, and region of origin. This works best for long lists or in establishments with knowledgeable customers and staff. A period of trial and error may be needed to fine tune the appropriate amount of information for your list.

Organizing your wine list properly can help generate sales, empower customers, and even take some of the burden off your guests. If there is any format to avoid, it is a hierarchy based on price. This forces the guests to think only of their budgets, and they will drop down to the price range they are comfortable with. They may be missing out on some incredible wines you offer that might be only a few dollars more.

For short lists of roughly twenty wines or less, it is easy to organize your list based on general style using a few broad categories: red wines, white wines, sparkling wines, and so on. You may need to use several categories that are more specific for a larger list. Two more specific options for organizing the wines are:

By grape variety	Cabernet Sauvignons and Cabernet blends, Merlots, Pinot Noirs, etc.
By region	French wines, California wines, Australian wines, etc.

For any wine list, and especially for longer lists or for those that include several lesser-known varietals, regions, and producers, the best option might be using a **progressive wine list.** A progressive format breaks wines up into different style categories, such as sweet whites, dry whites, soft reds, and powerful reds. Each category is then populated with the wines that match the description. If possible, all of the wines should be organized from one extreme to the next within each category. A short sentence can help to explain how the list works.

Example of a Section of a Progressive Wine List

Powerful Red Wines

Arranged from lightest to heaviest.

2003 Project 3000 Syrah—Lake County	$44
2004 Moillard Crozes-Hermitage—Rhône Valley, France	$28
2006 Ballentine "Old Vine" Zinfandel—Napa Valley	$30
2005 Hentley Farm "The Beauty" Shiraz—Barossa Valley, Australia	$72
2001 La Rasina Brunello di Montalcino—Toscano, Italy	$105
2005 Peter Franus Zinfandel—Napa Valley	$45
2005 Tamber Bey "Two Rivers" Cabernet Sauvignon—Napa Valley	$50
2005 Napa Wine Co. Cabernet Sauvignon—Oakville, Napa Valley	$42
2004 Page Wine Cellars Proprietary Red—Napa Valley	$62

The progressive format lets the customers know what kind of characteristics to expect, helping them to choose a wine. If they want a heavy, powerful red they simply move to the end of the list. They may have never tried a Brunello di Montalcino before, but from your list they can tell that the style of this particular brand falls somewhere between that of an Australian Shiraz and a California Zinfandel or Cabernet Sauvignon.

Your guests will be given points of reference to help them choose a wine, and servers will not have to guess at the style in which a wine is produced. In fact, if they know what style of wine will pair with a certain dish, they will have several different options to suggest using a progressive wine list.

Progressive lists do have their shortcomings, however. The main difficulty is that they require more work in the beginning, when tasting notes need to be compared on wines to arrange them into a hierarchy. Constant vintage changes and additions or deletions would also cause frequent edits to a list like this, as these new wines would need to be tasted, evaluated, and placed in their proper position on the list. In the end, the format of your wine list should be chosen based on the advantages and disadvantages for your establishment. Just remember that no matter what format you choose, this is how you will communicate your products to the guests that fill your tables.

Responsible Service of Alcohol

Selling alcoholic beverages is one of the main ways a restaurant or establishment can generate profits and build success. That said, the safety of your guests is the primary responsibility of any licensed establishment. One reckless action could cost you or your company fines or loss of your liquor license—or even worse, lead to the injury or death of a customer. Regardless of promotions or sales goals, the first thing to always keep in mind is the responsible service of alcohol. Part of being a professional is knowing how this is done. Several companies and government agencies offer liquor law training as well as classes and certifications for responsible alcohol service. Check with your local liquor-licensing agency for more information.

Summary

Selling wine, beer, and spirits effectively can make or break a restaurant or establishment. Several methods, techniques, and decisions can be used to maximize your sales and build a regular clientele. Beverage programs and wine lists are powerful tools to generate profit, but like all other aspects of your business they must be developed, managed, and maintained.

Review Questions

1. Educating your sales staff through regular training sessions and tastings is an effective way to increase wine sales.
   A. True
   B. False
2. The average industry markup for wine in a restaurant setting is 200%.
   A. True
   B. False
3. Your wine purveyors can be utilized in several ways to help you build wine sales.
   A. True
   B. False
4. It is always best to organize a longer wine list by price.
   A. True
   B. False
5. A progressive wine list is organized by:
   A. grape variety
   B. price
   C. region
   D. wine style
6. Which of the following is *not* a common size for a keg of beer?
   A. 5 gallons
   B. 7¾ gallons
   C. 10 gallons
   D. 15½ gallons
7. Which of the following price tiers would be served to a customer that did not request a specific brand of spirit?
   A. Well
   B. Call
   C. Premium
   D. Top shelf
8. What size bottle of spirit is known as a fifth?
   A. 500 ml
   B. 750 ml
   C. 1 liter
   D. 1.75 liters

Key Terms

up-sell
by the glass
markup
pony keg
half-barrel
standard pour
fifth
price tiers
well
call
premium
top shelf
wine list
progressive wine list

APPENDIX A

Answer Key

CHAPTER 1

1. **A.** True
2. **D.** Sugar + Yeast = Ethanol + Carbon Dioxide + Heat
3. **C.** *Saccharomyces cerevisiae*
4. **A.** Ethanol
5. **A.** True
6. **A.** True
7. **C.** Pest resistance
8. **A.** True
9. **B.** False (Acidity balances out the sugar or sweetness in wines, not tannins.)
10. **B.** Price

CHAPTER 2

1. **A.** True
2. **D.** Insect
3. **C.** 1976
4. **B.** Grafting
5. **A.** True
6. **C.** Iran and Iraq
7. **D.** The Romans
8. **C.** The Catholic Church
9. **A.** Louis Pasteur
10. **B.** False (California did not become the top state for wine production in the United States until the 1950s.)

CHAPTER 3

1. **B.** False (More stress will result in fewer grapes.)
2. **C.** less acid and more alcohol
3. **A.** True
4. **B.** *Vitis*
5. **A.** True
6. **A.** True
7. **D.** grapes were harvested
8. **D.** An exact genetic copy
9. **C.** A subspecies
10. **A.** Reproduction between two plants of the same species
11. **B.** Reproduction between two plants of different species
12. **D.** grafting

CHAPTER 4

1. **A.** Hand harvesting
2. **C.** red wines are fermented with their skins, white wines without
3. **A.** pressing
4. **A.** Hand harvest
5. **A.** True
6. **A.** True
7. **B.** Body
8. **C.** Adding a substance to a wine to remove cloudiness
9. **D.** Allowing a wine to age in contact with its dead yeast
10. **A.** Clarifying a wine by moving it away from sediment
11. **B.** Stirring up sediment and dead yeast cells
12. **A.** True
13. **C.** *méthode traditionale*
14. **C.** the addition of high-proof brandy
15. **C.** mold that attacks grapes and concentrates their sugar content

CHAPTER 5

1. **C.** Riesling
2. **D.** Chardonnay
3. **A.** True
4. **A.** Pinot Noir
5. **D.** Shiraz
6. **C.** Floral, depends upon *terroir*
7. **A.** Grapefruit, grassy, herbal, and hints of cat urine
8. **D.** Green apple, citrus, and mineral
9. **B.** Pear, pineapple, buttery, oaky, and spicy
10. **D.** Cherries, cranberries, earth, spice, and barnyard
11. **A.** Blackberries, meaty, smoke, and black pepper
12. **C.** Blueberries, cherries, chocolate, spice, and vanilla
13. **B.** Black currant, mint, bell pepper, and wet dog
14. **B.** Syrah

CHAPTER 6

1. **B.** False (A good pairing would seek to match the quality of the wine and the dish.)
2. **C.** a light pork dish served with an apple compote
3. **B.** Acid and tannins
4. **A.** True
5. **A.** Sour and salty
6. **B.** False (The protein is important, but the sauce, vegetable, starch, etc. could all be more important aspects of the meal when making a wine pairing.)
7. **B.** False (The dessert wine should always be sweeter than the dessert.)
8. **A.** True
9. **B.** False (Many white wines pair well to red meats, while many red wines pair well with white meats.)
10. **B.** sweet, white wines

CHAPTER 7

1. **A.** True
2. **A.** True

3. B. False (It is always best to taste wines from lightest to heaviest, so whites should be served before reds.)
4. C. without knowing anything about the wine
5. B. an individual leads a group of tasters through the sensory analysis of a wine
6. A. several vintages of the same wine are tasted
7. C. several different wines from the same region and vintage are tasted
8. D. several wines are shown by a winery, broker, or retail establishment
9. C. youth
10. A. age
11. B. darker
12. A. lighter
13. C. smell
14. A. True
15. B. False (Acidity can be sensed with taste and touch, but not sight.)
16. B. False (Intensity of aroma and intensity of flavor are actually indicators of quality in a wine, not age.)
17. C. Carbonation
18. A. grape skin thickness
19. B. False (A dry wine is one that has no residual sugar; a wine with high tannins would be described as tannic or astringent.)
20. C. Forepalate

CHAPTER 8

1. B. Tannins
2. A. True
3. C. less acid and more alcohol
4. A. Color
5. B. Body
6. A. True
7. B. 3 to 5 years
8. A. Cool climate

CHAPTER 9

1. A. True
2. A. Cool-continental
3. A. Cool-continental
4. C. Warm-Mediterranean
5. B. Temperate-maritime
6. A. Cool-continental
7. C. AOC
8. A. Bordeaux
9. B. Chablis
10. C. Médoc
11. A. Sancerre
12. D. Châteauneuf-du-Pape
13. C. Syrah and Grenache
14. B. Riesling and Gewürztraminer
15. D. Chenin Blanc and Sauvignon Blanc
16. A. Chardonnay and Pinot Noir
17. A. True
18. D. Chardonnay
19. B. False (Several different white and red varietals are grown in the Loire.)
20. B. Chardonnay

CHAPTER 10

1. C. Nebbiolo
2. A. Tuscany
3. D. Moscato
4. C. Veneto
5. B. Tuscany
6. A. Piedmont
7. D. None of the above (The Taurasi DOCG is found in Campania.)
8. C. Veneto
9. B. Tuscany
10. A. Piedmont
11. A. True
12. C. DOC
13. A. #1
14. A. True
15. A. True

CHAPTER 11

1. C. third
2. A. True
3. B. Tempranillo
4. D. DO
5. B. False (Only three appellations in Spain have been granted the DOCa status.)
6. C. Dry red wines
7. C. Dry red wines
8. A. Dry white wines
9. B. Sparkling wines
10. C. Dry red wines
11. D. Fortified wines
12. B. Verdejo
13. A. True
14. C. Winemaking techniques
15. A. Solera

CHAPTER 12

1. B. Ripeness
2. C. Rheinoceros
3. D. Lowest sugar content; normal harvest
4. A. Highest sugar content; made from raisins
5. C. Wine made from partially frozen grapes
6. B. Second highest sugar content; botrytised
7. B. False (Significant amounts of dry wine are produced in Germany in addition to sweet wines.)
8. A. boost alcohol content
9. A. Pinot Noir
10. B. False (An *Anbaugebiet* is the largest geographic area in German wine law.)
11. D. an *Einzellage*
12. A. True

CHAPTER 13

1. B. False (Port and Madeira, two fortified wines, are the most famous produced in Portugal.)
2. D. Touriga Nacional
3. A. *Denominação de Origem Controlada*
4. C. Bairrada
5. B. the Douro River Valley
6. C. the addition of high-proof brandy
7. D. Vinho Verde
8. B. False (Vintage Port is actually a bottle-aged Port and will spend a majority of the aging process in a bottle.)
9. B. during
10. C. cooked

CHAPTER 14

1. **C.** Grüner Veltliner
2. **B.** a scandal in the 1980s involving adulterated wine
3. **A.** True
4. **A.** style of dessert wine
5. **C.** Egri Bikavér
6. **A.** Furmint
7. **B.** Aszú
8. **A.** True
9. **B.** They lack an organized system of wine laws
10. **D.** "sour black"

CHAPTER 15

1. **B.** Australia
2. **A.** True
3. **A.** True
4. **B.** New World
5. **A.** True
6. **B.** New World
7. **A.** Old World
8. **B.** New World

CHAPTER 16

1. **D.** Zinfandel
2. **A.** Oregon
3. **B.** 75%
4. **C.** 85%
5. **B.** France, Italy, Spain, United States
6. **A.** California
7. **C.** Oregon
8. **A.** California
9. **B.** Washington
10. **D.** New York
11. **A.** California
12. **C.** Oregon
13. **D.** California, Washington, New York, Oregon
14. **D.** 90%
15. **B.** False (Wine is produced in all fifty states.)
16. **A.** Cabernet Sauvignon

CHAPTER 17

1. **C.** sixth
2. **B.** Shiraz
3. **B.** False (Because Australia is in the Southern Hemisphere, its climate is coolest in the southern areas.)
4. **A.** New South Wales
5. **A.** True
6. **C.** South Australia
7. **C.** Geographic Indication
8. **B.** 85%
9. **B.** South Australia
10. **D.** New South Wales
11. **A.** Western Australia
12. **B.** South Australia

CHAPTER 18

1. **C.** Sauvignon Blanc
2. **A.** True
3. **B.** False (Wine grapes are grown on both the North and South Islands of New Zealand.)
4. **B.** white
5. **D.** temperate-cool
6. **A.** North Island
7. **B.** 85%
8. **D.** Pinot Noir
9. **C.** 1970s
10. **C.** Central Otago

CHAPTER 19

1. **C.** trade embargoes
2. **B.** False (Due to the fact that South Africa is in the Southern Hemisphere, it will actually get warmer the further north one travels.)
3. **B.** Canterbury
4. **A.** the Wine of Origin (WO) laws
5. **C.** Dutch
6. **C.** Steen
7. **D.** 100%
8. **B.** 85%
9. **B.** Chenin Blanc
10. **A.** Pinot Noir and Cinsaut
11. **D.** Cabernet Sauvignon

CHAPTER 20

1. **A.** Cabernet Sauvignon
2. **A.** True
3. **B.** False (Chile ranks tenth in the world in terms of wine production.)
4. **D.** Pais
5. **B.** False (Chile's wine industry has actually had a large French influence.)
6. **C.** Carmenère
7. **B.** 85%
8. **C.** the Andes Mountains
9. **B.** False (In fact, Chile is the only wine-producing country in the world that has never had an infestation of *phylloxera* and is home to some of the purest grapevine stock in the world.)
10. **C.** Aconcagua Valley

CHAPTER 21

1. **C.** fifth
2. **B.** Spanish monks
3. **A.** True
4. **C.** 85%
5. **A.** True
6. **D.** Malbec
7. **A.** white
8. **C.** the temperate foothills of the Andes Mountains
9. **A.** Mendoza
10. **A.** True

CHAPTER 22

1. **A.** True
2. **C.** ice wine
3. **D.** Okanagan Valley
4. **A.** True
5. **C.** Valle de Guadalupe
6. **A.** dry red wine
7. **A.** True
8. **D.** Tannat
9. **A.** True
10. **A.** True

CHAPTER 23

1. **A.** True
2. **A.** Mesopotamia
3. **C.** the United States
4. **D.** Corn
5. **B.** False (Malting creates starch, not sugar.)
6. **B.** water
7. **B.** False (Hops give a beer bitterness, not sweetness.)

8. **A.** adjuncts
9. **B.** Mashing, boiling, fermenting, conditioning
10. **A.** True
11. **C.** wort
12. **B.** To carbonate the beer

CHAPTER 24

1. **A.** True
2. **A.** Ales
3. **B.** Lagers
4. **B.** Lagers
5. **C.** Not a difference
6. **A.** Ales
7. **C.** Not a difference
8. **A.** Ales
9. **B.** storage
10. **A.** Ale
11. **B.** Lager
12. **B.** Lager
13. **A.** Ale
14. **A.** Ale
15. **A.** Ale
16. **B.** Lager

CHAPTER 25

1. **C.** a mold that converts starch in rice into sugar.
2. **B.** parallel
3. **B.** False (Many top-grade sakés have small amounts of distilled alcohol added during pressing to help extract flavor.)
4. **A.** True
5. **D.** honey
6. **A.** True
7. **B.** wine
8. **A.** Southern Italy

CHAPTER 26

1. **B.** False (Fermentation creates alcohol, distillation simply concentrates or separates alcohol.)
2. **C.** 75%
3. **C.** 211
4. **A.** full-bodied and viscous
5. **C.** Heat exchange
6. **A.** True
7. **A.** True
8. **A.** Neutral spirits
9. **C.** Fruit- and plant-based spirits
10. **D.** Liqueurs and cordials
11. **B.** Grain-based spirits
12. **C.** Fruit- and plant-based spirits
13. **A.** Neutral spirits
14. **B.** Grain-based spirits
15. **C.** Fruit- and plant-based spirits

CHAPTER 27

1. **B.** False (Vodka is a neutral spirit, but tequila is definitely not.)
2. **D.** juniper berries
3. **A.** True (London dry gin)
4. **B.** Ireland
5. **A.** maintaining consistency
6. **C.** corn
7. **A.** malted barley
8. **B.** False (Since vodka is distilled to such a high degree, the sugar source is not as important as number of distillations, charcoal filtration, or the water added for dilution.)
9. **B.** Single-malt scotch
10. **C.** Puerto Rico
11. **A.** True
12. **C.** Kentucky whiskey
13. **A.** True
14. **C.** Añejo
15. **C.** X.O.
16. **B.** False (Cognac is a brandy produced from wine grapes, specifically the Ugni Blanc varietal.)
17. **A.** True

CHAPTER 28

1. **B.** Whoever ordered the wine
2. **B.** False (It is known as a waiter's friend.)
3. **B.** 60° to 65°F
4. **D.** 55° to 65°F
5. **A.** 50° to 60°F
6. **C.** 45° to 50°F
7. **A.** True
8. **B.** Reason to decant a vintage wine
9. **A.** Reason to decant a young wine
10. **B.** Reason to decant a vintage wine
11. **A.** Reason to decant a young wine
12. **B.** False (Depending upon style, beers should be served anywhere from 40° to 60°F.)
13. **C.** in a refrigerated area
14. **A.** True

CHAPTER 29

1. **A.** True
2. **B.** False (The average industry markup is anywhere from 300% to 500%.)
3. **A.** True
4. **B.** False (Organizing a wine list by price can limit a customer's choices.)
5. **D.** wine style
6. **C.** 10 gallons
7. **A.** Well
8. **B.** 750 ml

APPENDIX B

Pronunciation Guide

One of the most difficult aspects of mastering wine is being able to "speak the language." With thousands of industry specific and foreign terms used when discussing wine and alcoholic beverages, it can be dizzying at times to understand what you hear and speak intelligently about a topic. This guide is intended to help you phonetically pronounce some common (and some uncommon) terms used in this book, broken up by region and/or topic. Understand that this guide is set up for English-speaking readers, and while you may not suddenly sound like French or Italian is your "mother tongue," it will help to get you close to the native pronunciation.

COMMON WINE AND WINEMAKING TERMS

acetic *uh-SEE-tik*
amphora (s.) *am-FOR-uh*
amphorae (pl.) *am-FOR-ee*
anthocyanins *an-thoh-sy-uh-ninz*
appellation *ap-uh-LAY-shun*
astringency *uh-STRIN-jin-see*
astringent *uh-STRIN-jint*
Bacchus *BAH-kus*
Balthazar *BAHL-thuh-zahr*
barrique *bah-REEK*
battonage *bat-uh-NAHJ*
Blanc de Blancs *BLAHNK duh-BLAHNK*
Blanc de Noirs *BLAHNK duh-NWAHR*
botrytis *boh-TRY-tis*
Botrytis cinerea *boh-TRY-tis sin-uh-REE-uh*
botrytised *boh-TRY-tyzd*
carbonic *kahr-BAHN-ik*
chaptalization *chap-tuh-luh-ZAY-shun*
Charmat *shahr-MAT*
cilia *SIL-ee-uh*
cordon *kor-DAWN*
cuve close *KOOH-vay KLOHS*
Dionysus *dy-uh-NY-sus*
disgorgement *dis-GORJ-mint*
diurnal *dy-URN-uhl*
Enotria *eh-NOH-tree-uh*
ethanol *ETH-uh-nawl*
ferment *FUR-mint/fur-MENT*
fermentation *fur-min-TAY-shun*
goût de terroir *GOOHT duh-ter-WAH*
Jeroboam *jer-uh-BOH-um*
lagares *lah-GAHR-ez*
liqueur de tirage *lih-KUR duh-tee-RAHJ*
liqueur d'expédition *lih-KUR deks-pay-dees-YAHN*
maderized *MAH-duh-ryzd*
malolactic *mah-luh-LAK-tik*
méthode champenoise *meh-TOHD sham-pen-WAH*
méthode traditionale *meh-TOHD truh-dish-uh-NAHL*
Methuselah *meh-THOOH-zuh-luh*
Nebuchadnezzar *neb-yuh-kud-NEZ-ur*
olfactory *ohl-FAK-tuh-ree*
olfactory epithelium *ohl-FAK-tuh-ree ep-uh-THEE-lee-um*
panicle *PAN-ih-kul*
phylloxera *fih-LAHK-her-uh*
Rehoboam *ray-huh-BOH-um*
rosé *roh-ZAY*
Saccharomyces cerevisiae *sak-uh-roh-MY-seez ser-uh-VIS-ee-ee*
saignée *sahng-YAY*
Salmanazar *sahl-muh-NAH-zur*
sommelier *sah-mul-YAY*
sur lie *sur-LEE*
tannins *TAN-inz*
tartaric *tahr-TAHR-ik*
tartrate *TAHR-trayt*
terroir *ter-WAH*
Trichloroanisole *try-klor-uh-AN-ih-sohl*
veraison *ver-RAY-zun*
viniculture *VIN-ih-kul-chur*
viticulture *VIT-ih-kul-chur*
Vitis labrusca *VY-tis luh-BRUS-kuh*
Vitis vinifera *VY-tis vin-uh-FER-uh*

GRAPE VARIETAL NAMES

Agiorgitiko *ah-yohr-yee-TEE-koh*
Aglianico *ah-lee-AH-nee-koh*
Airén *ER-in*
Albariño *ahl-buh-REEN-yoh*
Aleatico *ah-lee-AH-tee-koh*
Aligoté *ahl-uh-GOH-tee*
Altesse *ahl-TES*
Alvarinho *ahl-vuh-REEN-yoh*
Aragonêz *er-uh-gah-NEZ*
Arneis *ahr-NAYS*
Assyrtiko *ah-sir-TEE-koh*
Athiri *ah-THEE-ree*
Auxerrois *awk-ser-WAH*
Babeasca *bah-bee-AHS-kuh*
Bacchus *BAH-kus*
Baga *BAH-guh*
Barbera *bahr-BER-uh*
Blanquette *blahn-KET*
Blauburgunder *BLAHW-bur-gun-dur*
Blaufränkisch *BLAHW-frahn-keesh*
Bombino Bianco *bahm-BEE-noh bee-AHN-koh*
Bonardo *boh-NAHR-duh*
Borrada Das Moscas *boh-RAH-duh dahs MAHS-kus*
Bouchet *booh-SHAY*
Bourboulenc *bor-buh-LAHNK*
Brachetto *brah-KEH-toh*
Braucol *broh KAHL*
Brunello *brooh-NEL-oh*
Bual *booh-AHL*
Cabernet Franc *kah-bur-NAY FRAHNK*
Cabernet Sauvignon *kah-bur-NAY saw-vin-YAHN*
Canaiolo *kan-eye-OH-loh*
Cannonau *kah-noh-NAHW*
Carignan *ker-ih-NYAHN*
Cariñena *ker-ih-NYAY-nuh*
Carmenère *kahr-meh-NER*
Catarratto *kah-tuh-RAH-toh*
Cencibel *SIN-suh-bel*
Cesanese *sez-uh-NAY-zee*
Chardonnay *shahr-duh-NAY*
Chasselas *SHAHS-lah*
Chenin Blanc *SHEN-in/SHUN-in BLAHNK*
Chiavennasca *kee-ahv-en-AHS-kuh*
Cinsault/Cinsaut *sin-SOH*
Clairette *kler-ET*
Colombard *KAH-lum-bahrd*
Cornalin *KOR-nuh-lin*
Cortese *kor-TAY-zay*
Corvina *kor-VEE-nuh*
Cot *KAHT*
Counoise *koohn-WAH*
Courbu *KOR-booh*
Criolla *kree-OH-luh*
Crljenak *kurl-JIN-ik*
Dobričić *doh-BRICH-ik*
Dolcetto *dohl-CHET-oh*
Dornfelder *DOORN-fel-dur*
Duras *DUR-uz*
Durif *DUR-if*
Esgana Cão *es-KAH-nuh KAHW*
Feinburgunder *FYN-bur-gun-dur*
Fendant *fin-DAHN*
Fetească Albă *feh-tee-AH-skuh AHL-buh*
Fetească Regală *feh-tee-AH-skuh ree-GAH-luh*
Fiano *FEE-ah-noh*
Fumé Blanc *fooh-MAY BLAHNK*
Furmint *FUR-mint*
Gamay *ga-MAY*
Garganega *gahr-gun-YAY-guh*
Garnacha *gahr-NAH-chuh*
Gewürztraminer *guh-VERTS-truh-mee-nur*
Godello *guh-DEL-oh*
Graciano *grah-see-AH-noh*
Grand Vidure *GRAHND vee-DUR*
Greco *GREH-koh*
Grenache *gruh-NAHSH*
Grillo *GRIL-loh/GREE-loh*
Gros Manseng *GROHS MAHN-seng*
Grüner Veltliner *GROOH-nur VELT-lee-nur*
Inzolia *in-ZOH-lee-uh*
Jacquère *jah-KER*
Johannisberg Riesling *joh-HAHN-is-burg REEZ-ling*
Kadarka *kuh-DAHR-kuh*
Kékfrankos *KEK-frahn-kohs*
Lambrusco *lahm-BROOH-skoh*
Lemberger *LIM-bur-gur*
Len de l'El *LIN duh-EL*
Macabeo *mah-kuh-BAY-oh*
MadelineAngevine *MAH-duh-leen AHN-juh-veen*
Malbec *MAHL-bek*
Malvasia *mahl-VAY-zhuh*
Mandilaria *mahn-duh-LIR-ee-uh*
Marsanne *mahr-SAHN*
Mauzac *MAW-zak*
Mavro *MAHV-roh*
Mavrodaphne/Mavrodafni *mahv-roh-DAHF-nee*
Mavrud *mah-VROOHD*

Mazuelo *mah-ZWAY-loh*
Melnick *MEL-nik*
Melon de Bourgogne *meh-LAWN duh-bor-GOHN*
Mencia *mahn-SEE-uh*
Merlot *mer-LOH*
Molette *moh-LET*
Molinara *moh-lih-NAHR-uh*
Monastrell *MAH-nuh-strel*
Mondeuse *mohn-DOOHZ*
Montepulciano *mahn-tuh-pul-chee-AH-noh*
Morellino *mor-uh-LEE-noh*
Morillon *MOR-ee-yahn*
Moscatel *mahs-kuh-TEL*
Moscato *moh-SKAH-toh*
Moschofilero *mah-skuh-FEE-luh-roh*
Mourvèdre *mor-VAY-druh*
Müller-Thurgau *MYOOH-lur TOOR-gahw*
Muscadelle *mus-kuh-DEL*
Muscardin *mus-kahr-DEEN*
Muscat *MUS-kat*
Muscat Blanc au Petits Grains *MUS-kat BLAHNK oh-puh-TEET GRAHN*
Muscat Canelli *MUS-kat kuh-NEL-ee*
Nebbiolo *neb-ee-OH-loh*
Negroamaro *nay-groh-uh-MAH-roh*
Nero d'Avola *NER-oh dee-AH-vuh-luh*
Nielluccio *nee-uh-LOOHT-see-oh*
Ojo de Liebre *oh-HOHday-lee-EH-bruh*
Pais *pah-EEZ*
Palomino *pah-luh-MEE-noh*
Parellada *per-ee-YAY-duh*
Pedro Ximénez *PAY-droh heh-MIH-nez*
Petit Manseng *puh-TEET MAHN-seng*
Petit Verdot *puh-TEET ver-DOH*
Petite Arvine *puh-TEET ahr-VEEN*
Petite Sirah *puh-TEET sih-RAH*
Picaridin *PEE-kahr-deen*
Picolit *PEE-koh-leet*
Picpoule *PEEK-pul*
Pignatello *pig-nuh-TEL-oh*
Pineau *pee-NOH*
Pineau de la Loire *pee-NOH duh-LWAHR*
Pinot Bianco *pee-NOH bee-AHN-koh*
Pinot Blanc *pee-NOH BLAHNK*
Pinot Grigio *PEE-noh GREE-zhee-oh*
Pinot Gris *PEE-noh GREE*
Pinot Meunier *PEE-noh moon-YAY*
Pinot Nero *PEE-noh NER-oh*
Pinot Noir *PEE-noh NWAHR*
Pinotage *PEE-noh-tahj*
Plavac Mali *plah-VAK MAH-lee*
Portugieser *por-tuh-GHEE-zur*
Poulsard *POOL-sahrd*
Primitivo *prim-uh-TEE-voh*
Prosecco *proh-SEK-oh*
Prugnolo *prooh-NYOH-loh*
Rabigato *rah-buh-GAH-toh*
Riesling *REEZ-ling*
Rivaner *ruh-VAH-nur*
Rkatsiteli *rih-kaht-suh-TEL-ee*
Roditis *roh-DEE-teez*
Rondinella *rahn-duh-NEL-uh*
Roussette *rooh-SET*
Roussanne *rooh-SAHN*
Rülander *ROOH-lahn-dur*
Sagrantino *sah-grun-TEE-noh*
Sangiovese *san-jee-uh-VAY-zee*
Saperavi *sah-per-AH-vee*
Sauvignon Blanc *SAW-vin-yahn BLAHNK*
Savagnin *sah-VAH-nyin*
Savatiano *sah-vah-TEE-uh-noh*
Scheurebe *SHOY-ray-buh*
Schwarzriesling *SHVAHRTZ-reez-ling*
Sciacarello *shee-yah-kuh-REL-oh*
Sémillon *say-mee-YAWN*
Sercial *SER-see-yul*
Seyval Blanc *SAY-vahl BLAHNK*
Shiraz *shih-RAHZ*
Silvaner *sil-VAH-nur*
Spätburgunder *SHPAYT-bur-gun-dur*
Steen *STEEN*
Sylvaner *sil-VAH-nur*
Syrah *sih-RAH*
Tannat *tuh-NAWT*
Tempranillo *tim-pruh-NEE-yoh*
Terret Noir *TER-et NWAHR*
Tinta Bairrada *TEEN-tah buh-RAH-duh*
Tinta Barroca *TEEN-tah buh-ROH-kah*
Tinta Negra Mole *TEEN-tah NAY-gruh MOH-lay*
Tinta Roriz *TEEN-tah HOH-reez*
Tinto Cão *TEEN-toh KAHW*
Tinto de Toro *TEEN-toh day-TOR-oh*
Tinto del Pais *TEEN-toh del-pah-EEZ*
Tinto Fino *TEEN-toh FEE-noh*
Tocai Friulano *TOH-ky freeh-ooh-LAH-noh*
Tokay (Fr.) *toh-KAY*
Torrontés *toh-RAHN-tayz*
Touriga Nacional *too-REE-gah nah-syoo-NAHL*

Trebbiano *treb-ee-AH-noh*
Trollinger *TRAW-lin-jur*
Trousseau *trooh-SOH*
Ugni Blanc *OOH-nee BLAHNK*
Ull de Liebre *UHL day-lee-EH-bruh*
Uva di Troia *OOH-vuh dee-TROY-uh*
Vaccarèse *vah-kuh-REZ*
Verdejo *ver-DAY-hoh*
Verdelho *ver-DEH-lyoh*
Verdicchio *ver-DEEK-yoh*
Vermentino *ver-min-TEE-noh*
Vernaccia *ver-NAHCH-yuh*
Viognier *vee-ohn-YAY*
Viura *vee-YOOR-uh*
Weissburgunder *VYS-bur-gun-dur*
Welschriesling *VELSH-/WELSH-reez-ling*
Xarel-lo *SZAHR-el-yoh*
Xynómavro/Xinómavro *ksee-NOH-mah-vroh*
Zinfandel *ZIN-fun-del*
Zweigelt *ZVY-gelt*

FRENCH WINE TERMS AND REGIONS

Alsace *ahl-ZAHS*
Alsatian *ahl-SAY-shun*
Angers *ahn-ZHAY*
Anjou *ahn-ZHOOH*
Anjou-Saumur *AHN-zhooh soh-MUR*
Appellation d'Origine Contrôlée *ah-pel-ah-SYOHN daw-ree-ZHEEN kohn-troh-LAY*
Arbois *ahr-BWAH*
Aube *AHW-buh*
Auxey-Duresses *OHK-seh-dooh-RES*
Avignon *ah-veen-YOHN*
Ay *EYE*
Bandol *bahn-DOHL*
Banyuls *BAHN-yulz*
Barsac *bahr-SAK*
Bas-Médoc *bahs-may-DAHK*
Batârd-Montrachet *bah-TAHR-mohn-rah-SHAY*
Beaujolais *boh-zhuh-LAY*
Beaujolais Nouveau *boh-zhuh-LAY nooh-VOH*
Beaune *BOHN*
Bergerac *ber-zheh-RACK*
Bienvenues-Batârd-Montrachet *byen-veh-NOOH-bah-TAHR-mohn-rah-SHAY*
blanc *BLAHNK*
Blanchots *blahn-SHOH*
Blanquette de Limoux *blahn-KETduh-lee-MOOH*
Bonnes Mares *BAWN MAHR*
Bonnezeaux *bah-nuh-ZOH*
Bordeaux *bor-DOH*
Bordeaux Supérieur *bor-DOH soo-per-YOOR*
Bordelais *bor-duh-LAY*
Bourgogne *boor-GOHN*
Bourgueil *bor-GYL*
Bouzeron *booh-zuh-RAHN*
Brouilly *brooh-YEE*
brut *BROOHT*
brut nature *BROOHT nah-TYOOR*
Buzet *booh-ZAY*
Cadillac *KAH-dee-yak*
Cahors *kuh-HOR*
Canon-Fronsac *kah-nohn-frahn-SAK*
Cassis *kuh-SEES*
Chablis *shuh-BLEE*
Chambertin *shahm-ber-TAN*
Chambertin-Clos de Bèze *shahm-ber-TAN-kloh-duh-BAYZ*
Chambolle-Musigny *shahm-BOHL-mooh-seen-YEE*
Champagne *sham-PAYN/-PAHN-yuh*
Chapelle-Chambertin *shuh-PEL-shahm-ber-TAN*
Charlemagne *shahr-lah-MAHN*
Charmes-Chambertin *SHARM-shahm-ber-TAN*
Chassagne-Montrachet *shah-SAHN-yuh-mohn-rah-SHAY*
château *sha-TOH*
Château Ausone *sha-TOH owh-SOHN-neuh*
Château-Chalon *SHAAH-toh shuh-LOHN*
Château Cheval Blanc *sha-TOH sheh-VAHL BLAHNK*
Château d'Yquem *sha-TOH dee-KIM*
Château-Grillet *sha-TOH gree-YAY*
Château Haut-Brion *sha-TOH oht-bree-OHN*
Château Lafite-Rothschild *sha-TOH lah-FEET RAWTH-sheeld*
Château Latour *sha-TOH lah-TOR*
Château Margaux *sha-TOH mahr-GOH*
Château Mouton-Rothschild *sha-TOH mooh-TOHN RAWTH-sheeld*
Châteauneuf-du-Pape *SHAAH-toh-noof-duh-POP*
Château Pétrus *sha-TOH peh-TROOHS*
châteaux (pl.) *sha-TOH*
Chénas *SHAY-nah*
Chevalier-Montrachet *sheh-vahl-YAY-mohn-rah-SHAY*
Chinon *shee-NOHN*
Chiroubles *shee-ROOH-bluh*
Chorey-lès-Beaune *shah-RAY-leh-BOHN*
claret *KLER-it*
clos *KLOH*
Clos de la Roche *KLOH duh-lah-RAWSH*

Clos de Tart *KLOH duh-TAHR*
Clos de Vougeot *KLOH duh-vooh-ZHOH*
Clos des Lambrays *KLOH duh-lahm-BRAY*
Clos Saint-Denis *KLOH san-duh-NEE*
Comblanchien *kohm-blahn-SHYEN*
Condrieu *KAHN-dree-yuh*
Contrôlée *kohn-troh-LAY*
Corbières *kor-BYER*
Corgoloin *kor-guh-LOYN*
Cornas *kor-NAHS*
Corsica *KOR-sih-kuh*
Corton *kor-TOHN*
Corton-Charlemagne *kor-TOHN-shahr-lah-MAHN*
Costières de Nîmes *kahs-TYER duh-NEEM*
côte *KOHT*
coteaux *KOAT-toh*
Coteaux d'Aix-en-Provence *KOAT-toh duh-EYE-ihn-pruh-VAAHNZ*
Coteaux du Languedoc *KOAT-toh doo-LAHN-geh-dock*
Coteaux du Layon *KOAT-toh doo-LAY-ohn*
Côte Blonde *KOAT BLAHND*
Côte Brune *KOHT BROOHN*
Côte Chalonnaise *KOHT shal-uh-NAY*
Côte de Beaune *KOHT duh-BOHN*
Côte de Brouilly *KOHT duh-brooh-YEE*
Côte de Nuits *KOHT duh-NWEE*
Côte de Sézanne *KOHT duh-say-ZAHN*
Côte d'Or *KOHT DOR*
Côte-Rôtie *KOHT roh-TEE*
côtes *KOHT*
Côtes de Blanc *KOHT duh-BLAHNK*
Côtes de Blaye *KOHT duh-BLY-uh*
Côtes de Bourg *KOHT duh-BORG*
Côtes de Duras *KOHT duh-DUR-uh*
Côtes de Provence *KOHT duh-pruh-VAHNS*
Côtes du Jura *KOHT duh-JUR-uh*
Côtes-du-Rhone *koht-duh-ROHN*
Côtes-du-Roussillon *koht-duh-rooh-see-YOHN*
crémant *kreh-MAHNT*
Crémant d'Alsace *kreh-MAHNT dahl-ZAHS*
Crémant de Jura *kreh-MAHNT duh-JUR-uh*
Cremant de Limoux *kreh-MAHNT duh-lee-MOOH*
Criots-Bâtard-Montrachet *kree-OH-bah-TAHR-mohn-rah-SHAY*
Cristal *kree-STAHL*
Crozes-Hermitage *KROHZ-er-muh-TAHZH*
cru *KROOH*
cru beaujolais *KROOH boh-zhuh-LAY*
cru bourgeois *KROOH boor-ZHWAH*
cru Classé *KROOH KLAHS-uh*
cuvée *kooh-VAY*
cuvée de prestige *kooh-VAY duh-pray-STEEZH*
cuvée speciale *kooh-VAY spes-YAHL*
de *duh*
dégorgement *day-gorzh-MAHN*
demi *DEM-ee*
demi-sec *DEM-ee-sek*
département *day-pahrt-MAHN*
domaine *doe-MAIN*
Dom Perignon *DAHM per-ee-NYOHN*
Dordogne *dor-DOHN-yuh*
doux *DOOH*
Échezeaux *eh-sheh-ZOH*
Edelzwicker *ED-ul-zvik-ur*
Entre-Deux-Mers *AHN-tray DOOH MER*
Epenots *ep-uh-NOH*
Épernay *ay-pur-NAY*
Ermitage *er-muh-TAHZH*
Faugeres *foh-ZHER*
Fitou *fee-TOOH*
Fixin *feek-ZENG*
Flagey-Echezeaux *flah-ZHEE-eh-sheh-ZOH*
Fleurie *fluh-REE*
Fronsac *frahn-SAK*
Gaillac *GAY-yak*
galets *gah-LET*
Garonne Estuary *guh-RAHN*
Gevrey-Chambertin *zheh-VRAY-shahm-ber-TAN*
Gigondas *zhee-gohn-DAHS*
Gironde *zhee-ROHND*
Givry *zhee-VREE*
Grands-Échezeaux *GRAHN-eh-sheh-ZOH*
Graves *GRAHV*
Grenouilles *gruh-NWEE*
Griotte-Chambertin *gree-AHT-shahm-ber-TAN*
Haut-Médoc *oht-may-DAHK*
Hermitage *er-muh-TAHZH*
Institut National des Appellations d'Origine *en-stee-TOOHT nah-syaw-NAHL dah-pel-ah-SYOHN daw-ree-ZHEEN*
Irouléguy *ee-rooh-leh-GHEE*
Juliénas *joohl-yeh-NAS*
Jura *JUR-uh*
Jurançon *zhooh-rahn-SOHN*
Kimmeridgian *kim-uh-RID-jee-un*
La Clape *luh-CLAHP*
Ladoix-Serrigny *lah-DWAAH-sehr-REHG-neh*
La Grand Rue *lah-grahn-ROO*

Lalande-de-Pomerol *luh-LAAHND-duh-PAAH-muhr-aahl*
Languedoc *LAHN-geh-dock*
Languedoc-Roussillon *LAHN-geh-dock roo-see-YOHN*
La Romanée *lah-roh-muh-NAY*
La Tâche *lah-TAHSH*
Latricières-Chambertin *lah-treet-see-ER-shahm-ber-TAN*
le mistral *lay-mee-STRAHL*
Les Bougros *lay-booh-GROH*
Les Clos *lay-CLOH*
Les Preuses *lay-PROOHZ*
L'Étoile *lay-TWAH*
Lirac *lih-RAHK*
Listrac *lee-STRAHK*
Loire *LWAHR*
Louis Roederer *looh-EE ROH-dur-ur*
Loupiac *looh-PYAHK*
Lussac-Saint-Émilion *looh-SAHK sant-eh-meel-YAWN*
Lyons *lee-YOHN*
Mâcon *mah-KOHN*
Mâconnais *mah-koh-NAY*
Madiran *MAH-dur-un*
maison *may-ZOHN*
Maranges *mah-RAHNZH*
Margaux *mahr-GOH*
Marsannay *mahr-sah-NAY*
Marseilles *mahr-SAY*
Massif Central *mah-SEEF sen-TRAHL*
Maury *moh-REE*
Mazis-Chambertin *mah-ZEE-shahm-ber-TAN*
Mazoyerès-Chambertin *mahs-zoh-YER-shahm-ber-TAN*
Médoc *may-DAHK*
Mercurey *mer-kyoo-RAY*
Meursault *mer-SOH*
Minervois *mee-ner-VWAH*
Moët & Chandon *moh-ET ee-shahn-DAWN*
Monbazillac *mohn-BAH-zee-yahk*
Montagne de Reims *mohn-TAHN-yuh duh-REEMZ*
Montagne-Saint-Émilion *mohn-TAHN-yuh sant-eh-meel-YAWN*
Montagny *mohn-than-YEE*
Monthélie *mohn-tah-LEE*
Montlouis *mohn-loo-EE*
Montpeyroux *mohn-pay-ROOH*
Montrachet *mohn-rah-SHAY*
Morey-Saint-Denis *moh-RAY-san-duh-NEE*
Morgon *mor-GOHN*
Moulin-à-Vent *moo-lan-oh-VAHN*
Moulis *mooh-LEE*
mousseux *mooh-SOH*
Muscadet *moohz-/mus-kuh-DAY*
Muscadet de Sèvre-et-Maine *moohz-/mus-kuh-DAY duh-SEV- et-MAYN*
Muscat de Beaumes-de-Venise *MUS-kat duh-BOHM-duh-veh-NEES*
Muscat de Frontignan *MUS-kat duh-frahn-teen-YAHN*
Muscat de Lunel *MUS-kat duh-looh-NEL*
Muscat de Mireval *MUS-kat duh-mir-uh-VAHL*
Muscat de Rivesaltes *MUS-kat duh-ree-vuh-SOH*
Muscat de Saint-Jean-de-Minervois *MUS-kat duh-sant-ZHAHN-duh-min-er-VWAH*
Musigny *mooh-seen-YEE*
négociant *nuh-GOHSH-ee-yant*
négociant-éleveur *nuh-GOHSH-ee-yant EL-uh-vur*
Nuits-Saint George *NWEE-sant-ZHORZH*
Orleans *or-lay-AHN*
Parsac Saint-Émilion *pahr-ZAHK sant-eh-meel-YAWN*
Passe-Tout-Grains *pahs-tooht-GRAHN*
Patrimonio *pah-truh-MOH-nee-oh*
Pauillac *poh-YAHK*
Pays Nantais *PAY-ee nahn-TAY*
Pernand-Vergelesses *per-NAHN- ver-zheh-LES*
Pessac-Léognan *peh-SAHK-lay-oh-NYAHN*
pétillant *pet-ee-YAHN*
Picpoul de Pinet *PEEK-puhl duh-pih-NAY*
Pic Saint-Loup *PEEK-sant-LOOHP*
Pomerol *PAH-mur-ahl*
Pommard *poh-MAHR*
Pouilly-Fuissé *pooh-EE-fwee-SAY*
Pouilly-Fumé *pooh-EE-fooh-MAY*
Pouilly-sur-Loire *pooh-EE-sur-LWAHR*
pourriture noble *pooh-ree-TYOOR NAW-bluh*
Prémeaux-Prissey *preh-MOH-pree-SEE*
Provençal *proh-ven-SAHL*
Provence *pruh-VAHNS*
Puligny-Montrachet *pooh-leen-YEE-mohn-rah-SHAY*
pupitres *pyooh-PEE-truh*
Pyrenees *PIR-uh-neez*
Quartes de Chaume *kahrt-duh-SHOHM*
Régnié *ray-NEE*
Reims *REEMZ*
remuage *rim-WAHJ*
Rhône *ROHN*
Richebourg *reesh-BOOR*
Rivesaltes *ree-vuh-SOH*
Romanée-Conti *roh-muh-NAY-kohn-TEE*
Romanée-Saint-Vivant *roh-muh-NAY-sant-vee-VAHN*

rouge *ROOZH*
Roussillon *rooh-see-YOHN*
Ruchottes-Chambertin *rooh-SHOH-shahm-ber-TAN*
Rully *rooh-YEE*
Saint-Amour *SAN tuh-MOR*
Saint-Aubin *san-toh-BEEN*
Saint-Chinian *sahngt-shih-NEE-yahn*
Saint-Croix-du-Mont *sant-KWAH-duh-MOHN*
Saint-Émilion *sahngt-eh-MEEL-ee-yahn*
Saint-Estèphe *sahngt-eh-STEFF*
Saint-Georges-Saint-Émilion *sahngt-JORDJ SAHNGT-eh-MEEL-ee-yahn*
Saint-Joseph *SAHNGT joh-SEHF*
Saint-Julien *sahngt-JOO-lee-yun*
Saint-Nicholas-de-Bourgueil *sant-nee-koh-LAH-duh-bor-GYL*
Saint-Romain *sant-roh-MAN*
Sancerre *sahn-SER*
Santenay *sahn-tuh-NAY*
Saumur *soh-MUR*
Saumur Champigny *soh-MUR shahm-peen-YEE*
Saumur Mousseaux *soh-MUR mooh-SOH*
Saussignac *soh-seen-YAHK*
Sauternes *soh-TERN*
Savennières *sah-ven-YER*
Savigny-lès-Beaune *sah-veen-YEE-lay-BOHN*
Savoie *suh-VWAH*
Savoy *suh-VOY*
sec *SEK*
Sèlections de Grains Nobles *say-lek-SYOHN duh-GRAHN NAW-bluh*
Sud Ouest *SOOHD WEST*
Tavel *tah-VEL*
Tokay d'Alsace *TOH-kay dahl-ZAHS*
Touraine *tooh-RAYN*
Tours *TOOR*
Vacqueyras *vah-kay-RAH*
Vallèe de la Marne *vah-LAY duh-lah-MAHRN*
Valmur *vahl-MUR*
Vaudèsir *voh-duh-ZEER*
Vendange Tardive *ven-DAHNZH tahr-DEEV*
Vielle Vignes *vee-YAY VEEN-yeh*
vigneron *veen-yeh-RAHN*
villages *vee-LAHZH*
vin *VIN/VAN*
Vin de Corse *VIN-duh-KORS*
Vin Délimité de Qualité Supérieure *VIHN duh-LIM-ee-tay duh-KAHL-uh-tay suh-PEER-ee-yuhr*
vin de paille *VIN-duh-PAH-yuh*
vin de pays *VIN-duh-PAY-ee*
Vin de Pays d'Oc *VIN-duh-PAY-ee-DAWK*
Vin de Pays l'Île de Béaute *VIN-duh-PAY-ee-il-duh-BOHT*
Vin de Savoie *VIN-duh-suh-VWAH*
vin doux naturels *VIHN DOOH NAHT-chuh-rehl*
vin de table *VIN-duh-TAH-bluh*
vin jaune *VIN ZHOHN*
vins *VIN*
vins du Centre *VIN duh-SAHN-treh*
Volnay *vohl-NAY*
Vosges *VOHZH*
Vosne-Romanée *VOHN-roh-muh-NAY*
Vougeot *vooh-ZHOH*
Vouvray *vooh-VRAY*

ITALIAN WINE TERMS AND REGIONS

Abruzzo *uh-BROOHT-zoh*
Acqui *ah-KEE*
Adriatic *ay-dree-AT-ik*
Aglianico del Vulture *AHG-lee-ah-nih-koh del-VOOL-tuh-ree*
Alba *AHL-buh*
Albana di Romagna *AHL-buh-nuh dee-roh-MAHN-yuh*
Alto Adige *AHL-toh AH-dee-jay*
Amarone della Valpolicella *am-uh-ROH-nee DEL-uh vahl-poh-luh-CHEL-uh*
Apennine *AP-puh-nyn*
Apulia *uh-PYOOH-lee-uh*
Asti *AH-stee*
Barbaresco *bahr-buh-RES-koh*
Barbera d'Alba *bahr-BER-uh DAHL-buh*
Barbera d'Asti *bahr-BER-uh DAH-stee*
Bardolino *bahr-duh-LEE-noh*
Bardolino Superiore *bahr-duh-LEE-noh sooh-per-ee-OR-ay*
Barolo *buh-ROH-loh*
Basilicata *buh-sil-ih-KAH-tuh*
bianco *bee-AHN-koh*
Bolgheri *bohl-GER-ee*
Bolgheri Sassicaia *bohl-GER-ee sah-sih-KY-uh*
Brachetto d'Acqui *brah-KEH-toh dah-KEE*
Brescia *BRESH-uh*
Brunello di Montalcino *brooh-NEL-oh dee-mahn-tul-CHEE-noh*
Calabria *kuh-LAH-bree-uh*
Campania *kum-PAHN-yuh*
Carmignano *kahr-mih-NYAH-noh*

Cerasuolo di Vittoria *cher-ah-SWOH-loh dee-vee-TOR-ee-ah*
Cesanese del Piglio *sez-uh-NAY-zee del-PEE-lee-oh*
Chianti *kee-YAWN-tee*
Chianti Classico *kee-YAHN-tee KLAH-see-koh*
Chianti Colli Aretini *kee-YAHN-tee KOH-lee er-en-TEE-nee*
Chianti Colli Fiorentini *kee-YAHN-tee KOH-lee fyor-en-TEE-nee*
Chianti Colline Pisane *kee-YAHN-tee koh-LEE-nay pee-SAH-nay*
Chianti Colli Senesi *kee-YAHN-tee KOH-lee suh-NAY-see*
Chianti Montalbano *kee-YAHN-tee mahn-TAHL-buh-noh*
Chianti Rufina *kee-YAHN-tee rooh-FEE-nah*
Cinque Terre *ching-kwuh-TER-uh*
Ciro *CHEE-roh*
Classico *KLAH-see-koh*
Colline Teramane *koh-LEE-nay ter-uh-MAH-nay*
Colli Orientali de Friuli Picolit *KOH-lee or-ee-en-TAH-lee deh-free-YOOH-lee PEE-koh-leet*
Conero Riserva *koh-NER-oh ree-ZER-vuh*
d' *duh*
della *DEL-uh*
Denominazione di Origine Controllata *dih-nahm-ih-naht-see-OH-nay dee-OR-uh-jih-nuh kahn-troh-LAH-tuh*
Denominazione di Origine Controllata e Garantita *dih-nahm-ih-naht-see-oh-nay dee-OR-uh-jih-nuh kahn-troh-LAH-tuh eh-gahr-un-TEE-tuh*
di *dee*
dolce *DOHL-chay*
Dolcetto d'Alba *dohl-CHET-oh DAHL-buh*
Dolcetto d'Asti *dohl-CHET-oh DAH-stee*
Dolcetto di Dogliani *dohl-CHET-oh dee-daw-lee-AH-nee*
Dolcetto di Ovada *dohl-CHET-oh dee-oh-VAH-dah*
Emilia *eh-MEEL-yuh*
Emilia-Romagna *eh-MEEL-yuh roh-MAHN-yah*
Est!Est!!Est!!! di Montefiascone *est-est-EST dee-mahn-tay-fee-ah-SKOH-nay*
Fiano di Avellino *fee-AH-noh dee-ah-veh-LEE-noh*
Franciacorta *FRAHNCH-yuh-kort-uh*
Friuli *free-OOH-lee*
Friuli-Venezia Giulia *free-OOH-lee vuh-NET-syuh JOOHL-yuh*
frizzante *frih-ZAHN-tay*
gallo negro *GAH-loh NAY-groh*
Gattinara *gah-tih-NAH-ruh*
Gavi *GAH-vee*
Ghemme *GIH-may*
Greco di Tufo *GRAY-koh dee-TOOH-foh*
Indicazione Geografica Tipica *in-duh-kaht-see-OH-nay jee-oh-GRAHF-ee-kuh TEE-pee-kuh*
Langhe *LAHNG*
Latium *LAY-shum*
Lazio *LAHZ-yoh*
Liguria *lih-GOOR-yuh*
Lombardia *lahm-BAHR-dee-uh*
Marche *MAHR-kay*
The Marches *MAHR-kay*
Marsala *mahr-SAH-luh*
Metodo Classico *meh-TOH-doh KLAH-see-koh*
Molise *MOH-lee-zay*
Montalcino *mahn-tul-CHEE-noh*
Montepulciano *mahn-tuh-pul-chee-AH-noh*
Montepulciano d'Abruzzo *mahn-tuh-puhl-CHEE-aah-noh duh-uh-BROOT-zoh*
Montepulciano d'Abruzzo Colline Teramane *mahn-tuh-pul-chee-AH-noh duh-BROOHT-zoh koh-LEE-nay ter-uh-MAH-nay*
Morellino di Scansano *mor-uh-LEE-noh dee-skahn-SAH-noh*
Moscato d' Asti *moh-SKAH-toh dee-AH-stee*
Oltrepo Pavese *ohl-TREP-oh pah-VAY-zay*
Oltrepò Pavese Metodo Classico *ohl-TREP-oh pah-VAY-zay meh-TOH-doh KLAH-see-koh*
Ornellaia *ore-nuh-LY-yuh*
Orvieto *or-vee-ET-oh*
passito *puh-SEE-toh*
Piedmont *PEED-mahnt*
Piemonte *pyeh-MAHN-tay*
Pinot Grigio Alto-Adige *PEE-noh GREE-zhee-oh AHL-toh AH-dee-jay*
Pinot Grigio della Venezie *PEE-noh GREE-zhee-oh DEL-uh vuh-NET-see*
Prosecco di Conegliano *proh-SEK-oh dee-kah-neg-lee-AH-noh*
Prosecco di Valdobbiadene *proh-SEK-oh dee-VAHL-dah-bee-ah-deh-neh*
Ramandolo *rah-MAHN-doh-loh*
recioto *reh-see-OH-toh*
Recioto della Valpolicella *reh-see-OH-toh DEL-uh vahl-poh-luh-CHEL-uh*
Recioto di Soave *reh-see-OH-toh dee-suh-WAH-vay*
riserva *ree-ZER-vuh*

Roero *roh-AY-roh*
Romagna *roh-MAHN-yah*
rosato *roh-ZAH-toh*
rosso *RAW-soh*
Rosso di Montalcino *RAW-soh dee-mahn-tul-CHEE-noh*
Sagrantino di Montefalco *sah-grun-TEE-noh dee-mahn-teh-FAHLl-koh*
Salice Salento *SAH-lee-cheh sah-LEN-toh*
Sardegna *sahr-DAYN-yah*
Sardinia *sahr-DIN-ee-uh*
Sassicaia *sah-sih-KY-yuh*
secco *SEK-oh*
Sforzato di Valtellina *sfort-SAH-toh dee-vahl-teh-LEE-nuh*
Sicilia *sih-SEEL-yuh*
Soave *suh-WAH-vay*
Soave Superiore *suh-WAH-vay sooh-per-ee-OR-ay*
Solaia *soh-LY-uh*
spumante *spooh-MAHN-tay*
superiore *sooh-per-ee-OR-ay*
Taurasi *TAW-rah-see*
Tignanello *tee-nyah-NEL-oh*
Torgiano Rosso Riserva *tor-zhee-AH-noh RAW-soh ree-ZER-vuh*
Toscano *toh-SKAH-noh*
Trebbiano d'Abruzzo *treb-ee-AH-noh duh-BROOHT-zoh*
Trentino *tren-TEE-noh*
Trentino-Alto Adige *tren-TEE-noh AHL-toh AH-dee-jay*
Tres Venezie *TRAY vuh-NET-see*
Turin *TOOR-in*
Tyrrhenian *tih-REE-nee-un*
Umbria *OOHM-bree-uh*
Valle d'Aosta *VAH-lay dah-AWS-tah*
Valpolicella *vahl-poh-luh-CHEL-uh*
Valtellina *vahl-teh-LEE-nah*
Valtellina Superiore *vahl-teh-LEE-nah sooh-per-ee-OR-ay*
Veneto *VAY-nuh-toh*
Vermentino di Gallura *ver-men-TEE-noh dee-guh-LOOR-ah*
Vernaccia di San Gimignano *ver-NAHCH-yuh dee-sahn-jee-mee-NYAH-noh*
Vernaccia di Serrapetrona *ver-NAHCH-yuh dee-ser-ah-peh-TROH-nah*
Verona *veh-ROH-nuh*
Vigna Vecchia *VEEN-yuh VEK-ee-uh*
vino *VEE-noh*
vino da tavola *VEE-noh duh-TAH-voh-lah*
Vino Nobile di Montepulciano *VEE-noh NOH-bee-lay dee-mahn-tuh-pul-chee-AH-noh*
vin santo *VEEN SAHN-toh*
Vulture *VOOL-tuh-ree*

SPANISH WINE TERMS AND REGIONS

albariza *ahl-buh-REE-zuh*
Alentejo *ahl-un-TAY-yoh*
Almansa *ahl-MAHN-zuh*
Amontillado *uh-mahn-tee-YAH-doh/-LAH-doh*
Andalucia *an-duh-LOOH-zhee-yuh*
Aragon *ER-uh-gahn*
Basque *BASK/BAHSK*
Bierzo *bee-ER-tzoh*
blanco *BLAHN-koh*
bodega *boh-DAY-guh*
Bullas *booh-YAHZ*
Cadiz *kuh-DEEZ*
Calatayud *kuh-LAHT-ah-yood*
Cantabrian *kan-TAY-bree-un*
Cariñena *ker-ih-NYAY-nuh*
Castilla-La Mancha *kuh-STEE-yuh luh-MAHN-shuh*
Castilla y León *kuh-STEEL-yuh ee-leh-YOHN*
Catalan *KAT-uh-lun*
Catalonia *kat-uh-LOH-nee-uh*
Cataluña *kat-uh-LOOH-nyuh*
Cava *KAH-vuh*
Consejo Regulador *kahn-SAY-hoh reg-yooh-luh-DOR-eh*
criadera *kree-uh-DER-uh*
crianza *kree-AHN-zuh*
Denominacione de Origen *dih-nah-muh-NAH-see-ohn day-OR-uh-jin*
Denominacióne de Origen Calificada *dih-nah-muh-NAH-see-ohn day-OR-uh-jin kah-lih-fih-KAH-duh*
Duero *DWEH-roh*
dulce *DOOL-chay*
Ebro *AY-broh*
El Puerto de Santa Maria *EL PWER-toh day-SAHN-tuh-muh-REE-uh*
Extremadura *ek-struh-muh-DOOR-uh*
fino *FEE-noh*
flor *FLOR*
Galicia *guh-LISH-uh*
Gran Reserva *GRAHN ree-ZER-vuh*
Hispania *hih-SPAHN-yuh*
Iberian *EYE-bir-ee-un*
Jerez *heh-REZ*
Jerez de la Frontera *heh-REZ day-lah-frahn-TER-uh*

joven *HOH-vin*
Jumilla *joo-MEE-yah*
La Mancha *lah-MAHN-shuh*
La Rioja *lah-ree-OH-hah*
Málaga *muh-LAH-guh*
manzanilla *mahn-zuh-NEE-yuh*
Meseta Central *meh-SET-uh sin-TRAWL*
Montillia-Moriles *mahn-TEE-yah moh-REE-les*
Murcia *MUR-shuh*
Navarra *nuh-VAH-ruh*
Navarro *nuh-VAH-roh*
oloroso *oh-loh-ROH-zoh*
palo cortado *PAH-loh kor-TAH-doh*
Penedès *PUH-nen-dez*
Priorat *pree-uh-RAHT*
Priorato *pree-uh-RAH-toh*
rayas *RAY-uz*
reserva *ray-SER-vuh*
Rías Baixas *REE-us BY-shus*
Ribera del Duero *rih-BER-uh del-DWEH-roh*
Ribera de Guadiana *reh-BEHR-uh day-GWAH-dee-aah-nuh*
Rioja *ree-OH-hah*
Rioja Alavesa *ree-OH-hah ahl-uh-VAY-zuh*
Rioja Alta *ree-OH-hah AHL-tuh*
Rioja Baja *ree-OH-hah BAH-hah*
rosado *roh-SAH-doh*
Rueda *roo-EH-duh*
Sanlúcar de Barrameda *sahn-looh-KAHR day-ber-ah-MAY-duh*
Scala Dei *SKAH-lah DY*
seco *SEK-oh*
solera *soh-LER-uh*
Tarragona *tah-rah-GOH-nah*
tinto *TEEN-toh*
Toro *TOR-oh*
Unico *OOH-nee-koh*
Valdepeñas *vahl-duh-PAYN-yuz*
Valencia *vah-LEN-shuh/-see-uh*
Vega Sicilia *VAY-guh suh-SIL-yuh*
Viñas Viejas *VEE-nyus vee-YAY-hahs*
vino *VEE-noh*
Vino de Calidad *VEE-noh day-KAH-leh-dahd*
Vino de Calidad con Indicación Geogrófica *VEE-noh KAH-leh-dahd kohn-in-duh-KAH-syohn jee-oh-GRAH-fee-kah*
vino de color *VEE-noh day-koh-LOR*
vino de la tierra *VEE-noh day-lah-tee-ER-uh*
vino de mesa *VEE-noh day-MAY-suh*
vino de pago *VEE-noh day-PAH-goh*
vino dulce *VEE-noh DOOL-chay*
Yecla *YEK-luh*

GERMAN WINE TERMS AND REGIONS

Ahr *AHR*
Alte Reben *AHL-tuh RAY-bun*
Amtliche Prüfungsnummer *AHMT-lish-eh PROOHF-unz-snooh-mur*
anbaugebiet *ahn-BAHW-guh-beet*
anbaugebiete (pl.) *ahn-BAHW-guh-beet-uh*
Auslese *AHWS-lay-suh*
Baden *BAH-din*
Beerenauslese *ber-en-AHWS-lay-suh*
Bereich (s.) *buh-RYK*
bereiche (pl.) *buh-RYK-uh*
Bernkastel *BURN-kahs-ul*
bocksbeutel *BAHKS-boy-tul*
Calmont *kahl-MAHNT*
Charta *CHAR-tuh*
Deutscher Landwein *DOY-chur LAHND-vyn*
Deutscher Tafelwein *DOY-chur TAH-ful-vyn*
edelfäule *EH-dul-foy-leh*
einzellage (s.) *EIN-zuh-lahg-uh*
einzellagen (pl.) *EIN-zuh-lahg-in*
Eiswein *ICE-vine*
erste lage *ER-stuh LAHG-uh*
erstes gewächs *ER-sterz guh-VAYKS*
erzeugerabfüllung *ER-zoy-gur-AHB-foo-lung*
Franken *FRAHN-kin*
grosses gewächs *GROHS guh-VAYKS*
grosslage (s.) *GROHS-lahg-uh*
grosslagen (pl.) *GROHS-lahg-in*
gutsabfüllung *goots-AHB-foo-lung*
halbtrocken *HAHLB-trahk-in*
Hessiche Bergstrasse *HES-eesh BERG-strahs-uh*
Johannisberg *yoh-HAHN-is-burg*
Kabinett *KAH-buh-net*
Landwein *LAHND-vyn*
Liebfraumilch *LEEB-frahw-milk*
Michelsberg *MEEK-uls-burg*
Mittelrhein *MIT-ul-ryn*
Mosel *moh-ZEL*
Mosel-Saar-Ruwer *moh-ZELL ZAHR ROOH-ver*
Nahe *NAH-heh*
oechsle *UKS-luh*
Palatinate *puh-LAT-uh-nayt*
Pfalz *FAHLTZ*
Piesport *PEEZ-port*

qualitätswein *kwah-luh-TAYTS-vyn*
Qualitätswein bestimmter Anbaugebiete *kwah-luh-TAYTS-vyn beh-SHTIM-tur ahn-BAHW-guh-beet-uh*
Qualitätswein mit Prädikat *kwah-luh-TAYTS-vyn mit PRAY-deh-kaht*
Rheingau *RYN-gahw*
Rheinhessen *RYN-hes-in*
Rheinpfalz *RYN-fahlltz*
Rhine *RYN*
rotwein *ROHT-vyn*
Ruwer *ROOH-ver*
Saale Unstrut *ZAHL-uh OOHN-shtrut*
Saar *ZAHR*
Sachsen *ZAK-sen*
Schloss Johannisberg *SHLOHZ yoh-HAHN-is-burg*
Sekt *SEKT*
Spätlese *SHPAYT-lay-suh*
süssreserve *ZOOS-ree-zerv*
Tafelwein *TAH-ful-vyn*
trocken *TRAHK-in*
Trockenbeeren-auslese *TRAHK-in-ber-in-AHWS-lay-suh*
Verband Deutscher Prädikats *VER-bahnd DOY-chur PRAY-deh-kahts*
Weingut *VYN-goot*
weissherbst *VYS-herbst*
weisswein *VYS-vyn*
Württemberg *VOORT-em-burg*
Zell *ZEL*

PORTUGUESE WINE TERMS AND REGIONS

aguardente *ah-gwahr-DEN-tay*
Alentejo *ahl-un-TAY-oh*
Bairrada *buh-RAH-duh*
Baixo Corgo *BY-shoh KOR-goh*
barros *BAH-rohz*
branco *BRAHN-koh*
Cima Corgo *CHEE-mah KOR-goh*
colheita *kohl-HEE-tuh*
Dão *DAHWN*
Denominação de Origem Controlada *deh-nah-meh-nah-KAHW deh-or-eh-JEM KAHN-troh-lah-dah*
doce *doh-CHAY*
Douro *DOOR-oh*
Garrafeira *ger-uh-FEE-ruh*
Indicação de Proveniencia Regulamentada *en-deh-kah-KAHW deh-proh-veh-NYEN-see-uh reg-yooh-luh-men-TAH-dah*
Madeira *muh-DIR-uh*
maduro *muh-DUR-oh*
Mateus *MAH-toohz*
Minho *MEEN-yoh*
Moscatel de Setúbal *MAWS-kuh-tel deh-seh-TOOH-bul*
Oporto *oh-POR-toh*
quinta *KEEN-tuh*
rosado *roh-SAH-doh*
seco *SEK-oh*
Setúbal *seh-TOOH-bul*
tinto *TEEN-toh*
vinho *VEEN-yoh*
vinho de mesa *VEEN-yoh deh-MAY-suh*
vinho regional *VEEN-yoh reg-yuh-NAL*
Vinho Verde *VEEN-yoh VERD*

AUSTRIAN WINE TERMS AND REGIONS

Ausbruch *AHWS-broohk*
Burgenland *BUR-gun-lahnd*
Districtus Austriae Controllatus *deh-STRIK-tus AHS-truh-ee KAHN-troh-luh-tus*
Federspiel *FEE-dur-shpeel*
Kamptal *KAHMP-tahl*
Landwein *LAHND-vyn*
Neusiedl *nooh-SEED-leh*
Neusiedlersee *NOY-zeed-lur-zay*
Neusiedlersee-Hügelland *NOY-zeed-lur-zay HOOG-eh-lahnd*
Niederösterreich *nee-dur-AHS-tur-ryk*
Pradikätswein *PRAH-deh-kayts-vyn*
Qualitätswein *KWAH-luh-tayts-vyn*
Riedel *REE-del*
Smaragd *smahr-AHK*
Steiermark *SHTY-ur-mahrk*
Steinfeder *SHTYN-feh-dur*
Styria *STIR-ee-uh*
Südsteiermark *SOOD-shty-ur-mahrk*
Tafelwein *TAH-ful-vyn*
Wachau *VAH-kahw*
Weinviertel *VYN-vir-tul*
Wien *VEE-ehn*

GREEK WINE TERMS AND REGIONS

Achaïa *ah-KEE-uh*
Aegean *uh-JEE-un*
Attika *AT-ih-kuh*
Cephalonia *kehf-aah-LOHAN-nee-yuh*
Crete *KREET*
Epirus *eh-PY-rus*
Epitrapezios Inos *ep-uh-truh-PEE-zee-ohs EE-nohs*

Ionian *eye-OH-nee-un*
Lefkada *lef-KAH-duh*
Limnos *LEEM-nahs*
Macedonia *mah-kah-THOH-nee-ah*
Náoussa *NAHW-suh*
Neméa *NEM-ee-yah*
Onomasía Proeléfseos Anotéras Piótitos *oh-noh-MAHZH-yah proh-eh-lef-ZEE-ohs AH-noh-ter-ahs pee-yoh-TY-tohs*
Onomasía Proeléfseos Eleghoméni *oh-noh-MAHZH-yah proh-eh-lef-ZEE-ohs el-eg-koh-MEH-nee*
Páros *PER-ahs*
Peloppenesos *pel-uh-puh-NEE-sus*
retsina *ret-SEE-nuh*
Rhodes *ROHDZ*
Samos *SAY-mahs*
Santorini *sahn-toh-REE-nee*
Thessalia *theh-SAY-lee-uh*
Topikos Inos *toh-PEE-kohs EE-nohs*
Zákinthos *ZAH-kin-thahs*

HUNGARIAN WINE TERMS AND REGIONS

Aszú *AHS-zooh*
Carpathian *kahr-PAY-thee-un*
Eger *EH-gur*
Egri Bikavér *EH-gree BEE-kah-vur*
Essencia *ehs-ZEN-see-uh*
puttonyos *pooh-TOHN-yohsz*
Tokaj *toh-KAHJ*
Tokaji *toh-KAH-jee*
Tokaji Aszú *toh-KAH-jee AHS-zooh*

OTHER EUROPEAN WINE TERMS AND REGIONS

canton *KAN-tun/kan-than*
Caspian *KAS-pee-un*
Caucasus *KAW-kuh-sus*
Commandaria *kah-mahn-DAH-ree-uh*
Cotnari *KAHT-nuh-ree*
Crimea *kry-MEE-uh*
Croatia *kroh-AY-shuh*
Cyprus *SY-prus*
Dobrogea *duh-BROH-jee-uh*
Dôle *DOHL*
Galilee *GAL-uh-lee*
Moldova *mohl-DOHV-uh*
Muntenia *MUN-tin-ee-uh*
Neuchâtel *nooh-shah-TEL*
Slavonia *sluh-VOH-nee-uh*
Slovenia *sloh-VEEN-yuh*
Sofiya *soh-FEE-uh*
Thracian *THRAY-shun*
Ticino *tih-CHEE-noh*
Transylvania *tran-sul-VAYN-yuh*
Ukraine *YOOH-krayn*
Valais *vah-LAY*
Vaud *VOH*

NORTH AMERICAN WINE TERMS AND REGIONS

Alameda *al-uh-MEE-duh*
Amador *AHM-uh-dor*
Arroyo Grande *uh-ROY-oh GRAHN-day*
Arroyo Seco *uh-ROY-oh SEK-oh*
Calaveras *kah-luh-VER-uz*
Carneros *kahr-NER-ohs*
Chalone *shuh-LOHN*
Chehalem *chuh-HAY-lum*
Chelan *shuh-LAHN*
Cienega *SEE-in-uh-guh*
Contra Costa *KAHN-truh KAHS-tuh*
Covelo *kuh-VAY-loh*
Dos Rios *DOHS REE-ohz*
El Dorado *EL duh-RAH-doh*
Eola-Amity *ee-OH-luh AM-uh-tee*
Guenoc *gweh-NAHK*
Lodi *LOH-dy*
Mariposa *mer-ih-POH-suh*
Mayacamas *my-uh-KAH-mus*
Mendocino *men-duh-SEE-noh*
meritage *MER-uh-tij*
Niagara *ny-AG-ruh*
Okanagan *oh-KAHN-uh-gun*
Ontario *ahn-TER-ee-oh*
Pacheco *pah-CHAY-koh*
Paicines *PY-see-nehs*
Paso Robles *PAH-soh roh-BLEEZ*
Puget *PYOOH-jit*
San Benito *SAHN beh-NEE-toh*
San Bernabe *SAHN buhr-NAH-beh*
San Luis Obisbo *SAHN loo-EES oh-BIS-boh*
San Ysidro *SAHN yeh-SEE-droh*
Santa Lucia *SAHN-tuh looh-SEE-uh*
Santa Rita *SAHN-tuh REE-tuh*
Santa Ynez *SAHN-tuh yeh-NEZ*
Shenandoah *shen-un-DOH-uh*
Tuolumne *tooh-UL-uh-mee*
Umpqua *UM-kwuh*

Valle de Guadalupe *VY-yeh duh-GWAH-duh-loo-pay*
Wahluke *wah-LOOHK*
Willamette *wih-LAM-it*
Yakima *YAK-uh-muh*

AUSTRALIAN/NEW ZEALAND WINE TERMS AND REGIONS

Adelaide *AD-uh-layd*
Barossa *buh-RAH-suh*
Coonawarra *kooh-nuh-WAH-ruh*
Fleurieu *fluh-REE*
Geelong *jee-LAHNG*
Geographe *jee-oh-GRAH-fee*
Gisborne *GIZ-born*
Grampians *GRAHM-pee-unz*
Grange *GRAHNJ*
Macedon *MAY-zuh-dohn*
Manjimup *mahn-jih-MUP*
Marlborough *MAHRL-buh-roh*
McLaren Vale *mik-LER-un VAYL*
Mudgee *MUD-jee*
Otago *oh-TAH-goh*
Padthaway *PAD-thuh-way*
Penola *peh-NOH-luh*
Pyrenees *PIR-uh-neez*
terra rossa *TER-uh RAW-suh*
Waikato *wy-KAH-toh*
Wairarapa *wy-ruh-RAH-puh*
Wrattonbully *RAHT-un-boo-lee*
Yarra *YAH-ruh*

SOUTH AMERICAN WINE TERMS AND REGIONS

Aconcagua *ah-kohn-KAH-gwuh*
Andes *AN-deez*
Bío-Bío *BEE-oh BEE-oh*
Casablanca *KAH-suh-blahn-kuh*
Colchagua *kohl-CHAH-gwuh*
Curicó *kuh-REE-koh*
Itata *EE-tah-tah*
La Rioja *lah-ree-OH-hah*
Maipo *MY-poh*
Maule *MAW-leh*
Mendoza *MEN-doh-zah*
Neuquén *NEH-uh-kin*
pisco *PEE-skoh*
Rapel *ruh-PEL*
Rio Negro *REE-oh NAY-groh*
Salta *SAHL-tah*
Valle Central *VY-yeh sin-TRAHL*

SOUTH AFRICAN WINE TERMS AND REGIONS

Constantia *kahn-STAHN-tee-uh*
Franschhoek *FRAHNSH-hook*
Klein Karoo *KLYN kuh-ROOH*
Paarl *PAHRL*
Stellenbosch *STEL-un-bahsh*
Worcester *WOR-stur*

BEER, SAKÉ, MEAD, AND CIDER TERMS

adjunct *AJ-unkt*
braggot *BRAH-gut*
Chimay *shih-MAY*
cidre *sy-DER*
cyser *SY-zur*
daiginjo *DY-gin-joh*
doppelbock *DAH-pul-bahk*
dunkel *DOON-kul*
esters *ES-turz*
framboise *frahm-BWAH*
futsuu-shu *fooht-sooh-ooh-shoo*
genshu *GIN-shooh*
ginjo *GIN-joh*
grist *GRIST*
hefeweizen *hef-uh-VYT-zen*
honjozo *hohn-JOH-zoh*
junmai *joon-MY*
koji *koh-JEE*
koshu *koh-SHOOH*
kriek *KREEK*
lager *LAH-gur*
lambic *LAM-bik*
Märzen *MAHRT-zen*
melomel *MEL-uh-mel*
metheglin *METH-uh-glin*
namazake *nahm-ah-ZAH-kay*
nigori *nih-GOH-ree*
Orval *or-VAHL*
pêche *PESH*
pyment *PY-mint*
Reinheitsgebot *ryn-HYTS-guh-boht*
Rochefort *ROHK-furt*
Saccharomyces uvarum *sak-uh-roh-MY-seez ooh-VAHR-uhm*
saké *SAH-kee*
Schwarzbier *SHVAHRTS-beer*

tokutei meishoshu *toh-KOOH-tay MY-shoh-shooh*
Westmalle *WEST-mahl*
wit *VIT*
wort *WURT*

SPIRIT TERMS

agave *uh-GAH-vay*
alambic *uh-LAHM-bik*
añejo *uh-NYAY-hoh*
aperitif *uh-per-uh-TEEF*
armagnac *AHR-mun-yak*
blanco *BLAHN-koh*
bourbon *BUR-bun*
brandewijn *BRAHN-duh-vyn*
calvados *KAHL-vuh-dohs*
cognac *KOHN-yak*
congeners *KAHN-juh-nurz*
cordial *KOR-jul*
digestif *dee-jes-TEEF*
eau-de-vie *ohd-VEE/oh-duh-VEE*
genever *JIN-uh-vur*
grappa *GRAWP-uh*
Islay *EYE-luh*
liqueur *lih-KUR*
mezcal *mez-KAHL*
mixto *MEEKS-toh*
oro *OR-oh*
piña *PEE-nyuh*
plato *PLAH-toh*
pulque *POOL-kay*
reposado *ray-poh-SAH-doh*
slivovitz *SLIV-uh-vits*
Speyside *SPAY-syd*
uisge beatha *OOH-skuh BAYTH-uh*

APPENDIX C

Important Spirit Brands/Distillers

VODKA

360 (U.S.)
42Below (New Zealand)
Absolut (Sweden)
Belvedere (Poland)
Blavod Black (U.K.)
Boru (Ireland)
Charbay (U.S.)
Chopin (Poland)
Cîroc (France)
Effen (U.S.)
Finlandia (Finland)
Fris (Denmark)
Grey Goose (France)
Hangar One (U.S.)
Iceberg (Canada)
Jean-Marc XO (France)
Ketel One (Holland)
Level (Sweden)
Popov (U.S.)
Prairie Organic (U.S.)
Pravda (Russia)
Rain (U.S.)
Reyka (Iceland)
Seagram's (U.S.)
Skyy (U.S.)
Smirnoff (U.S.)
Square One (U.S.)
Stolichnaya (Russia)
Svedka (Sweden)
Three Olives (U.K.)
Tito's Handmade (U.S.)
Tru Organic (U.S.)
Trump (Holland)
Van Gogh (Holland)
Vox (Holland)
Wyborowa (Poland)

GIN

Beefeater (U.K.)
Bombay (U.K.)
Bombay Sapphire (U.K.)
Boodles (U.K.)
Citadelle (France)
Gilbey's (U.K.)
Gordon's (U.K.)
Hendrick's (U.K.)
Plymouth (U.K.)
Seagram's (U.S.)
Tanqueray (U.K.)
Tanqueray No. Ten (U.K.)

WHISKEY

Irish Whiskey

Bushmills
Jameson
Old Kilkenny
Paddy
Powers Gold Label
Tullamore Dew

American Whiskey

Bourbon

Ancient Age
Baker's
Basil Hayden's
Booker's
Buffalo Trace
Bulleit
Early Times
Elijah Craig
Evan Williams
Ezra Brooks
Fighting Cock
Four Roses
Heaven Hill
Jim Beam
Knob Creek
Maker's Mark
Old Crow
Old Forester
Old Grand-Dad
Wild Turkey
Woodford Reserve

Tennessee Whiskey

Jack Daniel's
George Dickel
Gentleman Jack

Blended American Whiskey

Seagram's 7

Canadian Whisky

Black Velvet
Canadian Club
Canadian Mist
Crown Royal
Seagram's VO
Tangle Ridge

Blended Scotch Whisky

Ballantine's
Buchanan's
Chivas Regal
Cutty Sark
Dewar's
Dimple
Famous Grouse
Grant's
Johnnie Walker
J&B
Pinch
Passport
Teacher's
White Horse

Single-Malt Scotch

The Highlands and Speyside

Aberlour
The Balvenie
Cardhu
Cragganmore
Dallas Dhu
The Dalmore
Dalwhinnie
Edradour
Glenfiddich
Glengoyne
Glen Garioch
Glen Grant
The Glenlivet
Glenmorangie
Oban
Knockando
Knockdhu
The Macallan
Speyburn
The Speyside
Springbank
Strathisla
Tamdhu

The Lowlands

Bladnoch
Glenkinchie

Campeltown

Glengyle
Glen Scotia
Springbank

The Islands

Highland Park (Orkney)
Isle of Jura (Jura)

Scapa (Orkney)
Talisker (Isle of Skye)

Islay

Ardbeg
Bowmore
Bruichladdich
Bunnahabhain
Caol Ila
Lagavulin
Laphroiag

RUM

10 Cane (Trinidad and Tobago)
Appleton Estate (Jamaica)
Bacardi (Puerto Rico)
Cockspur (Barbados)
Cruzan (U.S.V.I.)
Flor de Caña (Nicaragua)
Gosling's (Bermuda)
Havana Club (Cuba)
Mount Gay (Barbados)
Myer's (Jamaica)
Pusser's (B.V.I.)
Pyrat (Anguilla)
Rhum Barbancourt (Haiti)
Ron Rico (Puerto Rico)
Zacapa (Guatemala)

Spiced Rum

Admiral Nelson's
Captain Morgan's
Sailor Jerry's

Flavored Rum

Malibu
Parrot Bay

TEQUILA

1800
Cazadores
Chinaco
Corazón
Corralejo
Don Julio
El Jimador
Gran Centenario
Herradura
Hornitos
Jose Cuervo
Las Trancas
Milagro
Patrón
Porfidio
Sauza
Tequila 30-30
Tres Generaciones

Mezcal

Monte Alban

BRANDY

Cognac

Courvoisier
Hennessy
Hine
Kelt
Martell
Otard
Rémy Martin

Armagnac

Darroze
Gélas
Laubade

Grappa

Nonino
Poli
Sibona

California Brandy

Christian Brothers
E&J
Germain-Robin

Mexican Brandy

Presidente

LIQUEURS AND CORDIALS

Herbal Liqueurs

Aquavit
Benedictine
Campari
Chartreuse
Damiana
Jägermeister
Kümmel
Metaxa
Pimm's
Strega
Unicum

Anise-flavored Liqueurs

Le Fée Absinthe
Libertine Absinthe
Lucid Absinthe
Metaxa Ouzo
Pastis
Pernod
Sambuca Romana

Fruit Liqueurs

99 Bananas (banana)
Chambord (raspberry)
Cherry Heering (cherry)
Cointreau (orange)
Grand Marnier (orange)
Hpnotiq (tropical fruit)
Ke Ke Beach (key lime)
Limoncello (lemon)
Midori (melon)
Pama (pomegranate)

Coffee Liqueurs

Kahlúa
Kamora
Starbucks Coffee
Tia Maria

Whiskey Liqueurs

Drambuie
Irish Mist
Rock & Rye
Southern Comfort
Wild Turkey American Honey
Yukon Jack

Cream Liqueurs

Bailey's Irish Cream
Carolans
Saint Brendan's Irish Cream

Miscellaneous Liqueurs

Aftershock (cinnamon)
Amaretto di Saranno (almond)
Bärenjäger (honey)
Cynar (artichoke)
Frangelico (hazelnut)
Galliano (vanilla, anise, and herbs)
Godiva (chocolate)
Goldschläger (cinnamon)
Licor 43 (citrus and vanilla)
Rumple Minze (peppermint)
St-Germain (elderflower)
Tuaca (citrus and vanilla)
Vermeer (chocolate)

APPENDIX D

Additional Resources

MAGAZINES AND PERIODICALS

Magazines and periodicals are a great way to keep current on trends and happenings in the global wine industry. There are several that feature articles about wines, wineries, winemakers, industry trends, food pairings, auction prices, travel to wine regions, and even the health benefits of wine. Many also critically review different wines, in some cases thousands per issue, providing tasting descriptions and often a critical score in terms of quality. Almost all have websites that allow users to search for different wine reviews, past articles, and up-to-the-minute wine news (membership fees often apply). The following is a list of some of the widely circulated wine-related magazines and periodicals in the United States with their companion websites.

Decanter (www.decanter.com)
Food & Wine (www.foodandwine.com)
The Wine Advocate (www.erobertparker.com)
Wine & Spirits Magazine (www.wineandspiritsmagazine.com)
Wine Enthusiast Magazine (www.winemag.com)
Wine Spectator (www.winespectator.com)

Beer and spirit magazines that feature information on beers, spirits, breweries and brewers, distilleries, and current industry trends are also gaining in popularity. Listed below are some popular examples.

Beer-Related
All About Beer Magazine (www.allaboutbeer.com)
Beer Advocate (www.beeradvocate.com)
Celebrator Beer News Magazine (www.celebrator.com)
Modern Brewery Age (www.breweryage.com)

Spirit-Related
Malt Advocate (www.whiskeypages.com)
The Spirit Journal (www.spiritjournal.com)

PROFESSIONAL CERTIFICATIONS

As in most industries, professional certifications are an important way to prove your knowledge and skills, and can be quite helpful throughout your career. There are several organizations in the United States that offer certification testing as well as educational programs and other activities. Listed below are some of the major certifying bodies as well as their websites to help you seek out more information. It is always best to research each to determine which best applies to your personal or career goals.

Court of Master Sommeliers (www.courtofms.com)
Society of Wine Educators (www.societyofwineeducators.org)
Institute of Masters of Wine (www.mastersofwine.org)
International Sommelier Guild (www.internationalsommelier.com)

Index

T